John Western 75

# SUFFOLK HOUSES

## *A Study of Domestic Architecture*

BY ERIC SANDON F.R.I.B.A., F.S.A.

with contributions by Stanley West, M.A., A.M.A., F.S.A.
& Elizabeth Owles, B.A., F.S.A.
Drawings by John Western
Photographs by Helen Sandon and Liza Whipp

*Richard*
*A memento of your stay in*
*Woodbridge, Christmas 1996.*

*Michael*

*Opposite: Giffords Hall, Wickham-brook, from the south-east.*

ANTIQUE COLLECTORS' CLUB

© 1977 Eric Sandon
World copyright reserved
First published 1977 by Baron Publishing Ltd.
Reprinted 1984, 1986, 1993

ISBN 0 902028 68 5

British Library CIP Data
Sandon, Eric
    Suffolk Houses: a study of domestic architecture
    1. Architecture, Domestic — England — Suffolk — History
    I. Title
    728′.09426′4   NA7331.5

Printed on Consort Satin
from Donside Mills, Aberdeen

Printed in England by
Antique Collectors' Club Ltd., Church Street, Woodbridge, Suffolk

FOR TERESA MARGARET-MARY ROSE

# Foreword

"Commoditie, firmenes and delight", how aptly does that Vitruvian description of well-being in architecture suit the inscape of the buildings which over the centuries of our Christian civilisation have complemented our Suffolk landscape in which it has been my unrivalled privilege to have been nurtured. This precious inheritance has been recorded in the following pages. For that Suffolk, and indeed a larger world beyond, must be ever grateful to Eric Sandon, not only for the scholarship with which he has endowed *Suffolk Houses,* but also for his insight of the essential unity of life of civilised man, rich or poor in wordly goods as may be, but rich in appreciation of the unity of life as we would wish to live it.

And who more aptly could have undertaken this happy and dedicated task than he who has done much to carry forward this tradition of 'commoditie, firmenes and delight' in our contemporary Suffolk scene?

Stradbroke
(Her Majesty's Lieutenant of Suffolk)

# Acknowledgements

I believe that the genesis of this book was in a conversation between Colonel Jimmy Langley and John Steel, but when in May 1971 I volunteered to write about Suffolk Houses it was with only the smallest notion of the size of the task that I had taken on. The initial plan of describing one hundred interesting houses slowly seemed less than adequate, in view of the lack of any single textbook on the subject of house building in Suffolk. It seemed plain that what was needed was an introduction in some depth to precede the description of a number of carefully chosen examples of houses of timber, plaster and brick. In reaching these conclusions I had the understanding and support of my publishers, Mr. and Mrs. John Steel.

Miss Elizabeth Owles, who has since succeeded Mr. A.R. Edwardson as Curator of Moyses Hall Museum, Bury St. Edmunds, promised to contribute an article on houses during the Roman occupation, and the County Archaeologist, Mr. Stanley West, to write about the housing at the Anglo-Saxon village of West Stow: Mr. Peter Warner has contributed two informative drawings of a typical house. With Mr. Edwardson I had an interesting exchange of views on the history of Moyses Hall. Lord Cranbrook kindly read through the section in my book dealing with 'Suffolk – the background of building' and the staff of the Reference Department at the Borough Library in Northgate Street, Ipswich, and the County Library, Woodbridge, were consistently helpful, and the same is true of the Suffolk Record Office, where Mr. V.W. Gray first drew my attention to the mid-fifteenth century contract for the supply of bricks to John Mannock of Giffords Hall, Stoke-by-Nayland, as well as that of 1553 to make bricks for Sir Edward North of South Elmham. To Mr. W.A.B. Jones of Hadleigh I owe the local Building Regulations of 1619 covering the 'Dividing of Cottages' and 'Against Thatching of Houses and Claye Chymneyes'. For the Library service of the Royal Institute of British Architects at 66 Portland Place, London W.1, I have nothing but praise. Local historians generally have been most helpful but there are two to whom I am specially indebted. The Rev. Dr. E.C. Brooks of Somerleyton contributed material on Herringfleet Hall and other historical houses in the vicinity, and first put me into touch with Audrey and Arnold Butler who allowed me to quote from their material on Somerleyton brickworks; Dr. Brooks has also shown me much personal kindness. With Hugh Paget, M.A., C.B.E., I have worked on the correlation of the structural evidence of Tudor House, Needham Market, with the devolution of this and the adjoining properties, of which Mr. Paget has made such an intensive study. He has provided an historical appraisal which sheds valuable light on the cloth trade, to which both churches and houses in Suffolk owe so much.

I must record also the help that I have received from abroad. Prof. Dr. IR. C.L. Temminck-Groll, B.I., who is on the staff of the Technical High School at Delft, is an authority on historical Dutch architecture. He has generously corresponded with me on the subject of the Dutch gables of East Anglia, and done much to elucidate difficult questions on the source of sixteenth and seventeenth century gable design in Suffolk. I have received help from Dr. J. Bauch of Hamburg University on the subject of dating timbers through the science of Dendrochronology. On the same subject I can only say how much I owe to the willingness of Dr. J.M. Fletcher of the Research Laboratory for Archaeology and the History of Art, of Oxford University, to provide information together with copies of papers which he has contributed in *Archaeometry, The British Oak,* and *Country Life.*

There is no doubt as to the source to which I am most of all indebted – the owners of Suffolk houses. I cannot praise too highly their readiness to allow their privacy to be invaded, their houses examined, photographed and drawn and their patience, furthermore, in reading and commenting upon my descriptive text. There is some bond that is quick to unite those who share more than a superficial interest in houses, and no interest which is more rewarding to share than where this bond exists. The writer on houses is thus in a position of special trust; those which he visits are, in almost all cases, family homes whose privacy must be fully respected. The fact that houses are described in this book in no way implies that they are customarily open to view. Where entry is permitted this is referred to in a separate list which describes arrangements existing in July 1977. It must be taken that houses not on this list are not open for inspection. House owners will not wish to have their names singled out individually, and will, I hope, accept this general expression of my gratitude. The one exception I must, however, make is that of John and Sylvia Le Comber of Read Hall, Mickfield, who have not only shown the customary courtesy of Suffolk householders, but John has also contributed the brilliant technical drawings of Read Hall which reveal so clearly the skill that went into the carpentry of timber-framed houses between the mid fifteenth and early seventeenth centuries.

To John Western I am also indebted not only for his drawings, but also for his patience in bringing out in them the required architectural qualities: his work being of an unusual sensitivity, he has succeeded not only in illustrating Suffolk houses but also in eliciting that special atmosphere of a certain brooding remoteness which, I feel, is unique to this county. For photography I must record my thanks to Baron Publishing, Liza Whipp and my wife, Helen, all of whom have made an invaluable contribution to this book. Although their pictures are not individually credited, their individual techniques are each of a high order. Where photographs have been obtained from other sources they are acknowledged.

The writing of this book has gone hand in hand with the business of running an architectural practice as well as an architect's home, and it has, inevitably, overlapped into both spheres. Without the tactful forebearance of my partners and associates on the one hand, and my wife and small daughter on the other, it could never have reached conclusion. Without my wife's help it could never even have been started, and she has partnered me on arduous trips over the length and breadth of Suffolk, taking photographs and recording the results of our inspections. There remains to be mentioned with a special word of thanks the labours of my secretary, Daphne Ward, who has come in for the immense task of typing and assembling the mass of material into the coherence of a single book.

# CONTENTS

# List of Colour Plates

# Introduction

I find that in the chronology of words an introduction was first described in the early eighteenth century as elementary instruction, or initiation in the knowledge of a subject. A little later in the same century it became known also as the action of introducing or making known personally: 'especially formal presentation of one person to another'. The whole of this book could be said to be no more than the first — an elementary initiation in the subject of Suffolk houses — and in that sense this is merely an Introduction to an introduction, but it could also be something of the second. Houses have personalities, like people, and the older and more mature are frequently the most interesting. This book is therefore also a presentation of personalities.

To exceed the limits of an introduction to so large a subject would need textbook treatment, which could easily run into volumes. Strictly speaking this is what is called for and why, I suspect, it has never been attempted. In an ideal world, regional studies of domestic architecture would be granted national bursaries, and, based on urban and rural parishes,[1] would systematically record and discuss historical houses: finally the whole survey would be evaluated in terms of architecture, archaeology and economic and social history.

To keep within introductory limits, the practical solution was to outline the most material aspects of house building, and to do no more than suggest the scope for further study. Even in this attenuated form, however, the material proved to be rich, complex and interesting.

The elementary starting point is the definition of terms:

a) *Suffolk:* refers to the whole of the administrative County Council areas of East and West Suffolk prior to the Local Government Act 1972; that is to say it includes the parishes of Burgh Castle, Bradwell, Fritton, Belton and Hopton which have been (alas) seceded to Norfolk under boundary changes.

b) *Houses:* the emphasis is not exclusively on the native or vernacular way of building, although this must share a considerable place in any stocktaking of local characteristics. The attempt is rather to underline distinct phases in the spectrum of building, extending from the late-mediaeval[2] to the modern. 'Houses' still remains an open ended category, for there are many gradations in the domestic scale that culminates with manor house and starts with cottage. There have been attempts to put houses into size groups, and in one recent classification they are divided into Great House, Large House, Small House and Cottage, corresponding to four groups of householders in a scale based on wealth and social status.[3] In practice, this is none too easy to apply, and in Suffolk it comes more naturally to think in terms of manor house, country house, farmhouse and cottage, with parsonage, town house and village house as the obvious corollary.

On what basis can material be selected? According to one estimate there are over ten thousand 'listed buildings' in Suffolk, but as the numbers tend to increase with new assessments, this total is probably an underestimate. The statutory listing and protection of significant buildings by the Department of the Environment is a relatively new feature of the contemporary scene (see Appendix vi). It is not always successful, either in the selection made, or in the protection given. The Grade I reserved for 'buildings of outstanding interest' has been a too exclusive category which covers about four per cent only of listed buildings, and is now due for reassessment. In theory all houses of special architectural and historic interest are included, but examinations have not always probed deeply enough. A recent survey of Stonham Aspall[4] uncovered one mediaeval and one post-mediaeval house, both of some interest but neither of them listed. Edgar's Farm, Stowmarket — a mediaeval aisled hall of the fourteenth century — was only discovered during an examination of photographs in the National Buildings Records. It is now described

1 i.e. the same basis as used by the Statutory List. Whilst one sympathised with regrets that were voiced at the disappearance of traditional boundaries under the Local Government Act of 1972, one could also be encouraged by the key role given to the *parish.*
2 For the term 'late-mediaeval' I am content to accept the definition given by Eric Mercer in *English Vernacular Houses* (op.cit.) viz: 'Late mediaeval is taken to mean the period from the late fourteenth to the mid-sixteenth century'.
3 cf., Professor R.W. Brunskill in his excellent *Illustrated Handbook of Vernacular Architecture* (Faber & Faber) pages 22-24 (see General Bibliography).
4 *The houses of Stonham Aspall,* a survey by David Penrose, B.A., and Peter Hill, M.A., published in The Suffolk Review *Bulletin of the Local History Council* in August 1971 (Volume 4, No. 1).

as 'a hitherto unrecognised class of structures, which may well find a place in the general history of North European as well as English roofs.'[1] The great majority of the houses discussed in this book are listed buildings and have been selected as significant examples in the grouping already proposed. Some of the religious houses converted into domestic premises after the Dissolution are grouped with parsonages.

In general, listed building entries consist of highly condensed descriptions of external and — to a lesser extent — internal architectural features, with an occasional reference to building history. The same is true, broadly speaking, of that remarkable source book on Suffolk buildings — Pevsner's *Suffolk* in *The Buildings of England* series. This series, covering forty English counties in forty six volumes, is designed on a more or less fixed plan. There is an introduction, dealing cursorily with the geological structure and building materials of the county, and then proceeding from pre-history to Anglo Saxon and Norman works, followed by a sketch of the principal events in church work, houses and other buildings in each succeeding century until the twentieth. Sir Nikolaus Pevsner is good at identifying the work of artists, architects and others, and each volume has an index of names. In his *Suffolk* volume he comments on the way in which material on local houses is scattered amongst various books, and it is one of the primary purposes here to bring such material together into a single volume. I have also collected as many references as possible in a General Bibliography.

I am solely concerned here with the domestic architecture of Suffolk, and it may be of interest to mention the methods used in the preparation of material. In practice there were three main work stages: 1) the Threshold Phase; 2) the Fieldwork Phase, and 3) the Assembly Phase. Phase 1 consisted of identifying material from personal research. In Suffolk five years ago (in 1972 to be precise), when there were thirteen rural districts, and separate urban districts and borough councils, it was relatively easier to screen these smaller areas for interesting houses. This stage took about eighteen months, and was succeeded by Phase 2, when selected houses were looked at and illustrated by drawings and photography. In Phase 3, the material thus prepared was assembled, and those two phases together occupied all of three and a half years.

The principles of introduction and selection helped to simplify the study, and by allowing a little more elbow room it became possible to discuss not only houses but some of their related aspects in greater detail. I have become increasingly aware of the importance of the *places* where houses are built; the lie of the land; water supply, aspect and outlook, and, particularly, communications — access to tracks, paths and roads. There is the connection between this local network and the wider geographical patterns of an area. These are the *organic* relationships in the siting of houses which are not only intensely interesting but of great importance in the study of building. It is for these reasons that I have devoted a short section entirely to the placing of houses in the landscape, whether singly or in settlements — hamlet, village and town. For those who care for such things there are always the more intangible relationships between buildings and places, such as those which inspired Gerard Manley Hopkins in his search 'for the law or principle which (gives) to any object or grouping of objects its delicate and surprising uniqueness',[2] and which led him to define such 'rich revealing oneness' by the word — *inscape*: at these things one can occasionally hint — and no more.

A study of architecture should have its own framework, or structure. It is frequently accepted that there is no more illuminating definition of architecture than that given by Sir Henry Wooton.[3] He succeeded in putting into Elizabethan English a description of 'well-building' borrowed from favourite Italian authors, which he rendered as *Commoditie, Firmenes* and *Delight.* These three qualities remain the source of 'well-building' and provide an equally acceptable basis for the study of both major and minor architecture. *Commoditie* — the planning of houses — is the subject of Section 3; *Firmenes,* or structure, the subject of Section 4; and *Delight* — the use of design — the subject of Section 5.

The planning of houses is the arranging of internal space, expressed in the shape of rooms and their functions as living spaces — places for cooking and eating, working, resting and sleeping. It is these arrangements which houses have been built

1 J.T. Smith, M.A., F.S.A., in *A Fourteenth Century Aisled House: Edgar's Farm, Stowmarket,* Proceedings of the Suffolk Institute of Archaeology, 1958, Volume XXVIII, Part I, page 61.
2 From W.H. Gardner's Introduction to *Poems and Prose of Gerard Manley Hopkins* (The Penguin Poets).
3 Sir Henry Wooton, M.P., born at Boughton Malherbe, Kent, in 1568, and died when Provost of Eton in 1639. He wrote his book *The Elements of Architecture* on returning to England after a long service in the Venetian Embassy, and it was published in 1624.

to provide at each and every level of society, and which are the material for historical planning studies. Early examples have been given by two authorities: Miss Elizabeth Owles, B.A., F.S.A., writes on Roman houses in Suffolk, and Mr. Stanley E. West, M.A. A.M.A., F.S.A., on the reconstruction of the Anglo Saxon village at West Stow. Later plans evolve more slowly over the centuries from the early tentative forms, gradually to become identified with the developing social patterns of manor house, farmhouse and cottage.[1] Suffolk is not unique in these planning trends, which are shared over most of East Anglia and much of lowland England.

In the structure of houses, the part played by local building materials is often mentioned but rarely pursued in much depth. It is well known that timber and brick were widely used in the building of Suffolk houses, and, to a lesser extent, flint. There are remnants of old forests sufficient to suggest the one-time profusion of oaks, chestnuts, and other trees that went into the building of our houses. There are the remains of clay-pits and brick-kilns[2] in sufficient quantity to show how widespread was once the use of clay in walling and the manufacture of bricks: lime pits also point to a once flourishing local industry providing the main constituent in mortar and plasterwork. A regional study is clearly incomplete without reference both to the nature and source of materials, and the methods used when employed in building. One of the glories of Gothic Suffolk was a superlative mastery in the handling of timber, and this is an achievement which we still do not comprehend in its entirety. The tendency is to specialise, and timber-framed techniques have recently become a species of separate discipline. The dating of framed houses, however, from visual evidence of timbers remains hazardous, owing to the reuse of old timbers which continued from mediaeval — and earlier — times: it is a subject in which generalisations are apt to be dangerous. The introductory purpose of this book will have been served by illustrating an authentic historical timber-framed house and discussing the method of frame erection and the carpentry jointing. Of comparable importance is the technique of building in brick, and Suffolk engaged with Norfolk in a sophisticated development of design in brickwork which rose to a peak before the middle seventeenth century.

When considering the design of houses, it is frequently difficult to determine why some are good to look at and some are not. It is usual in architectural studies to take certain laws of proportion and rules governing the choice of materials for granted, but in individual enquiry on houses there should be some thought given to objective qualities of design and workmanship. These would include character, suitability for purpose, proportions of the whole and of the parts in relation to the whole, materials and qualities of texture, colour, finish and execution. The mediaeval Suffolk manor house or farm exhibited a remarkable blending of these qualities. 'It grew out of the ground' — as Antonin Raymond once said of the farm-type he found in Japan in the early twentieth century — 'like a mushroom or a tree, natural and true, it developed from the inside function absolutely honestly; all structural members were expressed positively on the outside, the structure itself was the finish and the only ornament, all materials were natural, selected and worked by true artist artisans; everything in it and around it was simple, direct, functional, economical.'

A difficulty which writers on regional building frequently come up against is in drawing a distinction between building and architecture; it is a difficulty which can be avoided by accepting a simple principle: that most, if not all, extant domestic building — and this is true of Suffolk as elsewhere — is 'architecture' within the accepted meaning. This is not the same as saying it is the work of architects — for that would be obviously absurd — but that it has been given *architectural consideration.* The essential design decisions are architectural decisions: the choice of materials, the plan form, the length, the height, the span, the roof pitch and treatment of eaves, verges and gables, the number, height and design of chimney stacks, the number, size and proportion of door and window openings, and the placing of ornament or enrichment, e.g. around a front door or porch. At some point in every good house, or cottage, these details have been thought about and decisions — however perfunctory — have been taken. The *feeling* of bygone builders for the 'well-building' of houses — that is to say for houses with sensibly commodious accommodation, well-knit structures, good proportions, harmonious

1 For a detailed examination of the development of the last two, see *The English Farmhouse and Cottage* by M.W. Barley (1961. Routledge and Kegan Paul).

2 Nathaniel Lloyd makes the point that, at least as early as Elizabeth I's reign, the terms kiln and clamp were interchangeable, although some kilns were not clamps as the term is used today. cf. *A History of English Brickwork,* op. cit., page 31.

materials and direct, unpretentious character — lingered on in Suffolk even after vernacular traditions had been universally destroyed before the end of the nineteenth century.

There is a further difficulty — that of chronology. A traditional, but curiously little discussed, characteristic of householders was making do with old places. This, although generally true, was particularly the case in Suffolk. Thus one can find a surprising accumulation of historical strata in a single house, with the origins buried so deeply that it would seem an act of purest pedantry, for example, to proclaim a house fifteenth century when almost everything within and without is plainly eighteenth century. Nor is this tendency confined to the smaller houses; it can be found in far grander ones. Take Hintlesham Hall for example; here the red brickwork of Thomas Timperley — or some of it[1] — built in the reign of Queen Elizabeth I, can still be seen at the back and sides, overshadowed by the creamy white plastered front put up in the classical style by Richard Powys in 1720. Something similar took place at Little Glemham Hall, where the new classical red-brick façade replaced the front of the old Elizabethan house, the back being left standing with large sash windows cut into the Tudor brickwork. Examples such as these can be multiplied. The only sensible way when discussing a number of examples, is to adopt an alphabetical order and deal with the range of periods, when these occur, in each house individually.[2]

The last Section of the book — apart from Appendices — is called the Exemplar. The criterion for selection must have to do both with intrinsic interest and quality. In a regional study of vernacular buildings, considerations of planning and design are likely to take second place. In a study of domestic architecture we will be looking for evidence of capacity in craftmanship and design. An ideal Exemplar would trace modes of planning, structure and design through the centuries in an orderly chronological sequence, but, as already noted, Suffolk houses do not always lend themselves to such logical analysis. 'Pure' examples of each period are relatively rare. Questions of size and status also come into it: a mansion has a lot more to say than a cottage, and we would not expect to find them side by side in an Exemplar. Division into familiar house types will meet this difficulty; hence mansion, manor house, country house, farmhouse and cottage with the corollary of religious building and parsonage, town house and village house. Descriptions in the Exemplar tend to concentrate on the general architectural character of buildings in relation to site. I have throughout tried to avoid the use of unfamiliar technical terms but some have inevitably crept in.

In making a selection of houses to describe and illustrate, I have been very conscious of the strong claims for inclusion of the many that have been left out. In the last resort there is bound to be something subjective in questions of choice, and this is a dilemma from which — as far as I know — there is no escape. The problem of choosing a few examples of good modern houses with which to round off the list has, if anything, proved more difficult than selecting traditional examples.

I am only too well aware of the risk of inaccuracies in a study such as this, and would welcome my attention being drawn both to errors of omission and commission with a view to rectification in future editions. Truth is one and indivisible, and as necessary in architecture as in life.

1 It is mainly confined to a series of massive chimney stacks built against the external walls.

2 Each house is preceded by a map reference based on the National Grid Index following the series TL and TM derived from the 2½ inch Ordnance Survey (first series).

Drawn by H.Davy.

Engraved by J.Lambert

*Plate 1: Benhall Lodge, after a drawing by H. Davy.*

section 2

# Suffolk
## *the background of building*

**The Region**

A regional study of house building starts with the land itself. Suffolk is part of East Anglia which, historically, is the name of an Anglo-Saxon kingdom dating from about A.D. 500, made up of the Norfolk and Suffolk of today, and reaching into Cambridgeshire and the Isle of Ely to a frontier with Mercia along the Devil's Dyke. Geographically it is a crescent-shaped land mass surrounding a vanished inland bay which thrusts eastwards into the North Sea, as though seeking the hollow coast of the Netherlands. On the inner, westward side low outliers of the Chiltern Hills rise like a barrier against the Fens.

Within this crescent lie Norfolk and Suffolk, divided by the long river valley of the Little Ouse and the Waveney (see Figure 1).[1] In a lowland country there is a fascination about valleys and hills even when, as in Norfolk and Suffolk, the valleys may be shallow and the hills rise imperceptibly from their surroundings. But in this undramatic land we come occasionally upon breath-taking views, when, suddenly, a great tract of country is seen falling away into the blue and dim distance. Such moments may occur in the parishes of Depden and Rede, at 409 feet or so above sea level; in Wickhambrook, where Rookery Farm and Gate Farm are the highest farms in Suffolk, or at Ousden where the Fox Inn is the highest pub.

It is a land of farms, with some of the most intensively cultivated soil in England;[2] of only one city, but many boroughs, market-towns, villages and hamlets; of few main roads but a maze of by-ways, and of few important rivers but innumerable small streams. It is a land with a vigorous, windy climate, under enormous cloudy skies — but there are sunlit days in East Anglia when the wind is in the east, the glass stands high, and the light is so sharp and luminous that the clear sky seems to reflect the brilliance of the sea.

In the background of house building in Suffolk, there are three main factors:

1. Landscape    2. Building materials    3. Siting of houses

### LANDSCAPE

*Figure 1: East Anglia*

Suffolk — the land of the South Folk — is, as Julian Tennyson puts it, ' . . . the reverse of obvious. Just as to fathom the nature and qualities of a shy person you must employ a certain sympathy and persuasion, so to overcome the diffidence of Suffolk you must approach it with a receptive mind and discerning eye.'[3] And it is in just such a patient frame of mind that one must start by trying to comprehend the geography of this unspectacular region.

**The Boundaries**

The boundaries of Suffolk, as of any English county, are both physical and historical. The physical are mainly water-boundaries: the rivers Little Ouse and Waveney in the north, the river Stour in the south and the North Sea on the east.

**Riverside Towns, the Coast and Roads**

All important developments follow the course of the rivers. The towns are all riverside towns: Haverhill is on a tributary of the Stour, and Sudbury on the Stour itself; Bury St. Edmunds lies at the meeting of the Linnet and the Lark, and Ipswich where the Gipping joins the Orwell, with Stowmarket higher upstream; Saxmundham is on a tributary of the Alde, Halesworth on the Blyth, and both Beccles and Bungay on the river Waveney.

Of equal and, once, of great importance is the coast; for the coast makes Suffolk a maritime county, breeding a race of sailors and fishermen, a dour and stubborn race tutored by the treacherous North Sea. There was a string of ports and fishing villages all the way from Orwell Haven to Lowestoft — Orford, Aldeburgh, Thorpeness, Dunwich, Walberswick, Southwold, Covehithe — but over the centuries they were gradually silted up by the tidal drift or whittled away by erosion.[4] The towns that remain have the look of barnacles still clinging desperately to their seaboard sites, with tall grey church-towers giving an occasional landmark to seamen (Plate 2).

---

1 Nigel Heard has a graphic picture in his book *Wool: East Anglia's Golden Fleece*, showing the watershed of the Little Ouse and Waveney at Redgrave, separated only by the width of a road (see photograph on p.13).
2 In East Anglia — apart from Local Government — Agriculture is by far the largest industry; in Suffolk alone the number of farm holdings in 1967 was put at *6,291*, although the tendency is for the number of holdings to decrease and the average size of farms to increase.
3 *Suffolk Scene* by Julian Tennyson. (1939. London and Glasgow: Blackie) p.15.
4 The ancient fishing town of Lowestoft is also said ". . . to have been washed away at an early period by the ocean" — W. White, *History of Lowestoft* in his *Suffolk*, p.559.

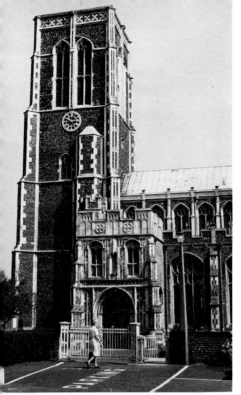

*Plate 2: Southwold Church Tower*
Simon Hicklin

## The Geology

1 Alfred Watkins developed the theory of straight trackways in prehistoric times in Britain in his book *The Old Straight Tracks* (1925. London: Methuen), and W.A. Dutt, author of *Suffolk* in *The Little Guides* series said that he had spent much time in testing the ley — or marker point — system, with surprising results. Watkins' theories received a fresh impetus by the publication in 1974 of Paul Screeton's *Quicksilver Heritage* (Thorsons), with sub-title *The Mystic Leys: Their Legacy of Ancient Wisdom.*
2 These road connections, together with the flourishing coastal ports, make it even more improbable that Bond, in his *Gothic Architecture in England*, should have claimed that even until the fifteenth century, "Norfolk and Suffolk were hardly an integral part of England; but severed from the mainland by rivers and fens more completely than Ireland is now from England" p.501.
3 *The Suffolk Turnpikes*, published by Ipswich and East Suffolk Record Office, Ipswich, 1973.
4 *A Survey of the Agriculture of Suffolk* by P.J.O. Trist, O.B.E., B.A., M.R.A.C., F.L.S., County Agriculture Advisor of Suffolk (1971, London: Royal Agricultural Society of England).
5 *Ibid* see pp.10-11, *The Last Glaciation.*
6 First published in the *Transactions* of the Suffolk Naturalists Society (Vol. 13 — Part 4, 1966) and included in Mr. Trist's book.

The coast inevitably played an historic part in the destiny of Suffolk. Once protected by the Roman military system, with fast roads serving the garrisons holding the Forts of the Saxon Shore, the coastline offered a constant temptation to raiders from overseas, and the infiltration of the Saxons was soon followed by invasion from Germany and Scandinavia as the Roman authority collapsed. The coast has remained a military risk all through history, as the surviving defensive structures show, but it has also promoted fruitful intercourse with Europe — for trade survives even wars — the ports serving the wool and cloth trade when Suffolk was in the forefront of national prosperity, and today promoting a substantial trade with the Continent.

The road system of Suffolk awaits thorough historical research. The whole network is complex and interesting, with the exciting possibility of hitherto undiscovered alignments across miles of country of sites or objects on the trackways of the people who lived here before the Romans came. If the Icknield Way is any indication, then there should be traces of similar old straight tracks elsewhere in a county as populous as Suffolk.[1] Whether or not the Romans made use of existing tracks can probably be established only by scientific archaeological research, using radio-carbon dating techniques: their most useful legacy was the Colchester-Stratford St. Mary-Baylham route, and on by the Pye Road straight through the centre of the county, and into Norfolk at Scole. This road anticipated the division of Suffolk into two halves, which became later a fact established by the Liberty of St. Edmund, and, very much later in time, by the separate administrative counties of West and East Suffolk in the nineteenth century. Many other portions of the sophisticated Roman military road-system of East Anglia are still in use in different parts of Suffolk.[2] A documentary history of the eighteenth and nineteenth century turnpikes has recently been prepared by the Archive Teaching Unit of the Suffolk Record Office.[3]

But the foundations of scenery lie in the structural contours, and in the soils. The soils of Suffolk are extremely complex, and have recently come in for unusually thorough analysis in Mr. P.J.O. Trist's study *A Survey of the Agriculture of Suffolk.*[4]

Broadly speaking, the main soil types are the Fens, the West Suffolk sands of the Breckland as far south as Bury St. Edmunds, which merge with the clay loams in the south-west. These are followed by the heavy soils of the boulder clay which cover the whole of central Suffolk. In the north-west occur the sandy clay loams, and in the Stour valley the sands and gravels which continue in the Sandlands, and end in the loamy sands north of Lowestoft. Mr. Trist has reminded us that in this county there is '. . . probably a greater variety of soil conditions than is found elsewhere in the British Isles'.[5]

The land structure of Suffolk is part of that great chalk outcrop which crosses England from south-west to north-west — from the Dorset Downs to the north coast of Norfolk — and finally reappears underlying the wolds in the extreme East of Lincolnshire and Yorkshire. It is this chalk sub-structure which makes Suffolk akin to Norfolk, and quite unlike the shallow parts of Essex, which lie upon the clays and gravels of the Thames Basin. In the time-scale of geological history, East Anglia is one of the most recent formations of Britain, with its cretaceous bed tilting downwards to the North Sea, and the recent Quaternary and newer Tertiary series overlaying the chalk in a coastal band from about Felixstowe right up to north Norfolk. From the glacial periods came the drift which eventually covered two-thirds of Norfolk and Suffolk with boulder clay; a cap varying in thickness from 226 feet at Wickhambrook to a few feet where the change to the coastal sands and gravels begins. It has been interesting to watch the chalk coming to the surface along the line of the new Claydon-Needham Market-Stowmarket By-Pass in the Gipping valley, where for several miles north of Claydon the new road embankments have been mottled white.

A typical cross-section of the county is reproduced in Figure 2.[6] From this it will be seen how the chalk appears in the west, and how the descending gradient of the chalk bed is covered by the thick bed of glacial drift gradually thinning towards Ipswich, where the crag appears in the river valleys and on the coast.

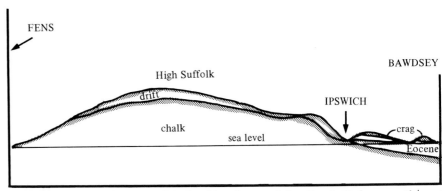

FENS

High Suffolk

BAWDSEY

drift

IPSWICH

chalk

sea level

crag

Eocene

*Figure 2: Geological section of the boulder clay overlying the chalk from south/west Suffolk to the coast (from section prepared by H.E.P. Spencer, F.G.S.).*

## BUILDING MATERIALS

The list of local materials is short. There is virtually no freestone in Suffolk, so any dressed stone found in houses — for example, in door surrounds or mullion-and-transom windows — has had to be imported. The soil yields only:—

**Chalk** that can be converted into lime for mortar, and, with an admixture of clay, into cement.[1]

**Clays** which not only promoted tree growth, and in some areas soil conversion, but also produce brick earth and material for walling.

**Flint,** mainly silica and often harder than quartz, found in layers in chalk as well as scattered in large quantities; the basic wall material of our churches and of many houses, especially in the west of the county, it was also used in foundations.

**Miscellaneous 'stones':**

**Septaria,** found in the London clay, a form of concretionary clay that was used by the Romans at Colchester, in the walls of Orford Castle, and at Little Wenham Hall.

**Coralline Crag,** a form of limestone found in coastal areas and, particularly, near Orford. It was used in the churches of Chillesford and Wantisden, and the Austin Friars seem to have done most of their building with it at Orford. Brown's Farm, Tunstall, and Stone Cottage, Snape, are comparatively rare examples of its use in houses.

**'Sarsens'** is the local name for glacial erratics or large-sized boulders, which were widely used by church builders in foundations and walls, and they have been observed also in flint and rubble-walled houses. Cautley thought that excavations in search of these boulders were made by 'the ancient builders'.

**'Ironstones'** are conglomerates of sand and gravel impregnated with iron once used in the walls of churches and other buildings.

**Timber,** mainly oak of the English variety, chestnut and beech for building in the earlier centuries. With the growing shortage of native hardwoods, softwoods were increasingly used and, together with hardwoods, were imported from Germany and the Baltic countries.

**Thatch.** The sedges, reed-beds and cornfields all provide building materials commonly used for roofing. The Anglo-Saxons thatched the roofs of their halls and huts at West Stow with corn-straw, and there is no reason to suppose that most of the roofs of Saxon and early mediaeval churches in Suffolk and Norfolk were not originally thatched.[2] Salzman tells us that in early times the outer covering of roofs was known generally as 'thack', and it was from that source that 'thatch' acquired its modern or restricted meaning of straw or reed roofing.[3] Thatching must have been the normal form of roofing for most buildings in Suffolk until the fourteenth or fifteenth centuries, when clay tiles began to come in. (Salzman quotes accounts for building the 'shire-house' at Ipswich in 1442, which includes '1300 tiles for roofing the house, at 4s. 6d.')

Suffolk builders, as we shall see, made a domestic architecture by the understanding use of these primitive materials. It is this remarkable achievement that underlies the deep harmony between landscape and traditional buildings.

1 The cement works at Claydon, originally a private Company known as Mason's Portland Cement Co. Ltd., started manufacture about 1890, and now belongs to the Cement Marketing Co.
2 Interesting figures of thatched churches in Norfolk and Suffolk in 1960 were quoted as 58 and 20 respectively by a correspondent to the *Times* (12.8.60) — the numbers have probably diminished in the ensuing years.
3 *Building in England* by L.F. Salzman, F.S.A. See page 223, and Chapter XV.

*Facing brickwork (Tudor).*

*Painted brickwork.*

*Suffolk pantiles.*

*Random-coursed flintwork.*

*Slate roofing.*

*Painted weather-boarding.*

*Thatched roofing.*

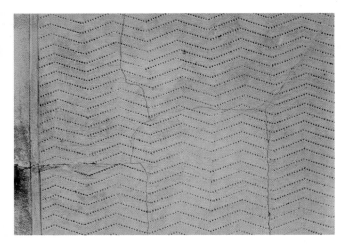

*Decorated plasterwork.*

*Clay plain tiles.*

*Vernacular building materials.*

It is somewhat surprising, in view of the extensive Roman occupation of southern East Anglia, that there is not more evidence of their dwellings. Miss Elizabeth Owles, B.A., F.S.A., the Curator of Moyses Hall Museum, Bury St. Edmunds, has kindly provided a report on the Roman occupation in Suffolk, with special references to domestic buildings, which is included at Appendix A to this Section.

The Teutonic folk, when they arrived in the early fifth century, were well versed in carpentry and timber building[1] (they were also accomplished boat-builders) and, fortunately, left traces of their wood-framed pit-dwellings in the form of holes in the ground. One of the most exciting developments in field-archaeology — under the direction of Mr. Stanley West, M.A., F.S.A., A.M.A., the County Archaeologist for Suffolk — was the start, in 1973, of the reconstruction of some dwellings at the Anglo-Saxon village of *West Stow* (797.713), some 5½ miles north of Bury St. Edmunds on the River Lark, and just off the Icknield Way. Mr. West kindly contributed a short article on the project, and this is included at Appendix B to this Section.

The study of movements begins *inside* the dwelling — where it is related to *commodite* — or planning — and goes outside the dwelling to the building site itself with its outbuildings, grounds, garden, plantations; and beyond this again, to the larger area of the property which, in the case of a farm, is a place of intensive work. Beyond the property, the movement follows the roads, tracks — and once, perhaps, the rivers[2] — to the various destinations with which the life of the dwelling unit is connected. Thus in every case movement-patterns provide plans or maps on which tracks can be studied between homes and outbuildings; between concentrated and dispersed work-sites, e.g. between barns, stackyards and cornfields; between the place of life and work, and between nearest neighbours, hamlet, village and church. Equally important will be the peripheral relationships between dwelling and boundaries of holdings, including ditches, watercourses and woodlands, and between local boundaries and parish boundaries.

The siting of houses in early times is clearly a complex study in which knowledge of peoples, their social groupings, economy, methods of growing food and systems of defence is essential; for this we are dependent upon archaeologists and historians. Looking at the broad picture, the majority of building sites in East Anglia will be found to have had their roots in agriculture and commerce. Methods of land tenure will have determined agricultural systems and these — in turn — the siting of buildings. In Suffolk generally the pattern will be found to differ from Norfolk, where there were more large landowners and fewer small freeholders. In the east of Suffolk the number of farms under 300 acres had been until recently, greater than those over this size, resulting in more farmhouses, as well as dwellings for employees.[3] William White noted in 1855 that the farms in Suffolk were not generally so large as in Norfolk, and there were 7,000 freeholders in his day, as against only 2,000 copyholders. These ownership patterns were reflected in the siting of buildings. In Suffolk we find many farms dotted about between market towns, villages and hamlets, particularly in the east of the county: further west this changes to a more nucleated pattern.

In the villages, hamlets and farmsteads dwelt the farmers and the labour force, and between these and the larger villages, market towns and boroughs developed a cross-fertilisation of economic services. From mediaeval times, until the decline of the cloth trade, these services included trades connected with the cottage-industries of wool-combing, the manufacture of hempen cloth and the spinning of fine worsted yarns, when 'There was scarcely a cottage which did not hum with the spinning-wheel, and hardly a street where you might not have counted weavers' workshops.'[4] For a long while the towns and settlements of Suffolk accommodated a work-force employed in the wool and cloth weaving industry as well as in farming, although many families would combine both: the women and children weaving and spinning, and the menfolk working on the farms and, no doubt, in their spare time on the loom or in combing wool. The prosperity of Suffolk during this period is reflected in the high development densities of urban and rural settlements.

*The village street, Kersey, Suffolk, looking south – Basil Oliver.*

### Agriculture, Commerce and Settlement Patterns

1 '... the Saxons brought with them to this country their own traditional methods of building *in timber*. They made little or no use of the stone buildings they found here, even those left empty by displaced local populations. They preferred to build their own timber settlements on other sites. They had indeed no word for building in stone: to build was *timbran*, i.e. to carpenter ...' cf. *An Introduction to Anglo-Saxon Architecture and Sculpture* by E.A. Fisher, M.A., D.Sc., p.24 (see Section Bibliography).

2 The close association of buildings with rivers is such a marked feature of Suffolk, and came about, no doubt, in early times when roads were bad and communications more difficult; small rivers offered an alternative means of transport, as well as water-power for milling and fulling and, of course, a supply of drinking water.

3 cf. *Agricultural Survey of Suffolk* by P.J.O. Trist, p.28. In 1968 Professor R. Emerson made the same comment in his *Suffolk – Some Social Trends*, p.8, '... the number of farms under 350 acres – indeed under 50 acres – is far larger [in Cosford, Melford, Gipping and Hartismere] than those of over 350 acres.'

4 cf. Eileen Power in *Mediaeval People*, p.149 (see Section Bibliography).

*Figure 3 illustrates typical Suffolk settlement patterns avoiding main roads.*

Against this background can be seen first the broad picture of settlement patterns in Suffolk, and then — successively — the larger centres and the relation of the big estates to these centres; the smaller centres in west and east; the villages and hamlets, and last the isolated buildings; Halls, with or without churches, and finally the farmhouses.

That there were once two Suffolks can be seen in the different patterns of roads, towns, estates and villages in the west and east of the same county (Figures 4 and 5). They were separated — broadly speaking — by the Pye Road (A140 — Ipswich/Baylham/Scole). To the west of it there is a general web pattern with Bury St. Edmunds at the centre. Of the ten major roads, seven converge upon Bury, and the secondary roads tend to fill in the web around the centre. To the east of it there is an irregular pattern of which the principal features are the characteristic Roman straightness of the Pye Road itself, and the rather meandering coastal road, keeping as close to the seaboard as the marshes and rivers would allow.[1] Of the twelve main roads, only five converge upon Ipswich, and only one secondary road from Diss through Eye and Debenham to Ipswich. The remainder serve both the coastal towns and villages and the country towns and villages. Closely linked with these broad road patterns are the settlement patterns.

There is an East Anglian tendency for settlements to avoid important roads. If we assume there to be about 500 villages and 400 hamlets in Suffolk, a total of some 900 settlements, it is worth noting that — even including the most populous road in the county from Ipswich to Gt. Yarmouth (A12) — there are not more than about 90 settlements on all the major roads of Suffolk. Most deserted are the Roman roads. On the whole length from Colchester to Norwich there are only 13 settlements, including Stratford St. Mary recently by-passed. On the Stone Street from Halesworth to Bungay (about 8½ miles) there are only a handful of houses and cottages, and a farm or two: long lengths of the road that went from Long Melford probably out to Dunwich are similarly deserted. But then in the whole of Suffolk today there are only 22 major (A) roads: secondary (B) roads are more numerous at about 43, and most numerous of all are the by-roads (un-classified) which, although difficult to enumerate precisely, can be put at about 1,500.

It is off the larger roads that the typical settlement patterns of Suffolk (and Norfolk) are to be found — in what appears at first sight to be a tangle of by-ways in secluded land areas (Figure 3). Inside these areas lie the villages and the hamlets. To begin with — in the west — they are more sparse, continuing the patterns of Cambridgeshire and North-east Essex; but then the characteristically tight development along the river valleys soon appears, with a knotty mesh of minor roads serving the settlements that lie between and on both banks of the Colne and Stour valleys. Similarly crowded is the country along the banks of most of the principal Suffolk rivers;[2] Gipping, Deben, and Waveney in particular. Each of the two other large areas — the upland and the coastal — has its distinctive settlement patterns. In the coastal there are the minor roads seeking to parallel the seaboard all

1 This is characteristic of English seaboard counties, and the coastal road system of Norfolk is the classic example of practically continuous roads keeping very close to the coast line, and joined every 5-6 miles by main or secondary roads from the interior.
2 Of the 500 villages of Suffolk I calculate that only about *150* are not on, or close by, a watercourse of some sort — brook, stream or river.

the way from Bawdsey to Boyton; between the Butley River and the Alde, and from Snape to Blythburgh, criss-crossed by small roads and tracks going to and from the coast; and a characteristic line of inland coastal villages – Alderton, Hollesley, Boyton, Orford, Sudbourne, Leiston, Westleton, Reydon, South Cove and Benacre. In upland Suffolk there are about 40 land spaces enclosed by A and B roads, within each of which is a network of minor roads (Figure 3): the pattern here is the lack of pattern – at almost every road junction there is a settlement, large or small, or an individual dwelling. All this has the look of natural growth, like the multiple veins in the fabric of large leaves.

### Bury St. Edmunds and Ipswich

The sites of important centres stem from a number of natural and other factors. Bury St. Edmunds had all the makings of a logical centre for the west of Suffolk; the site was in a river valley at the junction of the rivers Lark and Linnet, within three miles of the Roman road on its way north from Long Melford to Attleborough and beyond: it was an obvious place for a monastery, as well as a trading settlement. (When the body of the martyred Saxon King Edmund was brought to the monastery of St. Mary of Beadricesworth in the ninth century the greatness of its future was assured.) The destiny of Ipswich was assured by different means. The inception of Gipeswic in the seventh century was, we are told, the starting of some sort of trading station in contact with the Continent. The settlement not only had plentiful water supplies from numerous springs (e.g. Holy Wells and Cauldwell Hall), but also all the natural advantages of a safe port at the head of a river estuary, with a river penetrating some considerable distance into the interior and the Roman road from London and Colchester passing only about two miles away, making for Caister near Norwich: the coastal track from Yarmouth, linking all the ports and fishing villages, no doubt existed long before the making of the turnpike now known as the A12.[1]

### Estates around Bury St. Edmunds

Not unexpectedly the siting of country houses and estates around Bury St. Edmunds shows a markedly centripetal pattern, the direct result of that once-famed pilgrimage centre to which all roads naturally led. Furthermore the town was attractive in a way that Ipswich never was. William Cobbett – who admired Ipswich – was amusing about this in the Journal of his Eastern Tour in 1830: '. . . To conclude an account of Suffolk and not to sing the praises of Bury St. Edmunds would offend every creature of Suffolk birth; even at Ipswich, when I was praising *that place*, the very people of the town asked me if I did not think Bury St. Edmunds the nicest town in the world.'

A sketch map shows the principal landed properties in an inner and outer ring surrounding the town, the first at five miles distance from the centre, and the second at eleven miles (Figure 4). The great majority of these properties are lands once held by the Abbey of Bury St. Edmunds.

### Estates in the East of Suffolk

In contrast with this centripetal pattern in the west of the county, the siting of landed properties in the east of Suffolk follows a generally opposite and single linear pattern (Figure 5). A glance at the sketch map is sufficient to show the accumulation of sites along the historic route from Colchester through Ipswich to South Town (Great Yarmouth). This road served almost all the major and most of the minor country houses in the east of the county, and could well have been named 'The Social Highway'. To the north of it, with few exceptions, there were no large houses until the Waveney river-valley.

### Smaller Centres – West and East

The two halves of the county are divided also in the siting pattern of the smaller centres of population. In the west, Bury St. Edmunds seems to occupy a monopolistic place, admitting no rivals nearer than the extreme boundaries of its territory; Mildenhall about twelve miles to the north-west; Newmarket about the same distance west; and Thetford, for a long time part of Suffolk, again about twelve miles due north.[2] Between Bury and the Stour there is only one township about eleven miles south-south-east, but that of a once very considerable importance as a centre of the wool and cloth trade – Lavenham. The rest of the towns lie about sixteen miles to the south along the River Stour and on the borders of Essex: Haverhill, Clare, Long Melford, Glemsford, Sudbury and Nayland.

The pattern of minor centres of population in the eastern half of the county was no doubt influenced by the extremely asymmetrical position of Ipswich. The chief mercantile town of Suffolk – now an administrative District in its own right with a

1 It certainly appears on roughly the line of its present route in Hodskinson's Map of Suffolk (1783). The Act for amending the road from Ipswich to South Town was passed in 1785 (cf. Suffolk Turnpikes, *op.cit.*).
Lilian Redstone has an interesting note on the good water of Ipswich (cf. *Ipswich through the Ages*, p.42), linking the history of Cobbold's beer with that family's ownership of the springs at Holy Wells, previously part of the ancient hamlet of Wicks Episcope.
2 Ixworth, about six miles north-east, had once a market which – according to White's *Gazetteer* of 1855 – 'has long been obsolete', and the township must therefore have declined in importance.

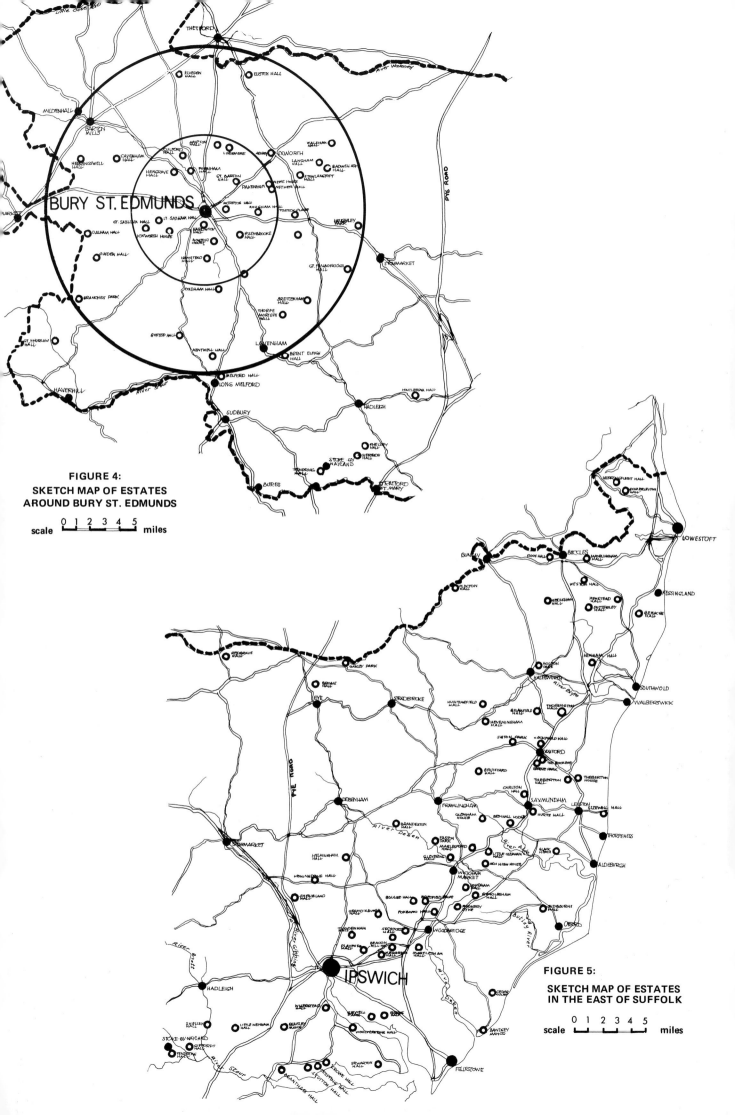

FIGURE 4:
SKETCH MAP OF ESTATES
AROUND BURY ST. EDMUNDS

scale 0 1 2 3 4 5 miles

FIGURE 5:

SKETCH MAP OF ESTATES
IN THE EAST OF SUFFOLK

scale 0 1 2 3 4 5 miles

1.

2.

*East Anglian Daily Times*

3.

*National Trust*

4.

5.

6.

7.

*Plate 3: Country houses round Bury St. Edmunds: 1. Hengrave Hall; 3. Ickworth House; 4. Great Saxham Hall. Country houses in East Suffolk: 2. Loudham Hall; 5. Marlesford Hall; 6. Little Glemham Hall; 7. Beacon Hill, Martlesham; 8. Grove Park, Yoxford; 9. Herringfleet Hall; 10. Somerleyton Hall.*

8.

9.

10.

far higher population (approximately 123,000) than any of the other six new Districts – is only ten ten miles from the Essex boundary in the extreme south of the county and about forty miles from Lowestoft, and not much less from Bungay and Beccles. Apart from this one curiously lopsided feature the situation of market-towns in the east of Suffolk was a model for an agricultural county in the days before mechanisation. No farm was further than about eight miles and the majority probably not more than five miles from the nearest market-town.

### The Villages

The sites of villages were in their turn related to the position of the smaller towns, and as each was a nodal point upon which roads converged, so also were the larger villages: some examples are Barrow, Hartest, Kersey, Walsham-le-Willows, Haughley, Coddenham, Grundisburgh, Stradbroke, Fressingfield, Peasenhall and Earl Soham. It is only necessary to turn the pages of William White's *Gazetteer* to see the self-reliance of villages such as these in the mid-nineteenth century, and the many goods and services which they offered to those living in surrounding villages and hamlets.

### The Hamlets

Related in their turn to the villages were the hamlets. It has not, perhaps, been sufficiently remarked that Suffolk – in common with many another – is a county of hamlets. Three kinds of hamlets can be identified: 1) the small community linked with the main village; 2) the group of hamlets which take the place of a village; 3) the isolated hamlet (Figure 6). The first occurs most frequently, and in both parts of Suffolk alike; Hartest has Mile End, Cross Green and Hartest Hill, all within less than three-quarters of a mile, and Hoxne has Green Street, Cross Street and Heckfield Green. The second group produces those rambling settlements with church and hall – or house of consequence – at one end, and, as at Wickhambrook, little clusters of dwellings with pretty names; Wickham Street, Malting End, Mole Hill, Attleton Green, Thorns, Cutt Bush, Boyden End, Meeting Green and Coltsfoot Green. Chevington is another example, with hall and church about half a mile south called Tan Office Green, but no distinct village as such. Edwardstone and Groton, north of Boxford are two further instances, in complete contrast to the compact nucleated villages of Monks Eleigh, Chelsworth and Boxford a little further north. Isolated hamlets of the third group are to be found everywhere, and it is these that can easily be mistaken from a distance for those single farmhouses which dot the Suffolk landscape; a tall plastered gable-end seen across the fields on a summer day, may well turn out to be only one of a group partly screened by trees.

These hamlets are extremely numerous. I have estimated that there are one or more attached to at least 150 villages in Suffolk, and that the total number of named hamlets exceeds 400 – not far short of the total number of villages in the county. They are obviously 'functional' in origin, those called *Green* – by far the most usual name – having to do, as already suggested, with the pasturing and security of animals. Only the trained eye may be able to discover the whereabouts of the original 'Green', since the majority have been enclosed and often built over.[1] The most common state of affairs is to find the hamlet consisting of one or two farmhouses with outbuildings, and perhaps a few cottages; occasionally a chapel, but seldom a church. The working hamlet was thus a small agricultural unit. After *Green* the most usual name is *Street,* but there is a wide variety which includes such descriptive terminations as Row, End, Gate, Hall, Tye (usually in the west and centre of Suffolk), Corner, Place, Ford, Cross, Heath, Bottom, Common and, more rarely, Watering, Moor, Boot and Stocks.

'Isolation' is a very relative term in what for a long time must have been a fairly thickly populated countryside. It must be taken to mean physical detachment from the nearest settlement. Excluding those farmhouses that are grouped in hamlets, there are still a prodigious number along roads of all types, not to mention those that lie well off the beaten track away across fields and perhaps on the edge of woodlands. Great Wilsey Farm (688 463), for one example, is about three-quarters of a mile from the hamlet of Little Wratting reached only by a long farm-road, or Mutford Hall, for another example, is again about three-quarters of a mile outside the village and half a mile off the nearest road. These buildings, in brick, or more often in plaster with brightly coloured walls surrounded by an assortment of farm buildings – roofs thatched or frequently pantiled (and, it must be added, now often cement-asbestos sheeted), walls tarred-weatherboarding or brick – usually backed

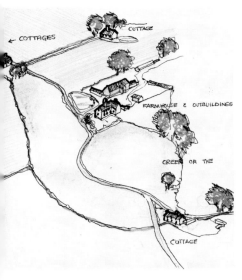

*Figure 6: Sketch of a Suffolk hamlet.*

1 *The Suffolk Landscape* by David Dymond; see pages 29-30 on Greens and Tyes. The same writer praises the value of Hodkinson's map of Suffolk of 1783 for the careful outline it usually gives for each common, and adds 'When the boundaries of ancient commons can still be identified (after about 150 years of enclosure), then they are among the most precious features in our landscape . . . '. cf. Introduction to the publication of Hodkinson's Map by the Suffolk Records Society, 1972.

by at least a substantial clump of trees, give to Suffolk one of its most distinctive features — that of a friendly, peopled landscape.

There are many Halls in Suffolk. Working off the 2½inch Ordnance Survey, I have counted no less than 584 (although this may well be slightly below the actual total and certainly does not allow for the many that have disappeared), as compared with about 360 in Norfolk. Could it be that these many Suffolk Halls had to do originally with the large number of Anglo-Saxon freemen given in Domesday survey?[1] The word *Hall* came from a common Teutonic source, meaning the residence of a territorial proprietor, a baronial or squire's hall. Related to the theory already noted that land enclosure in many parts of Suffolk began early, making holdings available to individual freemen, and there is a possible explanation for the exceptional number of Halls in the county. A further point to emerge from this study is the high proportion that are isolated. About two-thirds of the total lie away from villages and hamlets, occupying remote sites within their own lands. Such a significant number of isolated Halls seemed worth recording, and an attempt has been made to compile a list of these houses by name and map reference (see Appendix i).

**Churches adjoining isolated halls**

A further aspect of the same theory would be the provision of sites for the building of churches by the Anglo-Saxon landowners after conversion to Christianity. I was also very struck by the discovery of a large number of churches built on sites closely adjoining isolated Halls (Plate 4), and made a list of these with an approximate total of 100 (see Section 7, Appendix ii). This seemed to tally with the traditionally leading part played by the lord of the manor as patron of the local church, and, together with the great convenience of having the place of worship on the doorstep, would easily account for the existence of these churches next to manorial Halls. There are plenty of sites where, because the Hall was close to the village, the church was not inconveniently situated for the rest of the community: obvious examples are at Great Thurlow, Lidgate, Great Finborough and Brandeston. It must never be forgotten that the church played a much more important part in everyday life than it does today: attendance at Mass on Sundays, Feast Days and other Holy Days of Obligation was as much a duty of the faithful Christian as regular reception of the Sacraments, and to have the parish church close at hand would mean a great deal to any community.

*Plate 4: Sotterley Hall and the church built near the isolated Hall site after a drawing by H. Davy.*

It is to be expected that many of these churches would be found inside emparked estates, in common with a very general English tradition; but, in fact, this is not the case in Suffolk. There are only 28 examples out of a total of 100, although in the interesting case of Badley only vestiges of the original estate remain. One is tempted to think that one explanation at least is in the thrifty, hardworking, tradition of Suffolk landowners and farmers,[2] to many of whom farmland would have been more valuable than parkland.

1 'With no less than 7460, Suffolk had well over half the total recorded for the rest of England'. Norman Scarfe, op. cit., p. 150. It will not be overlooked that isolated Halls do not constitute the whole number of isolated dwellings, for there are many farms not going under the name of 'Hall' that are also indicated. By whatever name, most of these must have originated in the holdings of freemen.

2 Interesting comment on this point occurs in Alan Everitt's *Suffolk and the Great Rebellion* (1960. Suffolk Record Society) pp. 17 and 18. 'Enterprise was not confined to mercantile families in the towns, however; it was hardly less prevalent among the gentry themselves. All five brothers of Sir Thomas Barnardiston of Kedington were merchants: Nathaniel, Samuel, and Arthur in London, and Pelatia and William in Turkey. There can have been few families without close commercial connections, and in the agricultural exploration of their estates Suffolk landowners were as ardent as any.' This was, of course, Suffolk in the mid-seventeenth century.

*Plate 5: Moat at Bedingfield Hall – one of the many moats in Suffolk associated with a Hall.*

**Moated Sites**

Many of the building sites under discussion were moated, and the precise significance of the moat in relation to domestic buildings has still to be established.

The word *moat* is Middle English (c.1150-c.1450) but the origins of the moat are lost in antiquity. P.G.M. Dickinson, F.S.A., who was a *'moat-man',* would make only the guarded statement: 'Moats were placed round houses as a measure of protection but as, so far, no authoritative study of them has ever been written, their date is open to question.'[1] He added that it might be taken that many of them were thirteenth century, and this is confirmed by Stanley West from the evidence of the comparatively little excavation of moats undertaken in Suffolk. The fact remains that this is one of the most heavily moated of the English counties, the moats associated usually with buildings. There is a neglected subject here of intense local interest awaiting systematic survey.[2] The minimum constituent width of a moat has been agreed as fifteen feet, that it should contain an island or islands, and either has once held or still holds, water. The greatest concentration, of course, occurs in the Suffolk clay-belt, where I estimate, working entirely off the 2½ inch O.S. First Series, that there are at least 568 moated sites, and of these nearly two hundred are associated with a Hall (see Plate 5), either past or present: this is based on name, but there are, in addition, the castles, rectories, farms and houses by many other names – not to mention the sites shown simply as 'Moat' with no further qualification.

In the hope of promoting further interest, I am including in the Main Appendices the moated sites of Suffolk in the form of a list with map references (see Section 7, Appendix iii).

1 *Suffolk* in *The Little Guide Series*, p.34.
2 It is fortunate that the whole subject is now being given attention by the Moated Sites Research Group, of which the Secretary is Alan Aberg, M.A., F.S.A., of the Department of Extra-Mural Studies, Leeds University. The publication of a book on Moats is forthcoming.

27

# APPENDIX A

## Buildings during the Roman Occupation

*by Elizabeth Owles, B.A., F.S.A.*

Virtually nothing is known of the dwellings of the mass of the population of Suffolk during the Roman occupation. There seem to have been no walled towns in the County with public buildings, and regular street patterns, only sprawling, untidy settlements whose occupants were engaged in pottery making and metal working as well as agriculture. In 1973 considerable areas were excavated by the Department of the Environment across two of these settlements, Hacheston and Coddenham, in advance of road works, but the flimsy dwellings of the inhabitants had been almost entirely destroyed by the plough. At Hacheston an irregular ditch was interpreted by the excavator, Thomas Blagg, as the eaves-drip trench encircling an oval hut of some 5m by 4m. Only three post holes could be detected but it must have differed little from huts of pre-Roman date. Nearby, two areas free of the thickly clustering rubbish pits and again containing post holes, suggested buildings 12m by 5.5m and 9.5m by 7.5m respectively, which were at least rectangular. A roughly rectangular clay floor 3.2m by 2.8m with a central hearth may well have been a workshop. This was certainly the case with a similar though smaller, floor excavated by the writer in 1966 on the west of the A12. This had stone wall footings on three sides and was associated with pewter slag. In 1974 further excavations revealed a series of substantial post holes possibly a barn. At Coddenham also a portion of a timber structure was uncovered but again it was insufficient to ascertain its nature and extent. Another building with clay floor and sill beam construction is interesting in that it overlay pre-Roman huts. The villas at Park Street near St. Albans and Lockleys near Welwyn both overlay Iron Age huts but this is the first example from Suffolk.

This building can probably be classed as a villa: these can range from a small farmhouse to the country mansion of the local aristocracy. Romano-British villas are of two main categories. Firstly the timber aisled structure of the type used for large buildings, domestic and public from classical to mediaeval times. This was subdivided by partition walls and could combine the functions of house, byre and barn, a custom which continued on the Continent until recent times. The most sophisticated form consisted of a range of rooms, often linked by a corridor which could extend round a courtyard. The walls were generally timber framed with infilling of clay daub, standing on stone footings. The roofs were covered with flat tiles 33cm by 24cm, with upturned flanges, the joint was sealed by other tiles which resembled a drainpipe sliced longitudinally. Unexpectedly the Whitton Villa and the Stonham Aspall bath house produced a single diamond shaped slate. The windows were made of opaque green glass mortared into their frames. From the Hadleigh bath house came a diamond shaped lead object 8 centimetres long with a central perforation, this would be placed diagonally across the junction of a window grill; these grills may have held the glass or have served to exclude burglars. Walls were mostly covered with painted plaster. At Stanton Chair the design was elaborate and gaudy, at Stonham Aspall it consisted of a simple red lattice on a white ground, the door jambs being a plain Pompeian red; when the baths were redecorated the identical pattern was used again. At Capel St. Mary numerous tesserae less than one centimetre square were found made of red samian pottery, and blue, green and white glass, while three were enriched with gold foil. 100 yards

*Plate 6: Site of Roman villa at Lidgate.*

from the villa were more tesserae together with the glass cakes from which they were cut. This must have been a workshop of an itinerant craftsman from which it may be presumed that the tesserae came, not from some portable object,but from a wall mosaic like those in the 5th-8th century churches at Ravenna. This find is almost unique for Britain and it is tragic that the site was built over virtually unexcavated. Floors could be of beaten earth, of mosaics, tiles or *opus signinum,* a hard cement containing fragments of tile which gave it a distinctive pink colour. Mosaics are rare in Suffolk and mostly consist of coarse red tesserae. Only one of any quality has survived, that found in 1857 at Whitton and moved to Ipswich Museum; it consists of concentric patterned bands in red, grey and white. In general the rooms must have been heated by portable charcoal braziers, almost all the hypocausts seem to have belonged to bath suites.

Only one Suffolk villa, that at Exning, has been completely excavated (Figures 7 and 8). Here it was possible to trace the increasing prosperity and sophistication of the owner. A semi-circular hut of the late first century was succeeded by a timber aisled hall or barn dwelling 32m by 5.5m. This was gradually improved during the second century. The timber posts of the aisle were replaced by a flint wall, internal partitions were constructed, decorated with multicoloured panels on a yellow ground, and a bath house was added on to the north end. In the third century extensive rebuilding took place, a room was added at the south end boasting a mosaic pavement composed of coarse red tesserae and another room heated by a hypocaust. The Exning villa is the only one of aisled construction so far discovered in Suffolk, all the others fall into the second category.

Paradoxically the only villa in Suffolk of the second type, where the complete plan is known, is a site which has never been excavated: this is Lidgate where the wall footings are visible as crop marks. It is of orthodox winged corridor type some 51.8 metres long, standing with a buttressed barn in a rectangular enclosure (Plate 6). The villa at Redcastle Farm, Pakenham, was of the double winged type though lacking the refinement of a corridor; only half the building was excavated (Figure 9). The *triclinium,* or dining room, was apsidal and had possessed a mosaic pavement described in 1776 when it was first uncovered as 'of great beauty'. Unfortunately it was left open and damaged by cows and subsequent ploughing had completely destroyed it by 1953 when it was excavated by Ray Inskeep. The other rooms seem to have had earthen floors presumably covered by matting, though most had glazed windows and painted wall plaster. Fragments of box tile indicated the presence of a hypocaust but none existed in the area excavated. Two rooms were subsequently added to the north of the *triclinium* and presumably another pair to the west. Here again the site was occupied by a flimsy building which seems to date from the late first century shortly after the Roman conquest.

The villa at Stanton Chair seems to have been a large building of the courtyard type but one wing only was excavated. At the north-east end of this was a detached bath house, possibly stone built throughout, consisting of two hot rooms, an unheated dressing room and latrine. In the north-west corner were two apsidal rooms, evidently also baths since one had a lead waste pipe. These and the adjoining rooms all had floors of *opus signinum.* Between these two blocks was an aisled timber building containing corn drying kilns and metal working hearths.

Practically nothing is known of the other large Suffolk villa at Castle Hill, Whitton, two coarse tessell dated pavements were uncovered in 1932, and some disconnected walls. At Town House Farm, Hadleigh, a hypocaust was excavated in 1951 and at Ixworth a large heated room and three small unheated ones in 1877, both probably bath suites, possibly detached buildings to minimise the risk of fire. Two very small detached bath houses have been excavated by the writer, both probably belonging to timber buildings since no trace of rubble could be detected nearby. That at Stonham Aspall consisted of a heated room, a dressing room, both 3m by 2.4m, and two plunge baths, one 1.5m by 1m, the other even smaller. The bath house at Farnham consisted of a single cruciform room 5.5m square. It had been almost completely robbed but had been constructed of Coralline Crag. These two tiny buildings could be described as the last ripple of Roman civilisation on the fringes of the Empire.

In fact, Suffolk buildings in general make the County seem somewhat

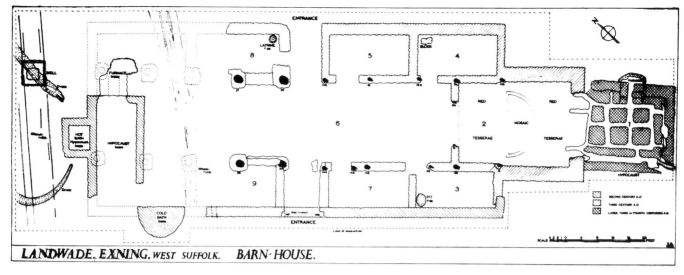

LANDWADE. EXNING. WEST SUFFOLK.   BARN·HOUSE.

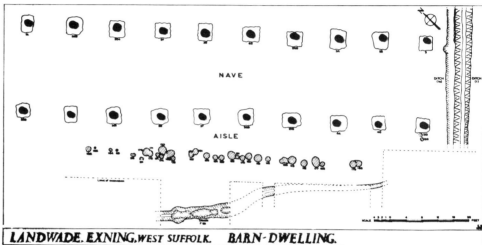

Figures 7 and 8: Drawings of the excavated Roman villa at Exning.

LANDWADE. EXNING. WEST SUFFOLK.   BARN·DWELLING.

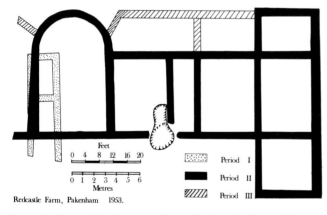

Figure 9: Plan of the Roman villa at Redcastle Farm, Pakenham.

impoverished compared with other parts of lowland Britain during the Roman occupation. This may be due, as Rainbird Clarke suggested, to savage reprisals after Boudicca's rebellion but the glass tesserae from Capel St. Mary and the Mildenhall treasure make it possible that it is due rather to lack of excavation. The new Suffolk Archaeological Unit may transform the picture in the course of the next few years.

Bibliography:
Icklingham papers, H. Prigg (1901) p.72-75. Castle Hill, Whitton, P.S.I.A. vol. XXI (1933) pp.1-23. Stonham Aspall, P.S.I.A. vol. XXX (1966) pp.221-251. Stanton Chair; Town House Farm, Hadleigh; Redcastle Farm, Pakenham; Exning and Farnham: unpublished notes and plans in Ipswich Museum. Plan of Stanton Chair, East Anglia, Rainbird Clarke (1960) p.20 Antiquity: Sept. 1971 XLV p.224.
Acknowledgements: My thanks are due to Thomas Blagg and Robert Mowat for information on the excavation at Hacheston and to Ray Inskeep and Ernest Greenfield who also supplied information on the Pakenham and Exning villas and gave permission to publish their plans in advance of publication.

# APPENDIX B

# The Anglo-Saxon village at West Stow

*by Stanley W. West, M.A., A.M.A., F.S.A.*

The excavation of the West Stow site had provided the most complete evidence so far for a settlement of the pagan Saxon period in Britain. The great value of the excavation is that we now have a fairly complete plan of the settlement and much new information concerning the structures, the artifacts, the economy and the social organisation of the settlement, which began before 400 A.D. while the Roman administration was still effective and ended with the abandonment of the settlement about 600-650 A.D. It would appear that a number of family groups were involved in the settlement and that these are recognisable in the grouping of the structures. Five or six 'halls' are strung out over the site, each associated with a number of smaller huts. The hall was the focal point of Anglo-Saxon life; the smaller huts were the workshops, weaving sheds, store houses and the sleeping quarters of the women and children.

All the buildings were constructed of wood and the only traces that remain for the archaeologist to interpret are the dark fillings of the post-holes and, occasionally, the charred remains of timbers when a building was destroyed by fire. The post-hole settings for the 'halls' show a simple rectangular outline, 30-35 feet long with large posts set fairly close together. With a central hearth and a door set in the south side, these form part of a long tradition of such buildings on the continent, where in fact they often incorporate another element of a cattle byre at one end. In terms of understanding these structures above ground however, there are considerable problems. The weak corners suggest gable ends and the strength of the building in the long walls, but the close packed posts, often irregularly placed, make it difficult to see how a wall plate could be attached and the necessary tie beams fitted. Buildings of this kind are the subject of a considerable debate at this time and details of their construction far from clear.

The smaller huts are recognisable as having a roughly rectangular or oval pit, about 12 feet long cut into the ground, with post-holes at each end. Because the pit is such an obvious feature, these buildings have been considered as 'sunken huts' or 'Grubenhäuser' and are normally reconstructed as a simple bivouac over the pit, with the living floor below ground level. The simplicity of such a structure is, however, far outweighed by other problems that such a reconstruction produces; of entry into the pit, of flooding and general dampness and of the decay and collapse of the walls of the pit itself. The evidence from West Stow has led to an entirely different interpretation of these structures. Two examples were found that had been burnt down accidentally and the charred timbers that remained showed that there have been both floor planks and wall planks. Three other huts had internal hearths on clay bases and two, overlapping the edges of the pit, must have been constructed on a wooden floor which had extended over the pit. With this evidence the unsatisfactory 'sunken hut' interpretation can be replaced with a more practical and convenient building in which the pit is floored over with stout planks, walls are established beyond the edges of the pit and the whole having a thatched roof dependant upon a ridge pole, purlins and tie beams (see Figures 10 and 11).

In 1973 the logical development of archaeological interpretation took place; that is, that the theories were put to the practical test. Although this is an expensive and time consuming exercise, there is great value in this approach, not only for the archaeologist but also as a dramatic, visual piece of 'living history'. The reconstructions at West Stow have been kept to the lowest possible level of wood-working technology to avoid unnecessary refinements; it is reasonable to suppose that a people with a long tradition of wood-working, for both houses and

*The first pair of reconstructed village houses, 1974.*

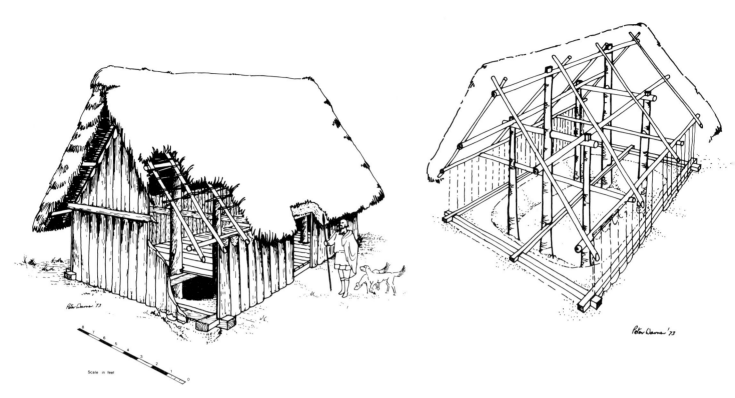

*Figures 10 and 11 show the reconstruction of a six-post house on the site of the Anglo-Saxon village at West Stow.*

boats, might be expected to have used squared timbers and close fitting planks of a more sophisticated kind than will be seen in the reconstructions now on the site.

The basic post-hole pattern of the so-called 'Grubenhäuser' consists of a central post at each end, with or without two secondary posts. Using the evidence of the two burnt huts, a wall height of about six feet and a thatch angle of not less than 45° can be used to arrive at the height of the ridge pole between the two central posts. A suspended floor would require a joist between the ridge posts and substantial support at ground level beyond the limits of the pit. Tie beams at the level of the eaves can be supported by the secondary posts, which, if taken right up to the roof, can support a further purlin at a point midway along the rafters. A lower purlin above the ties at eave level supports not only the lower ends of the rafters, but also the upper ends of the wall planks. In this way the walls are non load bearing and are simply set into a trench beside the outer floor joists and lashed to the lower purlin. The whole weight of the roof structure is thus borne upon the purlins and ties and the secondary posts.

In the reconstruction undertaken no nails or pegs were used, mortice and tenon joints only at the upper ends of the ridge and secondary posts and simple half-laps elsewhere. All the major timbers, the floor and the walls were of unseasoned oak; ash poles were used for the rafters and hazel for the woven base of the thatch, to accord with evidence from the burnt huts. The appearance of the building thus reconstructed is of a solid, rectangular, thatched house, twenty feet long internally, much more spacious and lighter than the bivouac type previously suggested. The entire floor space is usable and the pit under the floor could be used for storage or, in the case of the very shallow examples, merely be an air space both for insulation and the reduction of rot.

Several buildings have already been erected at West Stow. One, the traditional interpretation as a bivouac type, to compare and contrast with the second which is the new form. Eventually it is hoped to reconstruct a Hall and to recreate on the original site a living experiment in history which, based upon the archaeology of the period and employing only those tools and techniques available to the Anglo-Saxons will add immeasurably to a period of our history in which lies the roots of English village life and rural society.

Bibliography: *Interim report in Mediaeval Archaeology:* Vol. 13, 1969, pp. 1-20.
Acknowledgements: The reconstructions were undertaken by the West Stow Environmental Archaeology Group, based in Cambridge with financial aid from the Borough of Bury St. Edmunds on whose land the site is situated, Anglia Television and other donors, together with much information and advice from local craftsmen. The drawings of the re-construction of a six-post house were done by Peter Warner, B.A.

# Commoditie
## the planning of houses

To understand the planning of houses we need to understand the people for whom they were built, their place in society, their occupations and daily routine, and their ways of dressing, cooking, eating and sleeping. The ideas behind planning are those of 'commoditie' — or function — and the idea behind function is that of relationships; a building is said to work well when the several parts are related to the needs of the occupants — in a word, if it satisfies requirements it is *functional.* But needs change, and the special interest of planning lies in the way the traditional arrangement of houses was adapted to meet changing needs. These changes can only be understood through the causes by which they were prompted, and their consequences need to be observed in structure and design, as well as in planning. In this introductory survey of house planning the endeavour has always been to keep the human and sociological aspects in mind, and where this fails it is probably because too little is known about the people concerned.

*Evidence from Archaeology*

A certain amount can be deduced from surviving structures, domestic artifacts and the like, and modern archaeology has been notably quickened by a sense of history, and the wish to make the past *live*.[1] We now have a more vivid insight into the *modus vivendi* of, say, Iron Age farmers because of the comprehensive approach of schemes such as the Butser ancient farm project (dating to about 300 BC) being undertaken in Hampshire. Not the least fascinating aspect of the Anglo-Saxon village project at West Stow is the intention to recreate the life of the community who built and occupied these halls and houses: this would include crop husbandry; ploughing with oxen; making pottery; weaving hand-spun wool on wooden looms and using locally available plant dyes; basketry; woodwork and ironwork.

East Anglia from the early dates of pre-history was a densely wooded area with a succession of inhabitants possibly from the Eolithic, certainly from Palaeolithic times. We have also to remember that all through recorded history there has been a steady coming and going across the North Sea, and recent dating techniques suggest that the first settled agriculturalists were arriving in Britain circa 4000 BC.

Timber being plentiful, the most economical material for building was ready to hand, and it requires no effort of imagination to see the prototype of the Suffolk village in the timber-hutted settlements of the early people. But timber is a relatively snort-lived material, and the dwellings of these distant periods have disappeared almost without trace: occasionally a few relics may be uncovered indicating where the posts had been fixed and the blackened traces of a hearth, and, with good fortune, some domestic hardware. It is too early yet to talk about 'planning', but wherever there was a dwelling the nucleus of planning was there.

## EARLY HALLS AND HOUSES

Most of the Anglo-Saxon village dwellings are likely to have been small, and there is little doubt that the meanest cottages were mere hovels in which lived the serfs and villeins. Documentary evidence shows that houses would reflect social status, the hall of the lord being the largest and doubtless surrounded by a complex of outbuildings, and the homes of the freemen somewhere between the highest and lowest.

*The Hall*

The hall was evidently a place for communal gathering, eating and sleeping, and from a description of a residence in the Saxon Chronicles 787 – 1001 A.D.,[1], there were various other buildings in the vicinity: 'The chief building was the hall (*heall*) with the other apartments round it, the whole surrounded by a rampart of earth (*weall*) constituting a burgh (*burh*). The gate (*geat*) was an opening in the *weall*, but the entrance to any of the buildings within was called a door (*duru*).' This suggests a defensive settlement with a hall surrounded by smaller buildings, one of which would be the *bur* or ladies' sleeping-chamber — later to become the 'bower' or

1 Students of regional building in East Anglia will find relevant material, *inter alia* in the volumes published by the Norfolk and Norwich Archaeological Society, and the Proceedings of the Suffolk Institute of Archaeology. There have been many studies of early building sites and settlements.
2 Quoted by Edmund McClure in *British Place Names in their Historical Setting,* S.P.C.K., 1910, page 195.

*Figure 12: Royal hall of the Saga Period (from a conjectural reconstruction by Prof. Dr. Werner Radig).*

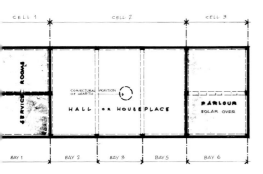

*Figure 13: Mediaeval houseplan showing bays and relation of cells within the building.*

1 cf. *Saxon Rendlesham* — Some preliminary considerations, by R.L.S. Bruce-Mitford, F.S.A. Proceedings S.I.A., Vol. XXIV, Part 3, 1948, page 239. He points out that the features of a seventh century Saxon hall, so far as anything is known about them, were taken almost entirely from the contemporary descriptions in Beowulf, and have been described by R.H. Hodgkin in his *History of the Anglo-Saxons*.
2 cf. *Norman Domestic Architecture*, a paper by Margaret Wood.
3 Suffolk Domesday (pub. Bury St. Edmunds, 1889) Vol. I, page 20.
4 The source, presumably, of the conventional — and somewhat disparaging — reference to the 'one-horse farm'.

'solar' of the mediaeval house — and others which would doubtless include kitchen, stores, and the quarters of the un-free. (In a later period, minor buildings would still be contained within the walls of the bailey of Norman fortresses.) There would be good reason for keeping wooden buildings apart from one another on account of the fire risk, which — with no chimneys or flues to collect smoke and sparks from fires on open hearths — must have been a constant hazard. If a single building went alight it would be possible to evacuate the occupants and beat down the structure before adjoining buildings caught fire.

It is probably reasonable to doubt whether, in Suffolk, the usual Anglo-Saxon hall was ever more than a strongly-carpentered but plain building; although at least one exception to this would have been the royal hall at Rendlesham. This could have been a large timber construction, reminiscent of a great mediaeval barn, but no doubt hung with patterned textiles or cloth of gold, the walls decked with shields and weapons, the gables carved and decorated. In addition to the hall itself, there would be in all probability a withdrawing room or ladies' bower, and some lesser buildings.[1] (See Figure 12.)

Thus we begin to form a picture of the early halls of Suffolk as built of timber and put together with upright posts and trussed-raftered roofs, of sizes varying with the degree of importance of the owners. The roofs would be either thatched, or tiled with wooden shingles, and the hearths usually on the floor in the centre, with apertures in the roof gables for the smoke to get out. Around the halls would be various out-buildings with varying degrees of dignity according to their function; later, the Christian church might be added, and around the church would grow up a feudal and parochial community. These would be the kind of settlements in the south-east of England which the Normans would find when they expropriated the Saxon thegns.

If we accept the principle of continuity, at least from the early Saxon period, there would seem to be every likelihood that the Normans both occupied the houses of displaced owners and built similar timber houses for themselves on new or existing sites. Although we are fortunate to have in Suffolk one of the 41 extant examples of Norman domestic architecture in England[2] — Moyses Hall, Bury St. Edmunds (c.1180) — little is known generally about Norman town or country houses as distinct from castles. There is evidence of timber framed aisled halls in the late twelfth century, and it would be reasonable to suppose that this was one of the types used by the Normans: others must remain hypothetical until further archaeological evidence can close the gap. We know for certain that the Normans lived in buildings called Halls, for these are frequently referred to in Domesday Book:[3] the following shows the rather indirect way dwellings are mentioned in the Survey, as though an adjunct in a list of livestock:-

| | |
|---|---|
| Cornard: Land of Earl Morchar's Mother | '. . . Always 4 horses at the Hall, and 18 beasts, and 80 hogs.' |
| Assington: Ranulph Peverell, | '. . . Then 6 horses at the Hall.' |
| Polstead: Suane of Essex, | '. . . Now 8 horses at the Hall.'[4] |

We can search the present parishes of both Great and Little Cornard in vain for any trace of Cornard Hall; although there *are* several moated sites and the two halls of Costens and Abbas. At Assington and Polstead we are perhaps on safer ground in attributing to the new Norman owners the sites of the present halls, although still much in need of archaeological guidance.

By the end of the twelfth century timber aisled-halls have been identified at Brome, as well as the first floor hall houses of masonry construction at Bury St. Edmunds and Framlingham. These two different ways of building are to be the main lines of future development and suggest a continuity that will lead, on the one side, through the later aisled-halls to the fully developed timber-framed manor house, and, on the other, through Little Wenham to the brick mansions of the early sixteenth century.

A typology of plan types should be possible at some point along both lines but scarcely until the end of the mediaeval period, because of slow growth and insufficient building evidence. The datum-line could probably be drawn conveniently at, or about, 1535, when the monasteries and religious houses of Suffolk were granted to laymen: this, for practical purposes, was the end of the mediaeval world and the beginning of a new and ambitious activity in domestic architecture.

Before attempting such a typology it is worth taking stock of some of the main features of mediaeval house-planning, viz:-

> Bay and cell system
> Aisled hall
> First floor hall
> Ground floor hall
> Screens-passage
> Chamber over hall

## BAY AND CELL SYSTEM

The word *bay* belongs to the Middle English period (c.1150-1450), and it used to be said[1] that mediaeval timber buildings normally were built in bays or half-bays, '. . . the bay being the space required to stable a yoke of Oxen – about 16½ft or one rod . . .'. Now the *rod* is another term for the *pole*, and the pole was the long wooden shaft 'fitted to the fore-carriage of a vehicle and attached to the yokes or collars of the draught animals' (cf. *The Shorter O.E.D. on Historical Principles)*. The late Middle English *perch* has the same meaning, and all three terms refer to what had become in the mid-fifteenth century a statutory measure of length – 5½yds or 16ft 6in. (5.025m).[2] The adoption of this form of measurement was doubtless the rationalising of an approximate dimension which had been in use over a long period in Anglo-Saxon – and earlier – building practice. (This is the more likely when it is remembered that in one form of long-house the cattle were housed at one end and the owners at the other.) But the term *bay* gradually ceased to denote a fixed measurement, and is now used to describe any regular space in a building plan between supporting posts, columns or piers.

The word *cell* refers to any single compartment, room, or enclosed space within a building. The mediaeval house plan is essentially the relating of smaller cells to the single large cell of the central hall (Figure 13), the dimensions of the cells being limited by economical timber lengths and span capacities.

*Figure 14: Type of hall house at Twente, Holland, after reconstruction of Dr. J.J. Vriend.*

## AISLED HALL

At an early date in pre-history, builders must have devised the idea of covering a larger space by supporting the roof intermediately on two rows of posts, thus forming a nave and aisles. This aisled hall form was used in Suffolk at the Exning villa during the second century (see Appendix A – Section 2) and this is unlikely to have been an isolated early use. The aisled form is known to have existed in Northern and Central Europe, where it is found in the Danubian culture, and is well-known in the Mediterranean classical period. On the other side of the North Sea the 'hallehuis' appeared in Holland before the Roman Empire, and plans show a marked resemblance to similar East Anglian structures (Figure 14). The plan is one with which we are especially familiar in parish church architecture, and to some extent in barns, where aisled construction alternates with other forms of post and truss. The interior of the Milden Hall barn – probably fifteenth century – shows well-developed carpentry with a trussed frame supporting common rafters: it gives a striking impression of the aisled form with its characteristic high 'nave' and series of bays along each side (Plate 7). Through such structures we can form a very rudimentary idea of the appearance of the halls of our ancestors.[3]

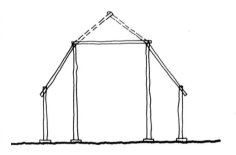

*Figure 15: Type of Scandinavian hall-building, after reconstruction of Dr. J.J. Vriend.*

The sequence of development remains extremely conjectural, and diagrammatic attempts at reconstructing sections and elevations are often so hypothetical as to be of little value: nevertheless some link of continuity must exist between the many structures found in England and on the Continent, and the conventional stages of development are worth recording if merely to show the general plausibility of growth from primitive forms (Figures 15 and 16).

## FIRST FLOOR HALL

Roger Bigod acquired the Framlingham property from Henry I, about 1100, and, according to the historians[4] immediately constructed a wooden dwelling

1 cf. Nathaniel Lloyd in *A History of the English House;* Introduction, page 5.
2 Since writing this, an interesting article by Mr. E.E. Bridges has appeared in the *East Anglian Magazine* (November 1976) on *The Village Pole,* in which the length of the *pole* is said to be 16 feet and to have been derived from actual feet measurement, the pole being kept in the village church.
3 One of the few aisled house forms in Suffolk occurs at Abbas Hall, Great Cornard (see Section 6).
4 *Suffolk* (Little Guides Series) by P.G.M. Dickinson, F.S.A., F.R.Hist.Soc., pages 32 and 33.

*Plate 7: The interior of the fifteenth century Milden Hall Barn.*

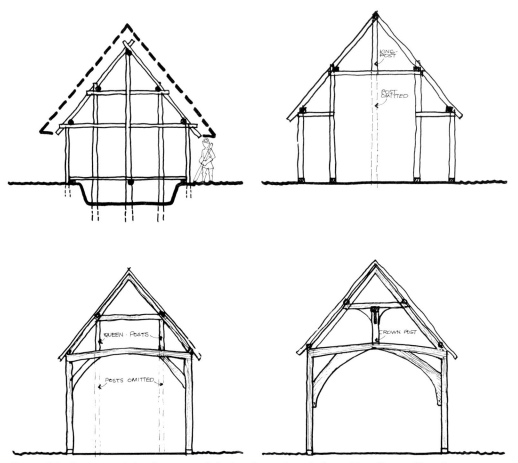

*Figure 16: Conjectural development of timber-framed roofs from West Stow village-house type —
period fifth to thirteenth century.*

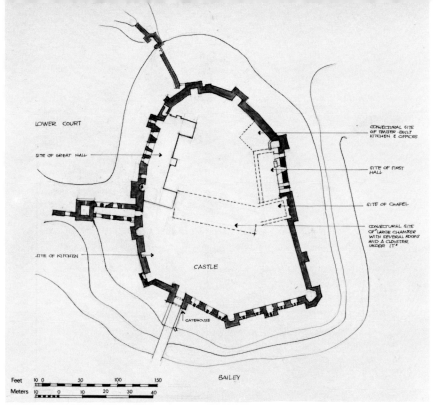

*Figure 17: Plan of Framlingham Castle.*

**Framlingham Castle**

which he protected by a palisade and ditch, with an outer bailey similarly protected on three sides and on the west by an artificial mere: some 40 years later, when the building would probably have become obsolete anyway, his son Hugh, first Earl of Norfolk, built a new complex in stone and timber, of which one of these buildings known — perhaps rather ambiguously — as 'the first Hall' could well have been among the first *two-storey* stone houses to be built in Suffolk, anticipating Moyses Hall, Bury St. Edmunds, by some 20 years (Figure 17).

Two interesting features of this project are: (1) Framlingham, as Raby and Reynolds point out, started as a fortified dwelling-house and only later became a 'castle';[1] (2) Hugh Bigod's complex was ambitious in size and solidity, comprising a two-storey block (N-S) with first floor hall, and a chapel (E-W) built of masonry, with kitchen and offices in timber north of the hall: it was of a size and importance to be compared with, say, Christchurch Castle, Hants, or the somewhat later Stokesay Castle, and, indeed, anticipated that series of fortified manor-houses which were built in England until the fourteenth century. It is only necessary to remember that Earl Roger built a new Great Hall (c.1200), on the opposite side of the courtyard, which could have been twice as large as that of his predecessor, and that this was joined to the chapel by a two-storey range 'containing a large chamber, with several rooms, and a cloyster under it, pulled down in the year of Our Lord 1700'.[2] The castle of today, although impressive is only a husk: at Bungay, Clare, Denham, Eye, Haughley, Ilketshall St. John, Lidgate, Lindsey, Milden and Otley — the remaining motte-and-bailey Castles — only archaeological research can tell us anything of once fortified dwellings.

**Orford Castle**

At Orford Castle (1165-66) only the keep survives, and this is military engineering pure and simple, intended not for the domestic life of an ambitious family but as a garrison stronghold for the King's constable. The planning of services and staircases is extremely ingenious, and the circular hall on the upper floor of the keep must have been handsome enough with its original lofty timber roof, and warmed by huge logs blazing in the great fireplace.

**Moyses Hall, Bury St. Edmunds**

'Moyses Hall' is something of an enigma. There is little doubt that it was built in the late twelfth century and of the same flint rubble with freestone quoins and dressings as used in the Abbey. The plan (Figure 18) consisted of a double compartment structure somewhat over 50ft (15.25m) square, of which only the east compartment at ground floor level survives: on this side there were originally openings on to what was known as Hog Hill, or Beast Market,[3] and on the south on to the Corn Market.

1 *Framlingham Castle* by F.J.E. Raby and P.K. Baillie Reynolds (1959. H.M.S.O.), page 5.
2 Ibid., page 8.
3 cf. *Moyses Hall Museum*, a guide book by A.R. Edwardson, F.S.A., page 1.

37

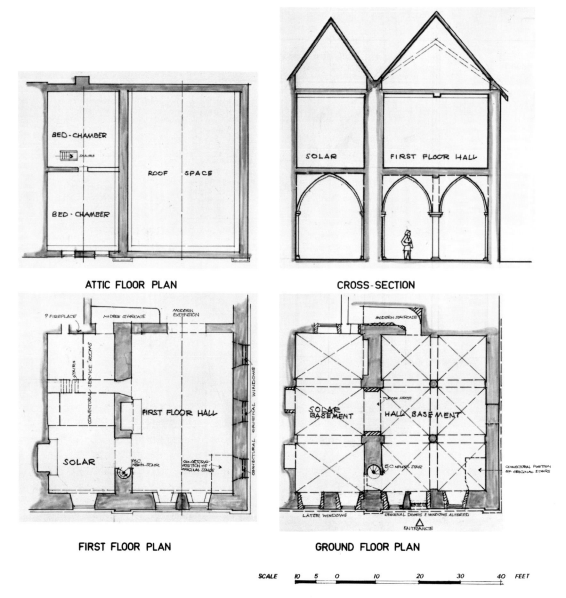

ATTIC FLOOR PLAN

CROSS-SECTION

FIRST FLOOR PLAN

GROUND FLOOR PLAN

SCALE  10  5  0      10      20      30      40   FEET

*Figure 18: Floor plans and cross-section of Moyses Hall, Bury St. Edmunds.*

The probability is that the building was devised by the same master-mason as then working on the Abbey and, certainly, the Barnack stone of the dressings is identical with that used in the Abbey at the same period, which came from a quarry owned, or leased, by Abbot Samson. These various circumstances seem to dispose of the tradition that this was ever a Jew's house or synagogue, and Mr. A.R. Edwardson, the Curator from 1954 to 1974, considered it extremely unlikely that, bearing in mind the attitude of the Monastic Church to the Jews in the twelfth and thirteenth century, the all-powerful Benedictine Abbey would have permitted a Jewish place of worship on this site.[1] The likelihood is that the building had connections with the Abbey, and passed eventually into the hands of local merchants: Mr. Edwardson thinks that the Jewish quarter of the town could well have been in 'Hethenmannestreete', once part of Hatter Street.

The accommodation at first floor level is that of hall and solar: the hall measured about 8m by 11.5m (26ft by 38ft) and the solar 5m by 11.25m (16ft by 37ft), with windows looking south on to the Corn Market. The kitchen quarters could have been west of the vaulted under-croft, but more probably in an annexe at the rear. There could well have been fireplaces in the thickness of the west walls or these two rooms before the present sixteenth century fireplaces were put in. The notable thing about this building is the storey-heights, which can be seen on the section (Figure 18); the ground floor, in particular, is a good deal more lofty than the usual undercroft of this period: the sad thing is that the restoration by Sir Gilbert Scott in 1858, together with a drab appearance, has almost given Moyses Hall outside the look of a dull Victorian building.

1 In 1956 the Secretary to the late Dr. Brodie, the then Chief Rabbi, called on Mr. Edwardson and agreed not only with the opinion of Frank Haes — who disputed the Synagogue theory in the Jewish Chronicle in 1896 — but also with Mr. Edwardson's own view that this was the result of equating Moyses with Moses in guide books to the town dating back to the early nineteenth century. The name Moyse is still current in Suffolk, as witness the P.O. Telephone Directory.

## Little Wenham Hall

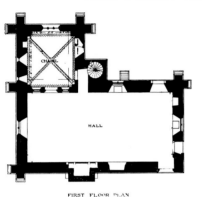

FIRST FLOOR PLAN

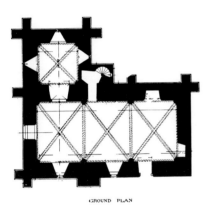

GROUND PLAN

SCALE _____ OF FEET

*Figure 19: Floor plans of Little Wenham Hall.*

1 cf. *The Borough of Bury St. Edmunds* by M.D. Lobel (1935. Oxford).
2 There are references to three stone houses in the Abbey Sacrist's Rental list of 1433/34 edited by M.P. Statham in *The Suffolk Review.*
3 cf. *Little Wenham Hall,* by F.A. Crisp, page 1.
4 These are the building dates attributed by Mr. D. Spittle in a letter to the owners dated September 15th, 1972.
5 I suggest timber-framing solely because these buildings have vanished with so little visible trace; there is perhaps the further point that by referring to the hall and tower only as built of 'lime and stone', it is implied that the annexe was built of other materials, hence probably timber. If correct, the chances are that the 'other rooms' could have been rebuilt more than once between the first build and the Survey of 1512.

We would like to know more of other stone-built town houses. Bury St. Edmunds is one of the relatively few examples of the Benedictine street planning of a walled town, the town plan being designed by Baldwin, a monk of St. Denys and a man of many parts, not only abbot but also physician, who died in 1098. M.D. Lobel[1] refers to Abbot Baldwin's wide experience both in England and on the Continent, and says that 'it will be surprising if his conception of urban life had not been of an advanced nature.' Lobel calculated that there were about 200 houses in the old *burh*, and that by 1087 there was a total of 542. At a later period (i.e. before 1198) we are told in *The Chronicles* of Jocelin of Brakelond that 'the Abbot purchased Stone houses, and assigned them for the use of the schools.'[2] Today the traces of Romanesque Bury, apart from Moyses Hall, are probably to be found only in the 'Norman' gateway, the Abbey ruins, some vaulted cellars and a few other building fragments.

The difficulty in discussing the planning arrangements of Little Wenham Hall is due to uncertainty as to the extent and disposition of other accommodation. This is a matter upon which the experts differ, although the general consensus seems to favour the first floor hall plan (for floor plans see Figure 19). Frederick Crisp who, with his brother George, bought the property in about 1884 (when the church had a tree growing out of it and the castle was used as a seed corn-store, with chickens occupying the ground floor) investigated the documentary evidence with a historian's thoroughness. In his printed guide, he refers to the earliest available description of the Hall in an *Extent of the Manor of Little Wenham* made 28 January 1512.[3] This contains a fairly unambiguous account of the contents of the site and its division into two parts. Part 1 was the inner part, and had 'a hall with a vault of lime and stone', and a tower of the same; and (6) different rooms joined on to the hall comprising kitchen, larder-house with other rooms 'under and above'. Part 2 was the outer part of the site with various farm-buildings and orchards, and 'the church there'. This survey of the property was, according to P.A. Crisp, made by Robert Brewse, the grandson of the first Brewse who acquired the property by marriage c.1440. There is no means of determining the extra accommodation that formed part of the original Little Wenham Hall, of which the building has been said to date from c.1260-8,[4] but, clearly, kitchen, buttery and pantry, and the like, would have been needed, and could have been in the form of a timber-framed annexe similar to that adjoining the 'first hall' at Framlingham Castle.[5] If we take the survey of 1512 to mean literally what it says, then the Tudor kitchen larder-house was at first floor level, with other presumably service-rooms below, and no doubt some sleeping chambers in attic accommodation above. This would only leave the main solar and the garderobe in all probability included in the first floor accommodation. It seems to be generally agreed that the only likely position for an annexe to the main hall is at the south-west angle of the building. The moulded stone string course which surrounds the outside walls just below window-sill level stops abruptly well short of the south-west angle, and again at the first floor door on the south elevation. This would not be conclusive of itself but the walls have the look of being disturbed and there are no angle buttresses at the south-west corner; the plinth is also missing hereabouts. The appearance of two unexplained doorways in the outer walls at first floor level and one at ground floor on the west, with an inscription over it dated 1569, further suggest that this has been the area of the principal alterations.

It is worth considering for a moment the earlier approach to Little Wenham Hall. In the absence of manorial maps, the antiquity of the road shown by Hodskinson in 1783 must remain conjectural, although by local tradition this has always been the old way to the house. It turns north off the Wenham Magna/Capel road for a short distance and then makes straight for the Hall along an avenue lined with clearly delineated trees, in thoroughly Tudor fashion. If this be accepted as the oldest approach, then shortly after crossing the bridge the road forked and one branch swung to the right, ascended a slight rise and then entered the Hall enclosure, presumably through a gateway in the 'fence' — later brick wall. This would be one of the three gates mentioned in the Survey of 1512 as giving access to the first part of the site 'all enclosed within three gates'. Once within the gate there would be the need for a courtyard with space for a vehicle and horsemen to turn round, as well as

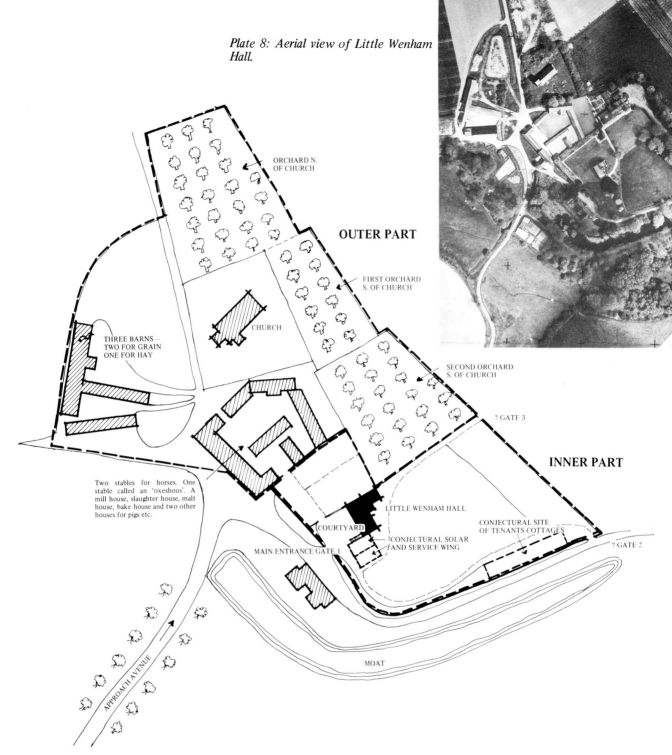

Plate 8: Aerial view of Little Wenham Hall.

ORCHARD N. OF CHURCH

OUTER PART

FIRST ORCHARD S. OF CHURCH

CHURCH

THREE BARNS – TWO FOR GRAIN ONE FOR HAY

SECOND ORCHARD S. OF CHURCH

? GATE 3

INNER PART

Two stables for horses. One stable called an 'oxeshous'. A mill house, slaughter house, malt house, bake house and two other houses for pigs etc.

LITTLE WENHAM HALL

CONJECTURAL SITE OF TENANTS COTTAGES

COURTYARD

CONJECTURAL SOLAR AND SERVICE WING

MAIN ENTRANCE GATE 1

? GATE 2

MOAT

APPROACH AVENUE

Figure 20: Sketch block plan of Little Wenham Hall.

1 cf. *Little Wenham Hall*, op.cit., page 3.
2 This is mentioned by Mr. Spittle in the letter dated September 15th, 1972.

access to stabling. This would be provided by the existing brick gateway between the Hall and the farmbuildings, now blocked up, but conveniently sited in relation to the hypothetical courtyard (Figure 20). An aerial photograph taken by the Department of the Environment on 25 September 1962 seems to suggest the actual location of this entrance area, and the way through to the stables (see Plate 8). There appear also faint traces of what could have been a staircase ascending in a straight flight to the doorway, which F.A. Crisp put as part of the alterations of 1565 (it is on this door that the word *'Vale'* is scratched, and the date 1584).[1] This staircase might have been sheltered by the pitched roof, the outline of which is said to have appeared on an illustration by Twiner and Parker in 1852.[2] If this assumption is correct, then the stairs would have been the main approach to the first floor hall, from which again there would have been access to other accommodation by the existing south door, clearly made long after the first building. (The door below with its pointed arch seems to have been the original.)

**The Mediaeval House Plan**

The mediaeval house develops a virtually ritual plan which remains almost static for about three centuries (Figure 21). Within the hall-house by the thirteenth century there is space for a sequence of functions, from the lower to the higher, in some ways as fixed as in the plan of the parish church. The entrance into the hall is at the 'lower' end, and roughly in the same position as that of the way into the church nave. 'Below' the entrance are the service rooms; buttery, pantry, brewhouse, dairy (the number of rooms depending upon the wealth and importance of the establishment): these will usually be floored over giving storage and, maybe, sleeping places for the lower members of the household. In a position that may vary in different regions between the 'upper' and the 'lower' end is the hearth,[1] the house-fire, where it has been since time immemorial. Above the hearth is the family table, varying from the simplicity of a trestle to the magnificence of a banqueting table, and, in important halls, both table and seating are on a dais. The most eminent seat — be it that of farmer, merchant, knight, noble or king, is, by timeless precedent, in the centre of the dais, and, as if to fix and to emphasize this pre-eminent place, the dais-beam spans the wall behind the table, or, as at Framsden Hall, was projected over the dais by means of the 'overshot' solar, forming a 'canopy of honour' enriched by carved woodwork and, no doubt, by colour. The similarity to the decorated roof over the rood-beam in the parish church cannot fail to be noticed, and is yet another reminder of the *Respublica Christiana* which pervaded mediaeval life.[2] Without pressing the analogy too far, one could reasonably compare chancel and chamber, the former reserved for the priestly office and the latter for the intimate life of the family.

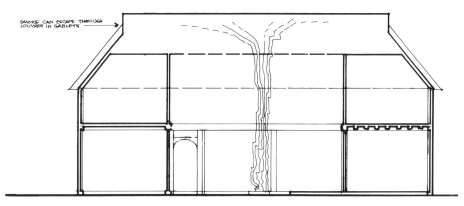

Cross-section on central axis

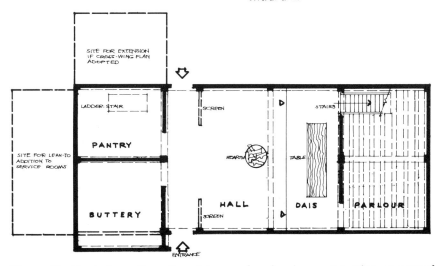

1 It has been claimed that in the south east the hearth was near the lower end of the hall, and in East Anglia towards the upper end, near the parlour. cf. *The Timber-Framed Buildings of Steyning* by H.M. and V.C. Lacey (1974). Introduction, page 14.
2 'All over Europe, there was one Church only. If a man were not baptised into it, he was not a member of society.' ... 'It was the Church which insisted that the poor did not have to fast as much as the rich, and which forbade servile work on Sunday. It was the Church which provided the poor with social services — free food and free hospital treatment. There was, for a long while, no other source of education.' cf. *Age of Faith* by Anne Freemantle and editors of Time-Life Books 1966 (page 12).

*Figure 21: Typical small mediaeval house plan showing cross-section on central axis (top) and the ground floor plan (above).*

*Plate 9: Autumn scene from the Grimani Breviary.*

*Figure 22: Early sixteenth century ladder for access to first floor.*

1 cf. *Framed Buildings of England* by R.T. Mason, page 30. 'The basic plan has normally a two-bay hall with two-storied accommodation at both ends: a parlour with solar above abuts at the high end, and service rooms (buttery and pantry) with a chamber above, at the low end.'
2 cf. *Wool: East Anglia's Golden Fleece* by Nigel Heard, page 64.
3 cf., op. cit., page 140.
4 ditto. Dr. Wood shows a photograph (pl. XXV opp. page 52) of the movable 'standard' at Ruffold Old Hall.

So prestigious was this pattern that even the meanest cote must claim to have its hall, and the irony of this was not lost on Geoffrey Chaucer, who starts the *Nun Priest's Tale* by telling of the narrow cottage where lived a widow, three daughters, three large sows, three cows and a sheep; '. . . full sooty was her bower, and her hall alike'. Small dwellings like this can frequently be seen in the landscape of mediaeval breviaries and books of hours. A good example is in the autumn scene from the Calendar in the Grimani Breviary: a single-storey cottage is on the edge of a cornfield; a peasant-woman stands in the open door at one end; the building is about 3m by 3.5m long (10ft by 12ft) with a height to eaves of probably not more than 2 metres (6ft 6in.); the roof is thatched and has two smoke-escape 'dormers' and what looks like a wicker-work stack poking out of the ridge; the little building has a timber box-frame, and the walls are evidently of wattle and daub, and perhaps whitened. The fact that there is one larger and one smaller 'window' on the side wall suggests two compartments, which by the late fifteenth century would be quite likely (see Plate 9).

The early hall-cottage of Suffolk would have been a similar building containing one simple apartment. Later, it would be found more economical to add extra space in the roof by raising the eaves level a couple of feet or so, producing a 'solar' or sleeping chamber in the roof, reached by a ladder. There is a ladder of this kind at Tudor House, Needham Market, dated 1530 (see Figure 22). With the addition of an 'upper end' parlour this could have been the typical mediaeval home of the small Suffolk farmer in the same period.[1] If there were two service rooms at the lower end, these might be the buttery — where the ale and bread and butter were kept, and the pantry — where would be the bacon and other dry household stores like meal and flour. Reached by a ladder, either inside or outside, was a loft-like apartment over the service rooms, open to the roof, which could be storeroom or another sleeping place. The furniture in the house was of the simplest possible: a trestle table, a few stools, wooden and pottery bowls, plates and cutlery; in the hall of a Suffolk farmhouse would almost certainly have stood also the spinning wheel, for carding, combing and spinning wool would have occupied the spare time of women and children, and helped to eke out the domestic economy.[2] Outside would be the woodstack, and the fire on the central hearth (or in a clay-lined pit) would be kept going for much of the time for cooking and warmth.

## SCREENS-PASSAGE

The entrances to a house are cardinal points in planning, and the 'screens-passage' is of much significance because, eventually, all that is left of the hall will have shrunk into this passage. The mediaeval system is to have a pair of doors opposite each other and as far away as possible from the upper end; these two doors are immediately next to the entrances to the service rooms, and are in a partition screening these rooms from the hall itself (see Figure 21). There are four stages in the development of this system:-

1. The aisled hall plan lends itself to the forming of barriers immediately next to the two outer doors, by filling in the space between the arcade post and the outer wall. The purpose of these barriers is a protection against draughts, and in this way there comes into being the speer truss, 'speer' meaning quite simply 'spur' or barrier. Margaret Wood argues for aisled-hall speer trusses at Little Chesterford and, possibly, Lampetts, both in Essex,[3] but says that most examples occur in 'aisled-hall derivatives.' This seems to be the case in Suffolk also.

2. If the speer truss begins in the thirteenth century in the aisled hall it lasts for another couple of centuries in the ordinary framed house: one of the finest in Suffolk must have been at Framsden Hall, c.1480 (see Figure 23). The derivation from the aisled hall form is suggested in the arrangement of the speer.

3. Screening can occur in two positions: (a) between the 'arcade posts', of the speer truss, where it starts by being movable;[4] and ends by becoming a fixture not unlike the chancel screen of a parish church, (b) the partition that separates the hall from the service rooms, where it is pierced by two and, sometimes, three door openings. At Bricett it is in the latter position with one pointed door

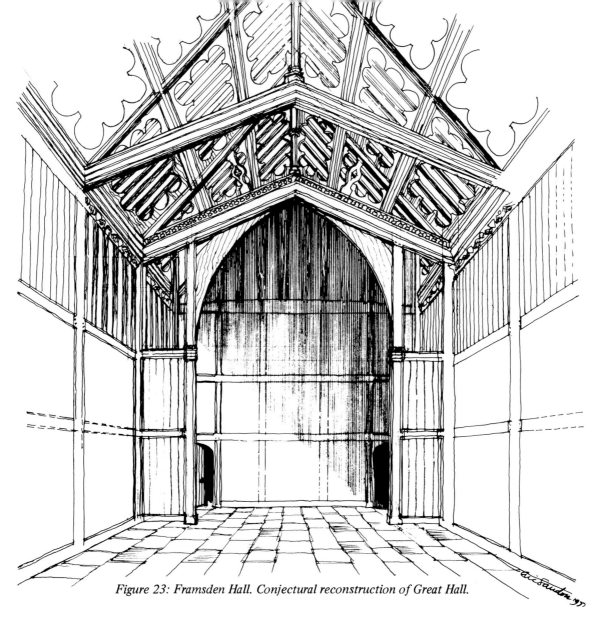

*Figure 23: Framsden Hall. Conjectural reconstruction of Great Hall.*

*Figure 24: Bricett Hall (formerly Great Bricett Priory). The thirteenth century screen.*

43

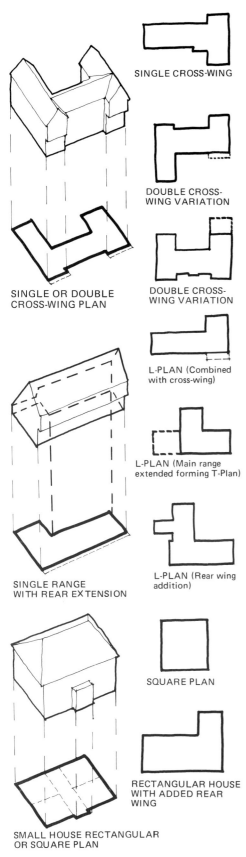

SINGLE CROSS-WING

DOUBLE CROSS-WING VARIATION

SINGLE OR DOUBLE CROSS-WING PLAN

DOUBLE CROSS-WING VARIATION

L-PLAN (Combined with cross-wing)

L-PLAN (Main range extended forming T-Plan)

SINGLE RANGE WITH REAR EXTENSION

L-PLAN (Rear wing addition)

SQUARE PLAN

RECTANGULAR HOUSE WITH ADDED REAR WING

SMALL HOUSE RECTANGULAR OR SQUARE PLAN

*Figure 25: Typology of house plans — small houses.*

1 The reconstitution of the screen and gallery at Hengrave Hall appears to date from early in this century, but gives a very fair idea of the traditional 'minstrel's gallery' over a cross-passage.
2 In Ogilby's drawing (inset in his Map of the Town of Ipswich dated 1674) Thomas Seckford's house in Westgate Street had a pair of towers with domed roofs and weathervanes, one at each end of the main elevation.

surrounded by dog-tooth ornament (see Figure 24). It is the same at Abbas Hall, Great Cornard, and elsewhere in Suffolk there are screens, usually in the speer truss position, as late as the sixteenth century when the hall has already been floored over, as at Langley's Newhouse, Hawkedon.

4. The Gallery appears over the screens-passage, as at Giffords Hall, Stoke-by-Nayland; although it is doubtful whether any of this is original it is in the right place at the lower end of the hall, with outer doors under the gallery opposite each other at both ends.[1]

## CHAMBER OVER HALL

Until the middle of the sixteenth century the high hall dividing the parlours and solars from the service quarters and stores was still the general rule. From the researches of M.W. Barley we learn that in Kent the downgrading of the hall had already begun by 1500, and that by 1570 flooring over was becoming general. For Suffolk, we await the results of similar research into probate Inventories, but my own experience suggests that the chamber-over-hall was happening by at least the beginning of the sixteenth century. If Clopton Hall, Wickhambrook, can be taken as a case in point, both the original hall and large parlours west of it have moulded ceiling beams and joists accepted as having been taken out of the earlier Hall, some little way off, and re-used here. This is interesting, because it would point to floored halls as early as circa 1480-1500. By the middle of the following century, the 'Great Chamber' over the hall was customary and the last appearances of the open hall in a great house must have been at Hengrave (c.1525) and, more surprisingly, at Brome (c.1580). The hall was floored over at Christchurch Mansion, Ipswich, Kentwell Hall, Redgrave Hall and Rushbrooke Hall — both the latter now demolished — and Seckford Hall, Great Bealings, as well as at Little Glemham, Hintlesham, Playford and Melford Hall — here the attic above the flat ceiling seems always to have been one long gallery. The hall remained the largest room of the great house, but it was no longer the focal centre of family life, and within the next hundred years would have become merely an entrance-place where the great staircase might be found, and from which there was access to the main living rooms.

## TYPOLOGY OF HOUSE PLANS

If the hall was, as we have seen, the kernel of the mediaeval house, it lay also at the root of structural planning. The hall was normally rectangular, the length dependent upon need and — to some extent — proportion, and the width governed by the practical limits of the span roof. It is roof span which has governed plan form from early times until this century, when, in spite of theoretical emancipation, the flat-roofed house shape is still related to practical span width. Thus the rectangular range suited to economical roofing is perhaps the most constant element in house planning.

It will be found that, although there are many variations in detail, there are remarkably few basic plan forms. The large early-Tudor house plan is an assemblage of rectangles; each rectangle represents a range and in most Suffolk houses this has a single — occasionally a double — pitched roof. These ranges are conjoined in the form of hollow squares, or E-, H- and rectangular U-forms. Apart from these basic shapes, the accenting of the angles of houses with octagons, bays, buttresses or — occasionally — towers[2] are merely incidental features. In the later plan forms the ranges have been consolidated into the mainly square or rectangular block, but can still be identified by the load-bearing spine walls, usually with chimney stacks, which play an important part in the job of supporting the roofs.

The smaller house will, as likely as not, start with a single rectangular range, as in the hall-house. In growing, it will often add a cross-wing, producing the L-plan by simply placing another rectangular range at right-angles to the first. Occasionally the smaller house will emulate the E-, H- or rectangular U-plan of the larger house.

A diagrammatic typology of house plans will clarify most of these points (see Figures 25 and 25a). Although many plan types are repeated, there is a division between Large and Small Houses. This division is accepted on the diagrams, in which basic plan types are associated with each group, together with variations.

## Quadrangular

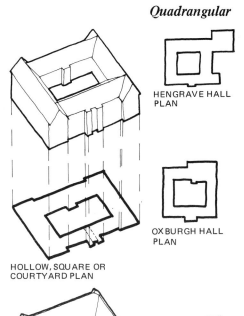

HENGRAVE HALL PLAN

HOLLOW, SQUARE OR COURTYARD PLAN

OXBURGH HALL PLAN

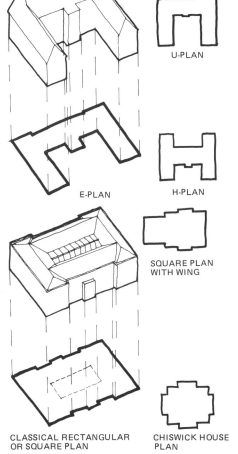

U-PLAN

E-PLAN

H-PLAN

SQUARE PLAN WITH WING

CLASSICAL RECTANGULAR OR SQUARE PLAN

CHISWICK HOUSE PLAN

*Figure 25a: Typology of house plans — large houses*

1 Sir John Summerson makes the point that the royal visits, so conspicuous a feature of Queen Elizabeth I's reign, dictated the continuation of the old courtyard plan in large country houses, where the wings provided the 'lodgings' required for persons of quality. (The 'lodging' comprised a suite of two or three rooms.) cf. *Architecture in Britain*, op. cit., page 28.
2 Avray Tipping (*English Homes*, Period II, Vol. I, page 202) calls Hengrave *Mediaeval* in plan *Perpendicular* in its details, but entirely *Domestic* in character.

## LARGE HOUSE PLANS

Compact groups of buildings around a hollow square can be traced at least to Roman origins, and have obvious defensive advantages, especially when increased by outworks such as walls, moats or ditches. The *castra* cannot be taken, without further question, as the origin of the quadrangular plan, but buildings planned in this way were evidently most numerous in the troubled centuries following the Norman conquest. The monastery, perhaps partly for the same reason, had adopted a similar plan. The devolution of the monastic plan into the courts and quadrangles of collegiate buildings is fairly obvious, but the influence of this plan on the larger Suffolk manor house is uncertain, and would be difficult — if not impossible — to prove. The fact remains, however, that monasteries such as Clare (figure 26), Great Bricett, Ixworth and Leiston were flourishing in the fourteenth and fifteenth centuries, and must have represented standards of amenity superior to many of the timber-built manor houses of the gentry. Castle building in East Anglia must have ceased well before the end of the fifteenth century, and there can have been few castles in Suffolk which house-builders would have wished to copy.

The system of building compactly round four sides of a square had, however, advantages other than the more obvious one of defence. There was first the possibility of greater economy, and this would have been a consideration for some secular and most religious houses. Furthermore, with a large household — either lay or monastic — the quadrangle plan made for easier management of the establishment, or control of the community. With increasing wealth and civility these earlier advantages might have ceased to influence the large landowner, but the earlier forms would persist for a while in the absence of any clear alternative.[1]

The principles of the domestic quadrangle plan seem to have been nationally consistent, and to recur wherever the grander houses were built on these lines during the reigns of Henry VII and VIII (see Figure 27). The approach was axial, and preceded by outworks in the form of gateways and walled courtyards, as at Melford Hall and Kentwell Hall; and a long straight drive, as at both Helmingham and Kentwell. The visitor approaching the main gatehouse was under surveillance from small cruciform or plain arrow-slit windows and, if pedestrian with acceptable credentials, would be admitted by the porter through the wicket in one of the pair of heavy wooden doors (as at Helmingham, Hengrave, or Giffords Hall, Stoke-by-Nayland). For an important cortège, the main doors would be opened and the procession would rumble into the open court within the buildings. The gatehouse would be flanked by a pair of towers ('For the purpose of chivalric display only' — Pevsner, on Layer Marney Towers in Essex).

The buildings around the quadrangle were habitually of single-room width in three ranges with simple pitched roofs to each range. These can be observed at houses as widely separated as Oxburgh Hall, Norfolk, and Sutton Place in Surrey. The fourth side, which contained the great hall, was invariably wider — especially if, as at Hengrave, the range was of double-room depth. The builders then had to decide how to roof these larger spans. At Hengrave this was done by constructing a pair of parallel roofs with an internal valley; a solution used later on at Hintlesham Hall. At Melford Hall the device adopted was a single span roof with a flat-roofed extension; at Sutton Place the roof was wider and pitched to a higher level than the adjoining wings: this produced an irregular silhouette which became increasingly unacceptable as the Italian preference for symmetry began to take hold of Tudor builders.

Nathaniel Lloyd claimed Hengrave Hall as an example of how the fortified castle developed into a great residence, and it is customary to point to Thornbury Castle in Gloucestershire, the unfinished 'palace castle' of Edward, Duke of Buckingham, from whom Thomas Kytson bought the Hengrave property.[2] The obvious points of comparison are the general plan form, the gatehouse and angle turrets and the moated site. (It seems more than likely that Kytson had seen Thornbury, and wanted both to imitate the stone finishing — which he did in white brick — and the Duke's fantastic quintuple-bowed bay-window.) Lloyd may well have been thinking in less derivative and more general terms, contrasting moated Hengrave with a great late fourteenth century castle such as Bodiam; but there is also the superficial resemblance to the plans of monastic priories — a resemblance increased by the

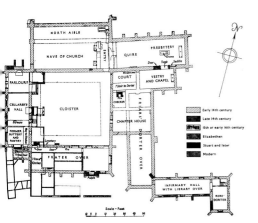

*Figure 26: Quadrangular plan of Clare Priory.*

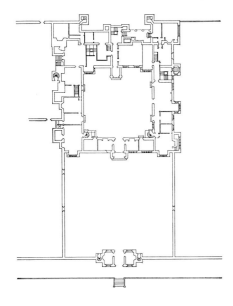

*Figure 27: Domestic quadrangular plan – Melford Hall, probably 1606.*

1 This is now the opinion of Mr. D. Spittle (vide, letter to owners dated November 21st, 1975) modifying the dating given in his article on Giffords Hall in Proceedings S.I.A., op. cit., 1965, Vol. XXX, Part 2, pages 183-187.
2 By 1278, the manor had passed to John Crow: cf. W.A. Copinger *The Manors of Suffolk,* Vol. 7, pages 123-133.

unusual feature of a cloister-corridor around three sides of the internal courtyard (see Figure 28).

In spite of seeming so obvious at first sight, the cloister-corridor had not previously been adopted in any Tudor house. A similar device appears early in the next century in the plans of Chilham Castle, Kent, (c.1616), attributed to Inigo Jones, and the corridor as such occurs fairly frequently in the plans of John Thorpe: in the latter's ground plan of Beaufort House, Chelsea, (c.1620), it divides the front rooms from the rear from end to end of the ground floor, where it is described as 'A Longe Entry throughe Alle'. The corridor became a normal feature of houses, large and small, during the seventeenth century, but in 1525 it was an innovation. In all the great quadrangular houses you had to cross the open courtyard in order to enter the hall, or make your way through a series of rooms in one or other of the two flanking ranges. At Hengrave the departure from the usual courtyard plan was to have the service quarters in a separate wing. This is believed to result from the decision to keep the kitchens and offices of the old de Hemegreth's house (see also Section 6). The practical advantages are obvious: instead of retaining only one range and the Great Hall, there were rooms for the use of family and guests on three sides of the central court. One of these was a 'Summer Parlour' facing east; another a 'Winter Parlour' facing south, and, additionally, there was a separate drawing-room and a household Chapel. All these rooms, and the Chapel, were entered from the cloister corridor. On the first floor the same plan gave access to the phenomenal number of over fifty 'chambers' or bedrooms, commencing, as Avray Tipping pointed out, with 'the Chiefe or Queen's chamber', and including one for the 'dayrye maid'. All in all, this was a big advance on the customary Tudor plan of one room leading out of another.

The courtyard plan of Giffords Hall has none of the architectural discipline of Hengrave. The courtyard itself is an irregular wedge-shaped rectangle, a good deal narrower at the west than at the east end, and this seemingly haphazard circumstance has never been entirely satisfactorily explained by historians. The buildings with which the courtyard is surrounded represent, in the differing fenestration and surface treatment, each successive generation's attempts at modernising the house.

The name most associated with the house is that of the Mannock family, who are said to have lived in the neighbourhood since the time of Edward III, and to have made a fortune in the cloth trade at Stoke-by-Nayland. Philip Mannock (b.1337) obtained the property from the Crown in 1428. As well as the gatehouse, dating from late thirteenth or early fourteenth century, there must have been other structures making it a habitable manor house. Archaeological investigation has not yet produced any evidence of these, and supposing that some were timber-framed, they may have left no trace, except, perhaps, in their siting. If the Mannocks were content to rebuild what they found, this could account for the irregular courtyard. There is no direct evidence of work by Philip Mannock, but his son John (d.1470) was evidently at work building – or rebuilding – the Hall, witness the contract dated 1459 for bricks (see Appendix B, Section 4). On structural evidence the timber-framed ranges east and west of the courtyard are likely to have been built in his time.[1] Whether his work included the great hall itself is uncertain, but it is known to be of brick construction: what is certain is the display on the gatehouse of the arms of Eleanor Goldingham (the wife of John) impaling Mannock, and Mannock impaling Goldingham. It is George (1467/8-1540/1) the son of Eleanor and John, who is usually credited with the re-building of the gatehouse, and on stylistic grounds it seems probable that the roof of the great hall was finished in his day (c.1500). A more exact dating of this splendid double hammer-beam roof may be possible following the recent extensive detailed photography discussed in Section 6.

Crows Hall is a fully moated site, possibly of great antiquity, with the remains of a single-storey brick gatehouse with flanking buildings, and a long brick gabled east range. This could have been the rebuilding in the early sixteenth century of an older hall of fourteenth century date, in turn replacing still earlier buildings.[2] There is enough brickwork standing on the north-west side to establish the existence of a complete frontage along the moat with – presumably – a matching brick gable ending the south-west wing. Beyond this, all is conjecture. It is supposed that the hall itself lay between the two wings, with a chapel at the east end, but there is nothing to go on in trying to trace the abutment of this building with the north-east wing. I imagine that this could have been timber-framed, which — like Gedding — would explain why it left no trace. (It is possible that aerial photography might provide clues not obvious from ground examination.)

## Moat Hall, Parham

In the case of Moat Hall, Parham (early sixteenth century) — originally known as Parham Hall — this seems also to have been a courtyard house[1] surrounded — in this case — by a system of double moats. Built sheer out of the moat, the foundations of the dismantled portion of the east wing are still visible, and it is possible to stand on the lawn and visualise the complete brick range continuing about a further 33ft (10,060mm) south. The outbuildings were probably of timber and plaster construction with an outer wall of brick, and formed the remaining two sides of the site, with the entrance through the present brick archway.

To recapitulate — the domestic quadrangle plan had an extensive ancestry which can be traced at least to Roman times, and from military origins and, possibly, monastic models, developed into a remarkable architectural form — practical as well as romantic, and unmistakably English.

## E- and U-Forms

The textbook account derives the E-plan from the quadrangular plan by the simple device of omitting one of the four sides.[2] The more romantic version ascribes the E to an occasional 'consciously devised . . . compliment to Queen Elizabeth by subjects prone to fanciful conceits and bizarre expressions of loyal devotion'.[3] Five years or so later than Hengrave, this plan is used at Barrington Court in Somerset, and evidently originates as a development from the mediaeval manor-house by adding a second cross-wing to the L-plan. Not a few factors probably produced the E-plan. Perhaps the first arose quite simply out of changed social conditions: the moated quadrangular house had afforded a measure of protection, but with the increasing centralisation of government in the sixteenth century, and new local powers of law and order,[4] there was diminishing need for the gatehouse, with its little squint windows and a porter to control the entrance, and — maybe — the drawbridge. The omission of the fourth side of the quadrangle at Caius College, Cambridge, is thought to have been deliberate 'lest the air from being confined in a narrow space should become foul'. Dr. Caius, who was the builder of the College (c.1557) is credited as the originator of 'this novel (and often copied) arrangement', in which a screen and gateway take the place of the fourth range. Pevsner speculates on Caius having seen similar courtyards at Chateaux, such as Bury (1520), on returning through France after taking his M.D. in Padua in 1541.[5]

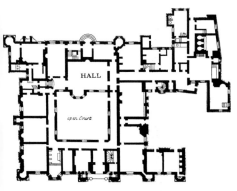

*Figure 28: Survey plan of Hengrave Hall.*

Christchurch Mansion (1548) was a notable example of this trend to more open courts: there were three main ranges (two-storied, with attic gables) and possibly no more than a screen wall and gateway before the single-storied range — shown on Ogilby's map of 1674 — was added during the reconstruction after fire damage in the early 1670 s. This trend was in no way peculiar to Suffolk, and appears almost universally in large Elizabethan houses — these, as Hugh Braun comments '. . . seem so alike as to appear as though they were planned by the same architect'.[6] They were, it is true, largely governed by three decisive shapes: the courtyard, E- and H-plans. In detail, however, there was considerable variety.

In terms of planning, we are still discussing the *hall-house*, albeit the old type with a difference. The hall itself was architecturally less spectacular when the plaster ceiling replaced the open carpentry roof (accepting the decor to be eighteenth century, compare the Banqueting Hall at Melford Hall with that of Helmingham). In terms of *use*, however, the hall was still as important in Elizabethan houses as it had been earlier: if the family had their private dining-room elsewhere, they could still stage a banquet when occasion demanded, and be seated with their guests upon the dais. The hall still remained the *climax* of the plan and the focal point of the entrance elevation, symbolised externally by the ornamental dress of the porch. With the opening of the courtyard to view, the porch had become the main feature in a geometrical paradigm of absolute symmetry. There could no longer be any question of an off-centre entrance to screens-passage and hall being allowed to push the porch slightly to one side, as had

1 cf. Parham in P.G.M. Dickinson's *Suffolk* in The Little Guide Series, page 277, and Avray Tipping in *English Homes,* Period II, Vol. I, page 54. Mr. Dickinson was more dogmatic about this than Mr. Tipping.
2 cf. *A History of Architecture* by Sir Banister Fletcher (ninth Edition) English Renaissance, page 786.
3 cf. *Tudor Renaissance* by J. Lees-Milne, Chapter X.
4 Lilian J. Redstone comments on the legal changes in Tudor Suffolk in Chapter X of her *Suffolk,* page 72 (see Section Bibliography).
5 cf. *The Buildings of England, Cambridgeshire* by Nikolaus Pevsner, page 63.
6 cf. *Elements of English Architecture,* Chapter 2 'The House Plan', page 86.

happened at Melford Hall (or Oxburgh Hall). This pre-occupation with symmetry coincided with – and was no doubt prompted by – the new Renaissance design.

Amongst the larger houses built in Suffolk on the lines of the E- and rectangular U-plans during the reigns of Henry VIII and Elizabeth I can be numbered:-

| | |
|---|---|
| Brome Hall | Playford Hall* |
| Glemham Hall, Little Glemham* | Redgrave Hall |
| Hintlesham Hall* | Rushbrooke Hall |
| Kentwell Hall* | Thornham Hall |

**Redgrave Hall**

Of these, only those marked * still survive, but Redgrave Hall was an example of the U-plan, from the researches of E.R. Sandeen[1] whose reconstructed plan of 1554 is here reproduced (see Figure 29). The overall length along the north of the house was about 34.5 metres (115 feet), the width of the three ranges about equal at 7 metres (22-23 feet), and the governing dimension of the three-sided courtyard about 13 metres (43 feet). (There is a distance of some 18 metres (60 feet) from the Dry Kitchen to the dais – a long stretch by modern standards.) The symmetry of the plan around the courtyard is notable: the main entrance was from the south and the doorway exactly central by dint of keeping the Screen/Pantry partition on the right hand jamb of the front door.

The Hall was not open to the roof, but was two storeys high and separated the first floor bed-chambers in the east wing, from those in the west wing, as well as the Gallery chamber. There was a large side-wall fireplace, as well as a small but unusual feature – a door of convenience from the dais to the garden. From the dais one entered the Great Parlour and thence the Little Parlour; two rooms corresponding to the summer and winter parlours of Hengrave Hall. The Great Parlour would have been a family Dining Room and the Little Parlour a Drawing Room, as indeed these rooms came to be called after the Jacobean era.

It would be a mistake to treat the plans of Tudor country houses as in some way of accidental derivation, and inferior to the calculated geometry of English Palladian architecture. The hollow square plan was, on the whole, a functional solution for the accommodation of a large family, staff and retainers, with ample room provided for guests. This plan continued in Jacobean usage, but mainly with a much smaller central courtyard. The only Suffolk example I have come across is the ground floor plan of an earlier Great Finborough Hall, built c.1656,[2] surveyed in 1794 and destroyed by fire in either 1794 or 1795. The hall was in the middle of the long side and already nothing more than a big entrance vestibule (the Stone Hall) whence started a circuit of the main rooms. To the left one went through the Tea-Room to the South Dining Room (a door from the Stone Hall gave access also to the extensive Service quarters); to the right lay the North Dining Room – presumably for summer use – and beyond was the Billiard Room and the main staircase (the game of billiards was mentioned by Shakespeare and Spenser); finally, one went past the foot of a smaller staircase to the Withdrawing Room. The interior yard may have had a well in the middle and, of the family accommodation, was over-looked only by the Billiard Room; otherwise it was surrounded by a service corridor and, with the one exception of the Study, the rest was for staff. In somewhat disorderly fashion a remarkable number of purposes were served: Butler's Pantry, Butler's Sleeping Room, Chandel Room, Preserving Room, Water Room, Ice Room, Milk Room, Pastry Room, 'Bak Hous', Knife Room, 'Pantrey', Kitchen, Servants Hall, Scullery, Meal Room, Larder, Laundry and so on through Stables, 'Coach Hous' and 'Brew Hous' – not forgetting the sanitary (?) conveniences: Powder Room, Iron Closet and two-seater 'Bog Hous'.

*Figure 29: Redgrave Hall – reconstruction plan of 1554.*

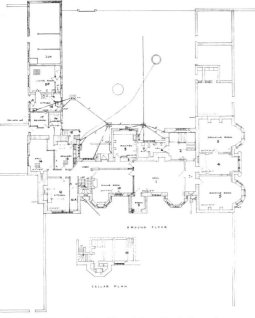

*Figure 30: Haughley Park based on a drawing prepared by Country Gentleman's Association.*

**H-Form**

One of the obvious drawbacks to the extended E-plan, dictated partly by one-room width ranges and single pitched roofs, was the distance from one end of the house to the other. Hintlesham Hall, built by the Timperley family during the reign of Queen Elizabeth, had a main range of some 100 feet in length and two end ranges of about 70 feet (29.0 metres and 21 metres). These dimensions were similar to those of Redgrave Hall and Rushbrooke Hall, started in the reign of Henry VIII. It was perhaps in Thomas Seckford's mind to have a house of more compact plan when he started on the re-building of Seckford Hall sometime about 1550. Two plans in the Thorpe collection are similar to that of Seckford Hall, and typical of the second half of the sixteenth century; the new shape is a central range with

1 'The Building of Redgrave Hall, 1545-1554', Proceedings of the Suffolk Institute of Archaeology, Vol. XXIX, part 1, pages 1-33; Ernest R. Sandeen, M.A., Ph.D.
2 This could have been the re-building of the Elizabethan House of Roger Gilbert, but I doubt it.

*Plate 10: Dalham Hall.*

cross-wings at both ends and a projecting porch on the north east — a combination of E- and H- (see Figure 25). It is not all of one build, however, and the history of the building is discussed later in Section 6.

For the fully-developed H-plan we have to wait until the early seventeenth century and the building of Haughley Park (see Figure 30). The date has recently been put as c.1620[1] and this is perhaps more credible for such an accomplished plan, owing something perhaps to the Seckford Hall of the late sixteenth century. The old quadrangular layout has been completely abandoned, as have the long ranges enclosing three sides of a courtyard within the building. The central range with its rear staircase wing is on the threshold of being widened to double room width, and the whole plan has set into a compact form which will provide a model for many gabled country houses of the same century. The architectural treatment is discussed more fully in Section 6.

### Classical

The term used here for the 'commoditie' of later Renaissance houses is 'Classical'.. The late English Renaissance has been defined as — A. Stuart (1625-1702) and B. Georgian (1702-1830)[2] and it is during this period that the plans of English houses adopt the basically square or rectangular shapes that we see, for example, in Plates I — LVIII of the Second Book of Palladio's *Architecture.* These 'Classical' plans can be found over the whole spectrum of domestic building, from manor house to cottage, and provide the neat symmetrical house fronts so familiar in towns and villages throughout Suffolk and the British Isles.[3]

Most large houses built from the late Elizabethan period until the Great Rebellion seem to have made use of the rectangular U-plan, or the H-plan. Examples occasionally come to light behind Classical fronts, as at Aspall Hall, near Debenham, or Polstead Hall, near Stoke-by-Nayland; in both these houses the Jacobean wings can be seen still at the back. When the resumption of domestic building began in the Stuart period, ideas had begun to change. In the late seventeenth century another generation of the Brooke family, who had inherited Aspall Hall in 1500, set about re-fronting the house in substantially the form we see today. The appearance is of a long simple rectangle.

If 1613, in a coat of arms in the dining-room window, be accepted as the date of the Jacobean addition to Cockfield Hall, Yoxford, then this house is strictly early Renaissance, and outside the period here called 'Classical'. We have only early nineteenth century engravings to show what the hall range was like before the Victorian re-modelling. This was a two and a half storey block with 'Dutch' gables to the east and crow-stepped gables to the west. There was a certain affinity with Somerleyton in the articulation of the bays by tall pilasters, and an even more haunting likeness to the early seventeenth century Holland Renaissance in the detailing, the overall use of brick, the steeply-pitched tiled roof with its dormer windows, and, of course, the decorative gables. The simple rectangular plan form has the new Classical look.

Complete early Classical houses of large size are not so easily found in Suffolk. Dalham Hall[4] is a good example of a large country house on the new model, with a square-plan central block of two and a half storeys, and flanked by single storey wings. It was built between 1704-5, on a prominent site above the Kennett valley,

1 *The Buildings of England — Suffolk*, by Nikolaus Pevsner. Second Edition, page 251.
2 cf. *A History of Architecture* by Sir Banister Fletcher, Ninth Edition, page 777.
3 To use the term 'Classical' in this restricted sense is, I am well aware, open to question, but it will probably convey to most people the meaning I wish it to have. It is wider than the 'Georgian' so favoured by estate agents, but narrower than the more scholarly definition of, say, Sir John Summerson, who would — rightly — date Classical back to the reign of Henry VIII. For a brilliant analysis of the whole period from the early Renaissance to the post-Waterloo Greek and Gothic Revivals, see his *Architecture in Britain, 1530 to 1830.*
4 see *Country Life,* Vol. LIV, page 280.

*Plate 11: Euston Hall.*
*(English Tourist Board).*

by Bishop Patrick of Ely (see Plate 10). The concept is the new classicism, in which the diverse ranges hitherto individually roofed have been brought together into a single block under one roof; to avoid an unseemly bulk this is hipped up to a central leaded flat above attic ceiling level.

At Euston[1] in 1666-70, Lord Allington seems to have accepted and re-modelled an Elizabethan hall on the old courtyard plan, retaining three ranges and building a screen across the south side. The house had the 'extruded corners' – to borrow Professor Summerson's description – of such great Elizabethan mansions as Burghley House and Hardwick Hall, with domed angle turrets (see Plate 11). Thus – if not in elevation, at least on plan – Euston, although re-done in the reign of Charles II, remains an Elizabethan mansion clothed in the new Stuart architecture.

What one notices in the plans of Classical houses in Suffolk is the thread of continuity with earlier features, such as the central porch, the advancing wings of the E-, H-, and U-plans, and the bay windows. In the late Elizabethan and Jacobean houses, the central feature of the entrance front was the porch running up to eaves level and above. In late Renaissance houses the centre-piece remains the focal point of the whole front, as it does in Palladian design where it has symbolic overtones – the noble proprietor's coat-of-arms within a pediment, flanked and pinnacled by sky-line figures representative of various virtues. The centre-piece may be broader, as at Sotterley Hall, where it is three bays wide and two storeys high with a pediment; or Benacre Hall, five bays wide and three storeys high with a pediment. In both these, the entrance 'advances a little', and the front door is absolutely central. (In neither are there coats-of-arms or figures, since eighteenth century Englishmen were less ostentatious of their nobility and their virtues.)

*Plate 12: Henstead Hall, after a drawing by H. Davy.*

The same process of translating into Classical norms the typical Elizabethan and Jacobean E-, and U-plans can be seen at work on a large scale at Sotterley Hall, and on a small scale at Gipping Hall (now demolished) and Henstead Hall, near Beccles (see Plate 12). Sotterley Hall has the form of a shallow H-plan with the addition, however, of slightly advancing centre-pieces on the entrance and garden fronts, which suggest a hybrid E. The narrow two-bay ends of the cross-wings have echoes of, say, Elizabethan two-bay gable ends at Rushbrooke Hall, and a more obvious similarity with those of Hintlesham of c.1720. Henstead Hall – much smaller and, doubtless, early nineteenth century – continues the double cross-wing plan but turns the ends facing the drive into three-storey bays. (Davy did a delightful study in his *Seats* of both this house and the somewhat similar Gipping Hall of earlier date: see Plate 13.)

The bay window has had, probably, the longest run of any domestic feature originating in the creative Elizabethan and early Jacobean eras. The name seems to have emanated from the window formed in the bay at the end of the dais in the

1 see *Country Life*, Vol. CXXI, pages 58, 102, 148.

*Plate 13: Gipping Hall, after a drawing by H. Davy.*

mediaeval hall. This tall window became a habitual feature of late sixteenth and early seventeenth designs (a remarkable use of narrow vertical bays occurs at Mockbeggars Hall, Claydon, of c.1621). For a time, in Stuart and early Georgian times, it was out of fashion in the mansion and larger country houses, but not at vernacular level; extremely attractive oriel bow windows (the term 'bow' refers to the curved bay) occur at Sparrow's House and No. 24 Fore Street, both in Ipswich, and of late seventeenth century date. By the second half of the eighteenth century, the bow and the canted bay window are back, and appear frequently in urban houses.[1] In the late eighteenth and early nineteenth century, they feature in country houses: a single-storey bow at Worlingham Hall, and a two-storey bow as the main feature on both the main elevations of Great Finborough Hall by Francis Sandys (1795).

## Heveningham Hall

The ground floor plan of the house Sir Robert Taylor designed for Sir Gerard Vanneck, in 1778, may be taken as an exemplar of the important changes that have taken place since the building of a large Jacobean country house such as Haughley Park some 120 years earlier:-

a) The central entrance has been fully exploited; whereas in the sixteenth century the porch was at one end of the hall, echoing the old screens-passage, in the later plan the hall extends left and right beyond the entrance.

b) The Hall has ceased to be a family room and has become a ceremonial place, with main staircase or — as at Heveningham — a prelude to a separate staircase hall. (An obvious analogy is the musical symphonic plan of the eighteenth century, in which the hall resembles an announcement of themes, and the principal rooms their development.)

c) The plan has become double-pile, i.e. two-rooms deep, with fireplace on the spine wall between the two; the traditional large open hall fireplace has been superseded by the smaller individual room fireplaces.

d) The rooms are arranged *en suite*, and the old parlours are replaced by apartments reserved for varying social and domestic occasions; dining-room, library, drawing-room and a small family dining-room.

e) The kitchen and service quarters are still remote from the main dining-room, although conveniently placed for service of meals to the small dining-room.

The floor plans of Heveningham Hall (see Figure 31) work on the principle of 'stacking' large rooms around a central circulating space — in this case the entrance and staircase hall.[2] An interesting point of comparison with Haughley Park is the corridor leading from the entrance hall through the middle of the service end of the house. The preoccupation of architects for the next two hundred years of house planning is with *circulation*. Rooms arranged *en suite* became increasingly less acceptable, and a substantial part of the history of domestic planning from the eighteenth to the twentieth

1 Hugh Braun in *The Elements of English Architecture* attributes the canted bay end to the dining-room during the early-Victorian period to the fashion (in middle-class houses) for giving dinner parties.
2 The most remarkable of all Suffolk mansion floor plans are those of Ickworth, which remain unique in the county. The evolution of the design has recently been traced by Dr. Tudor-Craig (cf. *Country Life,* May 17th, 1973, pages 1362-1365) and is discussed in Section 6.

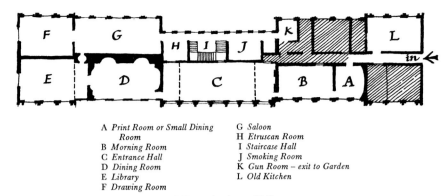

| A | Print Room or Small Dining Room | G | Saloon |
|---|---|---|---|
| B | Morning Room | H | Etruscan Room |
| C | Entrance Hall | I | Staircase Hall |
| D | Dining Room | J | Smoking Room |
| E | Library | K | Gun Room – exit to Garden |
| F | Drawing Room | L | Old Kitchen |

*Figure 31: Ground floor plan of Heveningham Hall.*

century is concerned with various devices for reaching one part of a house from another, without going through rooms to get there — in fact a history of entrance halls, staircase halls, vestibules, lobbies, corridors and passages.

*Later developments*   The problems of circulation in large Victorian and Edwardian houses were intensified by the need of ample space for entertaining large house-parties. Already at Heveningham there has been added to the older nucleus of hall, parlours and dining-room, the morning-room, library, saloon, Etruscan room, smoking-room and gun-room. A hundred years later, although the Etruscan room might no longer be in demand, there had been added the billiard-room, winter garden, conservatory and boudoir, together with extensive gentlemen's cloakrooms. And, as the reception rooms increased, so, likewise, by hierarchial progression, did the staff quarters; in a great Lutyens' house, such as Temple Dinsley, the floor area for these exceeded that of the principal rooms. The ground floor plan provides service room, kitchen, scullery, larders (kitchen and game), pantry, butler's room, house-man's room, chef's room, housekeeper's sitting-room, still-room and pantry, servant's hall and many stores-rooms. Furthermore there was a room for 'croquet mallets, etc.', and a large outside range comprising garages, workshop, kitchen and mess room (presumably for outdoor staff), and a racquet court.

## SMALLER HOUSE PLANS

The kernel of the mediaeval house has been seen as a near-standard sequence of parlour/hall/service, and although plans in the large size-scale could equally be traced to this original nucleus, it is probably in the smaller range that the connection is most obvious. In the following notes observations on the typology of plans continue with manor and country houses, followed by farmhouses, parsonages, town and village houses and, finally, cottages.

## MANOR AND COUNTRY HOUSE

One of the characteristics of Suffolk manors is to be numerous and small in extent, with the result that many smaller manor houses were built. Although not always called 'Halls', there are still a large number of halls originally built as manor houses, normally with landed property. These are the stem-source both of the later country house and, frequently, of the farmhouse. A systematic survey of the manor houses that still survive — in one form or another — in Suffolk would be a valuable exercise, and would distinguish between those which have become recognisably farmhouses and those — like Hemingstone Hall — that have remained, often after varying fortunes, as distinctive manor houses. The planning of the manor house can be traced to the mediaeval sources already discussed, and that of the country house in turn to the manor house, from which it is largely derived. In the course of development allowance must be made for the many outside influences which have successively changed the function and the pattern of house plans.

*Hemingstone Hall*   Hemingstone Hall (Plate 14), built by William Style in 1588, was the rebuilding, in brick, of an earlier timber-framed and plastered house with the addition of a two-storeyed porch in 1625. The plan is of the E-type with short cross-wings, the hall, with fireplace on the north side, occupying the centre of the house, the parlour to the west and the dining-room originally east, with the service quarters occupying part of the original house. The central range was one room deep until about 1730, when the space between the wings was filled in, making a double room width. (This was a Georgian device often used in the conversion of Elizabethan houses.) Hemingstone Hall is discussed in Section 6.

*Plate 14: Hemingstone Hall from the south-east.*

*Plate 15: Kenton Hall with moat.*

Kenton Hall (Plate 15), as Edmund Farrer wrote, 'must have been a large E-shaped mansion with the main block facing the east, but alongside the western length of the moat, having wings adjoining the northern and southern sides; thus the entrance, with its porch, would be immediately opposite the bridge, and the rest of the enclosure would be the forecourt of the mansion, as at . . . Kentwell Hall, in Long Melford, or Rushbrooke, near Bury St. Edmunds.' So all we find here today after the fire in 1919 is the southern cross-wing and a short length of main range running north-south, with the rest of the building modern, including everything above cornice level. The probability is that the surviving wing contained the parlours of the original house, when the hall was in the centre and the service rooms on the north side.

*Otley Hall*    Otley Hall, as it now stands, consists of about half only of the original hall-house, with later wings of sixteenth century build (see Plate 16). The hall itself finishes at the screens-passage, and in place of the buttery, pantry and kitchen there is a gable wall: it is this which gives the lop-sided look to this range, and a false

*Plate 16: Otley Hall from the east.*

impression to the plan. The first range could well have had a balancing cross-wing on the south side, as Edmund Farrer argued.[1] The unusual feature was the arcaded ground floor of the north wing open to the courtyard between the wings, where cock-fighting was traditionally held, followed later by more pacific games of bowls. (See Section 6.)

The smaller country house does not, of course, end with the decline of manors. As already noted in the pattern of estates in the west and east of Suffolk, houses cluster thickly around Bury St. Edmunds and along the coastal turnpike north east from Ipswich: the majority are country houses of the medium size. They are illustrated with charm in the pages of the *Excursions through Suffolk*, and in Henry Davy's *Seats*. There were many reasons for the growth of the later country house: increase in population; pleasant landscapes and fair climate; the rise of the middle class and of prosperous tradesmen; improvement of roads and the coming of railways. Already in 1813 we find F. Schoberl [2] concerned to prove, from figures obtained by Arthur Young, that the population of the county 'has much increased' between 1776 and 1795, and going on to deduce — 'Upon the whole . . . the climate of this county must be reckoned favourable; and it cannot but be extremely salubrious to judge from the mortality . . .' Reflections of this kind occur also in Kirby's *The Suffolk Traveller* and accompany the rising agricultural prosperity of the eighteenth and nineteenth centuries. As an admirer of scenery, Kirby — rather grandly — claimed the Orwell as 'one of the most beautiful salt-rivers in the world', and praised the hills on each side '. . . adorned with almost every object that can make a landscape agreeable: such as churches, mills, gentlemen's seats, villages and other buildings, woods, noble avenues, parks whose pales reach down to the water's edge, well stored with deer and cattle, feeding in fine lawns, etc. . . .'

*Foxboro' Hall*

Foxboro' Hall, Melton (see Plate 17), is a good example of the small estate on the outskirts of a village. Built about 1810 of white brick in the Classical style, the house is sited on rising ground with parkland on three sides, and fine views from the upper floors over the distant Deben estuary. It could be called the model of a gentleman's property of the period, having carriage sweep and shrubberies, stable yard and outbuildings, staircase hall, circular ante-room linking library and dining-room, and large drawing-room the whole width of a wing. The art of living in such houses reached considerable accomplishment during at least a century until, in the aftermath of two world wars, they ceased to play any longer the leading role in the community. Their 'commoditie' was considerable — shapely rooms, dadoed, and corniced with high ceilings, elegant fireplaces, large sash-windows — often

1 *E.A.M.*, Part 1, Jan-March 1929 (No. 7863).
2 *History and Topography of Suffolk*, op. cit., page 3.

*Plate 17: Foxboro' Hall, Melton.*                    Julian Stainton

french casements opening out on to terraces and verandas — and handsome staircases. The house was a hierarchial community from the head of the family down to the head-gardener's boy, and centred — in an age of lesser mobility than our own — upon the estate and properties: shooting, farming, and above all, the art of gardening, not only outdoors in rose-gardens, herbaceous borders and greenhouses, but also indoors in conservatories and plant-houses.

The succeeding generations of country house building were Victorian and Edwardian — periods remarkably little studied in Suffolk. One thinks of the estates west of Bury St. Edmunds, like Herringswell and Cavenham; of Nether Hall, Pakenham; and then almost immediately of Newmarket, with its ample red brick houses and black-and-white gable ends, the well-mown lawns, Wellingtonias and monkey-puzzles, and the immaculate racing studs. Holbrook Hall, a mile or so north of Waldringfield, was grandiose neo-Tudor of 1883 in dark red brick, and on a par with Brantham Court of 1850; neither have remained as private houses. There is little of Sir Edwin Lutyen's work in the country; some alterations at Stoke College, Brent Eleigh and Higham; an unusual establishment for fallen girls at Woolverstone (commissioned by Lady Berners) and a house at Snape. Near Leiston were the two small emparked estates of Old Abbey house and Theberton House — the former white brick and stucco, of the 80s, and the latter bizarre beaux-arts of c.1900.

This brings us to the more recent scene. Changes affecting the whole of national life may have appeared more slowly in traditionally conservative Suffolk, but the same forces have been at work; the decline of the squirearchy and the growth of rural democracy; the ending of village isolation through the motor car; the rise in wage rates and the increased cost of building — all of these gradually brought the building of the old-style country house to an end, not to mention the drying up of the local market in domestic service.

There are a few examples. In 1914, the architect, artist and poet, Cecil Lay built a country house at Aldringham in an ebullient, *art nouveau* style. (See Section 6.)

He contrived a galleried staircase hall of some originality in the centre of a complex H-plan built on two floors with an attic storey. In 1928, Edward Maufe — later to be architect of Guildford Cathedral — built Cousin's Hill for the Misses Tidswell, on a hillside west of Coddenham village with wide views to the woods of Shrubland Park and the Gipping Valley from the porticoed loggia.

In 1965 the rambling Victorian country-house known as Stratford Hills had become uninhabitable, and was pulled down with the exception of an earlier wing retained as a guest house. A modern house was built on the adjoining hillside [1]

1 In 1971, the new Stratford Hills was classified as a Listed Building under the conservation scheme which scheduled the entire Stour Valley as an Area of Outstanding Natural Beauty.

where the views lie south and west across the valley of the river Stour (see Plate 18). Here – curiously – the wheel has come full circle in returning to the hall-house plan. The hall is partly floored over and partly open at the dais end, and the idea of the dais is continued by a flight of shallow steps from the lower end of the room. The open part of the hall rises the full height of two storeys in the centre of the house, with a corresponding full height window (the modern oriel); it divides the Solar (in this case the owner's bedroom suite) from the Greater Chambers (the daughter's and guests' suites), and both from the Lesser Chambers (or staff suite); all three have access to a Gallery which – by tradition – is over the screen to the kitchen and service rooms. Below the gallery, the family and guests dine at a refectory table on the 'dais' by the great window, with its glazed doors opening on to the long south terrace (see Section 6.)

*Plate 18: Stratford Hills, Stratford St. Mary.*

In such ways can modern house-planning occasionally return to refresh itself from its original sources.

## FARMHOUSE

A farmhouse is the chief dwelling-house attached to a farm. As such it is distinguished by size and importance from the humbler dwellings on the farm, in which were housed the stockmen and labourers. The rise of the farmhouse to this degree of eminence is subject-matter for an historical survey, in which the origins would probably be traced to the 'dual-purpose' dwellings of antiquity. The later Suffolk farmhouse has little to distinguish it from the general run of halls and manor-houses, except for the proximity of farm buildings: the earlier farmhouse could be found corresponding to a European type in which the personnel occupied one end and the livestock the other. Hall-houses of a recognisably Saxon pattern where 'barn, cattle-stalls, stables and dwelling-house are covered by one roof',[1] are known to have existed in East Anglia as they still exist to this day in Holland and Germany. In Suffolk the probability is that sheep and dairy-farming on the mediaeval scale will have caused the abandoning of this dual-purpose type at a fairly early date, although continuing until as late as the sixteenth century to serve the needs of the smaller farmer and stock-breeder.

This long single-roofed building has been termed *langgeveltype* in Holland and *langehaus* in Germany.[2] The term *long-house*, from the same root, is frequently used (and misapplied) in this country. According to Eric Mercer the long-house appeared in its full and classic form about the middle of the sixteenth century in the uplands of Devonshire.[3] The English type generally has a through-passage dividing the part reserved for human beings from that allotted to animals; this passage gave common entry to both parts. The plan shape is invariably an extended rectangle. In its developed form the long-house was of two-storey construction with a chimney stack backing on to the through-passage, which effectively separated the living part of the house from the byre. It seems – understandably – to have become outdated by the eighteenth century.

There is a serious deficiency in classification of farmhouse-types in Suffolk, where the probability is that the long-house form continued to be used by small

1 cf. *A History of the English House*. Introduction, page 6, in which N. Lloyd illustrated 'a comparatively modern' Friesland house of this type, and also a plan of another homestead at Edam on similar lines.
2 The German farmhouse has been derived from two main groups: the West German *Wohnstallhaus*, and the East and North German *Zwiehof*, both of the hall-house. The former is – literally – 'dwelling-stable-house', and the latter 'double farmhouse'.
3 *English Vernacular Houses* by Eric Mercer (see General Bibliography), and see Chapter III, Dual-Purpose Dwellings, pages 34-50.

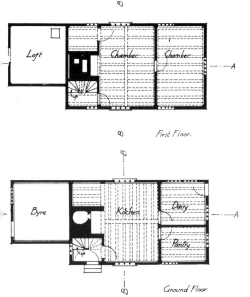

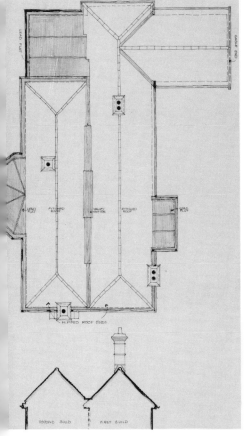

*Figure 32: First and ground floor plans of Wydards Farm, Cratfield.*

*Figure 33: Valley Farm, Heveningham.*

### Double cross-wing farmhouse

1 cf. P.S.I.A. vol. XXLV, Part I, 1947: *Restoration of a XVI Century Farmhouse in Suffolk* by Arthur Welford A.R.I.B.A. The kitchen, which with the chamber over, was heated by the chimney stack backing onto the byre.
2 cf. *English Vernacular Architecture*, op. cit., page 202.

farmers, but has since disappeared. Arthur Welford, A.R.I.B.A., gave an instance of this at Wydards Farm, Cratfield.[1] The original building, dated about 1540, consisted of a two-bay three-cell dwelling of two storeys, measuring approximately 8.5m by 5.5m (28ft by 18ft) with a two-storey annexe approximately 3.5m square (11ft square). The dwelling contained kitchen, dairy and pantry; staircase, two bedrooms and attic: the annexe is thought to have been a byre with a loft over (see Figure 32). If Mr. Welford was correct in identifying the annexe as a byre, this could have been a type of small Suffolk long-house, although not, of course, on the 'orthodox' through-passage plan. It remains to be seen whether other examples can be found.

It will be noted that Wydards was built as a two-storeyed house with floored attics, suggesting that, during the preceding forty years, the older plan form of open hall with storeyed and service accommodation in bays or cross-wings was being gradually superseded. The smaller farmhouse had probably to be content with a single general-purpose living-room-cum-kitchen, the open hearth being replaced in due course by the brick chimney stack. With rising prosperity the need for extra room would be met, as at Wydards, by adding a number of bays. There the original house had a one-and-half-bay kitchen, and a single bay divided laterally into two service rooms — dairy and pantry. Forty years later the half-bay, which was originally occupied by entrance-lobby, chimney-stack and alcove, had been cleared out, rebuilt, and added to the length of the kitchen. The dairy and pantry remained at the north-west end, but a new doorway had been made at this end of the kitchen; a new chimney stack had been built with a newel-stair and lobby on one side and a bread-oven and cupboard on the other; beyond these was a fine new two-bay parlour. The whole house was now of six bays, measuring approximately 9.5m in length and 5m in width (32ft by 17ft); a long narrow rectangle with a high-pitched roof (probably thatched at first and later pantiled). In its final form, with small windows, tall plastered walls and sharp gable-ends, it is instantly recognisable as one of the typical smaller farmhouses of central Suffolk.

The single-range plan remained, but there was a new tendency to promote the cross-wing addition. There are many instances to be found of the original single-range to which a grander and more ambitious cross-wing was added, often during the later reign of Henry VIII. The new wing can be identified by its greater height, embellishment of woodwork, spectacular ornamental brick chimneys, and decorative plaster ceilings. In addition to enlarging the original farmhouse, whether of the open hall or two-storeyed type, by a single cross-wing, there are other variants. Wings could be added at both ends, as at Moat Farm, Chevington[2] in this case apparently when the farmhouse was demoted to a pair of cottages. When the accommodation was extended in this way, the wing projections are seldom of equal length, and they need not be cross-wings in the accepted sense, but only annexes of which the roofs were 'crippled in' to the original. A wing could be added in the centre of the range at the rear making a T-shaped plan, although this is less often found than the L- or H-plan. Another range could be added parallel with the first producing a square or rectangular plan, as at Valley Farm, Heveningham (see Figure 33 and Section 6). This was frequently an eighteenth or nineteenth century device employed in the re-modelling of an earlier house. In cottages (see below) and occasionally in farmhouses, the second range was single storey, provided the 'baccus', and ran the length of the house to which it was annexed by a lean-to roof. The single storey annexe was occasionally merely a short wing projecting from the main farmhouse to provide a utility room. If this was dairy or cheese-room, it is likely to be found on the north or east side of the main house; if an extra parlour or sitting-room probably on the south or west, and with its own chimney stack. The single-storey porch is usually a later addition, as at The Grange, Chelsworth, where the porch is dated 1689, and was added to a late mediaeval dwelling.

The cross-wing plan is by no means always the result of later additions but can be an original build. Old Hall Farm at Hemingstone is an example of a completely framed timberhouse, probably built 1580±, designed as a two-storeyed central range with a pair of two-storeyed cross-wings, each having a large axial chimney stack at the rear of the wing. The result is architecturally pleasant. The plan is a departure altogether from the standard parlour/hall/service rooms sequence; the

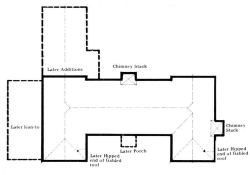

*Figure 34: Outline plan of Milden Hall.*

**The refronted farmhouse**

**Kitchen economy**

**Cheese lofts**

east wing contains the farmhouse kitchen, the central range service rooms, staircase and semi-basement, and the west-wing main hall or parlour. Milden Hall is one of the most interesting examples of a mainly symmetrical plan, dating to a first build of $1600^{\pm}$, and consisting of a long central two-storeyed hall range, flanked by a pair of equal cross-wings (see Figure 34). It seems likely that these wings are the original projection on the entrance side since they have massive late Elizabethan-looking chimneys (the tops have been much altered). At the rear, the wings project only a foot or so, and are gabled. In the mid-eighteenth century the front was drastically 'classicised', a columnar porch added, and the roofs hipped on the front of each cross-wing. The result is to give the farmhouse the look of a small Georgian mansion.

There have been no great number of new farmhouses built in Suffolk during the last hundred years, and a careful examination will show many seemingly Georgian, Regency or Victorian farmhouses to be old timber-framed structures refronted or partly re-built. The majority of Suffolk farmers seem to have been content to make do with the old, provided the 'front' could be made respectable by a new façade or a new range of rooms. At High House Farm, Bawdsey, the earlier farmhouse was dated about 1720, and on what remained of this was built (c.1820) a formal block, three-storeys high, in white brick. The pedimented front door opened into a hall, with a straight flight of stairs ascending to the first of the two bedroom floors, and on either side of the hall as a formal reception room, in the manner of the period, each with fireplace on the outside wall. From the front view it was indistinguishable from a private house of the same period.[1]

In sum, it may be said that the expansion of the farmhouse had been going on slowly ever since the Middle Ages. The motives were by no means always social ambition. In many a humble farmhouse they were prompted by domestic economy, where the need to make do and supplement ordinary returns called for extra working space. The memoirs of country life in the last century are only later versions of memories from the preceding centuries that have never been recorded. As Alan Jobson has pointed out,[2] *kitchen economy* was a great art 'based on that which had evolved in Tudor days', and the kitchen was 'the hub of the wheel of life', wherein was carried out 'baking, brewing, cooking, washing, curing, wine-making, laundering, candle and rush-light making, sewing and scouring, even to the cossetting of a sick animal'. But these many rural tasks have not vanished entirely without trace.[3]

Practically every dairy was in the farmhouse, as P.J.O. Trist reminds us,[4] until the mid-thirties, and in the eighteenth and nineteenth centuries large quantities of Suffolk butter were sent annually to London ('about 40,000 firkins' as F. Shoberl wrote in his *Suffolk* in 1813). Cheese-making seems to have declined after Tudor times when cheese was regularly exported by Ipswich merchants.[5] At High House, Otley, there is a cheese loft measuring some 5m by 12.5m (16ft by 40ft) with slatted windows for ventilation, and grooves inside the window frames for sliding shutters, and another example — from plenty still to be found — is on the first floor of the outbuildings at Bedingfield Hall. These cheese lofts will invariably be found on the north side of the building and were accessible both by ladder from the service rooms and from the first floor: cheese-making itself went on either in a separate cheese-house, or in the dairy, until after the process of salting and pressing when the cheeses were laid out in the cheese-loft for maturing.

## RELIGIOUS HOUSE AND PARSONAGE

Throughout the mediaeval period in Suffolk, there had been a continuous growth of monastic structures and religious houses built for practical works, as well as for prayer and contemplation; for education, study, training of clergy and care of the needy and sick. They were the corollary to the parochial churches, and part of the whole closely-knit fabric of Christian society of which we get such a graphic account in Langland's *Vision of Piers Plowman*.[6]

Historically they were recorded — not always reliably — by the *Victoria History of the County of Suffolk*,[7] and, at an earlier date, by Richard Taylor in his *Index Monasticus* of 1821. Taylor's map 'Exhibiting the Sites of the Religious Houses, Colleges and Hospitals in the county of Suffolk' is reproduced (see Plate 19). In the

1 G.M. Trevelyan in *English Social History*, page 472, commenting on this period ... Not only Cobbett but everyone else, complained that farmers were 'aping their betters', abandoning old homely ways, eating off Wedgwood instead of pewter, educating their girls and dashing about in gigs or riding to hounds. So many later refronted Suffolk houses look like the homes of fox-hunting farmers.
2 cf. *A Window in Suffolk* by Alan Jobson (1962) page 38.
3 There exists an extensive collection of traditional, domestic artifacts at the Museum of Rural Life, Abbot's Hall, Stowmarket.
4 *A Survey of the Agriculture of Suffolk* by P.J.O. Trist, page 221.
5 *Suffolk and the Great Rebellion 1640-1660* by Alan Everitt, M.A. Ph. D., page 17 '... The Rouses of Henham who owed their wealth to the export of Suffolk cheese in scores and hundreds to Calais, Boulogne and Berwick for the royal armies, or to London and the Low Countries in time of peace.' Lilian Redstone in her *Suffolk* (1950) also mentions that in Tudor times the county's chief contribution was in butter and cheese for virtually all the fleet.
6 The *Vision* is, as Neville Coghill once said, – 'one of the great Christian poems about humanity' ... 'every man's act and thought conforms with or disturbs the love and justice of God ... nothing can be considered in detachment from God.' (Introduction to H.W. Wells's version of Langland's poem 1938. Sheed and Ward).
7 Edition of 1907. Ed. W. Page, F.S.A. (London: Constable).

*Plate 19: Taylor's* Index Monasticus *map of Suffolk.*

59

*Index* we can discover the essential historical information on each of the Religious Houses, Colleges and Hospitals from commencement to dissolution; their situation, foundation, principal benefactors, the advowsons and impropriation of churches and other properties owned, the dedication, the valuation at dissolution, and the name of the grantee, as well as that of the owner in 1821. The interest of these foundations *before* their suppression belongs partly to the history of Roman Catholicism in Suffolk, and partly to the influence of their general arrangements upon domestic planning. Clearly a good deal more needs to be known about them, and the way in which conversion to private dwellings took place.[1]

In only a few cases have the sites of these religious houses come under systematic archaeological examination, and plans of the building been prepared. There remains a woeful lack of knowledge of the detailed planning arrangements of many of these houses, from which we could obtain some idea of their day-to-day routine. The subject is admittedly one that falls somewhat outside the scope of domestic architecture, but inasmuch as not a few were later converted to use as private houses, they became annexed to the history of Suffolk houses.

The history of the parsonage, or rectory, has still to be written at regional and local level. A study of those built in Suffolk would be a rewarding task, which would start with the mediaeval priest's house, wherever evidence can be found, and chart a course through the succeeding centuries. Examples would be needed in the immediate post-mediaeval period, followed by houses built in the Carolean era and in the reigns of William and Mary, Anne and the Georges, as well as in the prolific years of the Regency and Victoria, until the present day. After 1700, many ambitious parsonage houses were built in Suffolk: Kedington, loftily proportioned with seven-bay brick front, during the reign of Queen Anne (see Plate 20), Coddenham, four-square red brick Georgian, set on a knoll in an ample park, or Drinkstone, with a large and handsome classical rectory of about 1760 — to mention only three of the possibly thirty or more built in Suffolk during this period. A history of parsonages would be enlivened by character-studies of some of the more noteworthy clergy who had built or occupied these houses, and would follow the changing habits of church-going, and social life, in country and town. Such a task is not remotely within the scope of this work, nor within that of this present Section, where we are principally concerned more with the 'Commoditie' than other aspects of houses.

The mediaeval parsonage was probably to be recognised only by being a little better built than the ordinary house, but otherwise of the same materials as the rest of the village. For this reason, few examples are likely to have survived. The existence of a name, such as *Priest's House* (at Stratford St. Mary, for example), may have become attached to an old house on no very solid grounds. Normally the rectory could be expected to be somewhere near the church and when the living improved, or the old parsonage had deteriorated beyond repair, the tendency will have been to pull it down or largely rebuild. When the old (presumably timber-framed) parsonage at Buxhall in the Hall orchard west of the church was burnt down — so it is said — in 1703, a new site was chosen east of the church. The new house was built partly in brick and partly timber-framed; but, about 1852, the three sides visible from the village were refronted in fashionable Woolpit white-brick. The main ground floor accommodation consisted of a broad entrance hall with the seventeenth century staircase at the rear, a large drawing-room, study and dining-room, all facing the drive, together with kitchen and servants' room with a back staircase. The parsonage had become, socially and architecturally, one of the most important houses in the community.

From records, the mediaeval priest's house followed the customary plan of open hall, entered from the screens-passage, with buttery and/or kitchen at the lower end and parlour with solar over, at the upper. There were considerable differences in the size of the houses and the smallest could be of no more than three — occasionally only two — bays length. Later, in the same way as other hall-houses, a floor would be inserted, providing bed-chambers and storage at the upper level.

After the Reformation, parsonages became the homes of family men, but the accommodation remained similar, in most respects, to ordinary houses. Later the distinguishing feature came to be the study — the priest's room for parochial

## Parsonages

*Plate 20: The parsonage at Kedington.*

1 In the following, more or less substantial traces of original work remain in later conversions:

| | |
|---|---|
| Great Bricett: | Alien Priory founded about 1110 for Augustinian Canons, and granted by Henry VI in 1426 to the same college as Kersey Priory. |
| Ixworth Priory: | founded about 1170 for Augustinian Canons and dissolved in 1538. |
| Butley Priory: | founded in 1171 for Augustinian Canons and suppressed in 1538; the gate house remains. |
| Kersey Priory: | founded before 1190 for Augustinian Canons, dissolved in 1444 and granted to the College of St. Mary and St. Nicholas (later King's), Cambridge. |
| Campsey Nunnery: | founded about 1195 and dissolved in 1536. |
| Clare Priory: | founded for Austin Friars in 1248, dissolved in 1538, and recovered by the same order in 1953. |
| Welnetham Priory: | founded in 1273 for an order known as the 'Crutched' or 'Crossed' Friars, and dissolved in 1539. |
| Wingfield College: | founded in 1362 — 'The master and three others subscribed in the kings supremacy AD.1534.' (Taylor) |
| Leiston Abbey: | the New Abbey was founded in 1363, rebuilt in 1389, and dissolved in 1536. |
| St. Olave's Priory: | founded for Augustinian Canons, was dissolved in 1546 and became the home of the Jeryningham family; it is now a national monument. |

Small traces of Chipley Priory, Denston College, Battisford Preceptory, Woodbridge Priory and Bruisyard Abbey still survive in the present buildings.

60

business — a room often found in other houses but indispensable here. The place for the study was within easy reach of the front door, on the principle that the incumbent must — like the doctor — be ready to receive callers at any hour of the day or night. For this purpose — and because not all visitors might be welcome to the rest of the family — the study was usually found to be the first room on entry.

The parsonage plan has changed in one important respect only during the last thirty years or so — accommodation is no longer required for domestic servants, and with their disappearance go the 'back stairs'. There are no staff and therefore no longer any need to secrete their whereabouts. The kitchen has now become — for all practical purposes — the family dining room, and the garage has taken the place of the stabling, and, instead of being on the other side of a courtyard, has been brought as close as possible to the front door. It is no longer accepted without question that parochial church council and other meetings shall take place in the family living-room.

## TOWN AND VILLAGE HOUSE

The 'Commoditie' of town houses must be sought within the town plan itself, and begins with a study of the town map. This will show the characteristic street patterns and the layout of shops, houses and public buildings. Comparison with older maps will illustrate the rise and fall of properties over the centuries, and without a recognition of these changes, it is impossible to appreciate the original 'Commoditie' of older buildings. If, for instance, we study the plans of Nos. 12 to 16 Lower Brook Street, Ipswich (see Figure 35), it becomes clear that these were mainly a new build on the site of mediaeval houses possibly shown in John Speed's map of 1610. (No. 9 opposite, in contrast, kept much of the mediaeval framework when re-modelled during the eighteenth century.) That property values had evidently increased c.1760, when Nos. 12 and 14 were rebuilt, may be easily deduced from Joseph Pennington's Map of 1778: behind Nos. 12 and 14 there was the best part of a third of an acre of open garden, containing what appeared to be grass and fruit orchards, separated from St. Stephen's Lane by a distance of about 150 feet. The neighbouring houses as far as the junction with Dog's Head Lane were built, or rebuilt, about the same time, and the street, through which in mediaeval days flowed an open brook, would have been paved — after a fashion. Between Turret Lane and Star Lane there were large gardens on either hand almost as far as Foundation Street.[1]

That probate inventories can reveal, not only plans, but also ways of life, has been recently appreciated by historians such as M.W. Barley,[2] but already in 1948, a well-known local historian, Lilian J. Redstone, M.B.E., B.A., used this method to describe home life in Ipswich.[3] Thomas Bonner the blacksmith lived in a hall-house in St. Margaret's parish and died in 1583; he slept in the parlour (which would have been beyond the dais-end of the hall), but had three other bedsteads upstairs in the chambers (presumably at either end of the hall), and in his buttery were two querns, one of them for mustard, a boulting trough, two pails, a few tubs of various sorts and a washing bowl. Our special interest must be in relating facts such as these to the actual places where people lived, and it would have been useful to identify not only the parish but also the whereabouts of Thomas Bonner's hall-house. The widow, Margaret Lowe, who died also in 1583, lived in a hall with two tables and five chairs, and had a separate kitchen in which there were two tables, some stools, and a large variety of cooking utensils, together with 23 trenchers, probably of wood, four pewter platters and three pewter dishes. Her hall seems to have been floored over, for 'in the hall chamber a trundle bed was equipped with feather bed, flock bed and transom . . . two chests and a small press'.

These probate inventories are an invaluable guide to the accommodation, enabling us to follow through successive centuries both the rooms and their contents, and a further source of information will be local newspapers from the eighteenth century onwards. Houses will be offered for letting and sale and their contents and accommodation described, as in the example quoted by Miss Redstone from an advertisement for letting — 'the neat, compact and genteel residence in St. Peter's late in occupation of Mr. Notcutt', comprising a vestibule hall, a dining-room, parlour, store-room, kitchen and backhouse, three bedrooms, a

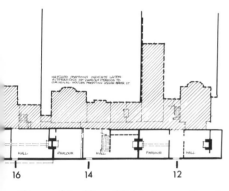

*Figure 35: Nos. 12-16 Lower Brook Street, Ipswich. Reconstruction of late mediaeval plans.*

HATCHED PORTIONS INDICATE LATER ALTERATIONS OF VARIOUS PERIODS TO ORIGINAL HOUSES FRONTING LOWER BROOK ST

HALL    PARLOUR    HALL    PARLOUR    HALL

16          14          12

1 Lilian J. Redstone in *Ipswich Through the Ages*, quoted how Monsieur de la Rochefoucauld had remarked 'rather amusedly' in 1784 how Ipswich people used to claim that their large number of gardens added to the health of the place.
2 *The English Farmhouse and Cottage*, op. cit., see General Bibliography.
3 *Ipswich Through the Ages* (see above) 1948 (East Anglian Magazine Ltd.) Chapter IX.

spacious laundry and three attics.

The urban plans of most smaller Suffolk towns and larger villages usually follow the meandering lines of mediaeval roadways, and there is a striking similarity in this respect between old Ipswich and the majority of townships, where the main difference lies often only in a greater street width and larger individual sites, e.g. Needham Market and Debenham. (Central Sudbury and Woodbridge, on the other hand, have noticeably narrow mediaeval streets.)

The impression given by these townships is one of a general uniformity imposed during the eighteenth and nineteenth centuries, and this is borne out by examination of individual houses. A good example — one of many — occurs in Sudbury. in 1725 the Gainsborough family are said[1] to have acquired a property in Sepulchre Street (later re-named Gainsborough Street after the famous painter who was born there in 1727). John Gainsborough must have set to work at once on a wholesale and extensive re-building of the premises. (This is discussed in more detail in Section 6.) The house was certainly of late mediaeval origins and one of many old timber-framed houses for which Sudbury was once famous. When re-built, however, its mediaevalism had been almost entirely disguised by a classical front in dark red and black brickwork.

In title deeds and local records are no doubt hidden the histories of innumerable town and village houses, but it is only rarely that systematic research has brought such history to light. The owner of No. 111 High Street, Needham Market, himself a writer and historian,[2] has traced the history of his house in considerable detail to the Tudor period, and with reasonable certainty to the reign of Edward IV. The plans of the house showing the successive building phases and other alterations are discussed in more detail in Section 6. The original hall-house adjoining the High Street had been floored over before the end of the fifteenth century, and the premises were then progressively enlarged by extending at the rear of the narrow site. It has been possible to connect the 'commoditie' of the house with its successive owners, and thus to open a vista of structural and social history connected with the business of clothiers and tradesmen.

*Plate 21: The Ancient House, Ipswich, from Illustrations of Old Ipswich by John Glyde, 1889.*

1 cf. Proceedings S.I.A., Volume VII, 1891, pages 1-16.
2 Hugh Paget, Esq., C.B.E., M.A., an authority on Anglo-Dutch relations.

Trade, it must be added, accounted for most of the celebrated town-houses in Suffolk. The well-known Ancient House in Ipswich (Plate 21) originates as a merchants' house in the middle of one of the busiest trading areas in the town — between the Butter Market and the one-time Fish Market. It has been traced to the Fastolf family as builders of the open hall-house in the late fifteenth century, certainly occupied by George Copping in 1570, a draper and fish merchant, and acquited from him by the Sparrowe family who traded in groceries and spices,[1] and who later carried out the extensive conversions of circa 1670 which included the phenomenal plasterwork.

When we can establish further local connexions between commerce and architecture, the pattern of change in houses will become more explicit: Alston Court, Nayland, is another interesting case of correspondence with the fortunes of a wealthy clothier, to be considered in Section 6.

## COTTAGE

The history of the planning of cottages will be found to centre upon one room — the 'hall', in its smallest and most tenuous form — a room of one bay's breadth, with a door and a window opening or two, which served for almost every purpose. These humble 'cots' survive only in pictures, and the latter-day cottage bears little resemblance to the dwellings of 'mud and sticks' which housed all but the poorest in society.[2]

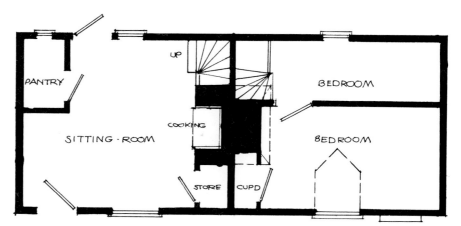

*Figure 36: Pair of farmworkers' cottages, c.1800. Left, ground floor plan; right, first floor plan.*

The Suffolk ploughwright would build his own cottage if his Lord would grant him the favour of a piece of land: see the petition of Thomas Rodgers endorsed by eleven signatures, dated 28th March, 1598, and addressed to Sir Thomas Kytson, his Lordship in London.[3] Thomas begs for licence 'to build himself up a cottage or poor dwelling place upon a piece of the common, next the east end of your pasture called Mare Close . . . ' There is small doubt — the petition having been granted — that this 'poor dwelling place' would have been built of such timbers as could be found, with some probably already used before, and the beam-filling of wattle and daub, the roof thatched. The accommodation would be a single hall, perhaps with the smallest pantry and buttery and over these a loft for sleeping, reached by a ladder.

Improvements at this lowest level of all were slow to follow. The addition to the hall of a couple of service rooms with a loft over, as found at Church Cottage, Pettistree (see Section 6), would be already a considerable advance on the single room. The next step would be the building of a chimney stack, but it might be a hundred years before this came to be put up against an outside wall to replace the central fire, where most of the cooking was done in a tripod-mounted stew-pot suspended over the hearth. The brick chimney was an amenity of consequence, making cooking easier and increasing the warmth and comfort of the room by getting rid of the smoke. Later on a bread-oven would be built alongside and sharing the same flue.

1 cf. *Ipswich Through the Ages*, op. cit., page 35.
2 cf. Appendix of Select Documents *The English Farmhouse and Cottage*, op. cit., page 271.
3 As footnote 2.

*A pair of plaster and thatch cottages at Ufford, 17th century.*

The awakening of social conscience on behalf of the labouring poor in the latter part of the eighteenth century is well discussed in *The Truth about Cottages.*[1] Plans prepared by John Wood, architect, better known as 'Wood of Bath' (1705?-1754) include two-room cottages, the largest about 4.5m by 3.5m (15ft by 12ft) and the smaller 4.5m by 3m (15ft by 10ft), each having a fireplace. And — remarkably in advance of his times — he proposed a lean-to at the back with an outside privy at one end, and the rest a wash-house entered from the living-room.

The farm cottage of the eighteenth century in Suffolk was still economically built of studwork and plaster, but usually had only a single general-purpose sitting-room with cooking in a brick chimney-opening. The stack was central and divided a single or double pair of cottages by back-to-back openings, often enlarged to include bread-ovens (see Figure 36). In the single cottage of this century and the next, the plan had a more or less central front door with a window on each side, and a chimney stack in the middle of the house (the best innovation of many centuries): the entrance was into a lobby against the stack; on one side was the kitchen — usually the largest room — with cooking range and bread-oven, and on the other the parlour, and a tiny corkscrew newel stair on the far side of the chimney stack leading to two bedrooms. In the east of Suffolk, in particular, the roof would often be carried down — 'cat-slide' fashion — to enclose the *baccus*. The nineteenth century landowner and farmer, when building tied dwellings preferred the 'double-dweller' for reasons of economy, with the resultant box-like brick cottages to be seen in most Suffolk villages. The cottages built in rows of four or more usually date from this period also.

*Terrace of brick and flint cottages at Wickham Market, late eighteenth century.*

1 John Woodford, op. cit., see Chapter 4 *Early Pattern Books*, pages 23-29.

*Trevor James*

# Firmenes

## the structure of houses

The structure of houses presupposes a selection of easily obtainable building materials. Traditionally the choice was limited by the stock that lay nearest to hand, and the range of choice was a certain index to the social position of the builder; only the really wealthy could afford to employ special craftsmen or unusual materials. Today, when it is only the wealthy who can afford to use local materials or conventional craftsmanship, the position is reversed and discontent is apt to be aimed not at restrictions but at excessive options in technique and materials, which seldom have any connection with the place of use. One positive aspect of this discontent is a revival of interest in the vernacular, and the wish ' . . . to understand, while there is time to do so, something of the forms and functions, origins and developments of English indigenous buildings.'[1]

In a section on structure in this introduction to the story of Suffolk house-building, the emphasis must first be given to local materials. These have been outlined already in Section 2, but only as 'raw materials', and the next thing is to see how they became used as building materials; for example:—

Wood as building timber[2]

Chalk as lime and cement.

Clay as lump, brick and tile.

Flints as masonry and ornament.

Reed and corn straw as thatch.

The miscellaneous stones, mentioned in Section 2, are too limited in quantity to need more than a passing mention if only to underline the need — in a region destitute of the material — for fetching freestone from elsewhere.

### WOOD IN BUILDING TIMBER

*Native trees*

'Before the Roman invasion of Britain the forest dominated the land. Two-thirds of the lowland and the gentler slopes of a spongy terrain were densely carpeted with oak, birch, Scots pine, ash, hazel, beach, hornbeam and maybe sweet chestnut'.[3] It is worth noticing how several of the common indigenous trees of Suffolk have become part of place names; e.g. alders at Alderton and Aldringham; ash at Ashfield, Ashe, Ashbocking, Badwell Ash; aspens at Aspall 'The aspen-tree nook'; birches at Barking = Berchingas 'Dwellers by the birch trees, and East Bergholt 'the birch-wood East'; elms in the Elmhams, and oaks at Copdock = Coppedoc 'The pollard oak',[4] and more obviously at Oakley and Okenhill. Tree names for houses — especially farmhouses — are a folk tradition, the three most used being elm, poplar and oak, with ash a close runner-up. (Can anyone say how many Poplar Farms there are in Suffolk?) From these names it would be easy to discover most of the main trees of Suffolk; acacia, alder, ash, baythorn, birch, cedar, chestnut, elm, fir, holly, maple, oak, pine, poplar, sycamore, willow and yew.

Oak is often thought to be the exclusive building material of mediaeval England. and it is obvious that enormous quantities were used in the Middle Ages (see Plate 22). Doubtless the churches had first priority,[5] and Cautley agreed that practically the whole of the woodwork in Suffolk churches is English oak: but also that a few mediaeval roofs were constructed of sweet chestnut.[6] There is no doubt that sweet chestnut was used in houses, and probably increasingly in the sixteenth century when oak supplies began to run short.

At the outset it is as well to be clear about *terms: wood* is the generic name for all that part of trees and shrubs which exists between the pith and the bark; *timber* is the name strictly referring to the tree when felled: thus it is correct to refer to buildings made of wood as 'timber-framed' and to all wood used in building as 'timber'. (The word in mediaeval documents for the clearing of forests by grubbing up trees and bushes in order to make them arable is *assart*, and by 1628 (O.E.D.) an

1 This is a quotation from Paul Oliver's introduction to the Arts' Council Exhibition English Cottages and Farmhouses 1975.
2 Sections of wood cut to size (or stone also for that matter) for use in building, are sometimes referred to as 'scantlings'. This is an ambiguous term, having at least three different meanings when applied to building-timbers:
a. Pieces of timber less than 5in. (or 4 or 6in., depending upon locality) in side or depth.
b. Any piece of timber sawn on all faces.
c. A dimension of timber.
For these reasons, the word 'scantling' is not used here.
3 cf. *Trees of the British Isles in History and Legend*, by J.H. Wilkes, page 9.
4 This and foregoing place-name derivatives occur in the Glossary to Lilian Redstone's *Suffolk:* others are to be found in Skeat, op. cit.
5 e.g. Salzman records how Henry III gave thirty oaks for the repair of the central tower of the monastic church at Bury St. Edmunds in 1251 (cf. page 240).
6 A. Clifton Taylor, in *The Pattern of English Building* mentions the traditional belief that chestnut was used in the roofs of Framlingham Church.

*Plate 22: Mature oak without foliage.*                    Forestry Commission

*Plate 23: Chester & Son's timber yard.*

### Seasoned wood and dating timbers

assart had come to mean a piece of land converted into arable by clearance.)

I would commend anyone interested in the connection between building timber and standing trees to search out the English oaks between fifty and a hundred years old,[1] and then to examine them closely in order to decide how they would best provide building timber when felled; which part of the tree would yield the long length logs needed for main structural components such as angles and intermediate posts allowing for the shoulders preferred at the head of such timbers for making an easier joint with the horizontal bressumers or tie-beams, and which parts could be relied on for shorter length timbers such as studs, floor joists, and rafters.

The traditional time for felling was in mid-winter or in mid-summer, because, as one old writer put it 'at these times the vegetative powers are at rest, or have expended all their most changeable parts in producing leaves, etc.' The traditional time for oak trees to arrive at maturity was 100 years. Times were when the wood for building timber was growing only a short way off,[2] but in later mediaeval days the builder would have to reckon with the cost of carting the felled timber considerable distances, and it is not difficult to imagine the heavy task this would have been for waggons and teams of oxen or Suffolk horses over bad roads in winter time.

It was once thought that old builders never used anything but seasoned wood, but a large amount had clearly never been seasoned, and one comes across plenty of examples of principal posts, joists and common rafters obviously used in a hurry from roughly prepared timber, the bark having been barely stripped off and the natural wood — waney edges[3] and all, put in much as it came to hand.[4] The presence of sapwood has always been a danger in building timbers: although, according to a writer in 1615: 'The sap is the life of the tree, as the blood is to man's body', once the tree had been felled the sapwood is liable to cause decay and invite infestation by beetles and woodworm. On the other hand, heartwood is much more resistant to decay and with the sapwood removed oak is practically indestructible, losing little of its strength through cracks and shakes.

I would guess that when mediaeval builders wanted seasoned wood, say for joinery, they would use the plentiful clear-running streams and rivers of Suffolk; water will flush out a lot of the sap when logs are kept submerged butt-end up-stream, and by comparison with sap the water dries out quite quickly, and after a short while the timber could be cut and dry seasoned. Natural seasoning takes place when timbers are stacked parallel to the ground, separated by thin wood strips to promote air drying. I imagine that the appearance of a timber yard cannot have changed much over the centuries and so include a photograph of Messrs. H.E. Chester & Son's yard at Needham Market (see Plate 23) taken in 1975.

The science of dating timbers has made considerable progress in the last thirty years, both in Germany and in England. The method known as 'dendrochronology' is already well-established for dating wood from archaeological excavations and historical buildings, and in Germany owes much to the research in the first place of Professor B. Huber at Munich and subsequently that of Professor J. Bauch and Dr.

1 It seems probable that oaks were often felled before maturity, i.e. at about fifty years if — as was probably the case in the sixteenth century — builders were short of timber.
2 cf. Salzman, page 237: 'At Peterhouse in 1438 they had only to step into the garden — to fell suitable trees, lop the branches and rough them up, to be carried, whole or sawn, to the framing place.'
3 Waney is the term used in the timber trade for splayed edges appearing at one end of a balk, caused by trying to cut too large a balk out of a log.
4 Harry Forrester in *The Timber-Framed Houses of Essex*, 1959, goes so far as saying that oak was not seasoned before use as a general rule, but used soon after felling and allowed to dry *in situ*, cf. page 21. He has allowed me to include the following description of felling oaks in the Middle Ages:
'Standing oaks were selected and felled with the narrow axe. If a tree was of large girth, usually it was cut around with the broad axe, the narrow axe then being used to work through the tough heart-wood. The branches having been lopped, those of growth suitable for braces and brackets were sorted out. Any splitting of big trees to workable logs was done by means of the axe and iron wedges. For cutting across large timber the twart-saw, managed by two men, was used.'

D. Eckstein at Hamburg. Recently this method has been applied to the wood panels used in the past by Dutch artists.

The following description of the dendrochronological method is taken from an article by Bauch/Eckstein/Meier-Siem: 'Dendrochronological analysis is based on the fact that trees in temperate zones develop characteristic, climate-determined series of growth-rings of different width, which corresponds in different trees of the same species in this temporal sequence and are unique within a certain geographical area. Because of the unique pattern of such a tree-ring width, characteristic standard curves, so-called 'tree-ring calendars', can be derived from already dated wood. Undated wood, in . . . buildings or otherwise, can be synchronised with the 'tree-ring calendar' if it belongs to the same period — such standard curves exist for oak and for fir, e.g. for Southern Germany, for oak from the northern plain of Germany . . . '[1] (see Figure 37).

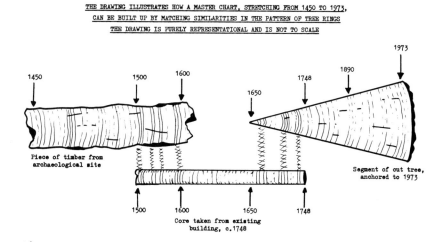

THE DRAWING ILLUSTRATES HOW A MASTER CHART, STRETCHING FROM 1450 TO 1973, CAN BE BUILT UP BY MATCHING SIMILARITIES IN THE PATTERN OF TREE RINGS
THE DRAWING IS PURELY REPRESENTATIONAL AND IS NOT TO SCALE

Figure 37: Dendrochronological chart (prepared by Richardson and Starling Ltd.).

This technique was applied to the timber of bell-towers and farmhouses in the area around Hamburg, and started with recent oak trees, from which data a mean curve (master chart) was plotted, that reaches from the present back to the year 1338 A.D. A large stable-building, called the 'Rieckhauses', near Hamburg, was submitted to forty dated 'probes', which established that timber in five age-groups had been used in the original structure, viz. 1533, 1542, 1565, 1663 and one doubtful group 1533 or 1542.

In England the development of these methods is being undertaken by Dr. John Fletcher at the Research Laboratory for Archaeology and the History of Art at Oxford. Dr. Fletcher has been identifying the ring-width chronology for south-east England for *slow-grown* oak from 850 A.D. to 1550 A.D. (with trees having upwards of 120 annual rings). In addition the results for recent oaks grown in Berkshire and Sussex have been published in *The British Oak,* (cf. 'Annual Rings in Modern and Mediaeval Times' by J.M. Fletcher). In *Archaeometry* 16, 1 (1974) Dr. Fletcher gives a reference curve for slow-grown oaks, A.D. 1230 to 1546.

## Radiocarbon dating

Tree-ring work has been used in conjunction with *radiocarbon dating* to determine the deviations which occur in early samples, and made it possible to calibrate dates to give a value for the tree date expressed in calendar years. Radiocarbon dating is, as Dr. Colin Renfrew put it in his *Before Civilization — The Radiocarbon Revolution* (see Bibliography), 'one of the most elegant contributions made by the natural sciences to archaeology'. Radiocarbon atoms, produced by cosmic rays from outer space, are assimilated into living things. Radiocarbon decays spontaneously, and after the death of the organism no more is taken into it. The decay process allows the remaining radiocarbon in the sample to be detected and estimated, and the 'surprising feature' of all radioactive decay processes is that, whatever the element concerned, they take place in the same, very regular way. This regular decay rate thus permits the calculation of the age of samples when their present remaining radioactivity has been measured.[2]

1 *Dating the Wood of Panels by a Dendrochronological Analysis of the Tree-Rings* in Nederlands Kunsthistorisch Jaarboek, 1972.
2 This account is based — with permission — on a largely verbatim transcription from the Appendix — *Radiocarbon Dating* — to Dr. Renfrew's enthralling book *Before Civilization*.

The traditional way of dating timbers — as well as other materials — is *inferential,* i.e. deductive analysis based upon comparative date such as the size and 'finish' of the sample, the colours and texture, and the existence of joints or mouldings or other features providing points of reference to previously dated work: to be fair, I think one should add the *intuitive* — or clairvoyant — instinct of old builders, who can 'tell' by the look and feel of wood both what it is and, roughly, how old. This ability — based it must be added on knowledge and experience — is dying out, and there are few architects today with the special insight into the nature of stone and brick of the late Donovan Purcell, who, it was said, could take a mediaeval brick in his hand and successfully date it to within ten years.

## CHALK IN LIME AND CEMENT

*Lime*

There is an interesting field awaiting research in the history of the extraction and burning of lime in Suffolk. On the old series of one-inch survey maps for Suffolk published in the 1830s chalk-pits and lime-kilns were often marked, and I have counted upwards of thirty when supplemented by the newer 2½-inch Ordnance series. Here again names are a useful guide, and there are frequent 'Limekiln' Farms (e.g. Brandon, 754 866 and Reydon 475 744); 'Limekiln' Cottages (e.g. Stowlangtoft, 941 693 and Reydon 471 768), and one 'Limekiln Plantation' at Culford (834 716). Not all of these will have been producing quicklime for building, because kilned lime had other uses in agricultural dressings, fuller's work and lime for whitewashing, but where lime-kilns are found close to brick-kilns, as at Brandon and Culford Park, we can be fairly sure that they had to do with building.

The extraction of chalk has a long history going back to Roman times, and Roman builders in Suffolk would have been quick to discover suitable sources of supply.[1] The main chalk quarries today are at Claydon, Great and Little Blakenham, Whitton, Coddenham and at Ballingdon, west of Sudbury, all of varying antiquity. Chalk lime derived from white chalk is produced by burning in a kiln; it is then quicklime, which greedily absorbs water in the slaking process, generating great heat and steam and leaving slaked lime as a fine white powder used in plasters and mortars.

*Cement*

Chalk mixed with clay (in proportion roughly 63% to 30%) produces cement, and the rivers Orwell, Gipping and Deben seem uniquely linked with the history of cement-making in Suffolk. In the middle of the last century, Pinmill had about fifty boats collecting and fetching from rocks near Harwich the stone needed in the manufacture of the so-called *Roman cement.*[2] This would have been Septaria (concretionary clay), much used, before the coming of 'Portland Cement', for its quick, hard-setting properties and strength, but really having nothing to do with the Roman variety and more correctly called 'Parker's Cement' after Parker, its inventor in 1796. (The whole exterior of that Gothic 'wonder' — Rendlesham Hall — was coated in Parker's cement, and I daresay this was also used at Crowe Hall, Stutton, to give the look of stone.)

Less than a century later the enterprising Mason family started the manufacture of Portland Cement at Waldringfield on the river Deben, and Humphrey Mason — brother of Eustace the last director of the family business — has lent me a photograph of the works in operation on the quayside (see Plate 24). The cement was made by mixing chalk — imported, rather surprisingly, by barge from the Medway in Kent — with the local clay.

About 1890, Frank William Mason of Northcliff, Felixstowe, had made chemical soil analyses of land in the Gipping valley, bought a farm from Mr. Wainwright, closed down the Waldringfield works and started a new Portland Cement factory at Claydon. Industry was already there in the form of lime-kilns and a whiting-manufactury immediately east of the navigable river Gipping, and conveniently along the valley ran the Eastern Union Railway — the new works were sited just west of the river and next to the railway station. Thus came into being about 1900 Mason's Portland Cement Co. Ltd., with the first rotary kiln put in during the 1914-1918 war, to be followed by a period of expansion and electrification, until in the mid-1940s the flourishing family business was sold to the Cement Marketing Company.

E CEMENT WORKS, WALDRINGFIELD.

*Plate 24: Mason's works at Waldring-field, 1909 (from a picture postcard).*

1 Vitruvius in his *De Architectura* details the making of *pozzolana,* a cement producing a mortar as strong as the aggregate giving the underlying strength to Roman walls, vaults and domes. cf. *Building Construction* by Martin S. Briggs in *A History of Technology.*
2 cf. William White's *Gazeteer,* edition 1855, page 218.

# CLAY IN LUMP, BRICK AND TILE

*Plate 25: Clay-lump wall in a farm building.*

Long before the clays of Suffolk were made into bricks, they gave a rough-and-ready kind of cement. Plastic clays — as their name suggests — can be moulded and worked when moist and, applied in a tacky state to a key such as wattle work, will adhere and harden on drying out; this was known to the earliest East Anglian builders and thought to have been much used in the walls of primitive structures. By the Middle Ages the technique used was wattle and daub[1] for the walling of timber buildings, and clay for the making of blocks or clay-lump. I suppose that by the eighteenth century clay-lump had gone out for houses but was still in use for farm buildings (see Plate 25). But the matter is not quite so simply decided because most cottages and farmhouses are plastered outside, and only a close examination will show whether the walls are built in the traditional wattle and daub or of clay-lump.

The way of making clay-lump is quite well known. Mr. P.J.O. Trist has a paragraph in his *Survey of the Agriculture of Suffolk*[2] with the following pleasant description: 'Pits were hand dug through the soil into the yellow-white clay subsoil which was loosened and covered with long straw. A horse was then led round and round to incorporate the straw into the clay. It was then lifted into a tumbril which two horses drew out to the farmyard where it was put into wooden box moulds to dry out as clay-lump brick.' These 'bricks' varied from about 18 inches long, 12 inches wide, and 7 inches deep to 17 by 8 by 6 inches: a sample of the latter taken from a cart-lodge at Great Bradley weighed — according to Mr. Trist — 46lb., and would be tiring to lay in any quantity and explain the diminished use when true bricks became plentiful and cheap.[3] According to Mr. H.E.P. Spencer, clay-lump was still produced at Wattisfield as late as 1930.

Clough Williams-Ellis in his *Cottage Building* (see Section Bibliography) — out-of-print, alas — would have it that, for no very apparent reason, the use of sun-dried bricks was almost entirely restricted to East Anglia, and added some interesting comments on clay-lump building by the Norwich Architect, Mr. Skipper:

'These lump walls are, of course, built on a base of brickwork, about 18 inches or 2 feet high to keep them free from damp.' '... the joints are generally stopped up and besmeared with a thin coating or almost a wash of clay.'

'A further stage in finish is to give the walls two or three coats of coal tar ... and the highest finish .... is to cast sand on the last coating of tar before it is quite dry, and then to colour or whitewash on this.'

The other advantages of clay-lump building — economy apart[4] — have proved to be first, *strength* — mature blocks taken out of an old building have had to be broken up with sledge-hammers; secondly, *endurance* — C. Williams-Ellis mentions buildings in East Harling, Norfolk, the oldest of 200 years or upwards and 'not a pin the worse' for wear; and thirdly, *insulation* — clay-lump walls are 'noted for being warm in winter and cool in summer.'

There seems no logical argument against the revival — in this age of inflation and compulsive DIY — of such clay building methods, either in solid walls plastered or in cavity work: a spontaneous as opposed to a spurious return to traditional methods, and well within individual control.

Suffolk — so much of which is clayland — has plentiful supplies of brickearth. The geological sequence of the county has been analysed and admirably set out by Mr. H.E.P. Spencer, F.G.S.[5] Mr. Spencer shows how the brickearths occur, over the Chalk and Thanet Beds, in the *Reading Beds, London Clay,* and *Norwich Brickearth;* in the Reading series are the coloured, plastic clays — grey or green (due to iron) with crimson blotches (due to haematite, ferric oxide), and these were used in the Great Cornard brickyard. 'London Clay was the raw material of brickmakers from Sudbury to Bramford.'[6] Aldeburgh and South Cove bricks are made from a marine clay of 'varve' type, deposited during a cold period following the crag period. This Baventrian clay occurs from Easton Bavents to Peasenhall and was used for brickmaking in former times: it is strongly micaceous showing 'spangles' in the brick. Colours in brickwork were produced by nature's own chemistry; the Norwich seam, having plentiful iron oxides, gives pink, rich red, and even dark blue when burnt at high temperatures; white bricks are caused by plentiful magnesia in the

---

1 'Wattle and daub': this form of clay walling is so intricately linked with timber-framed building practice that it will be discussed as part of that subject later on.
2 op. cit., page 66. Mr. Trist has a page of photographs showing 'old building materials formerly used in Suffolk'; viz. brick and flint, upper chalk clunch, clay-lump wall, and wattle and daub.
3 Average brick weights: Flettons 5-6lb., common stocks 6-7lb., best pressed bricks and wire-cuts without frogs 7-8lb., and 9-10lb. for Blue Staffordshires and some special bricks.
4 The cheapness of clay lump in 1849 is shown in the figures quoted by W. and H. Raynbird; viz: Lumps made at 5s. to 7s. per 100, and walls built at 10d. and 1s. per yard square at 1 foot thickness, including the pinning and foundation.
5 cf. *A Contribution to the Geological History of Suffolk* by Harold E.P. Spencer, F.G.S., published in Transactions of the Suffolk Naturalists Society (see Section Bibliography). Mr. Spencer has sent the following further notes. The Woolpit clay is of glacial origin. When the ice sheets melted, great quantities of water were liberated. In summer the force carried away coarse gravel and boulders which were deposited near the source. Smaller grade gravels were deposited further away, then coarse sand, fine sand and finally rock plant grade material in lakes. These deposits were seasonal, varves (layers) from masses of considerable thickness (as at Marks' Tey). They occur (the varved clays) at Boxford, Sudbury, and remants at Bramford with patches at Ipswich. The Woolpit clay originated in this way. It was assumed the white colour was due to the high proportion of calcium carbonate, but some magnesium could be due to the passage of the ice sheet over an area of magnesian limestone.
6 Ibid., Volume 13, Part 4, page 202.

London clays (supplemented by sulphur from the fuel used in clamp-burning). There is great natural beauty in the softly-mixed colours of early brickwork, e.g. Tudor period, and I recommend anyone interested in such effects to observe a section of the brickwork on the early sixteenth century tower of, shall we say, Ashbocking church. There is an overall diaper pattern of dark blue and the general effect is red; the joints are half-inch thick of creamy lime-mortar, but these rather roughly shaped bricks on close examination include shades of dark red, purple saffron yellow and chocolate brown — the very ground work of authentic *pointillisme*.

By what alchemy was the raw clay dug from pits transformed into bricks of such variety? The answer must be partly in the simple methods of the old brickmakers, and the traditional ways of making bricks. Bricks — from almost every conceivable angle — have been submitted to intensive study in recent times, with the result that a general continuity has been established in the typology of brick from the Roman period until the present century, and the period of obscurity narrowed from the end of the Roman occupation until the twelfth century.[1] The Romans bequeathed to this island the use of brick kilns and their potteries and tile kilns have been shown to have existed in over a hundred widely scattered places, with the main concentrations in the east, south east, and south Midlands.[2] The presence of extensive building in the third and fourth centuries has been put forward as a reason for the Tile Works at Melton, near Woodbridge. Occasionally there is the excitement of an authentic discovery, such as that at Byng Hall, Pettistree, recorded by V.B. Redstone in *The Annals of Wickham Market* published in 1896.[3] This refers to the discovery of a clay tile kiln thought to have been abandoned whilst in complete working order when Boudicca swept through this countryside (c.AD 61).

Miss Jane Wight confirms that there is no contemporary description of early brickmaking 'and what is known ... is pieced together from odd scraps of knowledge and a projection back of brickmaking processes in more recent times, when bricks were still shaped by hand and mechanisation was lacking — except for the pugmill, with horizontal beaters on a vertical shaft, used to mix the clay.' The rich variety of Tudor brickwork could be explained by rough moulds; the presence of pebbles, flints and shells; irregular firing surface marks coming from contact with straw, or, as Miss Wight suggests of the deep cuts in the face of bricks at St. Olave's Priory, Herringfleet, the indent of reeds;[4] and, of course, the natural and uncontrolled variety of coloured clays. The trade was always seasonal, and in its essentials conforms with Mr. Harley's Method (4)a in which wooden brick moulds were filled with tempered clay dried under cover and then burnt in a kiln or clamp; 'this was the basic method in use, with variations, from the later Middle Ages into our own times, from the thirteenth to the twentieth century'.[5] Perhaps the only innovation during this long period was the use of the moulding stock in the eighteenth century, which formed the hollow in the back of each brick known to most bricklayers as the 'frog', but called by the London Brick Company the 'indent'.

But the progress of brickmaking has been towards mechanical techniques of increasing sophistication, and the sequence in a highly automated modern brick factory consists of eight stages: 1. Crushing clay to size for grinding; 2. Reducing clay to size for screening in the grinding mill; 3. Conveying clay from silo to mixing plant; 4. Extruding brick-shaped columns of clay; 5. Loading stacked bricks into drying chamber; 6. Setting dried bricks on kiln cars; 7. Firing bricks in the tunnel kiln, and 8. Banding bricks into packs for despatch.[6] The resultant bricks are notable for their conformity of size, colour and texture, and this is the logical result when complete mechanisation takes charge; they are dependable but wholly lacking in the character of the handmade article of which Peter Catchpole of Colliers, Marks Tey, once said: 'Each (brick) is as individual as a fingerprint'.

By a first happy circumstance one — and one only — of the old private brickworks was still active on the Benacre Estate when material for this book was being assembled, and, by a second, the *Story of Somerleyton Brickfields* was written by Audrey and Arnold Butler, and published by Revd. Dr. Edward C. Brooks, the Rector of Somerleyton, early in 1975. These two circumstances are to

1 cf. *A Typology of Brick* by L.S. Harley, 1974. (See Section Bibliography.)
2 At Wattisfield the varved clay — rich in mica — was first used by the Romans for pottery. Other kilns were at Pakenham and West Stow.
3 My attention was kindly drawn to this by Mr. H.C. Wolton.
4 Mr. Harley says that he has seen and photographed reed marks also on early bricks from Walberswick, near Southwold, Suffolk.
5 Ibid., Journal of the B.A.A., Volume XXXVIII, 1974, page 66.
6 This sequence is mentioned in the description of the new brick factory at Nostell, near Wakefield, published by Ibstock Building Products Ltd.

*Plate 26: Filling the mould. Benacre brickworks, 1975.*

*Plate 28: Tunnel kiln, Benacre brickworks.*

some extent complementary, forming part of the history of Estate Brickworks in Suffolk.[1] At Somerleyton there was both blue and red clay. The clays were dug out in the autumn or early winter – in itself a sometimes hazardous operation – and loaded on to bogey-trucks to be pushed by two men along a light railway track. At Benacre the clay was mixed with loam from another heap, making a 'malm' – or artificial clay – and not broken down into a slurry as Somerleyton, but left to weather and temper until ready for use, when it was worked over with shovels, larger stones and impurities removed, and then puddled with water. In both works the next stage is the feeding of the prepared clay into the pugging mill, and at the Benacre works a diesel engine drives a hopper-fed mill which ejects plastic clay by means of chutes on to each of the three work benches.

*Plate 27: The hacks and hales at Benacre brickworks.*

It was then that the craftsmanship of the brickmakers was most apparent. Standing at his bench the brickmaker took sand from an often replenished heap in front of him, and sanded both the moulding stock (see Plate 26) containing the frog and the brick mould itself, to prevent the clay sticking; added a little water to the puddled clay if necessary, and then with a dexterous twist flung clay into the mould,[2] pressed it home and cleaned off the residue with the wooden 'strike'. The mould was then quickly reversed and the raw brick slipped onto a thin, flat, slightly larger than brick-sized board called a pallet, of which the brickmakers had always a stack ready by the side of their work benches. The loaded pallet was then placed on a long wooden soft-brick barrow ready to be wheeled to the hacks, or open sheds, where the drying took place. Also used in drying were hales, long dwarf sheds with movable wooden covers taken off in fine weather (see Plate 27).

The last stage is the packing of the bricks into the kiln which, at the Benacre works, took place about every five weeks in the brick making season, and the firing of the kiln which lasted for about 72 hours. This was a tunnel kiln some 35 feet long which had to be kept going continually throughout the 'burn', and the brickmakers were expert at throwing shovelfulls of coal the whole length of the firechamber (see Plate 28). Production between March and November was about 200,000 bricks. Before firing, the bricks had a strong sandy yellow colour, which turned afterwards into a bright clear red;[3] each brick weighing about 8lb. and measured 9 by $4\frac{3}{8}$ by $2\frac{5}{8}$in. (228 by 111 by 67mm).

The start, growth and decline of the brick industry in Suffolk is in great need of immediate study. The same centripetal tendencies which drove the cloth trade away from Suffolk, also destroyed the local industry in building materials. Today, with the closing of the Benacre works, there are only two private works in Suffolk making hand-made bricks: at Aldeburgh and at Sudbury. Many of the local brickworks used also to make roofing tiles, but not one is hand-made today. But the history of the brick industry is gathering its supporters, and there is in Suffolk a flourishing regional group of the British Brick Society (founded 1972). In conjunction with the British Brick Society, the British Archaeological Association

1 In an interesting letter, Mrs. Slater wrote to me about the remains of old brick buildings and a brickworks on four acres of her land at Easton, which, I suppose, is likely to have been the Estate Brickworks. From Mr. George Roper I heard that there was a brick kiln between Helmingham Church and School, and I think a Mr. Last was in charge, only about forty-five years ago. That would mean c.1928, and the site is still shown on the 2½in. O.S. in the Helmingham Estate. (See also Section 6.)
2 Mr. Harley comments: 'The physical effort is worth noting: each 'clot' weighs about 10lb. and this 10lb. of wet clay is flung into the mould every 30 seconds of a long eight hour day, making some 1000 bricks a day, each brickmaker using a total of 4½ tons of wet clay.'
3 Mr. Harley comments: 'I asked how it was that Benacre Hall is built (or faced) with 'white' bricks when the whole output of S. Cove works is red. The old brickmaker told me that Benacre Hall white bricks came from the old yard at Frostenden (not far away), long since closed.'

has formed a Brick Section. Time has a way of obliterating evidence more rapidly than seems possible, and what would have been relatively easy even 30-40 years ago – a register of Suffolk brickworks of, say, the last 200 years at least – is today fraught with difficulties. The ideal condition of local history would be positive knowledge of where and when the first bricks (and tiles) were made, and in what buildings they were used, coupled with the exact date on the artifacts themselves; shape, size, colour, characteristics, processes of manufacture and methods of use; on this groundwork of knowledge would be erected the historical superstructure in which the perspective of advance and recession would be apparent and related to techniques of fabrication and usage cross-referenced to structures in which these would be visible, this scaffolding of knowledge being extended century by century until the present date.

Needless to say a programme of these dimensions presupposes a degree of academic – and practical – interest, for which the conditions have hardly been favourable until this present half-century, with the result that lists of brickfields and brickworks in Suffolk can now be compiled, with difficulty, only from about 1740 onwards, and cross-referencing between maker and user – the works supplying the materials and the buildings in which they were used – is even harder.

### Brickworks near rivers

Perhaps there is one feature in the 'where' of brickmaking worth noting at this primary stage: in Suffolk about 70 brickworks have been recorded between c.1740-1800,[1] and all but 25 of these were to be found either on, or adjoining rivers. There are two possible explanations: (1) geological – the riverside clay would be easy to exploit because it can occasionally appear as at Stutton in '. . . a river cliff . . . half-a-mile in length, varying from 10 to 20 feet in height.'[2] Location would not always have been as favourable as this, but it is well known that mediaeval brickmakers used shallow deposits of clay frequently beginning with riverside or estuarine beds;[3] (2) transport – if many more rivers were navigable by barges of shallow draught, as may have been the case, then the proximity of waterborne transport would be an obvious advantage; it was one frequently claimed in eighteenth century advertisements: e.g. Harkstead kiln near Holbrook: 'the said kiln is near the River Stour, that bricks may be delivered into lighters, etc., and conveyed by water at an easy expence'; at Kingston, Woodbridge:– 'the kiln stands within 50 yards of Woodbridge River, where they may ship for any part of the Kingdom'; or a site at Beccles, with 'fine Brick Earth', and the 'convenience of a navigable river'.

### Roofing tiles

It was quite usual for Suffolk brickmakers to make roofing tiles; we have seen this happening at Somerleyton, and it was certainly the case at the Benacre works.[4] Apart from technical skill – and not much was required – the really important thing was good quality brickearth. In the main two kinds of tiles were made – plain tiles and pantiles. The difficulty for historians of mediaeval building has always been in knowing whether – as Salzman says – 'an entry of tiles (*tegule*) in a building account refers to roofing, building, or paving tiles, but those used for roofing are sometimes defined as 'thaktyle' or, more often, as 'flat (*plane*) tiles'.' From Salzman, again, we learn that roofing tiles were to be had at least from the beginning of the thirteenth century (London building regulations of 1212 give tiles as one of the materials that might be used in place of thatch).[5] But it is as well to remember that there was a precedent for the 'plane' tile in the oak tile, or shingle, and there is good reason for believing that wooden shingles were in use in Anglo-Saxon Britain, both for roof and wall covering. Harley gives the mid-twelfth century as the first date for British bricks,[6] and I see no reason why, by this date or soon after, clay roofing tiles should not also have been made.

The plain tile started as a humble slab of fired brick clay, quite flat, of a darkish red colour, with a size 'standardised' by Statute of Edward IV in 1477 as 10½in. by 6¼in. with a minimum thickness of $\frac{5}{8}$in.: later it came to be cambered (see Figure 38). In 1951, during the course of stripping the clay plain tiles from the roof of a Kentish hotel, one was removed with an inscription on the face 'Thomas Rack his tile June the 21, 1777', and on the back the name of the burner. These tiles showed no deterioration and were said to be in the prime of life and 'good for at least another 150 years' service.[7]

In the making, the clay was first pugged, and at Benacre this was once done by a

1 These are the brickworks or brickfields appearing in advertisements to *The Ipswich Journal*, starting in 1740 and ending in 1798, and represent the indefatigable researches of Mrs. E.M. Walker.
2 cf. *The Stutton Brickearth, Suffolk* by H.E.P. Spencer, F.G.S., in the Proceedings of the Geologists Association, Volume 64, Part I, 1953, pages 25-28.
3 cf. J. Wight *Brick Building in England*, page 140. Mr. Harley adds this comment: 'such estuarine or lacustrine clays seem to have been used to make the bricks for Little Wenham Hall c.1280.'
4 Mr. Rouse showed me one of the wooden moulds once used for making pantiles. The works also produced floor-paving clay tiles, usually known in Suffolk as 'pamments'.
5 *Building in England* by L.F. Salzman, F.S.A., page 229.
6 *A Typology of Brick* by L.S. Harley, page 71.
7 *The Clay Tile Bulletin*, Volume 1., No. 3, March 1951.

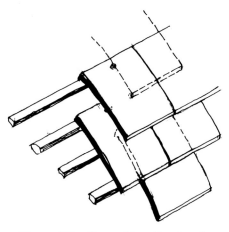

*Figure 38: Clay plain tiles (modern pattern has pegs as well as nail holes).*

*Figure 39: Clay pantiles on battens.*

horse walking round and round in a circle, pugging the clay in the pit in preparation for tile making (the same methods were used for brick clay before the days of the engine driven mill). The clay was washed and sieved, and then thwacked into a mould which had first been sanded — hence the expression sand-faced tile (or brick) — and later fired in the kilns.

Pantiles were an innovation in East Anglia although they were to become as much a part of vernacular architecture as the plain tile; their origins are in the Low Countries, and Professor Temminck-Groll (of the Delft Technical High School) considers that the so-called Dutch pantiles appear in Holland early in the sixteenth if not in the late fifteenth century. Pantiles were brought into East Anglia by Dutch and Flemish settlers during the seventeenth century, and then manufactured locally later in that century, or early in the eighteenth century.[1]

The size of pantiles decreed by Act of Parliament in 1722 (12 George I) as not less — when burnt — than 13½in. long by 9½in. wide and ½in. thickness was confirmed during the present century by British Standard Specification (see Figure 39). The characteristic colour of the Suffolk tiles was red — a red which varied from a dark terracotta to a bright yellow-red like that of a ripe blood-orange — and the brighter shade could be dazzling and especially exciting when seen on the roof of a black weatherboarded building.[2] In complete contrast was the black glazed pantile, often found in the coastal areas of Norfolk and Suffolk and very much a 'foreigner', having been once imported from the Low Countries. The upper surface of the tile was painted black, and then a glaze of either lead or salt was added, and made hard and transparent by firing.

## FLINT IN MASONRY AND ORNAMENT

The common flint, lying about the surface of the Suffolk claylands, was the bane of the arable farmer and a boon both to the roadmaker and the builder. The practice of stone-picking from the fields, as George Ewart Evans said,[3] had gone on for centuries; he describes how the stones were gathered in buckets and carried to a heap which was later picked up by one of the farmer's men responsible for carting the stone away in a tumbril for sale to the Highway authority.[4] Flint is the characteristic stone of chalk-based soils, endlessly turned up in the cultivation of fields and found in layers in the river beds and beaches of Suffolk and Norfolk and in inland gravel pits, a roundish sometimes freakishly shaped nodule with a surface colour grey-white, bright yellow or dark brown; a humble object until split open to reveal an interior bright as glass with black, cloudy, opaline and speckled colours. But the humble nodule is practically indestructible, and at Burgh Castle the walls, in rubble construction of enormous thickness, are faced with four courses of flint nodules to three lacing courses of wall tile in high-grade Roman cement. They are intact after about 1700 years of coastal weather. Such masonry was one case where Saxon architects copied their wall construction from Roman models. Norman engineers, too, made use of similar construction in the curtain walls of motte-and-bailey castles and in church building, as, for example, the stratified rubble walls of twelfth century Henstead Church, near Beccles.

The invention of flint decoration belongs to mediaeval East Anglian church builders who used it in panels framed by freestone on the outside of churches or other religious buildings. No unusual skill is needed — as Cautley said — to 'knap' or fracture flint,[5] the term 'knapped flintwork' is sometimes used for this type of church work but O.E.D. gives for 'knap' merely 'to snap or break by a smart blow', and this, as Cautley added, could be done by any skilled local workman. It was the next stage of shaping knapped flints into square or other geometrical pieces to which the name of 'flushwork' was given,[6] and for which special skills were needed. Norman Wymer once described the getting out and shaping of flints from the shafts at Brandon, and how the flintworker piled his flints round the top of the mine 'until he has a jag', or cartload, ready to be transported to the knappers.[7] The shaping of the flint took place as follows: 'When the uneven blocks of flint are well dried, the craftsman selects one and places it on his knee, and quarters it by giving a series of short sharp taps with his hammer, followed by a harder blow from the elbow, to break it into even square pieces.' I think it would be misleading to consider the Brandon flint-knappers as having a monopoly of this skill, which must

1 Dr. Clifton-Taylor quotes, cf. *The Pattern of English Building*, page 263, the granting of a patent by Charles I for 'the making of Pantiles or Flanders Tyles' as early as 1636. The date usually given is 1701, and the place, Tilbury, by a company in which Daniel Defoe had an interest.
2 I remember Mr. Rouse pointing out the red (unglazed) pantiles which had been on the roofs of the hacks at the Benacre Estate works for over a hundred years, and saying that a well made pantile is immensely strong and weather resistant: the strength must lie in the reverse-curves in much the same way as in the 'crinkle-crankle' brick wall.
3 cf. *The Farm and the Village*, 1969, page 57. T.D. Atkinson in *Local Style in English Architecture* mentions the laborious collection of flints for building from the surface of the fields, and quotes from Churchwarden's Accounts (of Cox) this entry at North Elmham in 1538: 'To the scolers for bred and drynk when they gathered stones, ijd.'
4 Ibid., pages 57 and 58.
5 op. cit., page 116.
6 I know of none who has perceived the visual qualities of flushwork so deeply as the Suffolk painter — Cavendish Morton. In his studies of church walls he conveys the rich and velvety depth of flint, not merely black and white but shot through with luminous tints of blue and brown, and heightened here and there with the rusty orange of lichens.
7 cf. *English Country Crafts* by Norman Wymer, (1946 Batisford.), page 112.

*Plate 29: Cutting reeds with an Alan scythe.*

## Thatching material

have been acquired by many country masons and tradesmen.

The thatched roof is as indigenous to Suffolk as the timber-framed wall, the brick, the clay-tile and the flint. The reason is not difficult to seek: reeds grow naturally in the verges and pools of the tidal river estuaries up and down the long coastline and in the swamps and shallow water of river valleys. A very long time ago the usefulness of this 'stout, durable grass'[1] for roofing was realised and it is still the most sought after of the thatching materials. The reeds may grow anything from 1 metre (say 3 feet) to 3¾ metres (12 feet) in length with long leaves and the characteristic purplish-brown plumy heads: winter frost kills and dries them, putting a crop at the mercy of the weather in a mild winter when only a few frosts can much reduce the yield. The traditional cutting season is between January and the second week in April and for centuries the reeds were cut with a scythe or sickle: the thatchers of today will convert an Alan scythe for the work (see Plate 29). Cutting is followed by drying — for the reeds must be bone-dry before they are bundled and baled with string — and then stacking ready for use; if damp they would merely generate heat on bundling and rapidly decay.

The cutting of reeds for thatching would be as natural as the digging out of soft yellow clays for walling, but it would only be arable farming which could produce the long straw wheat, oats, barley and rye considered suitable for roofing. We need old accounts to tell us more of local usage, as Salzman could quote, for instance, the purchase at Ripon in 1392, of barley straw for thatching, but gives no mention of East Anglia, where today only long straw wheat is thought to be satisfactory. But historians are agreed that in the best mediaeval practice unthreshed straw was used, which meant that the ears of corn only were reaped by sickle leaving a high stubble for the thatcher.[2] It stands to reason that threshing by flailing on the granary floor would damage the straw (destroying the continuity of the fibres as Innocent put it),[3] and it was reckoned that its life, as thatch, would be 'not much more than half that of unthrashed stubble'.[4] Today when the combine harvester breaks the stalks of the straw making it useless for thatching anyway, no exception is taken to threshed straw.[5]

Two further raw materials which became important parts of the thatching trade must be mentioned: sedge — the generic name for one of the large family of grasses growing in swampy places in parts of Norfolk and Suffolk — is sometimes to be seen in the ridges of thatched roofs where reeds are useless because they are too brittle for curvature. The sedges — being 'filamentous' or threadlike — are pliable, and sometimes preferred because they go better in colour and texture with reed thatch than the more usual straw ridging. Innocent quotes the sedge *cladium*

*Cottages on the Green at Cavendish, c.1910 – Basil Oliver.*

1 cf. Everyman's Encyclopaedia, page 375; the botanical name is *Phragmites Communis*.
2 cf. Salzman, op. cit., page 225.
3 cf. Innocent, op. cit., page 191.
4 cf. Salzman, ibid., page 225.
5 On March 15th, 1975 the *East Anglian Daily Times* carried a picture of thirty tons of wheat being threshed by an old Ransomes drum-machine at Boxted Hall Farm, near Colchester, for the use of Suffolk master thatcher Stuart Osborne.

*Plate 30: Fixing reed thatching to spars.*

*mariscus* growing in the Cambridgeshire fens as making, according to T.M. and M.C. Hughes '. . . a beautiful durable thatch', for its sharp serrated edges 'keep away birds and rats'.[1] The other material is hazel wood, which was traditionally used for the laths — or 'spars' — laid across and nailed to the rafters every 5-6 inches (125-152mm), being quite slender stuff about 1½in. by ¾in. (40mm x 20mm) to which the thatch was fixed by long tough strands of bramble (see Plate 30). Hazel is still part of the thatcher's stock-in-trade for broaches, the hair-pin like prongs used both in reed and long straw thatching which the thatchers like to cut the week before Christmas when the sap is down, and during the wet weather or slack periods shape into spars about 24in. long (610mm) with sharp points and a slight thinning at the waist for easier bending. The special merit of hazel is its long-fibred strands which withstands the typical sharp-wrist twitch of broach making.[2]

## BUILDING METHODS: TIMBER

In following the course of traditional house building, we have reached the point when the 'raw' materials have been converted to building materials, and are ready, as it were, in the yards and sheds of the builders and tradesmen for use on site. Supposing the first job to be the timber-framed house, the next question is as to the methods used.

Pending other and detailed studies, it seems more in keeping with the introductory character of this book to look simply at the *principles* of the developed form of timber-framed building in Suffolk. This purpose will have been served by taking and illustrating in isometric an actual example of a house of mid-fifteenth century date in order to show the structural framework, together with an added cross-wing of the early seventeenth, and some of the typical carpentry joints. Having established the main features of a building system which, although constantly developing, never departed far from basic principles, we can then discuss how the open hall gave way to the fully floored plan. But first to the tradesman himself, and the way a job was organised.

The carpenter is one of the oldest of the trades, and in mediaeval East Anglia — including Essex — the tradesman with responsibilities as great — if not greater — than those of the mason: he it was who designed and framed the high roofs of churches and halls, and built the manor houses, farmhouses and dwellings of almost the entire community. He was both 'wright' — a craftsman, according to Innocent, responsible also for other woodwork such as farm utensils and furniture — and 'wainwright', who made the large four-wheeled waggons, drawn by horses or oxen whose name came from the Anglo Saxon 'weanwyrthta'. The mediaeval Latin for

*Cottage at Stanstead, near Long Melford; sadly destroyed by fire in 1910 — Basil Oliver.*

### The Carpenter

1 op. cit., pages 213 and 214.
2 I owe a lot to the Chilvers family of Pettistree and their cheerful readiness for endless discussion on the craft of thatching and for the use of Plates 29 and 30.

Read Hall · Mickfield · Suffolk · circa 1450

John Le Comber Del. 1975

*Figures 40: Read Hall, Mickfield as it would have looked at the time of construction; exterior above, interior view left.*
*Figure 41: Crown Post at Read Hall.*

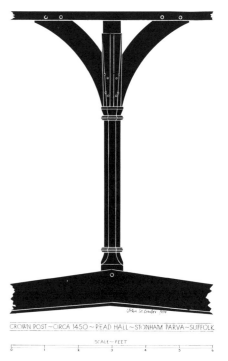

CROWN POST ~ CIRCA 1450 ~ READ HALL ~ STONHAM PARVA ~ SUFFOLK
SCALE ~ FEET

his name was *carpentarius*, but, according to Francis B. Andrews[1] he was sometimes *domifex* ('maker of houses'): and it is as the maker of houses that we are now chiefly interested in him and his methods.

The master carpenter would not be one to delegate his responsibility for the selection of standing trees for felling to any sub-contractor, and we may be sure that until at least the middle of the sixteenth century, he would himself make the choice for felling, and, with an expert eye, decide which trees would offer the best principals, curved brackets and braces, and from which trunks or limbs the large cambered tie-beams could be taken.[2]

*Erection of a small manor house*

Assuming the contract for the timber-framed house to have been agreed, how did the job proceed? The house I have chosen to illustrate in isometric is a typical small manor house of c.1450 (see Figure 40). It is based upon an authentic model, the old name for which has been lost but until recently has been known as Reads Farm, Mickfield. Now known as Read Hall, the early part is a Gothic hall house, comprising a central hall with service rooms to the east, parlour and solar to the west. The original parlour end went when the large seventeenth century chimney stack was built, and the cross-wing added in 1601. The structure of the cross-wing is shown separately but detached from the earlier house, whereas in fact it replaced the original parlour wing: in this way we can form a more complete idea of the original hall house built in the reign of Henry VI.

The order of building would have been somewhat as follows:—

(1)     The plan having been decided and the site chosen, the builder would next settle the overall dimensions, and proceed to work out the principal timber components. These would be settled by the number of bays, and in a four-bay house comprising a two-bay hall and single-bay service and parlour ends, there would be five principal posts to each side — two corner posts and three intermediate of a uniform height of about twelve feet. The main frame would be completed by the horizontal members — sill, middle rail and wall plate each about 265mm by 165mm (10½in. by 6½in.). The number of studs in the outer walls would be governed by the width of the bays between principal posts, and they average about 455mm (1ft 6in.) centre to centre, the parlour bay being one stud-width wider than the service bay.

The main partitions were to be at each end of the hall extending from floor to apex of roof, with at least one other partition dividing the service rooms into two.

(2)     The pitch of about 50° suggests that the roof was intended for thatching, but the possibility of tiling cannot be ruled out. The roof structure required three cambered tie-beams, one joined to each of the three principal posts, and the middle one to support a central crown-post (see Figure 41) which, in turn, would support a collar purlin and short collars at about two-thirds of the height of the rafters.

(3)     The carpenter would figure out the timber parts, and from experience could decide the number of main walls and roof frame components required (the *sizes* might have been agreed already with the employer), together with the secondary elements such as studs, braces, trimmers, floor joists and boards, rafters, collars, wind-braces, and crown-posts. He would also calculate his mullion windows, doors with arched heads and frames and ironmongery. His experience of assembling timbers would be ready to suggest the most suitable carpentry joints for the job in hand, and, being a practical tradesman, he might decide to make certain 'improvements' in jointing. (We owe to Mr. C.A. Hewett a study of Essex Carpentry which develops the hypothesis that different categories of joints can help to establish the dating of timber-framed buildings.)[3]

(4)     Fabrication (pre-fabrication) of the timbers would be done off-site in the carpenters' workshop. The various pieces could be cut to size and length and the mortises and tenon formed, and tried out. Sections of the framing would no doubt be roughly erected to make sure that they would fit well together in the final assembly. This done, the carpenter would use his 'prykng' knife to figure the principal timbers by means of Roman numerals (sometimes his own rather odd version), thus giving a key to the sequence of assembly by

1 *The Mediaeval Builder and his Methods*, op. cit., page 73. F.B. Andrews has much detail on organisation, trades and tools.
2 cf. *The Building of Redgrave Hall*, op. cit., page 5; in the second year of the work — 1546 — a carpenter was paid for 'felling of XL treys appoynted by Gybbon': in this case it was the master mason who decided which trees were to come down no doubt after discussion with the carpenter. In the Accounts of Little Saxham Hall, there is more than one reference to the hewing of timber and carriage to site.
3 cf. *The Development of Carpentry 1200-1700*, op. cit.

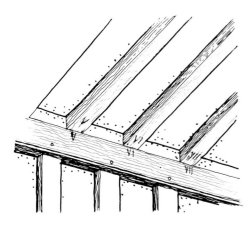

*Figure 42: Timbers numbered for sequence of assembly.*

1 The numerical sequence given to structural timbers are sometimes referred to as 'joint assembly marks'. As the timbers were erected in sequence, the existence of these marks forms a useful guide to the extent of the original build and, correspondingly, can indicate where subsequent alterations have taken place.
2 George Ewart Evans in *The Pattern under the Plough* has some interesting observations on 'house raising' on pages 30-33, and the customs connected therewith.
3 Salzman, op. cit., page 202. One of the remarkable qualities of a well made timber-frame was resistance to settlement stresses: it is not unusual to find structures where differential movements have caused a phenomenal degree of settlement – floors up one end and down the other – but, where the frame still holds together owing to the inherent strength of the joints. I suspect that the mediaeval builder knew a lot about shrinkages in clay subsoils, and that thatched roofs – which had no gutters – were relied on to keep the soil moist around buildings; troubles started when the thatch was replaced by tiles and this natural arrangement of preserving soil moisture was lost.

numbers on site (see Figure 42).[1] Pegs of oak heartwood would be got ready to lock the mortise and tenon joints, and the final peg-holes would no doubt be bored on site after the frame erection.

(5) One day the components, piled in long wains, would begin to arrive and be off-loaded on the site. By then the brick base, or plinth, would have been built ready to receive the ground-sill, and on a level site there would be about three courses of brickwork above ground and about the same number below (bricks in 1430 would probably cost 4s to 5s per thousand – a relatively expensive item).

(6) The ground-sill would next be assembled, jointed, and bedded directly on top of the base wall. The carpenter would have already decided the order of assembly, and at Reads this would probably have started at the east end by putting up the corner posts and the end girth (or wall-frame) comprising the sill, middle rail, wall-plate, studs and braces. (Sometimes the end girths were put up simultaneously.)

(7) The raising and setting up of the frame was a critical moment in the construction of the house. Whereas a carpenter with assistance could probably have coped with most of the work in a medium-sized house, the raising of the frame called for extra labour. This meant either the employment of temporary 'hands' (of which there are records: an employer in 1444 undertaking to provide two men for seven days at the 'rearyng' of the house or calling in farm hands), or even neighbours.[2] There is little doubt that the heavy principals were raised by poles and ropes, the poles serving subsequently as raking-shores until all the mortise and tenon joints had been secured. It is also evident that until the bressumers, floor, and tie-beams were in position, a certain amount of 'play' was needed, and for this purpose a kind of temporary – withdrawable – pin was used: only when the framework had thoroughly settled were the last peg holes bored and the joints finally pinned together.[3]

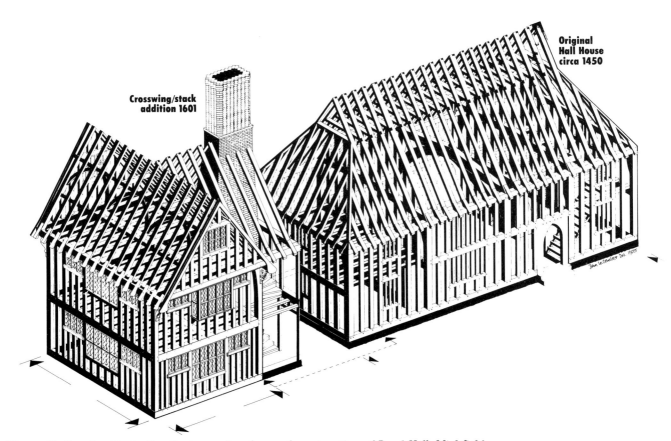

Crosswing/stack addition 1601

Original Hall House circa 1450

*Figure 43: Drawing illustrating the two major phases of construction of Read Hall, Mickfield.*

78

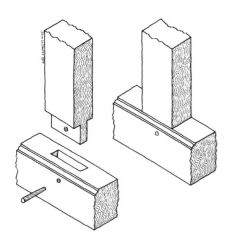

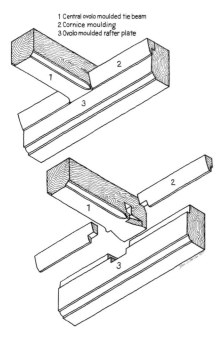

1 Central ovolo moulded tie beam
2 Cornice moulding
3 Ovolo moulded rafter plate

*Figure 44: Construction detail from cross-wing dated 1601, Read Hall.*

**Jettying**

1 O.E.D. (Historical Principles) traces the word jetty back to 1677, but Salzman can quote from a contract of 1405 (op. cit., page 205) for shops in Bucklersbury which requires that the first floor 'shall jut (gettabit)' on the north and south, the second floor only on the north; and Margaret Wood goes back even earlier and mentions a building at Coventry, of the late thirteenth or early fourteenth century, of three storeys, two of them projecting, and another at Salisbury with archaic, probably late thirteenth century, framing jettied on two sides (op. cit., page 222).

(8)   The door openings contrived within stud spacings would present no problem. Where the windows were unframed, as here, mullions, lintels, and trimmers would need to be assembled as part of the frame-raising.

(9)   It is difficult to be precise about the use of scaffolding. I suspect that mediaeval carpenters were so expert at the erection of frames that most of the work was done without scaffolding. Scaffolding — then as now — would be expensive and its use to be restricted as much as possible. In the pitching of the roof some kind of working platform would be needed, at least up to eaves level, on which the rafters, collars, and other roof timbers could be hauled, and from which the final pegging of mortise and tenon joints could take place at high level.

(10)  The last stage was to finish both ends and the 'internal gables' open to the hall, in order to provide support for the collar purlin. The crown post would then be mounted on the central tie-beam and the collar purlin run through from end to end of the roof, the carpenter making his scarfed joints as the work proceeded. After this the rafters were raised in pairs to be mortised and tenoned together at the head, and notched over the wall plate at the foot, and the collars secured. The roof was then ready for lathing and thatching (or tiling).

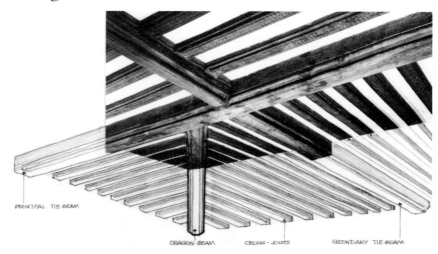

*Plate 31: Dragon beam at High House, Otley.*

One hundred and fifty years later, the new owner of Read Hall decided to improve the old house. The main alterations that were made c.1601 were first the addition of a cross-wing at the west (see Figure 44), then flooring over the hall and thirdly the raising of the roof rafting on the south side to permit of increased head room at the eaves at first floor level. The latter alteration enabled access to be made to the old wing from the head of the new newel staircase that was built adjoining a new brick chimney stack. The building of the cross-wing necessitated the removal of the last bay of the earlier house. In the nineteenth century the house was turned into tenements for farm workers.

The only jettying which occurs at Reads is that of gable overhang in the cross-wing of 1601, and although this could be a practical measure providing shelter for the wall beneath (or depth sufficient for a shallow bay window as at Monk's House, Glemsford), it was an obvious occasion for a pair of nicely wrought scrolled brackets on which the date could be carved. The 'jutty' or 'jetty'[1] is simply the projection of one storey or portion of a structure over that below, and occurs in all the timber-framed areas of Europe, particularly in towns. At the Manor of Got-Begot in Winchester there is a three-storey projection, from the upper windows of which it is almost possible to lean out and touch the wall of the building on the opposite side of a narrow lane, and this sort of thing was a commonplace in mediaeval towns. At first sight it may seem curious that no authoritative explanation of such a well-known feature has been given, but mediaeval carpenters were constantly experimenting and adapting their methods to overcome structural problems, and there are obviously many difficulties in putting one framed storey vertically on top of another.

Assuming two storey-height principal posts meeting a bressumer, together with a floor or tie-beam, there are three mortise holes to weaken the horizontal timber at a single point, and the same if the post is continuous and the bressumers housed into it from either side: in the worst case with short timbers there could be five joints. There is the further problem of the length needed for a full storey-height frame, and there would be every inducement to use shorter timbers. In this situation the carpenter soon hits upon the idea of jettying as a sound engineering solution: the floor joists are cantilevered beyond the bressumer a foot or so, the next storey sill is dowelled at the extremity of the joists, and the next storey-height frame built off this sill. A single mortise and tenon joint will take care of the junction of posts and studs with the bressumer, and the storeys can be built one over the other with economically short-length timbers. The secondary advantages are the useful enlargement of the jettied accommodation, the reduction of bending stresses in the floor joists, and the protection of the work below the jetty in the same way that eaves shelter a wall.

The carpenters then resolved the problem of continuing the jetty around the building by inventing the diagonal bressumer known as the 'dragon-beam'.[1] The dragon-beam (see Plate 31) provides quite simply for the floor joists to change direction at the angle of a building; an important provision because the joists are integral with jettied construction and will be laid flat about one foot apart each measuring 180mm (7in.) by 150mm (6in.), or thereabouts. The dragon-beam is always a structural engineering device and never decorative; it is determined by the need for continuity of stresses.

This is the right moment to discuss the finishing of the walls. There were various methods of 'beam-filling', i.e. of sealing up the spaces between studs and other timbers, and at Reads the traditional wattle and daub (or dab) was used (see Plate 32). Hazel wands of about 25mm diameter (1in.) were cut from woods and hedgerows and with the bark left on were lopped and trimmed to suit the size of the wall spaces. Slats of cleft (or riven) oak were notched or tenoned into the adjoining uprights to support the 'wattles' which were then fixed with hempen string or — sometimes — by tough bramble strands (as in thatching). This made a simple but effective plaster key ready to receive the clay walling. The clay was dug out from below the top soil and then well mixed up, or 'pugged', with the addition of water: it was sometimes trodden out by a horse as described under brickmaking. The clay was 'tempered' with chopped straw, or sometimes with cow-hair, and when mixed with water to a suitable consistency would be flung on to both sides of the wattle work by two men working simultaneously, one standing on the inside of the wall and the other outside. The outer surface would be scratched to form a key for a skin of lime plaster needed to protect the clay from surface moisture penetration, or excessive drying out.

(An alternative method was to fill the spaces between the upright timbers with clay-lump, but there seems to have been more use made of this in Norfolk than in Suffolk.)[2] The so-called 'brick nogging' only came in later Tudor times when bricks were cheaper and more plentiful, and when it was used as alternative to, or replacement of, wattle and daub. The idea behind herringbone brickwork was sound, because the brick tended to lock into the frame by natural gravity.

The surest evidence of external 'pargetting' *subsequent* to the first building of a timber-framed house is the rough nailing of laths over the timbers, and this occurs at Read Hall, together with interesting evidence of plaster lathing contemporary with the cross-wing of 1601, showing that the owner had decided beforehand to have the outside walls plastered. The beam filling consisted of the same wattle and daub work as the older wing but the surface of the timber frame had been deliberately rebated horizontally in about five positions to receive a kind of reinforcing lath. This rebate was about 48mm (1¾in.) wide by 15mm (⅝in.) deep and some 230mm (9in.) above the ground-sill as well as below and above the middle rail, and again about the same distance below the sill-trimmers of the window openings: it was regularly and evenly spaced and evidently done with saw and chisel at the preparation stage. The most convincing explanation was the purely practical one of strengthening the lath and plaster work close to its weakest points, viz., near the edge before meeting the adjoining timbers, showing that the wall surfaces were

*Plate 32: Wattle and daub in walling*

1 Margaret Wood suggests perhaps originally 'dragging-beam' (op. cit., page 222), and C.F. Innocent an ignorant corruption of 'diagonal-beam' (op. cit., pages 164-165).
2 An example of the use of clay-lump in a timber framed manor house of the late fifteenth century is Ufford Hall, Fressingfield.

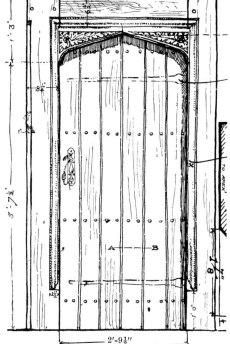

*Figure 45: Arch doorway (from a drawing by Basil Oliver).*

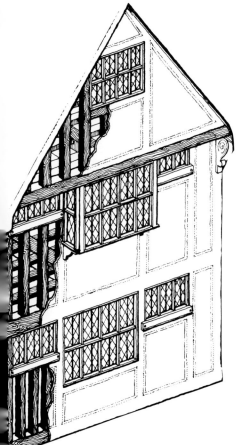

*Figure 46: Windows of 1601 at Read Hall.*

1 From O.E.D. (Hist. Principles) we learn that 'mullion' comes from the old French *moinel* or *moynel*, and would thus seem to date from before the middle of the twelfth century.
2 op. cit., page 185.
3 *A Typology of Brick*, page 70.
4 Which is rather disingenuous, by dating from Caesar's occupation. BC 54, to 1969 when these sizes were defined by British Standard Specification (B.S. 3921).
5 'Size is no real guide to the date of bricks' cf. Jane Wight op. cit., page 43; but Mr. Harley's *Typology* comes closer to correlation of size and date than any I have yet come across — not excluding Nathaniel Lloyd.

panelled out in pargetting with the main framing members.

At Reads the original doors had mostly disappeared after the house had been turned into tenements; this is a pity because there were at least four of importance two external doors to the screens passage and two internal to the service rooms. It is clear, though, that these openings were arch-headed and, as nearly as can be conjectured, the two-centred Gothic form fashionable in the second half of the fifteenth century (see Figure 45). The doors would almost certainly be of oak, and probably plain or moulded plank doors with carved decoration — maybe in the spandrils of the arches.

There were four distinct varieties of window:—

1) Plain rectangular mullion
2) Plain diagonal mullion
3) Moulded and framed mullion
4) Moulded and framed mullion and transom

The first belong to the original build and are c.1430; the second were intermediate, and the last two were used in the cross-wing of 1601. The first two[1] were unglazed window openings formed quite simply within the timber frame by leaving out a length of stud, and 'trimming' the opening with a timber head, or lintel, and a sill member: the first floor window-heads engaged directly with the wall-plate at the eaves. The size of the mullions was about 108 by 76mm (4¼in. by 3in.): they were tenoned and pegged into the lintels and sills.

The rectangular mullions were used in the parlour and solar windows, and the most interesting were those lighting the dais end of the hall. Opposite each other in the wall frames they were about 3m (10ft) high by just under 1.85m wide (6ft), and in two mainly equal halves divided by a middle rail in the wall frame; in each half there were eight lights about 150mm (6in.) wide. These details could be seen from the principal framing timbers remaining on the north and south walls, although the evidence of glazing or shuttering was inconclusive.

Frequent use must have been made of shutters for closing windows to judge from the number of cases where grooves exist above window openings. Where the window comes under a wall plate or rail, runners were formed by planting rebated battens top and bottom long enough for the shutter to slide clear of the opening.

In 1601 the new windows at Reads were glazed and were of two patterns that by then had become general. The windows in the new cross-wing faced south and west, and on each elevation consisted of pairs of small high-level windows adjoining central larger windows (see Figure 46). These windows were all beautifully made of oak with bold ovolo mouldings, and rebated to receive the glazing, for it must be remembered that this had to be easily detachable since it was customarily regarded as a movable fixture, to be taken out by owner or tenant on leaving. (Salzman quotes records of disputes in the fifteenth and sixteenth centuries over the removal of 'glas wyndowes' which were considered to be tenant's fixtures.)[2]

By the time these new windows had been put in, Reads had been drastically modernised; the old Gothic hall had disappeared, having been severed horizontally by a new floor and the upper part turned into a sleeping chamber; a new brick chimney had been built and adjoining this on the south side a newel stair, and in order to provide headroom on turning east or west into the bedrooms at the head of this stair, the whole of the south side of the old roof had been raised by some three feet making an irregularly shaped east gable end: attics were formed inside the roof area and the crown-post hidden within a new stud partition (see Plate 36).

## BUILDING METHODS: BRICK

The early history of brickwork in Suffolk still remains to be written. The Romans used brick in their later structures, and the brick story begins with a tile-like slab[3] such as can be seen in the walls of Burgh Castle. To make the broadest of generalisation, the history of English brick is the gradual achievement of a generally standardised artifact 8¾in. long by 4³⁄₁₆in. wide and 2⅝in. thick (222 by 104 by 67mm), a process which occupied 2,000 years[4] with such vagaries of sizes within this period as almost to defeat attempts to date bricks by size.[5]

The earliest authentic brickwork, not of Roman origin, is in Essex at

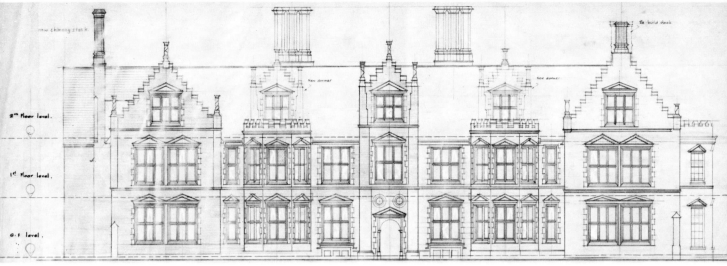

*Plate 33: Haughley Park, South-east elevation (from a drawing by Johns Slater and Haward, architects).*

Little Coggeshall Abbey (pre 1167).[1] In Suffolk, the round arches in the nave of Polstead Church date to the mid-twelfth century but their bricks *could* belong to a late fourteenth century reconstruction. Brick does not appear again until 1270-90 at Little Wenham Hall and thereafter at two priories: St. Olave's, Herringfleet, c.1300, and Butley,[2] c.1320; indeed, fourteenth century brickwork in Suffolk is mainly ecclesiastical. The gatehouse at Letheringham Abbey and those of Archdeacon Pykenham at Ipswich and Hadleigh (c.1490), some dated details in churches, and a few domestic buildings make up our scanty stock of fifteenth century brick.[3] From the start of the sixteenth century the numbers accumulate rapidly, and by the end of that century will have run into many hundreds. The new trend in brick was set by the larger houses — Assington Hall; Smallbridge Hall, Bures; Crows Hall, Debenham; Chilton Hall, Sudbury; Ewarton Hall; Gedding Hall; Giffords Hall, Stoke-by-Nayland; Haughley Park; Helmingham Hall; Hengrave Hall; Kentwell Hall and Melford Hall; Little Saxham Hall; Moat Hall, Parham; Redgrave Hall; Rushbrooke Hall; Seckford Hall and West Stow Hall — to recollect a few which suggest the almost spectacular appearance within a hundred years or so of an entirely new design idiom. Ernest Sandeen, writing of the building of Redgrave Hall, 1545-1554, said '. . . this was not a mediaeval house. To the Suffolk yeomen who passed it on the way to the market at Diss, it must have seemed as much a departure from their conception of a manor house as did the early architectural achievements of Frank Lloyd Wright to twentieth century Americans'.[4]

The walls of Tudor brick mansions must be seen as an elaborate architectural screen, the complexity of which can best be appreciated by measured drawings of the elevations. The east elevation of Sir John Sulyard's Haughley Park is illustrated (see Plate 33) and is worth discussing here as a technical exercise. It will be obvious that the setting out and controlling of the work called for a high degree of building skill, and the discrepancies in setting out — such as they are — can be called minimal. The length overall the front and cross-wings is approx. 35.25m (115ft 7in.), but the porch is not exactly central, the distance to the centre line from the west end being 17.40m (56ft 11in.) and from the east end 17.85m (58ft 8in.). The difference is made up partly in the width of the east wing gable, and partly in the wall space between that and the porch; it can be noticed on the elevational drawing. The point to be made is that the front was intended to be absolutely symmetrical, and that this was almost achieved — but not quite.

The job would start — as today — by setting out the building with pegs and lines and triangulation to establish true right angles at each corner; the foundations would then be dug deep enough to reach solid ground and probably a couple of feet wider than the wall thickness at the base which here was about 685mm (2ft 3in.). The trench bottoms would be filled with large flint stones well packed and rammed and grouted with mortar, known as *calion* (see Figure 47). The brick base work was then superimposed and brought up to the height of the plinth brick some 150mm or 230mm (6in. or 9in.) above ground level. Thereafter the work would continue by first building the corners, i.e. the angles at the extremities of the walls to a height of two or three feet, and these would then be plumbed. Timber scaffolding would shortly be set up, and the intermediate walls built between the corners, the

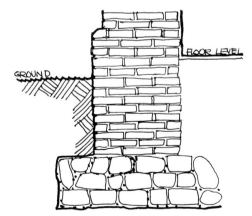

*Figure 47: Flint foundations with brick base work superimposed.*

1 cf. *Coggeshall Abbey and its Early Brickwork*, J.S. Gardner, M.A., J.BAA, Third Series XVIII, 1955.
2 The brick occurs in the cells of the rib vaults within the two extant wings of the Priory gatehouse.
3 Since writing this the Suffolk Records Office has turned up two fifteenth century contracts for the supply of bricks for domestic building (see Appendix B, to this Section).
4 op.cit., page 2.

courses being kept level by building their upper edges to a line strained between the corners.

The 'dressing' of doors and window openings in stonework can, I think, be regarded as a legacy of the native Perpendicular: it was a structural necessity in Suffolk church architecture with walls of flint rubble masonry, and the feature was continued in Tudor domestic work. The dressed work provides a valuable design contrast with walls of brick, and could occasionally be done in terracotta, as at Shrubland Old Hall with the suggestion of Layer Marney Hall, in Essex, as a source.[1] Stone was the more usual material, as at Hengrave Hall and Roos Hall, Beccles, but bricklayers soon became exceedingly skilful in imitating stone by the use of a type of Roman cement.[2] This was the technique employed at Haughley Park and at many another Tudor manor house in Suffolk where freestone was always difficult and expensive to come by. The elements intended as stone were prepared in moulded brick and tile, and then carefully plastered, the work often being so skilfully executed it is not always easy at first sight to be sure whether it is stone or not.

The wall thickness is reminiscent of rubble masonry, and at Haughley was maintained for the full height of the walls, only being reduced to single brick thickness in the crenellated parapets at the head of the bay windows, and on the raking line of the gable rafters. This ensured well splayed window sills outside and deep reveals to the windows inside, both important features of design at this period. The exact regulating of all these details was remarkably skilful, with a competent command of this new architectural system. Window heights were governed by the number of brick courses needed for the exact repetition of quoins in dressings to ground and first floor windows; the mullion and transom windows had to be built with moulded bricks, and moulded brick string courses were built in between to act both as tie and architectural feature, dividing the wall height to show the greater loftiness of the ground floor rooms. Twenty eight matching pediments were formed in moulded brick over windows and one over the opening to the porch. The porch — a typical tall narrow Tudor design — required pilasters, two string courses, three moulded brick finials and a crow-stepped gable; and two symmetrical bays were built between porch and cross-wings, each with four-light mullion and transom windows surmounted with crenellated parapets and ornamental dormer windows similar in design to the top of the porch. The crowning features were the triple-shafted octagonal chimney stacks, with ornamental bases and heads, eleven feet high overall.

## BUILDING METHODS: FLINT

There are two distinct ways of using flint in walls; the first is the solid wall of flint stones bedded in lime mortar and known as rubble masonry, and the second is to make use of flint as face-work, i.e. against the backing of another material — invariably brick, in Suffolk. The first of these is a traditional method going back — as we have seen — to Roman engineers and later used for most of the wall-work in Suffolk churches. Moyses Hall, Bury St. Edmunds, must be one of the few complete examples in this form of construction in domestic work although at Little Wenham Hall the lower part only of the walls, up to about 1.70m (5ft 6in.) in height, is of rubble masonry faced with a mixture of random knapped flint, clunch and brick. In this form of construction the work consisted of flint pebbles, bits of stone or any hard material that could be combined with the mortar matrix of burnt lime and sand. This, as Cautley said[3] lacked the quick setting qualities of modern cement, and therefore the speed of the work was governed by the time taken for the drying out of the mortar, '. . . if course were piled on course too quickly, there would be a tendency to 'slump' or 'bulge'. . . . For these reasons the work must have advanced slowly and it is possible that in the winter it was suspended altogether.' The average thickness of rubble walls was 1m (3ft 3in.).

It is important to distinguish between the structural wall and its facing. It was customary to lay the flints on the external face of the wall in regular horizontal courses, and much the same method was followed in domestic work. After the thirteenth century, domestic flintwork seems to disappear from view until well on into the sixteenth century when we find traditional walling still being used in a

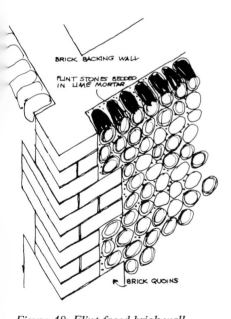

BRICK BACKING WALL

FLINT STONES BEDDED IN LIME MORTAR

BRICK QUOINS

*Figure 48: Flint-faced brick wall*

1 Discussed by Pevsner in his *Suffolk* op. cit., pages 387-388.
2 Made by the integration of suitable clays with chalk, in the ratio of about 1½ or 2 to 1, in a dry finely ground state and calcining the mixture and regrinding. Mixed with sharp sand the resultant rendering had quick and hard setting properties.
3 op. cit., page 16.

certain number of cottages and farm buildings, particularly in coastal areas as well as some way inland.

Flint became fashionable again in a roundabout way through the literary preoccupation with the antique which was part of the scenario of Romanticism; although nobody then, I imagine, would have seriously thought of building solid flint-rubble walls. Brick was plentiful and relatively cheap and could be used as a backing material to provide most of the wall thickness, usually 355mm (14in.), sometimes 460mm (18in.); the quoins at the angles of the building and the dressings to doors and windows could be done in red or white brick, and, more occasionally in stone and made to project some 115mm (4½in.), the flint facings being then bedded into the recesses thus formed (see Figure 48).

This second period went on into the early part of the nineteenth century, and is the true era of domestic flintwork. Flint was then much in vogue for the walls of villas, farmhouses, schools and cottages, and particularly in the north and west of Suffolk where it became as noticeable a feature of vernacular architecture as plasterwork had been before. Country builders – like the Kingsbury's of Boxford – bought gravel pits with plentiful flint seams, and the flints were sorted roughly both into sizes and colours suited to coursed pebble work and cleaned ready for use: for about 150 years flint pebbles were part of the builders' stock-in-trade. Fortunately we are spared in Suffolk almost all that random-faced work of large flints resembling Kentish Rag, where the joints are picked out in white mortar, and occasionally 'galleted' – i.e. dotted with small pieces of flint or stone.

## BUILDING METHODS: PLASTER

I must single out this trade because, after carpentry and bricklaying, plastering came third in the great trilogy of Suffolk building crafts. Salzman classifies daubing, rough casting and pargetting as constructional, and white casting or plastering as decorative. We have seen that wattle and daub is really an integral part of framed timber building and a job originally done by the carpenters. Pargetting, however, although strictly speaking another word for rough casting which, in Old French, was *parjeter* – to throw over a surface – came to mean something else in Suffolk; it could be said to have graduated from a rough, unskilled or semi-skilled process to that of a craft.

It is as a craft that we have come to look at it in Suffolk (see Plate 34). In a sense it is peculiar to the county or, at least, to a timber-framed region, in being only suitable for application to a lathed and timbered backing. Various reasons have been put forward for the plaster coat covering the whole – or nearly the whole – framed building, chief among them being the practical purpose of sealing the structure against draughts. It is obvious that, where a shrinkable material such as clay is put side by side with a more stable material such as wood, differential shrinkage will occur and, apart from overall frame movement, the former tends to move away from the latter. In spite of this I am inclined to think that with really well made wattle and daub protected by plaster externally, and so often by lime washing internally, shrinkage may have been less frequent than is supposed, or external lathing and pargetting would have come far earlier. (Salzman can record references to pargetting as early as 1285, continuing through the fourteenth, fifteenth and sixteenth centuries.)

The material itself is easily described: slaked lime, sand and hair, to which was added a certain amount of cow dung and road scrapings.[1] The actual workmanship is worth mentioning: indispensable to good class work was, of course, the lathing to provide a key, and we have seen how this was done at Reads. I have come across cases where the plasterer simply hacked over the surface of old daub and timberwork to give a key, but this is an inferior method: the best was floated on in at least two coats, the earlier one being 'pricked up' or 'roughed up' before the coat had set as a key for the subsequent coat. The older tradesmen would run a heap of fully slaked lime which, tempered over a long period, was a valuable part of their stock-in-trade.[2] As Professor Lethaby once said: 'The old material was well washed, beaten, stirred, and tested so carefully, and for so long a time, that, when laid, it was as tough as leather.' The cow hair was scraped from hides adding immense strength to the plaster body, and it was this innovation which gave the impetus to

*Plate 34: Pargetted house at Clare and detail (from G.P. Bankart's Theory of the Plasterer, 1908).*

1 cf. *The Art of the Plasterer* by G.P. Bankart, page 57.
2 This practice was continued in Suffolk until shortly before the last war when lime plasterwork was still done – mainly internally.

84

local schools of plasterwork in the late sixteenth and early seventeenth centuries.

## THE BUILDERS

The building of a large hall in the sixteenth century had become a complex operation and the Guild Lodges, in which the master mason or the master carpenter had undertaken both design and construction on traditional lines, were not ready for the upsurge of new ideas in the early sixteenth century. It is already clear from the accounts at Little Saxham and Hengrave that fresh methods were being tried, and that the scene was slowly being set for the beginnings of modern contracting. By 1505 the independent deviser had arrived on the scene with duties both of design and supervision, no longer a master builder in the sense of being a member of a trade Guild, but an independent 'professional' man,[1] whose functions, although not exactly stipulated, were clearly those of overseer and adviser — on his client's behalf — as to how things should be done. It was only one step from this for the term 'architect' to be revived — as it was by John Shute (c.1500-1570), the first Englishman to use this title.[2]

A system of directly employed labour and the direct purchase of materials will only work if records are accurately kept and all costs strictly controlled by proper agreements: it looks as though these duties were shared initially by overseer and clerk of works, and that sometimes both were done by one and the same person.

Gage, dealing with the '. . . bylding of the Manour of Hengrave', summarised as follows the picture given by fifteen successive annual accounts: 'The shell of the building within the moat was the work of John Eastawe, or Eastow, who executed it after some model seen by him at Comby. The bay windows, and probably the gatehouse, were the work of John Sparke, who, as well as Thomas Dyrich, the chief carver, and John Birch, the joiner, were artisans from London. The materials were derived from several sources: a great proportion of the brick was made on the spot, and large quantities came from the neighbouring kiln of the Abbot of Bury and others. Some of the freestone was brought from King's Cliff in Northamptonshire . . . The rest was supplied from the dissolved abbeys of Ixworth, Burwell, and Thetford. The old hall of the De Hemegraves, as well as several houses in the neighbourhood, furnished materials towards the building. The timber came chiefly from Comby and Sowe woods in Suffolk. Some of the lead was brought for the offices from the monastery of St. Edmund, dissolved after the chief part of the mansion was finished . . .'[3] (Note the use of second-hand material, doubtless timber, from old houses; a point already stressed.)

What none of these accounts tell us is the nature of the original agreements with the various trades and craftsmen concerned, and whether work was contracted for on gross quotation or whether simply paid for on a 'time and materials' basis. The system of gross contracts was, we are told,[4] common in the Middle Ages, and has continued in one form or another until the present day: here is where information on Suffolk contracting is still lacking. We need to know whether, for instance, in the building of eighteenth century mansions the owner himself acted as contractor or if the work was placed in the hands of a surveyor or architect, who then drew up schedules of various specialised items of building construction and called for tenders for these items from selected craftsmen.

It seems the small builder was already well-established in Suffolk by the mid-nineteenth century, although — curiously — the name of builder is everywhere linked with that of another trade — often joiner, sometimes bricklayer. In Ipswich, in 1855, there were 65 'Joiners and Builders' (their title in entries in William White's Directories): only very occasionally in one of the villages does one come across someone calling himself simply 'Builder'. There was a large market in building trades;[5] in Ipswich alone there were 15 blacksmiths, 28 bricklayers (none described also as builders) and plasterers, 24 cabinet makers (and upholsterers), 9 painters and decorators, and 28 plumbers, glaziers, and painters (of whom 10 plumbers were gas fitters). No carpenters are mentioned and for these we are told to 'See Joiners and Wheelwrights'; this was an interesting reflection from the days when the carpenter was the leading tradesman; in the towns, at any rate, he had become 'Joiner and Builder', although by this date construction in

1 It is interesting to notice that this trend goes back to the later Middle Ages, and F.B. Andrews (op. cit., page 9) quotes the plaint made in a sermon: 'For, take notice, in great building there is usually a single master builder who directs the construction by word alone and seldom does manual work.'
2 cf. *Concise Encyclopaedia of Architecture*, op. cit., page 302. Shute published in 1563 *The First and Chief Grounds of Architecture*, 'the earliest manual on the subject in English.'
3 cf. *History and Antiquities of Thingoe Hundred*, op. cit., page 214.
4 cf. *History of Building* by Jack Bowyer (1973. London), page 238.
5 It is good to see names in 1855 which can be found in today's Directories: Barton, Bennett, Catchpole, Chisnall, Gibbons, Goldsmith, Hayward, Green, Kerridge, and Weavers — in the County, if no longer in the Borough.

timber-framing — repairs excepted — must have practically ceased. The title 'Building Contractor' occurs in Suffolk trade directories for the first time in 1912.[1] Before then builders would sub-contract certain works to independent tradesmen of reputable quality when they had a new contract; for instance, when a house was to be built, a reliable bricklayer was engaged with whom the builder negotiated in advance the amount to be paid for the job: if the charge was considered too high he might agree a lower figure with another tradesman. This kind of sub-contracting has persisted since the Middle Ages. In the nineteenth century there started a new system with the contractor financing the whole building work and gradually forming his own permanent staff of various trades, the system which obtains until this day.

Careful accounting has always been an important side to successful contracting: by way of tail-piece two pages are reproduced from the account books of Robert Kingsbury, builder of Boxford (see Plate 35). The first is for work done at Assington Hall for John Gurdon, Esq. during February and March, 1829; various jobs evidently to do with running new cornices in plaster of Paris[2] and repairing an old celing. The firm of Kingsbury's did all the maintenance at the Hall until it was burnt down in 1957. The second is an 'inter-office' account for December 1831 and the whole of the year 1832 between the two brothers, Robert and Frederick Kingsbury, who were in friendly competition, each running a separate builder's business in the same town: Frederick's business was eventually acquired by the father of today's firm. The 'Lady Slate' used on 16th May is the smallest of the three common sizes of Welsh slates for which the names were 'Ladies' 400mm by 200mm (16in. by 8in.), 'Countesses' 510mm by 255mm (20in. by 10in.) and 'Duchesses' 610mm by 305mm (24in. by 12in.). The Bushels of hair used in July would be for plaster lathwork: 'Old Plain Tiles' were evidently still as useful a commodity as they are today. The Kingsbury family have been builders in Boxford since 1530 (in 1855 we can fine them described in White's Boxford Directory under BRICKLAYERS *And Builders* as 'Kingsbury Rt. B.,' and 'Kingsbury Fdk. and Brickmkr'.), but the family traces its origins to just before 1300 from Kingsbury in Warwickshire.

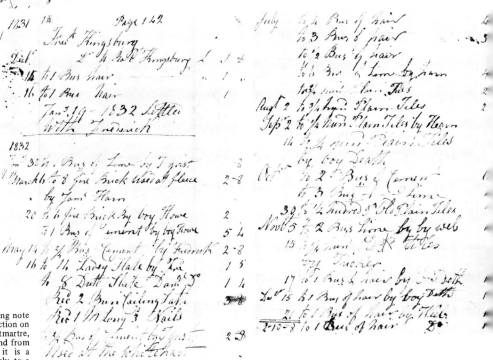

Plate 35: Pages from the books of the Boxford builders Robert and Frederick Kingsbury.

1 cf. Kelly's Ipswich Trade Directory, 1912.
2 'Plaster of Paris': Salzman has an interesting note on the history. It owes its name to its production on a large scale from the gypsum beds of Montmartre, outside Paris, and was imported into England from the early sixteenth century. Technically it is a calcined form of gypsum which sets quickly to a hard surface that can be polished, and being the only common plaster which expands on setting it is very useful in repairs.

# APPENDIX A

## *Alterations to timber-framed houses*

*Principles of construction;*
*Ground sills; Dating of*
*brickwork; Identification*
*of original structure*

*Plate 36: Crown-post at Reads revealed inside later partition*

**Planning Arrangements**

**Carpentry joints**

1 Donald Insall, R.I.B.A., in *The Care of Old Buildings Today* (1972. London: Architectural Press) uses a nice phrase '... a building's entire biography may be read and understood in its ancient timber framing.'

The mediaeval system of framed and trussed timber house building was based on a logical distribution of loads and stresses. The principle, as already noted, was that of providing for continuity of stresses in the main and secondary frame members. For this purpose all parts of the framework were interconnected by jointing them together and the house designed to be put up consecutively. Leading structural timbers were denoted by joint assembly marks. This is important to remember when trying to identify the original build.

Preservation from decay depended upon the detailing at ground level. The largest oak post driven into the ground will eventually rot by the absorption of moisture through the end grain, causing senile decay by local chemical decomposition. A timber sill laid directly on the ground, although presenting no end grain directly to the soil, will be subject to alternate wetting and drying (accelerated by the throw off of rainwater from the roof) and this over a period will promote wet rot. The heavy decay of ground sills often found even when mounted on brickwork results from excessive exposure to damp conditions.

The revival of brick in Suffolk seems to date from the mid-twelfth century, but few timber-framed buildings can have been mounted on brick plinths much before the late thirteenth century, the date postulated for Purton Green Farm, Stansfield, and these could presumably have been important houses. Brick can be dated fairly accurately by an expert, and whilst this is worth considering it must not be overlooked that a brick base may not be the original, and can well have been renewed, particularly as brick is subject to decomposition through alternate wetting and drying, and frost action.

The chances are high that a timber-framed building will have been altered many times during its history. In order to distinguish between original work and alterations, it is first necessary to identify the original structure.[1] Based upon a fairly standardised mediaeval plan with accommodation at one or both ends of a hall it should be possible to decide whether a given structure was an earlier open hall-house or a later floored house. This will provide the first step towards tentative dating. The roof must be looked at from inside for traces of smoke-blackening on rafters or plasterwork, as this will confirm the existence of an open hall with hearth (although not always conclusively since a primitive form of chimney flue may have been used). Cross-wings can be part of the original structure, as in the 'Wealden' type, but in Suffolk were frequently added at later stages to an original long-house.

In an open hall plan there is likely to have been a chamber at one end – parlour at the *upper* end and, usually, service rooms at the other, *lower*, end. A measured ground floor plan, in which the position of principal posts and beams is carefully shown, will form a basis from which original features and later alterations can be deduced. The same applies to cross sections (admittedly these can be more difficult to set up, and the optimum positions in which this should be done may call for professional judgement): in an open hall an exposed roof truss, possibly with king-post or crown-post is to be expected, and could be found buried within a partition, as at Read Hall, Mickfield (see Plate 36), or hidden within an attic as at Manor Farm, Saxted (see Section 6).

In carpentry every joint is calculated, and, generally speaking, no provision will have been made for a joint unless it was essential. Unoccupied joints suggest either that the timbers have been reused or that an original bit of the framing has been removed. Use joint assembly marks to check whether timbers are in their original place: these marks were invariably Roman numerals (Figure 42) in sequence;

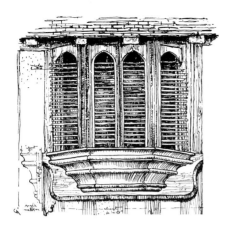

*An Essex oriel window, of which many examples are to be found in Suffolk – Basil Oliver.*

### Elevational changes

### Doors and windows

### Floors

interruption may be due to later alterations, or numbers out of sequence to timber having been reused from elsewhere. Examine *all* timbers with reference to:–

a) Appearance and surface finish (eg. adze or saw marks).

b) Type of finishes (eg. size, type and positions of chamfers and/or mouldings).

c) Type of joints and comparative sizes of, and spaces between, peg holes.

d) Continuity of members (eg. beams, bressumers, studs, braces, rafters) including assembly marks.

e) Unexplained cuts, joints, rebates, mortise or peg-holes.

f) Variations in stud sizes and spacings; also in those of rafters.

g) Transverse tension-braces in framed walls, and wing-bracing in roofs, and where missing.

h) Changes in wood, eg. chestnut or other hardwood or softwood in place of oak. This list is by no means complete, but suggests some of the main details to be considered in following original work and alterations. (Once this has been done a certain familiarity with the original carpentry methods and finishes will have been acquired, and this will help – even intuitively – in the detection of later workmanship by another hand. One of the pleasures in this kind of analysis is the growing ability to detect the difference between first-build and later carpentry.) *The golden rule is the importance of every single carpentry joint and joinery detail.*

Initial clues to the history of a building can be given by looking at external elevations.[1] Changes in plane of plastered wall surfaces, and variations in the height of roofs should be carefully noted; they may well be the result of builds of more than one period. These will be more obvious in exposed-frame structures, and can be confirmed by close examination of the carpentry. The existance of an original jettied floor between cross-wings may be seen inside where the originally set-back ground floor wall has been taken out, and a new outer wall built and, usually, plastered over. A good example of this occurs in the Old Guild Hall in St. Mary's, Long Melford. A Wealden type house may be one of those which has been disguised in this way.[2]

A plastered house may conceal original door and window positions, unless these can be seen from inside. The probability is that in a framed house, plastered over during the eighteenth or nineteenth century, doors and windows will not be in their original positions, and may be discovered only when plaster is removed. (Original door and window positions can usually be identified by the deliberate trimming of studs with timber lintels and sill members.) Windows may cause further problems. The original small fifteenth century mullions, for instance, may have been replaced by the larger mullion and transom type of the late sixteenth or seventeenth century. Details of these first windows may only be discovered if the later ones are taken out for repair, although there may well be clues in unrelated peg holes, or unaccountable rebates at the head of jambs of the framing timbers. An oriel or bay window may be a later insertion indicated by different detailing, and lack of correspondence with its surroundings.

Owners of a framed house often want to know whether theirs is one in which first floors belong to the original build, or whether they were put in later. The answer usually follows from an exact investigation. At Reads the open hall of the 1430 build was floored over in 1601, at the same time as the building of the axial chimney stack. There were, generally, only two ways of doing this. The first, as at Reads, was to support the outer ends of floor joists against the external walls and the inner ends on a central beam parallel with the latter; one end of this beam could bear on the brickwork of the new stack, and the other on a new lateral tie-beam across the centre of what used to be the open hall. In a two-bay hall this beam would continue from the tie-beam to the existing cross-beam at the end of the hall. The floor joists would then be run from wall to wall. The second way was the reverse of the first, and consisted in putting in *lateral* tie-beams, supporting these by new principal posts set in front of the older ones on the outer walls or notched into the latter, and then putting in new floor joists parallel with these outer walls (this was the method at Church Cottage, Pettistree).

1 The fourteenth century aisled hall within Edgar's Farm, Combs, near Stowmarket, was detected by these means.
2 cf. *The Timber-Framed Buildings of Steyning* by H.M. and V.E. Lacey; see pages 49 and 53 for details of two fine Wealdens discovered behind nondescript shop fronts.

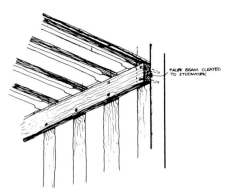

*Figure 49: False beam supporting later flooring at Ufford Hall, Fressingfield.*

**Roofs and chimneys**

In both cases the critical point is the 'seating' of the floor joists. The first case is more obvious than the second. At Reads, where the joist ends met the outer walls, a timber plate was cleated on to the framework to carry them, and this was hidden by an inclined oak board fixed to the wall. It was pretty obvious that this could not be original. Where the joists met the central beam this had been roughly notched to receive them, and it was only necessary to compare these joints with the original over the service rooms to see that two entirely different carpentry builds were involved.

At Ufford Hall, Fressingfield, the floor plate carrying the joist ends at the head of the ground floor was not so obvious, and could have been mistaken for part of the original framework. Close examination showed, however, that this timber was not part of the external wall frame and had been cleated on (see Figure 49). The same was true of the principal posts at Church Cottage, which could be seen to be a later addition.

These comments by no means exhaust the list of differences between a new and an original floor although in the latter case it is usually clear when the whole of the carpentry is contemporary. In such a floor existing beams and bressumers are carefully rebated to receive joist ends, the joists with chamfers or mouldings are neatly stopped off close to their supporting timbers, and beams are correctly seated and tenoned into principal posts naturally haunched to receive them. This is also true of jettied construction, and the absence of many an original sub-jetty wall has been revealed by the way in which the chamfers or mouldings on the joists cease, and the place of the missing bressumer at the head of the old wall can be seen.

These are often the least altered part of an original timber-framed house, making the careful examination of the interiors of roof spaces an absolute necessity. At Roydon Hall, Creeting St. Peter, I found an original pitched roof belonging to an earlier build hidden within the roof area, and completely surrounded by a later and higher roof. In the past builders did not scruple to make these changes when altering or adding to houses. At Aspall Hall, near Debenham, part of the first Tudor roof can be seen in the attics, spanning some 17 feet and supplanted by a new late seventeenth century roof with a combined span covering both the original house and an added passage way. Sometimes the whole roof was raised and rebuilt at a higher level, and this can be seen to have happened at Ufford Hall, and at the Neptune Inn, Fore Street, Ipswich. The walls have been heightened, and notching for the original rafter feet is partially visible lower down where the first wall-plate occurred.

At Read Hall, the north slope of the original roof over the first build was left undisturbed, but on the south side the rafters were taken down, except where they joined a cross partition (see Plate 37), the head of the wall raised by some couple of feet or so, and a new set of rafters put in. It was first thought that this was to give headroom for doors in the lobby at the top of the newel stairs, alongside the

*Plate 37: Raising of roof on south side at Read Hall, Mickfield.*

89

*Plate 38: Later addition of a chimney at Framsden Hall.*

*Plate 39: Ship Inn, Levington.*

1 This can be verified time and again simply by observation of the relative positions of axial chimney stack and front door, or porch (usually a later addition), on external elevations.
2 Since writing this Mr. W.A.B. Jones of Hadleigh has shown me two extracts from Building Regulations made in Hadleigh in 1619, and these are now added in Appendix C to this Section. The second, in particular, is interesting in forbidding the use of thatch for roofing, and enforcing the building of brick chimneys in place of those of 'lome or claye'.
3 *The Principles of Carpentry* by F. Tredgold.
4 A house at Hemingstone near Ipswich is said to have possessed papers referring to the purchase of half a wreck from the Strand at Ipswich for use in the building. Neither of these papers could be turned up nor the actual timbers examined because most had been destroyed in a fire.

chimney stack. Closer inspection showed that this was not strictly necessary, and the only conclusion seemed to be that this alteration was deliberately done to give increased wall height on the prominent south elevation, and more space for the large new mullion and transom windows.

Not only are the shafts of a chimney head of much interest, but also the position in the house of the stack itself. In existing Suffolk houses several alternative places were chosen for building the new chimneys. A large open hall, as at Framsden, could be divided into two rooms by a chimney in the middle, and a further stack built against the outer wall of what used to be the parlour (see Plate 38). A favoured position for a new chimney was between hall and parlour with back-to-back fireplaces serving each room. At Reads and at Langleys, Hawkedon, the screens-passage and entrances remained where they always had been, putting the front door remote from the two living-rooms; this, on the whole, was a better plan than in the later derivative in which the front door opened into a stack lobby between the two main rooms. An alternative was to build the chimney in the whole, or part, of the original cross-passage, providing either a single or a back-to-back fireplace; in the first of these cases another stack might be built on the end wall of the unwarmed room. A further alternative was on a side wall between two rooms in the angle of an L- or T-plan.

By no means all chimneys were built when converting open hall houses, for by the middle of the fifteenth century, possibly earlier, complete two-storey houses were being constructed on new lines without cross-passages (Clopton Hall, Wickhambrook is a case in point), and by the middle of the seventeenth century, if not before, the stack lobby entrance had become one of the commonest farmhouse plans in Suffolk.[1] Examine the timber-framing which adjoins the chimneys, particularly inside roofs, for evidence of alterations.[2]

## SHIP TIMBERS

'I have acquired a great veneration and respect of oak. I mean, of course, the common English Oak (*Quercus Robur*) which the old builders used for their houses, and also for their ships. Indeed, I found that most of the oak beams and studs in old houses were what are called ship timber, – old peg holes and mortises could be seen everywhere, and there were several cross-beams in the bedrooms which could only have come out of an ocean-going vessel. These timbers have sailed upon the Seven Seas, some as Merchantmen, others as Men-of-War.' This extract from *Suffolk Oak*, by H.J. Fane Edge (see Section Bibliography) puts, in those captivating sentences, the whole aura of romance that surrounds the idea of old ship timbers reused in framed houses. It is an idea in which we would all wish to believe but which, when search starts, proves to be one of the most elusive to pin down. There is nothing innately improbable about it. Until about 1840, when the use of wood had been practically superseded, English ships were all timber-built, and, at the end of their serviceable life were undoubtedly offered for sale in the shipyards and anchorages around the coast. Some were towed into backwaters and turned into dwellings, and others sold and broken up – builders would be amongst those who bought the timbers. Tredgold, in his classic work on Carpentry[3] when treating of the resistance of timber (Table VI – Experiments on the Stiffness of Oak Supported at the Ends), starts a table with 'Old ship timber'. This does confirm, indirectly, that such timber was available to builders in the mid-nineteenth century. The probability is that the cost of transporting loads of old timber across the country would tend to keep the area of distribution to within a matter of miles from the point of sale, and, therefore, to restrict use to fairly near the coastal port and navigable rivers.

The port authorities might be supposed to have old documentary records of the sale of vessels, such as men-of-war, for breaking-up, but the Docks and Harbour Commission of Ipswich could turn up no such evidence. References are supposed to exist for the sale of ships for use in house building, but I have been unable to trace any actual documents.[4] The Ship Inn at Levington has a licence that can be traced back to 1723, and a legend that the whole side of a ship was used in the building (see Plate 39); examination does not reveal more than the usual arch-braces which are, admittedly, hull-shaped, and some old reused beams. It has become clear that

Plate 40: United Reform Church, Walpole.

these investigations should be made in company with a historian of naval building, and Maurice Griffiths, author of many works on the history of ships and sailing, agrees that only an antiquarian knowledge of ship building could probably identify such timbers for certain. The difficulty is, of course, in distinguishing between a genuine ship timber and a reused building timber; for, as we have seen, there is a long tradition for taking down and reusing the components of timber-framed houses.

A well known, if unverified use of three ship's masts in supporting the roof of a building occurs at the United Reform Church at Walpole, near Halesworth (see Plate 40), built in 1607, and converted — as were other houses for purposes of Free Church worship — later in the seventeenth century and during the eighteenth century.[1]

# APPENDIX B
# Early Brick Contracts

### Suffolk Record office document HA 246: Brick contract with John Mannock

This indenture witnesseth that we Paul Frankryk and Henry Goodeman late of Shelley have bargained and bound themselves to make and to deliver unto John Mannock gentleman three score thousand bricks good and able of the great mould within the feast of Pentecost next following after the date of this writing, and to be told (counted) and set on a tass (stack) at the manor called Giffards if/that* it shall be made, and the said John to pay for the thousand twenty pence, and the said John shall pay at the beginning twenty shillings and at the making of twenty thousand twenty shillings, and when the said three score thousand is full made and delivered to the said John or his assignees, then the residue of the money to be paid content that is to them due. Unto the which convenant we the aforesaid Paul and Henry bind us in twenty pounds to be paid to the said John or his assignees at the said feast of Pentecost if the convenants on our part be not fulfilled and the said John bindeth him

to the said Paul and Henry in twenty pounds if he fulfil not his part. In witness of the which we put to our seals. Data apud (dated at) Stoke Neylond 16th day of November in the 38th year of the reign of Henry VI (1459)

Whereof the said Paul hath received the 16th day of December, 6s.8d.
Item received the 20th day of December, 6s.8d.
Item received by John my son on Corpus Christs Eve, 6s.8d.
Item received on Saturday before St. John Baptist, 6s.8d.
Item received on St. Peters Eve, 13s.4d.

(Signed) John Mannock.

* this word appears in the original simply as 'y' with an abbreviation mark above it. As such it is impossible to choose between the two possibilities here shown. It will be clear that the word is crucial to the sense of the whole document.

---

### Suffolk Record office document HA 12/B2/21/5: Brick contract with Sir Edward North.

Thys Indentyre made the x[t] daye of december in the syxt yere of the Raynge of ower Soverynge Lorde Edwarde the Syxt by the grace of god of Englond Fraunce and Irelonde Kynge defender of the faithe ande on earthe of the churche of Englonde and Irelonde supreme heade, Betewne Richarde Foxe off Sowthellmham in Cowntye of Suff' veman of thone partye and Thomas Gefferye of Luddham in the Cowntye of Norff' brykmaker, and Michaell Chanon of Felltham in the cowntye of Suff' brykmaker, and Robarte Gefferye of netshede in the cowntye Norff' of thother partye *wyttnessyth* that the saide Thomas Michaell and Robarte, hath convenantyde and grauntyde to and with the saide Richarde his executors and assyngnes, that they the said Thomas Michaell and Robarte thur heyers Executors Admynistrators or assyngnes shall well and workmanlye make or cause to be made at the Manor of the Ryght honorable Syr Edwarde Northe Knyght, of Sowthellmham aforeseyde, Eyght Skore thowsande brycke and thre skore thowsande thacke Tyle, and also

shalle performe fulfylle and make good all suche Number of bryke and tyle, as the saide Thomas ys be hynde at this present tyme, for the which the saide Thomas & his assyngnes hath Receyvyde monye for before the date here of, and shall well & perfyghtlye burne or cause to be brent the same Tyle & brycke, and the same so made and brent shall delyver or cause to be delyvered to the foresaide Sir Edwarde Northe to his Executors or assyngnes, One hole by tale, and so all the Reste to be delyvered by hole at the place where the clampe or clampes shall stande and be sett in maner & forme folowyng. Ths ys to saye on thyssyde the feast of Pentycoste next Ensewyng the date [hereof], ffortye and fyve thowsande brycke, and XV thowsande thake tyle, and at the ffeaste of Saynt Michaell Tharkangell next folowynge after the date here of, ffower skore thowsande brycke and tyle In full delyvery of the foresaide Eyght skore thosande brycke, and there (sic) skore thowsande thacke tyle, *and the sayde* Thomas Geffrey Michaell Chanon and Robert Geffreye do covenante & graunt

1 A Georgian example occurs at the Chapel on the Green at Hartest (cf. *A View into the Village*, op. cit., page 96).

by these presents that everye brycke of the forsaide Eyght skore thowsande beyng brent as aforesaide shalbe & conteyne in lenght Tene ynchis, in bredeth v ynchis, and in thycknes twoo & a halfe ynchis *and* every thacke tyle beyng also brent as a forsaide shalbe & contayne in lenght Tene ynchis & a quarter, and in bredeth vii ynchis & a quarter, *and* the saide Richarde Foxe Covenantyth and grauntyth to & with the said Thomas Michaell & Robart, that the forsayde Sir Edwarde Northe his Executors or assyngnes, shall fynde & deliver or cause to be delyverd Suffycyent woode, Sande, Strawe to and for the necessarye makyng & burnynge of the forsaid brycke and tyle, and also shall carye or cause to be caryed the Earthe beynge caste for the saide tylle, to suche place wher as yt shalbe wrought, *provyded* alwayes that of the saide Earth caste for the saide tyle shalbe within Six or vii skore of the place wher as yt shalbe wrought, that then the saide Earthe to be caryed to the said place at y$^e$ charge of the saide Thomas Michaell & Robart ther Executors or assyngnes, and the saide

Richarde Foxe covenanteth by these presents to assynge one convenyent horse alwayes to be on Redynes for the drawyng upp of the said Erth, and so make & dygge a pytte for the washynge of the said Earthe, and also to assynge the said Thomas Michaell and Robarte so muche Suffycyent woode as shall sarve for the dresyng of suche meat & drynke as the said Thomas Michaell & Robarte and their servaunts shall spende duryng the terme of makyng the said brycke & tylle, *and* the saide Richarde convenantyth by these presents to paye or cause to be payde to the sayde Thomas Michaell & Robarte thure Executors or assyngnes for every thowsande brycke & Tyle iii$^s$iiii$^d$, and the said Monye to be paide at suche tyme or tymes as nede shall requere for the chargis of the said Thomas Michaell & Robarte to be Susteynide in castyng and makyng of the said brycke and tyle, In *wyttnes* Wherof Eyther parteyes thone to thother to the presents Indenturs Interchangeable have putte ther Seales the daye and yere above Wrytten

# *APPENDIX C*

# *Hadleigh Building Regulations of 1619*

**Dividing of cottages**

35 Item that noe pson or psons that doth or shall hereafter inhabite or dwell wthin the said Towne or the limitts or pcincts of the same shall devide or parte any Cottages or dwellinge houses wthin the said towne of Hadleigh or any houses belonging to such dwellinge houses and convert any pte of such dwellinge houses or any houses or buildings belonging to such dwellinge house or houses to any severall dwellinge house or houses of habitacon without the Consent and allowance of the Maior & the greater pte of the Aldermen & the greater pte of the said Cheife burgessess in wrightinge under the Comon seal of the said towne first obteyned uppon payen of forfeite for evy month that any such Inmate or more families than one shall dwell or continewe in any dwelling house and for evy moneth that any such pson or psons shall continewe or maineteine any such pte of A dwellinge house or any house or houses belonging to A dwelling house so converted for or sevall dwelling house or house of habitacon without such licence as aforesaid the some of tenne shillinges

**Against thatching of houses and claye chimneyes**

37 Item for the better p(re)ventinge & more safe keepinge of the said Towne from danger of ffyer It is ordred that from hens forth such pson & psons which shall att any tyme hereafter repayer any house or houses adioyning to any dwelling house next the streete already built or buylde any house of newe within the said towne of Hadleigh in any of the streets from the further pte of Benton end to Stonestreete, or in the Angell Streete, the George Street Hillstreete, The Pounde Lane, The Markett place or Ducklane within the said towne (the houses there standinge for the most pte adioyninge near togither) shall cover such houses as shall hereafter be reared newe Covered or newe buylt with Tyle or Slate & not with strawe, Reede or any other Thache, And shall make such Chymney and Chymneys as they shall repayer or buylde in the said house or houses, all of Bricke from the foundacon or bottome thereof unto the topp of the Chymney & Chymneyes without such house & houses, and not of lome or Claye upon payne that evy such pson & psons for Coveringe or causing to be Covered any such house or houses with strawe Reede or thache & not with Tyle contrary to the forme aforesaid to forfeite to the said Maior Aldermen & Chiefe Burgesses to the Comon use of the said Corporacon for every fyve foote square of every Chymney soe buylt of Claye fourtie shillings, and to have the said Thache reared & pulled downe, and such Claye Chymney & Chymneys likewise pulled downe

# *Delight*
## *the design of houses*

A study of local design in domestic architecture must aim at giving:—

1) Characteristic use of materials
2) Design preferences
3) Design typology

My general thesis is simple: domestic architecture in Suffolk starts with timber-framed building, indigenous, but always accepting and making use of methods developed elsewhere; in this it is peculiarly well situated geographically to receive, adapt, and transmit ideas; this process of assimilation continues historically and results in a local architecture, first in timber-framed building and then in brick; this later submits to a general dilution with the spreading of a national vernacular in the eighteenth and nineteenth centuries, hastened by industrialism and the importing of machine-made building materials and metropolitan ideas. By the present century there is no longer any Suffolk vernacular architecture.

## REGIONAL CHARACTERISTICS AND TYPOLOGY

*Characteristic use of materials*     Suffolk — in common with its old partner in the Kingdom of East Anglia — slowly developed its own domestic architecture which, although sharing some general similarities with Norfolk, Cambridgeshire, and the Isle of Ely, had marked qualities of its own.

The same timber-framed building system with plaster infill or wholly plastered walls appears in each (and with a considerable southward extension into Essex and Kent), but, in Suffolk, there is a notable concentration of a building type, frequently hall-farmhouse, with a characteristic height, length and simplicity of shape that is immediately recognisable. In exposed framing, studs tend to be narrowly spaced and tension-bracing minimal.

Flint buildings appear everywhere in East Anglia, but with a special refinement of detail and architectural quality to be seen in the north-west, centre and south-west of Suffolk; red-brick building also, but with a local school, common to Norfolk and Suffolk, of compactly designed houses of the late sixteenth and seventeenth centuries with well resolved ornament and detail, and a vertical emphasis.

The white-brick school, again, is common to East Anglia, and Essex, but with an obvious concentration in Suffolk, where it was particularly popular in the eighteenth and nineteenth centuries. Plastered brickwork, however, is scarcely vernacular, tending either to stand in for stonework or to imitate rendered timber-framework.

The timber-framed and weather-boarded house is fairly general to East Anglia as well as the lowlands of South England, but, unlike Essex where it is widespread, only features in a minor way in the vernacular of Suffolk.

*Design preferences*     All who are interested in traditional houses will have their own views on the most characteristic features of local design. There is in Suffolk a limited number of characteristics which could be called constant by being common to domestic design, and which can be listed as *preferences*:

a) For simple building ranges, notably rectangular in form, with clear-cut roof shapes.

b) For vertical emphasis by simple means such as tall bays, porches or lofty gables.

c) For a predominance of wall over window.

d) For symmetrical arrangements of doors and windows.

e) For patterned and coloured wall surfaces.

Such a list makes no claim to be complete, and is essentially one calling for attentive study in order to probe the reasons for traditional preferences, and as a means of further understanding the mind of past builders (and, after assimilation, a

*Plate 41: The close-studded Guild Hall of Corpus Christi, Lavenham.*

means of improving modern house design?).

**Design typology**

Characteristic Suffolk houses are divisible into six wall-groups:—

Group A:    wholly timber-framed.
Group B:    partly timber-framed and partly brick.
Group C:    wholly brick.
Group D:    flint with brick dressings.
Group E:    pargetted.
Group F:    weather-boarded and miscellaneous.

Four of these six groups call for subdivision —

A.1:    exposed timber-framework with plaster infilling.
2:    timber-frame wholly or partly plastered over.
B.1:    external timber-frame, with brick infilling.
2:    part timber-framed (exposed or plastered over), part brickwork.
C.1:    facing brick with stone or plaster dressings.
2:    brick plastered to imitate stone.
D.1:    flint: solid masonry walls.
2:·    flint: faced only.

The A and B Groups are admittedly difficult to subdivide satisfactorily, since any one building can combine features from each (e.g. Otley Hall): an obvious example is the brick chimney which post-dates the earliest Group A types.

Then there is the C Group — wholly brick — and under C.1 we have to look at the development of local building design until this becomes diffused by the popularity of a national and more impersonal style in the eighteenth century, and finally peters out during the century that follows.[1] Certain features such as chimneys and chimney pieces, entrances, bay windows, gatehouses, gateways and garden walls can conveniently be put into an Appendix together with interior joinery.

In the F Group I include, along with weather-boarding, such oddities as houses with tile hanging (not indigenous to Suffolk), and mathematical tiling (imitation brickwork in tile form fixed to a timber-framed building).

Roofs are excluded from this typology because, on the whole, they are subsidiary to walls where the main design features occur. The chief contingency as far as a roof is concerned is a change of roofing materials, although this can mean also a subtle change of character — for example when a roof originally designed for thatching is covered with clay-tiles.

The tarred wall (i.e. coated with bitumen paint) is typical of the region, and frequently found in coastal areas where it is used to make brick, plaster, weather-board or lump walls more waterproof, but is incidental to building design.

The foregoing provides a certain framework, admittedly imperfect, for classifying the main design groups of Suffolk houses on the basis of their wall construction. These will be discussed now in fairly general terms, and later — in Section 6 covering individual houses — in a little more detail.

1 M.W. Barley ends the Vernacular Tradition at 1725, op. cit., page 243, although it could be argued that it persists in Suffolk in cottages and farm-buildings until at least the Regency.

# A. WHOLLY TIMBER-FRAMED HOUSES

*Generally*

As we have already seen, the design principle of the timber-framed system is continuity of stresses. There are clearly certain options in the way framed walls can be made to receive and transmit their loads which impinge on the field of design, and which have, therefore, not yet been considered. Methods differed between one part of the kingdom and another, and once it was seen that choice of design was constant over fairly large areas, it became evident that this could be used as a means of identification. It was on this basis that J.T. Smith worked out a theory of framed timber walls.[1] Without attempting to transcribe in detail the extremely interesting results, it is important to give a general summary. After a careful examination of national photographic records he concluded that from the middle of the fourteenth to the middle of the seventeenth century there were in England two major schools of carpentry, the eastern and the western, and it was the eastern which gave the lead. Of special interest to us is anything especially characteristic of Suffolk, and this occurs in the so-called close-studding.[2] Whilst this predominates also in Essex and Kent, it could be argued that the provenance was Suffolk, and although not so prolific in Norfolk, it combines with two other features to give an important distinction to Suffolk work; the absence of a middle-rail in the storey-height of the frame and a method of tension-bracing found otherwise only in Essex (although this feature may turn out to be less conclusive when more comparative data is available). At the moment we are not concerned so much with structure as with aesthetics, and have to recognise the strongly vertical emphasis given by close-studding unbroken by any middle-rail, in such fine buildings as the Guildhall at Lavenham; Giffords Hall, Wickhambrook; or Thurston End Hall, Hawkedon.

*A.1: exposed timber-framework with plaster infilling*

This is the purest of the types in the A and B Groups, and comes into the mainstream of Gothic house design. It is the type which illustrates the effective contrast between oak framing and plaster panelling in the way the original builders intended. It is the type with which we associate the finest framed houses of Suffolk, and in an extended history the succession from the earliest known to the latest examples of exposed timber framework would be identified and then discussed chronologically.

Away in the west of the county, the best example of exposed timber-framing and plaster is probably Giffords Hall, Wickhambrook, although the south front was plastered until fairly recently (cf. a photograph of 1907 in 'West Suffolk Illustrated').

There can be little doubt that the carpenters who put up this splendid manor house in the late fifteenth or early sixteenth century intended their work to be seen and admired. Giffords Hall, as Avray Tipping said[3] 'is quite Gothic in treatment. But ... Gothic of the last undiluted phase', and he maintained, in general terms, that East Anglia, although more open to continental influences than many parts of England, did not 'tincture its Gothic with Renaissance importations' until after the reign of Henry VII. The house, although later enlarged, remains a splendid example of oak close-studding, undisturbed even by diagonal bracing, and revealing all the elements of its structure — sills, bressumers, angle posts — with a lean and vigorous austerity which is typical of the best Suffolk timber work.

The other Wickhambrook houses have mostly been plastered, but can show superb carpentry internally, as we shall see under Section 6.

At Stansfield, three miles or so to the south-east, in addition to Purton Green Farm, is Elm Hall of the mid-fifteenth century in its earliest build, and a good example of oak close-studding, although, like Purton Green, much restored. Being brick-nogged this is one of the B Group houses — partly timber-framed and part brickwork — to be mentioned shortly.

Fine examples of close-studded work occur in the Brettenham, Preston, Lavenham area; Popples, Brettenham (see Section 6). Preston Hall has an architecturally distinguished version of the double cross-wing (see Section 6); Lavenham is a largely timber-framed town exhibiting stud and plasterwork in profusion, with the early sixteenth century Guild Hall of Corpus Christi — although considerably restored — remaining one of the supreme examples of close-studded construction in the Suffolk style (see Plate 41).

At Chelsworth, the Grange is an unspoilt group of timber-framed structures —

1 cf. *Timber-framed Building in England – Its Development & Regional Differences.* Art. Archaeological Journal Volume 122, 1965, pages 133-158.
2 It would not be inappropriate here to include the following extract from Holinshed's Chronicle written in the reigns of Henry VIII and Elizabeth I: *The Description of England*, Chapter XII, page 314.

The greatest part of our building in the cities and good townes of England consisteth onlie of timber ... In old time the houses of the Britons were set up with a few posts and many radels, with stables and all offices under one roof, the like whereof is to be seen in the fennie countries, and northern parts unto this daie, where for lack of wood they are inforced to continue this ancient manner of building. It is not in vaine therefore in speaking of building to make a distinction between the plaine and wooddie soiles: for as in these, our houses are commonlie strong and well timbered, so that in manie places, there are not above foure, six or nine inches betweene stud and stud; so in the open and champaigne countries they are inforced for want of stuffe to use no studs at all, but onlie franke posts, raisins, beames, prickeposts, groundsels, summers (or dormant) transoms, and such principals, with here and there a griding, wherewith they fasten their splints or radels, and then cast it all over with thick claie to keep out the wind, which otherwise would annoie them.'
3 *English Houses*, op. cit., Period II, Volume I, page 4.

house, barn and outbuildings dating from the fifteenth century — seen at special advantage from the village street north of the church, with which it combines to make a notable group of mediaeval buildings (see Plate 42). The towns and villages in this old wool and cloth weaving district have distinctively compact street developments, and Kersey, a little way south, is recognised as a little altered mediaeval community to which a touch of drama is added by the church on a hill high above the village street. The houses are of carpentry and brickwork, as well as a great deal of plaster.

To the south again lies Bildeston with streets of compactly developed weaver's houses, some much restored, but showing in combination a series of framed, close-studded, plastered and jettied houses. South again in Hadleigh are more tightly developed mediaeval street patterns of framed and plastered houses, some recently exposed close-studwork is to be seen in Angel, George and Benton Streets.

Along the Suffolk bank of the river Stour can be found close-studded houses in the old cloth weaving centres all the way from Stoke-by-Clare to Stratford St. Mary, and well exemplified at the latter by the Priest's House (the next door 'Gatemans' is thought to incorporate a weaver's house of 1334). They will be found at East Bergholt also, and in the surrounding country.

*Plate 42: The Grange, Chelsworth, view from the village*

Much of the half-timber work in Ipswich is either concealed behind plaster, has been much restored, as Nos. 7 and 9 Northgate Street, or has been destroyed. The house in Northgate Street (see Plate 43) shows in an interesting way how 'tincture of Renaissance ideas' could influence a wealthy merchant's building in traditional close-studded style in 1589, and must be discussed again in Section 6.

Close-studwork persists on either side of the Pye Road going north through the county; at Needham Market, Coddenham, the Stonhams, Cranley Green and Eye. And in the long clay-land belt of High Suffolk going north-east from the Pye Road, at Otley (both the hall-houses), Bedingfield, Laxfield, Fressingfield, Wissett and The Saints.

*A.2: timber-frame wholly or partly plastered over*

It will not escape the observant that by far the larger number of traditional houses are wholly or partly plastered over — too large a number for enumeration here. In current restorations there is a tendency to remove plaster and expose timber frames, but it would not be consistent with my arguments to approve the wholesale stripping of plaster. I am suggesting that the case for doing so depends upon a critical analysis of structure, and should be approved only when it is certain that the building is a good example of the school of Gothic carpentry before its decline, and then only when the timbers are intact, and by exposing them a fine building is restored to its original beauty. It must never be forgotten that after Elizabethan days new framed houses were designed to have plastered walls and that, with a dwindling stock of fine ornamental plasterwork (pargetting), there has to be an extremely good case for stripping this off in order to expose timber framework.

*Plate 43: Nos. 7-9, Northgate Street, Ipswich.*

Some explanation is needed why more old framed houses were not simply pulled down when Renaissance succeeded Gothic design, and although the O.S. 2½ inch shows the empty sites of many old halls and it is for historians to say when these were demolished, I suspect that the numbers taken down were greater before the first Elizabethan age than after. One reason would be economic: the peak of prosperity in the cloth trade had passed by the early seventeenth century, and the economy was becoming mainly agrarian. In 1600 there could have been something like five hundred halls and manorhouses, many newly-built or altered during the previous eighty years or so: it is unlikely that this total was increased by as much as one quarter during the ensuing 200 years.

## B. PARTLY TIMBER-FRAMED AND PARTLY BRICK

*B.1: external timber-frame with brick infilling*

Most of this work was in replacement of older 'beam filling', when bricks were easy to obtain and fairly inexpensive. Whether or not this was deliberate design during a transitional phase can be proved by looking closely at the studwork when opportunity offers: when there are carpentry indents providing for the horizontal laths so often used to support wattle work it is reasonable to assume the brickwork is a later replacement. Brick was a quite reasonable substitute for claywork, although not necessarily as waterproof because of porosity and today a single skin of brickwork is only regarded as satisfactory in cavity walls. The diagonal placing of bricks, although decorative, was also practical because, as already noted, the downward thrust tended to 'lock' brickwork into position.

Examples are fairly numerous and often effective, as at Thurston Hall (see Plate 44); Swan's Hall, Hawkedon (see Plate 45); Elm Hall, Stansfield; Great Bevill's, Bures; Fidget's Farm, Naughton; Otley Hall[1] and Otley High House. Brick nogging was frequently used in large farm buildings such as barns and stables, and there is a fine example of the former at Baylham Hall and of the latter at Bentley Hall.

*B.2: part-timber frame (exposed or plastered over), part brickwork*

This is a large group composed of earlier framed houses which have received brick additions, beginning with adjuncts such as porches, bays, and, of course, chimneys. Chimneys are best treated separately since they start either by being built inside or added on to older houses, gradually to become part of a new design idiom: it is a story which has been told before but will bear brief repetition.

Extensive use of brickwork in vernacular building (i.e. other than the small amount needed for raising ground-sills) begins to appear during the sixteenth century in the storey-height ground floor walls, gable-end walls, and two-storey porches and chimneys, as at Flemings Hall, Bedingfield. Chimneys sometimes combine with gable-end walls either in wholly brick houses, such as Wantisden Hall, or as at Moor Farm, Middleton (the B.2 Group). Brick features of this kind on otherwise plastered houses point mainly to a transitional phase which continues into the seventeenth century, by which time the vernacular brick house has

1 But not in the later restorations, when both brickwork and pointing are very unsympathetic.

appeared. At the lower levels of the building economy, the terraced and the single- or double-dwelling continues during the eighteenth century in timber-framing and plasterwork with the use of brick restricted to internal – very occasionally gable-end wall-chimneys.

Another feature is the cross-wing or extension built entirely of brick on to a timber-framed house, but more general is wholesale refronting in brickwork, and this is so prolific in Suffolk as to call for special comment.

## C. WHOLLY BRICK

*C.1: facing brick with stone or plaster dressings*

Discounting Little Wenham Hall which – as far as we know – was never copied, and which remains, as Pevsner described it, 'one of the *incunabula* of English domestic architecture', brickwork before the sixteenth century was probably found mainly but not entirely in church work and religious buildings. We know that monks were makers of brick, but have seen that in the reign of Henry VI (1459) bricks were also being made in Suffolk by tradesmen for use in private houses, and the supposition is that they could be had – at a price – even earlier in the fifteenth century. All the buildings in Suffolk with brickwork before 1450 given in Miss Wight's list[1] are ecclesiastical except Little Wenham Hall, but we need more contracts such as that to supply John Mannock with bricks for Giffords Hall, in order to point the existence of a secular brick architecture.

The picture begins to form of a native brick craft fertilised by immigrants from the Low Countries. From R. Freeman Bullen (East Anglian Miscellany, No. 5281) we learn that in 1436 alone applications for protection from the English Crown totalled nearly 1,200, and of these – mainly persons born in Holland, Flanders, or Germany – about 10% were living in Suffolk. Their trades were not always stated, but historians are agreed that bricklayers as well as brickmakers were amongst the settlers in East Anglia, and certainly Henry Herryson, dwelling at Ipswich in 1436 and 'born in Teutonic parts', was a 'brikemaker'.

So much was happening to architecture in England during the lifetime of Thomas Wolsey, the Suffolk-born Cardinal (1475-1530) that it is worth remembering his part as a 'fashion-leader' – as Miss Wight puts it. Wolsey preferred brick as we can see from the little that survives in the gateway of his incomplete school at Ipswich, and at Hampton Court he promoted a new style of domestic deisgn to which the English manorhouse, the mediaeval monastery, and – to some degree – the new classicism each contributed. The master whose name is connected with Wolsey's share of the work is Henry Redman (*fl.* 1508-29) who designed the Base Court and the West Gatetower. The remarkable feat here was the creation new-born of an English style of brick architecture founded upon the native Perpendicular Gothic – 'the noblest offspring of a single brain' – as John Harvey called it.[2]

*Plate 44: Diagonal brickwork at Thurston Hall, Hawkedon.*

*Plate 45: Another example of diagonal brickwork in timber-frame at Swans Hall.*

1 op. cit., pages 357-380.
2 *Gothic England – A Survey of National Culture*, by John Harvey, op. cit., page 135.

## Typology of brick houses

The history of house design in brickwork is almost as complex and extensive in Suffolk as that of timber-framed building, and like so many aspects of this introductory study calls for extensive research. We have seen where the brickearths are to be found and glanced at the history and the craft of brickmaking, as well as some of the methods of traditional brickwork and we have noted planning arrangements over a considerable scale of houses. It remains to take some stock of the ideas which prompted brick design. A few examples will suggest the scope of an inquiry:—

1 Hengrave Hall: stylistically one of the most interesting of the Suffolk mansions
2 Stepped Gables: a characteristic feature of Tudor brick mansions
3 Dutch Gables: a typical feature of seventeenth century brick design
4 Facade design: eighteenth century brick elevations in Suffolk towns and villages, and a trend continuing through the nineteenth century

### 1. Hengrave Hall

Wolsey could well be one of the formative influences behind an early sixteenth century brick mansion such as Hengrave Hall where, putting to one side Kytson's choice of white brick instead of Cardinal Wolsey's red, there is an obvious affinity of style with Hampton Court. Remember that both were moated and the loss is in every way incalculable — compare Helmingham or Oxburgh Hall, Norfolk. Then look at the general silhouettes; both turreted at every corner (Hengrave keeps its onion domes — at Hampton Court they have gone); similarly battlemented parapets; almost identical star-topped chimney stacks built of red brick with moulded brick patterns; nearly matching pinnacles and finials, and the same emphasis on the gatehouse entrance (Kytson's *tour de force* with three engaged bow windows resting upon empanelled coats of arms and supported by elaborate corbelling, all in heavily under-carved stonework), far outstrips that of Wolsey's entrance. What would be the provenance of all these themes? Art historians have combed the Continent for likely sources but we are still free to search for themes which obviously derive from English Perpendicular Gothic. Division of walls horizontally by stone string courses is a feature of Gothic churches, as, indeed, is the offset plinth; the large window openings can only come from the late Perpendicular when we can find any number of stone mullion and transom windows with shallow arch-headed lights of similar proportions (there is no need to look further than the south wall of the nave of Hengrave Church — and, for that matter, find there much the same crenellated parapets). The Hall windows have straight heads but the stone tracery and the label-moulds belong to church windows, as do the parapeted gable-ends, the gable-crosses being replaced here by small finials. The onion domes with finials are clearly — as James Lees-Milne called them — 'a relic of Gothic architecture'; at Hengrave the pair of cusped onion domes topping the gatehouse turrets almost exactly match the polygonal turrets on the four corners of the tower of St. Peter Mancroft, Norwich: the plain domes are simply shorn versions of the same. (I think it is these features in particular, together with the sharply pointed gables, that give Hengrave such an undeniably Gothic look.)

*The Gatehouse, Hengrave Hall*

This leaves the chimneys. It is possible that they were inspired by Hampton Court for this was building between 1515-1530, and could have been well advanced by the time Kytson started work at Hengrave in 1525. Somewhere he must have seen and admired red-brick moulded chimney stacks, and this would be more likely in London, especially since he employed several skilled craftsmen who came from there.

### 2. Stepped gables

The stepped gable can only rarely be found in East Anglian churches[1] and that could be one reason for its choice by Sir Arthur Hopton at Cockfield in about 1540 or Sir Nicholas Bacon for his Hall of 1554, but it was just as likely to have been a Tudor preference for spikey silhouettes, for this is how it seems at Roos Hall near Beccles. The ornamental gable becomes so important a part of the regional vernacular that a few general notes on the subject are called for.

The gable existed from the first moment that a roof was pitched, and architecture has traditionally thrived on the exploitation of features already present in structure. Looking back, for a moment, to East Anglian timber-framing, notice how walls acquired an aesthetic quality by close-studding; how window and door design was proportioned to the studwork module; how oversailing work was

1 It occurs in mediaeval brick Danish churches 'to be found in every town and village (where) the east end is invariably square, with a stepped gable.' cf. *The Cathedrals and Churches of Norway, Sweden and Denmark* by Francis T. Bumpus (London; 1908, page 23). Two examples of Tudor date in Suffolk known to me are St. Nicholas' church, Rushbrooke, and St. Andrew's church, Winston, where the porches are crow-stepped, and in the former the east gable also.

99

enhanced by the carved decoration of bressumers and the use of ornamental brackets, buttresses and corner-posts; lastly, how gable-ends were accented by the patterning of barge boards. Brick architecture had to find its own characteristic themes and one of the earliest was the ornamental gable.

One of the ways of emphasising the gable only possible in brickwork (or stonework) was by building the wall above the line of the roof, and then bringing it to the apex in a series of setbacks or steps (see Plate 46). Customarily the wall thickness of the gable above the roof line did not exceed two bricks, but can be brick and half, or single brick; and each setback or step needs a miniature roof of its own to throw off surface water, hence the use of copings in either stone or brick. This form of gable has been called stepped gable in English, *trapgevel* in Dutch, and *treppen-giebel* in German; the more romantic English name is crow-step or corbie-gable (supposedly for the bird foothold offered by these series of steps?). Historically it would be hard to date, but the European form antedates the English by as much as the widespread use of brick abroad precedes its use in this country, and wide distribution in Northern Europe suggests that it is incorrectly included amongst the so-called 'Dutch' gables.

*Plate 46: Stepped gable-end, Roos Hall, Beccles.*

English travellers crossing the North Sea in early mediaeval days would have seen brick stepped gables in most Northern European towns and ports; at Bergen, Oslo, Hamburg, Lübeck, Bremen, Antwerp, Ghent, Bruges; in most of the Dutch towns, and in moated castles in Denmark, Holland and Germany. Brickmaking revived in East Anglia in the twelfth to thirteenth centuries, and from the aftermath of the Black Death in the mid-fifteenth century, the immigration of tradesmen increased, and the Flemish settlers in Suffolk included weavers and clothworkers, and, as already noted, brickmakers and building tradesmen. Skills of many kinds had been coming into Suffolk ports for several centuries, and ideas from continental sources had a way of being fertilised here and fashioned into local forms — so it was in the architecture of brick and of the brick gable in particular. Comparisons can readily be made but exact copying is hard to find, and individual English counties seem to have invented their own versions.

At Cockfield the builders started the gable with the so-called 'kneeler' of four courses of oversailing brickwork (and a bonding timber) to bring the start of the stepping about ten inches away from the wall and level with the eaves; thence it ascended by six steps with moulded brick copings to an ornamental gable chimney, or by seven steps similarly coped to a decorative pinnacle in dormer gables. At Redgrave the individual steps could have been brick and half wide as against just over one brick at Cockfield, but in both the step height works out at about nine courses overall (i.e. including coping).

## 3. Dutch gables

It is possible to distinguish four periods in the development of the so-called 'Dutch' gable in East Anglia:—

A Late Elizabethan/Jacobean (c.1578-1623)
B Stua.t I (c.1623-1649)
C Protectorate (c.1649-1663)
D Stuart II (c.1663-1702 incl. William and Mary)

In the accompanying sketch diagram Suffolk gable-ends are compared with Dutch examples, to which they have a certain resemblance (see Figure 50).

Curved gables gradually succeed Tudor crow-stepped gables as the sixteenth century ends. Nobody, presumably, still believes that they acquired the name of 'Dutch' gables because they were the work of Dutch artisans, although the whole question of their origin in lowland England awaits a great deal more investigation. In Holland they have been effectively studied, and differing gable patterns have been grouped under familiar names such as *halsgevel* (lit. throated gable), *klokgevel* (klok = bell), *Tuitgevel* or *puntgevel* (pointed gable). No such general sub-division into types has been made in this country, if we exclude the attempt by C. Cudworth in the late '30s to distinguish five specific styles of East Anglian gables.[1] The majority of Suffolk and Norfolk gables are, in effect, *curvilinear,* not perhaps in the strict Gothic sense of continuously flowing lines (as in window tracery), but in their general geometrical shape. The exception to this is the pedimented top gable which is raised on a base of concave curves in thoroughly Italian Renaissance style, especially when, as at Christchurch Mansion, the bases of both pediments and curves are punctuated with stone ornaments; but this is fairly rare in Suffolk, and reminiscent of the pediments of classical brick mansions such as Raynham Hall in Norfolk, and Kew Palace in London. When all is said and done, however, the term 'Dutch' gable is the one most likely to stick; it is simple and everyone knows what is meant by it. The only trouble is that, quite apart from confused ideas on Dutch workmanship, it is still not entirely true.

First there is the difficulty over dating. The earliest East Anglian shaped gables seems to be those of the Manor House, Bracondale, in outer Norfolk, and dated 1578, and on top of the Elizabethan annexe to the King's Lynn Guildhall there is an odd pediment-shaped top gable, in stone, with concave and convex curves, which could also be about the same date. Whilst there are examples of curvilinear gables in Holland built between the middle and end of the sixteenth century, they are few in number when compared with the stepped gables then at the height of their popularity.

Secondly, there is the problem of source. It is not easy to find exact parallels in gable design between England and Holland, although every now and again there are obvious similarities. The brick gables of the town hall at Zierikzee in the province of Zeeland (1555), and another at Nes, on the island of Ameland (1625), are not unlike Red House, Knodishall, and Mockbeggars Hall, Claydon, respectively. It is arguable that these people out on the western seaboard of Holland had contacts with East Anglia aross the North Sea, but the case for exporting a gable design is tenuous, to say the least. Then there is the paradoxical fact that simplified forms of curvilinear gables akin to those in East Anglia can be found in the eastern provinces of Gelderland and Limbourg. The likelihood of any contact between these widely separated places is remote indeed. Even in their simplified form the Dutch gables make much use of stone dressings and ornamentation.

The tendency of Dutch and German steps is to be wider and higher; at Haarlem, for instance, early sixteenth century gable-end steps are twenty four courses high and three-and-half bricks wide, and this appears again in Haarlem in the early seventeenth century with five large steps rising to a central pinnacle, each step having a long flat moulded brick or stone coping. Urban development in Holland tends to be extremely compact (owing to scarcity of building land) and pyramidal gable-ends to appear in rows along the streets and water fronts. A good example of this is Cor Visser's quayside scene at Goes, Zuid Beveland (see Plate 47), although it is interesting to note one building in which the stepping is close to the typical East Anglian gable — ten steps high including the kneeler; but these high Dutch gables are produced by roofs often pitched to at least 60° in order to accommodate two attic storeys, and this, again, reflects the need to make the most of narrow building

*Mettingham Hall, Nr. Bungay, second half seventeenth century – Basil Oliver.*

1 *The Dutch Gables of East Anglia*, by C.L. Cudworth; the Architectural Review, March, 1939.

| Example | Notes | Example | Notes |
|---------|-------|---------|-------|

 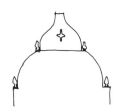

**MOCKBEGGARS HALL CLAYDON 1621**

*Compare with Hemingstone Hall of 1625. Resembles Dutch gable at Zevenaar Guilders (now Deventer Overjissel), early eighteenth century, as in above sketch.*

**WESTERFIELD HALL nr. IPSWICH 1656**

*Reverse curves occur in the Zaanstrech north of Amsterdam in eighteenth century wooden fronts, and at Zaandam in Holland. Compare also with Red House Farm, Knodishall.*

 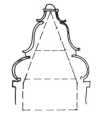

**NEWE HOUSE PAKENHAM 1622**

*Compare with House Bethlehem, Gorinchen, South Holland, of 1566, but gable much steeper and comprises three storeys, and is outlined with stone dressings.*

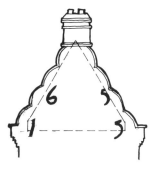

**MANOR FARM HERRINGFLEET 1655**

*Multiple-curved gable-end associated with the Waveney Valley. The design is said not to appear in Holland until late nineteenth century.*

*Notice the wrought-iron numerals corresponding with the Dutch 'Ankers'.*

**HEMINGSTONE HALL nr. IPSWICH 1625**

*Compare with Mockbeggars Hall, Claydon of 1621. Porch has gable, as above.*

*In Holland, porch gables are always simple as in above sketch.*

**METTINGHAM HALL nr. BECCLES c.1670**

*Compare with Shire Hall, Woodbridge for general similarity of arrangement without the frilly stone dressings and separate pedimented crown. This pattern of gable-end can be found in South Africa in eighteenth century.*

 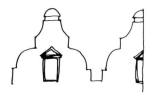

**WITNESHAM HALL WITNESHAM c.1625**

*Prof. Temminck-Groll calls the Witnesham Hall gable 'very Flemish' and compares with Zierikzee Town Hall of 1555: he considers both designs probably stemmed from pattern-books published in Flanders.*

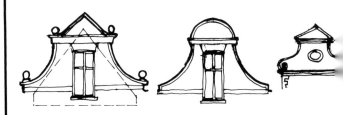

**CHRISTCHURCH MANSION IPSWICH 1674-75**

*Two differing types of ornamental gable-end showing Flemish influence. Raynham Hall, Norfolk, has gable-end as in sketch above right.*

*Figure 50: Examples of Suffolk gable-ends compared with Dutch.*

| Example | Notes | Example | Notes |
|---------|-------|---------|-------|

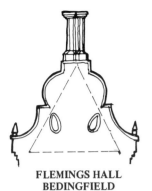

**FLEMINGS HALL
BEDINGFIELD
c.1650**

*Manor house dated to c.1550 but gable-ends assumed to be approximately one hundred years later, and to derive from Waveney Valley. In Holland the combination of a chimney stack with decorative gable is rare.*

**RED HOUSE FARM
KNODISHALL
1678**

*A variant of the Waveney Valley style found at Mettingham Hall but with gable summit in form of semi-circular headed pediment.*

**BOUNDARY FARM
FRAMSDEN
c.1650**

*Gable-end to small brick stable building adjoining farmhouse. Prof. Temminck-Groll comments that this design is to be found in the Eastern Provinces of Holland.*

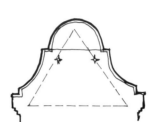 

**WENHASTON GRANGE
nr. HALESWORTH
c.1680**

*Design common in Holland in the eighteenth century but with much steeper pitch, as above sketch.*

**SHIRE HALL
WOODBRIDGE
c.1650**

*A comparatively rare Suffolk example of brick gable-end with outer stone dressings; in Holland the finishing of decorative gables with stone edges, cornices, and other ornamental feature is customary. Compare with grouped gables at The White Hart Inn, Scole, Norfolk, dated 1655.*

**DARSHAM HALL
DARSHAM
1679**

*Pediment over concave curves similar to Christchurch Mansion but less ornate. Popular in Holland in second half of seventeenth century, and frequent in Amsterdam, but steeper.*

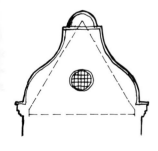

**WHITTINGHAM HALL
1653**

*Ogee curved gables were developed in the late seventeenth century. This type also appears in Holland in the late seventeenth and early eighteenth centuries.*

*A variant of the ogee gable occurred at Somerleyton Hall prior to the Victorian remodelling, as in above sketch.*

**HIGH HOUSE
HUNTINGFIELD
1700**

*A simplified version of gable-ends at Blickling Hall, Norfolk. More elaborate versions of this design are to be found in the Eastern Provinces of Holland.*

Plate 47: Water front at Goes, South Holland, from a woodcut by Cor Visser.

sites. In East Anglia the same need did not arise and most gables have lower pitched roofs — around 50° — and contain a single storey.[1] Nevertheless, the choice of small, regular, crow-steps can only be seen as deliberate on the part of local patrons and builders, and the result avoids the often bizarre effects seen in Netherlandish gables.

*Plate 48: Weston Hall, near Beccles.*

The gable-end did not lose its appeal to Suffolk builders as a decorative feature after 1600, but there is a transitional period before the so-called 'Dutch' gable makes its appearance. Weston Hall, south of Beccles (see Plate 48), is already moving towards a new compromise, and the old Gothic crow-steps look decidedly out of place, an uneasy relationship very marked where the pedimented attic window almost touches the stepped gable; wall planes are no longer divided by string-courses; the angle buttresses have been simplified and no longer have pinnacles, only squat brick caps; the chimneys are shafted but are plain octagonals. The date is the latter part of the sixteenth century, for John Rede died in 1605 — and is buried in Weston church. Like Roos Hall this is only part of a larger house but for a different reason; the missing centre-piece and North wing were burnt down about 1820: this is a pity because the central front entrance has gone which would have been an interesting detail. There would, too, have been confirmation of possibly two or three plastered dormer windows with circular lights and a strangely Stuart look (see Section 6.)

Thirdly, it is accepted by Dutch art historians that there were numerous and fertile contacts with Flemish culture, which powerfully influenced the Dutch Renaissance. Flanders was ideally placed to receive ideas coming in from Germany and France — and through France from Italy — and it was from this source whence came the architectural pattern books which were so avidly studied not only in Holland but also in Tudor England.[2] Professor Temminck-Groll, head of the Building Department of the Delft Technical High School, places the development of ornamental gables in Holland firmly within the context of Dutch history during a period in the very late sixteenth, and the first half of the seventeenth century, when the country became extremely wealthy. This was the time when many towns such as Amsterdam, Haarlem and Groningen were rebuilt and enlarged, and town councils were busy trying to compel the owners of timber-framed and thatched houses to replace them with structures of brick and tile — not always successfully, as G.L. Burke adds,[3] because the expense was still beyond the means of many citizens (fire regulations were extensive; no party walls were permitted; fire-break spaces were required between adjoining buildings, and it was even forbidden to paint a wooden front).

Professor Temminck-Groll draws attention to the way in which the new Renaissance forms came in during this period to develop typical Dutch variations on the old stepped gable form, the number of steps being reduced and the stone coping which protects the stepped brickwork adapting the top half of the classical

1 There is an unusual half-storey attic at Roos Hall giving two windows in the gable; and the gable steps total eleven; exactly the same number at Mutford Hall and Keir's Cottage, Mutford. At Cockfield Hall there are seven steps, and at Wantisden Hall twelve, both terminating in a chimney stack.
2 These architectural pattern books are well-known and the following were amongst the most influential:- *A Description of the Five Orders* by Hans Blum (1550. Zurich). *Perspective* and *Architecture* by J. Vredeman de Fries (1559 and 1563 respectively). Antwerp). *De Quinque Columnarum* and *Architectura* by Wendel Dietterlin (1593 and 1598 respectively). These references from Chapter VII of *Tudor Renaissance* by James Lees-Milne (see Section Bibliography).
3 *The Making of Dutch Towns* page 123 (see Section Bibliography).

cornice together with the widespread use of stone dressings. 'As soon as real architects came upon the scene, however, richer forms are introduced in the sixteenth as well as in the seventeenth century; they are rather rare of course. These richer forms, curvilinear and so on, are going to dominate the second half of the seventeenth century in a simplified form. Then very often you will find the forms which are comparable to those found in East Anglia . . .' I do think the above mentioned rare early examples of real 'new' architecture (based very often on the Flemish architecture books) have influenced both your simplified variations from the first half of the century, as (well as) our simplified ones from the second half . . . I think Flanders has been very important in the whole matter — probably from there individual streams developed.'[1]

When we return to East Anglia in the second part of the sixteenth century it is to find a similar rebuilding in full swing, and here also it was only the really wealthy who could afford to build in the new brick style. This was grafted on to the old Perpendicular Gothic — as has already been observed — and reached its most ebullient phase in the reign of Queen Elizabeth I, even though most people in Suffolk had to be content with a new or rebuilt timber-framed and plastered house, probably with the addition of a large new chimney stack or two, and maybe a brick gable-end or a porch. During this period Flemish ideas were being disseminated also, and it is not unlikely that cultured Dutch refugees who returned home after the persecution of Alva took with them ideas gleaned in England. It is, for instance, recorded that Lieven de Key, who was to create a new style of Renaissance architecture in Haarlem, was in England between about 1568 and 1591, and studied many of the brick mansions then being built. It is right to see this period as one of constant interchange between England and the Netherlands, when Dutch ideas were transplanted here and English ideas appear in Holland (Professor Temminck-Groll mentions a plaster ceiling in Brielle which looks very Elizabethan, and that Delft too had an example — which disappeared — and these are interesting for English influence on Dutch architecture).

The mood of the two countries was, however, very different after the early part of the seventeenth century. In Holland, following the founding of the Dutch Republic, this was a time of intense national self-consciousness, and of the growth of vigorous native schools of architecture and painting, borrowing ideas from Flemish sources and directly from the Italian Renaissance, but using them in a very Dutch way. In Suffolk it was a phase of a more reflective character, of unrest within the newly established Church, of diminution in the markets for Suffolk cloth in the Low Countries, of growing rivalry with Dutch traders leading to the First Dutch War in 1652, and of Civil War. It is scarcely surprising, then, that the domestic architecture of this period should be marked by sobriety of taste, nor that Renaissance forms imported from Flemish and Dutch sources should be stripped of most ornamentation and translated into brickwork with few stone trimmings. Gone were the spikes, pepper-pots, pinnacles, finials and honey-combed chimney shafts; the elaborate porches, bay windows, and long cross-wings; their place had been taken by the compactly designed house of either rectangular form, or with short cross-wings, surmounted by simple curvilinear gables. For the rest, walls were good honest red brick, often two-brick thick, in Flemish bond — after about 1630[2] — and occasionally diapered; the window lights larger and the thickness of mullions and transoms less; the classical rules of symmetry and proportion conscientiously applied, and the flourishes confined to classical columns or pilasters and pedimented door heads. All this fits well with the 'initial tendency of the county leaders to puritanism',[3] the mercantilist interests of both town and country, and the moralisings of Robert Ryece.

Further comments on the gable design of individual seventeenth century houses follow in Section 6.

*White Hart Inn, Scole, c.1655 — Basil Oliver.*

### Facade design

1 Letter to the author from Utrecht, June 1975.
2 Nathaniel Lloyd gives Kew Palace, 1631, and Raynham Hall, 1631-5, as early examples of the use of Flemish bond.
3 The phrase is Alan Everitt's from *Suffolk and the Great Rebellion*, page 15.

The street was a ready-made shop window for architectural display, and the history of taste and fashion is written in the facades that line the thoroughfares of English towns and villages. In Suffolk — as elsewhere — the advance from plainness towards display is linked with prosperity, and can be seen happening from the mid-fifteenth century. The merchants' houses then began to employ wood carvers to decorate features of timber-framed houses that hitherto had been plain: the bressumers, brackets below jetties and barge-boards. Ipswich — as has been said — was once celebrated for the carved angle posts associated with jettied houses (see Plate 49). But it was especially in front entrances and bay windows that ornament was most concentrated; and the prestige quality of the doorway to No.7 Northgate Street needs no emphasis (see below under Appendix A.) A hundred years earlier this might have been considered ostentatious, for in the mediaeval community the enrichment of entrances belonged to churches or guild halls, and the splendid doorway to the private house is an interesting reflection of growing secularism.

A classical example occurs just over the border, in Great Coggeshall, Essex, although the Paycockes were a Suffolk family of wealthy butchers and their house fits exactly with that class of tradesmen described by Harrison in the time of Queen Elizabeth, as 'Men of great port and countenance' . . .[1] The finest craftsmen were evidently employed to produce this expensive oak front, with its elaborate carving, and seven great bracketed bay windows.

I mention this background in order to give the brick facade its rightful historical setting. The keynote of the classical elevation is the front entrance which, in the grander house, is frequently part of an elaborate architectural centre-piece (as we saw at Loudham Hall — one small example only of a prevalent early eighteenth century fashion). The demonstrative doorway has, I suggest, obvious Tudor origins, and a long history of popularity from the sixteenth until the present century (it is only since the Second World War that the front door has been demoted and in the average modern house is often indistinguishable from an adjoining storey-height window. It could also be argued that the popular *bay window* — now on the way out — also originates as a Tudor prestige symbol).

Against this background one turns with renewed interest to historical streets. 'Facade collecting' could be a rewarding pastime, and the extent of a single style is suggested by the accompanying illustrations of 'Georgian' house fronts in Suffolk towns and villages (see Plate 50).[2] Part of the interest lies in trying to estimate whether the facade is integral with a Georgian-dated building, or whether, as in the case of The Fenn, Swingleton Green, near Monks Eleigh, it is a refronted timber-framed and plastered house.

There are only two of this group which appear to be completely contemporary — No. 2 St. Peter's Street, ('The Sailor's Rest'), Ipswich, and The Manor House, Stutton. The first occupies a corner site at the junction with Cutler Street, and is seen to advantage from halfway down Rose Lane, opposite. Speed's map of 1610 shows a gabled house on this corner, and Pennington, in 1778, the present block (the front range of which has survived the site redevelopment). It is a handsome building and the cornice with modillion soffit, and plaster quoins setting off red-brick walls, have a late seventeenth century look; so does the doorcase although this could easily be earlier in that century. The windows may have been altered, but the rather thin glazing bars suggest the mid-eighteenth century; in any case the date '1795' given above the entrance must be suspect. Gauged brickwork in arches over the windows, in panels below the first floor windows, and in the frame to the central window are repeated and developed in the other Ipswich examples. The Stutton house is somewhat unusual in a village by being of one build, and raises the — perhaps unworthy — suspicion of incorrect dating as 'mid-Georgian',[3] and the wonder whether it might be an essay in an earlier manner put up at a later date. It needs no specially expert eye to see something unusual in the Bildeston example. The discrepancy in the width of the facade on either side of the centre-piece is unorthodox by strict eighteenth century standards.

There are certain features which give Suffolk examples of the eighteenth century brick facade an almost stock quality. These could be listed as: a) ornamental central (or nominally central) doorway; b) emphasis on a feature above the doorway (at first floor or roof level); c) cornice above first floor windows (indicating eaves level); d) raised and coped parapet.[4] Within these general parameters the grammar of detail can vary between simple and complex, according to the architectural aspirations of the owner. The likely period within which work falls will, as usual, be suggested by the design of doorcases, windows, cornices, string-courses and brickwork — but with the important caveat that accurate dating within the normal span of styles can be easily upset by time lag. Mediaeval Suffolk gave a lead in

*Plate 49: The Old Coffee House, Tavern Street, Ipswich in 1815, with carved wooden angle posts. (From Illustrations of Old Ipswich by John Glyde, 1889.)*

1 cf. *English Homes* by Avray Tipping, Period II, Volume 1, page 12.
2 There are not many seventeenth century facades to be found, but the few there are (e.g. Bramford House, Bramford — brick, and The Willows, Earl Soham — plaster) are especially precious.
3 cf. Pevsner's *Suffolk*, op. cit., page 451.
4 I was tempted to add the *five bay front*, because it was so general in town and village houses of the eighteenth century that exceptions are noticeable, but exceptions there were — usually the *seven bay* front.

*The Fenn, Swingleton Green.*

*The Sailors' Rest, Ipswich.*

*House in the High Street, Bildeston.*

*The Manor House, Stutton.*

*Valley Farm, Heveningham.*

*Left: Cedar Court, Alderton.*

*Plate 50: Some 'Georgian' house fronts.*

timber-framed design and detailing, but Georgian and Victorian Suffolk imported ideas and went on with textbook designs when these were going out of fashion elsewhere. Thus there are many pitfalls in dating these later buildings to stress the importance of documentary local history in establishing ownerships and discovering records.

It is, however, the brick aspect with which we are mainly concerned in these notes. A facade design obviously much in vogue in the first half of the eighteenth century is based upon the use of header panels between windows. At Gainsborough's House, Sudbury; The Fenn, Swingleton Green; Linden House, Eye; and at Ipswich, No. 6 Lower Brook Street (five bays) and No. 16 Northgate Street (seven bays), there are examples of vertical header panels in a dark blue – almost black – brick.[1] In these houses the windows have quoins of red brick, with gauged red brickwork in arched-heads – plain or segmental – thus making a rather rich and dark colour scheme. At their best, in town examples, the mortar joints are black, or dark grey – and tuck pointed to give a more finished look. At both Sudbury and 16 Northgate Street, Ipswich, there are projecting sub-light panels of gauged brickwork to first floor windows, six and two courses supported by three and five triangular dentils respectively. In Lower Brook Street there are recessed panels to all windows, and a decorative feature to five of the thirteen window arches which, as far as I know, is unique in Suffolk brickwork (although at Pallant House, Chichester, attributed to Sir Christopher Wren something similar occurs): it consists of cutting the base of the brick voussoirs into shallow ogee curves on either side of the keystone.

At No. 16 there is an elborate cornice of gauged red brickwork, with tiny dentils and moulded bricks engaging with the central feature of Tuscan Doric pilasters which frame an arched first floor window. This, in turn, surmounts the curved pedimented head of the front doorcase, and is supported by the gauged brick surround to the door. The excellence of all this is undermined by the removal of original glazing bars from the windows, much lowering the quality of the elevation.

*Plate 51: The Red House, Cumberland Street, Woodbridge*      *Julian Stainton*

The Ancient House, Framlingham, late seventeenth century – Basil Oliver.

The occurrence of similar examples of accomplished brickwork in various parts of Suffolk raises again the question of building methods, and suggests the existence of specialist sub-contractors. These would have been accomplished artisans capable, not only of execution, but also of the complete design for a new front.[2] This is more than ever likely when the front was required simply as a facade to replace an original timber-frame, as at Gainsborough's House, and, to judge from plaster flanks just visible, at No. 16 Northgate Street also.

1 There is another in Bridge Street, Hadleigh, which I have since come across.
2 We now need chapter and verse on the employment of these itinerant sub-contractors in Suffolk, and more about their methods of work which, as already mentioned, appeared at Gainsborough's House, Sudbury, to consist of building a virtually independent brick facade against a local bricklayer's rough backing wall, without much attempt to bond the two together.

*Plate 52: Church Street, Southwold*                    Simon Hicklin

Another circumstance is a similarity of certain facades to those of the same period in Dutch towns. This is more marked where, as at the Red House, Woodbridge, the ground floor is raised to the level of the *piano nobile*, and the front door is approached by a flight of stone steps (see Plate 51). There is the same accent on the entrance to be seen, for example, in houses on the waterfronts of Amsterdam. Often surmounted by a *halsgevel*, there is usually some distinguishing feature to the first floor window immediately over the front door — maybe a balcony or a stone surround — and the same parapet, although this sometimes takes the form of an open stone balustrade. The comparison is closer where the window proportions are tall and rather narrow — an effect to which the dark vertical header panels contribute.

At the humbler level of small houses there is — in pursuit of possible Dutch influence — Church Street, Southwold (see Plate 52). Here the repeating pattern of gables and dormer windows has an indeterminate flavour of small streets in Delft or Haarlem. Much of Southwold was burnt down in a disastrous fire on 25th April 1659, and rebuilding must have started soon after and gone on for the next sixty to seventy years. There are records of Flemish weavers in the town, but none of building tradesmen, and in their absence it seems more likely that a seaboard, as opposed to an inland, way of building gave rise to this Dutch or Flemish impression. A local brick has been discovered bearing the impression of a cannon which could be commemorative of the 'victory' of Sole Bay, or of the siege guns — or *culverins* — said to have been presented to the town by the Duke of Cumberland after the battle of Culloden (1746). The habit of indenting a mark or pattern on locally made bricks was sporadic. Bricks made at Stoke Holy Cross bore the imprint of a cross, and, elsewhere, a brick with a reverse-S has been found: later the maker's initials were commonly imprinted (see notes on Somerleyton Brickworks, Section 4).

The presentation of an impressive face to the street was entirely compatible with Victorian ideas of propriety. In the collection of street facades there would be examples of 'neo-design' in Gothic and Classical, for the Victorians were quite uninhibited in impressing their varied tastes (for the picturesque) upon the generally quieter background of seventeenth century plaster and eighteenth century brickwork. In modern terms, the facade, as such, has been abandoned and the outward appearance of the building is merely one expression of the functional reasoning behind the whole design. As we have seen recently in Ipswich this can include wrapping a uniform glasscase around the whole building.

*C.2: brick plastered to imitate stone*

Plaster over framed timber building necessarily occupies a considerable place in Suffolk vernacular architecture from the seventeenth century onwards. Plaster, whatever its practical advantages, had for the Elizabethans the aesthetic merit of draping the bare bones of Gothic houses. The new classicism needed an unbroken

*Plaster ornament at Lavenham – Basil Oliver.*

wall surface to set off the stock features: quoins and rustications, columns and pilasters, architraves and entablatures; and plaster provided this plain background.

The history of external plasterwork in East Anglian building would start with the new Renaissance ideas, take second place in the seventeenth century whilst red-brick architecture was in the ascendant (but developed its own traditions of design and colour: for an example of seventeenth century stucco work on timber framing, see Cupola House, Bury St. Edmunds, and notes on pargetting below). It then began to cover up brickwork in the late eighteenth and early nineteenth centuries, just as it had covered timber framing in the sixteenth and seventeenth. Although stucco was used over brick to imitate stone it is scarcely comparable with pargetting, although both came from a common plaster stem.

It says a lot for the East Anglian brick school that pride in workmanship resisted stucco for so long. In the Brenta in Northern Italy the palaces and public buildings built in the sixteenth and seventeenth centuries were usually built of brick and stucco covered.[1] One good reason for delay in the advent of stucco is a local one, peculiar to East Anglia in general and to Suffolk in particular – the white brick.

The earliest example of the use of white brick must be Little Wenham Hall of c.1270-80. In 1538, white brick was used at Hengrave Hall to harmonise with stonework, but this remains a unique and original decision which no one, as far as I know, was to copy in East Anglia before Thomas Coke used a greyish-white brick for the outside walls of Holkham Hall (1734-61). White brick was the fashionable material for building Suffolk mansions in the latter part of the eighteenth century as can be seen from examples such as Benacre Hall (1763-4), Culford Hall (1790), Finborough Hall (1795), Marlesford Hall (c.1799) and Woolverstone Hall (1776).[2] It continued to vie with the use of stucco during the same period and well on into the next century. At a time when stucco was becoming fashionable, Benhall Lodge (1810), Great Glemham Hall and Beacon Hill House, Martlesham (1814 and c.1830), for example, could still be built of white brick, along with many villas and town houses.

*Plate 53: Hintlesham Hall refronted in stucco.*        Trevor James

1  A striking example is the Loggia del Capitaniato at Vicenza, 1571, from which today most of the stucco has peeled off to reveal the narrow brown bricks with which walls, columns and arches were built.
2  Dr. Clifton-Taylor in *The Pattern of English Building*, op. cit., page 233 quotes the view of Isaac Ware in his *Complete Body of Architecture* (London, 1756) on the superior advantages of white brick in 'the front walls of buildings'. This was probably the first time since the Tudors that the supremacy of red brick had been challenged.

The earliest stucco fronted mansion in Suffolk is probably Hintlesham Hall, which was acquired by Richard Powys in 1720, and radically Georgianised on the entrance side with a classical columnar porch and large double-hung sash windows. The Elizabethan brickwork was plastered and given quoins and string-courses around three sides of the approach courtyard, as well as the two end elevations of the wings facing the drive, leaving the outside walls in red brick (see Plates 53 and 54). Hintlesham Hall may have started the vogue for stucco work, for it appears at Great Saxham Hall, Herringfleet Hall, and Polstead Hall (the remodelling of a Jacobean house), all of the late eighteenth century, and continues into the early nineteenth century at Foxboro' Hall, Melton, and Sibton Park.

111

*Plate 54: Hintlesham Hall, rear elevation in red brick work.*    Trevor James

The use of stucco on a spectacular scale, however, must be reserved for Ickworth House. Mr. Gervase Jackson-Stops quotes from the letter written by the fourth Earl of Bristol.[1] In reply to the plea of his daughter that white brick be used for the exterior of the mansion, the Earl Bishop wrote, '. . . What! Child, build my house of a *brick* that looks like a sick, pale, jaundiced red brick, that would be a red brick if it could, and to which I am certain our posterity would give a little rouge as essential to its health . . . I shall follow dear impeccable old Palladio's rule, and as nothing ought to be without a covering in our raw damp climate, I shall cover the house, pillars and pilasters, with Palladio's *stucco*, which has now lasted 270 years . . . It has resisted the frosts and rains of Vicenza — *c'est tout dire* — and deceives the most acute eye till within a foot.' There can have been few house builders with more trenchant views on the covering for their walls, although, as The National Trust guidebook points out, in quoting from this letter, the Earl Bishop's confidence in the infallibility of stucco was excessive and the material has been a source of trouble ever since.

The next generation of stucco houses must be those in the Picturesque Taste such as Crowe Hall, Stutton (c.1820, see Plate 55), Rendlesham Hall (demolished 1949), but the Lodges still survive. The West Lodge is a remarkable Gothic invention with buttresses and pinnacles, niches, bar-traceried windows, crenellated parapets and four flying buttresses inside which the chimney flues are gathered over into a central shaft — and all done in stucco and Coade stone.

There was a modest blossoming of stucco architecture in many Suffolk towns and villages in the early nineteenth century. In The Thoroughfare, Woodbridge, are three notable examples: No. 40 (Barretts) with its pedimented and arched window-heads and pair of massive urns above shop window level, has been recently rescued from drab dullness by repainting an attractive shade of stone (there is this

*Plate 55: Crowe Hall, Stutton. The south front.*

*Chalk-rock and knapped flintwork at the Moot Hall, Aldeburgh.*

about stucco that, well maintained, it can be extraordinarily smart but, neglected, nothing is sadder or more shabby); Selwyn House, well-proportioned with three storeys and three of those balcony railings which Donald Pilcher referred to as 'highly standardised types ... which were distributed all over England and often abroad', representing one of the notable contributions made by 'mass production' to Regency architecture';[1] St. John's Lodge, at the junction of St. John's Street and The Thoroughfare (although this must be late eighteenth century with its heavy stucco rustications). The Castle and The Little Castle at the top of St. John's Hill have (sad to say) been demolished; they were 1805 and 1812 (according to Pevsner) and the former had a splendid example over a doorway of one of those grotesque heads designed and made locally of a composition similar to Coade Stone[2] – the only survivor of this group is, I believe, on the side of No. 29 The Thoroughfare (*Vogue*), facing the lower end of New Street. St. John's House, Castle Street, with its neo-Gothic stucco, has a thoroughly vicarage look (in fact it is not the Vicarage which is in white brick and just off St. John's Hill): it has white walls, vertical proportions, and groups of arch-headed windows and can be dated to 1830±.

An inventory of good stucco fronted houses (whether brick or timber) would be a useful corollary to that of pargetted timber-framed houses, and a way of drawing attention to their architectural qualities. The best stucco houses have a style and elegance which had disappeared by the end of the mid-nineteenth century, and the modern house, with its mechanical surface texture applied by the 'Tyrolean' spray, is a poor substitute.

## D. FLINT WITH BRICK DRESSINGS

The attraction of flint has varied at different times. To the mediaeval church builder it stood for indestructibility and permanence, and, with an exacting eye for design, was harmoniously linked in two or three different ways. Walls, with strength to be expressed and not refinement, were of roughly coursed flint stones set in a thick mortar bed; when refinement was called for, as in friezes and on buttress faces, then the same flints were squared and neatly coursed with quoins of dressed stone, and where ornamentation was needed, then the same flints could be knapped into geometric shapes and skilfully used as the bodywork in traceried panels of stonework. The aesthetic quality of one and the same material used in these different ways was specially attractive to the master mason, and remains equally so to us.

To the country builder putting up seaboard farms and cottages in East Anglia during the sixteenth and seventeenth centuries, it was a way of building strong walls with the sparing use of brick – still a relatively expensive material. The work went on slowly, but with low labour costs it was one of the cheapest methods to hand, stones needing only to be collected by barrow or in cartloads from nearby pits or shingle banks. The matrix was lime from local kilns, mixed with sand. Design was of the simplest: perhaps a pair of dwellings with a party wall and a central chimney, a parlour and a kitchen with a couple of chambers in the roof, lit by dormer windows. The wall-work then only had to be built to a height of eight feet or so, when the wood plate could go in and the roof pitched up to 50° or more with light rafters to carry thatch. Later, the wall height was increased, and a more economical form of roof could be framed for pantiles at a pitch of about 35°. Brickwork was only needed for quoins and arches over openings.

To the estate owner in 1800, with an eye to the picturesque and a copy of John Plaw's *Sketches for Country House, Villas or Rural Dwellings* to hand, the attraction of flint was an antique look combined with economy. His lodge or cottage could be built of studwork, lathed over and rendered with lime mortar, over which were scattered small pebbles. On more important occasions, the walls could be built of brick and faced with flint, as was done at Euston, when the new school was built in the early nineteenth century in a village which had been rebuilt by the third Duke outside the emparked grounds of the Hall (see Plate 56). The building was a schoolhouse of two storeys with a porch and a single-storey clasroom annexe, built about halfway along the village street, and parallel to the track which served all the cottages on one side of the two broad grass verges leading to the northern

*D.1: flint: solid masonry walls*

*D.2: flint: faced only*

1 Donald Pilcher A.R.I.B.A., a contemporary of mine at the Architectural Association, wrote one of the best-informed books on this period: *The Regency Style* (see Section Bibliography). Particularly relevant to our own times was his discussion on the 'mass production' of building materials such as ironwork and papier-mâché ornamentation. cf. Chapter III.
2 It was Arthur Legg, A.R.I.B.A., who investigated the history of these heads during his work on the first Statutory Lists.

park gates. A mixture of knapped and pebble flint was used in the walls, and the quoins and dressings were of white brick: all door and window openings had simple round-arch heads and window casements thick, white glazing-bars. The schoolhouse roof was hipped and the schoolroom gabled with one tall and two short windows in the gable-end; both roofs were covered with black glazed pantiles. The building — for all its simplicity — remains a model of scale, good detail and well associated materials.[1]

*Plate 56: The flint-faced schoolhouse at Euston.*

## E. PARGETTED

*Etymology*

The materials of which external plastering, or pargetting, are composed, and the technique of application have been considered in Section 4, and the derivation of the word has been traced to the Old French *par* = through, all over, and *jeter,* to throw or cast. The verb *parget* has meant many things, from covering a wall with plaster (in late Middle English) to decorating a surface with ornamental work of any kind, such as gilding, or, even, precious stones; it has also extended to painting or white washing walls in order to make them smooth or gloss them over. To *parge* a chimney flue was a term used in specification writing until not so long ago, and meant coating the inside of a brick flue with a mixture of lime mortar and cow dung. It was thus only one of the possible meanings of the word that came to be connected with ornamental plasterwork used, in general, externally, and to stand — as G.P. Bankart once said — for 'the decorative medium of the native English *'Playsterer'*.[2] In Suffolk it is fairly certain that nobody now uses the term to mean anything else.

In this sense pargetting is simply another word for ornamental plasterwork, both external and internal. To Bankart it stood for a school of plaster craftsmanship established in England during the late sixteenth and early seventeenth centuries. He himself traced its origins to the Italian craftsmen who decorated the outer and inner wall surfaces of Henry VIII's Nonesuch Palace,[3] but behind this lay a far longer tradition which led back to *sgraffito* and stucco work in Renaissance Italy, and, beyond this again, to the stucco plasters of ancient Rome, Greece and Egypt.

F.A. Girling once wrote a valuable paper on *Pargetting in Suffolk* for the Suffolk Institute of Archaeology and Natural History,[4] in which he started with provenance (pointing out that specimens of pargetting can be found widely scattered and mentioning examples at Maidstone, Newark, Banbury and Hertfordshire — in addition to the plentiful examples of Essex and Suffolk), and dealt with etymology, origin and function, and materials. Various kinds of patterns and their evolution were discussed, including string-courses and repeating patterns, plaster friezes, strapwork and geometrical patterns and floral ornament. Girling mentioned work at Church House, Clare; foliage at Lavenham; the Royal coat of arms in various places including Sparrowe's House, Ipswich, and coats of arms of Cavendish and Bayning at Hadleigh; seventeenth century oval decorative panels, and, finally 'colour

1  There is a general description of the estate-village of Euston in my book *A View into the Village* (see Section Bibliography).
2  *The Art of the Plasterer* by Geo. P. Bankart, op. cit., page 57 (see Bibliography to Section 4).
3  Ibid, page 45-47.
4  Ibid, page 57.

*Plate 57: Strapwork pargetting c.1610 at The Butterfly, Great Finborough.*

pargetting'. He evidently agreed with Bankart's view that the general run of plasterwork was carried out by the village plasterer or mason, who 'confined his humble efforts to his own particular radius of a few miles.'

This did not mean that 'foreign' plasterers were not called in for special wall or ceiling contracts, but it did mean that local plasterers would have been kept very busy in the sixteenth and seventeenth centuries ornamenting the exteriors of houses. And, it must be added the term 'local plasterer' could later also mean *bricklayer* in East Anglia (a slight variation on Bankart's reference to 'mason'). The old Suffolk 'brickie' was a man of parts, and before the days of trade demarcations, ready to turn a hand to flintwork, tiling or simple pargetting.

It is quite possible that, here and there, plaster work still exists that was carried out in the latter part of the reign of Queen Elizabeth I, although unlikely to be dated. The habit of enclosing initials or date — sometimes both — within an oval band or garland, does not seem to have started before the seventeenth century, where it continued at least until the early eighteenth century (e.g. plastered house in Polstead Street, Stoke-by-Nayland, dated 1713). The mistake is sometimes made of assuming that a pargetted date is that of the building of the house: this is improbable, as in the majority of cases the building is earlier and the date is that of the year in which the house was plastered. Such dating, in itself, is a valuable historical record to be carefully preserved: it raises also interesting questions as to the antiquity and structural history of the house behind the pargetting.

*Plate 58: Live-and-Let-Live Inn, Coddenham.*

The likeliest position in which to find early pargetting is internally, where, as at The Butterfly, Great Finborough, an original outside wall remains within a later addition. Here there is a farm probably dating from 1525$^{\pm}$, consisting of an original floored long house, a chimney with newel stair, and a stack lobby entrance on the east side once approached by a road from the Hitcham highway. A cross-wing was added later in the seventeenth century, but before this was done the old house had been plastered over with geometrical pargetting, probably about 1610. All of this has perished with the exception of a small portion enclosed within the later cross-wing (see Plate 57). Geometrical patterning of interlacing squares and circles was popular in the seventeenth century and some still can be seen on the one-time Live-and-Let-Live Inn, Coddenham (see Plate 58) dating to 1640$^{\pm}$. Bankart describes exactly how this was done by placing templates on the wood on the last coat but one, in borders and motifs — in this case imitation stonework and interlacing circles around a central square — and then rough casting around them up to the level of the templates. Here the plasterer obviously used two kinds of spiked impress on the roughing up coat, coarse for the main field, and a finer for inside the motif, in order to produce the pleasantly contrasting textured effects. It may well be one of the earliest surviving examples of geometrical pargetting in Suffolk.

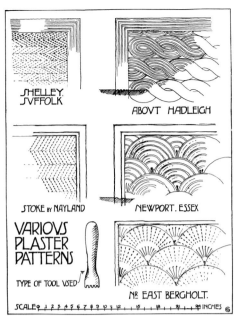

*Figure 51: Typical patterns in pargetting (after Edwin Gunn).*

The Butterfly parget is a combination of low relief (basso-rilievo) and scratch work (*sgraffito*). Pargetting in relief occurs internally in decorative wall and ceiling work (Tudor roses, floral patterns, suspended bosses, geometrical ribs and mouldings and so forth), and, to a lesser extent generally on outside work, often in combination with inscribed pattern.

Patterns in relief are commonly found as follows:—

    a) Geometrical and strapwork patterns
    b) Friezes and ribbon patterns
    c) All-over floral patterns
    d) Individual motifs
    e) Oval frames enclosing motifs

Geometrical and strapwork patterns such as those at The Butterfly are almost certainly Flemish in origin. The arrival in England of plasterers from the Low Countries must have coincided with the appearance of translations of the Flemish and German pattern books, and it is possible to trace many of these parget themes in relief directly to these sources.

The trail designs, such as the vine, seem to stem from Perpendicular Gothic sources, and together with honeysuckle and scrolled floral forms have a much longer history than the Renaissance. The oval frame composed of banded foliage must have become part of a local pargetter's stock in trade for roughly the same design occurs times out of number.[1] One of the wholly delightful aspects of Suffolk pargetting is the countrified form in which classical themes so often appear from the hands of local craftsmen.

Inscribed patterns are usually found within panels framed by indented mouldings, and amongst the patterns commonly used are:—

    a) Bird's foot
    b) Chevron
    c) Rope
    d) Scallop
    e) Fantail
    f) Basket-weave
    g) Dots

Basil Oliver includes in *Old Houses and Village Buildings in East Anglia* a drawing by Edwin Gunn, of various inscribed plaster patterns, which, although dated 1908, is as informative today as when it was first done, and is here reproduced (see Figure 51).

A good example of patterns both in relief and inscribed is at Walnut Tree Farm, Walpole. The parget was clearly done in 1708, and the date of the house is 1613 in a carved stone plaque with crest at the base of the chimney stack. The owner of the house in the early eighteenth century decided to have a broad decorative frieze across the whole upper part of the farmhouse front, and the work is still in excellent condition. About midway between the lower and upper windows a string-course was formed with rolled plaster mouldings, and between these an attractive vine trail ran from end to end of the house (see Plate 59). The space between the windows was divided into panels: two were picked out in relief, and the remainder consisted of impressed vertical rope (guilloche) pattern within a scratch moulded frame. The principal panel in relief was framed by a raised moulding (a repetition, in effect of the top moulding of the string-course) and contained a conventionalised oval garland, within which was a central rose surrounded by four floral stems and the initials I.C. In the spandrils were the numerals I 7 0 8, one in each corner.

The work at Walpole is every bit as fine as that at Yew Tree Farm, Finningham, which Pevsner calls 'perhaps the most handsome in Suffolk'.[2] There two large oval frames are arranged centrally on the plaster surface (quite plain except for scratch moulded panelling), and placed above and on either side of a porch (see Plate 60). East of the porch the oval is formed by a garland very similar to that of Walnut Tree Farm, but lacking the same finesse, and within the oval is a fig tree, bold, crude and lively. The oval to the west has a generous bolection-mould frame and contains a vine, with as much detail as the fig tree has little. Girling must have been right in thinking that the bunches of grapes were repetitions from a single mould,

*Plate 59: Early eighteenth century pargetting at Walnut Tree Farm, Walpole.*

1 Patterns from the same moulds can be found fairly close together as at Yoxford and Sibton. cf. Pevsner's *Suffolk*, page 512. But the best parget work was always done freehand, without resorting to moulds which mean, inevitably, sterotyped patterns.
2 *Suffolk*, op. cit., page 213.

but the whole of the vine could almost have been by another hand.

But we are not concerned here with technique, but only with decorative plasterwork as design and art.

Some pargetting could once have been picked out in colour, but, if so, little remains. Bankart tells us that geometrical patterning was sometimes tinted with bright colours, apple greens, ochre yellows, and earthy reds.[1] Girling mentions No. 99 High Street, Hadleigh, on both gables of which appear armorial bearings flanked by Tudor roses in a 'flamboyant design' with amorini. The coat of arms could be the Royal Arms of Charles I. The plaster date 1618 on one of the gables is, perhaps, more likely to be that of the house, or its restoration, and the pargetting to belong to the period 1623-1649. The whole of this old plastered house has recently been coloured Suffolk Pink, and the pargetted motifs picked out in colour.[2] One would hesitate to recommend wholesale recolouring of parget features, but, given knowledgeable guidance or evidence of original colouring the attempt can, with skill and judgement, obviously be successful.

In the redecoration of the pargetting at Sparrowe's House, Ipswich, it is the Royal coat of arms only that has been picked out in colour, and very correct and splendid this is above the entrance, in its red, blue, yellow and gold. The remainder of the figure work has been left uncoloured, and brought in with the white walls: if the whole sequence of the décor had ever been picked out in colour it would indeed have been 'more ornate and gayer than any other house of its date in England' – which is what Pevsner calls the pargetted decoration.

## F. WEATHER-BOARDED AND MISCELLANEOUS

'Weather-boarding ... represents the last phase of the timber structure characteristic of the middle ages ... It is a practical and inexpensive method, but usually decorative and effective' – in these two sentences Sir Albert Richardson and Donald Eberlein summed up the two principal aspects of weather-board used for the cladding of buildings.[3]

It would be quite understandable if, in an introductory study of Suffolk houses, no mention was made of weather-boarded houses. They are not a characteristic of the county and could scarcely be included as a representative vernacular type. This is not true of the neighbouring county of Essex, where weather-boarded houses are as plentiful as on the other side of the Thames, in Kent, Surrey and Sussex.

The immigration of ideas between English counties would make an interesting study, and just as timber-framing techniques developed in East Anglia appear to have spread westward in Kent and Sussex in an earlier age, so, in the case of traditional weather-boarding, a distributional survey would probably show the south-eastern centre of concentration to be in Kent, Sussex, Surrey, and Essex, with a thinning out into the adjoining counties of Hertfordshire, Cambridgeshire, Suffolk and Norfolk. Widely separated geographically, the western centre would be found in Wales, and, by a natural extension of the distributional approach, weather-boarding introduced by English settlers would be found concentrated in the New England States of America, where wood was the natural building material.

The distributional approach related to Suffolk would seem to show first a number of weather-boarded houses near the Suffolk/Essex border, in towns and villages adjoining the Stour. One example is Primrose Cottage on the Green at Long Melford (see Plate 61), a graceful small building dating to late eighteenth or early nineteenth century with weather-board walls and a timber-framed structure. The second area would be in the coastal zone with a number of examples dotted up and down the seaboard country from Trimley to Lowestoft, but examples turn up unexpectedly, such as No. 7 Church Street, Framlingham, with a Regency face on an earlier three-storey house (see Plate 62).

It is necessary first to distinguish between new architecture and maintenance. The usual way of making old timber-framed houses more weather tight in Suffolk was by coating them with plaster, but resort was sometimes had to covering them with weather-board. The second method was practicable as part of restoration or rebuilding, when new windows and doors were put in; otherwise problems of abutment and weathering occurred between walling and frames. This point is illustrated in the house in Station Road, Woodbridge, showing how boarding had to

*Plate 60: One of a pair of pargetted ovals at Yew Tree Farm, Finningham.*

*Plate 61: Primrose Cottage, The Green, Long Melford.*

[1] *The Art of the Plasterer*, op. cit., page 59.
[2] The owners, Messrs. Brett and Marston, consulted the Royal College of Arms, before colouring the armorial designs.
[3] cf. *The Smaller English House of the Later Renaissance 1660-1830.*

*Plate 62: Regency House, 7 Church Street, Framlingham.*

SASH WINDOW IN WEATHERBOARDED WALL :
JUNCTION OF SASH FRAME WITH BOARDING
COVERED BY ARCHITRAVE

*Figure 52 (above): Weather-boarding round a window.*

*Plate 63 (right): Houses at Thorpeness, 1911-14.*

fit tightly up to doors and windows in order to make a satisfactory joint (see Figure 52). The problem did not arise in blank gable-ends and is no doubt the reason for the fairly frequent weather-boarded — and often tarred — gable-wall. The maintenance of the weather-boarded seaside cottage was close to the upkeep of wooden boats, where the painting and pitching of timbers was part of normal routine.

The little house at Long Melford stands for the more architectural use of weather-boarding. It is this which we so seldom find in Suffolk compared with the Georgian examples of the later eighteenth century in the south east. By far the greatest use of weather-board in Suffolk was in timber-framed farm buildings — barns, stables, cart sheds and the like where it was, until this century, the standard walling material.

A revival of interest in weather-boarding in this century is worth mentioning. The design of pleasant faced cottages in vernacular style occupied the attention of architects during the early part of this century, and received a considerable impetus after the First World War, when resettlement housing was much in demand. It is a pity, indeed, that there were not more small houses like those built by the Felix Cobbold Memorial Trust between Ipswich and Hadleigh in 1908.

These had walls of stud and weather-boarding, painted white, with black window-frames, and red interlocking tile roofs, and they fitted unobtrusively and pleasantly into the Suffolk landscape. The same could be said of the houses designed by W.G. Wilson, F.R.I.B.A., at Thorpeness between 1911 and 1914, which combined stucco and black weather-boarded walls with red pantiled roofs, and well grouped along winding roads and stacked up in terraces on rising ground, they remain one of the convincing essays in a vernacular idiom (see Plate 63). The seaside village of Thorpeness is more successful in this respect than most of the residential estates put up in Suffolk since the Second World War (although it is permissible to be less enthusiastic over the use of neo-Tudor in the houses of The Whinlands, the red-brick Almshouses, and the West Bar).

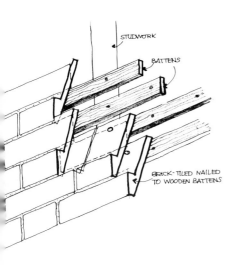

STUDWORK

BATTENS

BRICK-TILED NAILED
TO WOODEN BATTENS

*Brick-tiles known as mathematical-tiles.*

Like weather-boarding, the use of tile hanging as a wall finish is not vernacular to Suffolk. It is hard to say exactly why, because clay plain tiles were as plentiful in Suffolk as in Kent and Sussex, and are easily attached to battens which, in turn, can be supported both by timber-framed sub-structures, or by rough brickwork. The answer can only be in the field of taste and preference: Suffolk preferred either plaster or brickwork for the walls of farmhouses and cottages, and where we find extensive tile hanging, it is mainly used as a way of weather-proofing old walls or because of fashion. Stylistically, tile hanging goes with white rough cast and battered wall surfaces in the period roughly 1910-1930, when there was a return to the feeling for an unsophisticated, more truthful vernacular. It is associated with the work of architects like C.A. Voysey, P. Morley Horder and Ernest Newton. The mood of this period was well expressed by C.H.B. Quennell, F.R.I.B.A., when he once wrote in *The Studio:* 'It may be opportune, therefore, to remind readers that in this year of grace 1910 what is wanted is work suitable to our own time. A man in motor outfit, or arrayed as an aviator, is, to say the least of it, utterly incongruous in a mock Gothic hall'.[1]

A form of tile hanging seldom found in Suffolk, but worth mentioning in case further examples come to light, is the dummy brick, or so-called 'mathematical tile'. This is a clay tile made exactly to brick dimensions, but rebated and with a concealed nib for suspension, and holed for nailing to wooden battens. Nathaniel Lloyd quotes the *Dictionary of Architecture* of 1849, suggesting that brick tiles were probably employed many years before the introduction of the Tax on Bricks (1784-1850) which merely gave an impetus to their use for tax evasion.[2] These tiles were made both as headers and stretchers, and, well constructed, were practically indistinguishable from solid brick walling. Lloyd mentions the use of woodwork painted to represent quoins at the angle of buildings with mathematical tiled walls. Confirmation of use prior to 1784 seems to be given by the exterior 'bricking' of the timber-framed walls of Helmingham Hall by the fourth Earl of Dysart between 1745 and 1760.[3] The work seems to have consisted of battening over the sixteenth century timbers of the east front and then making dummy brick walls of the jettied portions between the gatehouse and the projecting bays at the north and south ends (see Section 6).

The area of greatest popularity seems to have been Sussex, Kent and Hampshire, but it would be worth recording all known examples of the use of mathematical tiles in Suffolk. The author would appreciate information of houses where these tiles were used.

## THE ARCHITECTS

Knowledge of the designers of houses in Suffolk follows an anticipated pattern. There is ample information on the nearer periods, but the further these recede into history the more sparse is the evidence. The mediaeval period has until recently remained an almost closed chapter, and so few names of master builders have appeared, not only in church but also in domestic work, that the theory of anonymous design has been fostered.[4] It is unlikely that many names of master carpenters associated locally with the building of timber-framed houses will ever come to light, but there is perhaps something more than mere 'academic curiosity' — as H.M. Colvin argued[5] — in finding out who they were. A great deal of the interest in Gothic house structures lies in workmanship, and to become familiar with the way in which a carpenter handled his wood, designed his joints, and carved his mouldings is but the first step towards a familiarity with the work of an individual. The chances are that the smaller 'masters' work will be found within definable geographical areas, and, if this is correct, then a certain style of carpentry will be one of the grounds on which it can be identified and dated. This has proved to be possible in mediaeval church work, but has never, I think, been seriously considered in relation to domestic buildings.

The search must be for contracts made in the earlier centuries between employers and carpenters for the building of houses, and it would be surprising if these could not be turned up in the archives of Suffolk towns. Lilian Redstone, as we have seen, quoted Ipswich examples, and Salzman reproduces thirty dating from the early fourteenth to the mid-sixteenth centuries, in which, in addition to the

1 *The Studio*, 1910, English Domestic Architecture.
2 cf. *A History of English Brickwork*, op. cit, page 52.
3 cf. *Helmingham Hall, Suffolk* by Arthur Oswald, Country Life, August 23, 1956, pages 379-380.
4 This myth began to be dispelled when Mr. John Harvey published *Gothic England* in 1947. The end papers disclosed a chart of English artists of the Gothic Period (1180-1560) which included masons, carpenters and carvers, and much of Mr. Harvey's book was aimed at dispelling the lack of interest in the artists of the past. It is significant that nowhere in Munro Cautley's great work on the Gothic Churches of Suffolk is there any mention of the names of individual designers, although a number can be traced.
5 In *A Biographical Dictionary of English Architects*, op. cit., page 10.

names of the contracting parties, details are often given of the accommodation, the sizes and types of rooms, and, occasionally, the required dimensions of the timbers. (Occasional corroboration of the reuse of second-hand timbers comes from these contracts.)

The title 'architect' was not used for the designers of these mediaeval houses, for the man in charge was the 'master of the building' — the exact equivalent of the German *Baumeister* which has remained the term for 'architect' in modern German. We have seen how, in contracts for the building of Tudor mansions, there was a master of the works who was responsible for engaging the different classes of tradesmen, and supervising the overall design to comply with his client's wishes, and we know the names of the men responsible for the building of Hengrave Hall, Little Saxham Hall, and Redgrave Hall. It remains for further research to bring to light the masters employed in the building of other Suffolk mansions, as well as the houses, outbuildings and warehouses in towns such as Ipswich, Bury St. Edmunds, Lavenham, Sudbury and Long Melford. The stipulations laid down in building contracts can be compared with such structures as still survive, not only giving an assured basis for dating (and also for comparative dating studies), but also information about the materials and occasionally the tradesmen providing specialist services. There is an extensive programme here awaiting local history researchers.

Whilst Suffolk cannot claim to be foremost in representative works by architects of national status, the great wealth of the county was accumulated at a time when few records were kept, and was poured out in a priceless contribution of parish churches and manor houses. The genius of Suffolk building had already achieved its climax before the outbreak of the Great Rebellion.

*Plate 64: Henham Hall (after drawing by H. Davy).*

The pattern of architects with national practices engaging in commissions of a moderate importance in Suffolk seems to be repeated through the succeeding centuries. This was the case on more than one occasion during the eighteenth century. Seven years after working at Euston Hall, we find Matthew Brettingham designing Benacre Hall for Sir Thomas Gooch, described by Henry Davy as 'a very good and substantial mansion'[1]; and so it looks in Davy's drawing, with its five-bay pedimented centre flanked by three bays on each side — two and a half storeys of a sober English Palladianism. In Norfolk, Brettingham had a hand in Holkham Hall, designed five Halls and four town houses in Norwich, and worked at Kedleston Hall — the home of the Curzon family — as well as on important houses in London. Robert Adam's work in Suffolk, accepting that he was not entirely responsible for Great Saxham Hall, seems limited to Moreton Hall (1773) and the Theatre and Market Hall (later Town Hall), Bury St. Edmunds.

James Wyatt (1746-1813), another architect of national reputation, had more important commissions in Suffolk. He designed the first Henham Hall (see Plate 64)

1 *Views of the Seats of the Noblemen and Gentlemen of Suffolk*, op. cit.

*Plate 65: Wyatt's Orangery at Heveningham Hall.*

for the sixth Baronet, Sir John Rous, following a fire in 1773 in which, according to Davy '... very little was saved from the flames, and the greater part of the books, pictures and furniture was lost in the general ruin.' Some five years later, upon the death of Sir Robert Taylor, Wyatt was commissioned by Sir Gerrard Vanneck to undertake a series of sumptuous rooms for Heveningham Hall. He designed the Orangery (see Plate 65) and improved other buildings also on the estate.[1] In the last sixteen years of the eighteenth century he had designed Culford Hall for the Marquess of Cornwallis, Sudbourne Hall for the Marquis of Hertford, and – seemingly – Nacton House for Phillip Bowes Brook, although the house of that name today was first built as a Workhouse.

Francis Sandys (c.1760-1830), possibly the son of an Irish architect, is found in Suffolk in about 1772 with an address in Bury St. Edmunds: in addition to a manifest architectural skill, he must have been an engaging young man, attracting the notice of the fourth Earl of Bristol and Bishop of Derry who brought him to Suffolk in order to carry out his new 'Palace' at Ickworth (see Section 6). It would be interesting to know the whereabouts of the office in Bury from which he conducted a successful practice until the death of his patron in 1803. A year later he moved to 23 Manchester Square, London.[2] His commissions included mansions at Great Finborough and Worlingham. Finborough Hall was designed for Roger Pettiward, whose classical tastes are reflected in Davy's encomium of the 'excellent library, some statues, Grecian vases, and a good collection of pictures' arranged in the 'handsome dining-room, library and drawing-room', as well as a saloon furnished with pictures by Wyck. Mr. Pettiward had a year previously obtained a design for his new mansion from a Mr. Richard Elsam, which (according to H.M. Colvin) was exhibited at the Royal Academy in 1804, although Francis Sandys' project of 1795 must by then have been completed. (It would be interesting if we could trace R. Elsam's two small 'Gothic houses' in Ipswich for Mr. Doughty, mentioned by Colvin as 'about to be erected' in 1803.)

1 See Huntingfield Hall and Valley Farm (Section 6). In addition to the Orangery Wyatt also designed the Temple in the park, and the pair of Lodges at the main south east entrance (now closed).
2 cf. Colvin's *Biographical Dictionary*, op. cit. page 526.

*Plate 66: Tendring Hall (from* Excursions in The County of Suffolk).

Sandy's patron at Worlingham Hall was another connoisseur — 'the talented, selfish, unlovable figure', who appears in an excellent monograph by Norman Scarfe.[1] The remarkable story of the remodelling of a seventeenth century mansion, with which both Soane and Sandys were connected, is retold in Section 6.

Soane's connection with Suffolk belongs to the years 1783-1791, following his unsuccessful trip to Ireland in pursuit of commissions promised by Frederick Hervey, Bishop of Derry: it is indeed rather ironical that his first design in Suffolk was not a Palace for a Bishop, but, seemingly, a cow house for George Smith of Marlesford.[2] But it was in domestic work in East Anglia that Soan (he adopted the final 'e' to his name after marrying Elizabeth Smith) first formulated his approach to classical design. In 1784 he built Tendring Hall, Stoke-by-Nayland, for Sir Joshua Rowley (see Plate 66), and this was far and away his biggest job in Suffolk (the house was demolished in 1960). In 1785, at nearby Nayland, he did some alterations in the church and designed new pews, as well as entrance lodges for Sir Thomas Gooch at Benacre Hall (not built). In 1786 he was preparing designs for Mr. Robert Sparrowe of Worlingham Hall (see Section 6), building Blundeston House for Mr. Nathaniel Rix, and doing work in the drawing-room of Herringfleet Hall (see Section 6). Between 1788 and 1791 he had commissions at Gawdy Hall; 81 Guildhall Street, Bury St. Edmunds; and at Wiston, where he built a small house near the church for Mr. Samuel Beachcroft, which is still there. But overshadowing these jobs was his surveyorship to the new Bank of England, to which he was appointed in 1788. It was the end of his connection with Suffolk and the start of his career as a leading English architect.

This period of the late eighteenth and early nineteenth centuries saw a number of larger projects in Suffolk. In eighty two years Shrubland Hall received the attention of three architects. In 1770-2 James Paine built a new mansion there for the Rev. John Bacon (is it possible that about the same time also he was building the square red-brick rectory at Coddenham for the same client, who was incumbent of this parish as well as inheritor of the Bacon property of Shrubland Park? The crest of the boar adopted by the Bacon family can still be seen at the Rectory, now re-named Coddenham House, see Section 6). Fifty eight years later, in 1830, Gandy, afterwards Deering, was at work at Shrubland on the south front for Sir W.F. Middleton, Bart., to be followed in 1849, the year before his death, by Sir Charles Barry (see Plate 67) on further alterations and additions for the same owner, including the Italian gardens said to be copied from those of the Villa d'Este at Tivoli, near Rome.

1 cf. Proceedings S.I.A., Volume XXVIII, 1959, pages 285-296.
2 cf. *Country Life*, January 8th, 1976. In an article by Pierre de la Ruffiniere du Prey, there is a reference to Soane returning from Norwich to London on June 19th, 1783, and making a detour via Marlesford Hall, where 'as a result of this visit the architect remarked in his daily notebook that he had received six guineas to cover expenses and his fee for the Cow house'. There is no doubt that this was actually built, for it is well remembered by the present owner of Marlesford Hall, who tells me that it was burned down in 1942.

*Plate 67: Shrubland Hall.*

On the Berners property at Woolverstone in about 1777 a Leicestershire architect, John Johnson, was designing the new mansion for his patron William Berners.[1] (Berners Street in Ipswich, dated 1836, owes its name to the same family.) The house is a miniature Palladian mansion with curving wings ending in pavilions, with an idyllic site above the west bank of the river Orwell. Twenty four years later Henry Hakewill, with widespread commissions nationally, was at work on designs for the remodelling of Rendlesham House for P.I. Thelluson, the banker, only the style is no longer Italianate but Tudor-Gothic. Another Hakewill[2] in 1859 was making extensive alterations to Stowlangtoft Hall in the Victorian Florentine style for Lt. Col. Fuller Maitland-Wilson.

A little prior to this Decimus Burton (1800-1881) was designing additions to Glevering Hall for Andrew Arcedeckne, a house already enlarged by another architect, John White, in 1792-3, and described by Davy as a 'very elegant and convenient country mansion'. Part of the older hall was left, a little south of the new one, to which it was attached. Decimus Burton had a fashionable practice in London, and is usually associated with the design of the Athenaeum Club and the archway to Buckingham Palace on Constitution Hill.

The later Victorian architects with few exceptions had abandoned both stucco and white brick, and were busy with serious neo-Tudor and Jacobean revivals in red brick. Ampton Hall is a good example, built in 1885, in imitation of a large Jacobean mansion, and closely paralleled by Hurts Hall, Saxmundham — neo-Elizabethan — of 1893 (by E.F. Bishop) replacing Samuel Wyatt's Regency house built for Dudley Long North ('altogether one of the most cheerful residences in the county' according to H. Davy — which is more than can be said of its successor). Another large neo-Elizabethan house is Brantham Court, built in 1850-2, by P.C.Hardwick, who specialised in railway station hotels and designed those at Victoria and Euston Stations. (This house has now been converted into flats.)

One of the greatest Victorian railway builders must have been Sir Samuel Morton Peto, who was responsible for the Eastern Counties Railway between Wymondham and Dereham, Ely and Peterborough, Chatteris and St. Ives, Norwich and Brandon, London and Cambridge and Cambridge and Ely. At Somerleyton he employed as architect John Thomas who started life as a bricklayer and has rightly been called 'a remarkable man'. He it was who transformed Somerleyton Hall as built by the last Sir John Jernegan (in the late sixteenth century) into a mansion — 'more Jacobean than any original Jacobean house' is Pevsner's phrase. It was the same John Thomas who also turned his patron's pipe dream of tenant's cottages round an open green into reality, taking Nash's Blaise Hamlet as a model for the new estate village of Somerleyton.

A few only of the architects of the High Victorian Movement[3] made their mark in domestic architecture, although a number worked on Suffolk churches, among them Edward Buckton Lamb who designed a rectory at Copdock, and Samuel Saunders Teulon who did the vicarage at Winston and rectories at Hollesley, Monk Soham, and Wetheringsett. Anthony Salvin is not admitted as one of the select company of those termed by Hal Goodhart-Rendel the 'rogue' architects, who specialised in irregularity and complication in design, but he is believed to have been at work at Helmingham Hall making alterations and additions in the early 1840s. The twin lodges on the Ipswich road could be to his design (see Plate 68).

Suffolk was more favoured with Edwardian hotels than country houses, but amongst the latter Bawdsey Manor must be counted amongst the notable: it was largely designed by Sir Cuthbert Quilter himself (about 1908) with the help of his friend Percy Macquoid (see Section 6).

Elveden Hall grew out of a Georgian mansion into an Oriental fantasy, and then in 1899-1903 was enlarged in a rather heavy-handed Italianate way by William Young, to become one of the largest of the country houses of Suffolk.

The work of Sir Edwin Lutyens in the county has already been briefly noted, but he built none of his great country houses here.

The recording of the life and work of local architects is strangely patchy, and satisfactory biographies of Suffolk architects of the nineteenth or indeed the twentieth century, are hard to come by. H.M. Colvin's *A Biographical Dictionary of*

*Hurt's hall after a drawing by H. Davy.*

1 J. Johnson had established his London office in Berners Street, in 1775 (acc. H.M. Colvin's *Biography*, page 323). He also designed Benhall Lodge for Sir William Rush, after 1781, but this was considered by Mr. Holland, according to Davy, as badly situated, and was therefore pulled down in 1810 and the present house built.
2 Possibly John Henry, given in D.N.B. as 1811-1880, architect.
3 Stefan Muthesius uses the phrase *The High Victorian Movement* to describe his recent book (see Section Bibliography).

*Plate 68: The twin lodges at Helmingham Hall, thought to have been designed by Anthony Salvin.*

*English Architects* ceased at 1840, with the founding of the Institute of British Architects. The only Suffolk-born architects I can trace in that Dictionary are Cottingham and Fulcher. Lewis Nockalls Cottingham (1787-1847), was born at Laxfield, the 'son of a farmer of an ancient and respectable family'.[1] Apart from the restoration and repair of churches, he seems to have done no domestic work in Suffolk. Of Fulcher little is evidently known, except that he designed the Bridewell at Woodbridge, was the inventor of a stucco 'equal to any ever invented', and published a book *Hints to Noblemen and Gentlemen of Landed Property, how they may build farmhouses, cottages and offices in a cheap and durable manner, without going to the timber merchant's yard for assistance.* (St. Albans, 1813.)[2]

The locally well-known architects of the Victorian era have not found their way into national biographies nor are complete records of their work to be had locally. The best documented are probably Frederick Barnes (1814-1898), John Shewell Corder (1857-1922), Brightwen Binyon (1846-1905) and Richard Makilwaine Phipson (1827-1884). There is the further problem of tracing domestic work as distinct from churches and public buildings, and even the R.I.B.A. Library, in the 'Grey book' reference series, does not possess a complete record of the houses designed by architects. Obituary notices are the usual source of information; F. Barnes, we are told, designed 'many houses in the Eastern Counties'; J.S. Corder became 'an authority on the construction of ancient houses, particularly those that were timber built',[3] and his best known restoration job is probably Little Wenham Hall, where he also designed the new Hall for the brothers Crisp; R.M. Phipson is said to have been extensively employed 'in domestic architecture, and examples given were Foundation Street Almshouses; Stoke Hall, Ipswich; Brandeston Hall, and other mansions'.

The scope for research is evident, and perhaps a start should be made locally by searching the original deposited plans in the local authorities' records. Under the 1875 Public Health Act, local authorities had the power to make by-laws controlling the construction of new buildings, and where this Act became operative building plans were required to be deposited at the local town hall or municipal offices.[4] It would seem probable, therefore, that from the late nineteenth century, building plans drawn mainly by local architects and surveyors were deposited at urban centres such as Ipswich, Bury St. Edmunds, Sudbury and Felixstowe. Thus the archives of local authorities may well prove to be the best source of information on the domestic architecture of recent history.

After men like J.S. Corder and T.W. Cotman, the names of the next generation of Suffolk architects are more familiar, although there exist no public records of the domestic and other works of W. Eade, E.T. Johns, William Brown, Henry

1 op. cit., page 153.
2 Ibid., page 218.
3 Several extremely knowledgeable contributions by J.S. Corder can be found in Proceedings S.I.A.
4 I am indebted for much of this information to Michael Talbot, Planning Officer of the Suffolk Coastal District Council, and author of a well documented article on the Felixstowe Conservation Area in the *East Anglian Daily Times*, August 8th, 1975.

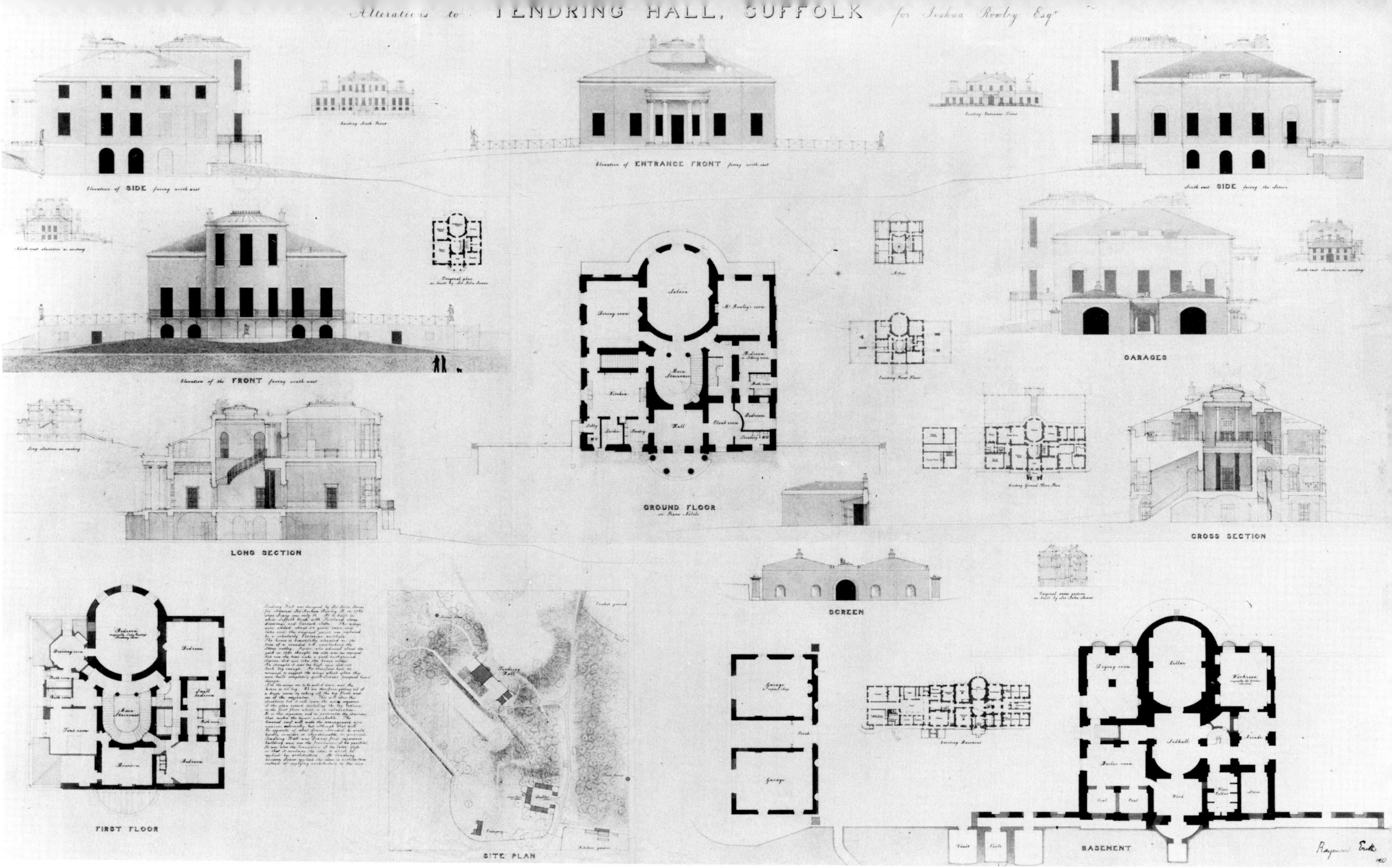

*Figure 53: Drawing by Raymond Erith of a proposed new Tendring Hall which was never built.*

*Jacobean staircase.*

*Mid-sixteenth century oak door.*

Wright, Raymond Wrinch, Arthur Welford, Cecil Lay, Munro Cautley and Leslie Barefoot — to name only a few of those no longer living. Raymond Erith (1914-1974) was not, strictly speaking, a Suffolk architect since he practised and lived at Dedham; as may be expected, he designed a number of houses in Suffolk, notably at Blackheath, Friston; two houses on the site of the old Walsham Hall at Walsham-le-Willows, and amongst others, several houses in the village of East Bergholt. He was a beautiful draughtsman, and one of his superlative sets of drawings was for a new Tendring Hall, Stoke-by-Nayland, which was never built. One of these drawings is here produced by kind permission of Mrs. Pamela Erith (see Figure 53).

This will serve as a reminder that much distinguished work has also been done in the country by outside architects, and that adequate records of architects' designs are incomparably more difficult to come by than works of painters and artists.

'... Even those who take an interest in architecture are generally content to think in terms of styles and periods rather than of individual creative achievement. The result has been to turn the names of our great architects into stylistic labels ... and to leave in undeserved obscurity the careers of many less celebrated but by no means uninteresting men'.[1] H.M. Colvin's lament is no less poignant at local than it is at national level.

# APPENDIX A
## Architectural features

This appendix provides the opportunity to group a number of features of general interest associated with houses, some of which have been touched on already but none discussed in detail.

The list should start with the fireplace, because, with the increase in brickmaking in East Anglia in the fifteenth century, the old open hearth in the middle of the hall was disappearing, to be replaced by the chimney piece.

The brick chimney lent itself to ornamentation when the stack broke clear of the roof and appeared on the skyline; hence chimney pieces and stacks should be next on the list.

Openings in the walls of houses for access and light adopted a special status, and have a long architectural history. The doors and windows of Suffolk churches were focal points of enrichment before they were emulated in Suffolk mansions and, with the Tudor passion for ornament, it was only natural that they should be given similar decorative emphasis in houses. (If rows of windows had not been fashionable towards the end of the seventeenth century there would presumably have been no Window Tax — that iniquitous money raising law introduced under William and Mary and not repealed until 1851.) The place of gatehouses and gateways, porches, doors and windows in the frontispieces of houses must be next on the list.

In an extended survey, account would have to be taken of the internal architecture of rooms; a development as extensive as, and more complex than, the external architecture of houses. In an introduction such as this, however, it must suffice to note such features as wainscot and carved woodwork, and to comment on ornamental plasterwork in walls and ceilings.

The staircase, which began by being a simple ladder, became a further symbol of opulence and status with the disappearance of the great hall and the opportunity for a ceremonial approach to the first floor. The status of the staircase still persists in folk architecture, although demoted in the modern house. There are good traditional staircases in many Suffolk houses.

The remaining features of architectural interest are those which surround the house. In the new era that followed the Wars of the Roses the surroundings of country houses became more open; there was no longer need for moats, although some may have continued to be dug in the early sixteenth century, and a new

*Garden House c.1700.*

*Parlour chimney piece, Bramfield Hall.*

culture of life out of doors came into being. The terrace with its ornaments and steps, the sunken garden, the tower, the garden house (the term 'gazebo' seems to date from about 1752), the fish house, the dove house and the brick garden wall — both straight and serpentine — with its piers and ironwork; these all belong to the extension of country house life into the immediate surroundings. Eventually the wall moved outwards and the area around the house was enlarged to include the home park; the gardens remained enclosed within walls and hedges, but the park reached the walls of the house and the grass remained unbroken except for the carriage drive.

The home park was used as the setting for architectural features; the temple, grotto, tea house, summer house, orangery — not forgetting the ice house — provided for diversions and tasks in the life of the eighteenth century country house at a greater distance from the house than in the seventeenth century. In the nineteenth century the great glass houses and plant houses are added, and the green house becomes a universal feature of houses large and small.

## CHIMNEY PIECES

A simple typology of chimney pieces commonly found in Suffolk houses, excluding surrounds or overmantels, could be set out thus:—

1. BRICK-facing
   - i    Straight opening with plain wood bressumer
   - ii    Straight opening with carved wood bressumer
   - iii    Arched opening with brickwork
2. BRICK-rendered
   - i    Straight opening with ornamental jambs and bressumer
   - ii    Arched opening with decorative finish
3. STONE (or marble)
   - i    Straight opening with decorative head and jambs
   - ii    Arched opening, moulded

The fireplace begins on the open hearth, with its immemorial ancestry, where it remains what Lloyd calls 'the commonest type of hearth during the mediaeval period'. The fuel is commonly wood, and the smoke gradually deposits an amorphous coating of charcoal carbon on the surfaces with which it comes into contact. In tracing the history of open halls this is always an important clue, and where it does not occur suggests that some sort of flue or fireplace was in use to get rid of the smoke.[1]

The hall fire begins by being the one for all purposes — cooking, light and warmth — but deviates in obedience to social trends. In the farmhouse the hall is the kitchen until the parlour begins to be the family living-room. In the great hall the kitchen was probably often in a separate place (as at Little Wenham Hall and Framlingham Castle). In Suffolk farmhouses, like Wydards at Cratfield, the kitchen could stay where it had always been, but the first brick chimney would be taken down to provide more room space and a new stack built with a large 'range opening' on the kitchen side and a more ornamental fireplace in a new adjoining parlour. There the kitchen opening was eight feet wide and high enough to get into (stooping) as there was a bread oven inside; to the parlour the opening was the more usual five feet or so, with an arched-head. This is the general pattern of houses in the small to medium group, one chimney serving two rooms with back-to-back fireplaces. In the larger houses there will be many more hearths (consult Hearth Tax Returns) and the fireplaces often built on outside walls, sometimes for calculated architectural effect.

The chimney pieces referred to in the simple typology and illustrated (see Plates 69) are all 'best fireplaces' found in the living-rooms, dining-rooms, and bedrooms of houses in the medium to large group. In character they closely reflect their period, starting austerely with the simple oak bressumer over a plain brick opening (at Abbas Hall this is about twelve feet long and large enough to stand or sit in). The simplest and most satisfying shape of opening is the four-centred arch which became general in the fifteenth century: this can be in plain chamfered or moulded brick or rendered in imitation stonework or in genuine stonework. But very soon

1 Lack of such a clue is not always conclusive, since an open hall may have been reroofed, or the original smoke-blackened timbers removed during the course of alterations, and so on.

the fireplace became more important when the oak bressumer would be moulded and carved; sometimes an arched-head was formed in the bressumer and the carpenters contrived a 'mason's mitre' at the junction of the brick and timber. The introduction of the owners' initials follows, as in the 'W' of William Wyard at Brundish Manor (see Plate 69). At Tudor House, Needham Market, when the new fireplace was built in the mid-sixteenth century, Thomas Aldus — the clothier — carved his merchant's mark in the centre of the bressumer over the opening. It is possible to see, at West Stow Hall and at Langley's, Hawkedon: at Otley Hall and at Moor Farm, Middleton, the embryonic overmantel (see Plates 69). In the first two this takes the form of a decorative painted panel; at West Stow an early Tudor strip cartoon continues round the sides of the overmantel. The Otley Hall mantelpiece, with its painted panelling containing coats of arms, grotesque capitals and arcading with pendant bosses, was soon to be translated into solid Jacobean wood carving, as at High Hall, Nettlestead. We need not be concerned here with the mantelpiece as such; the subsequent history of the fireplace is a return to greater dignity, simplicity and elegance, which came to a peak in the carved wood surrounds of the Robert Adam school.

*Moot Hall, Aldeburgh.*

## BRICK CHIMNEYS

Looking at Van den Wyngaerde's sketch of Hampton Court in its heyday is to be struck by the fanciful skyline crowded with towers, turrets, pinnacles and weathervanes in such profusion that the chimneys barely tell. It is difficult not to take the Tudor chimney as a *jeu-d'esprit*, the occasion for a display of showmanship at once very English and a shade eccentric — perhaps also a legacy from those spiky stone pinnacles and obelisks of late Perpendicular churches. Not to take too insular a view, the taste for romantic silhouettes appealed, Professor Rowse pointed out, to the deeper instincts of Northern Europeans in the Netherlands and France, as well as in England, hence Chambord and Burghley; '... the gables and dormers of Fontainbleau and Villandry as of Nonesuch or Gresham's Royal Exchange, the decorations and coruscations upon Anglo-Netherlandish monuments in our churches.'[1]

The chimney started as a wattle and daub smoke duct or a wicker work funnel parged with clay — 'a poor man's version of the built-in brick chimney' as Mason calls it.[2] By the comparatively late date of the first Hadleigh building regulations (1610), it is suggested that these clay lined chimneys were being built at the same time as brick chimneys. In the City of London regulations had been made as early as the fourteenth century that chimneys were no longer to be made of wood, but only of stone, tiles or plaster.[3]

We know that in Suffolk halls were being floored over after about the middle of the fifteenth century, and it seems probable that brick chimneys were being built inside timber-framed houses at the same time; these stacks took up a lot of space — often as much as the width of a complete bay, from 8-12 feet long and 6-7 feet across (2440-3650 by 1830-2130 mm) with enormous flues, and it was often necessary to build onto a house to make up for the loss of space. These chimneys must have had the same plain tops that we see today, and even when built on the side of a house, as at Clopton Hall, Wickhambrook — where they were obviously intended as an architectural feature (see Plate 70), the tops started plainly and were probably rebuilt in Elizabethan times. In the absence of any reliable record of the known invention of the first ornamental stacks, we are free to conjecture the arrival of immigrant tradesmen bringing samples of moulded and cut bricks from the Low Countries, and perhaps being brought to the notice of Thomas Wolsey, who — with his passion for building — would be quick to see the exciting possibilities of decorated chimney stacks. We do know, at any rate, that clusters of tall shafts — often as many as six or eight in a row — and each one differently patterned, were going up at Hampton Court Palace between 1515 and 1530, and that these were amongst the first in the country.

The work called for skilled craftsmen and the use of wooden moulds, often of considerable intricacy, in which the sections of brick could be cast. It was a craft

1 The Elizabethan Achievement A.L. Rowse (1972. London: Macmillan) page 135.
2 *Framed Buildings of England*, op. cit., pages 86-87.
3 Salzman, op. cit., page 99.

Otley Hall.

West Stow Hall.

Plate 69: Examples of chimney-pieces.

Below: High Hall, Nettlestead.

Clopton Hall, Wickhambrook.

Brundish Manor.

Below: Moor Farm, Middleton.

which was learnt by local bricklayers like Stephen Gaithorn of Gainescoln in Essex, who was employed at Little Saxham, and there were also the 'imported artizans' to whom Nathaniel Lloyd refers.[1] The free-standing ornamental chimney was designed from base to cap in clearly marked stages and rarely with any obvious break; in the case of polygonal shafts the main body of the stack, when clear of the roof, would be bevelled back to form geometrically correct bases, and the change of planes might be accented with moulded oversailing courses, possibly above and below; each gathering-in of the shaft towards its final shape of, say, octagon or circle, would be marked by a further moulding. The same process would be repeated in reverse as the head of the shaft widened out to the cap. These chimney tops could assume a variety of shapes: stellar, turreted, crenellated, occasionally enlivened by projecting 'nibs' at the angles, and were sometimes ingeniously linked by a continuous brick head for greater strength. The heights of the decorated shaft show a remarkable consistency, at around twenty-four to twenty-eight courses of

*Plate 70: Clopton Hall, Wickhambrook.*

*Plate 71: Thorington Hall, Stoke-by-Nayland.*

brickwork. Later, when no longer decorated, they can go soaring up to about forty courses as Thorington Hall, Stoke-by-Nayland, producing an overall height of over 20 feet above ridge (see Plate 71).[2]

The first astonishing chimneys — with their barley sugar twists and honeycombed surfaces — disappeared within about fifty years. They were followed by more sober shapes better suited to the mood of the following century. It is usually possible to distinguish late Elizabethan and Stuart work by the shafts of plain brickwork, often with four or five oversailing courses at the head, the stacks either single or joined — frequently diagonally — or combined in a single stack with 'saw tooth' sides. This is followed by a severely rectangular shape, as at Huntingfield High House, where a central stack has a recessed panel on each face and a cornice-like cap (date 1700, see Plate 72).[3] As the eighteenth century advances, the chimney as a design feature is gradually supressed and, according to Lloyd, 'decadence of chimney design (was) hastened by the invention of chimney pots of various forms'.[4]

## GATEHOUSES

To appreciate the military origin of the gatehouse we have only to see Framlingham Castle, dismissing for a moment the stone arch — which is Tudor — and visualise the Gate Tower as it was at the end of the twelfth century, perhaps with a simple Gothic arched opening and massive wooden doors fronting the drawbridge and the soldiery of Earl Roger Bigod peering through the crenellated battlements above. The different temper of England three centuries later is well conveyed by the changes made under the third Howard duke, the owner in 1524-47; the old drawbridge was taken away and the present brick and stone bridge

1 *A History of English Brickwork*, op. cit., page 82.
2 Frank A. Girling wrote an article on 'Some East Anglian Chimneys' in the *Brick Builder*, 20th January 1932, illustrated by nine exceptionally good photographs of Henry VIII stacks, all in Suffolk.
3 Lloyd shows a very similar example in *A History of the English House*, op. cit., page 350.
4 Ibid, page 350. Valentine Fletcher has devoted a book to *Chimney Pots and Stacks* (1968. Sussex: Centaur Press) and illustrates 80 pages of text with 40 photographs and over 300 drawings.

*Plate 72: High House, Huntingfield.*

*Plate 73: Framlingham Castle doorway with Howard arms.*

built and, at the same time, the original archway demolished to be replaced by a new dressed stone opening with coats of arms in the spandrels and — surmounting the doorway — a large flamboyant carving with the arms of the Howards (see Plate 73).

In this single embryonic example lies the character of Tudor gatehouses. They belong not to defence so much as to showmanship (although it might still have been quite useful, on occasion, to have stout outer doors which could be locked and bolted). Tudor ostentation is obvious in buildings, furnishings and costume; the Italians have a telling phrase for it — *far figura* — and main entrances in particular suggest something of this personal swagger, not only of the nobility and gentry, but also the country squire (sometimes with rather amusing results). By early Tudor times the gatehouse had become the 'decorative focal point' of the architectural frontispiece.[1]

The architectural themes of Suffolk gatehouses are easy to distinguish because they occur so invariably; the opening is central and arched and, coming towards the end of the Perpendicular period, the arch is shallow and four-centred; it is flanked by projecting bastions representing turrets, but only at Hengrave, Melford Hall and West Stow — I believe — do the turrets emerge as true octagons above parapet level. At Giffords Hall, Stoke-by-Nayland, they are merely three-sided screens. In height the gatehouses are usually two-storied, although Sir John Croftes contrived an attic floor at West Stow; there is nothing remotely comparable with the skyscraper Layer Marney gate tower in Essex, running up to eight storeys of service rooms.

The display of coats of arms was a reminder of the rank and ancestry of the owner, and much attention was given to silhouette at the top of the gatehouse. Both the stepped gable and the battlement parapet were in favour, rising to a central pinnacle of some kind: at Helmingham a lanky onion-topped brick terminal (a copy?); at Giffords Hall, Stoke-by-Nayland, a moulded brick pinnacle with a helmet top; at West Stow, a very Gothic looking pinnacle, niched, with cusped brick arches, supporting a heraldic animal displaying shield (the coats of arms below the attic window are those of Mary Tudor and Charles Brandon, Duke of Suffolk).

Suffolk gatehouses tend to be part of the larger mansion, as at Hengrave or Helmingham, but there are interesting variations like West Stow Hall, where the gatehouse was built to span a moat and connected thence by a two-storey gallery to the main house; or Gedding, where the gatehouse is all that remains of the Manor, and was converted into a dwelling in the seventeenth to nineteenth centuries. At Giffords Hall the gatehouse forms part of a range of earlier buildings. On a more

1 cf. *Tudor Renaissance* by James Lees-Milne, op. cit., Chapter X.

131

modest scale is the charming arched opening into the court at Crows Hall, Debenham. Brick is the usual material, although here — if nowhere else — was the obvious place for ornamental stone features.

## GATEWAYS

Gateways are quite separate from houses and can best be appreciated when supported by flanking walls, as at Stutton Hall, or at Wells Hall, Milden. It is important that the road, or path, should still be seen approaching and passing through the gateway, as at Stutton or Erwarton. At Wells Hall, the gateway is subtly demoted by the road no longer having any visible connection with the opening, verge and road alike passing by without a break. For the gateway was meant to mark the transition from a public to a private world.

Two types can be distinguished. The first — like Wells Hall — is the simple arched gateway, interrupting the course of a brick boundary wall with a flourish of pinnacles to announce an entrance for horseman or pedestrian (see Plate 74); or again — like the gateway of old Nettlestead Hall (now known as Nettlestead Chace) — the opening is a semi-circular arch within a pedimented frame, although there is now no trace of the original boundary walls (see Section 6). The second type is the tunnel gateway — as at Erwarton Hall or Stutton Hall (see Plates 75 and 76), where the structure is roughly square with a vaulted ceiling inside and the elevations are all symmetrical.

It is a curious fact that none of these gateways was large enough to admit more than a pedestrian or a mounted rider; indeed, at Stutton Hall the opening allows only two people to enter side by side. The conclusion must be that they were intended mainly for show, and that vehicular traffic used other entrances. In fact, this is what seems to have happened and whereas the latter are still in use, the gatehouses have ceased to have any practical function and become an academic curiosity.

The Wells Hall gateway has a distinctly ecclesiastical look and, with its buttresses, pinnacles and crenellated parapet, could easily be mistaken for the front of an early Tudor brick church porch; even the arch has a faintly Gothic shape. As such it breaks no new ground stylistically.

The Stutton and Erwarton gateways, on the other hand, raise interesting stylistic questions. Lloyd pointed out[1] the different characters of the outer and inner elevations at Stutton: the outer has a late Gothic arch springing from Renaissance capitals in stuccoed brickwork and surmounted by a very Perpendicular looking stepped gable, with honeycombed brick pinnacles and spiky onion tops; the inner has a more correct classical arch, flanked by coupled fluted pilasters with a semicircular pediment above, all originally in stucco up as high as the entablature. If Copinger is right, the manor had passed to Sir John Jermy by 1542 and if, as supposed, he was the builder of the Hall then the gateway must have been part of the job done in the '40s. The resemblance to Ewarton is really confined to the semicircular pediment on the garden site at Stutton with the two flanking pinnacles, and one on the top; in every other respect Erwarton is wholly different and designed to show off bricklayer's skill with its use of specially made segmental bricks to form the circular buttresses and the round pepper-pots, of which there are eight in this exceedingly small building. Lloyd dated it as 1590 and it could even be later, anticipating in some way the Dutch gables of the following century.

The Nettlestead gateway has deteriorated sadly since Henry Davy made his drawing in 1824 (see Plate 189). It was a more advanced attempt at classicism than at Stutton, and was done in stonework surrounded by rendered brickwork. The design somewhat resembles that of John Thorpe's porch at Kirby Hall, Northamptonshire, and suggests that the date, c.1572 or probably a little later, but before 1595, when the widow of Henry — third Lord Wentworth — is said to have married again and gone with her three children to live in Oxfordshire. The quartering of both dexter and sinister shields in the spandrels of the arch have been recorded and show the Wentworth connections with many distinguished families (see Section 6).

The brick gateway at Moat Hall, Parham, is part of the outworks of a

*Plate 74: Gateway at Wells Hall, Milden.*

1 *A History of English Brickwork*, op. cit., pages 312-313. Lloyd dates it as 1530, but it is more likely to have been about fifteen years later.

*Alston Court, Nayland. The earliest house from the courtyard.*

*Roos Hall, Beccles. View from the south-east.*

*Plate 75: Gateway at Ewarton Hall.*

*Plate 76: Gateway at Stutton Hall.*

*Plate 77: Detail of gateway at Moat Hall, Parham.*

*Plate 78: Gate piers belonging to the gateway of Parham House.*

double-moated site belonging to the once fortified manor house of the Willoughbys (see Section 6). Severely plain and set in high brick and masonry walls, the opening fronted a bridge across the outer moat but was large enough for vehicles; all traffic to the house still goes by this gateway. The brick is early Tudor in English bond, the arch four-centre Gothic, and the opening lined with stone quoins. In two high up niches are stone carved figures of 'wood-wose' (see Plate 77). Another arch stood at the entrance to the inner courtyard; of a later Perpendicular style in stonework, if we can go by T. Higham's sketch for the *Excursions through Suffolk*, and, according to one theory, brought here from the Priory Church at Campsey; it seems to have suffered the further indignity of being taken down, transhipped to the U.S.A. and re-erected there.

A few miles further along the valley towards Framlingham are two stone gate-piers belonging to the one-time gateway of Parham House, each about fifteen feet high and capped by a large stone ball (see Plate 78). The drive used to go in a straight line up the hillside from the valley, presumably entering the enclosure of the house through the gateway; in the valley, the approach road seems to have kept to the north side of the River Ore from Parham Church and village. (The student of brickwork will notice with interest that the minor road of today, a little west of the original drive, bridges the river at 'Bricklane Crossing' — a possible clue to the source of the bricks for the interesting Parham House.[1])

Until not long ago there used to be a Tudor brick gateway surmounted by a pair of stone eagles (?) on the south side of the road at the entry to the parish of Hollesley, about which there seems no recorded history. According to P.G.M. Dickinson, the brick gatehouse of Edwardstone Hall still survives in the grounds.

1 *E.A.M.* No. 6091 puts this as the house of the Warner family, built in the earliest years of the seventeenth century, which is a little earlier than the 1630-1650 postulated by Pevsner, cf. p.391, second edition.

although the Hall — which I believe was seventeenth century built, seems to have been demolished early in this century. (It was a good example of the isolated manor house with nearby parish church.)

These infrequent examples of the outworks of earlier mansions are all too vulnerable to decay in an age of extremely high maintenance costs, but when they are lost another valuable link in the history of the layout of country houses is destroyed. They have the same importance for students of architecture as the park and garden features mentioned later in this Appendix.

## PORCHES

The porch has both a religious and a secular history. Cautley has much to say about the church porch,[1] and it is probably seldom connected with the sacramental and legal purposes for which it was once used: he admits that the building of porches resulted from the wish that 'the discomforts of the church door ceremonies might be ameliorated by some sort of shelter'. A similar reason has obviously been advanced for the domestic porch, and Alfred Gotch could quote from the Liberate Rolls of Henry III's time (1232-69) giving orders for carrying out works to the various King's houses which 'nearly all point to making the house more comfortable'.[2] Some of these orders, which include the building of porches, are worth mentioning:—

Windows were to be glazed to prevent draughts, and were to be enlarged.
Porches were to be built to external doors.
Passages of communication were to be made from one building to another.
Roofs and walls were to be wainscotted.
Fireplaces were to be built.

The church porch rapidly became an occasion for the display of wealth and craftsmanship, particularly in the cloth churches such as Lavenham, Long Melford, Woolpit and Boxford; a little later the same tendency appears in the domestic porch. In Tudor times it is the natural sequence to the gatehouse, and this is well illustrated at Helmingham Hall. There, the axial approach starts about a third of a mile away at the entrance gates, dips towards the bridge over the park stream and then ascends the long double avenue of oaks, approaches and crosses the drawbridge and enters the gatehouse through the great Gothic doors. It then passes into the courtyard where the course of approach is still outlined in the pavings until finally it reaches the porch, stiff and upright as a sentry box between the rolled brick buttresses (see Plate 79).

The porch became the eminent point of entry to the private house, as at Crows Hall, Debenham (see Plate 80) and stayed so for some 350 years. Amongst the earliest is Shelley Hall, with a brick porch with front and rear entrances (see Plate 81). Charles Partridge[3] thought that Sir Philip Tilney built Shelley Hall between 1523 and 1532; the porch bricks average 9in. by 4¼in. by 1¾in. (228.6 by 108 by 44.5 mm) and could belong to an earlier period. The porch was flanked by engaged octagonal buttresses of which the main feature was a three-tiered set of niches on both sides of the opening, one to each face, and each with a trefoil head in moulded brick. The style is ecclesiastical late-Gothic and the front doorway has a typically Perpendicular four-centred arch, clearly of the same school as Giffords Hall at Stoke-by-Nayland or — for that matter — as the octagonal turret which was part of the porch covering the main entrance to the cloister at Leiston Abbey (see Plate 82). It is difficult to be sure what happened in the upper part of Shelley Hall porch, because it has been altered, but it had almost certainly two storeys and could have had three.

The tall narrow porch is so characteristic of the early Tudor mood. It is found again at Bruisyard Hall, where the height must be of the order of 40 feet (12.192m), about the same height as at Helmingham, and contained by rod-like angle buttresses. There are three storeys, the top being entered from the attics. There is the coat of arms and the sundial, the triple pinnacles with their pepper-pot tops and the crow-stepped gable. These brick porches have a thoroughly East Anglian flavour but the pattern of the tall narrow porch is national, and examples can be found in the oolite belt, where the type becomes vernacular and goes on well

*Plate 79: Porch at Helmingham Hall.*

1 *Suffolk Churches* by Munro Cautley, pages 48-54 (first edition).
2 *The Growth of the English House* (see Section Bibliography).
3 cf. *E.A.M.* No. 7012 — Shelley Hall: King: Aylmer: Tilney.

Plate 80: Gatehouse porch at Crows Hall, Debenham.

Plate 81: Rear entrance of porch at Shelley Hall.

Plate 82: Octagonal turret, Leiston Abbey.

into the seventeenth century (see Plates 83).

In Suffolk, the angle buttress was out of fashion after about the mid-sixteenth century and an interesting transitional example can be found at Thorpe Morieux Hall. The angle buttresses stop at first floor level and consort oddly with the diamond lozenge above the doorway and the mansard shaped gable which gives the top of the porch a Dutch look. Another transitional design occurs at Flemings Hall, Bedingfield, which is an engaging piece of work, suggesting a local builder left to put his own version of the current style. The vestigial buttresses are Gothic, and so are the arched doorway and the crow-stepped gable; the pediments are classical, and both the bull's-eye window and the three 'dunces caps' suggest Flemish details, but the tall narrow form is indisputably East Anglian. The bridge from label-moulds to pediments and from Perpendicular to classical details generally can be well studied in the brickwork of Seckford Hall, and in the porch on the south-west side of the Abbey at Woodbridge. This follows the first Seckford period, being dated 1564, and although one supposes that the same bricklayers were employed here, Thomas Seckford was obviously determined to do the job in a more classical way. He divided the tall, rather Gothic shaped structure into three strongly marked storeys, and flanked the doorway (round arches) and windows over with Roman Doric, Ionic and Corinthian pilasters in ascending order, all done in brickwork. But for all that the top gable and two pinnacles harked back obstinately to the Perpendicular. (Pevsner deduces from the asymmetrical placing of the porch that it was at one end of an original great hall.[1])

River House, Kersey, is another delightful case of country builders' brick classicism of early-Elizabethan date c.1560; round arched doorway, flanking buttresses, mullion and transom windows, pediments — one enormously elongated — and a convex-curved gable with three pinnacles. The broader proportions are already moving away from the Gothic towards something more Renaissance although, as seen at Witnesham Hall, the design is still a good deal less literate than the Abbey at Woodbridge. The work dates from about 1610; the idea of the three superimposed orders is there: the round arched doorway and the pediments — although with proportions all over the place — with one entirely new theme in the shape of the 'Dutch gable'.[2] Dutch gabled porches occur at Mockbeggars Hall, Claydon; Hemingstone Hall; Newe House, Pakenham, and these three examples are discussed under the individual house in Section 6.

1 cf. Pevsner's *Suffolk*, op. cit., (second edition) page 500.
2 See comments under 'Dutch gables'.

136

Plate 83: *Typical tall narrow early Tudor porch at Bruisyard Hall.*

Plate 83: *River House, Kersey. The round-arched doorway, c.1560, with flanking buttresses, pediments and pinnacled gable.*

Plate 83: *Left, Witnesham Hall doorway, c.1610. Right, porch at Flemings Hall, Bedingfield. Below left, the doorway at Thorpe Morieux Hall. Below right, mid-sixteenth century entrance porch at Woodbridge Abbey.*

*From a photograph by Angus McBean.*

*Plate 84: Fifteenth century doors at Helmingham Hall.*

*Plate 85: Entrance doorway, 7-9 Northgate Street, Ipswich.*

*Plate 86: Plank doors at Brundish Manor.*

*Plate 87 (left): Plank door at Framsden Hall.*

*Plate 88 (right): Gatehouse doors, Giffords Hall.*

*Plate 89 (below left): Doorcase, Manor House, Syleham.*

*Plate 90 (below right): Doorcase, Huntingfield Hall.*

# DOORS

The earliest function of the door was to screen the openings in a building, and the primitive door was evidently unfixed, being merely stood in position when the door opening had to be closed.[1] The next logical step in development was some form of hinge enabling the door to be opened and closed, and this required a fairly solid form of door structure. Mediaeval doors are still plentiful in Suffolk, the best examples being in church work. The principle used in construction was the frame supporting the face. Oak was the wood most widely used, and the usual church entrance consists of a pair of framed leaves with shaped-heads conforming with the arched masonry opening. In the developed fourteenth century door, the framing was moulded and rebated to receive panels invariably of oak planks, and the upper part a form of carved fretwork with ogival patterns. The gatehouse of the lord of the manor needed doors as robust as those of the church, and offered an opportunity for enrichment only slightly inferior to the house of the Lord. The gatehouse doors at Helmingham Hall (see plate 84) are evidently fifteenth century Perpendicular work, and believed to come from the earlier manor.[2] That they have been reused is obvious from their being hung behind a sixteenth century opening with its conventional four-centred arched head and carved spandril pieces. In addition to the framed face there is a massive rear frame to which the front members are clamped by square-headed blacksmiths' nails. (The door within a door is the wicket portal commonly used in important mediaeval openings, both lay and ecclesiastical, and most serviceable in controlling individual entrants.) The leaves are hung on hook hinges built into the masonry of the door opening.

Lower down the social scale, similar principles were used in the single leaf door of the merchant's house at 7 Northgate Street, Ipswich (see Plate 85). Unlike the Helmingham door, where there are stiles, muntins and top and bottom rails, it was not panelled. Here the place of the stiles, top rail and muntins is taken by moulded battens placed on the face and secured to ledges by round headed nails; these battens are both decorative and functional in covering the butt joints between the vertical planks. The door consists of four planks and five ledges, the top one being shaped to conform with the four-centred arch. This door with its restrained mouldings, diminutive spandrils and slender frame carried down to neatly carved column bases, is a good example of domestic Perpendicular work of the early sixteenth century.

The plank door, variously moulded and enriched, and unmistakably Gothic in form, was widely used in late-mediaeval Suffolk (Plates 86 and 87, Figures 54-56) until gradually supplanted by the panelled door. The gatehouse doors of Giffords Hall, Stoke-by-Nayland (Plate 88), come between the two, each leaf having six vertical panels containing linenfold not as yet fully developed, and rather awkwardly fitted into the Gothic arch, suggesting late fifteenth or early sixteenth century work. The doors are fully formed with stiles, muntins, middle rail and mitred mouldings to head of each panel. Transitional doors of domestic character were found at Norfolk House, Earl Soham, suggesting work of $1600^{\pm}$. The design seems to have been suggested by wainscot, consisting of three rows of three equal-sized panels divided by muntins and rails with scratch mouldings in the rails: each of the panels is fielded (see Figure 56). A more sophisticated pattern of similar design and period occurs at Instead Manor, Weybread, where the door panels — also nine in number — are separated by moulded muntins secured to rear framing by octagonal headed blacksmiths' nails (Figure 57). Note the height does not exceed 6ft 3in. and is often around 6ft 1½in. (the oak doorway from Church Farm, Clare, in the Victoria and Albert Museum is 6ft 2¼in. to apex of arch[3]). These examples show the trend towards the regular form of panelled door which has finally disposed of all Gothic traces by about the middle of the seventeenth century.

The classical doorway was to become the familiar idiom of Stuart and Georgian England, and often the main focus of enrichment in otherwise austerely simple elevations. The moulded six-panelled door is the norm (see Plate 91), although the number of panels may be increased to eight in a larger, more important opening. Builders' textbooks detailed conventional methods of framing together the rails and muntins, together with the varieties of panel; raised frieze, fielded, moulded, square and flat, bead and flush, and bead and butt. So standardised were these joinery

*Plate 91: Curved six-panelled door in Barking Rectory.*

1 cf. *English Building Construction* by C.F. Innocent, op. cit., pages 224-25.
2 cf. *Helmingham Hall, Suffolk* by Arthur Oswald, Country Life, August 9th, 1956. Creke Hall is the suggested source and the date early fifteenth or even late fourteenth century.
3 See sketch on page 31 of *Old Houses and Village Buildings in East Anglia* by Basil Oliver, A.R.I.B.A., op. cit.

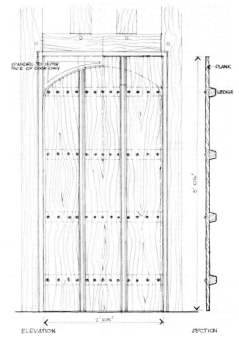

Figure 54: Ledged and moulded plank door of c.1450. Note door carried up behind arched head and frame formed by moulded studs. Note typically low overall height of door.

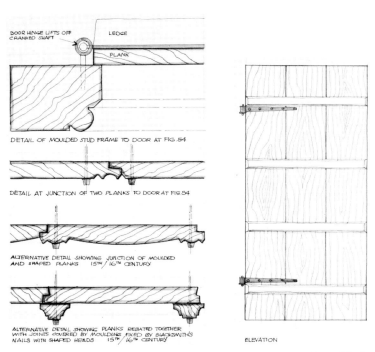

Figure 55: Reverse side of door in Figure 54, showing planted ledges for stiffening and hinges with lift-off shanks, and left, details of plank door construction.

methods that — together with the appropriate joints: single and double tenon, hanchion, and foxtail wedging — they were repeated in construction manuals until well into this century. The corollary to the panelled door was the panelled lining, in which the arrangement of the door was repeated. The crowning feature was the external doorcase. Suffolk towns and villages, as well as individual houses, from the seventeenth until the mid-nineteenth century, display a delightful variety of doorcases (see Plates 89 and 90). Revivalism produced some strange versions of Gothic and Classical doorways, and the modern reaction has been the machine-made, flush fronted, wood or metal door. Door furniture was another feature of both internal and external doors, and some examples are illustrated in Figure 58.

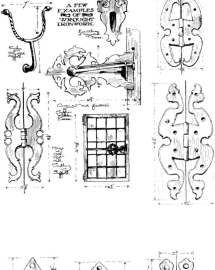

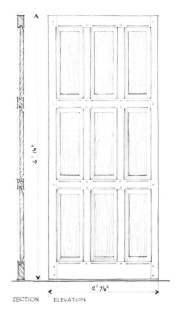

Figure 56: Front face of panelled door at Norfolk House, Earl Soham, c.1630. Note scratch mouldings on rails and fielded panels.

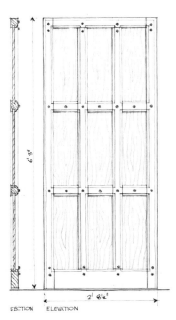

Figure 57: Front face of panelled door at Instead Manor, c.1615. Note continuous muntins joined to rails with mason-mitred joints. Some of the blacksmith nails to rails are purely decorative.

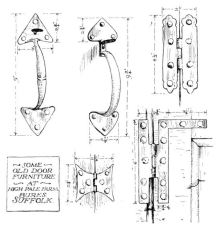

Figure 58: Wrought ironwork door furniture illustrated in B. Oliver's Old Houses and Village Buildings in East Anglia.

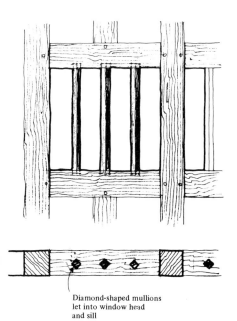

Diamond-shaped mullions
let into window head
and sill

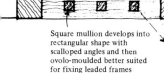

Square mullion develops into
rectangular shape with
scalloped angles and then
ovolo-moulded better suited
for fixing leaded frames

*Figure 59: Alternative unglazed 'windows' with square and diamond shaped mullions.*

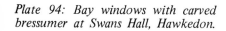

*Plate 92: Detail of a bay window with side-lights from the Guildhall, Lavenham.*

*Plate 93: An eight-light window with plastered jambs, mullion and transom, Yaxley Hall, Eye.*

## WINDOWS

The earliest domestic windows in Suffolk are probably those of Little Wenham Hall (c.1260-8) and Moyse's Hall, Bury St. Edmunds. On stylistic grounds the latter might well ante-date the former, for the original first floor windows to hall and solar have the Romanesque form of two-light separated by mid-shaft with solid tympanum above. First floor windows at Little Wenham are Early English in character with plate and bar tracery in hall and chapel respectively. These windows survive because they are in masonry structures, whereas in timber-framed houses the evidence of early windows is inevitably more scanty. At Purton Green Farm, Stansfield (conjecturally late thirteenth century), no original windows appear to have survived intact.

From C.F. Innocent we have it[1] that for centuries the term 'window' was used, not for the opening itself, but for the wooden shutters by which it was closed. Examples of head and sill members grooved for sliding shutters are fairly plentiful in old timber-framed Suffolk houses. The suggestion is that the 'window' was a square opening divided into one or more lights by vertical wood mullions (see Figure 59) containing, originally, no glass but, at best, oiled cloth stiffened by a criss-cross lattice work of osier. There are documentary references to windows of this type.[2]

The purpose of a window was twofold — to let in daylight and to provide ventilation. In halls with open central hearths the problem must always have been to get rid of smoke, and the window open to the air served this purpose, together with the smoke exits in the roof. The advent of window glazing corresponds with the development of the smoke stack and the chimney-piece, and is part of that progress towards more comfortable rooms which went with better fitting doors and windows, and the panelled wainscotting of walls. Fragments of the original early seventeenth century glazing were found in the attics at Read Hall, Mickfield, and

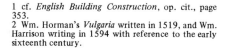

*Plate 94: Bay windows with carved bressumer at Swans Hall, Hawkedon.*

1 cf. *English Building Construction*, op. cit., page 353.
2 Wm. Horman's *Vulgaria* written in 1519, and Wm. Harrison writing in 1594 with reference to the early sixteenth century.

*Plate 95: Window at the Willows, Earl Soham.*

consisted of diamond shaped glass 'quarries' set in strips of lead ('cames' originally from *calamos*). These panels of glass were set in openings or casements and soldered to iron 'saddle bars'.

Salzman dates the reintroduction of glass into England from about A.D. 700 (glass had been used in the windows of Romano-British villas 150 years earlier), and although it took nearly a thousand years to become a commonplace of house life, he considers the usual idea of its rarity in mediaeval houses to be much exaggerated.[1] By the early sixteenth century the art of designing glazed windows was rarely shown to better advantage than at the Guildhall, Lavenham (see Plate 92). Other examples of early glazed windows are in Plates 93 and 94.

Leaded quarries seem generally to have been supplanted by rectangular leaded lights in the latter part of the seventeenth century, and to have promoted the vertical rectangular window. The cross pattern made by mullion and transom at The Willows, Earl Soham (early eighteenth century) is a fairly late survival of the type (see Plate 95). Then three-light windows, consisting of a fixed light on either side of an opening casement, becomes a standard type adopted in vernacular buildings throughout the eighteenth century until superseded by the wooden window. With lights commonly not exceeding .50m (20in.) in width, the proportions of these windows have altered little in the last 300 years (see Plate 97).

The narrow glazed panes of the earlier windows were determined by the available sizes of glass. Crown glass was sold in small panes, the biggest clear of the bull's-eye or bullion in the centre being no more than 18 inches square. The small rectangular leaded pane became the large rectangular pane contained by wooden glazing bars within the fashionable sliding sash windows. Dr. Tremminck Groll puts the first sash windows as appearing in Holland in 1686, in the Zeist Castle and at the country seat of William III, the Loo near Appeldorn. The double-hung sash window thus derives its proportions from the single-light leaded window, and in the accompanying illustration of the west front of Yaxley Hall, near Eye (see Plate 96), the leaded light windows to the ground floor windows of the 'Dutch' gable range are three panes wide by five panes high, compared with the wooden sash windows, which are three panes wide by four panes high. (There can be few elevations with a more representative collection of typical window types than Yaxley Hall, where side by side can be seen early seventeenth century mullion and transom windows with leaded lights — plain rectangular to lower and lozenge shaped to upper, eighteenth century double-hung sash windows, leaded casements with Gothic heads, and early nineteenth century pseudo-Gothic wooden casements with four square panes and ogival traceried heads.)

1  *Building in England*, op. cit., page 73.

*Plate 96 (below): Yaxley Hall, near Eye, from the West — a variety of windows.*

*Plate 97 (right): Porch gable, Clopton Hall, Wickhambrook. The window is three-light, with a fixed light on each side of the opening casement.*

*Plate 98: Cornice with angel frieze, Framsden Hall.*

*Plate 100: Grotesque head, Framsden Hall.*

*Plate 101: Another grotesque head at Framsden Hall.*

*Plate 99: Post with carved head of king, Framsden Hall.*

## DECORATIVE FEATURES

The enrichment of houses was a process in which wealth and leisure combined to promote the work of artists and craftsmen. The mansions and manor houses of England are a repository not only of architectural skills but also of talents in what Sacheverell Sitwell called 'the attendant arts'. The history of interior enrichment begins with the embellishment of churches, and in this respect Suffolk is better endowed than in domestic architecture. To begin with the decorative features of manor houses repeat those of churches; doors have carved heads and frames, tracery appears in windows, screens-passages borrow Gothic detailing, the moulding of beams, brackets, and the running patterns carved on bressumers are nearly identical in both. In mediaeval churches, walls were often decorated with fresco paintings, and in houses also; being perishable most have disappeared in both alike.

Framsden Hall contains some of the richest carved ornamentation to be found in any Suffolk manor house. The junction of the tie-beam roof trusses with the side walls is masked by an inclined moulded cornice, below which is a carved frieze of angels, alternately robed and feathered, and holding banners, which (at a guess) are cherubim and seraphim at their familiar task of praising the Holiest (see Plate 98). Arch-bracing comes to rest on strongly carved heads: in one case a superbly bearded monarch (Mr. John Harvey thinks this was probably intended to represent a 'king of olden times', see Plate 99). There is an iconography here waiting to be deciphered, possibly in some

*Plate 102: Hall interior, Roydon Hall, Creeting St. Peter.*

Plate 103: Late fifteenth century screens-passage hall, Otley Hall.

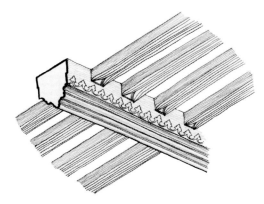

Figure 60: Swept chamfer to joist end, Otley Hall.

intentional hierarchy ranging from the celestial to the grotesque, in the heads of gluttons, sluggards and others (see Plates 100 and 101) in the great parlour behind the dais.

Roydon Hall, Creeting St. Peter, is notable for the deeply undercut Perpendicular type roll mouldings of the hall ceiling, and the complete continuity of beams and joists — an extraordinarily satisfying example of authentic mid/late sixteenth century carpentry. The wainscot is early Jacobean (see Plate 102).

There is a group of timber-framed houses near Woodbridge built — or rebuilt — between the late fifteenth and mid-sixteenth centuries, and, although inevitably altered during a long life — still have many features from their original build. All have deeply undercut roll mouldings to beams and ceiling joists; Basts at Grundisburgh and High House, Otley, with first floors jettied on more than one side, have fine exposed dragon-beams. The moulded joists to the earlier build at Otley Hall are especially good, with swept chamfers just before the junction with beam or bressumer, (see Figure 60); the latter have cresting on exposed sides which suggests a date of 1485$^{\pm}$ (see Plate 103). Panelling occurs in all main ground floor rooms in this part of the house, and in some first floor bed chambers. Although doubtfully contemporary, the quality is good and particularly the linen fold.[1]

The moulded and carved floor joists and beams in the hall and parlour of Clopton Hall, Wickhambrook, were taken from the older manor house and reused in the existing building. They are unmistakably Gothic in form, the beams with trail patterns of oak leaves, and the joists rib moulded with leaf pattern stop chamfers (see Plate 104). The work at Giffords Hall, Wickhambrook, is attributed to Clement Heigham in the late sixteenth century, and there is much excellent carved work in beams, joists and spandril pieces. There is a suggestion of different carpentry styles in the hall and the 'great chamber' over. The chamfer stops are dagger pointed in the former, and swept in the latter where there was much ingenuity in engaging the mouldings of the main and secondary tie-beams to preserve a flowing continuity. The ceiling of the bed chamber is cambered (a not uncommon feature in better class work of this period), and the spandrils of the arched-braces are vigorously decorated with leaves and flowers, amongst which appears the star of the Clopton insignia (the family keeping the lordship at the time of building). The work at Giffords Hall is, as Avray Tipping pointed out, untinctured 'with Renaissance importations',[2] remaining true to its native Gothic. Carpentry of comparable excellence appears in the Chantry Priest's House at Denston with a refinement of detail surpassing even the ornamental beams and joists in the earliest range of Alston Court, Nayland, although the vaulted wooden ceiling of the Solar there must be the richest of the kind in Suffolk.

All this fine carpentry work was intended to be seen, and, indeed, was an integral part of the interior treatment of important Gothic houses; where such ceilings have been plastered over, this will have been done later. The studwork of walls, now so

1 acc. Ralph Dutton, *The English Interior 1500-1900* op. cit., page 26, the term 'linen fold' does not appear to have been in use before the nineteenth century. The fifteenth century term seems to have been *lignis undulatis* or 'wavy wood'.
2 cf. *English Homes* Period II, Volume 1, Early Tudor, page 5 (see General Bibliography).

Plate 104: Parlour ceiling, Clopton Hall, Wickhambrook. Late fifteenth century.

*Plate 105: Late sixteenth century painted mural at Polstead Hall.*
G.B. Scott

*Plate 106: Early Tudor mural at West Stow Hall.*

frequently exposed, was largely intended to be covered, if not by wainscot then by sets of tapestry,[1] or a cheaper alternative fabric known as 'Steyned worke' of which there are documentary records. Little, if any, mediaeval tapestry survives in Suffolk, although the pair of framed wall tapestries at the Manor House, Bacton, might have been refixed there from an older house in the early eighteenth century. There remains painting direct on to studwork and plaster, of which a number of examples survive. One has come to light recently in the old Guildhall in St. Mary's, Long Melford, where painted figures cover both plaster and woodwork. The most complete is probably that at Polstead Hall, where an entire boarded partition some 20 feet in length is covered by black and white allegorical drawings — conjecturally the miracles of Hercules — in Italian Renaissance style (see Plate 105). Of frescoes on plaster, the most celebrated example is probably on the chimney stack in the gatehouse at West Stow Hall, with cartoons of the Four Ages of Man done in reddish brown and black (see Plate 106).

A popular Tudor decorative feature was the overmantel of the fireplace. Traditionally it was here that the coats of arms of the noble house owners were displayed, or some allegorical conundrum deciphered. At Langley's Newhouse, Hawkedon, the Clopton (?) star is included amongst other symbols in roundels and rectangles: this frieze is done in plaster and traces of the original greens, reds and blacks are still visible (see Plate 107). At Stutton Hall, the overmantel is of carved stonework (see Plate 108).

*Plate 107: Painted plaster frieze over fireplace at Langley's Newhouse, Hawkedon.*

*Plate 108: Carved stone frieze over fireplace at Stutton Hall.*

1 Acc. Dr. Margaret Wood, *The English Mediaeval House*, op. cit., page 397, tapestry was seemingly not in use until the fourteenth century. Dr. Wood's chapter on Interior Decoration is full of interest on the methods used to enrich mediaeval houses (pages 394-406).

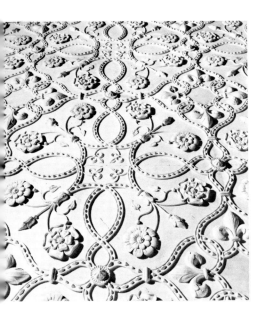

*Plate 109: Ceiling at Cockfield Hall, Yoxford.*

*Plate 110: Detail of ceiling, Clock House, Little Stonham.*

If it was the carpenters and joiners who had embellished the interiors of the better sort of houses until then, the reigns of Henry VIII and Elizabeth I increasingly favoured plasterers. Mural paintings had been done extensively in churches, but there was little or no decorative plasterwork until the interiors of houses were pargetted, and floors in interiors ceiled with plaster often extended down into friezes. The drawing-room at Cockfield Hall, Yoxford, has an extremely rich ornamental plaster ceiling in the geometrical fashion of the late sixteenth or early seventeenth century (see Plate 109). The extent of restoration at 7 Northgate Street, Ipswich, is indeterminate, but if the wainscot in the parlour is modern, the painted plaster frieze of roundels with portrait busts alternating with coats of arms (and, occasionally, Tudor roses) is likely to be contemporary, together with the moulded plasterwork covering the ceiling beams (see Plate 111). In the houses of merchants and smaller landowners, carved ceiling woodwork disappeared under plaster which was frequently ornamented with a pattern of individual motifs — flowers, thistles, monograms, and the ubiquitous rose. Examples are too numerous to mention, but the old manor house of Newbourne Hall has the characteristic Suffolk addition of a cross-wing of early seventeenth century date, on two of the ceilings of which are roses and lilies, and other motifs joined by patterned ribs. In a cross-wing of similar date at Clock House, Little Stonham, there is a ceiling divided into variously shaped panels by single ribs, the intersections being covered by plaster bosses with acorns and oak leaves (see Plate 110). Single motifs are centred in the panels and there is the occasional suggestion of Jacobean strapwork.

Somewhat similar in character to the Clock House ceiling is that in the drawing-room — originally parlour — at Aspall Hall, near Debenham, although the execution is of a higher standard, and the interlacing patterns on the beam soffits together with the fantail friezes on the vertical beam faces are notably excellent (see Section 6). Crowe Hall, Stutton, has remarkable plaster ceilings of two widely differing periods — in one of the principal bedrooms in the south-east range is seventeenth century work in high relief in which the design is controlled by moulded ribs and contains two remarkable elongated angel figures and a centre-piece, enclosed by borders with tied swags of fruit (see Plate 112). The first floor drawing-room, facing the river, is pure Gothic revival of c.1826, and has a decorated ceiling of which the centre-piece is fan tracery with pendants in the style of Henry VII's Chapel at Westminster Abbey (see Plate 113).

The bedroom ceiling must be one of the curiosities of Suffolk plasterwork, and could well be a vernacular copy of a design: Bankart shows a Jesse figure of similar style in a house at Dartmouth, Devon, done in the early seventeenth century.[1] For

1 cf. *The Art of the Plasterer*, op. cit., page 95. A similar curiosity in its way is the Rococo plasterwork at Browston Hall; very elaborate design and expert execution (see Section 6).

*Plate 111: No. 7 Northgate Street, Ipswich.*

Plate 112: *Seventeenth century bed-room ceiling detail, Crowe Hall, Stutton.*

Plate 113: *Drawing-room ceiling, early nineteenth century, Crowe Hall.*

complete contrast see the ceiling of c.1590 at Hintlesham Hall: very characteristic of later Renaissance design and, according to Pevsner, 'similar to work in Norfolk at Melton Constable and Felbrigg and 'among the best . . . anywhere in East Anglia.'[1] This degree of modelling in high relief was alien to the Adam brothers, who specialised in delicate geometrical patterns of low relief, and the use of 'light tints . . . to remove the crudeness of the white'. It was surprising to discover in an attic bedroom now occupying the upper part of the octagon at Great Saxham Hall, a neglected painted ceiling in the style of both Adams and Angelica Kaufman.

The best Adam work in Suffolk is by Wyatt at Heveningham Hall, and a faithful transcription of the Adam style: nowhere else in the county can we see late Georgian taste in interior decoration of comparable magnificence.

In the end, it is not magnificence which we should be looking for in eighteenth century Suffolk but the simple panelled rooms which, as Ralph Dutton points out, were better suited to the modest way of life of the country squire, the prosperous tradesman and the retired merchant than 'pilastered elevations and grand saloons'. Innumerable examples of these pleasant interiors exist, with their deep moulded skirtings, walls panelled above and below dado rails; shutterboxes in the panelled reveals of sash window openings, and broad well-proportioned doors with generous architraves. At Manor House, Bacton, the hall and three principal rooms are lined from floor to ceiling with unvarnished pine in broad, fielded panels — warm, rich and dark. At Loudham Hall, mouldings are more discreet, there are free-standing Corinthian columns in the entrance hall, and the panelling all painted white. The drawing-room at Great Saxham Hall is blue picked out in white.

1 cf. *Suffolk*, op. cit., second edition, page 273.

147

# STAIRCASES

*Plate 114: Mid-fifteenth century newel stairs at Read Hall, Mickfield.*

*Plate 115 (below): The staircase annexe at Otley High House.*

*Plate 116 (below right): The newel stair at Otley High House.*

1 The corresponding stairs at Moyses Hall, Bury St. Edmunds, were part of the alterations carried out mid-fifteenth century.
2 'Treads' and 'risers' are technical terms used in staircase joinery: the tread is the horizontal board supporting the foot and the riser the vertical board beneath the tread.
3 'String' is the joinery term for the timbers supporting the treads and risers on each side of a staircase: strings started by being 'closed', with the 'open' string — showing the sides of treads and risers — a later development.

The oldest domestic staircase in Suffolk is, doubtless, the newel stair at Little Wenham Hall.[1] The reason for its survival over nearly 700 years is due to construction in stone within masonry walls. The form is that of turret stairs, or vices — as they are sometimes called — in Suffolk churches, from which they were copied. The domestic newel stairs did not appear until brick became cheaper and more plentiful in the sixteenth century, when the staircase could be fitted conveniently into a small space between the lobby entrance and the principal chimney stack. The stairs could either be formed out of solid balks of timber, or, as at Read Hall, Mickfield, with four inch thick treads housed into the oak newel, and the risers of bricks and tiles plastered (see Plate 114). The newel was frequently of one continuous length taken from the bole of a young tree. The earlier stairs at Read Hall went out of the screens-passage next the main entrance, and were a single straight flight, probably of solid treads housed into wall strings, and steep. The ladder stairs at Tudor House, Needham Market, are, as mentioned earlier, dated circa 1530, and have been re-used between the new library and the gallery.

Before the internal staircase, access to the first floor in timber framed houses was by external steps, or ladder, usually at the back of the house. An example of this is at High House, Otley, where an otherwise inexplicable door occurs in the outside wall at first floor level. Outside stairs are thought to have been covered by a penthouse, or pentice, in much the same way as the steps to the galleries of early inns were covered by roofs. (A Tudor staircase of this kind is postulated at Little Wenham Hall.) By the sixteenth century these primitive devices were being abandoned in all but the humbler houses, and new internal staircases added. This was frequently achieved by a lean-to or gabled structure added at the rear. It is notable that at High House, Otley, this addition was immediately next to the older outside stairs door which was then blocked up. A square timber-framed annexe was built, measuring about nine feet each way and slightly bowed on the side parallel with the house to follow the curve of the steps around the newel. It is this type of structure that led to the term 'staircase', for it was quite literally a *case* for the enclosing of stairs (see Plates 115 and 116).

The newel stair continued to be used in cottages and humbler houses until the eighteenth century, although no longer with solid timbers but treads and risers framed together.[2] The stairway was not exploited for decorative display until Elizabethan times, and then usually in the grander house, prompted by foreign pattern books, fashions for sweeping clothes, and social ambition. The enclosure within a stair 'case' continued, as at Haughley Park, where the plan is still the Elizabethan one of a square open well stair contained by walls on three sides, in an annexe between wings. An enclosed well stair at Crows Hall, Debenham, probably dates from Gawdy ownership in 1595, and is of immensely solid framed construction, with heavy wall strings[3] and rails housed into circular newel posts rising the whole height of the stair well (see Plate 117). Similar design themes occur in the stairway at Roydon Hall, Creeting St. Peter, where the steps are worked from solid oak — the spandril panelling is later (see Plate 118). It is always worth looking

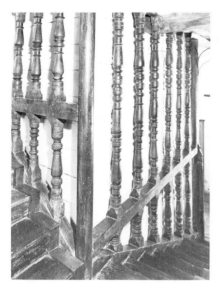

Plate 117: Detail of balustrade, Crows Hall, Debenham.

Plate 118: Balustrade, Roydon Hall, Creeting St. Peter.

Plate 119: Dog-gate to staircase, Shelley Hall.

Plate 120: First flight of stairway at Baylham Hall.

at the feet of Elizabethan or Jacobean stairs for traces of dog-gates: a fairly rare Suffolk example is at Shelley Hall where the original gate of c.1600, hung on hook hinges, is still intact (see Plate 119).

There are fairly plentiful examples in Suffolk houses of what James Lees-Milne described as '... the form so characteristic of the Jacobean house, great and small ... namely, the open well type of stair with prominent free newel posts at the corners, a balustrade and string.' This design of stairs Mr. Lees-Milne derives from Flanders, mentioning the Museum of the Plantin Morétus at Antwerp, where 'there ... is a staircase, dated 1570, of the sort we see most generally adopted in England thirty to forty years later'. A fine example is to be found at Baylham Hall, near Needham Market, where the centre of the house is occupied by a well, rising through three floors, and containing a flamboyant Jacobean stairway to be dated after 1626, when the property was bought by John Acton.

An interesting staircase enigma occurs at Hemingstone Hall (within a few miles of Baylham), where the design of the Baylham Hall newels (see Plate 120) has been almost exactly copied, but without the raking balustrade and the three-tiered finials (see Plate 121). One of the prettiest and — decoratively — most original open well early-Jacobean stairways is at Thorington Hall, near Stoke-by-Nayland (see Plate 122). This has closed strings on the outside and, presumably, an open cut string on the inside: the stairway is housed in the traditional case, and rises through three floors.

Plate 121 (right): Stairway at Hemingstone Hall.

Plate 122 (far right): Detail of newel post at Thorington Hall, Stoke-by-Nayland.

Plate 123: Bramford House staircase, c.1696.

Plate 124: Eighteenth century staircase, Milden Hall.

Plate 125: Early eighteenth century staircase, Loudham Hall.

Subsequent developments are towards an increasing 'lightness' of detail, already visible in the stairway at Bramford House of c.1696, and reaching an entirely un-Jacobean elegance at Milden Hall, where the new feature is the open string and elegantly carved consoles concealing the side of each step. Similar eighteenth century themes occur at Loudham Hall and elsewhere, until an ultimate unequivocal airiness is reached at Barking Rectory, and Worlingham Hall, near Beccles (see Plates 123-127).

Plate 126: Staircase c.1818, Barking Rectory.

Plate 127 (right): Double-flight stairway c.1800, Worlingham Hall.

150

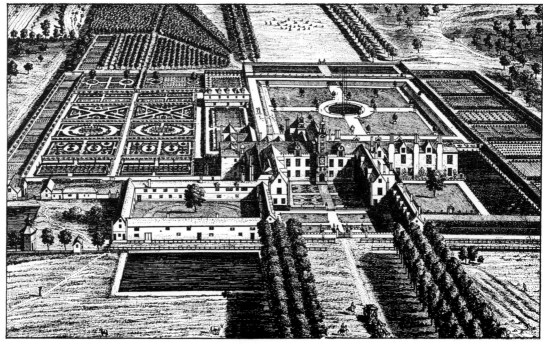

*Plate 128: Brome Hall, c.1580, after a drawing by Knyff.*

## GARDEN ARCHITECTURE

Amongst relatively neglected studies of domestic culture are those minor buildings and architectural works which embellished mansions, and town and country houses. The subject matter is sufficient for a book of its own, especially if landscape as well as works of 'garden architecture' were to be added. I use this term rather loosely, for the time being, to cover a variety of structures built separately and detached from houses. I suppose that the whole of this *genus* derives from the source to which Barbara Jones attributed 'follies . . . money and security and peace',[1] and does not therefore appear much before Tudor times. Certainly, if the outworks of Hengrave Hall, as described by Gage,[2] can be taken as typical of a great early sixteenth century house, they were manifold and complex ' . . . dovecote, grange, great barn, mill, forge, great stable, and various offices, separate kennels for the hounds and spaniels, and the mews for the hawks'. In addition to its great and little park there was a vineyard or orchard, gardens, hop

1 cf. *Follies and Grottoes,* by Barbara Jones 1953 London: Constable & Co., page 1.
2 cf. *The History and Antiquities of Hengrave*, op. cit., pages 16-17.

*Plate 129: Temple of Diana, Great Saxham Hall.*

*Kentwell Hall, Long Melford. View from the east.*

*Helmingham Hall, Helmingham. View from the south-west.*

grounds and hemp grounds; also fish ponds and a bowling alley. The grounds, Gage says, were 'laid out in the true Dutch style'. Knyff's prospect of Brome Hall *a vol d'oiseau* c.1580 (see Plate 128), shows a characteristic arrangement of the surroundings of a great house, with its moat, pastures, water gardens and courtyards, elaborately compartmented by brick walls, ornamental gates, piers and balustrades. None of this survives, and with the destruction of so many Tudor mansions their surroundings have perished also. Occasionally, as at Cockfield Hall, Yoxford, it is possible to recapture the ceremonial of approach through brick arches, gateways and courtyards. For the rest we have to accept such fragmentary evidence as remains: the occasional dovecote, or 'duffus', as at Kentwell Hall, Long Melford. The bridges spanning moats, as at Crows Hall, Debenham, and — remarkably — at Mary Tudor's beloved Westhorpe Hall, and the Elizabethan garden walls at Seckford Hall.

The last phases of great landscape and garden architecture were in the eighteenth and nineteenth centuries. Examples of the first can be found at Heveningham Hall, near Halesworth, and Great Saxham Hall, near Bury St. Edmunds (see Plate 129); the most spectacular example of the second is Shrubland Park, near Ipswich (see Plate 130). A complete record of works would include dovecotes, fish houses, garden houses, ice houses, obelisks and orangeries, pavilions, serpentine walls (see Plate 131), shell rooms (a fine example at Nettlestead Chace), tea houses, temples and terraces.

*Plate 130: Shrubland Park — terrace stairs and pavilion, c.1850.*

*Plate 131: Serpentine Wall at Heveningham Hall.*
**English Tourist Board**

# Exemplar
## Description of houses

The last Section of this book describes and illustrates a number of Suffolk houses, and is therefore entitled *Exemplar*. By grouping houses in the main categories of manor house, country house and farmhouse, with the related categories of religious buildings and parsonages, town and village house and cottage, we get a conspectus of the chief characteristics of each type. At the same time one has to recognise that few classification systems are entirely free of pitfalls, and this is specially true in the case of *manor houses*. The kind of problem that may arise is in identifying a particular house with a territorial manor; it can happen that a house built on manorial land is not *the* manor house; the original dwelling may have been pulled down and the description 'manor house' not be applicable to its successor. There may be no record to prove that an original manor house existed. Then there is the use of this word 'hall': it usually signifies a manor house but not invariably.[1] The frequency with which the name hall appears in Suffolk has already been commented upon and it is interesting to note that in Hodskinson's Map of Suffolk (1783) the word occurs approximately 221 times, as against the use of the suffix 'house' (7 times), 'lodge' (16 times) and 'farm' (23 times).

Comparable in status with the manor house is the *country house*. This description used as a term of reference is, I judge, fairly modern, and the name preferred by old gazeteer writers for the medium to large house in the country — usually with an estate — was 'seat'. The difficulty here is that the 'country house' may also be a manor house, or the successor to an original manor house — often enlarged, rebuilt and remodelled in such a way as to conform with the notional category of 'country house'.

The reason why so relatively few houses appeared with the suffix 'farm' in the late eighteenth century is doubtless explained by the prevalence of 'hall farms' in Suffolk. A large number of halls were then farmhouses, and have continued to be so-called: many were also manor houses. In a satisfactory architectural classification there must be a place, however, for the 'farmhouse', if only for the reason that it is one of the most easily recognisable of all building groups in the Suffolk countryside.

A distinct group is the vicarage, or parsonage, and many interesting houses come within this category of dwellings. There is an occasional overlapping with manor houses, as, for example, at Coddenham, where the vicarage was also a manor. It seemed appropriate to preface some examples in this group by including a few of the *religious houses* turned into domestic premises after the Dissolution, without implying in any way that these houses became parsonages.

The chief remaining class of houses must be those in town and village, and examples are grouped under the heading *town and village houses*. Dwellings in this class can have similar characteristics to those on open sites in the country, but take on a special interest where built on restricted sites and usually close to the adjoining street. Therefore it seemed important to include a few examples of special interest, such as Alston Court at Nayland and the group centred upon Tudor House, Needham Market.

The smallest dwelling is the cottage. The traditional Suffolk cottage, whether in town or village, has been little studied, but the introductory nature of this book has admitted the selection of a few examples only.

## MANSIONS

Helmingham Hall is the largest moated house in Suffolk. It is some six miles due north of Ipswich and lies on rising ground above the headwaters of a tributary of the River Deben. The character of the Hall is determined by an intimate association between site and building. The site is parkland with a carpet of bare and short

1 cf. Notes on Copinger's *The Manors of Suffolk*, Suffolk Record Office, County Hall, Ipswich. The author C.G.H. has valuable comments on halls in relation to manors: whenever two very similar or identical names occur, these are two separate manors unless it can be proved to the contrary (e.g. The Manor of Gelham is in Elveden, but *Gelham Hall* is in Wickham Market). He points out the use of the word 'hall' is often a kind of optional extra in the name of the manor, which is included or omitted in a very arbitrary way at different times (e.g. The Manor of Broughtons in Stonham Aspal is sometimes called The Manor of Broughton Hall, and there can be no doubt that it is the same manor which is meant).

*Helmingham Hall*
*TM 187 577*

cropped turf brushed across rising ground in the manner of a water colourist's foreground. Seen from the approach, the building rides alone in a sphere of clear space astride a slight summit: it is a composition in which the long two-storey house of warm earthy-red walls and roof — with the whitish accents of two widely separated bay windows and oriel centrepiece — contrast with the prevalent greenery of the park (see Plate 132). The skyline is cut by the severely straight ridged roofs, interrupted haphazardly by tall octagonal brick chimney stacks and the numerous finials of stepped gable-ends, and once, on the east range, by the conical roof of a white weather-boarded belfry.

When the great fourteenth century doors of the gatehouse are open, one sees through the arched opening into the interior courtyard, where the shaded porch reveals the original entrance to screens-passage and hall. The main approach is by an axial avenue, which does not appear in Hodskinson's map of 1783 but is shown in *Plans of Helmingham Park Estate* prepared by Isaac Johnson, Surveyor, of Woodbridge in 1802-3. The entry on the Ipswich to Debenham road is by a gateway with tall brick piers surmounted by black winged horses' heads of the Tollemache insignia, through gates brought here from the Dysart home of Ham House. The avenue, with its double row of oaks, runs straight as a rule across the park, descending to cross a stream and rising to reach the drawbridge in front of the Hall, a branch going off north to stables and outbuildings. The pair of neo-Tudor lodges,[1] overshadowed in summer by leafy oaks and neat as new pins in spite of their nineteenth century date, are a romantic reminder that a part of Helmingham Hall belongs to the mid-nineteenth century.

It is not easy today to visualise that earlier timber-framed hall of Lionel Tollemache, which conjecturally shared the same island site as the old manor hall built by the Creke family in Plantagenet times, and from which the gatehouse doors are thought to have come. It must always have stood in relative isolation in the deer park, surrounded by oaks which gradually acquired a legendary fame, and of which some were dated by the late Lord Tollemache as over 900 years old. Since those times the building history of the Hall was one of successive removes from the original structure, making it hard to believe that the waters of the moat had once —

1 These could be the work of Anthony Salvin, since much of the detailing is identical with the new west drawing-room range of 1840, although there is no documentary evidence to this effect.

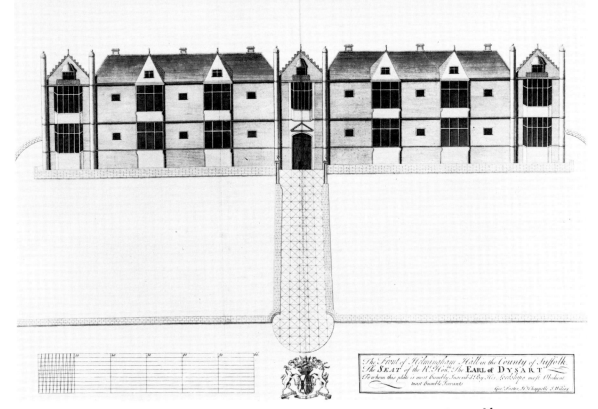

*Figure 61: The Front of Helmingham Hall in the County of Suffolk. The Seat of the R$^{t.}$ Hon.$^{ble}$ The Earl of Dysart. To whom this plate is most humbly Inscrib'd By His Lordships most Obedient most Humble Servants. Geo. Foster, Hy. Chappelle, J. Wilcox.*         *R. Parr Sculp*

as Arthur Oswald muses [1] — reflected the grey studwork and white plaster of typical early Suffolk manor houses. There is a tantalising lack of documentary evidence as to what this earlier hall looked like, and the only clue seems to be a drawing by Parr dated c.1745, which, although considered unreliable, is reproduced for its intrinsic interest (see Figure 61).

At the risk of over-simplifying the successive alterations, it can be said that they fall into fairly distinct phases. In the absence of indications as to earlier houses, the first would be the probable rebuilding of Creke Hall by Lionel Tollemache, who on succeeding to the property effected, in Oswald's words, 'a very extensive though not, perhaps, total rebuilding'. The new Hall occupied most of the island and, as already noted earlier on, was a fairly orthodox example of sixteenth century courtyard planning. The kitchen range was detached, as at Hengrave Hall, and was evidently joined to the house by a timber-framed covered way. It was not until Georgian times that further extensive developments took place, when the records suggest that the fourth Earl succeeded in giving the house the look of a then fashionable brick mansion with large sash windows. Half a century later the transformation to the Gothic taste was effected by Nash in partnership with Repton, and in 1803 Isaac Johnson included in his survey a little coloured drawing of the Hall in its new guise. The most inconceivable part of this was the covering of the whole exterior with 'a coating of cement', to give the effect of masonry in keeping with the Tudor-Gothic appearance. By that time the jettied first floors, both inside and out, had been underbuilt and most of the original timber-framed character effectively disguised. The wary eye can, however, still detect something peculiar in the apparently overhanging brickwork of the first-storey on the entrance range: the explanation is quite simply that the original upper timber-framed walls were battened and hung with 'mathematical tiles' ingeniously resembling brickwork. [2]

It was the alterations of 1840 under John, first Lord Tollemache, that gave the west front facing the gardens its present richly revivalistic-Tudor appearance. The architect is thought to have been Anthony Salvin, whose drawings of Helmingham Church are still in the R.I.B.A. collection, although none are still extant to prove his connection with work at the Hall: he was the architect for Peckforton Castle, Cheshire, built for Lord Tollemache in 1845. Since that date there have been few further changes apart from the internal improvements required to make the old

1 Arthur Oswald, F.R.I.B.A., described Helmingham Hall in great detail in five articles in Country Life between August 23rd and October 4th, 1956, and the help of this material is gratefully acknowledged.
2 These tiles are said to have been made at the Bulmer brickworks, near Sudbury, and were part of the fourth Earl's alterations to the exterior, when he faced it with brick and tiles, inserted sash windows and added a parapet to the roofs.

house more habitable. The interior, with its series of richly furnished rooms and family portraits, have all been described in detail by Arthur Oswald.

There is a tradition of brickmaking at Helmingham which is said to date from the sixteenth or seventeenth centuries. It may be that in the 1750s, when the fourth Earl was busy remodelling the house, it was the old brick kiln which was re-established. Arthur Oswald quotes a memorandum of 85,850 bricks and 33,520 tiles used at the Hall between 1745 and 1760. The site was about a mile north of the Hall and clearly marked 'Brick Kiln' on the first edition Ordnance Survey. According to Mr. D.W. Weedon, the descendant of four generations employed on the estate buildings, there was one domed brick kiln fired by coal and wood, producing about four thousand bricks at a single burn. The bricks (claimed to be 'the best in Suffolk') were strong, dark red in colour, and measuring 9 by 4 by 2⅝in. in hand-made wooden moulds they were also used for all the 'fancy work' at the Hall. The clay was 'pugged' in the old way by a horse walking round and round the pugging place. A systematic study of the brickwork at Helmingham Hall would disclose many unusual patterns, not least those segmental bricks used in the twin pilasters flanking the porch: if extended to the history of estate building on this property, it would disclose traditions of do-it-yourself work dating from Tudor times until the present day.[1]

*Plate 133: Hengrave Hall from the south-west*

## Hengrave Hall
*TL 824 686*

Hengrave Hall is one of the few survivors — but amongst these one of the most important — of that inner ring of large country houses that once surrounded Bury St. Edmunds. It could have vied with Helmingham Hall as the largest moated mansion in Suffolk, had not the moat been filled in during the late eighteenth century. The house was undoubtedly conceived by its wealthy owner as a Tudor *palazzo*, and in its design echoes of fortified castle building combined with themes from Perpendicular work — the turret tops of the gatehouse oddly reminiscent of Henry VII's pinnacles at Kings College Chapel, Cambridge, and finally there was the outburst of Italianate ornament over the entrance. Somewhere a model had been made which the overseer, John Eastawe, had seen, and which was to serve as a guide to the appearance of the new hall. Sir Thomas Kytson brought to the building methods which had helped to make him one of the wealthiest cloth merchants in London, and detailed accounts of the work of all trades were scrupulously kept. These are recorded by John Gage[2] in his study of Hengrave Hall.

The building started, seemingly, with the disadvantages of an existing site and house — the old, probably timber-framed, hall of the de Hemegreth's — but the necessity of throwing up a triumphal front elevation was brilliantly resolved by building a range 100 foot long across the whole south front of the moated site. This front can be detected at the east and almost as an elaborate screen of only one room depth with no cross-wing to back up a dummy gable put in to correspond with one at the other end of the house. Architecturally this 'screen' built in an

1 It was Mr. D.W. Weedon's great grandfather who transported the wrought-iron entrance gates from Ham House to Helmingham by wagon and horses. The last foreman of the Brick Kiln was — appropriately — Mr. Last, and the works were of necessity, but regrettably for posterity, destroyed in 1955/56.
2 cf. *The History and Antiquities of Hengrave in Suffolk*, by John Gage Esq., F.S.A. of Lincoln's Inn. (1822. London: James Carpenter, Old Bond Street, Joseph Booker, New Bond Street, and John Deck, Bury St. Edmunds.)

unusual combination of white brick and stone, was a balanced composition in which four massive turrets and two canted bays punctuated the long facade at regular intervals, and were accented horizontally by a ribbon of stone string-course around the whole building. It was this striking south front of which the heavily enriched gatehouse was the *tour de force* which Sir Thomas Kytson wished to see reflected in the waters of the moat — an added dimension that is now so sadly missing.

It is important to remember that in its present form Hengrave Hall is a remnant only (see Plate 133) — fortunately indeed a major one — of that whole complex of house, approach and outbuildings described by John Gage. The splendid south front was intended to be the impressive culmination of a long stately approach '. . . by a straight road raised above the level of the country, fenced in each side by a deep ditch, lined with a triple row of trees, and terminating at a long semi-circular foss over which a stone bridge led, at some distance to the outer court. This court was formed by a central lodge, the residence of the keepers and falconers, and by a range of low surrounding buildings used as offices, including a stable for the horses of pleasure. Beyond was the moat, enclosing the mansion . . .' Gage makes it quite clear that there was a bridge over the moat leading to the gatehouse, and round the east side of the house a drawbridge also, communicating with the church.

Although there is consolation in the amount of original work that survives, it would be of much value to the history of Hengrave Hall if the full extent of the eighteenth century alterations could be established. Apart from the demolition of the entire service range in the north-east corner, the front was also altered and it is well known that the three bays faced in stone between the gatehouse and the east angle turret belong to this period. If the plan of 1775 is accurate, it is possible that both the gable windows at the west end were enlarged from three to four lights in width, leaving only the oratory window unaltered and the first floor windows to the east of this. Internally there could have been extensive rebuilding at the same period; Dr. C. Hewett comments on the dimensions of the joists to the first floor[1] which certainly suggest post-Tudor carpentry.

The spell of the Kytson home is recaptured, however, in the family oratory above all, and in the inner courtyard also: in this oratory, with its great window of early sixteenth century stained glass depicting twenty-one biblical scenes, the proscribed Catholic faith was maintained with few breaks over many centuries. The courtyard, surrounded by a cloister-like corridor on three sides and entered only from one door, must always have been a place of quietude in a busy household (see Plate 134). The stone-faced walls with battlemented parapets, mullioned windows, and the one great carved stone oriel lighting the hall (specially commissioned from the master mason John Sparke) give to the interior of this courtyard a collegiate atmosphere. Apart from the Italian wall-head in the centre, there can be little here that differs from the days of the first founder of the Hall. (For comments upon other aspects of the planning and design of Hengrave Hall see Section 3.)

Ickworth House is sited within the park and well concealed except from near view. The entrance is first seen from the green on the west of the road entering Horringer and, beyond the entrance, the drive disappears in a ribbon of road through acres of short cropped turf, studded with great clumps of trees. It is the classic example of an English method which, as Viscount Norwich said in his introduction to the National Trust Guide (1973), was '. . . to lead by serpentine approach to sudden display'. Here it was an attempt to build one of the most ambitious Palladian houses in England. It is well enough known that the idea emanated from Lord Hervey's third and most remarkable son, Frederick, created Bishop of Derry in 1768, and fourth Earl of Bristol in 1779. Not the least incongruity was the ambition of a member of the Anglican bench of Bishops to build an Italian palazzo in a Suffolk park, open to bitter north and east winds.

His Lordship's first visit to Ickworth was in the winter of 1781-82 after he had inherited the estate. He was evidently disappointed by the flat Suffolk landscape, which he considered 'unsuitable for sublime architecture'. But he seems to have inherited also a building project and garden designs made by Lancelot (Capability) Brown between 1769 and 1776. Nothing came of the 'Plans and Elevation for an Intire New House' for which Mr. Brown charged £105 in 1781. The evolution of the

*Plate 134: Hengrave Hall — Courtyard*

*Ickworth House*
*TM 816 614*

1 cf. An unpublished report on the floors and roofs of Hengrave Hall by Mr. Cecil A. Hewett.

final project for a 'rotunda' with curving wings has been fully discussed[1] and it seems likely that the final scheme may have been designed by Mario Asprucci, son of the curator of the Borghese Collection in Rome and a comparatively unknown architect. It is difficult to see the idea of a house in the form of an enormous central oval (see Plate 135) as anything but an eccentric decision, or to believe that in the hands of a more able architect it would not have been considerably modified. The Earl Bishop had previously attempted a similar building, although on a smaller scale, at Ballyscullion in Ireland, but it had proved a disappointment. But the new design was finally approved and the site carefully and well chosen. The house was to be built almost in the centre of a level plateau, thus avoiding the problems caused by sloping ground. It was a fantastic building operation. To start with, a huge oval hole had to be dug out, and the soil disposed of. Within this oval was built the basement storey, with walls some 2.60 m (7ft 6in.) thick, diminishing to about 1.80 m (6ft) above.[2] Brick was used in this and in the construction generally, the majority of the bricks evidently having been made and fired in kilns specially set up on the estate for the purpose.[3] Ingenuity was used in gathering over the flues from perimeter rooms in the basement, and leading them up inside the thickness of the walls, together with those of fireplaces in rooms in the upper floors, to the more solid portions of the balustrades. In this way no chimney pots marred the classical silhouette of the skyline, and all that could ever have been seen was smoke issuing from the topmost crown of the domed roof. The work started in 1795, was nowhere near completion when, in 1803, the Earl Bishop died in Italy, without ever having seen his *palazzo* in Suffolk. The main rotunda was merely a shell covered by cupola roof: the wings, with the connecting galleries 'run up to the height of only three or four feet'. It was F. Shoberl who described this ten years later, leaving a vivid picture of the deserted site and unfinished buildings. The sheer vastness of the rotunda — 31.75m (104ft) in height to the crowning cupola and 27.50m (90ft) at the point of greatest diameter — seemed then, as now, overwhelming.

1 e.g. *Ickworth* published by The National Trust, 1976; *The Evolution of Ickworth* by Pamela Tudor-Craig, Country Life, May 17, 1973.
2 Once the basement storey of the great oval centre-piece had reached ground level, it must be supposed that this was used for planking and strutting the surrounding soil to form the area, followed by building the outer area brick walls.
3 Large clay pits, some now filled with water, lie about 600 yards west of the house.

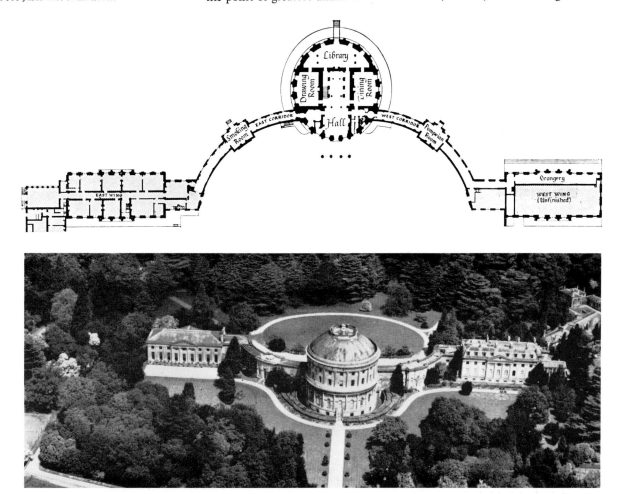

*Plate 135: Plan and aerial view of Ickworth House*

National Trust

The history of the completion of Ickworth House is well documented. The Earl Bishop's son (who became Marquess of Bristol in 1826) was moved to carry on with his father's unwieldly project, and work was finished in August 1829. But the house never achieved its high Palladian purpose, in which the 'rotunda' was to serve as the owner's dwelling, and the wing pavilions with their curving corridors, as galleries for the exhibition of superlative works of art.

There are days, at the end of a long fine summer, when the stucco in drying has lost all discolour, and under a clear blue sky the walls take on an almost Italian brilliance; then one is tempted momentarily to wonder how the house and gardens might have looked had the patron returned from Italy to Suffolk. Could he have realised his visionary ideal or would he have been disappointed a second time?

## MANOR HOUSES

*Aspall Hall*
*TM 172 654*

*Plate 136: Aspall Hall detail of original parlour ceiling.*

It is a natural spot for a settlement, being on a hill top with the land falling away on three sides and a river curling round from north to south — in this case the upper waters of the Deben, a little north of the market town of Debenham. When the broadly circular moat was dug, there was one entrance to the island on the south-east and another from the north-west. The antiquity of the site must await the archaeologist, for there is no evidence for the speculation that the Elizabethan hall of Edward Brooke (d.1541) replaced one of still earlier date. Some colour is given to the possibility of a house with the main entrance originally facing north, for there are the remnants of a U- or E-shaped plan with symmetrical wings, one of which with its *oeil-de-boeuf* windows still appears at the back of the house, suggesting a date of 1580 or somewhat later. The approaches could have been on both sides, the main entrance by drawbridge from the south-east,[1] with a secondary approach from Aspall Green by a road the vestiges of which still exist. From that side the house would have presented a pair of crow-stepped gables flanking an entrance courtyard with probably a central porch. If any proof were needed that it once belonged to a distinguished family,[2] this would be given by the ornamental plaster ceiling of one of the two original parlour rooms; this, which the Rev. Edward Farrer not unreasonably called 'one of the most elaborate and beautiful ceilings in the county', is intact and in excellent condition. It has double-moulded ribs with bosses, *fleur-de-lys,* rosettes, and running fantail friezes of great beauty, combined with intricately interlaced plaster ornament below the beams (see Plate 136). All this could be the work of 1600 or thereabouts. Further evidence is provided by carved oak wainscot of the same period, some of which is clearly still in its original position.

Had the house already been transformed in the classical taste when Temple Chevallier bought the property in 1702? The question is hard to answer, and one has to search for clues. There are two periods of sash windows on the south side; the first, with thick glazing bars, *could* date from the late seventeenth century, whereas those with narrower bars are unlikely to have been put in until some twenty to thirty years later. There is an interesting circumstance that Clement Benjamin Chevallier, who inherited the property from his cousin in 1722, is known to have made bricks some quarter of a mile away in the Deben valley, where the name of Brick Meadow still persists. Thus it seems possible that the Georgian work was part of a radical enlargement at this period, which produced the present unusually long brick front (see Plate 137).

The next alterations were to be equally radical, and took place in the early nineteenth century during the ownership of the Rev. J. Chevallier, M.D. This enlightened doctor had views on the treatment of mental illness far ahead of his own times, when the insane were a social disgrace and frequently housed in appalling asylums. Dr. Chevallier believed that mental illness needed domestic treatment, and to put his views into practice made numerous alterations including corridors between the wings and the raising of the entire roof to provide extra attic bedrooms for children and staff. The first floor he kept for his patients, some of whom had their own bedroom and sitting-room. The present south pediment would have been added as an afterthought by one of his predecessors, as it inhibited planning the attic bedrooms, but the enchanting little white bellcote immediately

1 Mr. P.M. Guild remembers being told as a child that there was once a drawbridge over the moat in front of the house, for the foundations could be seen when the moat was low.
2 The Brooke family are known to have been lords of the manor from c.1445 until c.1702. (W.A. Copinger, *The Manors of Suffolk:* volume 3, pages 217-220).

*Plate 137: Aspall Hall – viewed from the moat*

### Badwell Ash Hall
TM 006 691

*Plate 138: Badwell Ash Hall – detail of mid fifteenth century chimneys*

1 Mr. Norman Shield, a former owner, tells me that it was also shown on old maps as 'High House' in Gothic script, and since this was written, the new owners have reverted to the earlier name of 'High House'.

above this is probably of his date. The observant will notice the original central doorway filled in with a sash window on the south side, and two entrances with pretty early nineteenth century lattice work porches, which doubtless were part of Dr. Chevallier's replanning of the house. The moulded brick panels built into the base of the wall will have been preserved from the late Tudor chimneys.

Aspall Hall today is the seat of an active rural industry which has continued since – according to old MSS – the Chevallier family '. . . came from Jersey and brought hither with them the Spirit of Cyder-making'. They brought with them, indeed, not only the spirit but also the equipment, including the presses, and stones of the great circular trough, dated 1728, in which the apples were stored. In the peak season there is some reminiscence of a small *chateau* in the Gironde, immensely bustling activity proceeding within a stone's throw, but separated by the moat, from the old Hall. It will lie there, in the warm autumnal haze, with its rows of white sash windows and mellow diapered brick walls, waiting only, one feels to be engraved, in the French manner, upon the labels of its own bottles.

On the 2½ in. Ordnance Survey, this is shown as formerly 'High Hall', in the Gothic script used to denote an old house. The 'High Hall' may have been to distinguish it from adjoining halls, but the adjective is well suited to the site; this is high country and above the 200ft contour.[1]

The house was built on a by-road leading to Badwell Green off the road from Badwell Ash to Walsham-le-Willows, and is no more than five miles south of the source of the rivers Little Ouse and Waveney. Within fifty yards or so of the road, it suggests that it might have been a farmhouse, and this is certainly the impression given by the old Hall when its pile of dark red brickwork is first seen partly screened by farm buildings and trees. That this was once, however, a small emparked estate is quite apparent from the thirty acres or so of parkland south of the house, with some fine old oak trees, said to be three hundred years old.

We are discussing here the property of a gentleman-farmer, of which the farm formed part of an estate acquired by the Marsham family in the fifteenth century.

The building is composed mainly of three parts. There is an early two-storey range, with a later three-storey Victorian addition, and the remains of rather more than half of the brick hall. The earliest of these three structures is the east wing, which is a timber-framed building with wattle and daub, running east and west at right angles to the later hall (see Plate 139). The low eaves and steep roof pitch suggest a hall-house, of which only the two-storied service rooms remain. It would have been logical, and in keeping with the habitual tendency of Suffolk landowners

161

*Plate 139: Badwell Ash Hall — east wing*

*Figure 62: Badwell Ash Hall*

to make do with old premises, if the Marshams of that generation had decided to pull down most of the hall-house, keeping only the service accommodation, and in place of what had gone to build a house in the new brick style.

The new house was impressively symmetrical, consisting of a single range some 20m in length and 7m in width (65ft x 23ft), of three storeys in height with a centrally projecting staircase turret, flanked — to judge from the remaining south wing — by three bays, of which two were windows and the middle a very tall and architectural chimney stack. The first room on entry next to the staircase was evidently the owner's hall, and north of this a large parlour (in the demolished wing) and a way through to the service rooms and kitchen. The stairs went up in two flights to two floors of bedchambers. The design of the house invites immediate comparison with Roos Hall, Beccles (1583), with its angle buttresses, steeply pitched crow-stepped gable and pedimented mullion and transom windows. Certain features here, however, suggest an earlier date. The bricks, deep multi-red in colour and laid in the customary English bond, suggest the early sixteenth century, being, on average, 10in. by 5in by 1¾-2in. and laid with ½in. wide mortar joints. One of the notable features of the Hall is the richly ornamented chimney stack which could reasonably be attributed to the mid fifteenth century — that is to say, to the reign of Edward VI rather than that of Queen Elizabeth I (see Plate 138). The onion tops of the polygonal angle buttresses would go well enough with that period, and these circumstances suggest that Badwell Ash Hall antedates Roos Hall by thirty years $\pm$. The window design is reminiscent of Weston Hall, near Beccles, the large south-facing window of the hall consisting of six large lights below transom and six above, reducing to five above and below transom to the first floor, and four in a similar arrangement to the second floor. The window dressings, sills, mullions and transoms are of stonework, and not, as is so often the case, of moulded brick plastered to imitate stone. It is unfortunate that — supposedly in Victorian times — all the leaded lights were removed with a great diminution of design quality. The structure as a whole is of such regularity and competence as to suggest the work of an accomplished master brickmason, and the surviving part, although fragmented, is sufficient to indicate the impressive character of the original whole.

The owners of the Hall in Victorian times added the wing to the east in pedantic imitation of the original, copying moulded brick string-courses, battlemented parapets and crow-stepped gables but adding one feature for which there was no precedent in the earlier building — an axial gable-end chimney stack surmounted by three shafts. These were, however, ornamented as exactly as possible to imitate the original. It is a slight surprise to go into the east yard, and find the flank wall of this Victorian addition presenting double-hung sash windows of eighteenth century pattern to match those which were used in bringing the old timber-framed annexe up to date. It is also ironic that the old house, having been truncated in the eighteenth century, was again enlarged in the nineteenth century, and a little unfortunate that the addition occurred at such close quarters with the original brick architecture. The best position from which to admire Badwell Ash Hall is the south-west corner of the garden, where the earthworks suggest that the house might once have stood in a partly moated enclosure (see Figure 62).

**Baylham Hall**
*TM 093 517*

West of the River Gipping and between Nettlestead in the south and Stowmarket in the north, there is a long tract of high clay country in which villages are few and small but farms are plentiful. In this country are the manor houses of Nettlestead Chace, Tarston Hall, Badley Hall and Baylham Hall. It is upland country of arable fields and the remnants of old woodlands, in which the Halls are mostly remote from the main road that follows the river north from Ipswich to Stowmarket.

Baylham Hall faces uncompromisingly east from its hilltop towards the high country of Coddenham and Ashbocking several miles away. The site was evidently fully moated, for there is a quite well-defined island of some 150 yards square, roughly in the centre and towards the east of which the house is sited. House and outbuildings have evidently long coexisted, for there is a great brick and timber barn of about mid-sixteenth century date on the south, of some 35m (116ft) in length. The house itself has been so successively altered, enlarged, and then reduced in size that the original nucleus is difficult to determine: the probability is that it represents, in part at least, the rear wing. This is in the form of a brick built two-storey range, the roof of which was rebuilt, or considerably altered, when the front of the range was remodelled. Rising sheer out of the moat on the west (see Plates 142 and 143), this wing represented accommodation of which the first floor, at least, had substantial rooms with large mullion and transom windows. One oddity is the asymmetrical placing of the two windows on the west elevation,

*Plate 140: Baylham Hall — first flight of staircase*

*Plate 141: second flight of staircase*

*Plate 142: Baylham Hall from the moat*

suggesting that the width of the whole range was at some time reduced. Another clue to the earlier dating is the way in which an obviously Tudor chimney stack, containing the bases of triple octagonal shafts, has been incorporated in later work. On this analysis the rear range would be about $1540 \pm$ to which would have been added the staircase block and the front range about $1630 \pm$. The proportions of this later range are much loftier, as though the owner was deliberately seeking to make his high-standing hall a local landmark: there is a semi-basement putting the ground floor a *piano nobile* some 2m (6ft 6in.) above the surrounding ground, and, above that, two tall storeys with one further storey in the attic space. In the plan of the new seventeenth century front range, the Greater Parlour is the room on the south of the entrance, the main Hall in the centre with, probably, a Lesser Parlour in the demolished portion. Beyond the Hall lay the impressive staircase and, behind this, at a lower level, the service rooms.

In its heyday, and seen from the eastern approach, the Baylham Hall of the early seventeenth century must have been an imposing Jacobean brick mansion, with its lofty brick walls, Dutch gables at each end of the long front range, and rows of white mullion and transom windows. The stairs ascend through two tall storeys each with three flights of seven steps and two quarter-landings and were formed round an open well, from which the massive balustrading and three-tiered decorative newel finials could be seen to advantage (see Plates 140 and 141). Unspoilt, and in its original state, this is a *tour de force* of joinery.

*Plate 143: Baylham Hall – view from the south-west*

**Roos Hall, Beccles**
TM 415 900

Roos Hall lies within about half a mile from the centre of the town of Beccles, only some 500 yards from and slightly above the level of the River Waveney. The house is built in a space of level parkland, which has been connected with the owners of the Hall since mediaeval times (see Plate 144). The famous 'Hanging Oak'[1] is reputed to be over 500 years old. The present approach is an informal one, suggesting a service road winding round to the outbuildings of a great house rather than the ceremonial entry appropriate to the great hall once planned by Thomas Colby. The position of the mediaeval moat is apparent from what remains on the east side of the house, although now partly filled in and without water, for it is conjectured that an earlier hall stood within the moat on the same site, a part only of which is now occupied by Roos Hall.[2]

*Plate 144: The approach to Roos Hall*

*Plate 145: Roos Hall — detail of stepped gable.*

1 So-called from the grisly tradition that criminals were later executed by hanging from its branches.
2 The earlier hall could have been that of Sir Robert de Roos (fl.1321) and if timber framed, as seems likely, could have disappeared without trace, except that which archaeological survey might reveal.
3 The space under the roof was often used as a store by well-to-do Dutch merchants, and in Amsterdam, Haarlem and many other towns, the original hoist can still be seen protruding at high level.

The extent of the present house is confined to a single wing with ground floor living-rooms connected by a staircase to two floors of bedrooms above, and an attic storey under the apex of the roof. At right angles to this structure is a service wing of late-nineteenth century date. The disposition of these two structures is interesting because it will perhaps give a clue to the original intentions of the owner. It is well known that Thomas Colby was the builder and that the work was completed in 1583, for his initials (with those of his second wife?) as well as the date are on the lead rainwater heads. It is known also that a much larger house had been planned and, even if not known, this could have been conjectured from the planning dispositions of the present house. The owner would naturally have decided to start by building accommodation which he could use, and this, contained within the existing walls — although conjecturally only the parlour wing of a larger house — would have given him handsome rooms on two floors with secondary space above. The service wing, with kitchen, pantry, buttery, and other offices, could — in a fashion quite common with the Tudors — have been put in a separate wing of timber-framed and plastered construction. If built at the rear of the house, this wing would then have left the way open for the next stage, which — and this is a matter of pure conjecture — could have consisted of a hall range at right angles to the present building, to be followed by a service wing on the west. The mansion, when completed, would then have conformed with the E- or broad U-plan, comprising a central block and two cross-wings with an entrance in the centre.

The quality of the present work is enough to indicate that a mansion such as this would have been one of the finest of its period in Suffolk. A remarkable feature of what can be called the embryonic Roos Hall is its height. Apart from dramatic contrast with the flat site (doubtless a deliberate decision) the end-on gable is unusual in being much closer in character to the gable-ends of Dutch towns.[3] Apart from height, the designing is assured, and in comparison with neighbouring houses of a similar date, for example Weston Hall, is sophisticated in handling. The proportions are well judged, and the detailing as well as the execution of brickwork in polygonal buttresses, string-courses, stepped gables and chimneys are of a high competence (see Plate 145). It is this mastery of brickwork, in combination with verticality of form and a certain spare quality of appearance, which makes Roos Hall a notable successor to the austere carpentry of the tall Gothic houses of Suffolk, pointing to a brick style linked primarily with the Waveney Valley, but unique to East Anglia.

### Weston Hall, near Beccles
*TM 425 873*

In the early nineteenth century the house was still as built in the second half of the sixteenth century by John Rede who died in 1605. Within ten years of the death of his son Thomas, a good half of the Hall had been destroyed by fire.

The original Weston Hall was a brick built manor house of two storeys, with substantial attics, and built on an E- or H-plan, comprising a fairly long central range with symmetrical cross-wings at each end. The fire has left less than half the central range, unfortunately depriving posterity of the main entrance which, it must be conjectured, occurred almost at the point where the north gable-wall now stands. Thus we cannot be certain whether there was a projecting porch which would have completed the E-plan. The truncated building has been adapted to the purpose of a farmhouse (see Plate 146) with the addition of a rear service wing of later date. The full extent of the earlier house can be determined from the remains of brick base walls some 18m (60ft) further north.

The house has the look of country builders' work, entirely lacking in the sophisticated finish and detailing of Roos Hall, its nearest contemporary neighbour west of Beccles. It has, nevertheless, much charm and is built of a peculiarly soft rose-pink brick, offset by the cream stucco finished window surrounds. With great good fortune the main elevations to the Beccles road have been altered only by the introduction of one double-hung sash window in the return of the south cross-wing facing north. In every other respect the main fabric is exactly as it was left by John Rede's builder. The bricks would have come from some local source, such as the kiln between Redisham and Shadingfleet, about a mile west of the site; they were 9 by 4¼ by 2in. laid in English bond with ½in. lime mortar joints, with well made squint bricks for the polygonal buttresses which flanked the crow-stepped gable-ends. The builders' inventiveness seems to have given out at the top of these buttresses which terminate with dumpy little pyramids; nor are the chimneys adventurous, being octagonal with moulded bases, plain shafts and simply moulded

*Plate 146: Weston Hall – view from the north-east.*

166

heads. The inestimable advantage in all these details is the complete survival of the original work. The windows give some notion of the bold proportions used at this period for principal rooms: the main hall has twelve lights divided by mullion and transom with a height of close on 2m (6ft). The roof was no doubt always covered with plain tiles, and the eaves finished with oversailing brickwork consisting of two projecting courses mounted on two-course dentils.

The roof timbers were carpentered in oak and consisted of 7in. by 6in. principal rafters 6ft 6in. apart into which 5in. by 6in. purlins at 5ft 9in. apart were tenoned, giving a box framed structure supporting the common rafters. The principal rafters were collared together, and the roof soffit plastered for the benefit of more comfortable attics, which doubtless would be where the Rede household staff slept.

*Plate 147: High Hall, Weston.*

*Plate 148: High Hall – detail of plaster ceiling.*

### High Hall, Weston
*TM 428 869*

Opposite Weston Hall, on rising ground beyond the turnpike, the observant will notice what Suckling described as '. . . a small but curious edifice of red brick, built in a style of architecture prevalent in the time of Charles II, and marking the taste of Thomas Rede Esq., whose initials remain on the western front.' This Thomas was evidently a brother of the John Rede who built Weston Hall and who died in 1622 and was buried in Weston Church together with Anne Rede his wife by whom he had seven sons and seven daughters. High Hall is a rectangular structure of some 6.5m (22ft) long and 5m (16ft) wide, of two main floors and an attic storey (see Plate 147). According to Suckling,[1] it was originally much loftier, and this might account for the unusual detailing of the eaves at the gable-ends, and the unexpected appearance of a pantiled roof. The upper half of an exceeding tall chimney has also been rebuilt, and from its appearance would logically need the support of a further storey. There are rusticated brick quoins and arched-head windows with brick label-moulds. In the interior, some extremely good plasterwork survives in the main chamber at first floor, with moulded beams and panelled bays, an attractive floral trail pattern on beam soffit and a frieze with floral and fruit swags all round at the junction of walls and ceiling (see Plate 148).

### Flemings Hall, Bedingfield
*TM 193 679*

1 cf. *Histories and Antiquities of the County of Suffolk*, Volume I, page 98, by Rev. A. Suckling, 1846.
2 Copinger, cf. *The Manors of Suffolk*, op. cit., Volume 4, pages 16-19.

The territorial ownership of the Manor of Flemings, or Bucks, Hall has been traced to the reign of Henry III, and the name to then lords of the manor William le Fleming, or Adam le Fleming.[2] The antiquity both of the moats and the occupancy of the site by dwellings has still to be established, but it is only reasonable to suppose that this – as well as the adjacent Bedingfield Hall – is one of the oldest

Plate 149: *Flemings Hall, Bedingfield – viewed from the entrance*

Angus McBean

Plate 150: *Flemings Hall, Bedingfield – the south-east gable end*

Angus McBean

inhabited sites in the parish.[1] Both halls lie within half a mile of each other in settings very different in character; Flemings is a manor house on the edge of a by-road between Bedingfield village and Kenton, and separated from it only by the width of the moat, and Bedingfield Hall a farmhouse well secluded from passers-by.

The Flemings Hall moat system is based on a continuous rectangle about 210m in length and 33m in width, but sub-divided by a crossing giving the Hall itself an island site almost exactly 100 yards square (30m by 30m). This site is joined to the 'mainland' by a single brick bridge on the south-west side and the house was built approximately in the centre of the island, with a range of barns said to have been contemporary with the Hall[2] and at right angles to it, forming an L-plan. The moat walls were brick lined and it was what P.G.M. Dickinson called 'a strong moat': it suggests an originally defensive function, affording security for the manor house and outbuildings on one 'island' and possibly small dwellings and stock on the other. These circumstances could suggest that earlier owners were farming landowners, at least from the date of the moated construction.

With the change of ownership the Fleming connection ceased and under Bedingfields in the fifteenth century the nucleus of the present Hall was built of timber-frame and plaster, with a steeply-pitched thatched roof. The plan of this nucleus evidently conformed with the habitual mediaeval arrangement. Entered by the present doorway through a screens-passage (since dismantled and re-erected elsewhere) it opened into a hall with upper end at the south-east and, doubtless, a small parlour beyond (later rebuilt and enlarged), and lower end with buttery, pantry and kitchen. The hall itself would be open to the roof where the construction consists of crown-post truss longitudinally and laterally braced, with tie-beam arch-braced back to the wall posts. There is evidence of an early newel staircase for access to accommodation over the service area.

The Statutory List attributes the building of 'the outer-shell' of the house to Thomas Bedingfield c.1550. The brickwork as well as the design detail of the porch is compatible with this date (compare with Seckford Hall of c.1550, with which there are obvious similarities, e.g. moulded brick pediments, four-centred arched doorway and stepped gables). The bricking up of the ground floor walls may have been done at the same time, for it is difficult not to see this as a partly decorative adjunct confined, as it is, to the front of the house (see Plate 149). Although this was the age of great chimneys, the three groups of clustered octagonal shafts have only simply moulded bases and heads. These stacks were obviously added, that on the north-east being built against the outside walls to provide the hall with a fireplace, and those at each gable end for parlour and kitchen respectively; one of the four at each end is purely decorative. These chimneys are one reason for doubting an early dating, but there is also another.

The second doubt is the appearance of 'Dutch' gable-ends in the mid-sixteenth century (see Plate 150). The first East Anglian period is customarily considered to be c.1578-1623, and the most likely source of 'influence' would be the Waveney valley with its great brick houses such as Roos Hall, Beccles (1583), and Thorpe Hall, Horham (c.1550-80). The Flemings Hall gable-ends would fit with c.1600, suggesting a rebuild — for which the brickwork does not provide evidence. There are two possibilities: first that the general date of the brick additions is later than supposed, or secondly, that the 'Dutch' gables were the separate addition of a later Bedingfield. In the latter event there occurs here, as elsewhere in Suffolk, the curious retention of early Tudor label moulds over the window-heads belonging to a different textbook design to the slightly Baroque curves of the gables and oval 'horse-collar' windows. Perhaps this is yet another example of the conservative tendencies of local landowners.

### Browston Hall
*TM 499 017*

The site is below the 25ft contour and is in a shallow dell from which the land rises gently on all sides.

A red-brick house, subsequently plastered over, the original plan could have been H-form, consisting of a centre range with a pair of cross-wings. The house is now a rectangle, with a slight projection from between the original gables on the entrance side, and largely rewindowed. Floor levels can have changed also to allow for an attic storey, and this would explain the mezzanine landing on the main staircase, with a further flight going up to the west wing bedrooms. The plan had probably

1 This was the opinion of that knowledgeable antiquary the Rev. E. Farrer, F.S.A. cf. *E.A.M.*, op. cit., No. 7331.
2 cf. Listed building description, which gave them as consisting of 'a range of barns contemporary with the Hall alongside the road, forming an 'L' and consisting of a 4-bay, a 7-bay and a 4-bay linked together, timber-framed, part wattle and daub, part weather-boarded and thatched.' These have since been demolished.

169

*Plate 151: Browston Hall – orangery.*

*Plate 152: Browston Hall – doorway on the west side.*

always worked on the principle of grouping main rooms round the nucleus of an entrance hall, but the lobby and cupboards now separating the study, or library, from the staircase hall, and the room itself all seem to belong to an alteration phase which might plausibly be dated to the second half of the eighteenth century. That is the most likely period for the handsome front entrance, with its six-panelled door and reveals, console, brackets, frieze and cornice. It would also fit the fine staircase, with its pretty turned balusters at three per tread, each ending with a carved console. To the same period, equally, could belong the (now dummy) doorway on the west side, with its handsome panelled door and carved floral frieze above (see Plate 152).

If we can accept Suckling's attribution, then the other and, indeed, the most remarkable feature of the house – the plaster ceilings and wall decorations – was the work of 'the grandfather of the Rev. Edward Missenden Love', which would give a period of about 1785-90. In the late eighteenth century we would expect to find plasterwork influenced more by the Adam brothers than by the rococo of Louis Quatorze and Louis Quinze. It is something of a mystery how this exercise in the French taste comes to be found in a small house in a remote part of Suffolk, but there is always the possibility of itinerant plasterers coming into Great

*Plate 153: Browston Hall – stable building.*

170

*Plate 154: Ceiling in entrance hall.*

*Plate 155: Aurora in the dining-room.*

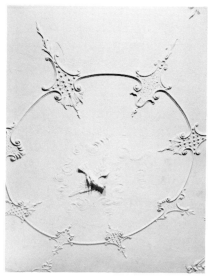

*Plate 156: A drawing-room ceiling detail.*

*Plate 157: One of the Four Ages of Woman.*

**Great Bevills, Bures**
*TL 909 349*

1 Acc. A. Percival, *The Dutch Influence on English Vernacular Architecture,* op. cit., this gable finish was known as 'mouse-tooth', from the Dutch *muisetenden,* a term used in the Dutch North American Colonies.
2 Bevills once formed part of Tawneys Manor which was centred at the top of Cuckoo Hill, half a mile to the east, but this had probably disappeared before Bevills was built. The name Bevills is thought to have originated from the name of the Beauvilles, a Norman family whose arms were recorded by Tillotson as being in the earlier stained glass windows of the nearby St. Mary's Church in Bures. The other four manors around Bures were Smallbridge Hall, Overhall, Cornerth Hall, and Sylvester's or Nether Hall, which for a period in the nineteenth and twentieth centuries was wrongly named Bures Hall. The Listed buildings description, however, calls Great Bevills itself 'a fine early sixteenth century manor house.'

Yarmouth from the Continent. In the entrance hall, the centre of the ceiling is occupied by a large rondel enclosing a massive eagle in flight, holding in one claw the chain of the pendant light fitting (originally candelabra? see Plate 154). Both drawing-room and dining-room have extensively decorated ceilings; in the former another, smaller, eagle with out-stretched wings surrounded by rococo ornament, and in the latter a dramatic Aurora ringed by rays and encircled by ribboned branches with little birds and medallion heads representing the Four Ages of Woman (see Plates 155, 156 and 157). The ceiling of the bay window is given over to a pastoral landscape with figures, including a round tower with conical roof and pennant flying, an obelisk, classical ruins, two cottages, a few trees and some pallisading.

From the carriage sweep one sees the screen wall with ball-capped piers hiding the service quarters beneath a superb beech tree, and a very Dutch-looking outbuilding (see Plate 153) with those tumbled-in brick gables familiar in seventeenth century Holland.[1] From the garden side there is a highly unusual orangery (see Plate 151) built as an annexe in the eighteenth century.

One of the difficulties of classifying houses by type is well illustrated at Great Bevills, and points to the changing status of many Suffolk houses. Great Bevills was originally built as a second family house by the Waldegrave family of nearby Smallbridge, who were kinsmen of the present owners, and it continued to be occupied by that family until the first half of the eighteenth century when the last of the Waldegrave family left the area. Subsequently for well over a hundred years the records show that there were many owners of the house, and judging by its appearance it must have become the home of a succession of superior yeomen farmers, with its old barns and outbuildings arranged behind the house just as they are today (see Plate 158). These changes may explain why seventeenth and eighteenth century maps fail to mark the house by actual name, but only with a dot, and it is not until the nineteenth century that the early Ordnance Survey and contemporary tithe maps name both Great Bevills Farm and its near neighbour, Little Bevills Farm. It would also account for the property losing any close identity with one of the five manors which descended from the original two of the Domesday Survey.[2] However, as a family house and a farm it was uncommonly well sited just outside the largish village of Bures St. Mary, with Sudbury only four miles down the road, and within a quarter of a mile of the then navigable River Stour. The place must always have had a comfortable climate, sheltered completely from the cold north and east winds by the hills behind, and facing almost due west over the river.

The original nucleus of the house is contained within the present considerably elongated structure, and was probably a hall-house with a screen-passage entered from about the same position as the present porch. The hall would have occupied

*Plate 158: Great Bevills, Bures. The house and outbuildings from the west.*

the first part of the present drawing-room, and had a parlour beyond with the service quarters taking the place of the present entrance hall and dining-room. The hall was probably built floored over, making this from the outset a two-storey house jettied on the west side; whether there were original gables and cross-wings could probably be established only by painstaking examination of the earliest surviving timber framing. Great Bevills has a special interest in showing that a well built, close-studded timber-framed house can be skilfully extended in exactly the same idiom, whether this be done one, or even three centuries later.

The first build could have been in $1500^{\pm}$ judging from the narrow stud spacing, the late Gothic window heads, trail carvings on the main bressumers and the type of moulding used on other beams, although the star-topped chimneys with their plain octagonal shafts suggest, if anything, that they were of an Elizabethan rather than a Henry VIII date.[1] The exterior detailing of the timbers, with such surviving original features as oriel windows and carved buttress brackets, imply a house of some distinction, as one would expect with its early Waldegrave origins, and they are more reassuring than the interior where so much alteration has occurred in common with many old family houses which have had to be adapted to meet the changing requirements of their occupants. The property could have become neglected in the nineteenth century in the same way as Seckford Hall, and required vision to see what could be done with it. It was the father of the present occupier who had both the vision and the scholarship to develop from this early nucleus such a remarkable extension of 'mediaevalism'.[2] Believing as he did from certain excavation work carried out around the house, that it had originally been substantially longer, he added a bay and cross-wings at the south end of the main range, and built the porch and the adjoining gable and the north and south crow-stepped brick gable ends, just as an earlier owner had done at Flemings Hall, Bedingfield. More chimneys were copied and the original wattle and daub probably replaced by brick-nogging at the same time. Whether all this was strictly desirable from a purist architectural point of view, the resultant house has certainly a considerable attractiveness.

To this brief sketch must now be added a mention of the landscaping of the grounds. The hillside rising behind the house became part of a grassy parkland. In a natural hollow to the south an Italian garden was formed with terraces, steps, urns and statuary. This conjuring up of a Mediterranean atmosphere in Suffolk was immensely helped, and perhaps inspired, by the warm and sheltered lie of the land below the steep hillside above the River Stour, and was much helped by the clever planting of the higher land that surrounds it.

Framsden Hall is one of many old houses on the Tollemache estate and is of manorial origin (see Plate 159). The site lies as high as anywhere in this part of the country and within half a mile of the River Deben to the north, and to the west there is that same stream which rises in the park of Helmingham Hall on its way to

1 Francis Steer, F.S.A., the well-known archivist, believed the house to have been built in the second half of the fifteenth century, although it was substantially altered from time to time after that. This ties in with the first occupant being Sir George Waldegrave who died in 1528. His father, Sir William Waldegrave, died the same year at Smallbridge, so presumably Sir George never moved out of Bevills into Smallbridge.

2 Pevsner used the adjective 'spectacular' for Great Bevills, 'made more spectacular by alterations and additions of circa 1912-20'. *Suffolk,* op. cit. He could reasonably have qualified this by excepting the rather unsympathetic Victorian additions at the rear, facing on to the gardens on the south side.

### *Framsden Hall*
*TM 206 601*

Plate 159: Framsden Hall. View from the north-east

join the river. An earlier hall is thought to have been on the same high land as the present one, and to have been surrounded by the moat of which three sides remain on the east side of the house.[1] The later Framsden Hall was built close to the road going east out of the village, and screened from it by farm buildings like many another Suffolk farmhouse, a great timber-framed and brick-nogged barn being within fifty yards of the front door (see Plate 160).

The building of the present house has been assigned to the Radcliffes in the second half of the fifteenth century, and the conversion to the Elizabethan taste by William Tollemache in the century following.[2] Thus the principal dates of the present house can be put as c.1480 and c.1580, and these seem to be supported by the evidence, although there are more signs of alteration of the earlier structure than of destruction by the later owners.

The Hall structure has been critically examined in recent years[3] and the main facts of the buildings have been established. The particular interest lies in the quality of the original building which was a hall-house of considerable richness, and to which no exact parallel has yet been discovered in Suffolk. The hall was a great height, about 9m (30ft) from floor to apex, and enough remains to justify the tentative sketch reconstruction (see Figure 23). The arrangement of the house was not in itself remarkable, consisting of a hall open to the roof within a central range of about 14m in length and 8m in width (approx. 46ft by 26ft), flanked by a pair of cross-wings. That on the east containing the parlour and solar projects about 2.5m beyond the main range at each end, but the opposite wing containing service rooms only about 1.5m to the south. There have been later additions to the service rooms, and the possibility is that, if any part of the earlier manor was destroyed, it may have been this end of the house: a Hall of such size required more substantial

Plate 160: Framsden Hall. A corner of the great barn.

1 cf. *E.A.M.*, op. cit., No. 6098. The Rev. E. Farrer contributed nine articles on Framsden Hall. He contends that the moat never enclosed the present house but that it completely surrounded the ancient home of the Montalts.
2 cf. *E.A.M.*, op. cit., No. 6116.
3 cf. *English Vernacular Houses* by Eric Mercer, Royal Commission Historical Monuments, first edition, 1975, page 202, and cf. *Framsden Hall* by Peter Hill and David Penrose in The Suffolk Review, 1974, Volume 4, No. 3.

space for catering than is suggested by the original service wing, with its two rooms of dimensions normally required for say a buttery and pantry. The kitchen itself might have been a detached structure. The accommodation at first floor level at both ends of the open hall must have been reached by separate staircases of which the positions have still to be located.

The Hall was entered not by the present front door, but at the extreme opposite end by two entrances at each end of the speer truss, with a pair of doors, giving access to the two separate service rooms, and kitchen, presumably, beyond. There are no traces of chimneys in the first build, and the hall would therefore have been warmed by a fire on an open hearth, probably in the centre near the lower end, for there are traces of smoke blackening in the roof timbers. The upper end would doubtless have had its dais below a projecting canopy of honour of which the construction survives, and the entrance to the parlour could have been at one or other side (the present door at the south end is eligible). The parlour ceiling is still remarkable and it is worth recording Farrer's description before much of it had to be removed: '... It is flat, and by beams and mouldings is separated into eight divisions, and then at every juncture there is a boss, or a portion of such, adjoining the walls and beams, and then others in regular intervening spaces. These bosses are beautifully carved, and consist of acanthus and other foliage, with a pendant in the centre, which is either a rose or a bunch of corn. These latter have now all disappeared, and but few roses are left; and then on the side walls at the base of every supporting beam is a carved face of a man, which from the drapery around the head might well be the representation of a monk. Sometimes the countenance is serious, in others full of mirth.'

Carvings of equal vigour and greater beauty were to be found in the hall itself At the summit of the side walls, at the point of springing of the great cambered tie-beams forming part of the roof trusses, runs a deep cornice consisting of two sections — the upper with deep roll mouldings and the lower with a frieze of angels carrying banners and punctuated by shields (see Plate 98). The type is similar to that of late Perpendicular church roofs, for example St. Mary's, Bury St. Edmunds, where there is a double frieze of angels with outstretched wings, and in the same way as church work these carved members were probably painted. Lower down the wall the main external posts are punctuated at a midway point by carved heads, both human and animal. One of the most striking of the human heads is that of a bearded and crowned monarch (see Plates 99-101).

One of the first changes to be made was the removal of a side wall bay where a full height window had been and, curiously since this was on the north side, the forming of an oriel window. (The head of this window is now visible above the first floor level.) Together with this went the opening of a new door both to the parlour and to the outside. Later Elizabethan alterations were more drastic. A large brick chimney stack about 3.5m long by nearly 2m wide was built in the centre of the hall, which was cut in two horizontally by the introduction of a beamed and joisted floor. The old entrance was suppressed and a new door the opposite end gave into a hall off which a newel stair ascended next to the first floor level. This floor was divided into bed chambers over which new timber-framed ceilings were inserted, providing an attic floor accessible by a corkscrew stair out of one of the rooms in the west wing. The original roof was thus entirely concealed from view, but fortunately has remained largely intact inside the attics, as can be seen from the illustrations (see Plate 161). In the parlour a massive stack was built against the east wall, providing a fireplace both here and in the great chamber above. It was no doubt about this period also that the service quarters were enlarged by the addition of a further two-storey extension of the existing cross-wing. The present staircase in the entrance hall is modern.[1]

The original manor house would doubtless have had its structural timber-frame exposed to view, with the wall filling consisting of wattle and daub. By the seventeenth century, however, the external plastering of timber-framed houses was general, and it may be that Framsden Hall then acquired its present appearance, together with mullion and transom windows and leaded lights which today suggest a characteristic Suffolk farmhouse, albeit of unusual girth and height, and oddly uncharacteristic as to dormer windows.

*Plate 161: Detail of head to speer truss concealed in attics.*

1 The house has been further modernised in recent years, and is still lived in by the Tollemaches.

*Plate 162: Ufford Hall, the south front.*

### Ufford Hall, Fressingfield
*TM 273 746*

*Plate 163: A detail of the Jacobean staircase.*

1 cf. *The Manors of Suffolk* by W.A. Copinger, op. cit., Volume 4, pages 35-37.
2 The surviving moat is deep and about 10.5m wide, with straight sides. The Hall was built about the centre of the island.

The Manor of Ufford Hall is named after Robert de Ufford, who was lord also of Ufford, near Woodbridge.[1] Ufford Hall is one of several isolated manor houses of which other examples within a mile or so are Wingfield Hall, Whittingham Hall and Vales Hall. It is about a quarter of a mile off the road from Dennington to Fressingfield and right on the south boundary between the parishes of Fressingfield and Stradbroke. The site is flat in a heavy clay country, and from the road the old house can be seen across the fields, surrounded with its barns and trees; it is perhaps best glimpsed in summer when the sun is shining on the south front, with its rosy ochre coloured plaster walls and dark tiled roof (see Plate 162). Probably once a fully moated site, what now remains are two substantial arms to east and west (see Figure 63), still tenuously joined along the south side but blocked on the north.[2] The First Edition Ordnance Survey marks other buildings in addition to the house, mainly on the west side, but does not show the farm track that goes south-west from Ufford Hall across the fields to join the nearest by-road.

The Hall has acquired some fame from its connection with the Sancroft family, dating back to the time of Edward I who granted the manor to Robert Sandcroft. It is recorded in the Statutory List as dated 1691, no doubt erroneously. There are many features which suggest that the Hall itself has been standing on its brick base since the early sixteenth century, undergoing many alterations and additions since that time. It is basically a long single range of close on 24m (78-79ft) by 5.5m (18-19ft), with nominal cross-wings at each end barely projecting on the south side, and only one at the back of the house (on the east side the other is prolonged by means of a lean-to). The structure is timber-framed with a steeply pitched roof looking as though it might once have been thatched, although now clay tiled. There is one large axial chimney stack towards the east end of the range, and another clearly added towards the west end of the south front: both chimney heads have been rebuilt and so give few clues as to date, although the base brickwork is clearly of Tudor origin. The windows look rather improbable in their manifest irregularity until it is seen that some are original early sixteenth century mullion and transom type, and others outward opening casements of the seventeenth century or later, which have taken the place of older windows. The most complete and striking of these windows is in the south parlour, with sixteen small mullion lights in a row, above a group of four central casements.

The house is two-storeyed, although originally it must have been an open hall-house with parlours at the east end and service rooms at the west. Access to the first floor at the east end must have been by stairs possibly removed when the

*Figure 63: Ufford Hall, Fressingfield.*

massive chimney stack was built (see Plate 164) and a new staircase formed in the angle of the building next to the east cross-wing. An unusual feature is the semi-basement at the rear of the east wing, with a lesser parlour on mezzanine level reached by independent steps. The new staircase was evidently put in in early Jacobean times (see Plate 163) and it was perhaps at the same period that the hall was floored over and the height of the central range increased by the building of a new roof.

The course of this alteration can be studied in the carpentry both above and below first floor level in the north and south walls, and in the roof construction of seemingly late sixteenth century date where this is exposed above attic floor level. Farrer maintained that the external wall construction was of clay-lump, but I have been unable to check this.[1]

The best moulded woodwork in the house is found, as would be expected, in the parlour, and has not been disturbed since its erection in the late fifteenth or early sixteenth century. The moulded cross beams have carved rib mouldings with leaf stop chamfers. The wainscot and mantlepiece on the west wall of this room were of early Jacobean date around 1620 and seemed to tie in with the staircase and other alterations already mentioned as of that period: unfortunately they were removed upwards of sixty years ago.

*Plate 164: The hall chimney-piece*

**Gedding Hall**
*TL 954 586*

Gedding Hall lies midway between Bury St. Edmunds and Stowmarket, in folded clay country threaded with little streams. The moated site has a logically defensible situation at the summit of ground rising from both east and west and south, where there is an affluent of the River Gipping, joined by water courses from the moat and four conjectural fish ponds lying east of the moat.

There is now no evidence — at least superficially — of the manor said to have been built by de Geddings in 1273, 'quadrangular, of great strength and moated'. What remains today is only the gatehouse, built some two hundred years later, buttressed by an assembly of buildings erected during the ensuing four centuries. It is this miscellaneous congeries which has inherited the name of Gedding Hall, and from these that the gatehouse itself, with its warm orange-brown brickwork, stands out with distinction. The original form, although variously altered, can still be identified. A slightly rustic version of the type of gatehouses being built during the reign of Edward IV (1461-1483), it seems to have been flanked on the west by some form of screen-wall long since dismantled, although of which some remnants remain immediately next to the house. On the east a difference in the detailing of the structure suggests that there may have always been some auxiliary accommodation abutting the gable-end. The gatehouse proper consists of the two customary towers on either side of an arched gateway, with principal chamber

*E.A.M.*, op. cit., No. 3631.

Plate 166: Gedding Hall – *from an engraving in* Excursions through Suffolk.

Plate 165: Gedding Hall – *the gatehouse.*

immediately over (see Plate 165). There were only two storeys, and the walls were finished with battlemented parapets, joined at each end to the base of stepped gables rising steeply to axial chimney stacks. (The original stacks have gone, that on the east being a nineteenth century rebuild unmatched by a very plain job at the opposite end.) If the gateway has not been altered then it was unusually lofty and belies a military purpose. The natural conclusion is that showmanship rather than defence was the object of the builders, although the small spyholes customarily provided in defensive gatehouses overlooking the entrance (and possibly an earlier drawbridge?) were retained. In marked contrast with the large gateway are the groups of narrow windows with arched heads arranged in pairs, and the central four-light window with cusped arched heads. Beneath these there is an unusual brick moulding, consisting of little balls at short regular intervals inset in a deep cavetto: this is a near-replica of the Decorated ball flower moulding found in Gothic work of the fourteenth century and a somewhat unique feature. Unmistakable traces of plaster, both here and elsewhere, suggest that this moulding and the window surrounds and mullions were originally plastered to represent stonework, a device frequently found in Suffolk houses of this period. An interesting contrivance – clearly original – is the pair of angled garderobes discharging at fairly low level into the moat.

The gatehouse had a pitched roof from the outset – also something of an unusual feature – providing an attic storey from which there was doubtless access to a flat roof behind the towers and the parapet. Examination of carpentry in the roof shows quite clearly how the later extensions were added, ending in the two rather clumsy gablets which perch on top of the towers. This may have been done about the same time as the adjoining range with the two Jacobean looking gables which appear in a delightfully romantic view of the house in the *Excursions* (see Plate 166).[1] These features, and the lean-to which then occupied the corner site on the moat were in turn swept away, probably in the late-nineteenth century when the hall became the property of Arthur Wakerley. It was he who in 1897 built the brick tower and the kitchen range at the rear.

*Gipping Lone*
TM 073 643

The historic home of the Tyrell family was remote even in a part of Suffolk where isolated halls are not exceptional. Gipping Hall lay off the road from Old Newton to Mendlesham, in the parish of Gipping, beyond Chapel Green and Farm. In 1860, the Hall was demolished, leaving only an empty space in a meadow to identify where it had once stood. The chapel apart, the only remaining trace of the

1 cf. *Excursions through Suffolk*, op. cit., Volume I, page 174 and facing page.

Tyrells is a house about a half mile further, on an isolated moated site in country singularly bare and open, but whose character in earlier days it is not difficult to imagine from the extensive remains of Gipping Wood.

*Plate 167: Gipping Lone from the south-east showing wings of two periods.*

It is this house which must have been renamed Gipping Lone only comparatively recently, for in the First Edition Ordnance Survey (1837) it was Old Vicarage or Coppings. There are traces of a moat to the east, but whether this was ever a fully moated site or whether earlier dwellings preceeded the now earliest surviving structure, remains unproven. The house is a composite of some three periods (disregarding modern additions) and the exact nature of its relationship with Old Gipping Hall has still to be established. Vicarage it may have been in the fifteenth century and possibly built about the same time as the chapel, as a house for the priest who served the Tyrell family: the earliest structure is compatible with a date around 1483. The circumstances which connect the murder of the Princes in the Tower with the building of the chapel, and the legendary hiding place of Sir James Tyrell in the Old Vicarage, must be left to historians to unravel.[1]

The house consists of two wings, the earlier at right angles to the moat and the later, joined by a simple abutment, making an L-plan (Plate 167). The first wing was a hall-house, with a parlour and solar at the east end, and service quarters to the west. That the hall was not floored over when built can clearly be seen in the large bedroom overhead, where the main tie-beams have been cut and taken out. The central beam spanning the open hall was clearly arch-braced, the mortise sockets remaining in the posts although the braces have been removed: this beam, in turn, could have supported a crown-post. It is difficult to be sure about the heating of the hall; the fireplace may have been where it is now, but I am inclined to think that it was built during the next stage, where the screens-passage had once been (this theory, if correct, would dispose of the alleged hiding place of Sir James Tyrell, which would not have been there until many years later). The second building period could have been in the reign of Henry VIII and would seem, appropriately, to have followed the restitution of all his estates to the son of Sir Thomas Tyrell, who is said to have obtained a special pardon on April 19th, 1507. The style of this second building was altogether more pretentious, and consisted of a two-storey range with a large central chimney stack dividing the ground floor into two large rooms. (This stack divided into four ornamented octagonal shafts above ridge level, and of these the original bases and the moulded brickwork remain, the heads unfortunately having been replaced by a single brick tie.) The house was timber-framed and probably plastered over with the possible exception of the west facing gable, where the timbers may have been originally exposed. This gable, facing the main approach, was ornamented by a richly carved bressumer incorporating the Tyrell coat of arms.

1 Mr. P.J. Turner, F.R.I.B.A. in *The Chapel of St. Nicholas, Gipping, Suffolk* (1931), gives little credence to the tradition of the Chapel being built in expiation of this misdeed, and quotes the Rev. W.H. Sewell, author of *Memoirs of Sir James Tyrell,* who considered after much study that Sir James' connection with the murder is 'utterly unworthy of serious consideration.'

Plate 168: Chimney piece in sixteenth century wing.

Plate 169: Chimney piece in original hall.

It seems most likely that the house was now for the Tyrell family, and that further embellishments were added in late Elizabethan days. These included oak wainscot and overmantels — one carved to display the Tyrell arms — and four rather splendid chimney pieces: óf the pair illustrated (see Plates 168 and 169), the carved stone overmantle in Renaissance style — again incorporating the family coat of arms — is in one of the bedrooms; the second at the south end of the original fifteenth century hall.[1]

Plate 170: Seckford — from a drawing by R. Loder, 1791.

**Seckford Hall**
*TM 253 484*

The house is sited at the upper end of a short deep valley running down to the River Fynn.[2] It is the least ostentatious of any of the sites of great Elizabethan houses in Suffolk, being entirely concealed from view except from the lane immediately north of the house. The land here rises, within about three quarters of a mile, from river level to the 100 foot contour and the house is built in the middle of the valley. In the early sixteenth century the river evidently traversed a marshy area before flowing out into Martlesham Creek, and — George Arnott tells us — 'Crossing the Finn was the sedgeford or Seckford, whence the name of Woodbridge's benefactor is derived'.[3] The first Ordnance Survey (1796-1805) confirms the existence of a drive, joining the main road from Ipswich to Woodbridge about a quarter of a mile above the Finn bridge, and going due north up the side of the valley. There is some suggestion of this drive entering an

1 It is not inconceivable that some of these chimney pieces came out of Gipping Hall and were refixed here during the last century.
2 This is the spelling on the 2½ inch Ordnance Survey, but George Arnott spells it 'Finn' in his *Suffolk Estuary*, and says the name is older than that of Deben, and means 'clear waters', (cf. page 104).
3 Ibid., page 104.

*Plate 171: Seckford Hall – south doorway.*  *Plate 172: Gazebo north of the Hall.*

enclosure which contained both the present lake and a forecourt on the south side of the house. Seckford Hall was evidently planned for entry from both north and south, and Robert Loder's drawing of 1791 suggests a grassed court crossed by a path to the north door (see Plate 170). Important visitors would, doubtless, be travelling to the Hall from Ipswich, and would use the southern approach, arriving in the courtyard between the wings of a mainly E-plan house. There they would be greeted by a modestly ornate centre-piece in which the Seckford coat of arms is displayed over the doorway (see Plate 171). All this would be thoroughly compatible with the fashionable way of approaching an important early Tudor house.

The ground plan (see Figure 64) shows a long central range balanced by wings at each end. There is little evidence to support the theory that the north porch originally projected and that the space between porch and cross-wings was filled in afterwards. Careful examination of brickwork shows that the same brick was used in the central range as in the gable-ends of the cross-wings, and there is no trace of irregular bonding where the two meet. During the rebuilding of the east wing in 1968-69, it was found that this wing had never been completed, although one can reasonably assume that the original 'platt' would have shown two balancing wings. The extent of the west wing was identified during the construction of 1975-6, and corresponded with the elevation shown in Robert Loder's engraving of 1791. The angle buttress was at a distance of some 32 feet from the corresponding buttress of the central gable. Returning to the middle range, the main entrances north and south were axial, and the disposition of rooms followed the mediaeval sequence of parlour/great hall/screens-passage/pantry/buttery and service rooms. The unusual feature is the extra space north of the fireplace wall in the great hall, inviting comparison with Hengrave Hall, where rooms also appear in this position. The difference is in the position of the staircases. At Seckford Hall the arched opening at the upper end of the hall was intended for the main staircase, and Arthur Welford postulated 'a sort of Pavilion with ogival metal roof and weathervane'.[1] This would have been balanced by a similar tower off the service quarters. Opposite the staircase arch in the great hall was an interesting alcove providing 'a kind of Solar or Lord's Room'; it was perhaps nearest to what today we would call a study. The fascination of the Seckford Hall elevations — apart from their mellow brick charm — must lie in the transitional character of details. The crow-stepped gables with their neat, small steps and flanking buttresses topped with bulbous pinnacles, hark back to Perpendicular Gothic, and the fantastically high octagonal chimneys with star tops to the ebullient brickwork of Henry VIII. The label-moulds of the window-heads in the central range suggest that this part of the house preceeded the building of the cross-wings — which turns out to be the case — for the latter adopt oddly proportioned pediments (which were often copied in the neighbourhood).

1 I am indebted to papers on Seckford Hall prepared by the late Arthur Welford, A.R.I.B.A., F.S.A., for this information, now held in the Seckford Library at Woodbridge. I have referred elsewhere to the probable appearance of the design originally intended.

181

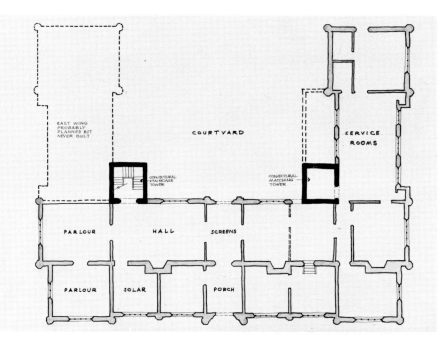

*Figure 64: Ground Plan of Seckford Hall*

The centre-piece of the south elevation is incomplete, lacking features above the level of the first floor window.

It is to 'Thomas the Settler' that most authorities attribute the building of the Seckford Hall of today. Lilian Redstone contributed a notable monograph on *The Seckfords of Seckford Hall,*[1] and Arthur Welford on the Hall building. It is difficult to disagree with his date of c.1550, or to disprove that an earlier timber-framed Hall was incorporated in the present structure. This older Hall is known to have existed until 1541. The new Hall was incomplete at the death of Thomas Seckford in 1588, but work on the west and east wings was carried on under Charles Seckford, his nephew who inherited it. It is said that the east wing remained unfinished owing to the untimely death of Charles Seckford at the age of 42. If it was occupied in an unfinished state is conjectural, although there is evidence suggesting that the roofed-in portion was destroyed some time between 1818 and 1855.

Interesting survivals of sixteenth century building works are the boundary walls and the so-called gazebo adjoining the Great Bealings/Woodbridge road (see Plate 172). The walls indicate the way in which the surroundings of a great Tudor house were architecturally separated into courtyards, orchards, gardens (see Plate 173), and so on. We are looking at brick garden walls built about the same time as the house. Compare, for instance, the bricklayers' X marks which appear on the moulded bull-nose bricks in an arched opening in the garden wall, with the main north door and the archway in the south wall of the great hall. The best general description of the Hall after the alienation by Seckford Gage in September 1709 is in a booklet written by Michael S. Bunn.[2] Mr. Bunn describes how the Hall was rescued from demolition when purchased in May 1940 by Sir Ralph Harwood, and the methods used in importing fittings and furniture from a wide provenance.

1 Two members of the Redstone family contributed to the history of the Seckfords: V.B. Redstone in *The Seckford Family and Seckford Hall* published in Proceedings S.I.A., Volume IX, page 359, and Lilian J. Redstone in *The Seckfords of Seckford Hall,* now in the Seckford Collection at the County Library, Woodbridge.
2 *A Short History of Seckford Hall and the Seckford Family,* available at Seckford Hall Hotel.

*Plate 173: View from the lake*          Lance Cooper

*Plate 174: Great Finborough Hall —*
*after a drawing by H. Davy, 1826.*

**Great Finborough Hall**
TM 015 581

In spite of many changes to the architecture of the house, Great Finborough Hall still occupies what has been described as one of the most delightful situations in the county. Lying to the south of Stowmarket, about two miles due west of Combs Ford, the house dominates a hillside which marks the end of a long stretch of high country. To north and east the parkland falls gently away to a small river valley. Behind the house lie church and village. In his delightful drawing, Davy well conveys the atmosphere of this new Hall built in the 1820s (see Plate 174).

*Plate 175: The stable building.*

*Plate 176: The south elevation from the garden.*

*Plate 177: The Hall after an engraving by T. Higham, 1818.*

The Manor was granted by Elizabeth I to Henry Gilbert, and there is an ornamental carved bressumer in the stables with the initials 'H.G.' The ground plan of the house, which was burnt down in 1795, suggests a seventeenth century house rather than the rebuilding of an Elizabethan one. Certainly the east gable of the stable block can be dated to about mid-seventeenth century both by design and brickwork. It is one of the few original 'Dutch' gables in Suffolk correctly coped with stonework in the Dutch manner. The rest of the stables seem to have been rebuilt, probably in the early nineteenth century, although the octagonal bell turret has a thoroughly Stuart look (see Plate 175).

The new house built by Roger Pettiward made a complete break with the past. He called in Francis Sandys, who may have been installed already in Bury St. Edmunds in 1795, having been brought over from Ireland by Lord Bristol, Bishop of Derry, to oversee the building of his new mansion at Ickworth.[1] They chose a new site about twenty five yards further north, and Sandys designed the small 'mansion' seen in Davy's drawing. It can still be recognised today (see Plate 176) — if overshadowed by the massive additions of Victorian and later owners. The plan was simple enough: a hollow square with semi-circular bays to entrance front (N) and garden site (S). The staircase hall occupied a central well which went right up through the house, with the principal rooms opening off. On the west was an orangery and probably a service annexe. There was a touch of Ickworth in the idea of a central stairwell, and some ingenuity in turning the top of the square hall into an octagonal dome, handsomely coffered and lit by a ring of window lights. (The looped theme in the glazing bars was a Sandys favourite, and occurs again in the staircase balustrade at Worlingham Hall.) This makes for a light interior in which the plain plastered walls set off to advantage the broad reeded architraves and *bas-reliefs* over door openings.

Externally it was a white brick house, plain but dignified. In Davy's drawing there is no trace of the odd stucco ornamentation round the south-east windows, which, together with massive moulded stone architraves surrounding both windows and doors, must be Victorian additions. The same is probably true of the semi-circular portico with its stone podium, steps and six Tuscan columns outside the front entrance. This is not to be seen in T. Higham's small engraving in Volume I of *Excursions* (1818), in which both north and south bows are to be seen as rather plain and simple, and the house has the air of a small classical pavilion at the summit of the park (see Plate 177). In spite of later alterations and additions there is much for students of Francis Sandys' work, both outside and in. The great modillion cornice (with 3ft overhang), which was such an important feature in the original design, has never been touched, nor have the shallow slated roofs, or the dome. The staircase hall also remains unspoilt, with its original cast-iron balustrade design and classical details. The gardens south of the house are beautifully maintained, and a statue and urns still remain, as does a charming garden house at the end of the orangery.[2] Half hidden by the later additions, the Pettiwards' noble coat of arms can be discovered at the east end of the garden house with its profoundly Christian motto *Crux Christi Lux Coeli.*

1 Possibly later in 1795, but certainly in early 1796, Sandys was in Italy, for he is recorded in *The Faringdon Diary* as having left Rome the beginning of April, and is now employed, as he says, 'in beginning to build a Palace at Ickworth for Lord Bristol', cf. Colvin's *Biographical Dictionary of English Architects*, 1959, page 526.
2 The garden house looks like Francis Sandys' work, or, if not, is close to his style and echoes the modillion cornice of the main house. His orangery seems to have been removed and replaced by the present design when the house was enlarged.

*Haughley Park*
*TM 004 619*

Hodskinson, in his map of 1783, draws Woolpit Wood very boldly, but 'Hawleigh Park' is much less distinct; there is his conventional symbol for a country lane, but the position of the drive does not agree with that of the first printing of the Ordnance Survey (Old Series — 1837). The drive in 1783 is faintly shown as going in a more or less straight line due north-east from the house and crossing the Bury road at the 10 mile point, continuing by the present lane straight into Wetherden village. This would have given an axial approach from the nearest village to the Hall much more in character with the Tudor style of the house. (Compare, for example, Helmingham Hall; Thwaite Hall; Nettlestead Hall and Badley Hall — all shown on the same Sheet VIII of Hodskinson's map.) By 1837, it is reasonable to suppose, the north end of the house had been remodelled in the Georgian taste with its bow windows and sashes and, doubtless, the enclosure formed with the long lawn and shrubberies. (It would be nice to connect this with the nine years of wedded life spent here by Sir George Jerningham after his marriage with Frances Sulyard — 1800-1809.[1])

Plate 178: Haughley Park, after an engraving in The Excursions, *1818*.

Plate 179: H. Davy's drawing of 1827.

The house is built almost, but not quite, at the highest point of the land hereabouts. The position was well chosen for aspect and prominence, and the large building in dark red brick can be clearly seen, framed by its trees, from Haughley New Street on the way west from Stowmarket. The entrance front faces slightly south of east and certainly observes the dictates of Robert Ryece in his Breviary of c.1602 that houses be built '... where they may be furthest seen, have best prospects, sweetest air and greatest pleasure ...' Sir John Sulyard could equally have remembered the advice of the influential Elizabethan physician, Dr. Andrew Boord: in a book of maxims on building published in 1549, that learned doctor recommended the chief prospects of a house to be east and west, and the site elevated. The probability is that Sir John preferred the easterly aspect and deliberately built the house where the land slopes gently down to the valley of the River Gipping, and afforded a considerable view over the countryside towards Stowmarket and beyond.

Once it has been established that Sir John Sulyard the second was the builder of Haughley Park, in c.1625, the comparatively sophisticated plan becomes more acceptable than at the hitherto suggested date of c.1554-1574. The original plan form (see Figure 30) was basically an H-plan, although the south-east porch projecting midway between the cross-wings has given rise to the idea that the house was an E-plan. The H-shape was, as Professor Summerson says,[2] easily one of the most popular types of Jacobean house, and Haughley Park has not been so altered that it is impossible to see the original plan. The story is one of an approximate return in recent times to something nearer the first house. This was based upon Elizabethan house plans of the second half of the sixteenth century, but with noticeable differences. There was a dining room next to the hall, which was already merely a large vestibule with a bay window reminiscent of the oriel: there was no

1 Information supplied by Norman Scarfe for inclusion in *The History of Haughley Park*. He has supplied valuable evidence that Haughley Park was built c.1625.
2 cf. *Architecture in Great Britain 1530-1830*, on page 44 Professor Summerson calls it 'the standard plan of the Jacobean period'.

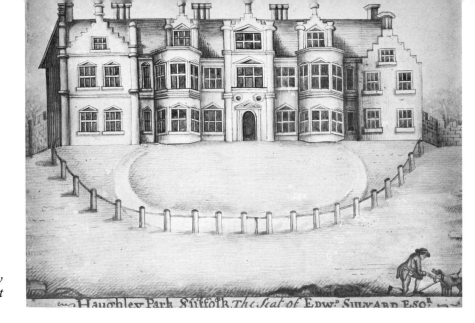

*Figure 65: Haughley Park in an early eighteenth century drawing – artist unknown.*

Haughley Park Suffolk. The Seat of Edwᵈ Sulyard Esqʳ

dais and probably never a screens-passage. Meals would be eaten in the dining room, served from the kitchen close by, with service quarters beyond. One crossed the hall to reach the family living rooms, and beyond the hall was a passage leading to the main staircase within its own well. The eighteenth century house plan is already there in embryo. During this century, or early in the following one, the dining room fireplace was taken out and turned into a doorway, a passage put in across the back of the dining room (doubtless to avoid domestic staff going through it on the way to answering the front door) and a pantry and cloakroom added between the rear wings. At the same time the family north wing was drastically remodelled. These changes can either have been made under the last of the Sulyards or, more probably I think, soon after Sir George Jerningham married Frances Sulyard. There is an engraving in *The Excursions,* based upon 'A drawing by Lady Jerningham'[1] which is careful to add one of the rounded bays on the north of the house (see Plate 178). This was published in 1818, but the Jerninghams had left by 1809, and thus these alterations were certainly done beforehand, and possibly in the early 1800s. There is every likelihood that the chimney stack serving the kitchen and the 'Justice Room' over was originally balanced by one opposite, on the north wing. When the 'Smoking-Room' and drawing-room were made, chimneys on the north wall were taken down, and the openings thus formed converted into bow windows. With these bright new additions, there were no scruples in blocking up all the windows on three floors in the east gable facing the drive, to put a chimney stack in their place. A balancing stack was added at the west end to provide a new chimney piece in the drawing-room.[2] All the mullion and transom windows in the east gable end are, therefore, dummies.

The high peaked dormers with their decorative finish which appeared along the top of each bay window on the east side of the house (see Figure 65) must have been taken down soon after the Jerninghams left, for they are conspicuously absent in Davy's drawing of 1827 (see Plate 179).[3] The altogether remarkable thing about the Haughley Park elevations of 1620 (see Plate 33) is their appearance of being so far behind the times. The tall pinch-waisted porch has proportions like that at Thomas Seckford's Woodbridge Abbey, built in 1564, and is topped with similar moulded brick pinnacles. The immensely tall octagonal chimneys with star tops appear at Seckford Hall of c.1550, as indeed do the pediments, mullion and transom windows, and the narrow stepped gables. By 1621 the so-called 'Dutch gable' had appeared in Suffolk at Mockbeggars Hall, Claydon, and a year or so later Hemingstone Hall had been remodelled in the Dutch style (c.1625). The five-sided bay windows suggest a certain Jacobean 'modernism', although the bay window as such is a standard feature of Elizabethan houses. Five-sided bay windows appear in plans and elevations in the Thorpe Collection, and provided splendid opportunities for the lavish display of glass as at Hardwicke Hall. They are amongst the graceful architectural features of Haughley Park. Only a certain innate conservatism of taste can, perhaps, explain the attachment of a Sulyard to the architectural fashions of an age two generations earlier.

1 cf. *Excursions through Suffolk,* Volume 1, facing page 168.
2 These very early nineteenth century looking chimneys are prominent at the right hand side of Davy's drawing of 'Hawleigh Park', published in 1827.
3 They were restored in the rebuilding of 1961-4.

186

## Thurston Hall, Hawkedon
TL 794 518

The same tributary streams that flow to join the River Glem, one through Wickhambrook and Denston villages and the other past Giffords Hall, Wickhambrook, pass just north of Thurston Hall, linking a distinguished company of manor houses, to name only Denston Hall, Hawkedon Hall and Boxted Hall within a matter of a few miles. Thurston Hall itself is one of a group of three in the tiny hamlet of Thurston End, of which the other two are Swans Hall and Hungriff Hall. The site, in a narrow valley, is some 50 feet above stream level in a country where the land rises steeply to uplands, and has a certain comfortable seclusion which seems reflected in the long gabled elevations with their silver grey timber framework and rose pink brick-noggings.

*Plate 180: Thurston Hall, view from south-east across part of the moat.*

The manor appears in Copinger under the alternative names of Thurstanton and Thursturston.[1] Farm it was by origin, and farm it has remained in spite of its manorial status, having the look of an originally fully moated site. The waterways can be followed alongside the minor roads on the south and east by which the site is enclosed, but on the north they are dry and overgrown. The impression is of a small island, moated to protect house and outbuildings, but this needs archaeological confirmation. The approach from the by-road to Hawkedon village passes the front of the house and from that point a track went due north-east towards Somerton and Hartest; both forded the stream in the valley.

The house consists of a long three-storey range with gable-ends facing south-east (see Plate 180) and north-west, of some 26m by 7.5m (84ft by 24ft 6in.) with a

1 cf. *The Manors of Suffolk*, op. cit., Volume 5, pages 245-249. Claude Morley has an interesting comment on the name: 'Thurstanestuna' of 1086 in Risbridge Hundred is correctly Thurstan's Farm, which is mangled into Thurstruston-hall and -end by Faden's 1783 map, and now telescoped into Thurston by the Ordnance; quite distinct from Thurston village.

*Plate 181: Early sixteenth-century chimney stack.*

*Plate 182: Carved bressumer over porch entrance.*

*Plate 183: General view of Thurston Hall from the south-east.*

cross-wing at the north-west end, the front entrance side having a three-storey porch and two gabled-bays: the third storey consists of attic space within the large roof (see Plates 183 and 184). The ground floor arrangement has at least one unusual feature. The entrance was originally by a door in the present position, which would, one supposes, have given on to a screens-passage with service accommodation to the left, and an upper end with parlour beyond at the opposite end of the hall. This is not the case now although the bay arrangement of the hall ceiling seems to include a passage. Farrer described this ceiling thus '. . . It is divided into three portions, by two very huge beams moulded and with stops; these beams going from the front to the back of the house. The centre portion is again divided up, also into three parts, by two similar beams, running from east to west'. South-east beyond the hall there is a way through to two rooms and a staircase; north-west the hall opens with a single way leading to another staircase and a single larger room, with service rooms in the rear of the cross-wing. Now on planning grounds alone one suspects alterations and not a first build. In a post-mediaeval house the entrance left on entry could be to a dining-room (e.g. Haughley Park) with service quarters beyond, but was more likely to have been direct to the pantry, buttery and kitchen. That was clearly never the case here, and taken in conjunction with detailing of the timber-framed ceilings quite different to the rest of the house, suggests that there may be some truth in Farrer's argument for alteration. These first three bays would belong to an earlier small manor house, dated at late fifteenth century, comprising the original parlour, the remainder being taken down (materials doubtless reused), followed by the building of a new hall nearly 12m long by rather more than 7m wide (approx. 39ft by 23ft 6in.) with new parlour beyond and next to this a staircase and way to service area. A small new room was built between the new hall and old parlour, with a staircase behind. This could be called the second stage build, and had provided a rather larger than usual amount of accommodation clear of the service quarters, which were at the rear of the cross-wing. The hall chimney stack dates from this period and points to a date c.1530-40; it is a magnificent affair some 2.5m wide at base and 12m high 'tumbled-in' in successive setbacks to a square summit on which are set four tall ornamental shafts in moulded brick above a diamond-pattern frieze (see Plate 181). The rear two shafts with their plain heads are the work of another bricklayer probably in the next century.

The third stage would be that dated by the carved bressumer on the porch entrance as 1607 (see Plate 182): there is little doubt that the porch is of later date than the previous structure for the cutting away of the structural timber-framed wall to form an opening internally into this. It would not be reasonable to accept this date as being contemporary with this detail, and no doubt other fairly considerable alterations were carried out at the same time on a change of ownership.[1] Farrer gives the devolution through the Everard family until the death of Ambrose Everard in 1595, when the old house had changed little from early Tudor times. If this can be accepted then it would make Richard Everard, Ambrose's elder son, responsible for the early Jacobean alterations, a young man whose wife was the daughter of John Laney of Ipswich and whose brother-in-law was Chaplain to the King. The work attributable to this period would include, beside the building of the porch, the replacement of the old stairs by the present balustraded staircase with its heavy urn-shaped newels, which goes up in six flights from ground floor to attic; the conversion of the kitchen into great parlour, and the panelling out of sundry rooms with wainscot.

The hall was substantially restored in the 1920s, when some of the carved woodwork, inside and out, was imported, the roof retiled and the ornamental barge-boards added.

*Plate 184: Thurston Hall: the south gable-end.*

**Huntingfield Hall**
*TM 342 743*

Huntingfield Old Hall is recorded as having been pulled down by Sir Joshua Vanneck after his purchase of the Heveningham Hall Estate in 1752. The Old Hall — if a contemporary drawing (see Plate 185) can be trusted — was a fortified dwelling with a three-storied gatehouse, castellated and having two angle turrets: within the walls were buildings forming at least two courtyards.[2] The drawing makes it clear that the old fortified manor house was on a sloping site with woods beyond, in just the same way as the present Hall.

*Plate 185: Huntingfield Old Hall from a contemporary drawing.*

1 Basil Oliver, F.R.I.B.A., in *Old Houses and Village Buildings in East Anglia*, op. cit., page 12, incorrectly took 1607 as the date of the building.
2 According to 'A.H.', author of the guide book *Huntingfield and its Church of St. Mary*, Michael de la Pole had been allowed to castellate the house by Edward III, putting the date of building into the fourteenth century or earlier.

Sir Joshua's farmhouse had – perhaps consciously – a hint of the earlier building in its design. The plan is L-shaped, the principal main range being the shorter and facing south-east towards Heveningham Hall, and the secondary range enclosed by a courtyard which is prolonged by a dairy and outbuildings. It was a model eighteenth century farmhouse, with the owner's accommodation at the south end and the stock at the north, easily accessible from within, and probably architect-designed. Sir Joshua Vanneck could even have designed it himself, with the help of Sir Robert Taylor, then retained for plans of the new Heveningham Hall. The sole problem is that of the principal elevation and the question – whether this was refronted by James Wyatt during the course of his Heveningham work when Sir Gerard had succeeded his father.

*Plate 186: Huntingfield Hall: The Wyatt front.*

Structural evidence points to two different periods of work at Huntingfield Hall, notably in a change of brickwork between the principal facade and the flanks of the front range. The front uses English bond and the flanks the then customary Flemish bond, a difference unlikely to have occurred in a single build. Furthermore the design and detailing of the front range is quite unlike the rest; in comparison with the routine handling of the sides it is a piece of surprising whimsy. Anthony Dale,[1] who described it as a 'rudimentary essay' in Wyatt's Lee Priory Gothic manner, calls it 'charming in its complete unreality'. The effect was, however, doubtless carefully calculated as a *trompe l'oeil* from the windows of Heveningham Hall, from which it would then have been visible – together with Valley Farm. This would explain both the newly fashioned Gothic style together with the altogether remarkable height of the front (see Plate 186), the parapet rising some ten feet or so above the level of the roof within, like some propped-up piece of stage scenery.

### Kentwell Hall, Long Melford
*TL 864 479*

The two Halls of Long Melford have entirely dissimilar sites. Melford Hall, built next to an affluent of the River Stour, forms part of that hierarchical group of church, almshouses and manor house surrounding the great Green which marks the end of the near mile long village street. Kentwell Hall, three quarters of a mile north of the church, is in upland country secluded from any but a near view (see Plate 187).[2] Both properties had belonged to the Abbots of Bury St. Edmunds, but the Kentwell estate seems to have passed into secular ownership in the thirteenth century,[3] and then, by marriage, to the Clopton family during the following century. The circumstances, which resulted in the building of Kentwell Hall, have still to be established in detail. There was an earlier house called Lutons or 'Kentwell' which may have been built outside a moated site that could date from the thirteenth century, and which might have contained an earlier manor house fallen into disrepair.[4] That would account for Kentwell Hall being within a moated site

1 cf. *James Wyatt* by Anthony Dale (1956. Oxford: Blackwell), page 211. The dates are given as 1776-1784.
2 The house is on the edge of the 250ft contour, and some of the highest ground hereabouts.
3 cf. S. Tymms, Proceedings S.I.A., Volume II. 19, pages 59-72.
4 Purely a hypothesis since, as Mr. Patrick Phillips says, no traces of any earlier house have been found there. It was P.G.M. Dickinson who attributed many of the Suffolk moats to the thirteenth century in the Introduction to his *Suffolk* in The Little Guide series (first edition. 1957), page 34.

*Plate 187: Kentwell Hall after an engraving in* The Excursions, *1818.*

which, in the 1550s, was scarcely likely to have been made by Sir William Clopton, the builder of the new mansion. It would have been entirely compatible with the period for the remains of an ancient hall to have been removed and a new house put up in its place. Building would have been going on c.1540-1550, whilst the family continued to live at Lutons, and was completed before the death of Sir William in 1562, for his mother's will, dated December 1st, 1563, mentions the 'new Mansion-house of Kentwell Hall'. Some time after that Lutons was probably pulled down.

Structural evidence points to the building of the new Hall in stages. The site — whether or not it had contained a dwelling — was certainly occupied on the west by a timber-framed barn, of which the basic date still has to be decided. This is the building now known as the Moat House (see Plate 188). The new Hall was sited immediately adjoining this in the western half of the island, in the form of a single range hall-house. As at Redgrave, where the hall was building in the period 1515-54, and at Melford Hall (c.1545-1554), the great hall was floored over to give a suite of bed chambers below roof level: unlike these, Kentwell does not seem to have been designed originally as an E-plan or courtyard house, in spite of the proximity of Melford Hall and Hengrave Hall. It is this circumstance which makes Kentwell unusual amongst Suffolk Tudor houses, and lends an added interest to the building, which only developed into the conventional E-plan of Elizabethan country houses by the addition, first, of the west wing and then, subsequently, of that on the east. The brickwork is fairly consistent between the centre of the west

*Plate 188: The Moat House at Kentwell Hall.*  *East Anglian Daily Times*

191

ranges, being multi-coloured and average 9in. by 4-4½in. by 2¼-2½in. (roughly corresponding to the Statute brick of 1571 which was 9in. by 4½in. by 2¼in.); and this is one factor suggesting that the west range followed fairly closely on the first build.[1] At that stage the accommodation evidently comprised, in the central range (from east to west), parlour, great hall, dining-room, staircase and service rooms, with access across a passage way to the earlier barn then serving as a brew-house. On the first floor the main solar, known as the state bedroom, was over the parlour, with a minstrel's gallery on about the same level at the west end of the great hall. Above this at higher level were the further bed chambers. The plan of the west wing suggests that more accommodation was needed for guests, and that this was provided on two floors with garderobes built out on the west side discharging into the moat. The east wing was the last main addition and built in a delightful two-inch brick with an orange red body, which clearly came from another kiln (with a conservative brickmaker still making the early Tudor long, narrow type); the accommodation seems to have consisted of two large rooms on each floor and a staircase hall. The present stairs are Jacobean of the seventeenth century, and said to have been introduced here during the remodelling of this wing c.1820, some six years before the fire which destroyed much of the interior of the central range.

The house, as it stands today, presents substantially the same face to moat and gardens as it did to the elder branch of the family whose dwelling it became after the death of Sir William Clopton and to their successors – the D'Ewes and D'Arcys. It was to Thomas Robinson, who followed the latter, that Kentwell Hall owes the three quarter mile long avenue of limes planted in 1678, leading from the north of Long Melford Green to the bridge over the moat. Earlier generations had approached the Hall from the east, for the main approach came off the Bury road in that almost straight line shown on the First Edition of the Ordnance Survey, and the near view of the house must have looked much as it does today from the same vantage points.

The stone gateway previously mentioned (see Plate 189) is the most tangible evidence to survive of the Wentworth connection with Nettlestead Hall, which ceased in 1645.[2] The remaining evidence lies in the site itself and what remains of a once considerable Tudor establishment incorporated in the house which today is known as Nettlestead Chace.

*The Nettlestead Halls –*
*1. Nettlestead Chace (formerly*
*Nettlestead Hall)*
*TM 089 493*

1 A clue as to the possible source of bricks is given by 'Kiln Farm' and 'Kiln Wood' about a mile north of the Hall.
2 cf. Copinger, *The Manors of Suffolk,* op. cit., Volume 2, pages 326-336.

Plate 189: Wentworth Gateway at Nettlestead Chace, after a drawing by H. Davy, 1824.

Plate 190: The Gateway as it now exists.

**Dexter Shield**

**on the Gateway of Nettlestead Hall.**

**Sinister Shield**

**on the Gateway of Nettlestead Hall.**

1. WENTWORTH.    2. DESPENSER.    3. CLARE.    4. GOUSHILL.    5. POYNTON.
6. OYRY.    7. TIBETOT.    8. BADLESMERE.    9. FORTESCUE.    10. STONOR.
11. NEVILL.    12. MONTAGU.    13. MONTHERMER.    14. HOLLAND.    15. TIBETOT.
16. DE LA POLE.    17. INGLETHORPE.    18. BRADSTON.    19. KIRKBY.    20. HARNEHALL.

1. WENTWORTH.    2. DESPENSER.    3. GOUSHILL.    4. TIBETOT.    5. BADLESMERE.
6. HOWARD.    7. TYRRELL.    8. HELION.    9. NORTOFT.    10. SWYNBURNE.
11. GERNON.    12. BOTETOURT.    13. ROLFE.    14. PARIS.    15. HAMOND.

*Figure 66.*

*Chace* is a now obsolete form of 'chase'.
In *The Suffolk Garland* of 1813, there is an article
by Mrs. F.J. Cobbold on *The Lily of Nettlestead*, in
which she writes '. . . till these few years past a very
considerable portion of the Old Hall was remaining
its pristine state'.

The site is one of that group of some hundred isolated Suffolk churches with nearby Halls, and here the Church of St. Mary is about two hundred yards from the house and near a small lake which could have been a Tudor fishpond and was known in the early nineteenth century as 'The Canal'. The First Edition Ordnance Survey (first printed 1837-40) showed a 'Parsonage' between the church and house. The Hall demesne, in its sheltered valley, lay along a small tributary flowing east to join the River Gipping. It was reached from the north by a lane between Somersham and Nettlestead, and from the south-east by an avenue from near Little Blakenham. Of the exact whereabouts of the one-time deer park — which has given the property its name of Nettlestead Chace[1] — there seems to be no record. Both the site and maps, however, show that the original Hall was at the south-east end of a roughly square enclosure which conjecturally would still have been surrounded by a wall in which was set the stone gateway that still exists (see Plate 190).

In 1824 Henry Davy drew, etched and published a drawing of the gateway but in the ensuing 150 years the condition of the stonework has sadly deteriorated, and the coats of arms in the spandrils are now illegible. The dexter shield contained twenty quarterings and the sinister shield fifteen, some of which are repeated in both shields (see Figure 66).

Of the Wentworth house there now remains insufficient evidence to decide its original form with any certainty. In Davy's drawing the only sign of Tudor work is in the base and part of the ornamental shaft of a chimney stack built into one of later date. This suggests a popular chimney design of the reign of Henry VIII, and could tally with the acquisition of the manor by the Wentworths during that reign.

The remains of a wing of the Wentworth house are evidently incorporated in the south range of the present house, where oak framework and Tudor brickwork are visible. Taking into account the period, and the formal approaches from two sides, the possibility is that the Wentworth house was of U-form with axial entrances on both sides of a central range, in just the same way that both the house shown by Davy and that which is there today have exactly symmetrical central doorways. The modern house in Davy's drawing could have been built where the main range of the original Hall was demolished, and only one of the two south wings retained as a service annexe.[2]

193

## 2. High Hall, Nettlestead
TM 087 503

*Plate 191: High Hall, Nettlestead, view from the south-west.*

## Otley Hall
TM 205 563

1 Pevsner, op. cit., says that 'High House' is Elizabethan 'and clearly only a fragment'. I cannot find evidence to support this assertion. He comments on irregularities in the porch with its two orders of Tuscan pilasters and missing top with which I concur.
2 The house may have been built for a Wm. Foorthe, Forthe or Forth, around 1600 (1590-1620) who lived in Nettlestead at the time, and whose father has a memorial slab behind the organ in Hadleigh Church. I am indebted to the present owner for this information which remains to be verified.
3 'One of the most interesting fifteenth century and early sixteenth century houses in Suffolk' is how Pevsner describe it. cf. *Suffolk,* op. cit., (Second Edition) page 386.
4 *The Manors of Suffolk* by W.A. Copinger, op. cit., Volume 3, pages 83-85.

On the highest point of land hereabouts (225ft contour) the small Elizabethan High Hall is well-named. It has already been mentioned as one of that congeries of halls occupying the highlands between Somersham and Stowmarket, which include Badley, Baylham and Tarston Halls, and the lane off which it is built does, in fact, turn into a farm track which continues across the fields to divide and link up with both the Halls of Baylham and Tarston. High Hall lies about midway between the prosperous cloth weaving towns of Hadleigh and Needham Market, and the surmise that it was built — or rebuilt — by a well-to-do clothier would seem entirely appropriate.

In the absence of the guide lines so often given by a knowledge of the devolution of the property through its various ownerships (so well illustrated in the case of No. 109 High Street, Needham Market — see Section 3), it remains to establish the historical clues revealed by the structure. The same preference for height with steeply pitched roofs can be seen here as at Baylham Hall, and there are certain similarities in the detailing of the mullion and transom windows.

The house of today consists of a pair of parallel three-storey ranges which are most apparent from the north-east aspect.[1] Linked to this is a two-storey service wing, the upper part of which was designed by the well-known Suffolk church architect, Munro Cautley, and added on in 1929/30. The double range has the appearance of contemporary work of early seventeenth century character, but on closer examination there are certain perplexing irregularities. The hipped roofs with gablets are highly uncharacteristic of Jacobean or earlier work in Suffolk, as, indeed, is the way in which the eaves of these roofs cut across the window heads on the north-east elevation. At the period in question brick gable-ends are to be expected, either crow-stepped or in the 'Dutch' style: here two timber-framed and plastered gables appear on the south-west elevation, one being converted into a gablet by a hipped lean-to roof. Similarly, on the north-east elevation two timber-framed and plastered gablets appear above hipped lean-to roofs: this elevation, instead of presenting the two symmetrical halves to be expected in an original build of this date, consists of two unequal bays with five-light mullion and transom windows on one side contrasting with four-light on the other. The placing of the pair of chimney stacks, with their triple octagonal shafts, is also curiously unlike an original build and suggests that they were fitted into an existing structure.

Taken together these, and other features peculiar in a first build of this period, strongly suggest that here is a timber-framed hall of the Elizabethan period, acquired by a well-to-do new owner in the early seventeenth century and extensively remodelled.[2] The original frame would have been largely bricked-in (except the gables already referred to) and extended by new work — thus accounting for the elevational irregularities, the chimneys added, and the old staircase taken out, to be replaced by the new well staircase of seven flights with its newel posts and turned balusters. The old house would have been further embellished internally by wainscot, of which one fully panelled room of the early Jacobean remains, four-centred arched fireplace openings and arcaded overmantels, again of which one is still there. The outside plank door on the south-west side, secured to its panelled framing with iron studs, would probably belong to the older house, as would a number of other doors internally.

Otley Hall is one of many moated manors in a clay country in which houses are sited on high ground, as witness the halls at Framsden, Helmingham, Ashbocking, as also Thistleton Hall, Clopton, now demolished. It is one of the relatively few houses in Suffolk listed as Grade I and is generally accepted as the important development of a late mediaeval building (see Plate 192).[3] This degree of importance, however, has only been recognised in the present century.

The earliest ownership is traced to the reign of Richard I, and the commencement of the Gosnold connection — with which Otley Hall is chiefly connected — to c.1454, when the manor was vested in John Gosnold, son of Robert Gosnold of Otley.[4] Copinger attributes much of the work in the house to Robert Gosnold, during the years of his ownership, 1470-1555. The Gosnolds seem to have lived here for about 260 years, the manor passing to the Rebow family in 1702.

The house, although still fairly extensive, is probably part only of an originally much larger dwelling, and it is worth searching Farrer's notes for the situation in

Plate 192: Otley Hall, east side beyond the moat.

the early 1900s. The quadrangular moat, within which the house had evidently been first built, remained only on the east with short returns westwards, as today, and as Farrer could see no traces of recent infilling, he concluded that this must have happened many years previously. His further supposition, that there was originally a range on the west of the central block, similar to that still existing on the east was pure – if not unreasonable – conjecture; the truth of this might be proved by excavation, although a timber-framed house can vanish leaving few, if any, traces. A house on these lines would have produced an H-plan, with entrance in the central range facing north. Evidently the doorway on the north side was then in use, for Farrer described it as approached by a wide path through a garden, 'which path was lined with tall shrubs', and was evidently entered from the by-road immediately north of the property. There remains the possibility of a still earlier approach, of a less cottagey kind, suggested by the First Edition Ordnance Survey for which the first field survey was completed between 1816 and c.1820 (although not published until 1837-1840). This clearly shows, by a double row of dots, the remains of an avenue nearly reaching the cross-roads in the middle of Otley village (the same convention for showing an avenue occurs elsewhere, e.g. Crows Hall, Debenham). This would have been more appropriate for a manor of the importance of the Gosnold family house, and is the sort of approach to be expected in the sixteenth and seventeenth centuries: it would have led to a courtyard – assuming the H-plan – between the wings. Farrer affirms that the present entrance was the work of Mrs. A. Sherston and was made by removing a newel staircase, turning the space into a hall with doorway, and forming a new drive in from the south. The stairs 'case' thus converted has obvious similarity to that of High House, Otley, and could well be contemporary, and, like the towering brick chimney stack, a mid-late sixteenth century addition to the earlier range.

Plate 193: A detail of close studwork at Otley Hall.

The plaster had already been stripped from the central fifteenth century range at the time of which Farrer writes, revealing the close-studded framework with jettied first floor, pair of eight-light mullion and transom windows, with intermediate lights at high and – originally – low-level. The carpentry, with its carved bressumer, delicately detailed arched brackets, ribbon windows and first floor oriels anticipates the Lavenham Guild Hall, and marks an important stage in the development of a recognisable Suffolk design idiom (see Plate 193). The house would have extended westwards with service quarters, the jetty continued and possibly a balancing gable, an early example of the two-storey house which was completely to replace the old open-hall plan. The interior was fitted up with a richness of wainscot and carved beam work (see Plates 194 and 195).

At the beginning of this century, also, the ground floor of the sixteenth century east wing was still open to the forecourt, and known as 'The Plahouse'. Supported on timber columns, with the overhanging first floor above, it provided a kind of cloister in which, traditionally, cock-fighting took place and later, games of bowls were played.[1]

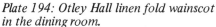

Plate 194: Otley Hall linen fold wainscot in the dining room.     Plate 195: Otley Hall, dining room chimney-piece and wainscot.

### Loudham Hall, Pettistree
*TM 308 542*

It does not often happen that a map and a drawing of a house are virtually contemporary, but this is the case with Loudham Hall; Hodskinson's map was published in 1783 and Isaac Johnson of Woodbridge drew the house in 1789 (see Plate 196). Both give useful witness to changes that have since taken place. In the late eighteenth century, Loudham Park reached to within a half mile of Ufford Mill and to the marshland bordering the River Deben; the main entrance to the drive was at 'Campsey Meer', and, after passing the front of the Hall, a back drive led to Ufford Church and village. This must be the roadway crossing the foreground of Johnson's drawing, in which Loudham Hall conveys the look of an aristocratic farmhouse, with a yard and outbuildings on one side and grazing cattle on the other – garden privacy being secured by a high brick wall.[2] At that date Sir William Chapman was in residence, and it can only have been some thirty to forty years since the house was rebuilt in the Palladian style.

The exterior transformation from an Elizabethan to a symmetrical classical mansion was more thoroughly done at Loudham Hall than it had been at Little Glemham Hall (c.1717) or Hintlesham Hall (c.1720). The rebuilding of the house kept largely to the original E-plan, reusing much of the old structure, and the only serious departure from symmetry was on the east where a five-bay wing projected in an asymmetrical and unclassical way from the side elevation. The general principle of the remodelling was to brick round the external walls and form the new door and window openings where they were wanted. Less immediately noticeable changes took place, however, in relation to room heights and window heights. The ridge level of the cross-wings in the Johnson drawing must have been about those of

1 *E.A.M.,* op. cit., Nos. 7863 and 7875.
2 The drive between Loudham Hall and Ufford village is said to have been a 'church road', enabling dwellers in Campsey Ashe to reach the nearest church subsequently to the demolition of Loudham Church (or Chapel).

*Plate 196: Loudham Hall, after a drawing by Isaac Johnson, 1789.*

*Plate 197: Loudham Hall, the south front today.*

the earlier house, but the roof could have been raised over the whole centre range to provide more impressive room heights. These changes were masked as far as possible by parapets, that of the centre being dropped at each end to meet those of the wings which were raised to meet them and given blind window openings for effect.

The inside of the house equally must have been radically altered, the original hall being turned into an entrance vestibule with dining-room on one side and drawing-room on the other, but a new staircase probably where the old one had been. The new stairs ascended to a mezzanine level corresponding with the original, and continuing to a gallery which ran the whole length of the first floor. It is tempting to see this as part of the Elizabethan house but, as the centre range was likely to have been of one-room depth between the cross-wings with a single-pitched roof, the matter is not so easily settled. The new roof plan was a hollow rectangle consisting of parallel ranges hipped into cross-wing roofs, surrounding a central lead flat. The service quarters must have been in the west cross-wing, and after the alterations remained in much the same place.

In the opinion of historians, the house was altered by Charles Wood, great nephew of Sir Henry Wood who was the owner of Loudham Hall at the latter end of the reign of Charles I and, according to Evelyn's Diary, 'an odd person' but extremely wealthy.[1] The rebuilding of the Elizabethan Hall would have started soon after 1730, and the exterior remains entirely in the early Georgian form which it was then given. The only exceptions to this are the later remodelling of the twin wings to the main front, and the alteration of four sash windows.[2] A comparison of the house today with Isaac Johnson's drawing shows how the single-bay projection of the wings was reduced to a break forward of about two brick widths (see Plate 197). The former sash windows were refixed in the new elevation, but not at a

1 cf. *E.A.M.*, No. 6395.
2 The central doorcase with its pair of Ionic pilasters and curved pedimented head is – *pace* Pevsner – identical with that shown in Isaac Johnson's drawing of 1789. (See Plate 198.)

Plate 198: The centre-piece with door-case, Loudham Hall.

Plate 199: Entrance hall at Loudham.

lower level as formerly, being now continuous with the remainder of the windows. The only other window changes must have been made at the same time, when larger sashes with narrower glazing bars replaced those of the dining-room and the first two bays of the drawing-room, and the number on the side elevation next to the wings was reduced from five to three. In the rebuilding the rather heavy brick quoins were completely omitted. The changes were probably all contemporary with the remodelling of the entrance hall which then received its screen of Corinthian columns and pair of apses (see Plates 199), and fireplaces in the Adam style appeared in the drawing and dining-rooms, and taken together suggest a date of 1790 or thereabouts.

The result of these later alterations has been to give subtly different characters to the front and — notably — the east elevations of Loudham Hall. Unified by the same pleasant rosy red brickwork the front has a certain classical sophistication, whilst the east still keeps that rather endearing early Georgian simplicity which appears so clearly in Isaac Johnson's drawing (see Plate 200).

Plate 200: Loudham Hall from the east.

### Preston Hall, Preston St. Mary
*TL 947 503*

The Hall holds the pre-eminent place in the small and scattered village of Preston St. Mary, a little way south of the church and separated from it by a stretch of water which is all that remains of a once moated site. Traditionally associated with the seventeenth century antiquary Robert Ryece and author of *Suffolk in the Seventeenth Century* — the so-called Suffolk Breviary (see General Bibliography), Farrer nevertheless came to the conclusion that the Ryece family owned two houses in Preston but neither of them Preston Hall.[1]

The manor house, backed by fine old trees, is tranquilly sited at the end of a grassy avenue of some hundred yards, open to the Lavenham road going south from Preston village (see Plate 201). The plan is principally of irregular cross-wing form, the central range having a considerably more extended wing on the east side. Structurally the house is timber-framed with closely spaced studs and a marked absence of tension bracing, the carpentry of the walls being fully exposed and not, as a late sixteenth century date might suggest, plaster covered. This slight sense of discrepancy is emphasised by the *croisonné* mullion and transom windows, which

1 Rev. Edmund Farrer was at some trouble to distinguish the whereabouts of the moat. In *E.A.M.* 5394 he wrote: 'the house faces west . ... though a great deal of the moat which once encompassed it has disappeared. On the south side some certain evidences of it remain. On the east side it is still there, but a mere ditch; on the north side there is a wide pond between the house and the church, and alongside the road westwards from which the house is approached the ground has been levelled, and there are no signs of there ever having been a moat at all.'

Plate 201: Preston Hall: view from the avenue.

*Plate 203: Star topped chimney stack.*

*Plate 204: Seventeenth century staircase.*

*Plate 205: Preston Hall — chimney-piece in entrance hall.*

1 Copinger says that Preston Hall in the reign of James I and Charles I was the seat of the great antiquary, cf., *The Manors of Suffolk*, Volume I. pages 183-187. See also *Robert Ryece of Preston, 1556-1638* by C.G. Harlow, M.A., B. Litt., in Proceedings S.I.A. Volume XXXII, 1971, pages 43-70.

were evidently remodelled in the early-mid seventeenth century, and, furthermore, by the hipped roof ends to the cross-wings. Pending more detailed examination of the roof structure, appearances suggest that this hipping back of the roof may not be contemporary with the first build, but, together with symmetrical refenestration and plastering — since removed — was the work of an owner wishing to give the hall a more 'classical' and less Elizabethan appearance in the century following (see Plate 202).

Given this supposition, the appearance of two impressive clusters of brick chimney shafts becomes more comprehensible, since they associate quite logically with the original timber framework, and were evidently an integral part of that first build. The hall stack is the most elaborate of the pair, consisting of four octagonal shafts with moulded bases and star tops, set upon a square podium of brickwork in the front of which, above the main entrance, is an inset panel containing moulded tiles conjoined to form a pattern of diagonal rosettes below a cornice of brick dentils — an oddly classical contrivance below such Gothic-looking chimneys. The

*Plate 202: Preston Hall: house from the south west.*

workmanship is that of a master bricklayer, and culminates in the ornate stellar caps at each angle of which protrudes a terracotta spike, or ray (see Plate 203). The rear range stack has six grouped octagonal shafts with plainly moulded caps, and an identical inset panel facing east (the tile module being five in length on the four-shaft, and eight in length on the six-shaft panel).

The house is considered to have been built on the site of an earlier hall,[1] and it is worth considering the changes in house design that had taken place when Preston Hall was erected in c.1575. The Hall was no longer open to the roof, but floored over and warmed by a comfortable open fireplace (see Plate 205), beyond this room, already much reduced in size from the older halls, lay the great parlour (now drawing-room) in the north wing with fireplace backing on to part of the hall; at the opposite end and in the east range, the lesser parlour, dining-room, staircase and service rooms. Each of the principal rooms, as well as kitchen, had its own fireplace. The staircase is not contemporary with the first build but would belong, I judge, to those seventeenth century modifications already mentioned (see Plate 204). From about this period also would date the square wainscot pattern in the bedroom of the south-east range. It could really be said that the subsequent English country house of medium size is largely there in embryo at Preston Hall.

## Shelley Hall

TM 027 381

The interest of its site, history and fragmental structure call for the inclusion of Shelley Hall in a book on Suffolk houses (see Plates 206 and 207). Bordering the water meadows beside the River Brett, it was built only slightly above flood level and immediately west of a square moat which could easily have been the site of an earlier building. Sir Philip Tylney is said to have bought the Shelley estate in 1523 and rebuilt the hall on a new site. This would date the earliest portions of the present house as c.1523-30, and would be compatible with the design of the north porch. The siting of the porch is evidently linked by a roadway skirting the edge of the water meadows with the church some 500 yards away. These are twin certainties in an otherwise somewhat obscure situation, establishing the functional relationship of church with manor house.[1]

Plate 206: Shelley Hall: Tudor and Edwardian work on east side.

Plate 207: A general view of the east side from the garden.

Of the house plan itself, there is the suggestion of a T-form, porch entering screens-passage with hall in the east and parlour (the present drawing-room) to the west, the staircase behind the parlour, and the service quarters extending in a single range beyond. By no means an orthodox late mediaeval plan, it is reminiscent of Baylham Hall (mid sixteenth century). The wing at the extreme south may have been a barn or store in the first build and only later brought into use with the house. The third generation Tylney, Philip — who is said to have entertained his kinswoman Queen Elizabeth I at Shelley Hall, August 11th, 1561 — could have added the massive triple shafted chimney stack with its moulded bases, plain shafts and spiky star-shaped tops at the south side of the hall (now dining-room, see Plate 209). Edmund Farrer compared the changes that had taken place in the years between his first visit — 1900 or earlier — and his last visit in 1923, when the house had been completely modernised. The infilling south of the porch of a one bay addition has the look of Edwardian work, and there are new chimneys and other alterations which suggest that about that time the old Hall was converted, as Farrer said, into a comfortable farmhouse. Before that date, however, and probably in the late eighteenth or early nineteenth century, the drawing-room had been remodelled in the Adam taste, and other works done in the principal living-rooms.

The ancient assets consist now mainly in delightful details. The brick porch is one, formerly open to east and west (leaving in question the treatment of the side facing towards the avenue), with the main entrance from the east. The doorway with deeply indented moulding has a four-centred arched-head flanked by polygonal buttresses, each with three tiers of arcading all in moulded brickwork.

1 cf. *E.A.M.*, No. 6980: Rev. Edmund Farrer adds that the small estate of Shelley did not often receive a visit from its medieval lords, the Tattershalls, Caillys and Cliftons, and quotes E.F. Davy writing in 1828 of heavy flooding five years earlier.

*Opposite: Giffords Hall, Stoke-by-Nayland. The Gatehouse front*

*Plate 208: Tylney coat of arms.*

*Plate 209: Shelley Hall — the dining-room.*

*Plate 210: Giffords Hall: view from remains of chapel.*

### Giffords Hall, Stoke-by-Nayland
*TM 019 375*

1 Rev. E. Farrer mentions one at Barnham Broom Hall in Norfolk, and 'an elaborate example at the foot of the great eighteenth century staircase at Bower Hall in Essex'. *E.A.M.*, No. 6988, April-June, 1925.
2 In the light of the Indenture of 1459, the evidence of local brickworks is of much interest. Within the Giffords Hall estate there is still a site known as 'Kiln Field', and just over the boundary of the parish of Stoke-by-Nayland the Ordnance Survey of 1838 shows 'Brick Kiln Wood' in the adjoining parish of Shelley. There can be no proof that these kilns were there in the mid-fifteenth century, but they give more credibility to the manufacture of bricks in the parish of Shelley by Paul Frankrik and Henry Goodman.

with cusped trefoil heads, very ecclesiastical and remarkably similar to the sixteenth century gatehouse at Leiston Abbey (see Plate 82). The buttresses may have terminated in ornamental finials in some conjecturally parapeted profile, and above the main doorway would doubtless have been the Tylney coat of arms (see Plate 208), the space for which was apparently bricked over when the superb carved stone panel was fixed on the end wall of the drawing-room facing the drive. The staircase is the original, a newel stair ascending in a brick 'case' with mullion and transom window light, and still possessing the dog-gate — a feature which I have come across nowhere else in Suffolk[1] (see Plate 119).

The life of the house must always have centred in the courtyard on the west of the Hall, where the stables and outbuildings were screened from the approach and entered through a gateway in a high brick wall. The development of the gardens may have continued since the seventeenth century, for it would have been about the turn of that century that the wall was built to screen small yards and outbuildings on the east of the house. It is from this side in mid-summer, with the moat beyond and the high herbaceous borders in the foreground, that the jumbled walls and chimney stacks of Shelley Hall are seen to their best and most picturesque advantage.

The present approach to Giffords Hall from Withermarsh Green seems to be of considerable antiquity, and — if Hodskinson's cartography can be accepted — there was in 1783 the same long, straight avenue from the Green to the Hall that exists today. He draws a double line of trees and, at the end of it, a miniature sketch of the entrance front, with its twin towers flanking the central gatehouse. The drawing emphasises more effectively than contour lines how Giffords Hall was built on a knoll some 100 yards above the River Brett, flowing past it to the east. One can see the favoured position of the property, protected by woods and rising ground to the north and on a sunny spur above the waters of Box, Brett and Stour; remote — as it still is — from the busy thoroughfare that leads from the London road through Stoke-by-Nayland and on to Sudbury, but within easy distance of larger centres. It is a site which seems especially appropriate to the tenacious struggles of the Mannock family to retain the Old Faith (see Plate 210).

Giffords Hall has too extensive a bibliography to need recapitulation. The problem of the irregular courtyard (see Figure 67) has already been touched on, and the reassessment of some hitherto accepted building dates, in the light of the recently found Contract for supply of bricks dated 1459.[2] An aspect of one of the chief features of the Hall — the carvings of the double hammer-beam roof — was fully revealed for the first time in 1974: with the erection of scaffolding for redecoration of the plaster ceiling, it became possible to take detail photographs of each of the carved spandrils. The astonishing richness and variety of ornamentation was then apparent, as well as the possibility of giving the roof a more exact date on stylistic grounds (see Plate 211).

The roof was designed to cover a hall space measuring approximately 34ft by

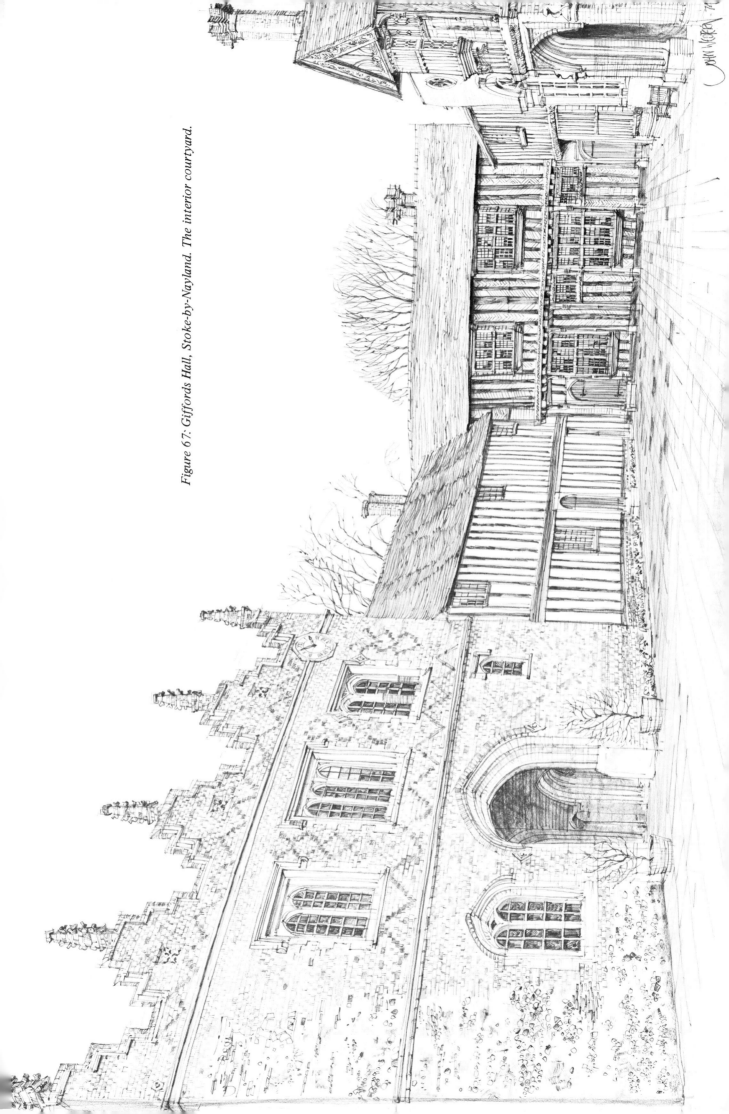

*Figure 67: Giffords Hall, Stoke-by-Nayland. The interior courtyard.*

*Plate 211: Giffords Hall, Stoke-by-Nayland: details of spandril carvings from great hall roof.*

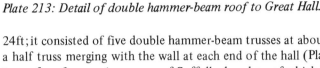

*Plate 213: Detail of double hammer-beam roof to Great Hall.*

24ft; it consisted of five double hammer-beam trusses at about 7ft 6in. centres, with a half truss merging with the wall at each end of the hall (Plates 212 and 213). This type of roof occurs in a group of Suffolk churches, of which Woolpit, Grundisburgh and Bacton are examples, and are illustrated in Munro Cautley's *Suffolk Churches*.[1] Cautley showed how the hammer-beam is essentially the sole-piece (timber laid across the top of the wall), projected into the church, with the wall-post and bracket tenoned into the underside: 'This arrangement transmitted any outward thrust on the roof plate to a lower position in the wall, made rigid the foot of the truss and reduced the span of the arch-bracing by allowing it to spring from the extremity of the hammer-beam.[2] There can be little doubt that the Mannocks employed experienced church craftsmen, and the similarity is striking. The use of the spandril piece — that broadly triangular section between the curvature of a shallow arch, the tie-beam and the vertical post — for a variety of carved *motifs,* was well exploited, and a conspicuous example is in the Needham Market church roof. At Giffords Hall, in addition to much Gothic foliage, there are many intriguing domestic objects: musical instruments, notably harp, lute, bell, and an early form of fiddle; chalices, or what Avray Tipping called 'covered cups',[3] parts of wooden wheels with spokes; bellows; flagon, mortar and pestle; a fish on a platter and a mouse entering a pitcher. There is also a crown, and what might be a sword belt, or arrow shafts, a singularly beautiful thistle and a pomegranate. It would be easy to point to the significance of many of these as Christian emblems, and this would not be in appropriate, in view of the strong attachment of the Mannock family to the Catholic faith.

The style and type of carving and ornamentation suggest work of c.1480-1500, and puts the Giffords Hall roof in the first rank of Gothic craftsmanship in Suffolk houses.

The head waters of the River Black Bourn rise somewhere near Walsham-le-Willows, and the stream flows through the middle of Stowlangtoft Park, about two miles south-east of Ixworth. It is typical heavy-land country, green and lush with dense woodlands, and the earlier hall builders sited their houses within about 200 yards of the river.[4] In 1783 there was a sizeable Green quite close to the house, which was then on the south side of the water and known as Stow Hall. This is clearly shown on Hodskinson's map, and Sir W. Rawlinson's name is written across the parks.[5] About a half mile north of the house, on the edge of Langham Thicks (then much more extensive) was shown the 'Brick Kiln',[6] Some forty six years later this house was still in existence, but the Green or common land had evidently been enclosed; in its place on the side nearest the house appeared a large sheet of ornamental water. Perhaps this was one of the further 'additional improvements' made by Sir Walter Rawlinson on inheriting the property. Twenty two years after the publication of the First Ordnance Survey, the house had finally disappeared. Its place was taken by an entirely new Hall built in 1859 upon the opposite side of the river.

The new Hall was built eight years after the Great Exhibition, and one might detect a tribute to Sir Joseph Paxton in the rather large conservatory with its vaulted glass roof sitting prominently on the south terrace. The principal influence

### Stowlangtoft Hall
TL 963 689

1 cf. *Suffolk Churches,* (first edition), pages 9, 97, 109.
2 Ibid., page 105.
3 *English Homes,* op. cit., Period II, Volume I, page 48.
4 There are likely to have been previous 'Halls' on a site of which the ownership can be traced to c.1200.
5 About the time Hodskinson was surveying, the older part of the first Hall must have been pulled down; we have this on the authority of F. Shoberl (*Suffolk,* 1813), who adds that in 1782, Sir Walter Rawlinson made great 'additional improvements'.
6 There are two historical references to bricks on the Stowlangtoft property: a) Amongst the Harleian MSS exists an agreement between Paul D'Ewes and George Peche, bricklayer, as to the building of STOW HALL in 1625. b) In the same collection is an original declaration of September, 1638, made by Robert Mallie of Stowlangtoft respecting the digging of clay for making bricks and tiles on STOW-digging, and that the dissolved Abbey of Ixworth never made any claim to Stow-digging, and that it was part and parcel of Stowlangtoft Manor.

Plate 214: Stowlangtoft Hall – entrance porch and tower.

Plate 215: The domed conservatory and house.

Plate 216: A detail of the stable buildings, Stowlangtoft Hall.

was, of course, that of Sir Charles Barry, who had already started a school of design in the Italian palazzo style nearly thirty years before, and who was then the most fashionable architect of the day. In 1854 – only five years before the building of Stowlangtoft Hall – Barry had been working on the remodelling of the house and gardens at Shrubland Park. Henry Wilson's aims were probably less ambitious, and his tastes more conservative: his rather ponderous country house was saved from utter dullness by the three-storey tower in the Florentine style, the domed conservatory (see Plate 215) and – perhaps unintentionally – the slightly bizarre stable buildings with their mixture of tall Gothic roofs and Italian features (see Plate 216). Approaching from the west, the drive led to a forecourt dominated by tower and porch (see Plate 214). It could be seen that the principal accommodation was contained within a symmetrical H-plan, good use being made of the Soane device of a deep recess above a porch. The porch led through a lobby into a large open hall, containing the main staircase and a showy marble mantelpiece (one of several in the Adam style). There followed a suite of principal rooms, study, library, drawing-room and dining-room where metropolitan plasterers – doubtless – had been brought down to do an ornamental ceiling in the rococo style. A covered way led to the conservatory, and this served to conceal the domestic offices from the south terrace. A separate block contained the kitchens and service quarters which, with various annexes, straggled out to the stable buildings. White brick was used for facing the whole house complex, red bricks appearing only in garden walls and in the outbuildings, and a hard oolitic stone for the decorative details. The amount of decorative work was limited. There was a balustrade theme appearing above the porch forming the skyline of the main block – since the roofs were flat – and at the head of the tower; there was a porch, with rather stodgy Roman Doric columns and heavy entablature. There was also the tower – the sole *folie de grandeur,* since it performed no useful purpose except, perhaps, housing the water storage tanks. Above an empty niche, the second tier of the tower displayed a carved stone panel with the armorial bearings of Henry Wilson: the next tier, above a heavy cornice, contained the open loggia with a pair of Ionic columns *in antis,* and a blind arch filled in with ornamental tiles and surmounted by a massive keystone.

The only other decorative concession was in the cambered segmental arches over the windows, where the absence of glazing bars – except, oddly, in the lower part only of those on the ground floor – contributed to that helplessly blank look of Victorian double-hung sash windows. The feeling that this large house has reached the end of an era is increased by dilapidated stonework, and the minimal maintenance of outbuildings and grounds. It was built, after all, well over a hundred years ago – a monument of mid-Victorian wealth and fashionable taste – and calls desperately for the *va et vien* of country house life; the elegantly costumed ladies and gentlemen strolling on the terrace; the gatherings of local landowners and country folk for the weekend shoots; bezique in the drawing-room and the candle-lit mahogany dining table.

Today the Hall is a house for the elderly.

*Plate 217: Crowe Hall, Stutton: view from the south west.*

### Crowe Hall, Stutton
TM 153 343

Mediaeval Englishmen built their houses with scant regard for orientation or outlook, being more preoccupied with defence than amenity. If this be so, then that group of Halls on the north bank of the River Stour, built to face south across the estuary, suggests the changing attitude of Tudor builders. From Brantham to Erwarton there is a succession of sites as enviable today as they evidently were in the sixteenth century: Brantham Hall, Stutton Hall, Crepping Hall, Crowe Hall, Erwarton Hall — not forgetting the Parsonage at Stutton, which must have one of the most beautiful river prospects of south Suffolk.

Crowe Hall is one of six manors in the parish of Stutton. The view of local historians that the Latimer building was early Elizabethan is, from the evidence of timber framework and an ornamental plaster ceiling closely matching one at Stutton Hall, likely to be correct. If plans prepared in 1824 can be taken as reasonably accurate, the earlier house was L-form, the main range running east and west with a wing at the western end running south in the direction of the river. The entrance was in the present position and could have led through a screens-passage into a hall with fireplace on the south wall, and two rooms beyond the upper end — possibly a lesser parlour in the main range, and a greater parlour in the south wing. The service rooms were on the east of the screens, with the kitchen occupying part of the present dining-room.

There is a strong possibility that the original house was extended in the late seventeenth century, and it could be at this period that the wing of the L was built — or remodelled. Two circumstances which point to this are, first, the unusually rich and elaborate moulded plaster ceiling in the great bed chamber at the south first-floor end of this wing, and, secondly, a nearby double-hung sash window of c.1700. It has been suggested that the same craftsman who was engaged on the plasterwork in William Sparrowe's house in the Buttermarket, Ipswich, might have been employed here. The problem would then be of reconciling a difference in dates of some fifteen to twenty years — perhaps no very formidable difficulty.

Within two years of acquisition George Reade had commissioned a local architect, Mr. Richard Beales of Lawford, Essex, to prepare plans for the complete transformation of the house in the Gothic style. These plans still exist and show the various alternatives submitted by Mr. Beales in the years 1823-4. Assuming the plans to have been agreed before the end of 1824, the work was in hand, if incomplete, on September 28th, 1825, when George Reade died prematurely at the age of 49. The possibility is, therefore, that the final stages of the work were carried out under John Page Reade, to whom the property then passed, and who lived until 1880.

The project was as sweeping as the then fashion for romantic mediaevalism, with the main feature a new two-storey bow ended wing having a lofty first floor drawing-room above a low basement. This wing was thrown out riverwards on the axis of the principal entrance and linked to the two existing wings by new extensions, from one of which emerged a battlemented turret (see Plate 217). The old Tudor and later walls were either rebuilt in brickwork, refronted in timber and plaster or simply plastered over, for nothing but a completely stucco appearance was allowed, even in chimney stacks. Buttresses proliferated, and there was one at every angle with the finial designs varying in succession around the building. Mr. Beales liked arcaded porches for in addition to the one which he designed as the main entrance from the north, he had proposed another for the west elevation which — perhaps luckily — was never built. Internally, the only changes of any consequence that have since taken place were the turning of the drawing-room and billiard-room into a single long living-room,[1] when the former breakfast-room was converted for billiards by adding a bow windowed end. The dining-room is unaltered and, as a former writer said, '. . . Claret coloured wallpaper, mahogany furniture, heavy cut glass and Victorian portraits complete the picture of a perfect and untouched early nineteenth century dining-room (see Plate 218).[2] Both ends of the room are curved, and, flanking the entrance are a pair of contemporary mahogany sideboards made by Maples of London, of which the receipted invoices are still held. It would be interesting to know the name of the plasterers responsible for the elaborately ribbed and fan vaulted ceiling in the drawing-room; the workmanship would have been extremely sophisticated for a local firm. The drawing-room possesses also all its original fittings; door frame in moulded plaster dated 1826, and fine chimney piece with cast-iron interior and basket grate, all in Perpendicular Gothic detailing; wall mirrors and an enormous ebony coloured *chiffonier*. A french casement at the south end opens on to the roof of the porch below, and from this vantage point can be seen the long silver ribbon of the Stour beyond the green meadows sloping down from the house. In bright sunlight, with its finials, battlements, and turret waiting only upon the floating of a baronial standard, the house suggests the passion of early nineteenth century builders for settings in the style of the Scott novels. On a misty autumnal day the impression is confirmed (see Plate 219).

*Plate 218: Crowe Hall: the dining-room.*

1 A stone chimney piece with moulded arch, of early seventeenth century date, has lately been uncovered in the former billiard-room.
2 cf. *Crowe Hall, Stutton,* by R.G.N. Country Life. Volume CXXII, pages 1434-5.

*Plate 219: Crowe Hall — the north side seen from entrance gateway.*

**Stutton Hall**
*TM 141 337*

In 1818 — or thereabouts — T. Higham made a captivating sketch for the *Excursions* (see Plate 220)[1] and so presented later topographers with a valuable record of the Hall before it was considerably enlarged at the turn of that century. The roof alone appears above the brick boundary wall but can plainly be seen as belonging to a house of moderately short range with a single cross-wing at the east end: three groups of ornamental chimney stacks — each with four shafts — break the skyline, suggesting work of Henry VII or VIII periods. The whole centre of the sketch is occupied by the walled enclosure with its battlemented top, decorative Tudor finials (octagonal buttresses with crocketted ogee tops) and extremely odd little gateway with four tall pinnacles clustered like candy sticks, stepped gable on the outside and semi-circular pediment inside. Away beyond the east corner of the wall, is the line of the distant River Stour reappearing again on the extreme west, and giving a very fair if somewhat romanticised version of the site. The artist conveyed sympathetically — and probably faithfully — the impression of a once stately home fallen to the lot of a remote riverside farmhouse.[2]

*Plate 220: Stutton Hall: after an engraving by T. Higham in* The Excursions, *1818.*

In order to reconstruct the house in the sixteenth century it is necessary to align the north gateway with an axial avenue (said to have been planted with oaks) from the Brantham road, the first requisite of an important Tudor gentleman's house being a stately approach. The History of the Manor also mentions '. . . some very fine oak and other trees extending from the house to the river.' Those who arrived at the gateway were evidently expected to dismount, for the opening was only of a size for pedestrians, their horses and equipage being led off to stables lying west of the house (see Plate 76). It is difficult to believe that there was not a formal entrance, beyond the gateway, into the great hall, which occupied the centre of the main range and was warmed by the large fireplace on the south wall. East lay the parlours in the cross-wing, and between this and the hall the newel staircase occupied its own projection on the south also. West lay the service quarters, the last of the three great chimney stacks presumably serving the kitchens. On the first floor were the bed chambers, for this was not the traditional great hall ascending into open roof, but a more modern Tudor house with continuous first floor. The present drawing-room will have been the great — or principal — bed chamber.

In the late nineteenth century, a bay was first demolished beyond the third stack and a new west cross-wing built with south oriel window under a massive gable overhang. In 1912 a further wing was added to the west and new fourth and fifth chimney stacks built, copying the original three (see Plate 221). During these alterations and additions, the earlier timber-framed and plastered structure was completely enclosed with brickwork, and there is a photograph taken in 1885 from the south side, showing what the old hall looked like, with its splendid brick chimneys abutting the plastered walls.

1 *Excursions in the County of Suffolk,* op. cit., 1818, facing page 150.
2 William White, in his *Gazeteer,* op. cit., ed. 1855, page 230, referred to it as '. . . now a farmhouse belonging to J. Tollemache Esq. . . .' The manor belonged to the Tollemache family from late eighteenth century until acquired by J.O. Fison Esq. at the sale 100 years later.

*Plate 221: Stutton Hall: general view from the south.*

Inside the house, the features that survived the modernisation were, mainly, a room over the hall wainscotted in contemporary chestnut or walnut with grotesque carving, the staircase, fireplaces and plasterwork. Some of the best plasterwork was in the great bed chamber – now the drawing-room – where there is a six-bay ceiling, each having beautiful interlacing rib work stemming from a central dropped pendant, with floral bosses and individual rosettes (see Plate 222). The beams are enclosed with finely moulded plasterwork and round the perimeter runs an elegant geometrical frieze. Outside, it is the original brickwork, in garden walls, buttresses, finials and ornamental chimney stacks which offers an invaluable contribution to the history of Tudor brickwork in Suffolk. There is a strong possibility that the brickearth was excavated and kilned locally, on account of the well-known existence of brickearth at Stutton Ness.[1]

1 cf. *The Stutton Brickearth, Suffolk* by H.E.P. Spencer, F.G.S., in Proceedings of the Geologists Association, Volume 64, Part I, 1953, pages 25-28.

*Plate 222: A detail of the drawing-room – formerly great bed chamber.*

## Chilton Hall, near Sudbury
TL 888 427

The road to Great Waldingfield climbs steeply out of riverside Sudbury to high clay-lands, where moats were plentiful. Two hundred feet above the town lies the Hall, a quarter mile off the highway at the end of a straight avenue. Originally within its own park there were (before the fire c.1800 which, as it seems, destroyed much of the Hall) no identifiable outbuildings.[1] A track leads further south to the even more remote parish church, with only an isolated rectory at some distance in the fields beyond.

Chilton Hall belongs to a class of manor houses which were originally intended as domestic strongholds surrounded by broad deeply-cut moats. The moat here was nearly a square of some 21.5m (70ft), with a width of about 9m (10 yds) containing an island site connected only at the south with the surrounding land by a triple-arched brick bridge (if the light modern footbridge spanning the moat on the east side be disregarded). To the approach from the north the house presented a flank wall of stark brickwork broken only by a single string course, and windows indicating a three storied house (see Plate 223). None of these are the original, but the size and position can be seen quite clearly where they have been blocked in, showing that the upper floor had large windows. A four-bay range of this castle-like structure remains with a tiled gable-ended roof and a service range of probably early seventeenth century date at the north end. At the south-east corner an octagonal angle tower of four storeys rises to about roof ridge level with a battlemented observation parapet. Tucked into the angle between this tower and the main range is what looks like a small garden garderobe structure.

The south facing gable-end (see Plate 224) has again been much altered. There is one mullion and transom window in brickwork at ground floor level -- not original -- and an extremely large blocked-in opening above suggesting an important reception room on the first floor. The gable over this has been rebuilt at some time, and the multi-corbelled verge with a band of parallel brickwork looks a highly un-Tudor feature. A polygonal brick angle buttress is obviously an original feature -- the only one of such to survive -- hinting at what the chimneys might have been. The west facing elevation of the main range is nondescript and only confirms the decline of this once important mansion 'into a farmhouse'.[2]

All that remains of the home of the Crane family is in that single east wing of what traditionally was an E-shaped house, extending, as Farrer suggested[3] to the walls of the moat on three sides, with a central courtyard between the wings and a porch leading into the great hall. This could have been another of that group of sixteenth century Suffolk mansions of which the end facing gables were flanked by angle turrets, as at Rushbrooke Hall and Kentwell Hall. West of the moat lay an extensive walled garden, and of this remain the Tudor brick wall with one delightful arched doorway and -- elsewhere -- three unusual niches which have been described as 'Ancient Archery targets', but may, indeed, be no more romantic than an arbour with seats from which to contemplate the gardens.

1 '. . . unless it can be supposed that the footings of two big buildings which I have uncovered are mediaeval barns. I have my doubts. Although the bricks are Tudor, I suspect they were reused in the nineteenth century.' From a letter from the Owner dated December 6th, 1976.
2 cf. Copinger *The Manors of Suffolk,* Volume I, pages 70-73.
3 *E.A.M.,* op. cit., No. 3466.

*Plate 223: The approach from the north.*

*Plate 224: The moat and south gable-end.*

**West Stow Hall**

*TL 817 708*

*Plate 225: Coat of arms of Mary, Queen of France.*

Prior to the Dissolution the history of this long, oddly shaped township is marked by discoveries of occupancy dating beyond Anglo-Saxon to Romano-British times. Situated in the extreme south-eastern corner, West Stow Hall is within 500 yards of a church probably upon the site of an early Saxon temple,[1] and not more than a mile from the Anglo Saxon village (see Section 2). The western boundary is on the line of the Icknield Way, and it is reckoned that at North Stow there was an important Saxon *healh* (hall). Until the year 1519 the Manor of West Stow had been the property of the Monastery of Bury St. Edmunds, possibly since its foundation, but, on March 25th of that year, it was granted to Sir John Croftes.[2] John Croftes was a member of the household of Mary, Queen of France, wife of Charles Brandon, Duke of Suffolk, whose Suffolk property was at Westhorpe. In compliment to his royal mistress, Croftes placed her achievement on the new gatehouse to his mansion of West Stow Hall (see Plate 225). He was knighted on October 2nd, 1553, the day after the coronation of Queen Mary, and the property remained in his family for at least another century.

By 1813, however, it had been reduced both in size and status, being then, 'used as a farmhouse'.[3] Early writers all told roughly the same story; that the Hall formerly surrounded a quadrangular court, was moated, and was 'well adapted by its interior arrangements to baronial customs and festivities.' From Copinger we learn, additionally, that the manor house of West Stow Hall was built on the site of the mansion house of Ginney's Manor, and that a 'fine wide moat . . . was filled up some years since' — presumably towards the end of the nineteenth century. The moast must therefore be presumed to antedate the gatehouse by some considerable time.

It is with such historical clues as these, backed by the remaining structural evidence, that the original mansion must be reconstructed. The route of the moat is fairly clear, suggesting that the house occupied most of the centre of an island. Unlike many Tudor houses, Sir John Croftes built a rectangular gatehouse towards the outside of the moat, and then connected it by bridge to the mansion. With numerous alterations, the essential form of this gatehouse is still intact, and remains a valuable document of early Tudor bricklayers' art. The proportions are narrow, and the height of the storeys emphasised by two octagonal angle turrets which closely flank the doorway and the three tiers of work above (see Plate 226 and John Western's drawing, Figure 68). There are similar inset panels with trefoil

*Plate 226: West Stow Hall – general view of the gatehouse front.*

cf. *Suffolk Names* in *E.A.M.*, No. 12551; notes by the late Claude Morley.
cf. Copinger *The Manors of Suffolk*, Volume 1, pages 403-412. The Manor included advowson of church, a watermill, a meadow and a fulling mill in West Stow.
cf. *History and Topography of Suffolk* by F. Shoberl (1813. London) page 194.

Figure 68: West Stow Hall,
near Bury St. Edmunds.
The Gatehouse from the east.

cusped heads as at the Shelley Hall porch and the Leiston Abbey gatehouse, label-moulds to window head openings and over the four-centred arched doorway, stepped gables, and an overall Gothic inspiration heightened by the Perpendicular onion tops to the turrets surmounted by grotesque little figures. No exact parallel can be found elsewhere in Suffolk Tudor houses.

Later in the same century the loggia-like colonnade in brickwork was evidently added to the bridge, as a base to a timber-framed brick-nogged superstructure which then joined the gatehouse to the main mansion, adding a considerable amount of extra accommodation. The central chimney stack no doubt dates from the same period, with its plastered brickwork internally on which the 'Four Ages of Man' were graphically — and wittily — frescoed.[1] Alike costumes and Renaissance frieze suggest a date of, say, $1575^{\pm}$.

In reaching conclusions about the Hall itself, present evidence suggests that there were single room width ranges surrounding a central court, and that the hall was entered by a doorway opposite the gatehouse. This extensive timber-framed structure is being uncovered by the present owner, pointing to a hall range parallel with the moat on the east side, with an upper dais end at the north, and beyond this the parlours in the north wing. South of the entrance — possibly with screens-passage — there must have been a service range forming the third side of the courtyard. The earlier structures were partly demolished and partly rebuilt by owners in the early mid-nineteenth century, who refronted the south range with white brick walls and sash windows in order to give this part of the building at least the appearance of a respectable farmhouse.

1 Compare with the 'Four Ages of Woman' in plasterwork to a ceiling of Browston Hall, near Lowestoft (see Plate 157).

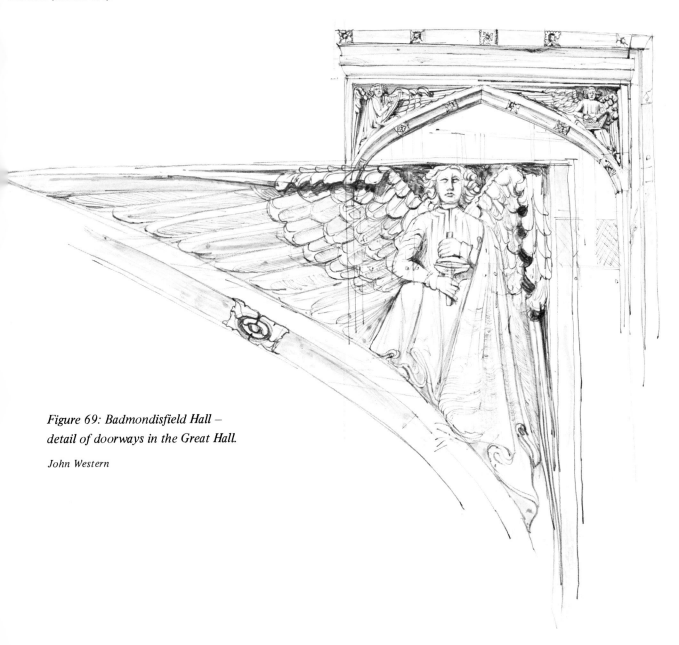

*Figure 69: Badmondisfield Hall —*
*detail of doorways in the Great Hall.*

John Western

*Figure 70: Badmon.lisfield Hall — the garden house beyond the moat.*

**Badmondisfield Hall,**
**Wickhambrook**
*TL 748 570*

The most northerly of the Wickhambrook manors, Badmondisfield (Bansfield locally) Hall was once a large establishment within a park which is said to have extended well into the neighbouring parish of Lidgate. Lying high, the Hall was built forward on an island site enclosed within the deeply cut moat, a great bastion of a house, with a manorial history traceable to the time of Henry I. Approached from biblical-sounding Genesis Green, and seen at the summit of ground falling to a long roadside pool, the old house excites curiosity. Skirting the property the road rises to an entrance seemingly as to any farm, with a way in through barns and outbuildings: before this, however, a drive turns off and circles round to bridge the moat, and, by a straight axial approach over pavings and brickwork, reaches the forecourt. West of this and between the inner and outer part of the moat, a narrow grass causeway leads to a graceful little summer house with white plaster walls and a Georgian porch and windows (see Figure 70).

On a near view the Hall is seen to consist of a substantial main range with east and west cross-wings; a lower range adjoins the east cross-wing, and chimney stacks are visible only at each end of the wings. The entrance is by a porch well off-centre (see Figure 71). The massing of elements is more complex on the south side, where a staircase annexe projects next to the west wing, and the east wing is seen to be much longer than the west with the space in between filled at ground level with a long conservatory or garden-room. None of this disproves the first idea of a hall-house, with the hall dividing the parlours from the service range, and further service accommodation in an annexe to the east. There have been as many vicissitudes, however, as changes of ownership, and the problem becomes one of deciphering the original elements.

Farrer claimed to have seen a sketch made in c.1825 of the house before it was re-roofed and altered in other respects,[1] which in the absence of more circumstantial evidence is worth mentioning. At that period the north elevation was multi-gabled, and, if Farrer's description is correctly interpreted, there was a two-storey gabled porch balancing a similarly gabled projection with a large ground floor bay window, and a further gabled dormer in the centre. The two existing

1 cf. *E.A.M.*, op. cit., Nos. 5583, 6544, 6548, 6557, 6567, 6569, 6573 and 6578.

*Figure 71: The north elevation – Badmondisfield Hall.*

*Figure 72: Badmondisfield Hall — the Great Hall.*

projections of the cross-wings were said at that time to have been '. . . not projecting, but flush with the rest'; this is difficult to credit because the cross-wings protrude too little from the main range to have made it worth any builder's while to do this after the original build. Given the generally conservative character of late-mediaeval house design these details could fit well enough with the plan of an important manor of 1500± and seem to be corroborated here and there from documentary sources. The entrance porch gave on to a screens-passage of similar girth which ran the whole width of the hall; on the left were the double-arched openings shown in John Western's drawing (see Figure 72). Curiously, Farrer does not mention *twin* archways, although describing the music-making angels in the carved spandrils (see Figure 69) — which he dates as late fifteenth century — and suggesting a chapel built elsewhere on the site as the probable source. The larger of the two openings enters upon an early staircase, and the smaller gave access to the service area. The hall itself was entered from the screens through a pair of semi-circular arched openings, and above the passage was the balustraded minstrels' gallery — this work was evidently Early Carolean. The hall was floored over and the loads carried on four round pillars about 4.5m (15ft) high, and walls lined nearly 3m (10ft) high with wainscot: at the far end was a central doorway opening into the west wing. The fireplace was doubtless in the present position on the south wall but Farrer omits to mention it. Thus we have all the elements of a conventional late-mediaeval plan; hall with fireplace and upper and lower end, the upper having an oriel bay window and opening into a greater and lesser parlour (now dining-room and drawing-room), and the lower doubtless into buttery and pantry, with the kitchen in the barn-like annexe beyond, which is still very much as originally built. An unusual feature was the Chapel over the porch, reminiscent of the *parvise* sometimes built over a Church porch, and entered here from the gallery above the screens-passage:[1] this is associated with Sir George Somerset who acquired the manor by inheritance, c.1540.

Two hundred years or so later, when the property was in the hands of the Warner family drastic alterations took place which were designed to get rid of all those spiky Gothic gables and give the Hall a more sober look. A photograph of the north elevation (published in the *East Anglian Daily Times* on February 17th, 1975, together with a letter from Mr. Bradbury P.F. Clarke) shows the old gabled roofscape replaced by the hipped roof of today, enormous double-hung sash windows to the front of each cross-wing, a completely flattened central range elevation in which only the old mullion and transom windows survived within plastered walls, and a new pedimented frame enclosed the round-arched front door. At this period the Georgianising of the interior must have gone ahead also, the hall wainscot being removed, and elsewhere painted over, and eighteenth century joinery put in. The old house had evidently been the customary one room depth, with the bed chambers reached by separate staircases at each end of the hall. In the Warner alterations the rear of the house was remodelled to provide a first floor passage between the cross-wings, and the roof extended both to accommodate this addition and the garden room behind the hall by means of a lean-to. Later on when the pillars had been taken out, a huge new open fireplace was built in the hall, and the tie-beams supported by the rather clumsy arched braces to be seen today: at the same time (c.1908) a new staircase ascended south out of the hall to the first floor passage. The post-war phase, which Pevsner called 'a drastic mid-twentieth century beauty treatment', amounted really to no more than a laudable attempt to recapture both outside and in some of the original late-mediaeval atmosphere of an old Hall that went back as far as the early sixteenth century, and is likely to have been the rebuilding of a still earlier Gothic hall, of which a few traces still remain.[2]

### Clopton Hall, Wickhambrook
TL 761 547

Clopton Hall, Wickhambrook, has probably the highest site of any manor house in Suffolk. On the edge of the 375 foot contour, the land falls away on three sides, and the house stands well up on the skyline above the Bury road: '. . . rather lonely and bare', as Farrer commented, 'for most of the timber which once must have surrounded it has been removed.'[3] Locally it is maintained that the original approach was by a trackway off that road, leading to the Hall, Clopton Green and a number of cottages, and this could be something of considerable antiquity for an unmistakable ley makes almost due north to the moated site of old Depden Hall. At

1 This information appeared in V.B. Redstone's paper *Chapels, Chantries and Guilds in Suffolk*, published in Proceeding S.I.A., op. cit., Volume XII, part 1, 1908, and is quoted by Rev. E. Farrer in his *E.A.M.* articles. The interesting history of the Badmondisfield Hall mediaeval Chapel, and its successor in the manor house is too extensive for inclusion here.
2 A good example is a plank door in one of the two openings originally under the screens-passage, which could easily be of fifteenth century date and is remarkably intact with its hinges and fittings.
3 cf. *E.A.M.*, op. cit., No. 7219.

*Haughley Park, Haughley. View from the south-east.*

*Plate 227: Clopton Hall, Wickhambrook – the house from the south east.*

*Plate 228: Porch to west elevation.*

Depden Green just beyond that Hall there was a meeting of many tracks, and this high point could well be comparable with that of Clopton Hall as the site of an early settlement. There are the remains of a large moat with a circular earth rampart some 730m (800 yd) further south, obviously reached from Clopton Green by a trackway now become the minor road ending in the valley below Giffords Hall. Here stood an earlier hall closely connected with the history of the present Clopton Hall, and only 180m (200 yd) or so east of Giffords Hall.[1]

There were several small manors in this large parish, and the three usually grouped are Badmondsfield, Gaines, and Clopton which Copinger calls the Manor of Clopton Hall or Chappeley Manor. The builder of the present house was a lowlander who took the name of Clopton and settled there in the sixteenth century, and was connected with the cloth trade.[2] The materials came mainly from the adjoining moated Hall when this was demolished early in the 1500s, and the way in which carved oak tie-beams and floor joists were reassembled in the new house can clearly be seen on close examination. The plan consists of a main range about 18m by 5.5m (60ft by 18ft) running south-east/north-west, with, originally, a single wing projecting on the west making an L-shape. Later on, infilling took place between the wing and the main range. The accommodation consisted of a central hall flanked by greater and lesser parlours with kitchen and service rooms at the rear: corresponding with the rooms below were the bed chambers above. If the

*Plate 229: The triple chimney stacks from the north east.*

1 Rev. E. Farrer (above) comments on the frequent close proximity of early manor houses, and quotes the example of Brome Hill and Somer Hall in Norfolk within 300-400 yards of each other.
2 There is a privately printed study of the Clopton family entitled *The Ancestors of William Clopton,* by Lucy Lane Erwin.

221

*Plate 230: Detail of the Hall ceiling.*

*Plate 231: Detail of Hall doorway at Clopton Hall.*

planning was remarkable only by its transitional character between the open hall-house and the newer two-storey Tudor manor house, the elevational design was more unusual. This consisted of a triple-gabled front of a classical regularity with an entrance (the porch is later) exactly in the centre and windows balanced one above another, making a perfect prototype for innumerable smaller houses to be built to this same pattern. In contrast to the somewhat prosaic front (see Plate 227), the rear elevation has a touch of drama in the three large brick stacks with their ornamental shafts in groups of two, three and four, carefully related each to the ridge line of the front gables, to each of which they provide a strong vertical accent, seen from the front (see Plate 229).[1] From the back the dramatic quality has been lessened by the infilling that took place between the wings, leaving only in view the full height (some 12m or 40ft overall) of one of these superb monuments of Tudor brickwork.

The hall, on entry, is found to be a rectangular apartment of some 6.5m length by 5.25m width (21ft by 17ft 3in.) with door (see Plate 231) at each end leading to the two parlours, and another opposite to the new staircase. With a storey-height approaching 3m (over 9ft), the richly moulded oak tie-beam and ceiling joists are not oppressive. There are twenty four of these moulded joists each with ribbed mouldings and feathered stop chamfers, and the twelve used in the outer part of the ceiling clearly belong to an earlier jettied form of construction (see Plate 230). The main tie-beam can be seen to be of sawn oak and did not belong to the earlier house, being put in to provide the necessary support for the older joists. The oak wall studs at 6ft by 4ft are closely spaced at average 11in. centres compatible with an early Tudor date. The great parlour contained the same number of moulded ceiling joists, and the tie-beam has three parallel runs of a floral trail pattern which could be dated as far back as 1400. The original staircase went up to a small landing on the west side of the house next to the chimney stack, giving access to a cheese loft as well as the principal bedrooms. The charming two-storey porch seems clearly to have been removed from elsewhere and refitted here (see Plate 228).

### Giffords Hall, Wickhambrook
TL 771 538

This house is called after the same Gifford family who bestowed their name on that other and more extensive property at Stoke-by-Nayland. Both were the halls of Manors but their devolution followed very different courses, the latter passing to the Mannocks in the early fifteenth century, and the Wickhambrook house in the fourteenth century to the Cloptons and subsequently, until the mid seventeenth century, to Highams.[2] In common with many of the manor houses of Suffolk it became a farm in Victorian times. Later it seems to have been sold and divided into 'tenements', until finally rescued in 1904 through purchase by Seymour Lucas, R.A., and then carefully restored and modernised by a Mr. Fass who built the new north wing: 'in complete, although not deceptive, harmony with the old work'.

The site is in the remote south-east corner of the large parish of Wickhambrook, at the end of a by-road nearly a mile off the Haverhill-Bury St. Edmunds road, in a folded county where old houses are plentiful, and many like Purton Hall, Cordell

1 I have raised elsewhere the doubt whether these ornamental shafts were contemporary with their bases, but this in no way detracts from their design quality.
2 cf. Copinger, *The Manors of Suffolk*, op. cit., Volume 5, page 304.

Hall and Purton Green Farm can be reached only by unmade farm roadways. It is fully moated, the island within measuring some 98m by 80m (300ft by 240ft), accessible only by a single triple-arched brick bridge. Compared with Clopton Hall, some three quarters of a mile off, the site is sheltered, the land falling steadily to a little valley through which runs one of the many affluents of the River Stour. Across the fields to the south it was not more than a mile and a half to the Priests Chantry at Denston.

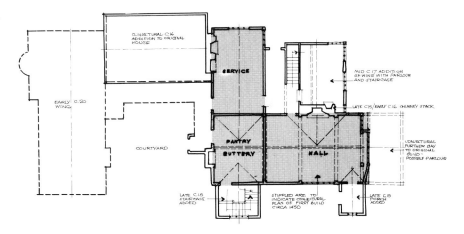

*Figure 73: Giffords Hall floor plan.*

The hall has the long axis running approximately north-east/south-west, and close to the eastern arm of the moat, although with space enough for a terrace walk below the walls and nowhere built sheer out of the water (see Plate 232). That this building replaced one or more of older date can be deduced from the historical evidence of those who are mentioned as dwelling here in earlier centuries, as well as from certain unusual architectural features. The plan (see Figure 73) is irregular by normal late mediaeval standards, consisting of a main range off which two wings protrude on the east side, with a service range tacked on asymmetrically at the north end. Accommodation in the main dwelling consisted of four rooms on each of two floors, for there was no evidence of a hall house converted to two storeys by the insertion of a floor, everything pointing to an original two-storey build. The first structure, on approaching the house, is a two-storey porch, the door being sheltered from prevailing winds by an entry on the north side: at right angles to this entrance is the doorway into the main range, and immediately ahead the door habitually opposite a screens-passage entrance.[1] The only suggestion of passage way

1 This can only be seen externally for the doorway has been covered up inside by later wainscot.

*Plate 232: Giffords Hall, Wickhambrook – view from the south-east beyond the moat.*

*Plate 233: The chimney-piece in the great bed chamber, Giffords Hall.*

*Plate 234: Carved spandril in the great bed chamber.*

is in the obviously narrower width of this bay compared with the remainder in what is now an open hall. It is reminiscent of Otley Hall where the screens-passage was left isolated alongside an end gable-wall, although there we have good reason to believe that the parlour accommodation was pulled down, together with another range. If the same thing were to have happened here, the addition of another bay or so would restore the ground floor to something like the usual sequence in a building of single room width of this period. There is singularly little evidence of a newel stair said once to have been in the south-east corner of the hall. The longer one looks at the structure the more the feeling grows that alterations have been more numerous even than those normally accounted for. If the hall chimney stack was not part of the first build, and was built later — as occurred so commonly in early timber-framed houses — then the wing at the rear of stack could also have been an addition, and the hall lit from both sides in the way normal at the period. In that event ascent to the first floor would probably have been by a newel stair in the angle between the hall and dining-room ranges, the latter having been originally the kitchen (with the service wing logically extending from it). The plan would then have been of L-form, and *if* — very tentatively — the parlour had been south of the hall, with the buttery/pantry at the opposite end, we would be back at the near normal late mediaeval plan. The circumstances that arouse suspicions are: the timbers in the chimney stack bay have clearly been disturbed in a way that would not have occurred had this been a contemporary structure. The stop chamfers of the moulded ceiling joists in the hall have been lost when the main bressumer was moved forward, and both the moulded timbers and bressumers in the great bed chamber have equally been disrupted. Now if there is one aspect of the master carpenter's work at Giffords Hall that is especially outstanding, it is the 'flow' and continuity of the framing and the mouldings, which rises to a pitch of perfection in the great bed chamber (see Plates 233 and 234). If this is true internally it must also be so externally, admitting that the carpenter's work there is plain — even austere. With this reservation it seems all too clear that the framing to south gable of the main range has been altered at some time; the way in which the semi-bay window at the end of the hall has been formed is noticeably clumsy, both outside, where the oversail of the first floor is crudely bracketed at one end and splayed back at the other, and inside where shouldered posts — put in on both sides to support the main bressumer over the large fourteen light window — are singularly lacking, with their coarsely bevelled angles, in the refinement of the moulded work generally.

The highly tentative conclusion could be that the first build was indeed of the mid-late fifteenth century owing to the pronounced Gothic character of the structure and detailing, and that perhaps a century later, c.1590, further alterations were carried out possibly by Thomas Higham. These were: the second projection roughly balancing the porch on the west side, the new chimney stacks, possibly enlargements of some already built,[1] and the second wing on the east side. In that case the shortening of the main range at the south end would have been done at the same time, and existing windows refitted there.[2] The infilling between the east wings to provide space for a more stylish staircase would be late Stuart period, doing away with the newel stairs somewhere in that part of the house. Thereafter little would have been done until the present century for Giffords Hall could have entered its long period of decline with the Chinery occupation in the late eighteenth century — a decline so dramatically arrested in the early years of this century, and a reversal of fortune maintained ever since, not least under present ownership.

1 The two stone fireplaces would have been imported: that in the hall is fairly nondescript late Tudor, but the one in the great bed chamber is a remarkable essay in late fifteenth century Gothic, and remains one of the surprising enigmas of the Giffords Hall building history. Where did it come from and when was it installed?
2 I am well aware that these conclusions differ radically from those put forward by Mr. Hope Bagenal, F.R.I.B.A., for a visit of the Suffolk Institute of Archaeology in 1947, but the whole question deserves further study.

# COUNTRY HOUSES

### *Cedar Court, Alderton*
*TM 345 429*

The site is on the extreme edge of the Parish of Alderton, the boundary with Hollesley skirting the farm buildings north of the house. On the edge of the 25 ft contour, this is the first high ground due west of Shingle Street and the water meadows. In 1783 there was a wooded area between the contour and the Hollesley road, and in this area was built Cedar Court, known earlier as The Cedars - after the magnificent Lebanon cedars in the front garden. A map of the estate dated August 4th, 1826 proves that the site of the 'mansion house' in 1826 was the same as the Cedar Court of today. So we have a gentleman's residence, with farm, in a favoured position sheltered from the east by woods, on the edge of the marshes, and within a comfortable ride of the market town of Woodbridge. In 1688 this property belonged to Edmund Woodroffe. There are records of occupiers until 1720, when James Woodroffe, then of Mitcham, Surrey and Charity, his wife, sold the property to Robert Watts. The impression is of frequent changes of occupant between these years, and probable deterioration, until a new owner - either Mr. Watts or his successor - sets about a thorough reconstruction of the premises in the mid-eighteenth century (see Plate 235).

*Plate 235: Cedar Court – elevation to drive.*

This new owner had definite ideas on the planning, design, and landscaping of a country residence. It seems probable that the earlier entrance from the Hollesley road was directly opposite the front entrance, and that this was closed and a new drive made through the woodland from the south. The grounds in front of the house were then reclaimed as a area of open lawn, surrounded by fine specimens of trees and shrubs. That this had already been done by 1805 is clear from the early printings of the 1-inch Ordnance Survey. Dissatisfied with the flatness of the site and the lack of elevation of his house above ground level, a sunken drive was formed in front of the entrance, giving a raised base to the house with a flight of six steps up to the front door (see Plate 236).

Half the original seventeenth century house was demolished with these alterations and replaced by a symmetrical front range with a central doorway. This gave access to a staircase hall with left and right a dining-room and morning-room respectively. Considerable skill was used in transforming what must have been a fairly dull seventeenth century 'tenement' into an impeccable small Georgian mansion. It was of regular rectangular form, the hipped tiled roofs being sunk behind the parapet walls. From the front the east and west chimney stacks balanced each other, with six and four flues respectively, and the three dormer windows of the attic bedrooms were carefully centred on solids and voids below. The front was in five bays, widest in the middle bay where occurred the door case and the

*Plate 236: Detail of front entrance.*

225

Venetian window. The door case comprised thrice-fluted pilasters, entablature, and a broken pediment finely moulded, enclosing an arched door opening with decorative fanlight. The touch of the same designer is evident in the detailing of the Venetian window, where the double keystone crowns the single one over the fanlight below, and the architrave of the arched window head is delicately moulded. A strongly detailed, simple modillion cornice in stone surrounds the whole building one course above the rubbed brick flat arches of the first floor windows. The upper and lower sash windows are of identical proportions, each with twelve panes and fine sash bars (the details suggest a date not earlier than 1750). The sills are stone. The brickwork is of good quality, deep red in colour, with tuck pointed mortar joints, and dimensions are 8 by 4 by 2¼in., and therefore close to the typical mid-eighteenth – early nineteenth century brick[1].

The house block was supported in front by flanking garden walls (disturbed on the west), and the whole of the large rear garden enclosed within high brick walls, that on the east being serpentine – doubtless for fruit growing. Beyond the north wall were the farm buildings and below, the marshes.

The Manor House was probably built in the 1720s, and the interior will raise more interesting questions about the structural history of the house than the comparatively little that remains of its former architecture. The present plan curiously resembles that of a seventeenth century farmhouse, of single room depth with a cross-wing making an L-shaped house. The front facing the road would suggest a square plan, but the cross-wing is Victorian and, superficially, there is no trace of any further eighteenth century work at the rear. The cellar could have been there in 1620, to judge by the deeply undercut Perpendicular-type mouldings of the beams and joists. The walls of the principal bedroom are panelled from floor to ceiling with oak linen fold wainscot of a similar date. There are painted panels in the overmantels of two of the early eighteenth century chimney pieces in ground floor rooms, and from one of these we get a very different version of the Manor House from that of today. The painting (said to be by T. Bardwell, and dated 1730) is of an elegant country-house which, to judge by the rows of young trees, has been recently landscaped, say within the last ten years (see Plate 237).

**The Manor House, Bacton**
*TM 044 666*

1 cf. *A Typology of Brick* L.S. Harley, page 76.

*Plate 237: Overmantel painting of the Manor House, dated 1730.*

Plate 238: The Manor House, Bacton —
the front elevation.

The house is separated from a country road by a grass courtyard enclosed by brick walls; the walls next to the road being swept down from two angle piers crowned by stone eagles to a lower level, in order to give a better view of the front. There is the suggestion of a moat, at least on two sides of the house, crossed by a bridge opposite the front door, on which are wavy classical figures in the Palladian style. Approached in the picture by two fashionably dressed ladies with a pet dog, the bridge is flanked by a pair of lamp standards. The house is unmistakably the present one, although with the addition of many features, of which the chief are a pair of pavilion like, single-storey, extensions at each end, making a symmetrical front of some architectural pretension. This is supported to one side by a charming stable block with clock tower and bellcote, a cottage and other outbuildings, a great deal of post and rail fencing, and several handsome five-barred gates — not to mention the double tree avenues. None of these remain, and it is only the front elevation which survives (see Plate 238), somewhat inappropriately approached by a gravel path between rose beds.

The house seems to have been built by George Pretyman, who died in 1732,[1] although the coat of arms in the pediment appear to be that of his son (see Plate 239). After a hundred years the house had come down in the world, and by the middle of the nineteenth century was a farmhouse. The then owner is recorded as demolishing all except the main block, and it was he who probably built the present dull, red brick rear wing, with its large farmhouse kitchen.[2]

There is still much to admire in the quality of the detailing and workmanship. The front doorcase, with its broken semi-circular pediment, encloses the same bust of Mercury as in the Bardwell painting, and the tall, unusually narrow sash windows of identical height in both storeys combine to give a lofty character to the design which was evidently intended by the original builder - with a certain elusive Dutch classical character. The front walls are in Flemish bond with dark blue headers and exceptionally deep rubbed arches with marked white keystones surmounted by moulded brick capitals - all in all, some of the best eighteenth century brickwork in Suffolk. The eight-panelled front door, and all internal joinery, is original. Two large tapestried panels on the landing are, sadly, almost too worn to be deciphered. The Jacobean wainscot could have belonged - like the carved timbers in the cellar — to the earlier Pretyman manor house.

Plate 239: Detail of Pretyman coat of arms in pediment.

1 cf. *Suffolk Manorial Families* by J.J. Muskett (1908. Exeter: Pollard), who says that George Pretyman 'rebuilt Bacton Manor House on a new site'.
2 This would have been prior to 1858 during the ownership of Mr. Edward Cooper, ibid., No.5011, page 103.

**Bawdsey Manor**
*TM 337 379*

Plate 241: The White Tower from entrance courtyard.

Plate 242: The Jacobean tea-house on the terrace.

The building of Bawdsey Manor is romantic: before it was built the peculiar bleakness of that spit of land at the mouth of the River Deben can be gathered from the Ordnance Survey of 1838, when the only buildings on the coast were Martello V and a Battery, with 'Life-boat Huts' on the river. The sandy track from Woodbridge via Alderton led to Bawdsey village and ended at the ferry. The area takes on a momentary interest from White's description in the Gazeteer of 1850 of a local industry in coprolite, used as a fertiliser by Suffolk farmers. Thirty five years later there seems to have been only a cottage left standing next to Martello V, when the Quilter brothers, shooting over the ground as the guests of Lord Rendlesham, discovered the Bawdsey peninsula. It was then that Sir Cuthbert Quilter made the spontaneous decision to live there one day, and from that decision sprang Bawdsey Manor. Beginning as a seaside house, it grew with the family and its fortune.

There was never any special plan, and the Manor developed from that first small house; built for the children's holidays, they would have driven there from Hintlesham Hall via Ipswich and Felixstowe, crossing to Bawdsey by boat, as the roads from Woodbridge over Sutton Walks were unmade. Then one day the family decided to have the house enlarged and make the Manor their home. The story goes that eight architects were employed to prepared elevational designs, somewhat regardless of what lay behind. In the end it was Sir Cuthbert himself who finally determined the details of the house, with the help of his friend Percy Macquoid; curiously enough, it appears that everybody forgot the staircase. The only cohesive part of the design was the Red Tower built in brick, and finished in 1895 (see Plate 240). Later new designs were prepared for the entrance when corridors were needed to link the new White Tower across the front with the Red Tower. The entrance front was built in stone together with the White Tower c.1908 (see Plate 241) which was to house the grandchildren and intended as a balancing feature to the

1 Mr. Macquoid was a pioneer authority on English furniture. His history of it was published early in the century in four parts, and later in collaboration with Ralph Edwards, he was responsible for the first edition of *The Dictionary of English Furniture*.

Red Tower. The onion domes capping the turrets of the White Tower could have been influenced by Kytson's Hengrave Hall, which Sir Cuthbert had once toyed with the idea of buying.

From the front door, which led into the staircase hall, there was a way into the great hall, with its massive Italianate chimney piece, and another to the garden-room with its large glass windows, where mimosas flourished, and doors led to the south terrace. At the end of this terrace below stood the Jacobean tea-house (see Plate 242) the walls of which were lined with coloured tiles from Southern Italy. Through the great hall, with its organ gallery, was the way to the dining-room and the large French drawing-room: but the billiard-room found itself on the first floor in the east wing. Turning right on entry led to the Red Tower containing three rooms on each floor, the largest on the ground floor being Sir Cuthert's sitting-room. This was panelled in exquisite reproduction linen fold wainscot and the upper part of the walls covered with Spanish leather of red sealing wax colour, embossed with lions and *fleur-de-lys* in gold. From here, as well as from the many windows above, the views along the coast to Bawdsey Haven, with Felixstowe and Walton beyond, were superlative.

It was Lady Quilter, with her affection for Italian gardens, who made the remarkable quarter mile walk of cliff terraces. These were reached through artificial tunnels built of materials from the demolished Martello tower. Removed by gunpowder, this produced a perfect round garden, where, by one of the most imaginative touches, a rose garden was made from which the sea could not be seen but was always heard. Behind a mixed tree belt lay the typical Edwardian gardens: in the centre was a two acre walled garden with glass houses on two sides, and, at the end of the main axis, a very beautiful orangery modelled on that at Hintlesham Hall (see Plate 243).

The Manor was supported by a large establishment, and for some thirty years had more than taken the place of that earlier local industry. Sir Cuthbert planted over two million trees on an estate which eventually covered 10,000 acres, rebuilt most of Bawdsey village, built new farmhouses and restored the church. He owned and operated two large cable steam ferries (see Plate 244), because Felixstowe, with its railway station, was the main contact with the Manor: Woodbridge was usually out of touch, but there were occasions, such as Cricket Week, when the yacht went up the river to Woodbridge to fetch the guests with their immense collection of luggage.

THE GARDENS, BAWDSEY MANOR

*Plate 243: Bawdsey Manor. The Orangery in the walled garden.*

*Plate 244: The steam-ferry from Bawdsey to Felixstowe.*

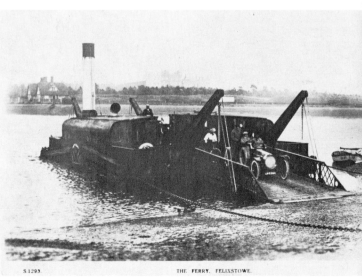

S.1293.                    THE FERRY. FELIXSTOWE.

229

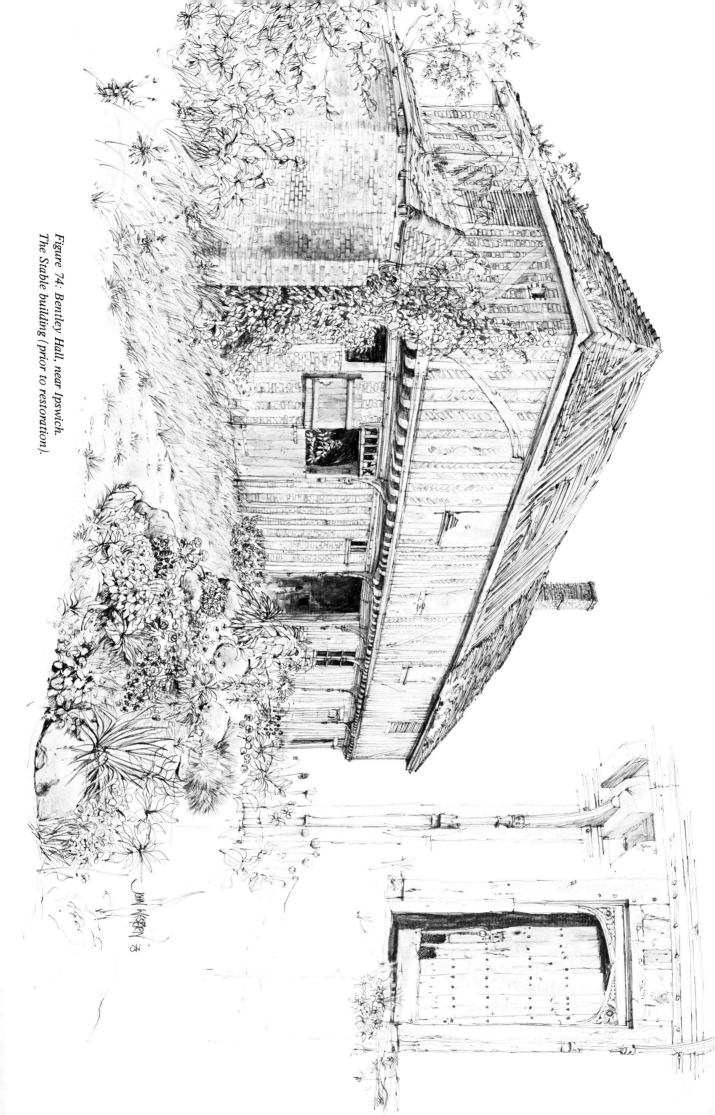

Figure 74: Bentley Hall, near Ipswich.
The Stable building (prior to restoration).

**Bentley Hall**
*TM 118 383*

In 1973, prior to the restoration of Bentley Hall, John Western made a drawing of the attractive old stable building which stands to the south of the Hall itself. Even in its then dilapidated state the excellent architectural quality of this building is visible. Single range in form, the long ground floor storey is oversailed by the projecting superstructure with its simple hipped roof. The timber-framed construction consists of closely spaced vertical studding with brick-nogged walls, and three entrances on the north side, two at storey-height and one — clearly a door of importance — at the west end having a four-centred arched head and spandrils carved with Tudor roses and foliage (see sketch detail in Figure 74). The jettied overhang is emphasised by singularly graceful arched brackets, which engage with carved Gothic capitals and are supported by slender carved wooden buttresses. This detailing is comparable with that of the Guildhall at Lavenham, and the date suggested for this structure of c.1526 is probably about right. Farrer considered the use of this building to be intended 'far more for the use of retainers than for horses',[1] and the first floor could have offered both sleeping quarters and loft space, as, for example, at Whittingham Hall, near Fressingfield.

**Bramfield Hall**
*TM 399 736*

Lying within a mile or so of Heveningham, Bramfield claimed two manors, one of Bramfield Hall and the other of Brook Hall.[2] Both these lay to the north of Walpole Lane outside the village proper, and neither was connected with the *new* Bramfield Hall. There is a reference to this new hall having been first the Vicarge House (it is indeed just across the road from the church); a timber-framed and clay plastered building, 43ft in length and 17ft in width, with a thatched roof. These dimensions correspond closely with those of the central range of the present house, and, with the added circumstance that timber framing and wattle daub were discovered during alterations earlier in this century, point to the likelihood that this nucleus was the original parsonage. It is known from church registers that the Rabett family were established here in 1561, and they acquired, enlarged and transformed the old Vicarage into a Tudor brick 'Mansion'.

The earlier dwelling on this site was no doubt an open hall house with the usual upper and lower ends, together with stables and other outbuildings (the sizes are recorded) which have long since disappeared, probably being built over. Under the Rabett development, cross-wings would have been added to the original nucleus, the plan thus becoming H-form. The new mansion house would have retained an open hall in the centre, with a chimney on the west side which has since been bricked up. The parlour range was in the north cross-wing, with, as Christopher Hussey conjectured, a staircase in the north-west corner. The original partitioning in this wing can be seen from the arrangement of the moulded ceiling timbers of mid-sixteenth century date in the drawing-room which retains its original Tudor fireplace. The south wing can have changed little, at least in plan, with a dining-hall at the south-east end and the rest service quarters. We are, therefore, discussing a Tudor and not a Georgian plan, and the clever change from what was probably a gable-ended two-storey house with attics, into regular three-storey eighteenth century elevations on three sides but not the back (see Plate 245).

*Plate 245: Bramfield Hall — elevation to drive.*

1 cf. *E.A.M.*, No. 6141, page 79.
2 cf. Copinger's *The Manors of Suffolk*, Volume 2, pages 21-23.

Plate 246: Bramfield Hall —
Serpentine garden wall.

The facing brickwork is rather rustic in character but, unmistakably Tudor. It is laid in the customary English bond of the sixteenth century, and only the rubbed work in the flat arches over the window openings is obviously later. The quoins of Tudor work in both cross-wings were evidently kept, and between these the new windows put in, the walling then being carefully made good with old bricks: the change can be seen particularly clearly in the varying colour of bricks and mortar between wavy vertical lines on the fronts of both cross-wings. In the recessed portion between the wings, changes are difficult to detect, and I would not be surprised if this three-storey wall with its five bays and elegant central doorcase, were not completely rebuilt with old bricks. The classicising of the Tudor house may well have been spread over nearly a century. The clue to this is the central doorcase, the detailing of which is much earlier than that of, say, internal doors and panelled shutters, and dates from the Queen Anne period (1702-1714). Evidence like this points to another generation of Rabetts again bringing the house up to date in the later Georgian style, when the early eighteenth century work would have been considered *vieux jeu*. In this they could well have been influenced by the Taylor/Wyatt work at Heveningham Hall next door, and, indeed, mantelpieces at Bramfield Hall are remarkably similar.[1]

Looking critically at the exterior today, one is struck by one or two unusual details; the peculiar position, for instance, of the lead rainwater heads in the angles of the entrance front much lower than normal, suggesting that they could once have been at eaves level of the original Tudor roof, and the irregular and very un-Georgian positions of the chimney stacks. In the internal alterations the open hall was partly floored over, and divided into a staircase hall with a nice galleried landing and, on the ground floor, a library, with a short passage leading to the drawing-room. The rest of the work must have been the forming of new bedrooms on first and second floors, the refitting of the house with panelled joinery, and the improving of the kitchen quarters with servants hall, pantry, gun room, dairy and larder. The Rabetts, who carried out these successive changes, must have been well advised, for the work, done with considerable skill and taste, resulted in one of those admirably simple but dignified Georgian country houses uniquely to be found in the British Isles. It is sad to reflect that the family fortunes evidently declined in the nineteenth century, for before they parted with the property in 1899 the Rabetts had sold half the balustrade of a finely marquetried staircase to America. In recent years the house has been restored as nearly as possible to its former glories.

**Great Saxham Hall**
TL 791 628

Plate 247: Great Saxham Hall — *after an engraving in* The Excursions, *1818.*

Great Saxham is one of these properties which lie so plentifully around Bury St. Edmunds, having descended to secular ownership through the Dissolution of the fantastic wealth in land and property of Bury Abbey. Some four miles west of the town, it adjoins Little Saxham where the mansion of the Lucas and Crofts families

1 They could have copied the Heveningham Hall serpentine wall also, for there is a nice version in 4½in. brickwork in the garden (see Plate 246).

*Plate 248: Great Saxham Hall. The elevation to the drive.*

once stood. To leave Bury on the Westley road is to follow the River Linnet until this turns away south into Ickworth Park, and to enter a richly planted and folded country of halls and villages. Drives lead off this road to Little Horringer Hall, Ickworth Park, the Little Saxham Hall of today, and finally, to Great Saxham Park. The Hall lies high, and the grounds are comfortably wooded, with artificial lakes in a long dell and a stream crossing the park from east to west. The owner in the late eighteenth century is said to have spent 'considerable sums in embellishing the grounds under the great Mr. *Capability* Brown'; and there is an engraving from a drawing of c.1818 showing the unfenced drive ascending in smooth curves through a parkland of close cropped grass, tree clumps and distant woodland to a house front devoid of any trace of artificial gardening — all that Mr. Brown could have wished (see Plate 247).[1]

It was Sir Thomas Kytson who acquired the property after the Dissolution and sold it to John Eldred for £3,000. John Eldred is known to have been 'a considerable Levant merchant' and an Alderman of London, and the house that he built at Great Saxham traditionally acquired its picturesque name of Nutmeg Hall from his connection with the spice trade. The Eldreds owned the Hall until c.1745-50, when the property was sold to Mr. Hutchison Mure, younger son of the Mures of Caldwell, Renfrewshire. As a Scot with rebuilding in mind, it would be natural for him to approach the Adam brothers, whose successful architectural practice started in Edinburgh. The first set of plans was dated 1763 (it would be interesting to know whether this was the start of the Adam brothers' connection with Bury St. Edmunds, where Robert subsequently — 1774/80 — designed the new Town Hall and did several other jobs). In 1779 the old Jacobean hall was burnt to the ground, and in that year the second design was prepared by Robert Adam. The new house was erected north-west of the old one and as recently at 1961 it was said to have been 'from a plan by Mr. Adam'. Mr. Scarfe has, however, recently produced interesting evidence that Mure did not adopt either of the Adam plans, but had 'a very good house built from plans of his own'.[2]

The drawings in the *Excursions* are fairly reliable, and if the sketch of c.1818 by J. Grieg is no exception, it has notable differences from the house today (see Plate 248); it shows it as finished in accordance with plans done by J. Patience of London, probably a pupil of Soane.[3] (Mure sold the property in 1793 to Thomas Mills who evidently did the main rebuilding after taking over an unfinished mansion. Gage says that Mure had only 'built the centre'.) There was an engaging classical simplicity about this house, with its low-pitched slated roofs and unadorned openings surmounted by bas-relief panels.[4] Everything points to a massive Victorian attack under a later generation of the Mills family, when pediments were put over all windows, bow windows added below and balconies above, and a rare assortment of chimneys appeared above the balustrades following the replacement of the pitched roofs by lead flats.

1 Brown died in 1788 and his work at Great Saxham Hall must have been almost his last commission.
2 cf. Proceedings S.I.A. Volume XXVI, part 3, pages 230-231.
3 cf. H.M. Colvin, *Biographical Dictionary of English Architects 1660-1840*, (1954), page 446.
4 These panels were of Coade Stone and two remain in their original places; the others were taken down with later alterations but still stand in the porch of the Hall.

Plate 249: Great Saxham Hall — the elevation to the garden.

*Painted octagonal ceiling at Great Saxham Hall, after Angelica Kauffmann.*

*Hemingstone Hall*
*TM 142 538*

It must have been this period when the first floor octagon (said to have been the music room) was lost: two-storeys high, with a ceiling beautifully painted *à la* Angelica Kauffmann, this was an unmistakably Adam feature (see marginal detail).[1] By c.1900 a floor cut the height in half, the lower made into two bedrooms, and the upper into staff cubicles. Thereafter the staircase was taken out and replaced elsewhere, the back of the drawing-room turned into a cloakroom, and a truly hideous wing built out into the garden: these two later barbarities have been removed, and proper restitution has been made to the drawing-room.

In the grounds the ornaments of eighteenth century taste still stand (see Plate 129 — architecturally inestimable — but, with the Hall, unlikely to survive for more than a few years unless their more than local significance is understood, and underpinned by a more appreciative national exchequer.

A tributary of the River Gipping rises in the parish of Ashbocking and runs west to join the river near Bosmere Hall. At the midway point is Hemingstone Hall, built in a small sheltered valley, and facing south. The stream is bridged where it passes beneath the drive to the house, just off the by-road that links Hemingstone village with Shrubland Park and Coddenham. Behind, the land rises steeply into woods and, in front, more slowly in arable fields to the skyline. It is a natural building site and was evidently appreciated as such from an early date, for there was a timber-framed house here — possibly one of several predecessors — before the present Hall was built. The approach is axial as befits a Tudor country house, and a double drive parts before reaching the flights of steps that conduct the porch.

In Hemingstone Hall we have a house that has been successively altered over many centuries, with insufficient documentary evidence, as yet, for the exact succession of change to be established in detail. The earliest work that survives in the eastern part of the present house is compatible with a date in the early fifteenth century. In 1551 the manor was held by Townshends of Raynham Hall, Norfolk, and it may be that under their ownership an earlier timber-framed house was altered and enlarged by the addition of a brick dwelling in c.1557. The connection of William Style with the property is well established, and the date of his work has been put at 1621; he is known to have died in 1655.[2] It is his alterations and rebuilding that have given Hemingstone Hall its present distinctive look of an ample, Dutch gabled, Jacobean house (see Plate 250). The irregularities, where they appear in the plan and elevations, are those likely to arise from the remodelling of an existing structure. The plan is consciously based upon the Elizabethan E, but without the regularity of an original build; there is one bay to the left of the porch as compared to two to the right of it. The windows vary considerably in size and position, and on the east side there is an extension where part of the old timber-framed building was kept as a service annexe. The arrangement of rooms

1 There is a domed first floor drawing-room in the Adam designs for the Deputy Ranger's house in Green Park, London (cf. *Works in Architecture of Robert and James Adam* (Tianti: London) Volume III, pages 16-17).
2 cf. *The Manors of Suffolk* by W.A. Copinger, Volume 2, pages 316-319.

*Plate 250: Hemingstone Hall. The elevation to the drive.*

*Plate 251: The Jacobean porch.*

### Herringfleet Hall
*TM 481 993*

1 The bricks have the look of local reds, and there was a brick kiln less than a mile away in the early nineteenth century: although there is no evidence of this being there in the sixteenth century, it would be only reasonable to suppose that the bricks for the new Hemingstone Hall came from some such local source.
2 The Listed Building description mentions that the old timber-framed wing was bricked over and the sash windows put in, also in the mid ninteenth century.
3 It is due to the researches of Dr. E.C. Brooks, Rector of Somerleyton, that the people chiefly responsible for Herringfleet Hall can be connected with the building that exists today.

departs from the traditional in that, although the porch entered the great hall, and the chief parlour occupied the west cross-wing with a staircase well at the rear, there was in addition to a separate dining-room east of the entrance an unusually large number of service rooms.

The architectural features that remain from William Style's work on the exterior are, in addition to the main gables, the porch with its stucco entrance simulating stonework and much of the brickwork.[1] The porch, with its stilted Tuscan Doric pilasters, arched doorway and triangular pinnacles, is an excellent bit of country builders' classicism, delightful in the naivety of its proportions and detail (see Plate 251). The great loss is, of course, the original windows; these would have been of brick mullion and transom with leaded lights, and would probably have been plastered to imitate stonework. The only original early window to survive is a timber mullioned opening belonging to the Elizabethan house, and still exposed at first floor near the Georgian alterations.

In 1741 the space between the cross-wings of the E-plan was filled in by a new brick range with double-hung sash windows, giving the rear of the house a charming, if inappropriate, early Georgian elevation. Sash windows appeared also on the west, where they still remain north of the Jacobean chimney stack (the chimney heads were all ruthlessly Georgianised). It is difficult to imagine why the front was not refenestrated at this period, and this may indeed have happened, for there has been a great deal of alteration of brickwork. The present windows are of mid-nineteenth century date, and will have been put in by members of the Martin family who occupied the hall from 1750 until 1953.[2]

At that date the house lacked the advantages of the well designed gardens which have since contributed so much to giving Hemingstone Hall a setting worthy of its place in the heritage of Suffolk houses.

The Ordnance Survey of 1837 gives Manor House Farm, Herringfleet as 'Old Hall', and the 2½ inch Ordnance Survey as 'formerly Manor House'. About a quarter mile east was the by-way which linked Somerleyton with the St. Olaves/Bradwell road and, shortly before reaching this, a drive went west through the middle of a woodland leading both to Blocka Hall and an unnamed house in the woods. This house, which was to be the new Herringfleet Hall, was a lodge or shooting box, and went with a property of some 1,700 acres that had attractions for game shooting. Exactly how the property was acquired by Hill-Mussenden has still to be explained. Dr. Brooks[3] thinks that sporting rights had a lot to do with the vicissitudes of ownership in the mid-late eighteenth century. After 1778 it had become part of the estate of Hill-Mussenden's successors.

The new Herringfleet Hall (see Plate 252) originates with the inheritance of the property by Carteret's eldest son, John, in 1778 and his romantic marriage with

*Plate 252: Herringfleet Hall, view from the south-east.*

Elizabeth Death, the captivating daughter of a local Herringfleet farmer. Enthralled with his young wife and her social ambitions, John set about enlarging the shooting box which Copinger — writing in 1848 — understandably refers to as 'glorified'. If we stand next to the orangery and look east, this is the neat small range with six symmetrical windows — the one in the middle on the ground floor had probably taken the place of a door (see Plate 253). Judging from the fenestration, it would have been built c.1730. In front of this small house was built a completely new square range on two floors, with a three-sided bay at the south-west corner. This was clearly to enhance the size of the dining-room, and permit of larger parties to be seated around the table. Structural evidence suggests that — apart from the entrance front — the new south range, the adaption of the old shooting box, and the adjoining stable building at least were completed before 1788. The first entrance front was probably a plain brick elevation with five sash windows and a simple porch containing a pair of Grecian Doric columns *in antis.* (It is uncertain when the brickwork was first painted white — possibly later, during the alterations of the 1830s.) On entry, a fair-sized passage led to the staircase hall, with — on the right — the morning-room, and a vaulted lobby giving access to the domestic offices and study. On the left was the drawing-room, followed by the dining-room, which was

*Plate 253: The original house between the Orangery and the later addition*

entered from the staircase hall. This was the *pièce de résistance*. The stairs, broken only by quarter-space landings, swept up in a continuous flight to a galleried landing: above this the square well became an octagonal dome surmounted by a cupola surrounded by window lights and — by a touch of fantasy — one circular rosette window to catch the late afternoon sun (see Plate 255). It may have been during this period that the architect John Soan (as his name was then spelt — later to become Sir John Soane) was called in to design the drawing-room, or — more likely — to redesign a room already there. His scheme involved blocking up and making a dummy of the east window. The shallow niches are characteristic of his

*Plate 254: The drawing-room with niches by Soane.*

*Plate 256: Herringfleet Hall — one of a pair of entrance lodges.*

*Plate 255: Staircase hall with dome.*

1 cf. *Biographical Dictionary of English Architects* by H.M. Colvin (1954), page 557.
2 Since this photograph of the east elevation there have been alterations to the porch.
3 According to *Historical and Topographical Notices of Great Yarmouth* by Drury, 1826.

work (see Plate 254), and so is the frieze pattern, and also the subdued curve over the larger of the three niches. The job at Herringfleet Hall was probably one of those 'modest commissions, chiefly in East Anglia', to which H.M. Colvin refers, and which established Soane in practice.[1]

The next phase of the improvements' seems to have taken place in the second quarter of the nineteenth century, and included the new stuccoed entrance elevation.[2] This can be seen to have a markedly more sophisticated character than other architectural exteriors of the house and is unlikely to have been the work of a local architect or builder. One sees J.F. Leathes, 'whose rich and numerous paintings ornament the apartments',[3] as a man of taste and not improbably as one who might have commissioned his new entrance from a reputable architect. Although in the Regent's Park style of Nash, it has a possible look of Decimus Burton, who was, after all, working at Glevering with A. Arcedeckne in 1834-5.

The orangery appears to be late eighteenth or early nineteenth century, with its five well proportioned arched window openings and glazing bars; and, no doubt, the walled kitchen garden and crinkle crankle (serpentine) brick wall also. To the same period belongs the so-called 'North Lodge', with its white brickwork, painted stucco pilasters, and handsome pediment carried on Greek Doric columns. The lodge (see Plate 256) can just be discerned at the foot of the drive on the first edition Ordnance Survey. Herringfleet Hall then seems to have remained undisturbed for the next forty years, and not until 1873 was the house again enlarged under Col. Hill-Mussenden Leathes. This enlargement could have included a double pile range to the north of the main block, and additional outbuildings. This would put the rear elevation facing the drive as Victorian, albeit in careful conformity to the generally Georgian character of the house. On January 15th, 1919, the Hall was bought from Major Herbert de Mussenden Leathes by Sir Savile Crossley, first Lord Somerleyton, in whose family it has remained since. At that time the outer porch was added and the building put in good order for the tenancy of Sir Thomas and Lady Jackson; in 1974 the house was successfully improved by Mr. Tom Watson.

*Plate 257: Thorpe Hall. View from the south.*

*Plate 258: Detail of staircase to attic floor.*

**Thorpe Hall, Horham**
*TM 212 738*

Architecturally one of the most accomplished small Tudor brick dwellings in Suffolk, the history of its erection remains enigmatic. There is the surprise of finding such a complete and sophisticated structure at the end of a farm track, all of half a mile from the road between Stradbroke and Eye. Not normally visible, it can be seen by the observant on a bright winter's day like some strange brick tower across the fields (see Plate 257 and Figure 75).

It is a double moated site, and Thorpe Hall was built centrally in the larger of the two. The height from ground to top of chimney stacks is some 55ft, the length nearly 57ft and the width 25ft 6in.: thus the vertical proportions of the design are virtually contained within a square. The plan is a rectangle, with a projection of equal size on both the north and south sides each less than 10ft in width, and standing out about 7ft 6in. from the main walls, and joined at ridge level to make a cross-wing. The impression is of gabled look-out towers on each face, of which the three main windows are in the upper storeys, and the uppermost only just below ridge line at nearly 40ft above ground. In the lack of any certainty as to the original purpose of the building, these heights, and the corresponding visibility from the upper windows, have probably given rise to the tradition that Thorpe Hall was intended as a hunting lodge. Allowing for the high ground on which it is built, there must always have been a commanding view of the countryside, even when this was more densely wooded, as would no doubt have been the case in Tudor times.

The planning was extremely simple. Apart from the two axial porches connected by a hall passage, there was a pair of rooms on each of three floors with an axial chimney stack at the gable-ends. Above the third floor a further small stairway ascended to the upper part of the roof space (see Plate 258). On each floor the room to the east of the entrance was larger than the one opposite, producing an interesting and slightly asymmetrical elevation (25ft from the porch to the end wall on one side and rather less than 22ft on the other). There is some doubt as to the exact position of the original staircase. It could have been a newel stair in the southern projection. (It is worth noting that no window was provided in the lower part of the south projection, and this would be compatible with the staircase having originally occupied this space.) Alternatively it is possible that the stairs have always been in their present position, although they intrude rather awkwardly into the rooms west of the central hall. In a plan of such formality there would be no room for kitchen and other offices, and it is unlikely that these would have been in an annexe immediately adjoining the west gable-end as they are today. The present two-storey wing could have been built in the late eighteenth or early nineteenth century to replace service quarters at a distance from the main house. There is plenty of precedent for these being separated in Tudor times. A garderobe

*Figure 75: Thorpe Hall seen from the south-east.*

providing sanitary disposal from the main west bed chamber on the first floor was, by means of a vertical duct in the thickness of the brick wall; it is scarcely likely, therefore, that kitchen premises would have abutted the base of this wall.

The exteriors present symmetrically grouped windows on each elevation, each window being mullioned and transomed with curved arched heads, and each surmounted by a pediment such as we find, for example, at Roos Hall, Beccles (1583). At the top of each gable-end there is a pair of *oeil-de-boeuf* window openings. Each stack consists of a group of four octagonal shafts with moulded bases and star-shaped tops, but otherwise unornamented. Roofs are of clay plain tiles, the eaves being carried on a moulded brick cornice. The brickwork is in English bond, and the mullion and transom elements of the windows were done in brick and covered with plaster: it is almost certain that the pedimented window heads would also have been plastered originally to represent stonework. In all probability local bricks were used for the construction, and old maps show a brick kiln about a mile and a half away at Athelington, suggesting that some such source provided for the original build.

In the absence of any conclusive documentation, the building suggests a date in the period 1550-80 and clearly belongs to the Waveney Valley school of brickwork of which Roos Hall, Beccles (1583), is such an outstanding example, and to which in its lofty proportions and good details Thorpe Hall has a marked resemblance. After considerable depredations of its original character, including the removal of the lead light windows, sympathetic restoration is going on under the present ownership and Thorpe Hall is recovering much of its uniquely distinguished Tudor character.

**Polstead Hall**
*TL 988 382*

Seen from the hillside opposite, Polstead Hall (see Plate 259) and Church provide an idyllic picture of Georgian country house and village church in the intimacy of a small parkland setting. The site is favoured by the land, which falls away south to the River Box and north to the road and 'Polstead pond', which separates the park from the little village climbing steeply a further hillside. This is some of the prettiest secluded country hereabouts, with Boxford about two miles to the west and Stoke-by-Nayland not much above a mile to the south.

The existence of a group of sharply pointed gabled roofs on the north side of the Hall draws immediate attention to antecedents certainly Tudor, and probably, as suggested by Harley, part of the remains of an early sixteenth century building (see Plate 260). An exacting measured survey might well indicate the existence of a central timber-framed range, and clarify stages of successive alteration. This could take into account details such as mullion windows (uncovered during restoration by the present owners), and stud and plaster walls in the structure at first floor level; it might indicate whether a large chimney stack and a Tudor fireplace were

*Plate 259: Polstead Hall – the south elevation.*

*Trevor James*

240

*Plate 260: Sixteenth century gables to north elevation.*

*Plate 261: Polstead Hall – detail of wall painting in bed chamber.*
G.B. Scott

contemporary with the first build, or were later additions. A remarkable feature of the house, in the form of a wall painting in one of the bed chambers, has been dated by Professor Eve Baker as between 1550-1560; in her opinion, the only other painting in a secular building and in a comparable state of preservation, is in the Golden Cross Inn, Oxford.[1] A portion of the painting is reproduced (see Plate 261): the theme is uncertain but has been given the attribution of 'The Labours of Hercules'. This could have been an embellishment of the house under the Waldegraves, whose family home was at Smallbridge Hall, Bures, and who were lords of the manor here until, according to Copinger, it was sold in 1598 to John Brand, John Gage, and others.[2] John Brand was a clothier of Boxford, and it is quite likely that a well-to-do merchant would have set about improving the old manor house, thus accounting for the Jacobean additions already mentioned.

The process by which Tudor Polstead Hall was transformed into a Georgian mansion does not seem to have remained on record. It could have taken place under a later generation of the Brand family, conjecturally in the early eighteenth century (c.1730-40). It is known that when the property passed to Thomas William Cooke, the architect, William Pilkington (1758-1848), was employed between 1816-19 on what H.M. Colvin refers to as 'improvements'.[3] Three years is quite a long time for work of this description, but it may have consisted in adding the window bays and the Palladian porch to the south front, and building on a wing to this side of the house (now vanished), containing a ballroom with bedrooms above.

The charm of the south facade of Polstead Hall lies in its elongated proportions in relation to height, the well-placed windows, and the effective punctuation of the long front by the two two-storey canted bay windows, and the single-storey porch with its inset Tuscan Doric columns. The solids and voids of the balustrade parapet are neatly related to the spacing of wall and windows below, and indicate that, allowing for alterations, the house has been well served architecturally.

### Worlingham Hall
TM 443 903

A certain taste for seclusion could easily be attributed to the earlier builders who settled on a site only a little higher than the level of the Beccles Marshes and well back from the road out of Beccles to Lowestoft. On Hodskinson's map of 1783 it looks as though Worlingham Hall was built on Beccles Common, but there must in fact have been a considerable marshy area between the two. The owner's name appears as 'R. Sparrowe Esq.', a comparative newcomer, for it was barely thirty years since he had bought the property from Sir Thomas Robinson, who, in turn, had purchased from the descendants of John Felton. Whether there was an earlier manor house on the site does not seem to have been recorded, for Joshua Kirby's *Suffolk Traveller* simply says: 'The hall is a neat Mansion, and was for some time the seat of John Felton Esq. . . .' This would date the house to the late seventeenth century, and originate yet again the familiar story of a Suffolk house successively altered by subsequent owners (see Plate 262).

As so often happened, the remodelling concentrated upon the three sides of the house most likely to be seen (compare with Little Glemham Hall, Bramfield Hall, Polstead Hall, etc.). Walking round to the back of Worlingham Hall, with its

1 Remains of a full-length wall painting can be seen at the Old Guildhall, Little St. Mary's, Long Melford, the painting being continuous across both plaster and studwork as at Polstead Hall: only a small section, however, remains.
2 Copinger, Ibid., pages 178-181.
3 cf. *A Biographical Dictionary of British Architects* (First Edition 1954), page 457. Pilkington had both a town and country practice and, in addition to work in London, altered several country houses. In 1812 he had designed Clermont Lodge, Suffolk, for Lord Clermont (not traced): cf. H.M. Colvin, above.

241

*Plate 262: Worlingham Hall, after a drawing by H. Davy, 1826.*

structural complexity of red-brick building, it is only too evident that an older house had been pulled about in order to conform with a later plan. This impression is confirmed by a visit to the cellars where the bricks are 2 inch, varying from 8¾-9in. long, and 4¼in. wide:[1] the building period could well be 1680-1700.[2] Kirby's 'neat Mansion' was evidently a red-brick house, with a large hall, part at least of which was retained in the next building phase.

Robert Sparrow — later writers, like Shoberl, drop the 'e' — seems to have lived in the house as he found it, and his son Robert to have thought about alterations some twenty years after his father's death (c.1765). This Robert, who Norman Scarfe describes as a 'talented, selfish, unlovable figure'[3] then approached the architect John Soane (who had just *added* the 'e' to his name after marrying Elizabeth Smith in 1784) with the commission to prepare plans for extensive alterations. Marcus Binney relates the story of Soane's unsuccessful projects,[4] and how he only received payment for the drawings eleven years after Sparrow had received them, and then only after persuading the Revd. Norton Nicholls, who had introduced him to Sparrow, to remonstrate with his client. Unfortunately no copies

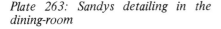

*Plate 263: Sandys detailing in the dining-room*

1 'The Restoration', as L.S. Harley says, 'is the period of change from generally 2 to 2¼ inch thickness to 2½ inches or a little more' cf. *A Typology of Brick*, page 75 (see Section 3 Bibliography).
2 According to Page's *Suffolk Collections*, Felton died in 1703.
3 In a fascinating essay *Whitney and Read: Two Regency Estate Agents* (with a short account of the Worlingham Estate 1755-1851). Proceedings S.I.A., Volume XXVIII, Part 2, pages 185-196.
4 cf. Country Life article, March 12th, 1970.

of these drawings seem still to exist, for they would have revealed the plan of the original house (of which Soane made a survey in December 1785), and also the extent to which his successor, the Irish architect, Francis Sandys of Bury St. Edmunds, made use of them. (Sandys was architect to the Earl Bishop of Bristol at Ickworth, and to Roger Pettiward at Great Finborough Hall.)

His civic work apart — and the similarity of the front of the Athenaeum, Bury St. Edmunds, with that of Worlingham Hall is too obvious to have escaped notice — it is Great Finborough Hall that can best be compared with the latter. Both have an unadorned simplicity of external design and detail which contrasts with a considerable richness of interior. In both Sandys made use of the device of a central staircase hall ascending to roof level and top lit by a lantern, although the design at Worlingham was far more elaborate and, indeed, impressive. There he made use of an octagonal stair well surmounted by a domed and coffered ceiling which rose to a central lantern (see Plate 127): in this he placed an Imperial staircase dividing after the first flight and ascending, with mezzanine landings, to the main bedroom floor. A theatrical effect was contrived by balustraded openings from the high level landings into the stairwell, as though designed as a setting for an *opera buffa* — an unreality further heightened by the fact that the elegant pair of doors within the pedimented doorcase on the first landing open not into a ballroom, but a cupboard. The looped theme of the staircase balustrade is employed at Great Finborough Hall where it also appears in the glazing of the lantern light. Francis Sandys, in his lesser way, shared something of Soane's ability to simplify classical ornament, and to give it an unmistakably personal and contemporary flavour (see Plate 263).

*Grove Park (formerly The Grove), Yoxford*
*TM 391 690*

A comparison of the house is drawn by T. Higham in the *Excursions Through Suffolk*, c.1818 (see Plate 264), and as it stands today shows how remarkably little it has changed (see Plate 265).

*Plate 264: The Grove, after a drawing by T. Higham in* The Excursions, *1818.*

*Plate 265: The house today from the same viewpoint.*

It is not always remembered that the valley of the River Yox has been called the 'Garden of Suffolk'. Today, it is probably the river more than the 'garden' that is better known on account of the graphic symbol of the Ox fording the stream at the entrance to the village. Grove Park was acquired by Mr. D.E. Davy in the later eighteenth century. There are structural details of brickwork and timber bressumers in the north wing that suggest a house of the early/mid eighteenth century. It is clear that an architect was employed, although the designs are scarcely pronounced enough in character to suggest who this might have been; there are reminiscences of Matthew Brettingham's Benacre Hall, but he died in 1769, and James Wyatt is scarcely a candidate, although he was working at Heveningham Hall in the 80s and, according to some accounts, the 90s. The design of the staircase (see Plate 266) has affinities with that at Bramfield Hall, particularly in the detailing of balusters and a similar pattern of decorative console to the outer string; as this house was being modernised about the same time, there is a possible clue from that direction.

Plate 267: Grove Park, the stable building.

Plate 266: The staircase hall

In the drawing by Higham the earlier north wing is discreetly omitted, and as it cannot be said to enhance the later design, there was something to be said for leaving it out. That apart, the only alteration seems to be the addition of a small pedimented portico in front of the main entrance doorway (a little too diminutive in scale to be completely effective). The project took the form of two long principal facades, that of the east entrance front and the other a westerly facing garden elevation. These were employed as screens for the older work and boldly asserted the change of scale from three storeys with small sash windows to two-storey with tall proportional sashes of twelve panes each. The recession between the front wings is a successful device and more convincing than the side elevations where the pediment has a woefully unsupported look.

The change from red to white facing brick between the older and later structures underlines the change of design and period, and the family in the early nineteenth century must have been well satisfied to be the owners of one of those small classical mansions, set in open parkland in the best traditions of Capability Brown which appear so frequently in the pages of the *Excursions,* and in the drawings of Henry Davy of Southwold. As a tailpiece there must be mention of the charming stable building at Grove Park which echoes the classicism of the house (see Plate 267).

# FARMHOUSES

In a county with over 6,000 farm holdings there can be no lack of examples of farmhouses, and these will be found to cover almost every period of building from the earliest known timber-framed structures to those put up in the last decade of this century.

The examples are, with a few exceptions, traditional timber-framed and plastered houses (see Plate 268), and date from the late-mediaeval to the early seventeenth century. The exceptions are seventeenth century brick-built houses, and none are later than the late eighteenth century. Valley Farm, Huntingfield, is an earlier timber-framed house which may have been refronted by Wyatt when he was at work on the Heveningham Hall estate for Sir Gerard Vanneck. It points to the problem of consecutive dating to which I have already referred, and which greatly affects farmhouses. There are many many cases to be found, all over the county, of houses so drastically refronted as to be entirely misleading in appearance. Examples of this kind have been excluded from this Section generally.

Then there is the vexed question of status. W.A. Copinger[1] can write rather slightingly of manor houses that have 'deteriorated' into farmhouses, but this is extremely misleading. For one thing, we never see anything derogatory today in a manor house in use as a farmhouse; for another, it must be apparent that, in a mainly agricultural county, many estimable old manor houses have been farmhouses ever since their foundations: Crows Hall, Debenham, could be taken as a case in point. It may be objected that, according to the method of classification adopted here, houses such as this should find themselves included under the heading of 'manor houses'. I would only plead that a manor house had many different faces, and could equally be in a sophisticated milieu, such as the manor house of the Earls of Bristol in Bury St. Edmunds. A building of that character could appear in my classification as a 'town house', just as a manor house with a distinctive farming character would appear as 'farmhouse'. In the section that follows I have, for these reasons, included a number of farmhouses which are manor houses, but whenever this occurs and they are known to be of manorial status, the fact is mentioned.

*Plate 268: Boundary Farm, Framsden.*

## The Moat Farm, Badingham
*TM 301 652*

The building of the present farmhouse in Tudor times (see Plate 269) does not exclude the possibility that it replaced an older dwelling elsewhere within the moated site. The new farmhouse must have been one of those being built in the parish of Badingham not long after the Nunnery of Bruisyard was granted to Sir Nicholas Hare in 1538. The house consisted of a single range of two storeys with attic quarters, and the accommodation downstairs was a 'house-place', a parlour and service rooms, and upstairs the best bed chamber, or solar, over the parlour and probably two further chambers over the house-place. The arrangement of bays from

1 cf. *The Manors of Suffolk*, op. cit.

*Plate 269: The Moat Farm: the south front across the moat.*

the east suggests a two-bay parlour, two further and narrower bays, the first of which was the entrance and the second part of the house-place with a further wide bay as far as the gable-end. There was a stack at the west end of the house, with, doubtless, additional service rooms beyond under a lean-to roof.

The next stage might have been in the early seventeenth century when a new large axial chimney stack was built between the parlour and the house-place, with an entrance into a lobby where the newel staircase, backing on to the stack, ascended to a first floor landing with doors at each side to bed chambers. At the same time as these changes, a new cross-wing was built at the west end replacing the older service rooms by a new 'baccus' with pantry and dairy and stairs to the new bed chambers above. At some time after this, the roof, originally thatched (as can be seen from the oversailing courses at the bottom of the chimney stack) was replaced by clay plain tiles, and the old house-place divided into two small rooms.

*Plate 270: Pargetting feature above the porch at The Moat Farm, Badingham.*

The original building, measuring some 14.5m by 5m (48ft by 16ft 6in.) was entirely framed in oak off a sill-piece set upon a low brick wall,[1] and was always a floored structure: the carpentry was regular and the timbers massive and well-shaped, with chamfered sides. Some original plank doors remain but the windows were all replaced in later centuries. The wall frames had probably been plastered over in the seventeenth century, but the pargetting is modern — the porch also.[2] All the structures at the rear of the house, and beyond the cross-wing are recent additions and the pargetting is modern (see Plate 270).

### Badley Hall, Badley
*TM 061 558*

In his drawing, made in 1973, John Western recorded not only the essential facts of latter-day Badley Hall, but also the tenuous atmosphere of past splendour (see Figure 76). From that vantage point it can be seen how the Hall had a main range with steeply-pitched roof, from the north gable-end of which still protruded the sawn-off ends of wall plates, a two-storey porch to the west, and a short wing running out eastward. Beyond this wing are the barns and farm buildings. A modern

1 The bricks will have been kilned locally, probably on the Rous' estate and possibly at Dennington where there are known to have been brick kilns.
2 Both the pargetting and the porch were designed by the author for the late Archibald Rose, C.I.E., who acquired the farm in 1931.

*Figure 76: Badley Hall, nr. Needham Market.
View from the north-east.*

75

annexe on the south does not appear. The property is some two miles south of Stowmarket, and in secluded country lying west of the road to Needham Market. Approached today by a winding farm road which turns off the main road at Badley Hill, the Hall in its heyday was reached by a near mile long avenue running absolutely straight from the Gipping valley, which Farrer says was called Badley Walk.[1] Traces of this avenue are still visible.

*Plate 271 (a): Detail of carved bressumer on north gable-end.*

*Plate 271 (b): Detail of carved bressumer on east elevation.*

A proposal that the house, which may well be mid-sixteenth century, was originally of E- or H-plan does not seem to be very solidly based, as structural indications are that the east wing is likely to have been a later addition to a single range, two-storey, hall-house.[2] There can be little doubt that the main hall with, presumably, upper end parlour and bed chambers, was dismantled, and that this accounts for the sawn off wall-plates and the improvised appearance of the north gable-end of the house. If the present porch was roughly in the centre, then the house could easily have been twice its present length. Farrer quotes the *Ipswich Journal* of March 2nd, 1759, advertising the sale at Badley Hall of 'the framework of a building about 60 feet long and 18 feet wide, the whole of good sound oak . . .', together with a number of doors, and windows, etc., and suggests that this was the great hall. His view, that the carved bressumer on the lower part of the otherwise blank, plastered gable was once the support for a gallery at the lower end of the hall, seems to be a distinct possibility; the top moulding is pierced at short, regular intervals by dowel holes, compatible with the tenoned joints of balusters (see Plate 271).[1] The chimney stack on the main range is doubtfully Elizabethan. and likely to have been a later addition, possibly when the building had been turned into 'tenements' and the hall was no longer used. An unusual late seventeenth or early eighteenth century feature is the flagged path, some 50 yards in length, enclosed within brick walls, which leads from the west porch to an entrance gateway (see Plate 272). This gave on to the roadway going north from the Hall, and must have become the main entrance, to judge from its ample proportions and solid brick piers, capped with stonework and ornamental pineapples.

*Plate 272: The original main entrance to Badley Hall.*

1 *E.A.M.*, Part II, April-June 1917; Part III, July-Sept. 1917.
2 Note the uncoordinated junction between this wing and the adjoining carved jetty beam, with its delicately carved and bracketed oak buttresses.

**Bedingfield Hall**
*TM 198 677*

Historians argue that Bedingfield Hall was not a residential manor, in the same way as Flemings Hall or Redlingfield Hall, and there is a suggestion that at some period in its history it may have become separated from the manor.[1] The moat must be one of the most impressive in Suffolk. It has been estimated to contain an area of about four acres, measuring over 200 metres on each side of a generally rectangular shape, and originally rounded at the corners. The walls are deep, all of 2 metres from ground to water level with a width of some 8 metres and it was, when examined in 1974, filled with extremely clear water, in which the white plaster walls and tall brick chimneys were perfectly mirrored. The moat opened into ponds

*Plate 273: The two ranges facing into the courtyard.*

at two corners and at one point connected with a fishpond, which occupied part of the centre of the island parallel with the south-east range of the Hall; its full extent has not, I believe, been accurately surveyed nor archaeologically examined.

The interest of Bedingfield Hall now centres in two building ranges, one running parallel with the south-western side of the moat, and the other running south-east of slightly wider girth and higher roof line. Thus there were two dwellings at right angles, each facing outwards to the moat and inwards into a courtyard (see Plate 273). The explanation hitherto of the function of these two structures is the one which assigns to the south-western range the role of chief farmhouse of a non-residential manor, and to the south-eastern an adjunct of later date providing

1 cf. *E.A.M.*, op. cit., No. 7331: Bedingfield Hall by E.F. Botesdale.

*Plate 274: The south-western range facing the moat.*

better living-rooms and bedrooms than in the earlier range, although this is not borne out by the evidence.[1] The building on the west side remains a useful guide to an Elizabethan Suffolk farmhouse, although in external appearance it is disappointing in detail owing to changes probably in the late seventeenth or early eighteenth century. These probably took place at the same time as work was going on to the building on the east side of the courtyard.

The farmhouse wing is the type of dwelling to be seen on many sites in the east and centre of Suffolk, a long simple rectangle with steeply pitched tiled roof. It is timber-framed and plastered externally, of two storeys with a length of 21-22m (65-70ft) and a girth of 5-6m (16-18ft). The ground floor arrangement consisted of a dairy (later converted to double garage) at the north-west end with a cheese room over. This is still reached by the original staircase and contains the oak flooring and the suspended shutters to two unaltered open mullion and transom windows, exactly as put in by the builders in the sixteenth century. The north-west window projects slightly, oriel-wise, with a moulded sill member, and, together with the long dairy window below was obviously carefully designed to give a good appearance to the main gable facing the entrance side of the house. The disposition of rooms can be figured from the position of the great four-shafted ornamental chimney stack externally. This indicates entrance to a stack lobby, probably with newel stairs — as is the case here — with living-room on the south side and kitchen on the other, each having back-to-back fireplaces, with a further fireplace in each of the principal bed chambers over. Beyond the kitchen were service rooms leading through to the larder. There was sleeping space on the first floor and storage in the attics to which the newel stair ascended. It is one of the great assets of Bedingfield Hall that there are so many unaltered original carpentry and joinery details belonging to a large Elizabethan farmhouse, the life of which it is not at all difficult to reconstruct.

On the maps it is shown as 'Poplars Farm', but on a recent change of ownership the name reverted to the colloquial Suffolk for poplar trees — 'Popples'. The site was evidently fully moated, suggesting that it has been built on since earlier centuries, but much of the moat has since been filled in and, today, it is the western arm, and a short part of the southern arm, that still exist (see Plate 275). In a parish of mainly roadside farms, Popples — together with Ryece Hall — must be among the largest,[2] but moats appear to have existed only at Roses Farm and Poplars Farm.

The buildings on the site suggest work of at least three centuries; the fifteenth, sixteenth and twentieth. Of the earliest of these there is probably no more than a

### Popples Farm, Brettenham
TL 953 527

*Plate 275: The western range flanking the moat, Popples Farm*

1 Originally there was no access between this range and the other, the junction being added as part of the work in the succeeding century. A similar occurence of two wings conjoined at a corner is to be found at Brundish Manor. Mr. D. Penrose suggests that the old structure was an aisled hall of which half remains. The theory of a non-residential manor is, therefore, now likely to be much less tenable.

2 The Ordnance Survey shows no less than twelve farmhouses in Brettenham, and there may well be others.

*Plate 276: The modern addition on the east, Popples Farm.*

two-bay range surviving at the north end. This suggests that an older house may have been partially demolished and the long seven-bay range added in $1540^{\pm}$, as an evidence of considerably increased prosperity. The accommodation would then have consisted of a large house-place or hall — with parlour at the south end separated from the hall by a back-to-back fireplace. The pantry and buttery would have been in the older rear annexe, and a short wing built out to the east — and subsequently largely modernised — could have been added at the end of the sixteenth or early in the following century. This wing has now been adapted for entrance and staircase, and balances a further dining-room wing built since the last War, when the house was carefully modernised under the direction of Mr. Marshall Sisson, A.R.A., F.R.I.B.A. As a part of this work the elevations on the east side of the house were finished in traditional plasterwork with pargetted panels (see Plate 276). The remaining sides of the house have been altered only in respect of modern casement windows, and retain accomplished carpentry with narrowly spaced studs. The chief enrichment was concentrated at the south of the main range, in the gable-end facing towards the road, and there can be no doubt that both the owners and the carpenters intended their work to be seen — and admired — by passers-by. The use of tension bracing, with its diagonal timbers, was practically excluded from the work, stiffness being produced by close studding and jettying the first floor over the ground floor frame. The roof was pitched up steeply to take thatching, and this, weathered, as a good reed will, to silver grey, blends with the natural grey weathering of the unstained timber-work to give an extraordinarily clear statement of the appearance of a traditional timber-framed Suffolk farmhouse.

In his drawing of the south gable-end (see Figure 77), John Western shows the main elements of the most consciously 'designed' part of the house; the division into three tiers of the vertical studwork, with the horizontal lines emphasised by roll-mouldings, the varying sill levels, and the brickwork forming a 'base' to the central ground floor window.[1] The ribbon windows are reminiscent of the Lavenham Guildhall, and it is almost certain that — before the addition of the east wing — they continued along the east side of the house in exactly the same way as they do on the west. The carpenter enriched the ground floor sills with a carved trail pattern of foliated leaves, and the oversail of the gable beyond the first floor window by a pair of very Perpendicular-Tudor ornamental pendants, linked to the main bressumer line over by narrow carved spandril pieces. There are, as yet, no 'foreign' classical elements to confuse the pure Gothic tradition of house building which, in Suffolk, continued well into the Elizabethan era.

1 Compare this five-light bay window with that in an identical position in the centre of the roadside gable-end at Swan's Hall, Hawkedon; where, however, there is considerably more enrichment and the detail of the carving shows very clearly the influence of the Flemish pattern books.

251

Figure 77: Popples Farm, Brettenham. Jettied south gable-end.

Plate 277: The two ranges facing into the entrance courtyard – Brundish Manor.

**Brundish Manor**
TM 264 703

Superficially there is a marked resemblance between the structural relationship of the two wings of Brundish Manor and those of Bedingfield Hall. Two ranges, one long and one short, meet at an angle forming an L-shape, with a moat on the outer side and a courtyard on the inner (see Plates 277 and 278). The Manor House, however, is within twenty yards of the road and separated from it by little more than the width of the moat. Still appearing on the 2½ inch Ordnance Survey as 'The Poplars', it forms one of a group of houses that together make up the hamlet of Brundish Street. The country hereabouts is high and flat, and the soil the deep clay of High Suffolk; moats are plentiful and there are at least seven moated houses within a couple of miles. It is deep farming country, and Brundish Manor was evidently built as the house of a gentleman farmer. In spite of the name, it was never a manor house, although evidently part of the manorial property of Brundish Hall.[1]

The entire structure is timber-framed on a brick base wall and is now plastered over; assuming the relatively early date of the main north-south range and the consistently good carpentry of the exposed studwork internally, it seems probable that the timberwork would originally have been exposed. The absence of a diagrammatic scheme of framing accounts for the odd appearance of the long narrow mullioned oak windows on the gable-end facing north-west towards the road (see Plate 279). There is a design problem here which effects many early timber-framed houses where the wall openings, mainly windows, can appear singularly odd and unrelated, especially when they are of varying sizes, without the supporting grid of framework. A good example of this kind is at Basts, Grundisburgh, where the wing adjoining the first build was subsequently plastered over, with results similar to the gable-end under discussion here. The remainder of the Brundish Manor windows are mainly of late seventeenth or early eighteenth century lead lights with mullions and an occasional transom, although a few earlier oak mullions appear on the secondary range. This range is of later build, and, as can be seen from the height of the first floor windows, the roof was raised to provide

*Plate 278: View from the north-east across the moat.*

1 cf. Copinger, op. cit., Volume 4, pages 22-23. Copinger gives the devolution from Robert Malet, the Domesday tenant-in-chief, to the Willoughbys, who were owners in the fifteenth and sixteenth centuries until it passed to Anthony Wingfield, who sold to Anthony Rous.

*Plate 279: Brundish Manor — the gable-end facing north-west.*     *Plate 280: Later passage to first floor.*

*Plate 281: Original moulded plank-door.*

more accommodation. The appearance of entirely thatched roofs is a great asset, by pointing to the type of roofing which was widely prevalent before plain tiles became more plentiful during the sixteenth century. There are no ambitious chimney stacks, although, since the main chimney in the north-south range was contemporary with the structure it is likely once to have been decorative and to have been rebuilt later. A seventeenth century date would account for the second stack which was built to serve the original kitchen, and could have been an addition to the earlier structure.

The planning of this range was on fairly orthodox late mediavel lines. The screens-passage entered the hall, at the upper end of which there was the chimney and fireplace, and on either side of the stack a lobby leading to the parlour at the north end of the range. There must have been a newel stair in one of these lobbies leading to the two main bed chambers, for there was certainly no passage in the first build and they would have been accessible only by these means (see Plate 280) There was originally no connection with the sleeping chamber over the service end of the house, and access to this was gained by a steep staircase for which the timbers used to form the stair-well in the first floor framework can be clearly seen On the ground floor this must have been the farmhouse kitchen, with, doubtless, a small buttery and pantry separating it from the screens-passage. At a later stage, the service quarters were transferred to the secondary range.

The same good quality evident in the structural framework is to be found also in the joinery. The oak ceiling joists are rib moulded and each terminates with a spear point in which the mouldings are gathered 'like the end of a fold of linen'. The moulded plank doors are original, and have shaped heads of fifteenth century pattern, with Tudor roses carved in the spandrils (see Plate 281). Farrer also drew attention to the original iron hinges and fitments on these doors, and to the sad circumstance that wainscot with which the parlour was formerly panelled, had been stripped out early in this century. Brundish Manor seems then to have been a farmhouse *tout court,* with most of its excellent craftsmanship covered with limewash and plaster, and it was evidently at that time that the panelling was seen coveted, sold and removed.[1] In spite of these depredations the Manor House admirably maintained, is still an excellent guide to the taste and structural skill of late mediaeval builders in Suffolk.

1 Acc. Farrer, the then owner told him '... it was a perfect example of a complete room, with frieze, mantelpiece, and even pegs for the coats and hats.'

*Figure 78: Hempnalls Hall, Cotton. View from the west prior to restoration.*

## Hempnalls Hall, Cotton
### TM 082 675

It is easy to see how such an interesting old manor house could come to be forgotten, in its out-of-the-way corner of the parish of Cotton (see Figure 78). The boundary of the parish runs within one field on the east, and the house itself is a good three quarters of a mile from the village and approached, together with Willow Farm, by a winding farm road. There is another way from the north, known as The Avenue, which would seem to date from the heyday of Hempnalls Hall in the sixteenth century; it was described in the sale particulars as 'a fine old elm avenue 250 yards long'. Vestiges still remain along the broad straight grassed way, although the avenue itself has been cut down and the distance to the road is probably nearer a quarter mile, but the lush grasslands and large elm trees which surround the property continue to give Hempnalls Hall a remote, deep country feeling. The name is attributed to the family of Hemenshall, or Hemenhale, belonging to the village of that name — or Hempnall — in the county of Norfolk. The site is moated, and in conformity with its origins, the moat could have been made in the thirteenth century: the island within the moat is comparatively small and square, measuring rather less than 16 metres each way, although in an overgrown condition it was difficult to do more than guess that the width was about 5 metres. Access seems originally to have been by a wooden bridge. The house consisted of a main single range occupying the south side of the island, with a short rear wing, the front entrance to the main range being on the north. The chief architectural feature externally[1] was the splendid Elizabethan gable end which, at a date of circa 1590, is likely to have been an addition as at Flemings Hall, Bedingfield. There were pairs of window openings, since blocked up, to rooms on each floor, and the gable ascended with four crow-steps to the wide base of a pair of octagonal chimney shafts. For Suffolk stepped gables these are unusually wide and high, being much closer to sixteenth century patterns in the Netherlands. The rear wing, with its triple diagonally set chimney shafts rising from a massive base, has the look of being an addition in the seventeenth century — probably together with the wing itself.

## Roydon Hall, Creeting St. Peter
### TM 084 585

Not of manorial status (the nearest Manor in the parish is that of Brazier's Hall), Roydon Hall possesses nevertheless an architectural status which would do justice

*Plate 282: A picture postcard of Roydon Hall, c.1930.*

to any of the smaller manor houses of Suffolk (see Plates 282 and 283). By some curious anomaly the parish boundary between Creeting St. Peter and Earl Stonham passes across the yard at the back of the house, and takes in both rear wings as well as most of the moat which has the look of being once roughly square and including the hall and barn within the island. The site was well chosen in the centre of a forward spur of the 175ft contour, the land falling away slowly to the south and west in the valley of the Gipping River. The nearest hamlet is the scattering of cottages called West Creeting Green, just over a quarter mile away, with the church — in this most scattered of parishes — alone with a Rectory house in amongst fields half a mile south of Roydon Hall.

The following notes were taken at Roydon Hall in September, 1973:—

1 Internally the original fittings seem to have suffered from considerable depredation and neglect.

## A. Externally

### Elevation

(1)  The stack, 8ft wide at base by 3ft projection, the whole structure being clearly additional to and built up against the frame.

The brickwork is unusual, starting with a moulded base at 2ft 6in. above ground level. Bricks 8¾in. by 4¼in. by 2in. Joints average ⅜in. At 10ft above ground level there is a change – up to that height Bond Eng. with diapers of dark headers, each taking 9 brick course for complete diamond, and 4 diamonds in each row, 3½ rows in all: above the bond changes to stretcher and continues for remainder of height. The stack is tumbled in 5 times starting about 10ft above bond change line. Originally there was an Elizabethan stack. The present reduction in width at fourth tumble is modern and ugly.

(2)  Structure to E of stack is probably Victorian or Edwardian; bricks uniform red 9in. by 4½in. by 2½in. with average ½in. mortar joint – bond Flemish.

(3)  The small lean-to structure to W of stack is stretcherbond of same brick as stack and the moulded plinth appears, although there is a vert. straight joint between this and stack. (*NB* The garden wall brickwork: bricks are 9in. by 4¼in. by 2in. pretty well identical with stack and there is partial diapering – suggesting this is contemporary with the stack. The diaper appears again clearly on W boundary wall abutting the SW corner of the house and going straight to join the end of the barn – where it stops.)

(4)  The W stack (of same vintage as the S) but somewhat smaller and very truncated – prob. the outer skin in red and white alternate courses was someone's fancy work much later, although the upper part looks like a simple Tudor job.

(5)  The E stacks; one sticks out of the SW wing on the yard side and is cemented over; the other is on the gable of the NW wing in 'header bond' of C16 - C17 ? vintage. The other stack from the kitchen is entirely modern.

## B. The Moat

Two sides of the original moat extant – long arm on the S/N axis with a short arm on the E/W axis at the S end. It was a good wide moat – average 30ft.

## C. Roof examination

As guide to sub-sctructures, the following phases appear:–

1st  A wing SE at rt angles to existing long SW block: of this there remains fragment of a former oak roof of king-post variety, arch-braced in long direction only on to a runner. This appears to have ended at about the NW wall line of the long SW block, but as it has been cut off inside the roof, could have gone on further toward SW cross-wing fashion. There is no evidence of another roof joining this at rt angles on either side and so this could be the remains of the earliest long-house on the site running NE/SW – the span equivalent to the present wing, viz. approx. 18ft (mid C15).

2nd  A large oak framed structure of 5 bays running SE/NW at rt angles to above. It was the erection of this structure that necessitated the mutilation of the old roof referred to above. It appears that the plan of the house was transformed into an L. The central 3 bays of this structure undoubtedly served a large hall (possibly without an intermediate floor?). Anyway there was a large 3-bay room with a ceiling some 2ft or so higher than the existing rooms with ornamental plasterwork. Conjecturally the solar end was at SE and the service at NW.

3rd  The alteration of the phase 2 work, the lowering of the ceilings and forming of 3 bedrooms with ornamental plasterwork.

4th  The C18/C19 alterations when the whole of the original roofs were straightened up and new rafters laid over the old and the house retiled, etc., etc.

## D. Internally

The Parlour/Hall/Service sequence can be detected in the existing ground-floor plan, with the addition of further accommodation at each end in the form of rear wings.

The roof structure examination indicated an earlier single-range (?) hall running NE/SW which was incorporated in the later structure – an extensive rebuilding, attributed by Farrer[1] to a Capt. Flick between 1595 and 1600, who also traces a James Rivett as living in a house on the same site in 1568: presumably it is this house which was built into the new work at the end of the century.

If this is acceptable then, in the interior fitting out of the new Roydon Hall by the new owner, excellent tradesmen were employed. The quality of the wainscot, deep roll moulded joists and beams (see Plate 102), staircase (see Plate 118), doors and hinges, and plasterwork at first floor ceiling level is high.

The unusual feature seems to have been the existence of a lofty first floor room with partly domed and ornamental ceiling corresponding in size with the hall below. The house was 'Georgianised' – fortunately only externally – in late eighteenth or early nineteenth century when the present roof, external doors, sash windows, etc. were made.

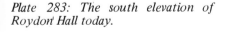

*Plate 283: The south elevation of Roydon Hall today.*

1  cf. *E.A.M.,* op. cit., No. 4214, page 33.

*Plate 284: The bridge, the moat and the Gatehouse.*

Claude Morley saw secrecy as the key to the position of Debenham, like so many early Anglo-Saxon settlements hereabouts, and the conjunction of streams in a valley a natural site for dwellings.[1] From the west the River Deben flowed in, to change direction where it met the Aspall affluent and flow south-east, swelled by three further streams rising in the surrounding uplands. It was on the most easterly of these uplands that Crows Hall was built, and if secrecy was the origin of Debenham, defence was clearly that of this farming outpost. The site had been chosen on the summit of ground rising from the Deben valley, little more than a mile away from the township, to which it was linked by tracks and a single roadway, ending where the buildings began. For practically the last half mile it straightened into an avenue – doubtless a Tudor device – where, enclosed by broad green margins, the road was flanked by the double row of oaks which still identify the site of Crows Hall on the skyline above the Deben valley.

The moat system was complex, and the only portion still completely intact is that forming the island on which Crows Hall itself is built. There is a supposition that this may have been only one of three or more moats, within which were enclosed outbuildings and stock, for the extensive farming tradition is coexistent with, and no doubt originated in, the first dwellings and buildings on the site. The hall moat measures somewhat over 90 metres each way (say 100 yards) and forms a square island accessible at only one point, and, logically enough, at the extreme end of the western approach road. Of the earliest buildings on the island there are now no traces but, with a manorial history extending to 1086, when the first Norman

*Plate 285: West gable-end and moat.*

1 cf. *E.A.M.*, op. cit., No. 11832: Suffolk Names –
Debenham.

owner was Ranulph Peverel (behind whom stands the powerful but shadowy figure of the Anglo-Saxon Lord Seaxa), the site can have been occupied from earliest times. The Records of the Star Chamber,[2] mention a chapel at Crows Hall in 1519, and, if a chapel then there was — as Farrer commented — 'certainly a great deal more.'[2] Timbers from some of these earlier buildings may well have been reused later, together with doors, and it is here that scientific dating by radio-carbon testing, or dendrochronology, might yield valuable information.

When so much of this great establishment remains, there can only be disappointment that so little is left of the actual Tudor Hall, which evidently replaced the older buildings in the mid-sixteenth century. It is Sir Charles Framlingham who has always been identified as the most likely builder, for it is his coat of arms which appears above the gatehouse entrance, with Neville quarterings (see Plate 284).[3] Historians of the Tudor period have supplied much detailed information on the devolution of the manor of Crows Hall, and all this is well recorded. Less attention has been given to the architecture and layout of the buildings, due partly, no doubt, to lack of direct evidence as to the original plan. The situation at Crows Hall is in some ways the reverse of that at Roos Hall, near Beccles; there the tall, narrow brick range, not dissimilar in proportions, remains one wing of an uncompleted mansion — at Crows Hall the solitary range is all that is left of a once much larger establishment. One of the letters in the Verney Papers, dated November 15th, 1658, says of Crows Hall '. . . the seate is good and pleasant and that old house (in my conceit) excells the Louvre and Escuriall.' This letter was written in November of the year in which Oliver Cromwell died (September 3rd, 1658), and could scarcely have been put like this if, as popular tradition has it, much of the house had previously been destroyed by Cromwellian cannon. The Gawdy family had then been in possession since 1595, and in 1657, the then Lady Gawdy's eldest son was married, and the entertainment at Crows Hall was obviously delightful, and lavish. These chance records point to the house being very much of a going concern in the late seventeenth century, and from another reference in the same papers we know that there was attic space, called 'vane roof', above the 'dining chamber', for this was occupied at the time of the wedding by Lady Gawdy and 'all her family of women'. The remaining north wing was clearly neither a parlour nor guest chamber range, and can only have been the service rooms below, with sleeping chambers above: the probability is therefore that the 'dining chamber', or hall, abutted this range and must have been sited at right angles to it — in other words parallel with the porch range. This can only mean a courtyard plan, with the remaining south wing providing parlours and accommodation for guests and possibly family, and completing the fourth side of the square (see Figure 79). The retaining wall of brick to the moat, along the west side of the island, would have provided a base for another wing about equidistant from the centre, as well as for the rest of the gatehouse range.

Against this background one would expect sixteenth century Crows Hall to present an ornate facade at the avenue's end, with a pair of similar gable-ends, supported by polygonal angle buttresses capped with moulded brick finials, flanking the single-storey range in the centre, the gatehouse and its buttresses and pepper-pots (see Plate 285). The front facing east, judging by the surviving gable, may have been fairly plain. Until further evidence comes to light, the destruction of the east and south courtyard buildings cannot be satisfactorily accounted for, although the possibility that some, at least, of these structures may have been timber-framed would explain why no traces are left. A fire — not apparently extensive — is recorded in 1814.

In the work that does remain there is much of quality. The brickwork is excellent, and enriched by an overall diaper of dark 'headers'.[4] Some sixteenth century mullion and transom windows remain in recessed brick frames, of which the heads on the west elevation are slightly cambered. The staircase of late Elizabethan work has already been illustrated, and is, I believe, without any exact parallel in Suffolk. On the first floor, there is good Stuart wainscot and some unusual marquetried doors (collectors' pieces imported from elsewhere — possibly abroad?), and also a number of plank doors with frames which could easily have come from a late fifteenth or early sixteenth century building (perhaps the earlier

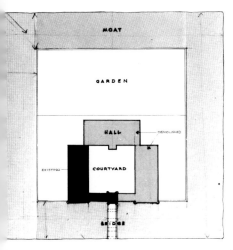

*Figure 79: Conjectural block plan of the original Crows Hall.*

1 cf. *The Manors of Suffolk*, Volume I, page 202.
2 cf. *E.A.M.*, op. cit., No. 6284, page 40.
3 Ibid., page 43.
4 The bricks were probably made quite close to the house in a spot known as 'Brick Kiln Close', adjoining which is a field called 'Brick Kiln Meadow'.

Figure 80: Elizabethan Barn, Crows Hall, Debenham.

Hall?). The oak roof construction is exactly as it was left by the carpenters in the middle sixteenth century, with heavy principal timbers about every 7 feet connected by purlins, which support common rafters about 14 inches apart: all the roof timbers have scratch joint assembly marks about 4 inches in length.

Any description of Crows Hall omitting the 100ft long stable building immediately west and south of the moat would be incomplete (see Figure 80). This was, by any reckoning, a major architectural feature amongst the outbuildings, being in brickwork which could antedate the building of the Hall, and divided into two storeys and a hay loft, the lower storey providing stabling and the upper — conjecturally — accommodation for retainers. It was certainly there across the yard when Lady Gawdy wrote a letter to Sir Ralph Verney of Claydon, Bucks, lamenting that Crows Hall 'is as dirty as Claydon without dors.'

## The Butterfly, Great Finborough
TM 003 563

*Plate 286: The main north/south range and the cross-wing.*

*Plate 287: The house from the south-east.*

1 The origin of 'Butterfly' is uncertain. According to the Rev. H. Copinger Hill (d.1948) the local name for the *fleur-de-lys* form used in the pargetting was 'butterfly'. There is a 'Butterfly Hall' at Attleborough in Norfolk, but the owner tells me that it was renamed thus early in this century on account of the prolific quantity of butterflies in the neighbourhood.

The name is on the maps as 'Butterfly Farm',[1] and, to judge by the buildings, it was a small working farmhouse deliberately sited in the middle of lands, the greater part of which, in Copinger's day, were in the neighbouring parish of Buxhall. Outwardly unpretentious, it is one of a type deeply-rooted in the building history of Suffolk, preserving a mute record of the changing fortunes of successive owners through many centuries. That there was, first of all, a single range with gable-ended roof is evident, both from documents and structure (see Plates 286 and 287). This is the long arm of a T-plan running north-south, and may well correspond with the house mentioned in the will of William Copinger, September 3rd, 1436, under the description of 'a tenement called Cordes in Finborough Magna'. With an oak sill set above ground on a few courses of brickwork, and a solidly framed oak superstructure, the essentials of this range could well date from the reign of Henry VI. The likelihood is, however, that the house-place was floored over when the chimney stack was built in the following century, and the newel stair put in on the east side of the stack accessible by lobby at both ground and first floors. Thus the first plan has not greatly changed; there was always a parlour at the south end of the range with a sleeping chamber above (reached by a ladder?) and, centrally, a house-place or hall, where the cooking and all the general work of the farmhouse went on. Beyond this, in the bay now occupied by staircase and store, would have

*Plate 288: The elevation of the north cross-wing.*

been a small pantry and buttery and, possibly, a lean-to giving a 'baccus' as this would not have interfered with the decoration of the upper part of the wall, and, doubtless, the gable-end also, with pargetting in the late sixteenth century. There was certainly always a doorway at this end of the house and it is unlikely to have been the main entrance, which, supposedly, has continued to be in the present place entering the house-place at the lower end on the west: above this there would have been more sleeping or storage space.

The next work stage was the building of the cross-wing at the north end, completing the top of the T-, and the structure suggests that this could have been done in the middle of the seventeenth century — possibly during the ownership of John Ransford of Great Finborough (see Plate 288). The new wing provided a kitchen and a large parlour at the west and east ends respectively, separated by a large chimney stack with back-to-back fireplaces. On the first floor three further rooms were added, very sensibly connected by a passage which opened on to the landing at the head of the new stairway. The addition was built in the same traditional way as the original structure, with an oak timber-frame set on a base of brickwork, the stud wall infilling being wattle and daub, completely plastered over outside. Since that date there have been alterations of a minor kind, chiefly the addition of windows (compare Ayliffe's drawing (see Figure 81) with Plate 286 taken from roughly the same position), and numerous repairs to chimneys and roofs, which have been retiled. The present owner has himself renewed defective plasterwork using traditional methods, and an account of these is given below. The difference in results compared with the use of modern quick setting renderings or plasterwork has to be seen to be believed.

### Repair of Plaster using original methods.

Walls constructed with wattle and daub or clay-lump can be repaired very satisfactorily by using materials similar to the original.

The mixture consists of three measures of clay to a half measure of hydrated lime. Sufficient water and chopped straw are added to this.

The clay should be dug from below the level of the top soil. Material from old walls can be used as an alternative.

The straw should be chopped roughly into 6in. lengths — smaller pieces can also be added. It will in fact be difficult to add too much straw, but straw must be well mixed with the clay so that it is covered.

The clay and lime should be well mixed together on a flat hard surface as in making cement. The consistency and the amount of straw to be added is a matter of experience in use. If there is too much straw or if there is too much water the material is difficult to use.

The chopped straw is scattered over the clay mixture and trodden into it with some water being added as required, until by repeated additions of straw and subsequent treading the working consistency is achieved.

To repair holes in existing work moisten the area to be repaired as the clay combines more easily with a wet surface. Larger areas for repair may require replacement of wattles. The material can also be used on lathes, including repairs to ceilings, providing the layer is not too thick and well-lapped around the lathes.

The initial packing and smoothing can be done by hand providing rubber gloves are worn as protection. Floats or trowels are used in finishing, bearing in mind at all times the need to match existing work.

*Figure 81: The Butterfly — after a drawing by Ayliffe.*

**Castling's Hall, Groton**
*TL 972 433*

Situated on a by-road between Groton village and Lindsey, in the midst of farming country, Castling's Hall seems to have been somewhat eclipsed by the numerous old houses in the surrounding country, for it is rarely mentioned in Gazetteers.[1]

The house is one of those that suffered the vicissitudes of 'Georgianisation' in the eighteenth or nineteenth century, when the jettied first floor seems to have been underbuilt, sash windows put in, and the whole exterior plastered over. Not only was the late-mediaeval character camouflaged but the timber-framework heavily cut about in the process, and the recovery of a good deal of the original character is due to the purchase of the property in the 1920s by Mr. Herbert West, and the efforts of Basil Oliver, A.R.I.B.A., his architect (and author of *Old House and Village Buildings in East Anglia* (see General Bibliography) himself an East Anglian). In view of the unusual interest of the record, it is worth quoting from the article which Oliver published describing the restoration: ' . . . Sufficient evidence came to light to enable me to know what the fenestration of the lower floor was like in Elizabethan days, although I had to guess the size and position of the upper windows . . . As to the high window lights many of them were found complete, some damaged and others missing . . . A certain amount of new work was inevitable but it was only done where absolutely necessary . . . It would have been impossible

*Plate 289: A general view from the south-west.*

1 Pevsner gives only the parish church of St. Bartholomew, and the motte called Pytches Mount in Groton Park.

*Plate 290(a): Detail of carved sills and buttresses.*

*Plate 290(b): Detail of carved bressumer.*

*Plate 290(c): Detail of a carved bracket at Castling's Hall, Groton.*

to complete the damaged lights otherwise, but elsewhere all new oak window frames, mullions, etc. are quite plain, being merely splayed and rounded internally, to differentiate the new work from that which is authentic. Where it was necessary to continue and complete the carved transoms this has been done in plain oak. A certain amount of conjecture as to the original design was unavoidable, but there has been no falsification. Anyone can see what is old and what is not, yet at a distance the whole appearance of the house is harmonious and pleasant'.

Few people would disagree with Mr. Oliver, but in detail the results do illustrate the hazards of conjectural restoration (see Plate 289). There is the inescapably 'cut off' look of the west gable end due to the lack of a balancing cross-wing which at Great Bevills, Bures, for example (a comparable restoration job), satisfactorily contains the intermediate fenestration. Nor is the detailing of the porch so successful as Great Bevills, where the gabled roof manages to avoid overlapping the first-floor overhang. Farrer thought there had been a balancing cross-wing [1] in Elizabethan days, as well as a two-storeyed porch, but does not give any ground for the statement. These features would have been quite compatible with a late Elizabethan manor house. They would also account for the missing parlour and solar end, which would have occupied the west cross-wing, and restore the plan to proper order with the pantry, buttery and service rooms at the lower end of the hall in the east cross-wing. The present entrance would be in the correct position.

What we now see is the substantial rebuilding of an older timber-framed manor house, with a great deal of the material being reused (a decorative example being the reuse of Tudor-Gothic buttresses and brackets below the jetty, and a structural example in the present dining-room — old service room — which, as Farrer observed, has roughly hewn beams 'which do not cross one another exactly in the centre'). Some of these details were extensively photographed by Liza Whipp and are reproduced here (see Plate 290). The exact modular relationship between main upright timbers at bay centres and the window units, together with carving, suggests that the close studded framed walls were intended to be seen, and that, above the jetty, the same close studwork would have continued until it met the line of the first floor windows. (The absence of this studwork is again one of the rather unconvincing aspects of Mr. Oliver's restoration.) The old house may have been lit by windows on both sides, which would explain the need for extensive fenestration on the south side when William Clopton added his massive chimney stack on the north, with its triple shafts and elaborately detailed stellar tops.

Pending documentary research, one is left to guess that the west wing was demolished in the eighteenth/nineteenth century, perhaps when Castling's Hall was disguised as a Georgian farmhouse. The farm buildings themselves press closely on the house along the north side, and may always have done so — another reason for concentrating so many windows on the south.

1 cf. *E.A.M.*, op. cit., No. 5717.

264

## Swans Hall, Hawkedon
*TL 796 512*

*Plate 291: A general view of the house from the south-east.*

During the reigns of the Tudor sovereigns, and particularly between 1500-1600, there is plenty of evidence, not only in Suffolk but elsewhere, of immense building activity. During this hundred years old houses were demolished and rebuilt, remodelled, and added to. A favourite form in this county took the practical course of retaining an old range, built, say, during the preceding century but adding a wing in the new style. This is largely what took place at Swans Hall, where the rear range was a timber-framed farmhouse put up during the fifteenth century by country carpenters, using massive sections and arch-braces. Built on to this later, in such a way as almost completely to conceal the old house, was a five-bay range running east towards the approach road, where it finished with a very showy gable-end (see Plate 291). Examples can be multiplied; something similar took place at Poplars Farm, Brettenham, and at Earl Soham a swagger new wing was added to Rookery Farm during the reign of Henry VIII, c.1530, again running towards the highway.

At Swans Hall, the oak framework is fully exposed in both the earlier and later ranges, making a study of the progress in carpentry methods, during the hundred or so years that may separate them, a rewarding exercise. The little that remains of the

*Swans Hall, Hawkedon – Basil Oliver.*

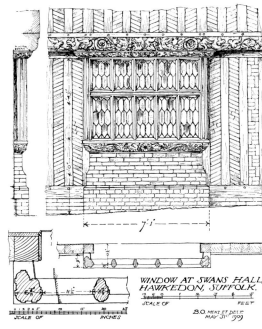

*Figure 82: The parlour window after a drawing by Basil Oliver.*

265

old house suggests that the hall, parlour and solar were probably demolished, leaving only the service rooms. To this was butted the new range with a two-bay hall or house-place, a chimney stack bay, and a further two-bay parlour, the great bed chamber being above the latter, slightly jettied over the room below. In the roof space there were attic rooms and a further jetty in the gable-end: at the opposite end, the new roof was 'crippled in' to the old with eaves and ridge both well above their previous levels. The setting out of the framework shows the complete mastery achieved by carpenters in the mid-late sixteenth century. The whole system is clear and logical; a brick wall some five courses in height supports the oak sill, and off this are framed both the principal posts and the intermediate studs divided horizontally into two at storey height by a bressumer or middle-rail, and then taken up to the wall plate at roof level. The principal posts engage with trusses in the roof frame, supporting horizontal purlins which, in turn provide support for the common rafters spaced at about the same intervals as the wall studs. The position of the collars is indicated on the gable, where the horizontal tie also serves as a lintel for the window. Windows and doors are all determined by the modular spacing of studs, which, it will be noted, are uniformly eight in number with the exception of the chimney stack bay — where they reduce to five — and the first floor jetty where they are increased by one.

The carpenters — in conformity, no doubt, with the instructions of the building's owner — reserved their skill in fancy work for the gable-end facing the roadway. The principal features were the double jetties which oversail, each accommodating a 'boxed-out' shallow bay window. The parlour window was

*Plate 292(a): Detail of bressumer over ground floor bay window, Swans Hall, Hawkedon.*

beautifully drawn by Basil Oliver[1] and his sketch is reproduced (see Figure 82). It will not escape the observant that he reproduced the lozenge design of the lead quarries used in the window above — compare with Plate 45 — and not that of the ground floor window where the lozenge proportions were skilfully reduced to give *four* below transom and *three* above. The intermediate rail, or bressumer, on turning across the end elevation was gracefully carved with a running foliage pattern and grotesque heads, two of which flanked the initials of the owner — 'W.A.' — and his merchant-mark (see Plate 292).[2] Below the gable proper there is a further carved bressumer, the overhang of which rests at each end on the projection of the wall plates, which, in turn, are supported by ornamental brackets. Engaging with these brackets are carved spandril-pieces, each of which terminates in a decorative pendant flanking the upper chamber bay window — a device not unlike the arrangements in a similar position at Popples, Brettenham. Also reminiscent of Popples is the brick base to the ground floor bay window shown in Oliver's drawing.

That house can boast no such fine octagonal chimney shafts which, although not entirely axial, would seem to be part of the same build as the rest of the work and have excellent star-tops. When viewed together with the gable end they appear to accent the verticality of the whole design, and confirm the impression that craftsmanship of a high order went into the addition to Swans Hall. The house was long in the family of Abbot, and Copinger includes the 'Manor of Swans Hall' in his inventory of Suffolk Manors.[3]

1 cf. *Old Houses and Village Buildings in East Anglia,* op. cit., page 11.
2 In a note in *Merchants' Marks in Suffolk* (Proceedings S.I.A., Volume XXIX, 1962, page 115) F.A. Girling says these initials may stand for a member of the Abbot family, and adds that the carving is very similar to a bressumer at Highlin's Farm, Monks Eleigh, date 1594, and of another at Brettenham dated 1587 (? Poplar Farm, where there are resemblances in the carved window sills, spandrils and pendants, but with none of the Flemish influence which appears at Swans Hall). Although a William Abbot paid the subsidy in 1568, Girling concurs with Farrer in dating the Swans Hall carving to 1590-1600.
3 op. cit., Volume 5, page 250. It would be appropriate to add that Swans Hall is mentioned in an American book by Bond: *Genealogies of the Families of the Early Settlers of Waterstown, Massachusetts;* a will of 1531 refers to a 'tenement with appurtenances called Swaynes at Hawkedon'. Farrer doubted whether this could be Swans Hall (cf. *E.A.M.,* April-June 1927, No. 7448).

*Plate 292(b): Detail of bressumer at gable overhang.*

*Plate 292(c): Detail of carving to ground floor bressumer.*

### Valley Farm, Huntingfield
*TM 343 735*

*Plate 293: Distant view of Valley Farm from entrance gate to Heveningham Hall.*

The valley is that of the River Blyth, and the farmhouse borders closely the water meadows in amongst which the river here winds through a broad, open landscape. From the west drive entrance to Heveningham Hall, the 'classical' front is ideally situated to catch the eye on the opposite slope of the valley, as though built for that purpose by one of the great eighteenth century landowners of the Hall (see Plate 293). It is these circumstances which have, perhaps, given rise to the notion that James Wyatt, who succeeded Sir Robert Taylor as the architect of Heveningham Hall, had something to do with the 'classicising' of the Valley Farm (see Plate 294). His work at Huntingfield Hall has already been touched upon, and this is thought to have included also the rebuilding of the Rectory at Heveningham.[1] In the case of Valley Farm, authorship is open to question on stylistic grounds. Basically this could be an Elizabethan timber-framed farmhouse, single range, of L-plan, for the timber-framed construction is plain to see.[2] The roof was probably a plain pitched structure with gable-ends, and eaves at a lower level as in the north-west wing. The alterations were fairly drastic: a completely new range was added to the south side of the main range, forming a 'double-pile' plan, and, in conjunction with the remodelling of the north side, the whole was covered by a double roof system, the ends of both the original and the new roofs being hipped to give a more classical look. The roof slopes met internally in a central valley gutter, and chimneys were all brought into a rather heavy white brick conformity. The new plan thus added a suite of three new reception rooms on the ground floor, with three large bedrooms above, and a new, flat-roofed staircase annexe on the north

1 Anthony Dale, in his study of Wyatt, op cit., says that this is likely. The Rectory is in white brick, and more of a textbook classical job than Valley Farm: there is a central pedimented gable into which the blind arch over the first-floor window goes, and this window has a balustraded panel beneath, and below this is a Greek Doric porch in stucco — the front of the house is flanked by fluted pilasters.
2 A will, discovered hidden in the house, is dated April 21st, 1578, and although not directly connected with property at Heveningham, the date is nevertheless not without interest.

*Plate 294: The south elevation of the new range.*

complete with tall Palladian windows having a scalloped arched head (see Plate 295). The front door which adjoined the staircase projection was a plainly detailed job, in contrast with the doorway and french casement in the centre of the bay on the south side. Apart from the eaves cornice, the only other decorative architectural features were the staircase window and the five-sided south bay with its central doorway and decorative arched fanlight, flanked by composite columns and surmounted by a broken pediment. It is difficult to imagine the young James Wyatt being satisfied with such comparatively routine design work, and another possibility suggests itself. There can be little doubt that when the first Sir Joshua purchased the Heveningham Estate in 1752, the Valley Farm must have presented a fairly drab aspect from the other side of the river. It was clearly occupying an important site in the landscape surrounding the Hall, and if, as Anthony Dale suggests, Sir Robert Taylor was employed to rebuild Heveningham Hall at some time between 1752 and 1776, it would have been only natural for the first baronet to consult him on other estate properties. That this happened in the case of Huntingfield Hall is on record, for it is known that Sir Joshua demolished the old Hall and built a new farmhouse.

*Plate 295: The entrance elevation and staircase projection, Valley Farm, Huntingfield.*

Much the same thing could have happened at Valley Farm, except that here the Elizabethan farmhouse was kept and simply refronted by the addition of a new range. The detailing has the look of early George III work, and, for all we know, Taylor may have given local builders a plan for both farmhouses to be built or remodelled in the way Sir Joshua wanted. Sir Gerard Vanneck, on succeeding to the property is thought to have dismissed Taylor, and engaged Wyatt. They considered the plain front of Huntingfield Hall a wasted opportunity — offering as it then did the prospect of a distant *trompe l'oeil* — and Wyatt was commissioned to do a new design. Valley Farm, with its new simple 'classical' front in painted stucco, was acceptable and was left untouched: that is perhaps a slightly more plausible conjecture than the supposed Wyatt connection — until disproved by new documentary evidence. At all events the farmhouse itself remains much as it was left in the mid-eighteenth century.

**Red House Farm, Knodishall**
TM 410 633

The appearance of 'Dutch' gables in Suffolk in the seventeenth century is an interesting moment in the history of local domestic architecture. These many curved shapes stem from that same reaction to strict classicism which goes by the name of 'Baroque', and which, in the Netherlands, coincided with the defeat of Spain. There, the design of gable-ends was far more extravagant and picturesque than in England, where the mood of the country was very different to that of Holland, at least until the Restoration in 1660. More imaginative shapes appear in Suffolk in the last part of that century, and Red House Farm, Knodishall, is a case in point. We shall have to wait on documentary research to establish how it came

*Plate 296: Red House Farm: the south-west elevation.*

about that this farmhouse, in an out-of-the-way part of a remote coastal parish, came to be built in this fairly sophisticated Dutch style (see Plate 296).

It is the plan form, of Elizabethan E, that raises a doubt as to whether this was not the rebuilding of an earlier house (see Plate 297).[1]The use of this design would have been somewhat anomalous under Charles II, for the date given by tie irons (the equivalent of Dutch 'ankers') is 1678, unless, as at Christchurch Mansion, Ipswich, an Elizabethan house already existed. The handling of the principal facade, facing south-west towards the roadway, is exceedingly 'architectural', with the general verticality offset by horizontal string-courses. Built in warm red brick in English bond, there is a pair of symmetrical three-storey gables to the end of each cross-wing, flanking a tall narrow porch (rather less than half the width of each gable-end). The porch is as high as the adjoining gables, and it is this verticality combined with narrowness which gives it the specially Dutch flavour (see Plate 298). The gable with semicircular top appears in both Amsterdam and Haarlem, often in conjunction with inverted curves (these are usually taller and steeper), and the brick-on-edge coping can also be found there, although generally in late sixteenth or early seventeenth century examples. There was quite a fashion for these inverted curves in Suffolk gable ends towards the end of the seventeenth century; examples are, Westerfield Hall (1656); Mettingham Hall (1670); Christchurch Mansion (1674-75); Darsham House (1679) and Wenhaston Grange (c.1680). In none of these, however, does the niche appear, and in the Red House porch there are no less than three, the topmost containing (according to the Statutory List) a statue of St. Agnes. The pair in the second tier are blind and

1 The appearance of roughly shaped ceiling cross-beams internally – e.g. in the dining-room – coupled with the size of the chimney piece openings, adds to the suggestion that here was an Elizabethan farm house skilfully remodelled towards the end of the seventeenth century. There is, of course, no trace of earlier work in the chimney heads, which are all of that uniformly plain design one would expect to find at that later period.

*Plate 298: Detail of the central porch.*

*Plate 297: A corner of the dining-room.*

plastered internally, as they are on the south facing gable of the Shire Hall on the Market Hill at Woodbridge. There is a blank rectangular panel between this pair of niches, suggesting that this was intended for an inscription. The carved stone panel is a typical feature above doorways in seventeenth and eighteenth century Dutch architecture, and it does appear that one of the few alterations that have been made to the Red House was the blocking up of a doorway immediately beneath the panel, and its replacement by a window. Perhaps an inscription over the door had been intended?

The windows are indeed contemporary, and are excellent examples of the slender mullion and transom type with rectangular leaded lights, which preceded the double-hung sash window. (They are nearly identical with those at Westerfield Hall, near Ipswich.) The boldly cambered brick arches over the head of the window seem exactly complementary to the shallow curves employed in the gable designs. The only design feature — delightful in itself — which is unresolved when it meets the front edge of the gable end, is the bold cavetto plaster cornice running round the eaves of the roofs on three sides of the internal courtyard between the cross-wings.

## Letheringham Lodge
*TM 276 570*

*Plate 299: South-east view across the moat.*

*Plate 300: Detail of corner post.*

1 The north pair of corner posts are only visible in the building internally.

Within a couple of miles west of Wickham Market, along the twisting course of the River Deben, are the two large estates of Glevering and Easton, the sites of Letheringham Hall and Priory, Godwin's Place and Letheringham Lodge. Local history suggests that the fortunes of all these properties have been interlinked. Those of the Manor go with the Priory founded by the Augustinians on the south bank of the Deben in 1200, with which the Lodge is by legend associated. History by word of mouth puts the Lodge as connected with the Priory, and once used by 'monks' (i.e. the Black Canons) as some sort of annexe.

The house occupies a moated site on the higher ground (see Plate 299) above the little tributary stream of the Deben called Potsford Brook; in this valley runs the track of the Roman road from Baylham to Yoxford. 'The Drift' goes up the hillside to the Lodge, passing a great barn built probably before the seventeenth century and, continuing past the house, goes on as a footpath to the Deben valley, joining the road to the Hall and the Priory. Prior to the Dissolution, the Hall is known to have been the seat first of the Boviles and then of the Wingfields (lords of many manors in the county), but of the occupancy of the Lodge there seems to be no actual record until the early seventeenth century.

The moat measures rather less than 45 metres each way (say 48 yards) and roughly in the centre is a structure in the form of a square. At each corner are massive oak posts with a girth of 560mm (about 20in.), and set at approximately 8 metres (26ft 6in.) on a shallow base of brickwork.[1] These corner posts (or 'teazles') were hewn out of well-grown oaks, roughly squared, and ornamented at about

*Plate 302: Detail of the Jacobean staircase.*

two-thirds of their height with triple arches surmounted by scalloped cresting, suggesting Perpendicular work of 1460 $^{\pm}$ (see Plate 300). Above this 'capital' the natural outward growth of a tree-limb was shaped into an arched bracket designed to support the end of a 'dragon'-beam. Thus there was a symmetrical structural arrangement of four bracketted posts, one at each corner, supporting diagonal (or 'dragon') beams which, in turn, were carried by a central shaft of brickwork containing fireplaces and flues: this terminated in a single chimney stack. The roof is hipped back to the central stack on the south side and this was probably repeated originally on the north side also, making a tall, regular-sided building with a pyramided roof rising to a stack at the apex. It must have resembled a small shire hall — rather like a miniature two-storey version of the Guildhall at Thaxted (where a similar form of framed construction is used). The purpose of this building is still obscure. There was evidently one large room on each floor with a fireplace, and Farrer described 'a spiral staircase of very early date' leading to the attics, which were divided into 'dormitories' with a great deal of wainscot: none of this now exists — but could have contributed to a tradition of monkish use. Tradition supplies two further stories: first that it was built as a hunting-lodge, and secondly, that it was the Shire Hall of Wickham Market which, when taken down in the late seventeenth or early eighteenth century was rebuilt here.

The structural evidence points to a building of the mid-late fifteenth century (possibly replacing one of earlier date on an already moated site) to which a wing and staircase annexe was added in the early seventeenth century, and which was then progressively 'de-mediaevalised' in later centuries, until it finished up with the very non-committal plain plaster walls and sash windows of today. To judge from the position of a four-light mullioned window with Gothic arch-headed openings in the first floor passage, there could have been a window, or a pair of windows of this type in the middle of each elevation in the upper jettied walls of the original building. There would presumably have been similar windows to the ground floor, and, possibly, a centred doorway on the south side in the present front door position, reached by a bridge over the moat (see Plate 301). The second bridge, on the west side, would fit with the extension of the house which, the initials 'E.W.' and the date of 1610 over the side entrance suggest, may have been built for Elizabeth Wingfield, the widow of Sir Thomas Wingfield who died in 1609. A careful look at the roof structure of this wing confirms that it was built on to an earlier framework, and this could not have happened if the main building were only erected in, say, the early eighteenth century.

*Plate 301: Letheringham Lodge — approach from the west by a bridge on the moat.*

JOHN WESLEY 73

The Jacobean work produced not only a superbly simple brick gable-end on the north side of the house, which descends sheer into the waters of the moat and is terminated by an intricately clustered group of four chimney stacks (see Figure 83), but also a robust and well detailed oak staircase in three flights with turned newel posts and balusters (see Plate 302).

*Mettingham Hall*
*TM 366 897*

The parish of Mettingham lies between Bungay and Shipmeadow, and borders the River Waveney in the north: immediately to the south lies the country of 'The Saints'. The most important site in this small parish is Mettingham Castle, containing the remains of the fortified manor house which went under that name, and owed its origin to Sir John de Norwich, 'who obtained license from Edward the Third, 21st August 1342, to castellate his residence here in reward for his services in the French wars.'[1] About half a mile to the north is Mettingham Hall, off the main Bungay/Beccles road and on a lane which leads to a double moated site, and then continues east to join a farm road called Beech Lane off which another lane branches, one way to Castle and College and the other to Shipmeadow village. Up here on high ground (100 feet above river level) moats must have been made a good deal earlier than the building of the present Hall. One of the advantages given to Mettingham Hall by the moat system is the provision of a house site on its own, and away from the farm buildings. The Hall, with its orchard and garden, faces south and is close enough to the moat to be reflected in its water (see Plate 303). The main architectural features are still intact, although there have been some rather makeshift alterations of recent years.

The plan is of modified H-form, having a longer central range and shorter cross-wings, with the general appearance of having been built c.1660. It is only when certain details are assessed that this date is called in question. There is the odd circumstance that the south-east gable is timber-framed and barge-boarded, and that attached to it is the remnant of a structure which is not cohesive with a mid-seventeenth century build: then there are the star-topped chimneys of the west chimney stacks which have an Elizabethan and not a Carolean character. A further cause for comment is the remarkable discrepancy between the handling of the entrance elevation and that on the south side facing towards the moat: the former is a highly orchestrated architectural piece with absolute regularity of fenestration and only one later feature in the Gibbsian eighteenth century front door, whereas the latter makes no such attempt and chiefly consists of fitting windows and a door opening around the girth of a massive chimney stack — the sort that looks as though it had been added to the outside wall of an earlier hall. Details such as these, and an extensive survey might reveal others, raise a doubt as to whether this is not a house of a century earlier extensively remodelled later on. A history of this kind is, as we have seen, quite normally compatible with that of many Suffolk houses, where the owners were reluctant to demolish completely and start over again or

1 cf. Proceedings S.I.A. op. cit., *Mettingham Castle and College*, by C.R. Manning, Volume IV, Part 2, page 77.

*Plate 303: South side facing the moat.*

*Plate 304: Detail of Dutch gable-end.*

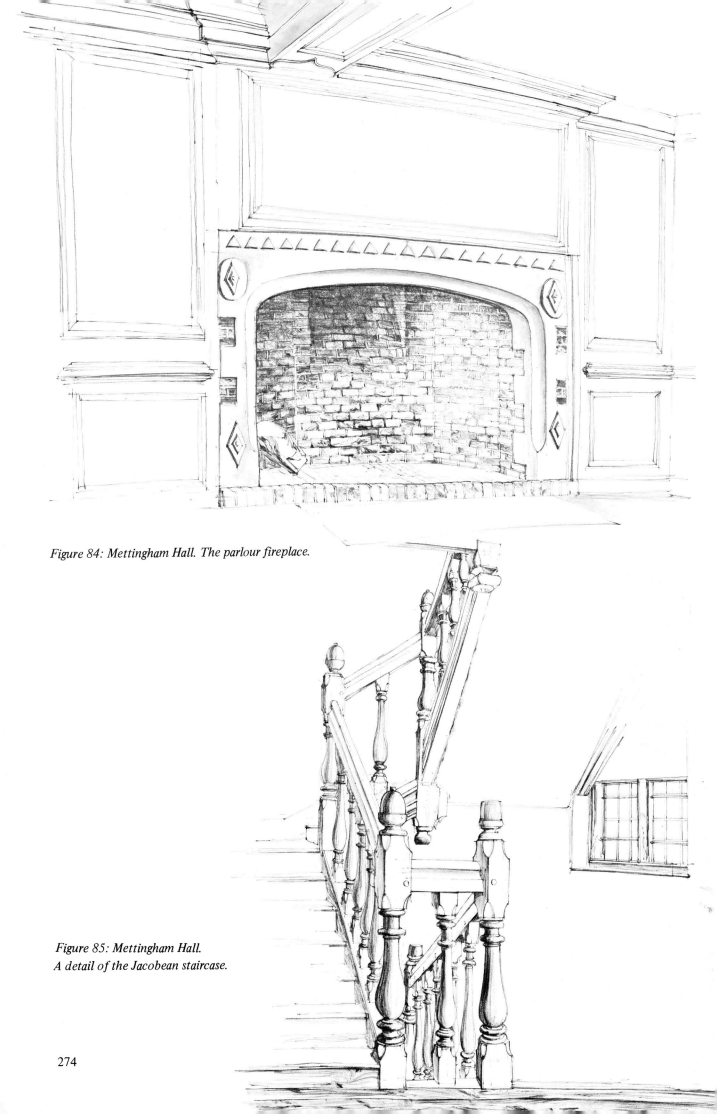

*Figure 84: Mettingham Hall. The parlour fireplace.*

*Figure 85: Mettingham Hall.*
*A detail of the Jacobean staircase.*

274

prepared to make do with and alter what they had. These tentative conclusions apart, the brickwork is of good quality in English bond, and the design and detailing shows considerable competence.

The window heads are boldly arched except below eaves (and in the centre part of the south elevation), and the springing of the arches to the ground floor windows is linked by a string-course consisting of two courses of brickwork with a third dentil course immediately beneath. This string course is continuous around the building, as far as the junction with the south-east gable, and is carried over the arched heads of the ground floor windows: the same feature is repeated over the first and second floor windows but without a supporting string course (see Plate 304). The windows have a number of the original mullion and transom pattern casements, filled in with rectangular leaded panes, of much the same detail as at Red House Farm, Knodishall, and Westerfield Hall. Chimneys are nondescript with the single exception of that to the west elevation with its star-topped twin shafts, which consort so oddly with the formality of seventeenth century design.

John Western made a drawing of two interesting features internally. The plan — which one supposes could have been the traditional central hall, with dining and service rooms at the east and parlour at the west — provided rooms which featured in the general mid-seventeenth century remodelling. The parlour fireplace again looks like late-Elizabethan or early Jacobean design (the flue connects with one of the star-topped stacks) done in plasterwork, diamonded and quoined (see Figure 84). On the whole it is unlikely that this was contemporary with the gable-ends any more than is the well staircase, with its early Jacobean looking newel posts and balusters (see Figure 85). These two details, taken in conjunction with the panelling out of the parlour walls, suggest that, subsequently to the first build, at least three periods are present at Mettingham Hall; the late sixteenth/early seventeenth century of the chimney stacks, fireplace and staircase; the mid-seventeenth century remodelling of the exterior, and the eighteenth century doorcase, fielded panels, cornice and dado rails of the parlour. The harmonious coexistence of different schools of design is, after all, one of the most time-honoured and endearing characteristics of English houses.

*Moor Farmhouse, Middleton*
*TM 417 677*

In East Anglia the tall and narrow gable in brickwork facing the road or street always invites comparison with houses in the Low Countries. Those on the quayside at Goes, in South Holland (see Plate 47) present their different varieties of stepped gable to the passer-by, and one wonders whether this tendency was not imported into Suffolk with the Flemish and Dutch bricklayers who, from as early as the reign of Edward III, had been coming here. The tradition of the decorative elevation to the roadway was certainly well-established by the fifteenth century, and during the two succeeding centuries innumerable examples occur all over Suffolk. One thinks of Waveney valley houses, such as Roos Hall, and those in the narrow streets of Beccles. Here at Middleton the nearest house which invites comparison is Cockfield Hall at Yoxford, less than two miles away. There Sir Anthony Hopton was building in the early 40s of the sixteenth century a new house with gatehouse and outbuildings, all with crow-stepped gables and a variety of decorative chimney stacks. It is likely that when Thomas Pynnowe's will was proved in 1506, 'all that messuage called Pynnowes beside Middleton Moore'[1] had been built some years earlier, and was a single range timber-framed and plastered farmhouse of two storeys on the east side of the common land still called Middleton Moor (see Plate 305). That it contained a hall is evidenced by the will of Thomas Pynnowe's grandson — another Thomas who described himself as 'of Middleton, yeoman' — for he bequests 'my table in the hall'. The service rooms must have been north of the hall and, presumably, the parlour at the south end. It could well be this Thomas who altered and improved the south part of the old farmhouse, after inheriting the property c.1545, and it would not be unreasonable to suggest that bricklayers, who may still have been at work at Cockfield Hall later in the reign of Queen Elizabeth, came down the road, and were happy to add this substantial gable-end in brickwork as the crowning feature of Thomas Pynnowe's alterations. As a substantial yeoman, who was able to bequeath to his wife Maryene lands and tenements in Middleton, Fordley, Westleton and Yoxford (and to his son his feather bed as well as hall table), he was able to afford a new parlour and best bed chamber. To achieve this,

1 The will was in Latin, and this transcription was made by Rev. E. Farrer, F.S.A., in *E.A.M.*, op. cit., No. 5091. See also a delightful description of the Pynnowe wills in Allan Jobson's *A Window in Suffolk*, pages 20-23 (1962. London: Robert Hale).

*Plate 305: Moor Farmhouse – the general view from The Moor.*

*Plate 306: Gable-end detail.*

1 Since writing this, I have observed that the flat ball motif in brickwork occurs in the pilasters of High House, Parham, admittedly in a different context but similar in detail.

276

the original south end of the house must have been put temporarily out of commission, and the carpenters brought in to raise the whole framework, put in new floors and ceilings, and raise the height of the eaves and roof sufficiently to include an attic chamber. At the same time the bricklayers were at work on raising the gable-end and forming chimney pieces in each of the three new rooms. The decorative brickwork was of a plainer character than at Cockfield Hall – as befitted a yeoman farmer – but still extremely handsome (see Plate 306). The gable end had five windows, two to each of the ground and first floor rooms and one to the attic chamber (sadly, these were later taken out and all except one, which now has a modern casement, were bricked in). Above each of the four main windows, the bricklayers invented ornamental emblems of two types (which, as far as I know, are unique[1]): above each of the ground floor windows this consisted of a straight run of moulded brick supported by four brick dentils, and above this three raised panels, 9 inches wide and 4 bricks high, engaging with a three quarter brick circle top and bottom. (The straight moulding has been lost above the two ground floor windows.) A similar design was used above the first floor windows, except that there the little brick panels were reduced one brick in height with a single circle above. The attic window opening was left severely plain. Finials were used to flank the gables, and resemble the bases of those at Cockfield Hall without any decorative terminals – perhaps they were never intended? The detailing of the crow-steps is pretty well identical also, at one brick width and six courses high, each step having its own moulded brick coping. (The one curious feature of the gable brickwork is a change of bond roughly at the base of the second from top crow-step: brickwork of English bond, the courses change to stretcher bond, giving a subtly different, although very effective character to the broad base on which are set the three chimney shafts – approx. 2.4 metres or 7ft 10in. wide.) The chimneys are independent and octagonal throughout, proceeding from moulded bases to plain shafts which were plainly never intended to be cut off straight, having probably lost some height as well as moulded heads.

Of the chimney pieces, the richest and most interesting was in the best bed chamber (see Plate 69). Above a brick opening with shallow, cambered arch (interestingly enough – again in stretcher bond), occurs an ornamental plaster panel with mainly foliated and floral motifs, with large Tudor roses in two spandrils, reminiscent of themes used in local pargetting. The design motifs suggest that, if this work was contemporary with the remainder, then a late- Elizabethan date is correct. It must have been this chimney piece which gave much satisfaction to Thomas and his wife as they lay in their feather beds.

**Mutford Hall, near Beccles**
*TM 482 874*

The old maps do not give any positive evidence of an approach to Mutford Hall from the east, and yet it is this way that the main front faces, with its central doorway between cross-wings surmounted by the date 1607 in floreated iron figures (Dutch style). There are traces of a connection by farm road with Rushmere Hall, a little over half a mile to the east, and the principal farmhouse of that small adjoining parish. Rushmere Hall, like Mutford Hall, is on the edge of the Hundred River. Those who came by that road, would have arrived at what was clearly designed to be the main elevation of an important Jacobean farmhouse, and not, as they do today, at the back of the house — interesting though this is (see Plate 307).

*Plate 307: The rear elevation facing west.*

It is not difficult to discern here yet another example of that process of decay and rebuilding characteristic of many houses in Suffolk during the sixteenth and seventeenth centuries (and continuing, indeed, in a diminished way until present times). The earliest surviving structure at Mutford Hall is in the south cross-wing, and is represented by a two-storey timber-framed and plastered range, some two metres out of alignment with the new cross-wing which it was evidently intended to continue (the explanation of this is not immediately evident). True, the west-facing gable end of this range was added in brickwork at the same time as the rest of the rebuilding, but it is clear, from the evidence of structure, that this is part of an earlier house — doubtless the previous Mutford Hall. (What we need to know is how many times earlier Halls had been rebuilt already, and this is where a scientific analysis of timbers might help by establishing the earliest dated specimens.)

The building of today shows few changes since late-Victorian days, when the roof was retiled(?), new windows and other fittings and finishings introduced, and a lean-to built along the west side between the wings, giving easier access to the two ends of the house. The work of 1609 consisted in adding a form of modified two-storey H-plan to the remaining range of the older house, and erecting a solidly brick-built structure (18 inch main walls on a plinth 22½ inches thick), with a

*Plate 308 (below): An angle of the main east elevation.*

*Plate 309 (below right): The house from the north drive.*

steeply-pitched plain tiled roof, the fireplaces all being on outside walls. In consequence of this, there are a number of very tall external chimney stacks (although not all of seventeenth century date): two of the earliest of these have detached octagonal shafts with moulded bases and triple-offsets to the main chimney-heads, similar to those at Weston Hall, a little south of Beccles (see Plates 308 and 309). The gable ends built at this period are all narrow crow-stepped (generally one brick width and five courses high) and, in the case of the gable added to the earliest range, combined with a pair of twin-shafted diagonally joined stacks, which, as they are on octagonal bases must be the later rebuilding of stacks originally matching those previously described. In the early seventeenth century there was probably one large hall occupying the centre, with parlours in the north cross-wing (and a hay loft in the rear first floor) and service rooms in the south. In the principal parlour the heavily moulded ceiling beams were left exposed when most of the rest of the interiors were Victorianised. Surviving from some still earlier period, and suggesting that prior to 1609 there could have been an Oratory in the house, is a roundel of stained glass (of the Norwich School?) about two feet in diameter depicting Saint Veronica, surrounded by the text 'Ecce vidimus eam non habentem speciem neque decorum aspectus ejus ... ', in part a quotation from Isaiah, chapter 53, which occurs in the liturgy for Holy Week. There is surely some wider significance in the biblical texts to be found in Suffolk houses in frescoed inscriptions, painted panels and stained glass.

Leaving Mutford Hall and its fine site overlooking the Hundred River and the county beyond, there is to be seen across the fields, on returning to the village, a dwelling with the look of ancestry related to the Hall. Consisting of a single timber-framed and plastered range with a steep pantiled roof, it has a brick crow-stepped gable at the west end of similar design to the Hall, once ornamented with terracotta finials. There is a central brick chimney stack of that early seventeenth century 'saw-tooth' pattern to be found on the cross-wing of The Butterfly, Great Finborough (see Plate 288). (Here the chimney head has clearly been rebuilt and the stack shortened in the process.) The windows have been modernised, but those on the gable end have simple plastered label moulds. This dwelling is called Keir's Cottages, and was labelled Grade III in the first Statutory List; it was one of the cottages of the Mutford Hall holding and evidently rebuilt at the same time as the Hall itself (see Plate 310).

*Plate 310: Gable-end of Keir's Cottage.*

**High House, Otley**
*TM 212 549*

*Plate 311: High House and moat from the south-west.*

A good deal smaller than, perhaps, better-known Otley Hall and in quite another part of the parish lies the High House (see Plate 311), on a by-road leaving the village street nearly opposite the church, dipping to cross a stream and then rising to the edge of that high plateau on which the house stands, before continuing to link with the road from Clopton to Monewden. From this elevated ground the eye scans the country falling steadily south to Woodbrige and the distant coast-line, and confirms the simple logic of a farmhouse up here being named 'High House'.

*Plate 312: The north range with cheese-room windows.*

It is only since 1928 that the house has appeared as it does today. Prior to that it was a very ordinary looking plastered dwelling, of one long range but having a splendid ornamental clustered-shaft chimney stack two thirds of the way along the roof; at the rear was a decrepit looking wing with immensely long slatted windows. At some period in the early nineteenth century, the farm must have changed hands. Its late-mediaeval character was then almost completely removed by refenestration, plasterwork and interior alteration. In 1925, when purchased by the Schofield family, the road front had three large four-light casement windows and a batten-door below, and over each of these a window of corresponding size to the first floor. The upper part of the plastered wall slightly overhung the lower, and the south gable end was blank except for a partial overhang of the upper storey supported by brackets from within a blind recess. At the back was the staircase projection with studwork and brick nogging, and between this and the rear wing a lean-to with pantiled roof. All this information was recorded photographically by the new owners in 1925-6. There are plenty of farmhouses on Suffolk by-roads of similar appearance and amongst them many, no doubt, in which the routine fronts hide a late-mediaeval timber-frame with mullion openings blocked up or cut about in order to accommodate later windows. Where a decorative brick chimney stack survives, as here, the way is open to a passer-by to surmise the original form of the dwelling. To the Schofields, with their son Sydney, an architect at Christ's College, Cambridge, even a slight familiarity with old framed houses in Suffolk might have sufficed to suggest what might lie behind the conventional exterior. The position of the stack would indicate two rooms of smaller dimension at the west end, which might turn out to be respectively parlour with solar over; next, the distance between the stack and the doorway would suggest the hall, and, with walls and roof of this height, probably floored, with bed chambers above; the door entering the hall at the lower end and, immediately next to it, probably a partition with an entrance into the remaining room, which, to judge by a further chimney at the rear, was the kitchen. The high roof would point to useful attic space. The rear wing must then be scullery and dairy on the ground floor, and the long slatted openings above an unusually long cheese-room (see Plate 312). An analysis of this kind could have been made by simply walking round the outside when, incidently, the close studded brick-nogged annexe at the back would suggest an addition, of no later than the sixteenth century, to an earlier house.

That, in brief, is the basis of what was actually discovered, but the quality of the craftsmanship within could not have appeared fully until the later alterations and fittings were stripped out. Some of the excitement when this happened can be felt even in the formal letter written by Sydney Schofield to the Rev. G.H. Round-Turner on January 20th, 1926 on the subject of the deeds, in which he says '..... I wish you could have seen the High House since the repairs were started — we

*Plate 313: Cambered ceiling in a bed chamber at High House, Otley.*

have made all sorts of interesting little discoveries .....' Many of these must have occurred with the stripping of whitewash from ceiling timbers, when the exceptionally good quality of the carpentry would have come to light. Workmanship of a high order went into the moulding and assembly of the timber components for the ceilings of important rooms, and the hand of the same tradesmen can be seen throughout. The structural principle was to run the principal tie-beams from north to south with a secondary beam on the longitudinal axis of the rooms right through the range. A single tie-beam spanned the centre of hall and parlour, and parallel with this ran the floor joists — a visually satisfactory arrangement. Mouldings adopted a more or less uniform principle throughout the house, consisting of a roll, or roundel, either single, as in the bed chamber ceiling joists; double, as in the first-floor ceiling beams and the ground-floor ceiling joists; or treble, as in the main tie-beams to hall and parlour. In a Gothic house such as this, the moulded timbers combine function and decoration, and are an essential part of the visual impression given by the whole work (see Plate 313). An unusual form of moulded arched bracket was used to give extra support between the tie-beam and the principal posts of the hall, and a cambered bressumer over the hall fireplace was carved with a running acanthus pattern. A dragon-beam occurs in the parlour, running from the principal tie-beam to the south-west corner (see Plate 31), and enabling the carpenter to give a larger jetty to the west gable-end, and a smaller one to the south range as far as the east corner (this accounts for the change in plane of the plasterwork on the south front). Another interesting feature was the cambered timber ceiling given to one of the smaller bed chambers where an aromatic chestnut seems to have been used, and the effect is reminiscent in a small way of the great bed chamber at Alston Court.

The newel stair, with its timber-framed and brick-nogged case was, presumably, an addition (see Plate 116), and there is the unexplained appearance of a doorway at first floor level immediately next to it, suggesting that there might have been an external covered stairway to the first floor in early days. Internally the stairs are as originally built in the sixteenth century, consisting of solid wedged shaped treads, supported by equally solid risers, housed into a central newel post which is nothing more nor less than a straight tree trunk shaped up for the purpose and given an ornamental finish at the top. Finally a cheese-room of such unusual dimensions must be mentioned: measuring some 12 metres in length and 6 metres in width (approx. 39ft by 19ft), it occupied the entire upper floor of the rear wing, and on the wide oak floor boards were stacked the cheeses. '..... the herd of cows kept on the property ..... must have been large to have necessitated so huge a room', as Farrer commented.[1] The windows were open latticed, and the grooves in which the wooden shutters ran can still be seen.

If Farrer was right,[2] High House could have been built by Richard, one of a family of Ermegards with an ancestry of 200 years in and around the parish of Otley, who is recorded as living there in 1524. The building — or was it a rebuilding? — could therefore have been done about the end of the previous century.

1 cf. *E.A.M.*, op. cit., No. 7344.
2 Ibid., No. 7348.

## Moat Hall, Parham
### TM 315 605

*The gateway, as illustrated by Basil Oliver, before it went to America.*

For a manor house as celebrated as the Moat Hall, the site is extraordinarily reclusive. Until at least the middle of the last century known by the name of 'Parham Hall', no visible means of access at all appears on Hodskinson's map of 1783: in the first printings of the Ordnance Survey in 1837, on the other hand, there is clear indication that the present approach from Silverlace Green altered course after about quarter of a mile before branching to the Hall, and continued straight on down the hillside in a south-westerly direction, crossed the River Ore at a ford, and came into the centre of Hacheston village, going more or less directly on to Blomville Hall. The Hall is still approached by the same route from Silverlace Green, but the roadway turns abruptly north and reaches the house only after passing the many farm buildings and entering the gateway (see Plate 314). It lies almost due south of Parham Church and just below the 100ft contour, the grassy slopes of which rise steeply from the moat on the north side (see Figure 86).

Copinger traces the devolution of the manor from the time of Henry II, until it came into the hands of the Willoughby family in the fourteenth century, and the assumption is that the present Hall is on the site of an earlier dwelling occupied by William de Ufford (d.1382), the builder of Parham Church.[1] The building of old Parham Hall has been attributed to the Willoughby family, and on stylistic grounds it would seem probable that the builder was the father of that Sir Christopher who was created first Baron Willoughby in 1546 and who had inherited the estate in about 1527. This — if the historians concur — would put building into the period 1498-1527. Oliver compared the detailing of the carved stone gateway before this was shipped off to America[2] — with that of the upper windows of the first floor hall, and was convinced that they were both contemporary and late fifteenth century early Tudor.

*Plate 314: Brick gateway with 'wood-wose' in niches.*

From the approach side Moat Hall gives little away (see Plate 315). There is the long timber-framed and plastered wing running south, looking like any run-of-the-mill Suffolk farmhouse, and of indeterminate age. The only features which suggest an early building are: (1) the bevelled brick angle, containing arched windows, of what could be taken for a staircase turret, (2) a bulky chimney stack with ornamental star-topped shafts, and, (3) a tall mullioned window with narrow vertical lights and arched heads. On passing round the building to the north and east sides, it is seen that these features are at the rear of a single range of which the front facing the moat is infinitely more elaborate. What is now standing must be two-thirds only of an originally symmetrical composition in brickwork. Consisting of one chimney stack and two tall vertical bay windows, the remains of foundation walls suggest that there was once a third bay and a matching stack at the south-east

1 cf. *The Manors of Suffolk*, op. cit., Volume 5, pages 152-157.
2 There was some discussion in *E.A.M.* about this gateway (cf. No. 8381) and according to the theory of the then General Secretary of the Suffolk Institute of Archaeology it was part of a canopied tomb, intended for the grave of Robert Lord Willoughby at Mettingham, but for some reason never conveyed there. Tipping thought it might have come from Campsey Priory.

Figure 86: Moat Hall, Parham.

*Plate 315: Moat Hall, Parham from the entrance drive.*

*Moat Hall – Basil Oliver.*

**Thorington Hall,**
**Stoke-by-Nayland**
TM 013 354

end. The roof is scarcely likely to have looked the same when the house was first built,[1] nor the bay projections to have had plastered gablets: it is evident from the twin bases of the chimney shafts, indented with blind trefoliated arches, that a pair of octagonal shafts have been removed, and the heads of the bay windows seem to call for battlemented brick parapets. The inestimable value of the Moat Hall exterior lies in its brickwork detailing, both in the general bonding and diaperwork of the walls, and the particular handling of the mullion and transom window openings. These were evidently all arch-headed, plain in the ground floor bay window, and with cusped trefoils in the upper windows: they were all done in moulded brickwork intended for a Roman cement finish to simulate stonework, and would repay any architectural student as a subject for a measured drawing study. When completed there would have been more than a touch of magnificence about the exterior of this Willoughby brick mansion, built well before the dissolution of the monasteries in the Gothic idiom. One searches in vain for any parallel in Suffolk — or indeed elsewhere.[2] There is a hint of the tall, narrow triple towers of Beckley in Oxfordshire, but the major contribution of Moat Hall is in bay window design, and this must be one of the earliest examples of a type increasingly developed and increasingly popular until at least Jacobean times.

The internal arrangements are no longer very clear, and the staircase on the south side was evidently a sixteenth century addition to give easier access to the first floor, where the remaining bay windows at least seem to have lit a large and splendid bed chamber.

The River Box flows south within thirty yards of Thorington Hall, which stands at a junction of the Stoke-by-Nayland/Higham road with a by-road going north to Withermarsh Green. It is the Hall house of a roadside hamlet known as Thorington Street, and, built so close to the corner, is the most conspicuous feature of this tiny settlement. Its earlier character of a working farmhouse has been subtly lost in the subsequent restoration in spite of the obvious gain in architectural quality (see Plate 316).

Both plan and structure suggest that originally the house may have been of smaller and less pretentious proportions, possibly of T-plan, with a central range and a single cross-wing at the west end. Whether this is so can probably be determined only by an exact study of the carpentry within the roof and elsewhere, but there can be little doubt that the first build was in the late Elizabethan period, say 1590$^{\pm}$. Without recourse to carpentry study, this is suggested by stylistic details — notably the barge-boards and bay window on the north elevation, and the immensely tall star-topped chimneys. The four-light bay window, with its canted side-lights and adjoining three-light mullion windows at high level is extraordinarily close in design to the fenestration on the Lady Street elevation of the Guildhall at Lavenham; the arched brackets and the buttresses, however, have gone, and the solid moulded sill member replaced by four small moulded sub-sill brackets of

1 Tipping talks about 'the very homely re-roofing and re-windowing' and makes a parallel between the windows and chimney shafts on the south (sic) side and those at West Stow, amongst other examples. An inexact parallel one would think, since the work at West Stow could have been anything up to forty years later.
2 Pevsner mentions a possible similarity at Earl Soham Lodge, where there are 'traces of sixteenth century canted bays of brickwork overlooking the moat'.

*Plate 316: Thorington Hall — seen from the Stoke-by-Nayland road, from a photograph by Basil Oliver c.1910, prior to restoration (see Plate 71).*

incipient Renaissance design, replicas of which appear beneath the ends of the projecting wall plates where these engage with the barge-boards. The latter have a very Gothic double-billet moulding, repeated on the bressumer, beneath the projection of which the bay window was neatly fitted. The massed groups of stacks, three to each side, making a six shafted chimney with moulded octagonal bases and elaborate star-tops, is a feature of East Anglian brickwork with roots deep in Perpendicular architecture (see Plate 317). A *croisonné* mullion and transom window immediately below the first-floor bay window is a reminder of the changes that must have taken place in the early to middle period of the next century.

One plausible explanation of the next phase at Thorington Hall would be a change of ownership about the time of 1610-20, when the old stairs — which could have been of the ladder pattern — were taken out and the case built out on the south-east side to enclose a new stairway. This superbly designed multi-flight staircase, with its beautiful carved newel posts has already been illustrated (see Plate 122).

The next substantial changes would have taken place at the end of the seventeenth century, to which period (c.1690) must be attributed the second staircase in a hall entered from the south, and in a wing which invites speculation on account of different proportions. This, although timber-framed and plastered like the rest, is unlikely to be contemporaneous owing to a different roofing system at a higher level than the range to the west. It is where this wing joins the conjecturally earlier work that occurs the elaborate classical doorcase with its scroll-pedimented head, which, in turn, is practically opposite the brick gate piers with ball caps set in the brick boundary wall on the roadside, and presumably of the same period. These details together pose the possibility that this part of Thorington Hall was an addition intended to give a 'classical' end to the house, a proposal strengthened by the plain axial chimney stack of the eastern cross-wing.

The whole house was repaired under the direction of the architect, Mr. Marshall Sisson, F.R.I.B.A., in 1937 and acquired by The National Trust in 1941.

*Plate 317: The rear view of Thorington Hall from a photograph by Basil Oliver, c.1910.*

### Clock House, Stonham Parva
*TM 114 612*

On the Ordnance Survey the name is 'Clock House Farm', and farmhouse it has evidently been since an early date. The property is within a half-mile of the Pye Road with lands on both sides of a lane which leaves that road at Little Stonham village, going west to church and Hall, and then north towards Mendlesham. It is a roadside farm, the house facing east and separated from the approach only by the width of a narrow lawn. No signs of a moat appear.

The present farmhouse is agreeably proportioned and pleasant in appearance, if giving little of its history away — only a quadruple stack of Henry VIII vintage

*Plate 318: Clock House, the elevation facing east to the road.*

appears above the roof and the central two-storey projection looks as though it might be a late-mediaeval porch (see Plate 318). Like the rest of the house, however, it has been plastered over and made respectable with double-hung sash windows of the late eighteenth century style. Looking more closely, however, it will be seen that there are a pair of four-light mullioned windows with diamond quarries which could be of the early sixteenth century, but they are very small and the eaves unusually low on either side of the central projection. The suspicion grows that we are looking at an early hall-house with numerous later accretions, which might include even the cross-wings and the centrepiece as though these were intended to give the fashionable look of an E-plan house.

Indoors, the threads are not so easy to disentangle. The original nucleus of the building does turn out, however, to be a hall-house, confirming the comparatively low eaves level externally. The entrance doorway opens into a room below of some 6 metres in length by 4.5 metres in width (approx. 19ft 6in. by 14ft 9in.), which a single glance at the room above shows to have been a hall open into the roof and floored over later on. This early hall was a two-bay unit with one central truss consisting of a massive cranked tie-beam (cut out of a 16 foot oak tree trunk) supported at each end on principal posts and by a pair of 15 inch deep arch-braces

*Plate 319: Detail of tie-beam and crown-post.*

meeting at the apex and giving the appearance originally of a shallow arch spanning the entire hall. Above the centre point of the tie-beam was mounted a short octagonal crown-post with beautifully moulded base and capital which provided the seating for four small arch braces, one pair engaging with the lateral collar, and the other with the longitudinal collar runner — an extremely satisfying example of Gothic carpentry (see Plate 319). Pevsner dates this as early fourteenth century, but compared with the generality of Suffolk roofs of this type, it might be safer to opt for a mid/late fourteenth if not a fifteenth century dating. The earliest recorded date is a will of 1483 made by Thomas Crowe, and accounts for the early name of the house as Crows or Crowes.

Thereafter an indenture dated 1577 and a series of wills give a remarkably full documentation of ownership until the early twentieth century — and often, whilst it would be the purest guesswork to attribute to successive owners the changes that were obviously wrought, it would not be unreasonable to credit Blomvyles with the first stage alterations. The mediaeval farmhouse might well have consisted of parlour/hall/service rooms sequence, the latter being in a cross-wing at the north end, giving the house a T-plan. If there was a chimney then it could have been an improvised affair, for traces of smoke blackened roof timbers are not to be found. About 1530$^\pm$, one conjectures, there were alterations at the parlour end when a new chimney stack was built right through the house, and the parlour extended. The new stack culminated in a four-shafted head of circular form in moulded brickwork on skilfully designed octagonal bases: the shafts were decorated alternatively with rose and *fleur-de-lys* and capped with moulded and battlemented tops — amongst the best examples of its kind in Suffolk (compare with Badwell Ash Hall). In 1577, Arthur Blomvyle, yeoman, sold to George Harrison of Debenham, yeoman, and the connection of the former family with the property seems to have ceased until the mid eighteenth century.[1] The new owners, one postulates, could have built the new great parlour at the south end, decorating their bed chamber above with the superb ribbed ornamental plaster ceiling with oak leaf and acorn bosses, and floral centrepiece which still exists — if in fragmentary form (see Plate 110). At this point the hall would have been floored across, the new porch added and the cross wing effect created at the south end. (There must have been some sacrifice of comfort in achieving the loyal E-form, for the new front door opened right on to the fireplace, and perhaps explains why, at a later date, the front door returned to somewhere near its original place at the lower end of the hall.)

There is a list of the goods and chattels in the house in the year 1625, when Mrs. Alice Atye made a deed of gift, and as these are inventoried room by room it is possible to link all with those that still exist — with the exception of the 'clock chamber'. This, in addition to 'one bedsted, one coverlett, one fether bed and bolster, one truckle bed, a pair of Drymalls (?) and two stills', contained 'one clock with a bell'. My own guess would be that in place of the present hipped roof over the porch (which is out of character with the architecture) there was a gable, in which there was a clock face — in much the same way as at Bruisyard Hall — with a bell chamber behind, and it was from this that Clock House derived its name.

Farrer puts the house in the hamlet of Mells.[2] In the north-west corner of the parish, it is within 500 yards of the River Blyth rising in the high claylands of Cratfield and Ubbeston, and flowing through Heveningham Park and Walpole village to join the Wissett tributary below Halesworth, less than a mile away. Basically a long timber-framed range 17 metres by 6 metres (approx. 56ft by 20ft) of two storeys with habitable attics, the plan is L-shaped with a rear wing and all of a contemporary build dated late fifteenth or early sixteenth century. The name 'Grange' has been used to connect it with the Abbey of Sibton, to which it would have served as an outlying farmhouse with barns, etc., used for storing tithes, and by whom it might have been built. The chimney stack towards the west end of the front range could be a mid-sixteenth century addition, suggesting that the Grange had been sold off c.1550 and the new chimney then built, since it is improbable this would have been added by the Abbey (plate 321).[3] Given a well-to-do owner in the early eighteenth century prompted to remove the farmhouse look (still visible at the rear — see Plate 320), this would account for the refronting of the north and west elevations most visible from the road in dark red brickwork (see

*Wenhaston Grange*
TM 388 758

1 The late owner, Brigadier R.R.B. Hilton, who was intensely interested in the history of the house, showed me a letter from a descendant of the Bloomvyles (the name was variously spelt until it reached the modern Bloomfield), written in 1965 and quoting a reference in the Visitors' Book of Stonham Parva Church to the effect that Bloomfields had owned Clock House from 1520 to 1916. This is not entirely borne out by the documentation of wills.
2 cf. *E.A.M.*, op. cit., No. 7435. Rev. E. Farrer contributed three articles in all to *E.A.M.* on Wenhaston Grange (Nos. 7435, 7440 and 7445), and attributed the later alterations to Captain Hall, owner in 1680 — a dating which seems slightly premature for the work in question and by comparison with similar alterations to other old Suffolk houses.
3 The chimney stack has triple stacks on the north and a single stack on the south which looks like an afterthought with its separate base corbelled out from the main stack: otherwise it would be a most unusual arrangement. The moulded brick ornament is intricate and different to each separate shaft.

*Plate 320: Wenhaston Grange. View from the garden.*

*Plate 321: The ornamental brick chimney stack.*

Plate 322). A date of $1702^{\pm}$ would fit the Queen Anne appearance then given to the main range, with its eight bays, doorcase with segmented hooded pediment, and windows with wide sash-boxes and thick glazing bars: it would also suit the convex and concave shapes of the 'Dutch' gable at the west end (a pattern common in the Low Countries in the early eighteenth century, although with roofs of steeper pitch). The refitting of the front range internally included pannelled wainscotting, doors and architraves, new fireplace surrounds and staircase alteration, all of similar period. The alteration of the braced frame construction to admit a south passage on the first floor, giving separate access to bed chambers, would presumably date from this time also. The only major changes in architectural character since then have been the addition of a lean-to on the west of the service range, and the removal of three dormer windows with hooded pedimented heads on the north roof slope belonging to the eighteenth century refit.

*Plate 322: The Queen Anne front.*

287

**Westerfield Hall**
*TM 175 484*

Seen beyond the pond and its tangled brushwood, the Hall is a reminder of that long distant period when Norwegian invaders came here from eastward and bestowed upon this clearing in the forest north of Ipswich a name meaning 'more to the west', to which the Anglo-Saxon *feld* was added, producing the 'Westerfield' of today. Modern Ipswich has crept close to this village of one time farms and cottages, to the north of which lies Westerfield Hall and Farm, a complex of red-brick buildings rebuilt — one suspects — and developed in the mid-seventeenth century. Architectural enterprise on this scale was not usual during the Protectorate and, if the date of 1656 on the north gable of the outbuilding adjoining the barn be taken as including the Hall and its buildings, then works were finished just before the Restoration.

The special claim of Westerfield Hall is an H-plan house seemingly of one contemporary build, and of considerable architectural purity (see Plate 323).[1] It invites stylistic comparison — inevitably — with Christchurch Mansion, of which the upper walls and gables were rebuilt in 1674-5, only eighteen years later than the Westerfield house. At Ipswich the pedimented gable-tops and concave curves appear, although not in association with the convex curves of Westerfield, and the outlining with a projecting double course of brick is similar. The pedimented window heads of the latter appear also at the Mansion (although above first floor — and not attic — windows), and the mullion and transom windows were employed in each, although of a more sophisticated character at Ipswich. If the dates had been reversed, then Westerfield Hall might have seemed a complementary offspring of the Mansion, but the latter was rebuilt afterwards, in a style then a little out of date. At Westerfield the projection of the symmetrical cross-wings is already slight, and fifty years later they may have disappeared in favour of the uniform front, articulated, most likely, by a columnar centrepiece. The house remains an example of a moment in the seventeenth century development of brick architecture in Suffolk which is both valuable and irreplaceable.

*Plate 323: Westerfield Hall — the east elevation to the Ipswich road.*

**Witnesham Hall**
*TM 177 508*

Many pages of the *East Anglian Miscellany* have been given up to tracing the devolution of Witnesham Hall, and the latest in the series appeared under the initials 'S.M.W.M.'[2] These historical researches have opened up a time scale for the origins of the house taken back as far as the fourteenth and fifthteenth centuries, when the Brewes were the principal family and likely to have been the builders of the original Witnesham Hall. As an example it is very close to that self-imposed exclusion of houses which have been altered almost out of recognition in Victorian times (see Plate 324), but there are certain good reasons for its inclusion. The porch, with its three-storey triple-pedimented door and window openings, flanked by pilasters and topped by a triple curved gable-end, is a virtually untouched 'original' and important in the history of Dutch-gables in Suffolk: it is as well to

1 The slightly anomalous features are the detached circular chimney shafts with the dentilled heads, which seem to hark back to the Jacobean, although the absolute symmetry of disposition seems to point to their being contemporary with the rest of the build.
2 cf. *E.A.M.*, op. cit., No. 11744 *et seq.*

*Plate 324: Witnesham Hall: the south elevation.*

include an illustration giving this in its setting. The external elevations which accompany the seventeenth century porch are dated 1844, and can be read as an elaborate mid-Victorian screen around the ancient core of the house.[1] Even the chimney shafts were rebuilt, but their moulded bases are of Tudor brickwork, and within the house the heavy-beamed timbers of the early sixteenth century are visible, together with a Jacobean staircase and overmantels.

The indications are that basic structural framework is of timber construction, which could be of $1450^{\pm}$, erected as a single range roadside farmhouse just east of the Witnesham/Ipswich road. The hall is central, and, with a height to eaves of about 4.5 metres (say 15-16ft), could give the dimensions appropriate to an originally open hall-house. Floored over later, this would account for the small mullion and transom windows just below eaves level giving a height of about 1 metre (say 3ft 3in.) above the level of the floor. The hypothetical arrangement would then be an open central hall, with two-storey accommodation at each end, the hall entrance being at the lower end and enclosed by a passage of which the vertical boarded and panelled screen formed part.

### Red House Farm, Witnesham
*TM 186 503*

1 This elevational screen was not complete, however, for at the back of the house there are remains of the earlier plasterwork over timber-framing, with rusticated pattern work around windows, and a brick – or stone – overall pattern filling.

*Plate 325: Red House Farm: crow-stepped gable and diapered brickwork.*

*Plate 326: Rear elevation with plain brickwork and brick-nogged studding.*

*Moat Farm, Badingham. Early sixteenth century farmhouse with later cross-wing, timber-framed and plastered, originally thatched.*

*East End Manor, Stonham Aspal (formerly Morgan's Far Mediaeval farmhouse, timber-framed and plastered w double cross-wings.*

*Cordell Hall Farmhouse, Stansfield. Elizabethan timber-framed and plastered farmhouse, with double cross-wings and central gable.*

*Boundary Farm, Framsden. Timber-framed and plaste Tudor farmhouse with single cross-wing.*

*Old Hall Farm, Hemingstone. Elizabethan timber-framed and plastered farmhouse with double cross-wings.*

*Green Farm, Bredfield. Elizabethan farmhouse remode in eighteenth century, timber-framed and plastered, v pantiled roof.*

It is not difficult to visualise the influence exerted by Seckford Hall (c.1550) at Woodbridge, and the Withipoll mansion at Ipswich (1548-1550), with its overall wall pattern of diapered brickwork, and to see in such buildings the source of inspiration for the later bricking up of old timber-framed and plastered houses such as this (see Plate 325). There can be little doubt that the owners of the Red House (was that the new name which it was christened after its transformation into a red brick building?) in the mid-late sixteenth century embarked upon an ambitious programme of modernisation. The work included the remodelling of the cross wing at the parlour and solar end of the house in the later Seckford style (c.1580), complete with angle buttress, crow-stepped gable, and large pedimented window-openings (these have unfortunately been altered, and filled in with nineteenth century type casements); a new chimney stack with back-to-back fireplace between parlour and hall, and the bricking over of the original timber-frame (this outer skin suffered from inherent weakness, causing cracking and necessitating repairs and rebuilding). The new parlour ceiling was enriched with ornamental plasterwork. That these alterations and additions were designed to impress the world without the farm gates is evidenced by the rear of the building, where plain bricking up was resorted to and the back elevation of the cross-wing was left in studwork with brick-noggings (see Plate 326). All this followed faithfully the Tudor traditions of facade show.

### Manor Farm, Saxtead
TM 263 657

Saxtead Green is a hamlet the best part of a mile from village and church, and the Green itself straddled the route of the Roman road going north-east from Baylham to Peasenhall and Yoxford, with an off-shoot of the Green branching to the east. This broad grassed area, some 100 yards wide, seems to have been eroded in length over the centuries, for in Hodskinson's map of 1783 it can be seen continuing as far as Saxtead Lodge, and must have provided extensive grazing for the householders whose farms and cottages lay along each side. Chief amongst these was the Manor Farm, with a moated site which must once have totally enclosed an island upon which the house was built (see Plate 327). The site was entered by a single bridge, of which the position is probably unchanged, and the barn and buildings were close to, but outside the moat.

*Plate 327: View across moat from the south-east.*

The moat, doubtless, antedates the Manor Farm, for the earliest part of the present house probably dates only from the mid-fifteenth century or a little before. Then it could have consisted of a single range with a gable-end facing south on to the Green, slightly over 6 metres wide (approx. 20ft), containing a hall, or house-place, in the centre open into the roof, with pantry and buttery at the north end (and, probably, a lean-to addition), and, most likely, a small parlour at the south end. The house-place itself was fairly generously sized as befitted a house of consequence, some 8 metres by 6 metres (say 26½ft long by 19½ft wide), and the hearth smoked up into the roof where traces of soot blackening can still be seen. The space was divided in length into two bays by a central arch-braced tie-beam at a height of some 3.3 metres (about 10ft 8in.) above the floor, and was entered by the present doorway. This was at the lower end of the hall and immediately next to the service room: at the upper end would have been the dining place of the family, with the cauldron over the fire near the centre of the hall. There would probably have been a small parlour — possibly single bay — behind the dais, but of this there is now no trace. The sleeping chambers would have been at one or both ends of the hall reached, doubtless, by ladder stairs.

Life could have gone on like this since about the middle of the fifteenth century — or even before, if the primitive crown-post can be taken as an index of a fairly early build (see Plate 328) — until well on into the sixteenth century. By that time bricks would be increasingly plentiful and within the means of the well to do yeoman farmer, and large chimney stacks were going up everywhere in the manors and farmhouses of Suffolk. To build a brick chimney here necessitated pulling down most of the parlour, for it would require a ground area of nearly three metres square. What seems to have happened was this: in order to avoid getting too close to the moat at the south end, about 1 metre was subtracted from the hall in order to bring the base of the chimney in, and still allow enough space both for it and a good-sized parlour of two bays measuring about 5 metres (say 16ft 8in.) in length. This accounts for the difference in the length of the two hall bays (now dining-room), that to the south being about 1 metre shorter. At the base of the stack were back-to-back fireplaces to warm both parlour and hall, and on the west side a newel stair was constructed with access from a lobby between these two rooms with a doorway opening out into the orchard. A partition was built at the lower end of the hall — roughly where the screens-passage would have been in a mediaeval house — and the service rooms extended into a new wing built either then, or not long after, in which was the kitchen with a second brick chimney. Adjoining this was a brick floored annexe which could well have been used for stabling. The newel stair between hall and parlour went up to a landing off which gave the new — and best — bed chamber above the parlour, with its own fireplace. Opposite this was a door to the two new bed chambers which had been formed by flooring over the hall: the tie-beam with its arch-braces and crown post being built into a partition, and an opening cut into the centre for a doorway (see Plate 329). Later on this door was blocked, and a passage formed along the west side by the dangerous expedient of cutting off the end section of the tie beam complete with arched brace. The upper part of the crown post disappeared above the ceiling. At the far end there was access to the rooms previously over the service area below, and from these to others in the east wing, probably connected later on by a staircase into the kitchen.

That in brief is the building development of a fifteenth century farmhouse to which the first clues were given by the low eaves in the middle and the higher eaves and ridge line of the obvious addition adjoining the moat. A careful tracing through of timber internally will go a long way to completing the story.

*Plate 328: Early crown-post within attic roof at Manor Farm, Saxtead.*

*Plate 329: Tie-beam showing base of crown-post in a bed chamber.*

*Figure 87: Columbine Hall, Stowupland, west view from moat.*

## Columbine Hall, Stowupland
TM 067 608

In addition to Philip de Columbers from whom the name is derived, the manor has passed through the hands of some distinguished Suffolk families; Hotots, Tyrrells, Gardiners, Careys who were connected with the Hunsdons of Huntingfield, Poleys, Ashburnham, and Bobys, until the beginning of this century.

Although the house today is lacking in notable architectural qualities, either within or without, it is not lacking in the charms of a secluded site and a wide moat enclosed with trees, which at certain times and seasons give Columbine Hall a romantic fascination (see Plate 330). The house itself does much to promote this, being built directly out of the waters of the moat on two sides, with its timber-framed and plastered walls lodged on a deep brick base, and having a continuous jetty along the whole of the west and much of the north side — giving the building somewhat of the look of a vessel at anchor (see Figure 87). The earliest part was evidently a single range built along the north side of the moat which here measures about 64 metres, and on both the east and west sides about 71 metres.

*Plate 330: The jettied west elevation above the moat.*

(The site was once completely moated but has been filled in on the south.) This single range extended as far as the west corner of the island and seems to have comprised a floored hall house, with the hall in the centre and parlours and service rooms at the west and east ends respectively. Above the brick revetment which contained the moat, and provided a basement wall off which the carpenters could build, it was timber-framed. The jettied first floor was clearly supported at the north-west corner by an angle post, and the massive arched bracket supporting the outward projection of the dragon-beam, and springing off a moulded base at a depth of rather more than one metre below. The joist ends appear above the head of the first floor frame at regular spaces of about nine inches, suggesting that the close studwork was intended to be seen, and that within this the windows would have the modular relationship which today is lacking. At various periods these windows have been renewed, and, at a guess, the original range was probably extended by the building of the west wing in the early seventeenth century, when the zigzag patterned brick chimney stack was built between hall and parlour, and the external walls plastered over, and mullion windows replaced by casements.

The first simple plan of the house has become complicated by internal alterations in the form of passages, and the sub-division of rooms, but one of the most interesting changes of purpose seems to have taken place in the north-east corner which, it is hard to believe otherwise, was originally intended as a larder. This, which is about 3.6 metres by 2.4 metres (say 12ft by 8ft), seems to have been equipped for devotional purposes as a house oratory in the early seventeenth century, with an ornamental plaster ceiling in which angels intermix with floral patterns and *fleur-de-lys,* within a trail border of vines and grapes.[1] The corollary of this change would have been to transfer the kitchen and dairy to the new west wing, where they would remain until in Victorian times a new wing was built on the south-east side of the house.

Surrounded by rich green meadows and old trees, there is much that still suggests an imparkment of the fifteenth century, and within this a moated manor house which, in slowly declining from its former status, has preserved an atmosphere of indefinable timelessness.

1 cf. *Columbine Hall, Stowupland*, in *E.A.M.*, No. 3879.

294

*A row of timber-framed thatched and plastered cottages, eighteenth century.*

# COTTAGES

A great deal of history in the building of small dwellings is seen in the following two structures, which although widely separated, are remarkably alike in many features. They are chosen from amongst innumerable examples, in order to illustrate certain basic differences which determine the cottage type as opposed to the farmhouse. The accommodation provided was of the most primitive kind, and, to begin with, it was little more than a shelter with four walls and a roof. Aggregation of amenities was a slow process, and most valuable being a brick chimney stack; if extra space was needed it was often latched on by means of a lean-to.

**Birch Cottage, Coddenham Green**
*TM 125 568*

Birch Cottage was built on a patch of ground surrounded by fields, 300 yards away from the end of a lane serving the hamlet of Coddenham Green. The track system suggests that it was a dependence of a farm just under half a mile away — Whitegate Farm — and, possibly, erected by a freeholder for a foreman or stockman. The cottage is a timber-framed structure on shallow brick footings (see Colour Plate), just enough to raise the sill-plate above the ground and so preserve the woodwork from early decay. It is of three bays 9.4m (nearly 31ft) overall length. The height of the wall frame from underside of sill-plate to top of wall-plate measured 3m (9ft 10in.), and the overall height from floor level to top of rafters 7m (23ft). In trying to decide the original form there were the usual conundrums.

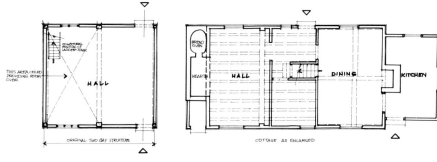

*Above: Birch Cottage, Coddenham Green, ground floor plans.*

*Neo-Tudor cottage, near Barking, c.1890.*

295

*Cottages in Angel Lane, Woodbridge.*

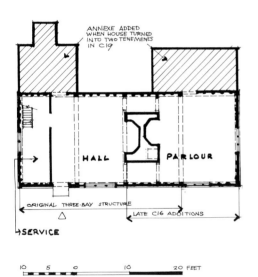

*Church Cottage, Pettistree, ground floor plan.*

It was evident that it had once been a two-bay structure, nearly 6m square, with wall-plates connected by tie-beams: these were still in position at both ends but missing in the middle, resulting in a sag at the top of the wall. The roof was collared at about 2m (6ft 6in.) above the tie-beams, and the rafters were stiffened by arched wind-braces neatly carpentered in pairs between each of the principal timbers. The ground floor was ceiled over, but the first floor was clearly not the original, as could be seen from the joints between the principal posts and the ends of the supporting beam; furthermore the ground floor headroom had been reduced to less than 2m (6ft 6in.) when the floor was put in. A reasonable deduction is that in this small dwelling – practically square with a steep thatched roof – one bay was a hall open to the roof, and the other was ceiled between tie-beams providing a sleeping chamber in the roof space (see plan). Access to the latter would have been by ladder in the floor opening now used for stairs. As there is neither smoke-blackening of rafters nor any signs of renewal of roof, there was probably always a chimney stack at the south end, although not necessarily the one that is there now with its large open fireplace and bread-oven. The sudden appearance of black weatherboarding at this end of the house suggests that this was a false gable wall put up at a later stage. There was probably only one main stage of later alterations, and, assuming the original cottage to have been built $1650^{\pm}$, this could easily have been about a century later. Then the two extra rooms were added at the north end, the staircase put in and from the landing a doorway cut through the tie-beam of what had been hitherto the end gable wall (a triangular-shaped iron tie, improvised by the blacksmith, went over the doorway to compensate for the loss of strength). A second chimney stack was built on the new gable wall, and a lean-to baccus added, through which the cottage is now entered: the earlier door had been on the west side, but this must always have been inconvenient, and went largely out of use. Thus the cottage ended up by having a parlour with bread-oven at the south end, a pantry (later bathroom) and lobby in the middle, a kitchen-cum-dining-room, and a baccus at the north end: at each end on the floor above were bed chambers and in the middle a staircase landing and another small bedroom. Drinking water was provided by the pond until the middle of this century.

*The Cottage, Kersey, c.1550.*

## Church Cottage, Pettistree
### TM 298 549

*Plate 331: Church Cottage, Pettistree, view from the east.*

Church Cottage, Pettistree, more nearly resembles a small farmhouse, and, being built within a stone's throw of the church in half an acre of ground, conveys the impression of having been a dwelling of better quality such as might have housed the Clerk of the Parish (see Colour Plate). It was a three-bay timber-framed structure (see Plate 331), consisting of a two-bay hall open to the roof, and a single-bay with service rooms at the south end, and built probably at least a century earlier than Birch Cottage. The sill-plate was raised well above ground on a brick base, and the standard of carpentry and jointing was generally superior. The cottage must have been much improved at Elizabethan times, for it would be probably in the late sixteenth century that a large brick chimney stack was built in the centre and a further bay added at the north end (see plan). At the same time the hall was ceiled, together with the extending northward. The plan that resulted was a somewhat smaller hall with its south service rooms and a large open fireplace taking the place of the old open hearth, which, for half a century or more had been smoking up and blackening the rafters, before finding its way out through a kind of lattice work flue in the apex of the roof. The original access to the first floor remained at the south end, and a new stairs must have been built in the lobby at the back of the stack rising to a small bed chamber next the chimney and a further, and larger room over the new parlour. In common with many another old dwelling, Church Cottage must have later declined in status, for in the nineteenth century it was turned into two tenements, each with a brick built baccus at the rear, and a shallow well for drinking water.

In comparing these two cottage dwellings with others, there is a remarkable conformity of dimensions and structural principle. The timber-framed Suffolk cottage seems for several hundred years to have remained consistently of

*Brooke Lodge, Kettleburgh.* John Western.

*A pair of timber-framed thatched and plastered cottages, early eighteenth century.*

rectangular plan, with a cross span ranging between approximately 5 and 5.6m (16ft 4in. and 18ft 4in.), bay centres between 2.8 and 3.1m (9ft 3in. and 10ft 2in.), and a height overall the wall girth — measured from the underside of the sill-plate to the top of the wall plate — of around 3m (9ft 10in.). The roof pitch remained fairly constant between 48-50 degrees as long as thatch was used: immediately plain tiles, followed by pantiles, became cheaper and more accessible, roof pitches declined as walls increased in height to a minimum sufficient for two storeys of around 2.2m (7ft 3in.). The basic rectangular plan is found in both cottage and timber-framed farmhouse, but there is an addition of bays and wing annexes in farmhouses, together with a significant difference in the height of the wall girth — measured as above. This will extend to 4.5m (approx. 14ft 10in.) or more, for two storeys and, in many cases, attic space as well. The remaining differences are those that reflect the humbler status of the cottage in contrast with the farmhouse, and which appear not only in the smaller scale of the former, but in the diminished quality and size of features such as doors, windows and chimney stacks. In the use of materials, however, they remain recognisably of the same family.

*Late eighteenth century cottages, Quay Street, Orford.*

*Church Cottage, Pettistree. Mid-fifteenth century dwelling with later alterations. Timber-framed, plastered and thatched.*

*Tudor cottage at Dalham. Timber-framed, plastered and thatched.*

*Birch Cottage, Coddenham Green. Mid-sixteenth century structure with later addition. Timber-framed, plastered and thatched.*

*Cottage at Swilland. Late mediaeval dwelling, timber-framed, plastered and thatched.*

*Cottages at Euston. Timber-framed, plastered and thatched. Dating from late-seventeenth century.*

*Brick and flint cottage, Middleton (now known as The Stone House). Pebble faced walls with white brick quoins of the early-nineteenth century.*

*Brick cottage, Great Saxham. The so-called Tea-house, built in the late-eighteenth century and used as a gamekeeper's cottage.*

*Figure 88: The Gatehouse, Butley Priory.*

*Butley Priory*
*TM 376 492*

Of all the religious houses in Suffolk converted to secular usage after the Dissolution, none have caught the imagination quite so much as the gatehouse of Butley Priory. A ruin until the reign of George II,[1] it was converted into a dwelling in 1737. This involved building new walls on the south side and raising all the old walls to the height of a uniform roof springing, filling in the gaping window openings with glazing, forming fireplaces and chimney stacks. It also meant carrying out innumerable masonry repairs; putting in new floors and a new staircase, and, finally, pitching timber-framed roofs to the main high level as well as to the secondary roofs, and providing slated covering. The house owes its present form to the partnership between Dr. M.J. Rendall who had retired in 1924 from the headmastership of Winchester, and his architect, Mr. W.D. Caroe, in his day one of the leading authorities on English Gothic, who was commissioned to undertake the restoration soon after Dr. Rendall acquired the property in 1926.[2] John Western made the drawing (see Figure 88) of the Priory from the north-east in 1975, showing the approach side and the great Armorial in carved freestone set amongst neatly knapped squares of flint. More than this, he caught something of the massive scale of the gatehouse piled up into the clear sky of this remote corner of coastal Suffolk. The principal feature of the interior at ground floor level is the original carriage-way converted into an arched and vaulted hall, the vaulting infilling being of stonework. On either side of this magnificent chamber are two smaller rooms, each of about 6 metres square (say 20ft square), that on the west now designated as drawing room, and on the east as kitchen. Both these rooms are covered with quadripartite rib and panel vaults, the panel fillings being of fourteenth century brickwork. The panels are shallow domed shape in form, and carried out in stretcher bonded brickwork beautifully executed where the original remains. These vaulted ceilings are amongst the finest examples of brickwork of this period in Suffolk.

The Priory, founded before 1195 by Theobald de Valcines, occupied a secluded corner of the River Deben a mile below Wickham Market, in a site of great natural beauty. The story of its devolution until eventual suppression in 1536 is well-enough documented. After that date, when the grantee sold it to a Mr. John Lane of Loudham, the history is obscure. Most of the Priory seems to have been demolished or turned into farm-buildings, and in 1855 Wm. White gives the occupant as John Walker Miller. A timber-framed mill building had evidently existed since mediaeval times (see Plate 333) and, together with the adjoining house, is likely to have been more or less continuously occupied. Lying north-west of the priory ground, it was built on a mill stream taking the spill water from Decoy Pond, itself of mediaeval origin, and can well have provided a living for many generations of millers until it ceased grinding corn in 1950.

*Ashe Abbey, Campsey Ashe*
*TM 317 545*

In the priory grounds, only the barn (see Figure 90) still stands and a building shown on a plan of the Priory published in 1790 as 'The Dwelling House'. The barn evidently incorporates part of the range of buildings west of the cloister, of which the exact function has still to be determined. The house, which is now known as 'Ashe Abbey', must have formed part of the complex of religious buildings on the site at the time of suppression. The purpose for which it was built is uncertain, and also the use to which it was put by new owners. There is some reason for believing that it was larger than at present, and that it may have been the chaplaincy attached to, but built at a short distance from the main claustral buildings.

In 1962, when the present owners decided to make it into a habitable dwelling, there remained little of original work in the exterior apart from the flint rubble masonry walls and a stone doorway on the east side of late fifteenth or early sixteenth century date. The chimneys were later, although that on the east may well have been added before 1536. The great interest of the interior centred upon the roof construction. Spanned by a single immense beam — cut from an oak tree

1 Butley Priory was one of thirteen Suffolk houses of Augustine or Black Canon, and described in some detail in Richard Taylor's *Index Monasticus* of 1821. 'This priory', he says, 'was enriched by the contributions of a number of noble and pious persons: besides great possessions in Suffolk and Norfolk, it had an interest in, or the patronage of, 11 churches in the latter county, 23 or more churches and 'chapels appropriated in Suffolk, one in Lincolnshire, two in Essex, and one in London; 14 or more manors, two rabbit warrens, and a mill at Chesilford.'

At the Dissolution it was granted to Thomas Duke of Norfolk in 1540, who sold it in 1544 to William Forthe of Hadleigh, '. . . in consideration of the sum of 910£ 2s. 3d.' In 1821 it belonged to the trustees of Lord Rendlesham and, at that time, 'much of this monastery is preserved; the gatehouse is nearly entire' — suggesting that it may have been uninhabited at that date and again becoming dilapidated. In later years, and until 1924, it seems to have been used as the vicarage of the parish.

2 See also Hugh Farmar's *The Cottage in the Forest* (London: Hutchinson), in which Chapters 10 and 11 discuss the history of the Priory. He mentions also Dr. Rendall's genius as a gardener. In addition, see the article by James G. Mann on Butley Priory, in *Country Life* of March 25th, 1933.

*Plate 332: Detail of queen-post and tie-beam.*

*Plate 333: The mill-house.*

*Plate 334: The modern annexe.*

*Plate 335: The patio through a Tudor doorway.*

*Plate 336: Ashe Abbey – detail of queen-post.*

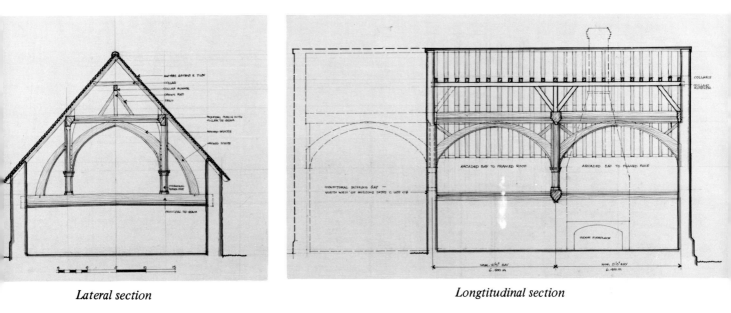

*Lateral section*

*Longtitudinal section*

*Figure 89: Ashe Abbey – cross-sectional roof details.*

*Figure 90: Ashe Abbey. The barn – formerly conventual building.*

303

of nearly 11 metres (35 feet) long — the house had an open hall with walls of only about 4 metres high (13 feet), covered by a single pitched roof with gable ends of about 6 metres measured from springing to apex. It was a feat of carpentry. The roof loads were evenly distributed between walls and tie-beam, to which they were transmitted by means of a composite truss. This consisted of two posts of queen-post type mounted on the tie-beam, which, in turn, carried the weight of a pair of massive longitudinal purlins connected by a further high-level tie-beam supporting a crown-post which engaged with a collar and collar runner (see Plates 332 and 336 and Figure 89). The purlin loads were transmitted to crown post and walls by arcaded arch-bracings. (The whole of this roof structure has survived the best part of 580 years with scarcely any opening of the timber joints.) There was no evidence of mortice holes in the soffit of the main tie-beam which would have pointed to a load-bearing stud wall below. On that evidence the space was intended to be open, and this would be compatible with a room used as a hall or refectory.

The problem then became the lack of other accommodation. If this had been the chaplaincy, there would have been sleeping quarters as well as a kitchen and service rooms. If, as seems possible, a further bay had been removed on the north side in the late eighteenth or early nineteenth century, this might account for the absence of sleeping quarters (dorter). The building could then have consisted of the two-bay refectory (frater) in the form of an open hall, with a two-storey annexe — sleeping quarters above and service rooms below. The kitchen might well have been in a detached structure (as it still is in the modernised house).

The recent alterations (see Plate 334) aimed at leaving the maximum clear space open from ground to roof apex in order to reveal the mediaeval timber roof construction. The eighteenth and nineteenth century windows and doors — a very miscellaneous lot — were removed and replaced by new joinery in natural hardwood, with the intention that externally this would weather silver-grey to tone with the flint faced walls. The two-storey wing replaced a late eighteenth or early nineteenth century kitchen annexe. A south-facing terrace patio was formed between the buildings, close to the mill stream (see Plate 335). In character the new work was frankly contemporary, but related by form and texture to the original structure.

*Clare Priory*
*TL 769 449*

The traditional founding of Clare Priory by friars of the Augustinian Order in 1248, and its subsequent devolution until the suppression of the house in 1538, have been well recorded. The story of the house appeared in a delightful study by Mr. K.W. Barnardiston in 1962 — *Clare Priory — Seven Centuries of a Suffolk House* (Cambridge: Hagger & Sons). That story ended, in a remarkable way, with the return of the house, in 1953, to the same religious order for whom it was first built and endowed.

*Plate 337: The western guest-house range of Clare Priory.*

*Plate 339: The rear view of the guest-house range.*

*Plate 338: The rear of the guest range from the ruined church.*

The original building complex centred upon a nearly square cloister (see Figure 26) measuring 24.5m (80 ft) by 22.25m (73 ft). Along the north side ran the church, comprising nave with a north aisle and choir some 36.5m (120 ft) in length. On the west was the three-storey building lacking authenticated history but normally considered as the cellarer's domain, partly for storage of provisions and partly for guests — therefore reasonably assigned as guest-house. On the east the two-storey structures seem to have contained a ground floor chapter-house with ancillary rooms and on the first floor the friars' dormitory (dorter). Adjoining this to the south side was, evidently, the friars' refectory also at first floor level, approached by a staircase at the west end. To part of the basement of this structure have been assigned kitchens and lavatories. Further east lies the long building called on St. William St. John Hope's plan 'Infirmary with library over'.

Of this original complex only two habitable buildings remain, (1) the two-storey building west of the cloister and (2) the 'Infirmary'. The first was converted into domestic premises after the Dissolution (see Plates 337, 338, 339 and 340). The second has recently been converted for use as a chapel (see Plate 341). The cellarer's domain, being well constructed of rubble masonry, later embellished by brick chimney stacks, and having a staircase annexe on the east side, made a good house with little alteration. The plan at the time seems to have been the customary mediaeval one of central hall with screens-passage, the parlour being at the north

*Plate 340: The group of buildings from the south.*

*Plate 341: Clare Priory. The infirmary building, now the chapel.*

end, the buttery and pantry below the screens to the south, together with a way through to kitchens in the adjoining building. The hall was ceiled, with bed chambers above, where, the guests were accommodated.

A special interest of Clare Priory must be the continuous occupation of the guest-house, with its development into a comfortable Tudor house. Seen from the drive it is a two-storey building, of four bays, and an attic storey with large dormer windows. The front has a series of triple off-set buttresses rising all the way from ground to eaves, and dated as of fifteenth or early sixteenth century construction. There is a main gable range with two rear wings, a secondary range at the south end, and on the east a gable porch and two small gable annexes. The chimneys were Tudor and Jacobean additions. That on the west side, between the central pair of dormers, does not appear on J. Kirby's engraving of 1748, and although of Elizabethan form was evidently added in the succeeding century. The windows were narrow mullioned lights with arched heads. A few survive on the west elevation, together with the off-centre doorway (indicating a screens-passage entry) and beautiful carved fifteenth century door, with a small central wicket.

## Abbas Hall, Great Cornard
*TL 901 405*

Three roads leave Sudbury on the east, and between the two going roughly due east and south respectively lies the parish of Great Cornard, containing two extremes of population density. That part of the parish which is contiguous with the town is now — to use the unattractive description coined in the 60s — an 'overspill' area. Under the Town Development Schemes the parish was chosen to receive population from the Greater London Council area, and a concentrated housing scheme appeared between the years 1961 and· 1974. The eastern lands of the parish are, in contrast, thinly populated and strangely remote, and it is here that Abbas Hall is to be found. The name of Abbas stems traditionally from 'Abbess', the property being in the ownership of the Abbey at Malling, Kent, during the reign of Henry VIII.

Structurally, the building awaits thorough survey and technical assessment. Its interest lies in belonging to that comparatively small group of aisled halls that have come to light in Suffolk in recent years. Difficult to recognise at first — and externally revealing nothing of its antiquity — it will be found still to contain the essential components of a two-bay aisled hall form. At some time — probably on passing into secular ownership after the Dissolution — the central hall was floored across at a height of about 2.5m when the strutted heads of the principal posts became enclosed in the bed chambers (see Plate 342). A new timber-framed wing was built at the east end, and an immense chimney stack along the line of the screens-passage.

Facing the back of this stack are a pair of sharply pointed timber arches with capitals and shafts (see Plate 343), mutilated in some of the original carving but

*Plate 342: Strutted head of principal post in a bed chamber.*     *Plate 343: Arched openings to service area, Abbas Hall.*

recognisably more primitive than the group of arches that occur in a similar relation to entrances in the Prior's house at Great Bricett priory. It can be conjectured that, as in the latter, these were the entrance to service rooms, and that they probably fronted screens at the west end of the hall. A similar lack of refinement is characteristic also of the roof carpentry, and this, together with the use of massive timber sections, could point to an early dating. A late fourteenth century date has been suggested but this remains to be substantiated. Scientific techniques might be called in to give a date difficult to establish correctly by inferential methods.

The house has been basically altered little since the change of ownership after the Dissolution, when it seems to have turned into a small farmhouse, and its external appearance gradually conformed to a typical Suffolk dwelling with plastered walls, casement windows, plain-tiled roofs and plain chimney heads.

*Ixworth Abbey*
*TL 929 704*

The disposition of the property in the early seventeenth century is shown on the accompanying detail from an eighteenth century estate map of the Manor of Ixworth dated 1620-24,[1] on which the draughtsman included both the ground floor plan and an elevational drawing of the priory (see Figure 91). Mrs. Joy Rowe, the present owner of Ixworth Abbey, who is working upon the history of the foundation, contributes the following description of the devolution from 1538, together with notes on the structural alterations:

'At the Dissolution the priory buildings and manor passed by exchange to Richard and Elizabeth Coddington. Their manor of Cuddington adjoined Nonesuch Palace (near Ewell, Surrey) and was 'acquired' by Henry VIII to extend the palace bowling green and tennis courts with the promise of appropriate recompense. The stone from the priory church was bought by Lord Keeper Nicholas Bacon and carted to Redgrave, while the lead from the church roof was bought by Sir Thomas Kytson for his house at Hengrave. The domestic (claustral) buildings were adapted for use by the Coddingtons as simply and inexpensively as possible. The frater was divided by an inserted floor and the dormitory left untouched to serve as a long gallery. The house passed in 1624 to Dame Elizabeth Coddington's grandson, Sir John Caryll, and from him to the Nortons of Southwick, Sussex. In 1680-95 the main hall and dining-room were added and the dormitory-long gallery divided (by wainscot and panelling) into more conveniently sized rooms. In 1821 the frater (south range) was halved in length and the north hall constructed by filling in the south corner of the original cloister walk and garth. The new front was faced with grey brick. The buildings were coloured ochre with marl from a pit in Ixworth. Where red brick was used in sixteenth century additions, some seems to have been locally burnt and some bought from Sir Thomas Cornwallis's brickworks at Brome.'

*Plate 344:  A general view of Ixworth Abbey from the south.*

1  I am much indebted both to Mrs. Joy Rowe for drawing my attention to this map and to Mr. & Mrs. John Cross for permitting it to be photographed.

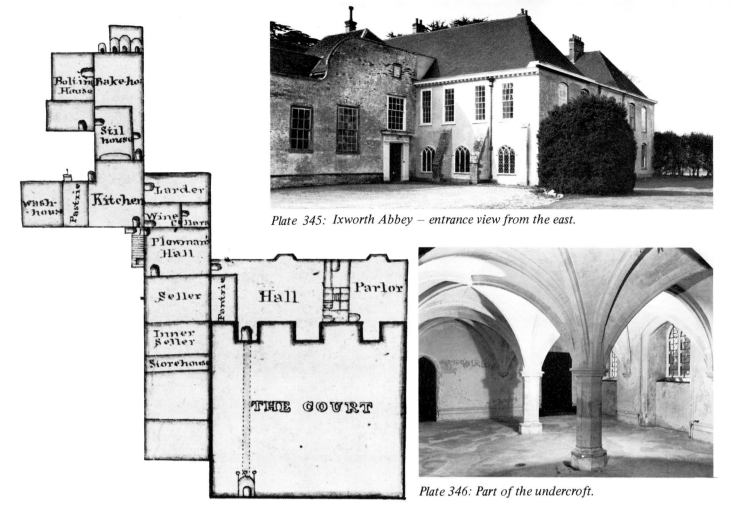

Plate 345: Ixworth Abbey – entrance view from the east.

Plate 346: Part of the undercroft.

*Figure 91 above and below: Part of an eighteenth century estate map of Ixworth Manor.*
*Courtesy of Mr. John Cross*

It has become increasingly evident that both Coddingtons and their successors in title did not destroy the surviving monastic structures so much as conceal their appearance. The interest of Ixworth priory lies in the way premises, originally intended for the occupation of a prior and between fourteen and eighteen canons, were adapted for secular and domestic purposes during the succeeding centuries. (See Plates 344-346.)

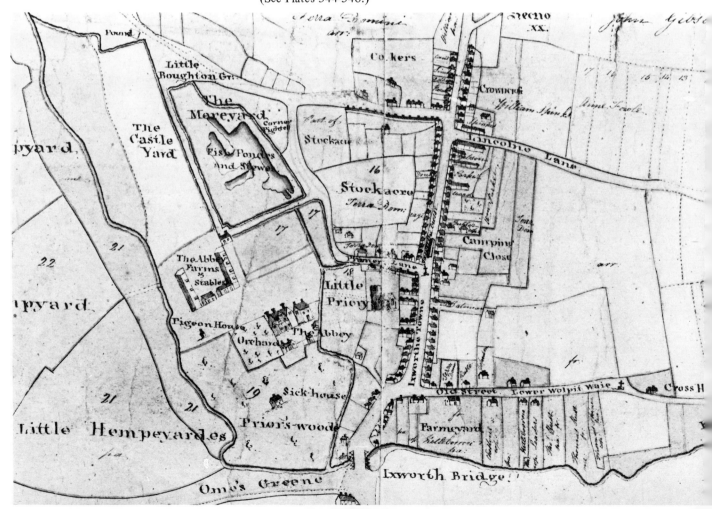

## The Old Rectory, Badingham
*TM 312 678*

*Plate 348: Early Georgian staircase.*

*Plate 349: Staircase at The White House, Badingham.*[5]

The period in the established Church between the mid-eighteenth and mid-nineteenth centuries reached a peak of affluent and comfortable living — at least in lowland England. The younger sons of landed families frequently took holy orders, and with their social background and university training were often interested in art and architecture. The Old Rectory — as it is now called — at Badingham is a satisfying example of these trends, about half a mile from church and village, with its garden, woods and meadowland of some forty acres, built on high ground with ranging views south and west over distant country (see Plate 347).

The whereabouts of an earlier rectory are not known, but, certainly until the time of the Dissolution, the priest was probably housed in a timber-framed dwelling of only slightly better quality than others in the village, and in fairly close proximity to the church. What is known is that Dr. Ward, the Rector in the late seventeenth century, 'made his way home after sermon' — as Lilian Redstone put it[1] — 'to a comfortable eight-roomed house', but whether this was on the present site or, indeed, forms part of the present building, it is difficult to be certain. Local history goes on to record that Dr. Barrington Blomfield (who had been born in Badingham when his father was the Rector), on succeeding to the living in 1727 set about building 'a "neat" Rectory House with twenty rooms not far from the church.'[2] That there have been substantial changes since Dr. Blomfield's days is apparent, the whole of the front range having been added about a hundred years later. At the rear of the Old Rectory are the remains of earlier buildings some of which could date from the late seventeenth and early eighteenth centuries. Dr. Blomfield's house, one would judge, must have been of red brick, for when the new front range was added in white brick, the old brickwork was refaced to match the new brick.[3]

William White in his Gazetteer of Suffolk records the next developments by referring, in his edition of 1855, to 'the commodious Rectory house which he (the then Rector — Rev. Robert Gorton) much improved about 15 years ago.' A date of 1835-40 is perfectly compatible with the sophisticated design of the front range, which consists of twin brick bays flanking a central porch and punctuated by well-proportioned sash windows with fine glazing bars. The sole non-contemporary feature is the frieze of small windows just beneath the eaves of the slated roofs, where these are hipped forward over the bays, and believed to have been added — with considerable skill — by a recent owner[4] for the sake of the far-reaching views to be had from that height above ground. The ends of this new range were dexterously done with pilasters, enclosing three storeys of windows and achieving a pedimented effect in the gable end. The contrasts between the nineteenth century work and the simpler eighteenth century house can be seen here side by side.

Within doors, the joinery of the front range is contemporary, with high skirtings, moulded mantelpieces, broad architraves enclosing panelled doors, and, as in the staircase hall, panelled and painted wainscot. The staircase itself is in the early Georgian style, faultlessly done in mahogany with heavy swept handrail and shaped consoles at the end of each tread (see Plate 348).[5] The difference between the two builds is further emphasised by a change of level with steps leading from the front to the rear halls, and in the kitchen — almost certainly belonging to an earlier house — a particularly massive chimney stack with range opening.

*Plate 347: General view from the south-east.*

1 In her unpublished paper: *Badingham — A Land of Moats and Halls* (1940), which can be seen in the Seckford Collection in the County Library, Woodbridge.
2 Ibid. Miss Redstone says '20 bedrooms', but probably meant a 20-roomed house.
3 This was cleverly done by building an outer skin of 4½in. brickwork with snapped-headers to carry on the bond of the new work.
4 W. Bridges Adams, Esq., the well-known Shakespearian impresario and producer, who lived at The Old Rectory until 1948.
5 It is not inconceivable that this staircase had been taken out of the earlier house and reused here. A comparable example can be found nearby at The White House, Badingham: it could be contemporary, with its pairs of moulded baluster to each tread — one plain and one twisted — but lacking the ornamental consoles and having a much lighter handrail (see Plate 349).

## Barking Rectory
TM 077 537

In 1818[1] Rev. Davy applied to the Bishop of Norwich to build a new parsonage. There is a tradition that this was designed by Sir John Soane, which I have been quite unable to substantiate, although the design is obviously in the Soane manner, and could well have been influenced by the book which he published in 1788: *Plans, Elevations and Sections of Buildings erected in the Counties of Norfolk and Suffolk.* Davy's architect was Mr. William Brown of Ipswich (a member of the same family as the well-known Ipswich firm of builders' merchants of that name), and the house, which was first estimated to cost £2,550, finished by costing nearly £4,000.[2]

*Plate 350: Barking Rectory — the view from the church.*

*Plate 351: The Rectory seen from the drive.*

The site chosen was some 350 yards north of the church, on open rising ground with a south aspect. The plan was compact and formal, the front entrance in the centre of the south side, with a vestibule which opened into an octagonal hall extended to accommodate an elliptical staircase, ascending in one flight to the first floor landing and gallery — a touch of the dramatic in an otherwise conventional enough interior. Left and right of the hall doors opened into drawing-room and dining-room respectively — doors which, on entry, were found to form part of bowed ends to each room, and which were themselves beautifully constructed pieces of curved joinery. The Rector's study was across the hall and behind the drawing-room — an arrangement promoting a lack of privacy which would today be frowned upon. A door opposite the study, on the other side of the hall, led into a back passage in which a straight flight of stairs went up to the staff bedrooms which were in the west wing. The best bedrooms could be entered mainly off the landing gallery, and faced south and east.

The rectory was built in red brick, which appeared on the north and west elevations, but was faced in Suffolk whites on the south and east (see Plates 350 and 351). The bond was Flemish and the bricks 2½in. with narrow joints in lime mortar to match the brick colour. With the intention of crowning the rise with high walls, the roof pitch was kept low and slated, with wide overhangs: chimneys were as inconspicuous as possible. The general character of the exterior clearly aimed at dignity and sobriety, the one exception being in the pedimented centre-piece with its tall inset Tuscan Doric columns *(in antis)* built of brick and finished in stucco, which enclosed a curved arch-headed front entrance with slender fanlight. There was a hint of *piano nobile* in that flight of shallow steps ascending to the entrance, and the heads of basement windows just visible above ground level: furthermore the approach had a certain elegance in the drive, which came curving up the hillside and turned off into a carriage sweep in front of the house, before continuing to the stable yard at the rear. From the back one could see how use was made of the Soane device of two projecting wings, partly filled in by a single storey ground floor block with flat roof, the wings being prolonged by low outbuildings to form an enclosed yard with entrance from the north.

1 Mr. Vane tells me that there is reference to the earlier parsonage during the incumbency of Samuel Marshall, 1687-1700. At the Archdeacon's visitation in 1691 he was admonished for pulling off the lead from the chancel roof "insomuch that the rain runs down into the chancel". The lead was used to repair the parsonage, which indicates the poor state of the house. I am greatly indebted for historical information on the history of Barking Manor and the building of the new Rectory to Mr. John Vane of Tarston Farm, Darmsden.
2 cf. *The Ipswich Journal*: '. . . the excellent, substantial and highly respectable Parsonage House (at Barking) at an expense of nearly £4,000.'

## Buxhall Rectory
### TM 003 577

*Figure 92: Buxhall Rectory before the removal of the vine-house — from a drawing by Wm. Ayliffe.*

*Plate 352: Buxhall Rectory and church today.*

*Plate 353: Crest on rainwater-head.*

It can be said at once that there are few more delightful compositions in Suffolk than the Church of St. Mary juxtaposed to the classical-looking Rectory backed by its great trees; a composition which has probably altered only during the past century by the removal of the large vine-house in the angle between the two buildings (see Figure 92 and Plate 352). This is the *new* Rectory, for its predecessor was in the hall orchard west of the church.

In 1703 the old rectory was said to have been struck by fire and demolished, and seven years later the new parsonage house was built by the Rev. Thomas Hill (1678-1743). It is this house which betrays its presence only on the approach side by the tall groups of single, triple and quadruple octagonal chimney shafts, and at the rear by the remains of timber-framed and plastered work, together with some windows of the period and a brick gable-end. For a design in the reign of Queen

Anne, the new rectory must have been curiously old-fashioned, judging by such details as remain. The plan was evidently an L, with the day-rooms occupying the middle and south end, and the service rooms the north, which adjoined the stable yard and outbuildings. The traditional hall had by this time become more of an entrance vestibule and the staircase a feature of some importance. The likely arrangement of the ground floor can be guessed from the east elevation, with its interesting attempt at giving a more Palladian appearance to the older house. This takes us to 1852, or soon after, when Rev. Copinger Gooch succeeded the Rev. Charles Green, having already changed his name by deed poll to Hill a year after his marriage to Emily Pyke, daughter of the Rev. George Pyke of Baythorn Park, Essex. It is probable that Mrs. Hill had a hand in the remodelling of the Rectory, for in appearance it much resembles her old home at Baythorn; this would also account for the Georgian look in early Victorian times. Apart from extensive alterations to the look of the main rooms,[1] the house was then given a rounded bay at the south end, the cornice and parapet, and the rows of twelve-paned sash windows. The best job possible was made of the four bay centre-piece, but the front door had to remain obstinately off-centre because of the dining-room. The whole of this refronting was done in white brick (9in. by 4½in. by 2¼in.) in Flemish bond, the bricks no doubt coming down by road from nearby Woolpit (the only exception to this was the retaining of a red-brick plinth, of which the bricks seem to be those of the early eighteenth century). On the lead rainwater-heads the Rector embossed the Hill-Copinger crest (see Plate 353).[2]

1 The earlier staircase in the Jacobean style was not altered.
2 cf. *History of the Parish of Buxhall*, op. cit., page 60: Crest, on a chapeau gu turned up, erm., a demi lion passant, or, between two dragon's wings expanded of the first, each charged with two bars, erm.

**Coddenham House
(formerly Vicarage)**
TM 129 544

In May, 1775, Parson Woodforde, 'the famous diarist', spent a week at Bosmere house and, as he had done ever since going up to Oxford University, recorded the events of each day in his diary. In the afternoon of May 12th, he went with his host to Shrubland Park and drank tea with Mr. Bacon. The next day, together with his host's daughter, they went to visit 'another Mr. Bacon, brother of the other gentleman and a clergyman also who lives at Coddingham, and there we drank tea this afternoon and played at Quadrille at three (d?) per fish. He has a very pretty house indeed, lately built (see Plate 354).[1] The 'very pretty house indeed' was the new vicarage at Coddenham.

That an earlier parsonage existed on the site is still local tradition, and is said to have been a little to the south of the present house, on the tennis courts. There can be little doubt that this was the manor house implied by Joshua Kirby in 1735 as going with the Vicarge manor, nor that this was part of the property of the Bacons, who had been for a long time lords of the manor at Shrubland Park. There is a carved stone plaque embedded in the west wall of the present house with the (graphic) Bacon crest, and the date 1630 (see Plate 355) suggesting that this might be the date of the earlier vicarage.

The new Coddenham Vicarage was on the edge of the 100ft contour, with parkland falling away east toward the village some quarter mile distant (see Plate 356) and in sight of the beautiful Church of St. Mary. It was − and still is − a ravishing prospect, obviously much admired in the eighteenth century, for the drawing-room and principal bedroom (now music room) both looked this way, and shared a three-sided bay with windows which take full advantage of the view. In 1770 the appearance of the Vicarage was much altered by the presence of a further storey (with the inclusion of the basement, four storeys in all). This added, beneath a shallow-pitched slated roof, a series of small sash windows above those of the main bedroom floor, making a remarkably commanding looking house. The reasons for taking away this top storey can only be guessed, but since it consisted presumably of bedrooms for the staff, a later incumbent must have decided that they were better housed in an independent wing. It is this which was added to the west side of the house, and where the Bacon plaque was refixed.

Plate 354: Coddenham House - the entrance from the south.

Plate 355: Bacon crest.

Plate 356: Landscape view east from the House.

The Vicarage was planned and built on spacious lines, and the fundamental decision must have been to place the main day-rooms above a semi-basement on a *piano nobile*. This, in accordance with the best English Palladian traditions, was reached by a flight of stone steps from the drive, and entered by a broad panelled front door with arched fanlight, enclosed within a columnar porch of the Ionic order. To right and left of the entrance hall were dining-room and study respectively, and, beyond, the drawing-room; the kitchen was sensibly placed on the other side of a passage behind the dining-room. A wide balustered staircase with swept handrail rose at the end of the hall to the main landing.

1 For this information, I am much indebted to the article contributed by Mr. F.H. Erith to *The Suffolk Review*, bulletin of the Local History Council, in Volume 4, No.4, Winter 1975/76, pages 173-186.

312

**The Grange, Chelsworth**
*TL 981 478*

To the observant this must be one of the most familiar scenes in Chelsworth: travelling east from Monks Eleigh there comes into view, shortly before reaching the village centre, the weatherbeaten church with its unusually short, high nave and rather squat tower and — looking, as somebody remarked, rather like a village — that rambling assortment of brick walls, stud and plaster and plain plaster house walls, tarred weather-board and plain plaster gable-ends, pantiled and plain tiled roofs, and miscellaneous shaped and sized chimney stacks, that goes by the name of The Grange (see Plate 357). The River Brett, as it goes twisting through this 'picturesque and well-wooded valley',[1] makes a loop around the spot where the church is built and, immediately north of the church, The Grange.[2]

The Grange has a complex plan, the result of numerous additions, but the original house was evidently L-shaped, the main range running north-south with a cross-wing at the north end (see Plate 358). This followed an arrangement to be

*Plate 357: View of The Grange showing the complex of house and outbuildings.*

found in farmhouses of the mid-fifteenth century, in which there was in the centre a hall open to the roof, with a high level tie-beam supporting a crown-post, which, in turn, supported a collar runner with strut bracing in four directions. There is a similar carpentry system at The Clock House, Stonham Parva; The Manor Farm,

1 cf. William White's *Suffolk Gazetteer*, op. cit., page 623. In 1855, the alternative name was 'Chellesworth', which was somewhat closer to the Anglo-Saxon *ceoriesworth*, which Claude Morley translated as 'Husbandman's property'.
2 *Story of a Little Suffolk Village* by Geoffrey R. Pocklington, privately printed in 1956.

*Plate 358: The Grange from the front.*

Saxtead; and, I believe, at Stonewall Farm, Hemingstone. These halls would, doubtless, have had open hearths, the brick chimneys are usually later, and, judging by the zig-zag or 'saw-tooth' pattern of the central stack, the Grange chimney was one of that breed built in the seventeenth century, of which examples have already been noted at The Butterfly, Great Finborough, and Columbine Hall, Stowupland.

*Plate 359: Jettied gable-end, The Grange.*

*Plate 360: Porch — The Grange, Chelsworth.*

At either end of the central 'house-place' occur two-storey rooms, and here they take the form of a parlour at the south with a principal bed chamber above, contained in a short jettied cross-wing construction. At the north end of the hall there is the less usual feature of a small room, which Farrer believed was called the 'keeping-room', comparing it with one at Fordley Hall, near Saxmundham: the rest of the north wing of the L was occupied by service rooms and kitchen, with bed chambers above. At a later date, maybe in the early sixteenth century, a further cross-wing was attached to that at the south end, presenting a jettied gable-end towards the church (see Plate 359). Further outbuildings must have been added on the west side during that century, with a separate barn-like building forming eventually an enclosed courtyard on that side of the house. The latter building with its chimney may have been a malting and brew-house. This may have been the trade of the Green family, to whom it is reasonable to attribute the building of the small porch at the entrance to the house on the east side. The gabled seventeenth century porch is somewhat of a rarity in Suffolk, although there is another example of an earlier, more florid, pattern at Long Melford, dated 1610. Both are timber-framed and open roofed with sides open for a short depth just below the eaves, and both have ornamental barge-boards with a carved inscription on the front. The Grange porch is particularly charming both in scale and detail, with its turned balusters adjoining the central doorway and returning on each side, at eye level, and its pargetted panel with central cartouche enclosing the inscription 1698 (see Plate 360).[1] The ornamental barge-board with its billet edge-moulding appears to have been superimposed by modern timbers. If this was the work of Farmer Green, then it may have been the crowning touch to various alterations and improvements, including the renewal of windows in the then fashionable narrow mullion and transom idiom inset with rectangular panes of leaded glass.

The main road from Barnby through Carlton Colville enters the parish of Oulton after crossing Oulton Broad, and following a turning to the west, that of Flixton, passing Flixton Old Hall and Flixton House. The road then continues to Blundeston and the first by-road to the east skirts a substantial property called 'The Villa' on the Ordnance Survey First Series of 1837, and on the 2½ inch map 'Blundeston Lodge' (but is today, in fact, H.M. Prison). In William White's *Gazetteer* of 1855, it is evidently this which was described as Blundeston House: 'a handsome mansion,

**Blundeston House**
*TM 512 969*

1 Not 1694 as given by Pevsner in *Suffolk: Buildings of England Series* (second edition), page 164.

*Plate 361: South view from the garden.*

*Plate 362: Blundeston House —
columnar porch.*

1 op. cit., page 534.
2 1961. Studio Books: London. In a letter written
to the present owners, Miss Stroud says that there
are numerous notes on the backs of Soane's drawings
as to the timber and materials to be used.

with about 70 acres of well-wooded pleasure grounds, and a lake of 16 acres'.[1] The
property which tòday, however, is called Blundeston House lies at the junction of
the next by-road going east, and it is this which was designed by Soane for
Nathaniel Rix. Finished in 1786, it is one of the smaller of the commissions which
occupied Soane in East Anglia between 1783 and 1791 (see Section 5). The house
has been associated with 'The Rookery, Blunderstone', where David Copperfield in
Charles Dickens' great novel passed many poignant hours during his youth.

In addition to Tendring Hall, Stoke-by-Nayland, for Sir Joshua Rowley, Soane
built two small country houses in Suffolk during these years, and both show his
meticulous attention to detail and finish. The front of the smaller of these — Wiston
Hall, Wissington, near Nayland, for Samuel Beachcroft — appears to be unaltered;
of red brick, it is a variation on the conventions of a typical Queen Anne design. At
Blundeston House the idiom was more Italianate, and the plan form more complex
(see Plate 361). There was a central three-storey range ẁith a shallow pitched
hipped and slated roof, and the original plans show a slight central recess on the
rear elevation from which projected a low-storey wing — kitchen below and nursery
above — and a single-storey dining-room projection in front. The effect intended on
that side of the house was unfortunately lost when the low wing was built up to the
level of the main roof, and the appearance was not enhanced by a Victorian
greenhouse built in the angle between the wings. In *The Architecture of Sir John
Soane,* Dorothy Stroud[2] quotes Soane as saying in his *Works* of 1788, that the
brick walls were to be rough-cast. This was not done, and the red brickwork in
which the house was built was merely painted over, losing inevitably with lapse of
time and lack of maintenance the intended Italian whiteness. Miss Stroud
comments on the Greek Doric columnar porch which is not shown on the surviving
drawings, but is probably contemporary (see Plate 362).

In the external detailing of Blundeston House, there is a notable refinement at
the eaves, which were kept very slim and sharp by reducing the fascia to the
utmost, and giving the wide overhang decorative support by the console brackets in
pairs at regular intervals. The white brick chimney heads, in contrast, were rather
ornate and heavy and one wonders whether the Victorians did not have a hand in
these. It is the back of the house, with its enclosed stable yard and outbuildings
which, apart from a modern lean-to, still preserves in the elevation the Soane touch,
particularly the upper part, where the large lunette window in the central recess is
an original and satisfying feature.

It is still possible not only to appreciate the quiet architectural qualities of this
small country house but also to see that it was the dwelling of a man of taste.
Remarkably unchanged internally, with its original joinery in staircase, doorways
and window frames, ceiling cornices and so on, it must be remembered that the
surroundings now bear little resemblance to those of the late eighteenth century.

The early editions of the Ordnance Survey emphasise the remoteness from Ipswich of villages such as Whitton and Bramford, and with the coming of the railways it is possible to visualise the dramatic impact in a county where hitherto transport was solely by means of roads and rivers. In 1838, for instance, the main link between Bramford and Ipswich was a lane in which, shortly after leaving St. Matthew's parish, there were scarcely any buildings until the outskirts of Bramford village, where the first house was The Lodge. Twelve years later, the topography is unaltered but the Eastern Union Railway has reached Ipswich, and between Chantry Park and Handford Bridge a new line cuts north to Norwich. Bramford now has a railway station and bridge, and the main line is in full view of the church and the distinguished village property of Bramford House.

*Plate 364: Chequered brickwork front, Bramford House.*

Beyond the river bridge at this period there was a group of timber-framed cottages fronting the lane to St. Mary's Church, a mill house on the Gipping, and Bramford House, mainly hidden behind its high brick wall. In front was an open meadow, for the school had not yet been built. The cottages are still there (Group II statutory listed buildings), probably dating from the sixteenth and seventeenth centuries but it is no longer easy to imagine Bramford House as another, if larger, building in timber-frame and plaster. The structural evidence does, however, suggest that this could have been a single-range, timber-framed house, parallel to the road, with plaster gable-end facing towards the river — an open garden in front and a yard with outbuildings at the back. Pending historical research, the size of the property suggests that this was a house of quality, possibly even of manorial status, for — according to Copinger — there were at one time seven separate manors, of which the largest was probably Bramford Carlton[1] with Bramford Hall as manor house. The Bramford House property occupied most of the land on the north side of the street leading into the village proper with a tail parallel to the river.

In the late seventeenth century, a major rebuilding of Bramford House took place.[2] The arrangements suggest that the precedent set by the earlier house was continued, with a gateway opening off the street (see Plate 363) and only footpath access to the front entrance: vehicles and horsemen were to enter the premises, as they had probably always done, off Mill Lane, where the yards and stables were to be found. The idea seems to have been to convert the older timber-framed premises into a new brick building in the classical taste (see Plate 364). Some thirty or more years after the Restoration there was already a vogue for brick facades with chequered brickwork, of which examples can be found in Ipswich, Hadleigh and elsewhere. The general theme was a flat rectangular front, with central doorcase and a length of either five or seven bays, with sash windows one above the other, the intervening walls being in red brickwork in Flemish bond and dark blue/black

*Plate 363: Entrance gate to Bramford House.*

1 cf. *The Manors of Suffolk,* op. cit., Volume 2, pages 264-269. Bramford Hall has been demolished in modern times. The remaining manors had the picturesque names of Lovetofts, Normans or Beverties, Overtye, Frickets, Weylands and Kentons.
2 Pevsner quotes dates of 1693-4, according to deeds.

headers. At Bramford House there was a completely new facade of seven bays, this range being built in front of the older one. There was a large entrance hall and staircase, with a day-room at either end, and a similar plan on the first floor, the central three bays being occupied by a galleried landing. The front may have been carefully calculated for the effect from the street, the upper floor being the only part visible above the garden wall. The doorcase would be seen framed between the tall gate piers, where there are still fittings belonging to iron gates (it is possibly because this doorcase was not considered sufficiently impressive that the porch with Ionic columns was added during the eighteenth century). The lower part of the walls would only be seen on entry, and it was perhaps for these reasons that the chequer-board enrichment was only used to the first-floor walls above a string-course. The beauties of the facade are, in fact, concentrated in the upper part, culminating in a richly detailed cornice with bold lion masks on the guttering. Below this, with its carved bed-moulding, is the broadly overhanging cornice supported by groups of ornamental modillions; here there was a nice by-play between bricklayers and carpenters, for where there are four courses of dark headers below there are four modillions above, and where three a corresponding three modillions.

The impression, on opening the front door, was one of a comfortably pine-panelled interior set off by a suitably elegant mahogany staircase (see Plate 123), an impression confirmed by the panelled day-rooms with their carved wooden mantelpieces, marble interiors and hob-grates.

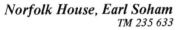

### Norfolk House, Earl Soham
TM 235 633

*Plate 365: Norfolk House – the front.*

*Plate 366: The west side showing the staircase annexe (later extended to form a porch).*

The siting of this dwelling at the foot of the drive leading to the sixteenth century Lodge combined with ample ground space, suggest that it has been historically a house of some importance in the village of Earl Soham. Prior to restoration two doors facing the street may have given the impression that it was once a pair of tenements, but there is nothing to suggest that this was ever the case. On the contrary the building seems to have been enlarged from a comparatively small nucleus by a substantial addition at the north end, together with a back-house, and later by a modern kitchen and bedroom on the same west side. With ground approaching a half acre, the property could have been allotted to a tenant of standing by the lord of the manor, and the building itself confirms the impression of a well and strongly carpentered timber-framed house.

The earliest part consisted of a three-bay structure of two storeys, the bay at the south end being underbuilt with a cellar the full width of the house. The entrance was at the lower end of a two-bay hall, in the position of a screens-passage in a large house, with a doorway in the corresponding position on the opposite side. To the south of this were the service rooms, ladder staircases down to the cellar and up to

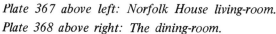

Plate 367 above left: Norfolk House living-room.
Plate 368 above right: The dining-room.
Plate 369 left: Landing at head of the newel staircase.

Plate 370: Brick, timber-framing and exposed thatch in bedroom.

the first floor, being later replaced by an easier stairway with winders. There would have been a fireplace at the north end, and the hall was the general purpose living-room where the cooking was done. The purpose of the cellar was clearly storage, and it could have been used in connection with brewing, the latter 'baccus' with its chimney being a malting house. On the first floor there were a pair of good-size bed chambers. The roof carpentry was designed for thatching and the tradition has been maintained until this day. This house could reasonably date back to 1540<sup>+</sup> (see Plate 365).

The next stage was the addition of a sizeable parlour, with bed chamber above measuring about 5m square (approx. 16ft square). Before this was built the first chimney would have been taken down and replaced by an altogether larger brick stack with back-to-back fireplaces on both floors. The new structure was strongly framed in oak timbers, and the structural principle was a main tie-beam from stack to outer wall into which the floor joists were notched on the short span. Access to the first floor was by a newel stair built out on the west side (see Plate 366 and cf. High House, Otley). The original entrance was superseded by a new door which entered a baffle-lobby in front of the chimney stack on the east side facing the street; there was evidently the intention that callers should be received first in the new parlour. The handsome carpentry of this room has been fully revealed in the recent restoration. In the bed chamber above a higher ceiling was put in, the coving being decorated with an ornamental plaster frieze of which some traces still remain. The addition to the older house can be seen in the change of ridge levels north of the chimney stack, and the date of this work could reasonably be assigned to the mid-seventeenth century.

There still existed one or two iron casements in wooden mullion and transom windows, with rectangular lead lights of this period, and these were taken as a pattern in the replacement of the more miscellaneous wooden casements of later date. Similarly in the case of new doors, an existing seventeenth century panelled door was taken as a model where replacements were required. The modern kitchen wing was accepted and improved by new windows and an adequate range of contemporary equipment, and bathrooms contrived at both north and south ends of the house.

In the final stages of restoration the external plastering of the walls was renewed, except to the north and south gables, where the original timber-framing was once again exposed. The plastered walls were given a pargetted finish by a scratch pattern within engraved mouldings. Finally a simple thatched porch appeared over the original entrance, the later doorway having been removed.

The careful eliciting of the natural expression of good workmanship, which gives the house its distinguishing quality, has been more than justified by the results,[1] not least in the interior of the rooms (see Plates 367-370).

1 It is to be hoped that the allocation of Grade III in the Statutory List will be raised, in the course of revisions now in hand by the Department of the Environment.

## Linden House, Eye
TM 146 739

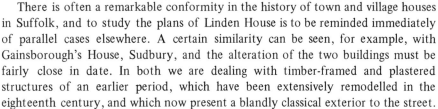

*Plate 371: The front of Linden House to Lambseth Street.*

*Plate 372: Doorcase to central doorway.*

There is often a remarkable conformity in the history of town and village houses in Suffolk, and to study the plans of Linden House is to be reminded immediately of parallel cases elsewhere. A certain similarity can be seen, for example, with Gainsborough's House, Sudbury, and the alteration of the two buildings must be fairly close in date. In both we are dealing with timber-framed and plastered structures of an earlier period, which have been extensively remodelled in the eighteenth century, and which now present a blandly classical exterior to the street.

In the case of Linden House, the oldest part of the building could be of the middle sixteenth century, and the structural dimensions suggest the possibility of an L- or U-plan. This might have taken the form of a hall of about 9m by 5m (30ft by 16ft), and service rooms at the south. Between hall and parlour a chimney stack could have been built in the early seventeenth century, which would account for the mass of brickwork, about 2.5m by 2m (8ft by 6ft 6in.), separating these two rooms. A further stack could have been added between kitchen and service rooms at the other end of the house. (There is everything about the size and shape of these two chimney stacks to suggest that they antedate the eighteenth century work by near a century.) The size of the property, with its numerous outbuildings and considerable acreage, give it the look of a village farmhouse a little way out of the centre, which, perhaps on a change of ownership in the early 1700s, was turned into a smart town house (see Plate 371).

The way in which the change took place can be studied both from outside as well as from within. It will be seen that a new brick skin was built around the three sides of the house visible from the roadway, the back being left timber-framed and plastered. In fact, the entire range adjoining the street must have been a rebuilding in 14 inch brickwork, with a new hipped roof, and, at the same time a similar roof was constructed over the rear range, each roof having dormer-windows at the hipped ends and one central dormer on the east side to light attics. All this can be seen from the south-east corner (see Plate 373), including the way in which the front parapet comes to a stop at the ends, and a normal eaves appears at the sides, underlining the facade character of the street elevation. The facade is skilful enough, although lacking in the sophistication of proportion and detail of the Gainsborough House front. There are seven bays, three on either side of a centre-piece composed of a tall moulded wooden doorcase with fluted pilaster and a segmented pediment over a frieze with metopes and triglyphs (see Plate 372): above this a semicircular-headed window enclosed with an arch and keystone in rubbed brickwork and flanked by brick pilasters (lacking any proper base). The windows are all equal sized twelve-paned sashes, with wide frames brought forward almost to the face of the brickwork, and well constructed flat arch-heads of rubbed brickwork. The brickwork is of that variegated pattern fashionable in the first half of the eighteenth century in Suffolk. The window openings are picked out in red quoin-work which continues beyond sill level down to plinth and intermediate string-course respectively and the parapet copies the theme with blind panels of header brickwork matching the windows below: between quoins all brick is in dark headers throughout the facade. The infelicities of detailing and proportion all suggest that this was the work of country builders, but it is none the less charming

319

Plate 373: South-east view of Linden House from the garden.

on that account. The date of the remodelling could be put as 1730+

The rear view of the house is the outcome of numerous alterations and additions, engaging in that haphazard way when there is a harmony of materials and scale of details, such as doors and windows. In plan there were a series of rooms all much of the same size; entrance hall, drawing-room, study, dining-room, staircase hall and kitchen. The same was true of the bedrooms, with the exception of that over the dining-room which had been enlarged and was propped on two iron columns, until the dining-room was also increased to the same size. The drawing-room had an extension to the south and, in Victorian days, french casements opening into a conservatory. The joinery throughout is all of a piece with the remodelling, and of examplary early eighteenth century quality.

## Basts, Grundisburgh
TM 225 512

Plate 374: Basts from the south-west.

Plate 376: Moulded beams and joists.

This tall, three-storeyed timber-framed structure, with its double jettys and triple hipped roofs is hard to place in the hierarchy of old framed Suffolk houses (see Plate 374). The outside appearance suggests that it once stood alone at this corner of the village of Grundisburgh, the short side facing the road, and the long side the church a hundred yards away. There seems remarkably little cohesion between this building and the wing to which it is joined on the east side, and the lack of any obvious relationship was even more apparent when the latter had the timber-framework exposed — as it was after the restoration by Mr. Arthur T. Bolton, described and illustrated in Country Life, October 7th, 1922. From the plans of the ground floor in 1920, before the work was done, it was evidently then a farmhouse with a long kitchen in the middle, and a large dairy and scullery at the east end. This is confirmed by the name of Weir Farm, by which it had been known for some time,[1] before the new owners returned to the ancient name of Basts, with historical connotations dating to the fourteenth century.[2]

On a closer view, two distinct stages in the building appear. There is little or no resemblance between the carpentry of the three-storey structure and that of the wing by which it is joined (see Plate 375). The division occurs between the two, and the difference in workmanship makes it quite clear that the latter was an addition. Both plans and structure show that the original dwelling consisted of a hall and parlour, with two floors of bed chambers above, but the subsequent alterations have, unfortunately, removed evidence of earlier features, such as staircase and service rooms. Despite these drawbacks, and the loss of rich linen fold wainscot recorded as having been in the main rooms, it is soon evident that the early house was a singular example of Gothic workmanship. The interior was a highly organised system of exposed beams and joists (see Plate 376), all carved with deeply undercut roll mouldings of Perpendicular type of remarkable consistency, extending to the detailing of mullion windows and doors. (Some of these are likely to be replacements when the house was restored.) The house itself was unusual, consisting of a ground floor structure, measuring some 8m by 5m, surmounted by two storeys jettied on three sides, each side oversailing the one below by some 400mm (about 1ft 5½in.). Each wall girth was close-studded, and limited tension bracing occurred only on north and south upper storey faces. The long wall to the upper storey on the west side presents an unbroken row of studs. There is said to be a drawing by Henry Davy, dated 1838, in the British Museum Davy Collection, showing this side surmounted by three gables framed off the upper wall, when the appearance somewhat resembled the Thaxted Guildhall with its pair of hipped (originally gabled) roof ends facing the Market Place. There is, perhaps, more than a hint of late-

1 The author of an article *Note on the History of Bastes or Basts, commonly called Weir Farm House,* in Grundisburgh, Suffolk, published in June, 1923, considered the name to be comparatively new, and probably dating from the building of the small dam or weir in the stream running between house and road.
2 cf. ibid: 'one William Bast was Prior of Woodbridge 1345-1350. Another William Bast, possibly the Prior's father, earlier in the XIVth Century held lands in the Parishes and Manors adjacent to Grundisburgh'.

*Plate 375: The south elevation to the garden at Basts.*

*Plate 377: Angle post carvings at Basts.*

1 It is true that at Basts there was some substantial brickwork below ground, which must have been part of the first build, for the foundations are said to have gone down five feet below ground with walls 760mm (2ft 6in.) thick, suggesting cellarage since filled up.

mediaeval guildhall in the design of Basts, and when related to the family responsible for the building, the possibility that this was deliberate cannot be over-ruled.

The first floor angle post at the south-west corner facing the road is inscribed on one face with the merchant mark identified with that of a Walle or Awall, and on the other with a salt-cellar (see Plate 377). In his *Merchants' Mark in Suffolk*, F.A. Girling, F.S.A., identifies this mark with that of Awall, with a date of ?1510. This Awall must have been John, who married Margery Chance, but both had died by 1501, according to a wall memorial in Grundisburgh Church. A smaller house is said to have stood on this site in John Awall's time, and historians seem to have assumed that it was Thomas, the son of John, who rebuilt the house early in the sixteenth century. It is known that this Thomas went to London, and became a member of the Salters' Company, and presumably for this reason the work at Basts has been attributed to him, but the merchant mark adopted by Thomas, although a variation on that of his father, was neither the same nor is it the one carved on the corner post. It seems, therefore, that John Awall was the builder of Basts and that he was, like his son, a member of the Salters' Company of the City of London. A late fifteenth century date would seem to be more appropriate also on stylistic grounds, and there is a parallel to be found in the corner post at Letheringham Lodge, where occurs a similar carved capital with scalloped cresting dated 1460$^{\pm}$. It is worth noting that Letheringham Lodge is the nearest surviving example of a timber-framed structure with a continuously jettied first floor, and that the use of brickwork is there restricted to a central chimney stack. It could be argued from their positioning that the present stacks were an addition — possibly by Thomas Awall — to his father's House.[1] The zig-zag ornament on the detached chimney shafts, just visible behind the roof of the east wing, has the look of Henry VIII work, and, as Thomas made his will in March 1530-31, could have been finished shortly before his death. The same could be true of the infilling of the ground floor storey with diaper-patterned brickwork, for close examination shows that of the pair of west ground floor windows, that at the south end has been reduced from six to five lights, and the bricking-up could be the reason.

The second stage was evidently the addition of a timber-framed east wing, a four-bay single-range structure with attics, and a short section at the junction with the first build. The old house could scarcely have accommodated a large family, and the successors of Thomas Awall may have been dependent upon the property for their living: those circumstances could explain the new wing with provision of extra rooms and arrangements needed for a farmhouse. Barns and outbuildings would have then been added doubtless in the places where they are today.

## Alston Court, Nayland
TM 975 343

Plate 378: Alston Court and the church.

Nayland is one of those small cloth weaving towns that line the River Stour from Clare to Dedham, whose wealth accounts not only for a succession of great churches but also for some of the finest timber-framed houses. The narrow curving streets are lined with facades of timber and plastered construction, many with jettied oversails above the pavements. Eighteenth and nineteenth century fronts of brick may indicate the desire of later owners to present a more fashionable countenance to the street, but often conceal a timber-framed structure. According to Claude Morley, Nayland comes from the Old Norse *Eyland,* pointing to the earliest settlement believed to be Court Knoll near a bend of the river, a circuit of higher ground above water level for which a prolongation of the course of the Roman road at Great Horkesley appears to make directly, but inconclusively, since, as Prof. Margary says, beyond that point 'its course is quite unknown for five miles.'[1] The possibility of an older ley cannot be entirely dismissed.

It is across some such old route that Alston Court lies, for the village street, which here opens out in a little centre, once branched off towards the river, going between the two wings of the house. To Farrer[2] we owe first the devolution of the house from the cloth making family of Payn to the Alstons, until, with the decease of the last member of that family in the late nineteenth or early twentieth century, the ownership passed to Fenns — relations by marriage: secondly, the identification of those many coats of arms which appear in the stained glass mullioned windows of the house.

The Payns house, or rather houses, for it is a complex of interlocking structures, lay nearer than most Nayland houses to the river, and must, as a result, have been a valuable site. It must be remembered that the Stour was navigable in the fifteenth and sixteenth centuries, and that close access to water offered not only transport for raw materials and finished articles, but also water for washing wool, before weaving[3] and for cloth fulling. Tipping suggests that it was the father of John Payn who, in the late fifteenth century built himself a house in the lane leading to the church (see Plate 378), basing this upon structural evidence.

With the building of a new dwelling or the rebuilding of an old one, this house would have marked an important stage in the fortunes of the family. What is now the east wing of Alston Court was then a single house of one-room depth, gable-ended to the church lane and running towards the river, in three ranges, the first with the parlour, then the principal apartments, and the kitchen with service rooms. Behind these again it is only reasonable to suppose warehouse and storage, in much the same way as merchants' houses adjoining the docks at Ipswich were built in a more or less continuous range, the end nearest the quayside being the warehouse. This house, it must be understood, reflects the taste of a fifteenth century merchant who had made his way up in the world, and was now able to call upon experienced craftsmen to embellish his home. It presented a well-braced gable to the church lane, in which the first floor was jettied far enough over the ground storey to contain an ornamental bay window of fourteen narrow lights, separated by ribbed mullions and divided by a carved transom, with two similar lights on each

Plate 379: The hall, now the dining-room.

1 cf. *Roman Roads in Britain I* by Ivan D. Margary, op. cit., pages 223-4.
2 cf. *E.A.M.,* op. cit., Nos. 3678, 3683, 3688, 3693 and 3700.
3 Lord Camoys, the present owner of Alston Court, drew my attention to the importance of Nayland as a village where wool was washed before weaving.

*Plate 380: Carved halberdier.*

*Plate 381: Moulded and carved joinery in the great bed chamber.*

*Plate 382: The new hall, Alston Court.*

1 cf. *Alston Court, Nayland*, in *English Homes*, op. cit., Periods I and II, Volume 2, pages 197-206.
2 These walls were painted but it cannot be stated definitely that the ceiling was ever decorated to correspond with the walls.

return. Within was the parlour, which Mr. Payn would doubtless use as an office when customers came to discuss purchases of cloth; next came the hall (see Plate 379) or 'house-place', as Tipping reminds us[1] it would more often be called in a yeoman's dwelling. Entered from the lane between the houses, there was a lobby adjoining the chimney stack where a newel stair went up to the bed chambers. It was in this hall that Christopher Hussey identified the little carved wooden halberdier (see Plate 380) as wearing the costume of German mercenaries, brought over to England by Edward IV in 1471, this date being 'compatible with the character of this feature as well as being borne out by the crowned initials of Edward IV on the solar window cill.' Finally, the stairs ascended to the solar over hall and to a lesser bed chamber over parlour. It is the solar, or great bed chamber, that in its ceiling conveys better than anywhere else in the house the consummate craftmanship in moulded and carved joinery that a wealthy merchant could command in the late fifteenth century (see Plate 381). Today this woodwork has lost all the colour with which it was originally picked out and heightened, and the effect, although still delightful, is of course lacking in the glowing richness of its original appearance.[2]

The developments in the days of John Payn, the next generation of clothiers following the death of his father, are somewhat obscure. It was probably in his time (c.1524) that the lane between the houses was blocked by the building of a new hall (see Plate 382) adjoining the parlour of the east range, with a further parlour on the west, followed either by the remodelling or rebuilding of that earlier house which had hitherto been on the opposite side of the lane. This had the effect of creating a long narrow courtyard enclosed between the two parallel house ranges, with a single exit to gardens, orchards and river at the south end.

The main purpose of the ground floor accommodation was evidently to provide cellarage and improved kitchen quarters, together with another small eating-room at the south end. Reached by a separate staircase, the first floor of this western range provided a series of bed chambers. Later alterations concentrated upon giving the elevation of this second house a classical appearance by the use of a fielded and panelled front door under a narrow canopied hood of c.1730, and, adjoining this, a pair of sash windows in a plastered wall, the upper one in the Venetian idiom. The scope of the twentieth century alterations was described in detail by Charles J. Blomfield in an article in *The Architectural Review* of May 1907. The external attractiveness of Alston Court lies in the way these various alterations and additions blend like the different styles that lie side by side in the streets of Nayland.

## Tudor House, Needham Market
### TM 087 552

*Plate 383: Tudor House, left, with Clare Cottage.* Elm Studio Ltd., Ipswich

*Watercolour of Tudor House by Leonard Squirrell.*

The majority of the smaller townships and larger villages of Suffolk reached their greatest prosperity during the height of the cloth trade in the fifteenth century, and by the middle of the century that followed had achieved a settled urban plan. The streets, lanes and alley-ways existed, and a closely-knit pattern of development had come into being which was to persist through succeeding centuries. In the main it was only the appearance of buildings that changed thereafter. The High Street, Needham Market, for example, follows a typically mediaeval plan in which houses crowd together presenting a more or less continuous row of fronts to the street, their backyards and gardens straggling out behind in irregularly shaped strips. The pattern is mediaeval and it is a case of not being taken in because so many fronts are eighteenth or nineteenth century; behind these may lie, as at Tudor House, a complex history of mediaeval building.

The house is in the heart of the High Street, opposite the south porch of the church, a position of considerable importance in harmony with the wealthy clothiers by whom it was owned and developed in the fifteenth and sixteenth centuries. The brick frontage, with its central doorway flanked on each side above and below by late Georgian sash windows and pilasters, is the achievement of early nineteenth century owners anxious to conceal a mediaeval ancestry (see Plate 383). Within, the same maxim applied, and it has only been the keen historical sense of the present owner that has brought to light so much that had long lain hidden. The building was found to have three main phases, of which the part fronting the High Street was, not unexpectedly, the oldest. The site, in comparison with many others, was extensive; it occupied a frontage of 12m (39ft 6in.) and at the rear possessed a walled garden and orchard of about one rood of land. It was clearly a property of substance.

A careful survey suggested that in the late fourteenth century there had been a hall-house with a pair of cross-wings both possibly jettied at first floor over the street. The earliest owner about whom much is known is John Flegg, an eminent clothier from Norfolk who settled in Needham Market and prospered exceedingly, for, by 1476, the Fleggs owned or occupied over thirty properties in Needham and Barking. The principal residence of the family always appears to have been Tudor House which was occupied by the eldest son in each generation. A wealth of information about this and other properties and possessions is provided by John Flegg's voluminous will of 1473 and from then onwards, the history of the house is remarkably well documented.

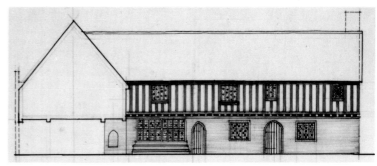

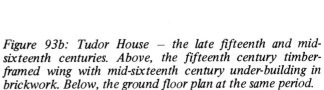

Figure 93a: Tudor House, Needham Market in the late fourteenth century. Above, the conjectural elevation to the High Street. Below, the ground floor plan.

Figure 93b: Tudor House – the late fifteenth and mid-sixteenth centuries. Above, the fifteenth century timber-framed wing with mid-sixteenth century under-building in brickwork. Below, the ground floor plan at the same period.

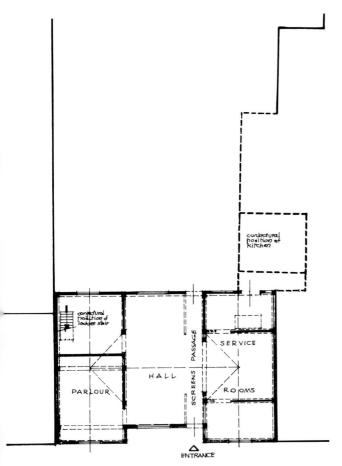

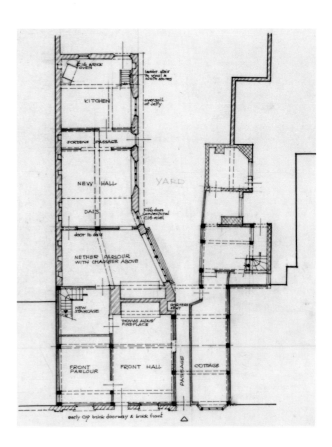

The dyeing of the cloth is the only process in its manufacture and preparation which appears to have been carried out on the premises and John Flegg owned a shop (in which he sold his 'mercery ware') elsewhere in the town, so the house in its first stage appears to have been almost entirely domestic in character.

John Flegg and his wife Agnes evidently lived in some style in their open hall, having a parlour on the south side; an entrance from the street immediately adjoining the present side door, with a screens-passage (leading to a further door into the yard behind the house) and the service rooms beyond (see Figure 93a).

John Flegg's eldest son, of the same name, died in 1500, leaving provision, in his will for his eldest son, Robert, to inherit Tudor House and for his widow, after his death, to live in the house also, occupying 'my nether parlour and the chamber above.' From this we learn that the extension of the house to the rear (at right angles to the High Street) was carried out between his father's death in 1474 and his own in 1500 (Figure 93b). It took the form of two parallel wings, separated by a

*Plate 384: Tudor House — the two lofts converted into a library.*

passage way, the northern wing (now forming part of Clare Cottage) measuring 6.70m (22 ft) and the south wing 18m (59 ft) in length. This latter wing incorporates, on the ground floor, in addition to the 'nether parlour,' a long hall, divided into a dining-room and a service area, and, on the first floor, in addition to the 'chamber above,' two lofts, one above the other, which were doubtless used for the storage of wool and bales of cloth respectively.

The property passed by marriage from the family of Flegg to that of Gardiner early in the reign of Henry VIII and in 1536 Thomas Aldus acquired it through marriage with Elizabeth Gardiner. By the time the 'Great Re-building' — as Professor Hoskins calls it[1] — which followed the Dissolution of the monasteries, was starting, ambitious building schemes, prompted by the greater plentifulness of brick, were going on all over Suffolk. In this third phase of building, a large brick chimney was built with back-to-back fireplaces, one into the front hall and the other into the 'nether parlour' in the extension to the rear. This extension took up most of the yard and, in order to let in as much light as possible, the outer wall was splayed and given a large mullion and transom window. The screens-passage was closed off from the old hall and a way through made to the yard. At the passage end of the new chimney stack an embrasure was made in which the porter could sit and check the passage of goods in and out (warming his back the while in winter). The timber-framed jettied first floor on the north side of the main rear wing of the house was retained but Thomas Aldus was doubtless responsible for the brick facing of the rest of this wing and for the two handsome early Tudor doorways now giving access to the dining-room and to the kitchen respectively.

The work included the bricking around the window in the parlour (compare the sub-window brick-work with Swans Hall, Hawkedon). The author of all these improvements, Thomas Aldus, left his merchant's mark incised in the centre of the beam over the chimney piece in the front hall.

In the reign of Elizabeth I the property passed to Thomas Colchester and thence to his brother, Roger Colchester who left it to his sister's son, William Coleman (described at his burial as 'a ritch Clothier of Needham'). His grandson, of the same name, who died in 1694, was the last of a long line of clothiers to own the house.

The attempted 'classicising' of the house in the early nineteenth century may be attributed to the Alexanders, a Quaker family who founded one of the first private banks, in Needham Market, in 1744. Under the present ownership of Mr. Hugh Paget, C.B.E., M.A., himself a historian, not only has the devolution of the house been traced, but its latent beauties revealed and enhanced by careful restoration and the conversion of the lofts into a library (see Plate 384).

1 cf. *The Making of the English Landscape,* op. cit., pages 119-123.

### Newe House, Pakenham
*TM 932 673*

Built in the last years of the reign of James I, by Sir Robert Bright, and dated 1622 over the entrance, Newe House must be amongst the first group of distinguished brick houses to be found in Suffolk villages. The site is a little more than half a mile from the course of the Roman road which is known to have travelled from Bildeston to Ixworth, and probably led off the main Colchester-Norwich road.[1] The house is within 500 yards of the village street and the Church of St. Mary, situated on ground rising fairly steeply from the watercourse known as Pakenham Fen. It is well enough screened from the road to offer few glimpses to the passer-by, especially in summer when the tree belt that separates the drive from the road is in leaf. The main entrance elevation faces a little north of west, and lies parallel with the road, the drive leading up to a carriage sweep in front of the entrance, before continuing to stable buildings at the rear (see Figure 94).

1 cf. *Roman Roads in Britain, I,* op. cit., page 226.

*Figure 94: Newe House, Pakenham.*

In order to appraise the importance of Newe House in the history of brick domestic architecture in Suffolk, it must be remembered that it was built three years before the date now attributed to the building of Haughley Park by Sir John Sulyard (c.1626). The latter house is in a markedly more Elizabethan idiom, commencing with the traditional E-plan and ending with those enormously tall chimney shafts and decorative brick finials which marked the *fin de siècle* style of the sixteenth century. There is none of this at Newe House, where the main range is a simple rectangle from which the only projections are the porch and the flanking chimney stacks at each gable end. It is a good deal simpler than the rumbustious White Hart Inn at Scole, which springs immediately to mind as a possible parallel. There the Dutch gables are far more showy, five in number, and each crowned with a pediment, and the wall surfaces are broken into horizontal and vertical divisions by means of string courses and pilasters, angles being rather eccentrically emphasised by quoins (above the first floor string course only) and gable-end chimney stacks greatly elaborated with the addition of niches with statues. The special charm of Newe House lies in its purity, and the scrupulously neat handling of only a few simple elements. The main accent of the design is, in keeping with a Suffolk characteristic, an emphasis on verticality. The front entrance is raised five steps above drive level, creating a slight *piano nobile*. It is a five-bay facade of an exact symmetry, the porch of two storeys being central and balanced by a pair of mullion and transom windows – three- and four-light respectively on each side – the window-head level being emphasised above ground and first floor windows by a bold cornice in moulded brickwork broken only by the porch. The five-bay rhythm is subtly changed to three above the upper string course, where the second floor windows on either side of the porch are axial, not on the windows below but on the intervening brick piers, thus producing a three-bay superstructure, with four-light mullion windows and a small top attic window within the ornamental gable – in the Dutch manner. The Dutch gables are a combination of segmental curves supporting a single straight step, from which rise two ogee curves to a narrow straight head.[1] The least successful of the features in this interesting front is the group of lunettes forming the five-sided porch parapet.

The only other enrichments on the front are the pediments, one above the entrance doorway, the others over each of the porch windows in the upper storey, and the coat of arms above the porch opening. The grouped chimney stacks have detached diagonal shafts coming off rectangular bases with cleverly arranged offsets.

Newe House represents a new direction in the development of domestic brick architecture in Suffolk. It is substantially more advanced than Mockbeggars Hall at Claydon, built in the previous year, and suggests that Flemish influences had been well assimilated by local tradesmen, and, when used with restraint, could produce a local idiom of high architectural quality.

## Gainsborough's House, Sudbury
### TL 873 413

Within little more than a stone's throw from the Market Hill stands the house of which John Gainsborough came into possession in 1722. It stood in a road with the sombre name of Sepulchre Street,[2] leading west from the market place down to the River Stour, which here performs the great arc within which most of old Sudbury town was built. There was at that date a straggle of houses along the roadway leading to Stour Street and Mill Hill, some of which, like the Chantry and Salters Hall, had been built in the fifteenth century. For a town property the Gainsborough acquisition was extensive, containing above two acres of orchard, garden, paved yard and 'estate of building'.[3] The land must have reached most of the way to Gregory Street on the west, in which stood the old mother church of Sudbury close above the river. It is virtually impossible to reconcile the structure shown as 'Gainsborough's Birth-place' in Geo. Finden's romantic late eighteenth century drawing, with the building of today, but it can be accepted as an impression of the old houses that once stood on the north side of the street (see Plate 385). It is quite certain, however, that Thomas Gainsborough's father had acquired a late mediaeval property, and that it was of timber-framed construction with wattle and daub panel filling.[4] The task of converting this probably dilapidated old house into a gentleman's residence must have daunted a lesser man, especially when it is remembered that John Gainsborough was already father of a

1 It is important to notice that the Dutch gables are backed by pitched roofs, hipped into the main gable road a little below ridge level; these are not therefore merely ornamental features propped up from the back, as are some of their Dutch counterparts, by long stay rods.
2 It was named after the Church of St. Sepulchre which, before the Reformation, had stood at the junction of Sepulchre and Gregory Streets with Stour and School Streets.
3 cf. sale particulars of January 16th, 1792, when Messrs. Boardman and Oliver, 24 Market Hill, Sudbury, offered the property for sale by auction.
4 This was proved in 1975 when it was possible to examine the outside of the east gable end exposed during the course of works to the adjoining property.

family of eight children. There appears to be no record of where the family had been living, but Gainsboroughs are known to have been in Sudbury for over two hundred years by the early eighteenth century,[1] and cramped surroundings may well have prompted the purchase and alteration of a larger property in the town.

*Plate 385: Engraving of 'Gainsborough's Birth-place', by Geo. Finden, late eighteenth century.*

From such structural evidence that does exist it can be conjectured that the house was of the late-fifteenth — mid-sixteenth century, and that it had first been a single range building parallel with the road, having a pitched roof and gable-ends. (To that extent it agrees with Finden's drawing.) This dwelling would have a 'house-place' to the west and a parlour to the east with an entrance in about the present position; at the rear it could be expected there would be some form of annexe with service and store room. The hall and parlour were ceiled, with bed chambers on the floor above. To this old house certain additions must have been made in the early seventeenth century, when a second range was added to the first and chimney stacks built. One fireplace served the parlour (it is the back of this stack which protruded into the lobby opposite John Gainsborough's front door). The other warmed the hall and may once have backed on to a kitchen, but if so this was altered by the later staircase. At this time, also, the workshop range could have

*Plate 386: The classical frontage — Gainsborough's House.*   *Richard Burn*

1 cf. *Thomas Gainsborough*, a bibliography 1727-1788 by Isabelle Worman, page 11, (1976. Terence Dalton: Lavenham).

been added at the first floor back, and possibly at ground floor also. It was already a weaver's house on which John Gainsborough set to work in 1723.

The first decision was completely to rebuild the front range, leaving only the timber and plaster end gables, Tudor chimney stacks, joisted ceilings and such partitions as happened to come in the right places. The main objective was to put up a swagger facade to the street, and, behind this to arrange the main day rooms and bedrooms as best as possible. The whole of the old timber-framed wall was taken down and rebuilt in brick, and it would be interesting if any contemporary papers could be turned up to throw light on how this was done. The work seems to have proceeded by first building a backing wall of rough 9in. brickwork (reducing to 4½in. in the window openings), and this could have been done by relatively unskilled bricklayers. It was followed by employing a master tradesman to add the outer brick skin to the whole front. The result, despite some structural weakness, was supremely successful, and John Gainsborough must have had the satisfaction of producing one of the most sophisticated classical house-fronts in Sudbury (see Plate 386). The theme was the decorative contrast between very dark, almost black headers and rich red quoins and rubbed work in the segmental arches over the window heads, the whole design being contained between broad pilasters at each end and a boldly projecting cornice in moulded brick over the head of the first floor windows. The well detailed centre-piece was a white doorcase with Doric pilasters, an elegant fanlight and simple entablature.

In complete contrast with this textbook exercise in classical propriety is the rear of the house facing into the garden, with its delightfully inconsequential set of windows — weavers, eighteenth century sash and early-nineteenth century Gothic — and the oddly assymmetrical projection of the bow-ended wing, which must have been added after Gainsborough's day. The house still seems to epitomise the engaging atmosphere of the Gainsborough family, and the good-natured, idealistic father, who went bankrupt when Thomas was six years old but survived, with the help of his family and friends, and went on to become a postmaster of the town, a burgess and 'a highly respected person in the community'.[1]

The head-waters of the Wissett tributary rise in the southern highlands of the parish, and flow south-east to join the River Blyth just above Halesworth. In the valley about a quarter of a mile beyond the church lies The Grange, on a steeply falling site close to the road. The Wissett valley marks the end of that territory lying south of Bungay and Shipmeadow called 'The Saints', and a road close to The Grange climbs into the high country of Rumburgh, and the many saints associated with the South Elmhams and the Ilketshalls.

The Grange at Wenhaston, a few miles away, has already been connected with the Cistercian abbey of Sibton, and there might be a case for linking The Grange at Wissett with the Benedictine abbey of Rumburgh, about a mile to the north. It is not improbable that it was once a small farmhouse owned by the priory, which held the advowson of Wissett church, that of Holton and several others locally.[2] This is country where farms congregate thickly, and between the Grange and Rumburgh Common today there are no less than nine. We need documentary search, however, to establish the antiquity of the name, but even should it prove to be of more recent origin, there are still reasons for connecting this interesting small dwelling with Rumburgh Abbey.

In the structure at least three phases can be seen. The earliest consists of a single timber-framed range on a south-east/north-west axis built about 8 metres from the roadside, measuring about 14.25m by 5.66m (46ft 8in. by 18ft 6in.). To this has been added a short wing projecting on the south-west side, and modern extensions at the back, the chief of these being at the east end and, finished in plaster, with oak framed lead-light windows and a roof of Suffolk pantiles (see Plates 387 and 388).[3] There are circumstances about the main range that need explaining. Work of two kinds can be seen on the south-west elevation where there is a change both in the framing system and the spacing of studs. The portion to the east consists of two clearly defined bays of narrow spaced studs, one bay marking the place of the chimney stack. The rest of the range as far as the front wing contains the open hall and service rooms, and has more widely spaced studs. Beyond this point the wing has replaced the original front wall.

*The Grange, Wissett*
*TM 364 795*

*Plate 387: The earliest structure with extension at The Grange.*

1 cf. *Thomas Gainsborough*, Ibid, page 14.
2 cf. Taylor's *Index Monasticus*, op. cit., page 85. Runburgh was one of the small priories which were suppressed before the general Dissolution, and was given by the King to Cardinal Wolsey for his college at Ipswich in 1528.
3 We have it from Farrer: *Some Old Houses in Suffolk*, volume 6, page 11, that this work together with the restoration of the house — previously adapted to three tenements — was undertaken by Mr. Seymour Lucas, R.A. (See General Bibliography.)

Plate 389: Thatched roof and exposed studwork, The Grange, Wissett.

The entrance is on the side facing the road, and could have been approached by a path coming up directly from the roadway, although, if so, the old route was lost when a brick retaining wall was built right across the front. The only entrance, apart from the drive at the north end, is now by a door in the wall at the extreme opposite end of the building.

The entrance into the house is through a modern porch into a screens-passage. To the left of this is a pair of oak-framed pointed arches, somewhat resembling those in a similar position at fourteenth century Abbas Hall, Great Cornard. The hall is screened on the right with a later addition, and the arches give access to the former buttery and pantry, now converted into kitchen premises. The house-place is open to the roof with a central tie-beam and crown post, and opposite is a large brick chimney stack. At each end there are two storeys, and this sequence of rooms clearly indicates a mediaeval hall-house. The east end would be a parlour and solar, and, at the north, service rooms with sleeping space or storage over. The different construction already noticed could therefore be systematically related to the change of function between the centre and the two ends of the house. The wing in front must be a later addition.

An unusual feature occurs in the parlour, where the shouldered heads of the principal posts at each end of the principal tie-beam are carved with the emblems of the Passion. That to north has the Sacred Heart surmounted by three nails and based upon pincers and hammer, and, to the south, the Crown of Thorns flanked by nails with another in the centre base. There seems to be no exact parallel to these carvings elsewhere, although religious motifs occur not infrequently in late mediaeval houses: Framsden Hall comes immediately to mind. It is these emblems which promote the idea of The Grange being in some way related to the nearby Abbey of Rumburgh, although this must be a matter for conjecture in the absence of historical or documentary evidence. The dwelling could have served as a guest house to the Abbey, in much the same way as the New Inn at Sibton served Sibton Priory. Both are on the edge of the highway.

After the general Dissolution and the downfall of Cardinal Wolsey, properties in his ownership must have been redistributed by the king, and if The Grange was, indeed, attached to Runburgh Priory, it is likely that after 1530 it had passed into secular hands. During the succeeding fifty years it must have been modernised by an owner who left his mark carved on the bressumer of the hall fireplace.[1] Farrer has the story that the late sixteenth century wainscot, with which the hall is panelled, was taken out when the house was converted into cottages, and refixed when it was restored.[2] This tends to confirm a change of ownership, and suggests that the south-west wing was built about the same time also, together with the new chimney stacks (the plain head of the principal stack looks, however, like a nineteenth century alteration). The roofs remain thatched, as they must have been since the beginning, and, together with the exposed studwork, combine to suggest much of the appearance of a mediaeval hall-house (see Plate 389).

1 The mark is not one recorded by Girling or Elmhirst, cf. Proceeding S.I.A., Volume XXIX, Part I.
2 op. cit. E.A.M.

# TWENTIETH CENTURY HOUSES – a Postscript

Twentieth century houses in Suffolk show two major design trends. The first is a continuation, the second a radical reinterpretation of traditional norms. The traditional plan was based on the rectangle and the intersection of rectangles; the structural principles were timber-framing, followed by load-bearing masonry walls, with elevations which, in both cases, expressed these principles. In able hands such formulae continued to produce pleasant and distinguished buildings. At the lower end of the scale, however, they led to the banal and nondescript bulk of modern housing. Radical reinterpretation has concentrated on more imaginative plans, using up-to-date structural techniques to create freer and more open house design. This has been made much easier by abandoning pitched roofs, using the structural framework and reducing static partitions to a minimum.

The following illustrations start with an example of Sir Edwin Lutyens' work of 1901, and continue roughly in date order to show a typical revivalist example by J.S. Corder which stems from the movement started in the late nineteenth century by the Webb-Morris partnership. Also included are two relatively rare houses in the art nouveau style by the Suffolk-born architect, Cecil Lay. In the inter-war period it was mainly the revivalist trends that were developed, although an outstanding example of the "functional" style of the thirties is King's Knoll, Woodbridge. The remaining houses have all been built since the last war and, with one exception, illustrate the attempt to create a genuinely contemporary architecture using accepted traditional materials such as timber and brickwork.

*Above and below: 'Corners' (formerly Woolverstone House), Woolverstone, designed by Lutyens for Lady Berners, 1901. Situated on a secluded site between the Shotley Road and the river Orwell, the house is built on a courtyard plan, being approached through a carriageway in the centre of a single-storey entrance range – a device employed to give an effect of greater size and importance to a comparatively small house. The top picture shows the Lutyens' chapel at 'Corners'.*

*Below right: A rare example of an art nouveau building – 'Raidsend', Aldringham, designed by the Suffolk-born architect, Cecil Lay, F.R.I.B.A., in 1912. In plan traditional, in elevation it has engaging eccentricities: extremely tall windows, highly stylised curved gables, the swept curve of the porch canopy – these are the hallmarks of art nouveau. Reminiscences of Suffolk pargetting come from innumerable but carefully controlled groups of fruit-and-leaf motifs above and between the windows.*

*Below: Another Lay design at Colts Hill, Aldringham (since altered by the addition of a pitched and tiled roof). Designed in the 1920s, it was a tentative move on Lay's part towards a freer form of house design, and is a strong contrast to the house at Raidsend.*

*Below: A studied attempt to reproduce the character of a typical early Elizabethan Suffolk manor house – the J.S. Corder house at Little Wenham built in 1912 with a timber frame and plaster appearance. The method of construction, however, was not that of the mediaeval builders – oak studs and bressumers are planted on brick walls; plaster panels between the timbers are formed by rendering on brick.*

*Above: The marriage of an ideal site and exciting house in the new-style: King's Knoll, Woodbridge, designed by Hilda Mason, A.R.I.B.A., built in 1933 and situated on a spit of land running down to Kyson Point, near the junction of Martlesham Creek with the river Deben. Original tall columns flanking the centre-piece have been removed to make way for the later sun-room addition.*

*Above: House in the High Street, Bildeston, designed by John Weller, A.R.I.B.A., 1960. The house recedes from a front gable-end to a rear service range. Painted brickwork in the forward planes contrasts with weather-boarding at the rear.*

*Above and right: House off Church Walk, Aldeburgh, designed by Mr. H.T. Cadbury-Brown, O.B.E., R.A., A.R.C.A., A.A.Dipl., F.R.I.B.A., and Mrs. Cadbury-Brown, 1963. Built in an area already surrounded by two-storey dwellings, the architects decided to place the house quite close to adjoining development, but to adopt the principle of brick garden walls and build no higher than the top of these. The top picture shows the entrance courtyard.*

*Left and below: Stratford Hills, Stratford St. Mary, 1960, designed by Eric Sandon, F.R.I.B.A. (job architect R.A. Miller, F.R.I.B.A.). The new Stratford Hills has links with the late-mediaeval tradition of jettied first floors confirmed by the timber-framed superstructure. Inside there are obvious echoes of the mediaeval open hall which separated the two-storey ends of the house.*

*Colin Stubley*

*Above and right: Tye House, Monks Eleigh, designed by Eric Sandon (job architect P.D. Lennard, A.R.I.B.A.), 1969. The site is surrounded by the 225ft. contour and seemed to dictate a traditional Suffolk dwelling in the main form of the house. Open through two storeys in the centre, the wings are joined by a gallery crossing the hall on the north. Plastered walls, sharply pitched gables and roof of second-hand plain tiles, are reminiscent of Suffolk manor house building, but there the comparison ends, particularly in the window detailing which is contemporary in character.*

*F.E. Rust*

*Above: Long Wall, Acton, designed by Philip Dowson, O.B.E., M.A., A.A.Dipl., R.I.B.A., 1964. Set in a rolling landscape on a gentle slope with distant views, the plan was organised to relate the building to the landscape. The openness of living spaces to the exterior has achieved a natural relationship with the countryside surrounding the house.*

*Above: Longlands, Nettlestead, designed by K.G. Pert, F.R.I.B.A., 1964. New forms, traditional methods – there is nothing haphazard about the placing of walls and windows; each face of the house follows a regular modular grid. The structural frame is as regular as in mediaeval carpentry and the windows placed within the spaces dictated by studs.*

*A general view of Long Wall, Acton, from the south.*

*Colin Westwood*

*John Penn*

*Above: House at Westleton designed by John Penn. The plan consists of a living space with rooms at each end, backed by service and other rooms. A spiral staircase ascends to a long first floor space, divisible by sliding and folding partitions. A more complex plan than that used at Beach House, Shingle Street.*

*John Penn*

*Above: Beach House, Shingle Street, designed by John Penn, M.A., A.A.Dipl., A.R.I.B.A., 1969. The plan is based on an open space divisible by sliding, folding partitions, around a central service core. The architect calls this a 'temple plan'.*

# section 7 — Appendices

## I. Isolated Suffolk Halls.

The following is a list compiled from the 2½ inch Ordnance Survey (First Series) giving the names and map references of dwellings under the name of 'Hall', that lie in open country and are not attached to towns, villages or hamlets. The basis of the compilation is that used for the National Grid and Reference system, in which the vertical (Eastings) line precedes the horizontal (Northings) line. The referencing follows the East to West direction, and the list is divided into two groups corresponding with the National Grid Index. The first group, commencing with Hanchet Hall 643.460, and ending with North Hall, Hepworth 980.763 is in the TL series. The second group, commencing with Bobbits Hall, Holton St. Mary 047.362, and ending with Burgh Hall 496.046 is in the TM series. Where individual houses are discussed in Section 6, this is indicated by an asterisk.

### TL SERIES

| Name | Map Ref. |
|---|---|
| Hanchet Hall, Hanchet End | 643.460 |
| Haverhill Hall | 663.442 |
| Moon Hall, Haverhill | 667.440 |
| Boyton Hall, Lt. Wratting | 674.467 |
| Little Bradley Hall | 686.523 |
| Wamil Hall, Mildenhall | 695.744 |
| Undley Hall, Lakenheath | 695.817 |
| Cotton Hall, Kedington | 708.456 |
| Floriston Hall, Wixoe | 720.434 |
| Pinhoe Hall, Hundon | 733.483 |
| Hundon Hall | 745.497 |
| Clopton Hall, Poslingford | 766.498 |
| Houghton Hall, Cavendish | 786.466 |
| Cavendish Hall | 794.459 |
| Colts Hall | 794.477 |
| Barnardiston Hall | 713.504 |
| Cowlinge Hall | 713.525 |
| *Badmondisfield Hall, | 748.570 |
| Denston Hall | 758.525 |
| *Clopton Hall, Wickhambrook | 761.547 |
| *Giffords Hall, Wickhambrook | 771.538 |
| Hall, on site of Depden Hall | 774.568 |
| Beech Hall, Depden | 780.568 |
| Purton Hall, Stansfield | 781.535 |
| Elm Hall, Stansfield | 785.517 |
| Stansfield Hall, Stansfield | 788.513 |
| *Swans Hall, Hawkedon | 796.512 |
| Hungriff Hall, Thurston | 796.517 |
| *Thurston Hall, Hawkedon | 794.518 |
| Needham Hall, Gazeley | 721.656 |
| Desning Hall, Gazeley | 735.633 |
| Aspal Hall, Mildenhail | 702.773 |
| Brandon Hall | 770.863 |
| Wood Hall, Sudbury | 877.428 |
| *Chilton Hall, Sudbury | 888.427 |
| *Kentwell Hall, Long Melford | 864.479 |
| Acton Hall | 891.455 |
| Pickard's Hall, Rede | 804.554 |
| Rede Hall | 806.577 |
| Doveden Hall, Whepstead | 822.589 |
| Manston Hall, Whepstead | 834.567 |
| Rivett's Hall, Hartest | 846.528 |
| Spring Hall, Stanstead | 844.505 |
| Blooms Hall, Stanstead | 863.502 |
| Coldham Hall, Lawshall | 865.558 |
| Nether Hall, Gt. Welnetham | 874.593 |
| Seymour Hall, Stanningfield | 884.557 |
| Great Welnetham Hall | 882.592 |
| Bradfield Hall, Bradfield Combust | 896.574 |
| Pepper's Hall, Bradfield Combust | 898.557 |
| Little Horringer Hall | 818.629 |
| Gt. Horringer Hall | 833.625 |
| Nowton Hall | 861.605 |
| Necton Hall, Gt. Barton | 881.674 |
| *West Stow Hall | 817.708 |
| Elveden Hall | 825.797 |
| Culford Hall | 833.704 |
| Livermere Hall | 877.713 |
| Corn Hall, Bures St. Mary | 911.358 |
| Roper's Hall, Bures St. Mary | 917.359 |
| Smallbridge Hall, Bures St. Mary | 929.331 |
| Farthing Hall, Nayland | 945.353 |
| Gedding Hall, Assington | 940.368 |
| Turk's Hall, Boxford | 955.391 |

| Name | Map Ref. |
|---|---|
| Coddenham Hall, Boxford | 953.399 |
| Peyton Hall, Boxford | 967.387 |
| Scotland Hall, Stoke by Nayland | 997.369 |
| Tendring Hall, Stoke by Nayland | 993.357 |
| Rockalls Hall, Polstead | 997.389 |
| *Abbas Hall, Great Cornard | 901.405 |
| Holbrook Hall, Great Waldringfield | 916.451 |
| Brandeston Hall, Little Waldringfield | 914.468 |
| Down Hall, Great Waldringfield | 927.434 |
| Nether Hall, Little Waldringfield | 928.464 |
| Abbot's Hall, Brent Eleigh | 926.473 |
| Siam Hall, Newton | 938.409 |
| Lynn's Hall, Edwardstone | 936.436 |
| Slough Hall, Little Waldringfield | 939.444 |
| Milden Hall | 944.463 |
| Marls Hall, Brent Eleigh | 943.472 |
| Wells Hall, Milden | 946.474 |
| Water Hall, Kettlesbaston | 963.495 |
| *Castling's Hall, Groton | 971.434 |
| Boyton Hall, Monks Eleigh | 974.466 |
| Lindsey Hall | 982.448 |
| Raven's Hall, Lindsey | 988.461 |
| Evan's Hall, Polstead | 996.417 |
| Sampson's Hall, Kersey | 995.433 |
| Earl's Hall, Cockfield | 909.535 |
| Cockfield Hall | 909.544 |
| Sutton Hall, Bradfield Combust | 905.570 |
| Raw Hall, Bradfield St. George | 905.590 |
| Frog's Hall, Lavenham | 918.503 |
| St. Clare Hall, Bradfield St. Clare | 919.578 |
| Broom Hall, Bradfield St. George | 916.597 |
| Abbot's Hall, Bradfield St. George | 935.583 |
| Down Hall, Preston St. Mary | 944.517 |
| Brooke Hall, Felsham | 948.562 |
| Brettenham Hall | 957.529 |
| Ryece Hall, Brettenham | 957.546 |
| Hammond Hall | 962.598 |
| Wetherden Hall | 972.510 |
| Stanstead Hall | 983.537 |
| Cockerell's Hall, Buxhall | 988.577 |
| Clopton Hall, Rattlesden | 985.599 |
| Fazbourn Hall, Buxhall | 997.567 |
| Wood Hall, Buxhall | 993.588 |
| Shelland Hall | 995.597 |
| Rougham Hall | 911.641 |
| Nether Hall, Pakenham | 928.669 |
| Old Hall, Pakenham | 929.688 |
| Hessett Hall | 930.615 |
| Maulkin's Hall, Pakenham | 937.680 |
| Beaumont's Hall, Pakenham | 945.675 |
| Little Haugh Hall, Norton | 953.666 |
| Old Hall. Tostock | 964.640 |
| *Stowlangtoft Hall | 963.689 |
| Elmswell New Hall | 972.642 |
| Norton Hall | 970.654 |
| Elmswell Hall | 984.644 |
| Rockylls Hall, Shelland | 998.606 |
| Shackerland Hall, Badwell Ash | 993.685 |
| Troston Hall | 901.718 |
| Lark Hall, Little Fakenham | 902.761 |
| Rushford Hall | 926.813 |

| Name | Map Ref. |
|---|---|
| Bardwell Hall | 940.727 |
| Wyken Hall, Bardwell | 965.717 |
| Stanton Hall | 978.733 |
| Reeves Hall, Hepworth | 978.759 |
| North Hall, Hepworth | 980.763 |

### TM SERIES

| Name | Map Ref. |
|---|---|
| Bobbits Hall, Holton St. Mary | 047.362 |
| Clay Hall, Copdock | 098.394 |
| Braham Hall, Brantham | 100.335 |
| Great Copt Hall, Chelsworth | 000.493 |
| Whatfield Hall | 016.473 |
| Overbury Hall, Hadleigh | 023.403 |
| Aldham Hall | 040.445 |
| Poplar Hall (Farm), Aldham | 041.465 |
| Maskells Hall, Offton | 045.490 |
| Hintlesham Old Hall | 065.438 |
| Bleak Hall, Somersham | 077.479 |
| Hintlesham Hall | 084.438 |
| Loose Hall, Hitcham | 001.530 |
| Boyton Hall, Gt. Finborough | 029.576 |
| Charles Hall, Battisford | 033.537 |
| Chilton Hall, Stowmarket | 040.595 |
| Battisford Hall | 056.546 |
| Sheepcote Hall, Creeting St. Peter | 064.585 |
| Willisham Hall | 070.506 |
| Crow Hall, Willisham | 076.503 |
| Braziers Hall, Creeting St. Peter | 074.587 |
| *High Hall, Nettlestead | 087.503 |
| Tarston Hall, Baylham | 081.519 |
| *Roydon Hall, Creeting St. Peter | 084.585 |
| *Baylam Hall | 093.517 |
| Sparrow Hall, Creeting St. Mary | 095.561 |
| Mutton Hall, Wetherden | 003.637 |
| *Badwell Ash Hall | 006.691 |
| Wetherden Hall | 020.641 |
| Old Hall, Haughley | 032.649 |
| Bacton Hall | 030.656 |
| White Hall, Old Newton | 054.619 |
| *Columbine Hall, Stowupland | 067.608 |
| Newton Hall, Old Newton | 068.619 |
| Cotton Hall, Cotton | 067.651 |
| Stowupland Hall | 079.604 |
| *Hempnall's Hall, Cotton | 082.675 |
| Crowland Hall, Walsham-le-Willows | 010.702 |
| Honeypot Hall, Wattisfield | 017.741 |
| Old Hall, Walsham-le-Willows | 025.713 |
| West Hall, Rickinghall inf. | 030.735 |
| Facons Hall, Rickinghall sup. | 043.735 |
| Abbot's Hall, Botesdale | 049.730 |
| Rob Hall, Gislingham | 051.710 |
| Redgrave Hall | 054.770 |
| Pountney Hall, Mellis | 081.738 |
| Swattisfield Hall, Thornha Magna | 088.720 |
| Wortham Hall | 084.789 |
| Mellis Hall | 091.742 |
| Old Hall, Belstead | 119.397 |
| Brantham Hall | 121.339 |
| Tattingstone Hall | 141.374 |
| Hubbards Hall, Bentley | 134.391 |
| *Stutton Hall | 141.337 |
| Crepping Hall, Stutton | 148.340 |
| *Crowe Hall, Stutton | 153.343 |

| Name | Map Ref. |
|---|---|
| Alton Hall, Stutton | 156.361 |
| Bond Hall, Freston | 167.388 |
| Nether Hall, Harkstead | 191.341 |
| Burstall Hall | 103.450 |
| Lt. Blakenham Hall | 103.483 |
| Bramford Hall | 113.467 |
| Belstead Hall | 128.413 |
| Mockbeggars Hall, Claydon | 133.487 |
| Pannington Hall, Wherstead | 144.403 |
| Thorington Hall, Wherstead | 144.410 |
| Gusford Hall, Ipswich | 140.423 |
| Akenham Hall | 158.495 |
| Pond Hall, Gainsborough, Ipswich | 181.411 |
| Deerbolt Hall, Earl Stonham | 113.584 |
| Shrubland Hall | 126.526 |
| Mowness Hall, Stonham Aspal | 125.599 |
| Barham Hall | 138.509 |
| Crowfield Hall | 137.576 |
| *Hemingstone Hall | 142.538 |
| New Hall, Crowfield | 163.583 |
| Cockfield Hall, Witnesham | 176.504 |
| Abbot's Hall, Pettaugh | 174.591 |
| Laffits Hall, Pettaugh | 173.596 |
| *Helmingham Hall | 187.577 |
| Bocking Hall, Helmingham | 180.589 |
| Newton Hall, Swilland | 194.517 |
| Westwood Hall, Stonham Aspal | 107.625 |
| Thwaite Hall | 109.678 |
| Wood Hall, Stoke Ash | 108.698 |
| Fleed Hall, Stonham Aspal | 111.611 |
| Waltham Hall, Stonham Aspal | 117.626 |
| Brockford Hall, Thwaite | 113.673 |
| Mickfield Hall | 134.627 |
| Read Hall, Mickfield | |
| Brames Hall, Wetheringsett | 138.673 |
| Ulveston Hall, Debenham | 149.633 |
| Hestley Hall, Thorndon | 145.683 |
| Old East End Hall, Stonham Aspal | 155.604 |
| White Hall, Debenham | 154.625 |
| Old Hall, Debenham | 155.645 |
| Poplar Hall, Winston | 163.619 |
| Debenham Hall, Debenham | 162.626 |
| *Aspall Hall, Aspall | 172.654 |
| Blood Hall, Kenton | 185.647 |
| Kenton Hall | 187.652 |
| *Crows Hall, Debenham | 192.628 |
| *Bedingfield Hall | 198.677 |
| Thornham Hall | 103.718 |
| Gardiner's Hall, Stoke Ash | 125.709 |
| Yaxley Hall | 125.736 |
| Goswold Hall, Thrandeston | 125.756 |
| Braiseworth Hall | 132.706 |
| Rook Hall, Braiseworth | 133.727 |
| Stuston Hall | 138.783 |
| Occold Hall | 150.707 |
| Cranley Hall, Eye | 153.728 |
| Brome Hall | 155.764 |
| Benningham Hall, Occold | 167.709 |
| Denham Hall (Farm) | 180.737 |
| St. Edmunds Hall, Hoxne | 178.771 |
| Beaumont Hall, Harkstead | 205.339 |
| Erwarton Hall | 223.352 |
| Broke Hall, Nacton | 225.391 |
| Old Hall, Shotley | 237.357 |
| Stratton Hall | 244.388 |
| Levington Hall | 241.393 |
| Morston Hall, Trimley St. Martin | 258.385 |

| Name | Map Ref. |
|---|---|
| Grimston Hall, Trimley St. Martin | 259.366 |
| Kirton Hall | 269.399 |
| Blofield Hall, Trimley St. Mary | 281.353 |
| Capel Hall, Trimley St. Martin | 289.375 |
| Tuddenham Hall | 201.488 |
| Playford Hall | 214.477 |
| Foxhall Hall | 229.437 |
| Grundisburgh Hall | 223.499 |
| Kesgrave Hall | 233.464 |
| Bucklesham Hall | 256.421 |
| Brightwell Hall | 252.435 |
| Kembroke Hall, Kirton | 265.413 |
| Little Haddon Hall, Sutton | 278.475 |
| Methersgate Hall, Sutton | 289.468 |
| *Otley Hall | 205.563 |
| Bastings Hall, Framsden | 295.579 |
| Moat Hall, Otley | 229.557 |
| Hasketon Hall | 238.513 |
| The Hall, Charsfield | 236.565 |
| Monewden Hall | 246.594 |
| Boulge Hall | 254.527 |
| Hoo Hall | 256.594 |
| Foxboro' Hall, Melton | 277.515 |
| Glevering Hall | 295.575 |
| *Framsden Hall | 206.601 |
| Thorpe Hall, Ashfield | 201.623 |
| Suddon Hall, Monk Soham | 201.658 |
| Bedfield Hall | 227.664 |
| Braiseworth Hall, Tannington | 245.671 |
| Tannington Hall | 247.688 |
| Kettleburgh New Hall | 270.603 |
| Elm Hall, Dennington | 291.666 |
| Athelington Hall | 207.712 |
| Monks Hall, Syleham | 202.783 |
| *Thorpe Hall, Horham | 212.738 |
| Vales Hall, Fressingfield | 253.787 |
| *Ufford Hall, Fressingfield | 273.746 |
| Whittingham Hall, Fressingfield | 279.783 |
| Chippenhall Hall, Fressingfield | 281.760 |
| Metfield Hall | 296.787 |
| The Hall, Weybread | 240.801 |
| Thorpe Hall, Mendham | 274.803 |
| Walsham Hall, Mendham | 280.831 |
| Withersdale Hall, Mendham | 281.801 |
| Middleton Hall, Mendham | 287.836 |
| Pettistree Hall, Sutton | 303.445 |
| Sutton Hall | 306.451 |
| Peyton Hall, Ramsholt | 319.412 |
| Shottisham Hall | 317.437 |
| Boyton Hall | 384.465 |
| Frogs Hall, Boyton | 387.469 |
| *Loudham Hall | 308.542 |
| Bloomville Hall, Hacheston | 304.592 |
| Ashmoor Hall, Campsey Ash | 318.558 |
| *Moat Hall, Parham | 313.605 |
| Naunton Hall, Rendlesham | 325.533 |
| Marlesford Hall | 323.585 |
| Little Glemham Hall | 346.592 |
| Blaxhall Hall | 350.576 |
| Wantisden Hall | 361.523 |
| Farnham Hall | 366.599 |
| Dunningworth Hall, Snape | 388.574 |
| Parham Hall | 315.605 |
| Okenhill Hall, Badingham | 307.666 |
| Fiddler's Hall, Cransford | 317.640 |
| Colston Hall, Badingham | 317.673 |
| Cransford Hall | 327.653 |
| Badingham Hall | 327.698 |

| Name | Map Ref. |
|---|---|
| Sweffling Hall | 337.646 |
| Bruisyard Hall | 334.663 |
| Rendham Hall | 353.660 |
| Hurts Hall, Saxmundham | 389.625 |
| Carlton Hall, Saxmundham | 383.643 |
| Boats Hall, Ubbeston | 314.709 |
| Turkey Hall, Ubbeston | 311.731 |
| Ubbeston Hall | 327.728 |
| Linstead Hall | 322.762 |
| *Huntingfield Hall | 342.743 |
| Snows Hall, Peasenhall | 352.705 |
| Heveningham Hall | 351.734 |
| Chediston Hall | 370.777 |
| Wissett Hall | 381.786 |
| South Elmham Hall | 308.833 |
| Flixton Hall | 304.858 |
| Docking Hall, St. James, S. Elmham | 312.806 |
| St. Peter's Hall, S. Elmham | 336.854 |
| Upland Hall, St. John Ilketshall | 334.881 |
| St. Margaret's Hall, Ilketshall | 357.841 |
| St. John's Hall, Ilketshall | 363.873 |
| The Hall, Mettingham | 368.987 |
| Spexhall Hall | 378.813 |
| Ilketshall Hall, St. Laurence | 375.857 |
| St. Andrews Hall, Ilketshall | 388.868 |
| Ringsfield Hall | 393.876 |
| Sudbourne Hall | 408.513 |
| Iken Hall | 407.558 |
| Raydon Hall, Orford | 430.505 |
| Hazlewood Hall, Friston | 435.588 |
| Friston Hall | 405.603 |
| Fordley Hall, Middleton | 407.669 |
| Darsham Hall | 410.696 |
| Theberton Hall | 433.663 |
| Old Hall, Westleton | 439.698 |
| Holton Hall | 407.784 |
| Wenhaston Old Hall | 416.746 |
| Thorington Hall | 423.733 |
| Henham Hall | 452.782 |
| Reydon Hall | 482.783 |
| Redisham Hall | 403.858 |
| Walpole Hall, Weston | 420.869 |
| Weston Hall | 425.873 |
| Brampton Hall | 415.833 |
| Harmony Hall, Weston | 432.867 |
| Ellough Hall | 445.871 |
| Uggeshall Hall | 457.814 |
| *Mutford Hall | 482.874 |
| Rushmere Hall | 493.873 |
| Benacre Hall | 505.838 |
| *Roos Hall Beccles | 415.900 |
| *Worlingham Hall, Beccles | 443.903 |
| Wade Hall, North Cove | 473.904 |
| Block Hall, Herringfleet | 475.991 |
| *Herringfleet Hall | 481.993 |
| Somerleyton Hall | 493.977 |
| Carlton Hall, Carlton Colville | 509.904 |
| Flixton Old Hall | 518.957 |
| Bradwell Hall | 503.055 |
| Hopton Hall | 515.006 |
| Hobland Hall | 510.017 |
| Fritton Old Hall | 476.002 |
| Belton Hall | 485.023 |
| Burgh Hall | 496.046 |

## II. Isolated Suffolk Halls with adjoining Churches.

The following is a list compiled from the 2½inch Ordnance Survey (First Series) giving the names and map references of Halls, with nearby Churches, that lie in open country and are not attached to towns, villages or hamlets (except in the parochial sense). The basis of the compilation is that used in Appendix I. Where individual houses are discussed in Section 6, this is indicated by an asterisk.

### TL SERIES

| Name | Map Ref. | Name | Map Ref. | Name | Map Ref. |
|---|---|---|---|---|---|
| Great Bradley Hall | 673.532 | Ousden Hall | 735.596 | Westley Hall | 824.647 |
| Great Thurlow Hall | 683.504 | Kedington Hall | 705.472 | *Hengrave Hall | 824.686 |
| Dalham Hall | 724.626 | Denham Hall | 756.618 | Nowton Hall | 861.605 |
| Hargrave Hall | 766.607 | Wangford Hall | 750.830 | Rushbrooke Hall | 891.612 |
| Chevington Hall | 789.603 | Culford Hall | 834.704 | Alpheton Hall | 873.505 |
| *Gt. Saxham Hall | 791.628 | Euston Hall | 898.786 | Boxted Hall | 821.506 |
| Lidgate Hall | 723.581 | Fornham Hall | 840.684 | Brockley Hall | 827.557 |

| Name | Map Ref. | Name | Map Ref. | Name | Map Ref. |
|---|---|---|---|---|---|
| Shimpling Hall | 858.513 | *Buxhall Hall (Rectory) | 003.577 | Redingfield Hall | 187.707 |
| Stanstead Hall | 843.494 | *Finborough Hall, Gt. Finborough | 015.581 | Hoo Hall | 256.595 |
| *Chilton Hall, Sudbury | 888.427 | Onehouse Hall | 017.593 | Boulge Hall | 254.528 |
| Acton Hall | 893.454 | Harleston Hall | 016.604 | Orwell Park | 267.397 |
| Newton Hall | 919.412 | Gt. Bricett Hall | 038.508 | Letheringham Abbey | 268.586 |
| Assington Hall | 935.388 | Ringshall Hall | 044.528 | Monk Soham Hall | 214.653 |
| *Polstead Hall | 988.382 | *Badley Hall | 061.558 | Tannington Place | 240.676 |
| Brent Eleigh Hall | 942.483 | Creeting St. Peter | 080.577 | Brandeston Hall | 248.603 |
| Bildeston Hall | 985.492 | Battisford Hall | 056.546 | Kettleburgh (Old Hall) | 265.607 |
| Nedging Grange | 998.483 | Willisham Hall | 071.506 | Lt. Glemham Hall | 346.590 |
| Semer Manor | 998.468 | *Barking Hall | 075.536 | Carlton Hall | 383.653 |
| Lindsey Hall | 998.445 | Woolney Hall | 099.578 | Hurts Hall, Saxmundham | 389.625 |
| Edwardstone Hall | 941.421 | Dagworth Hall | 042.615 | Linstead Hall | 317.763 |
| Thorpe Morieux Hall | 944.533 | Gipping Hall | 073.636 | Ubbeston Hall | 325.727 |
| Kettlebaston Hall | 965.503 | Burgate Hall | 080.756 | St. Cross, S. Elmham | 308.833 |
| Hitcham Hall | 984.513 | Harkstead Hall | 196.354 | All Saints & St. Nicholas | 329.828 |
| Tostock Hall | 959.634 | Woolverstone Hall | 195.386 | Barsham Hall | 397.897 |
| Hunston Hall | 976.683 | Belstead Hall | 126.413 | Knodishall Hall | 425.629 |
| Langham Hall | 978.691 | Rise Hall, Akenham | 148.488 | Holton Hall | 403.780 |
| | | Stutton House | 161.345 | Ringsfield Hall | 404.883 |
| **TM SERIES** | | Wherstead Hall | 165.408 | Redisham Hall | 405.860 |
| *Giffords Hall, Stoke by Nayland | 019.375 | Crowfield Hall | 143.578 | Brampton Hall | 435.815 |
| *Shelley Hall | 027.381 | Ashbocking Hall | 169.546 | Sotterley Hall | 459.853 |
| Higham Hall | 036.353 | *Witnesham Hall | 177.508 | Frostenden Hall | 479.818 |
| Lt. Wenham Hall | 081.392 | Swilland Hall | 188.530 | Henstead Hall | 491.859 |
| Naughton Hall | 023.490 | Lt. Stonham Hall· | 112.602 | Somerleyton Hall | 493.975 |
| Aldham Hall | 041.445 | Winston Hall | 179.617 | Flixton Old Hall | 518.955 |
| *Nettlestead Chace | 089.493 | Thornham Hall | 104.718 | Oulton Hall | 510.935 |

## III. Moated sites of Suffolk.

The following is a list compiled from the 2½inch Ordnance Survey (First Series) giving the name or description of moated sites, and map references. The basis of the compilation is similar to that used in Appendix I, with the exception that moated sites are grouped under individual Ordnance Survey sheet numbers. Where individual houses are discussed in Section 6, this is indicated by an asterisk.

| Site | Map Ref. | Site | Map Ref. | Site | Map Ref. |
|---|---|---|---|---|---|
| **SHEET TL 64** | | **SHEET TL 76** | | Moated Site, N. of Conyers Green, Gt. Barton | 887.681 |
| Site of former Rectory, Lt. Wratting | 690.476 (?) | Site of Barrow Hall, Barrow | 763.640 | Fornham Hall Farm, Fornham All Saints | 837.678 |
| Great Wilsey Farm, Lt. Wratting | 687.463 | Small Moat, W. of Barrow | 757.638 | Aldridges, Fornham All Saints | 837.678 |
| Moated Site N. of Fox Inn, Withersfield | 657.484 | Desning Hall, Gazeley | 735.633 | *Hengrave Hall, Hengrave | 824.686 |
| Hall Farm, Withersfield | 658.477 | Chevington Hall Farm, N. of Church, Chevington | 788.603 | Site of Lt. Saxham Hall, Lt. Saxham | 807.633 |
| Site of Castle, Haverhill (?) | 658.458 | **SHEET TL 77** | | Site of Lt. Horringer Hall, Horringer | 818.628 |
| Haverhill Hall, Haverhill | 663.442 | Aspal Hall, Mildenhall | 702.775 | Site of Rushbrooke Hall, Rushbrooke | 891.612 |
| Moon Hall, Haverhill | 668.440 | Barton Hall, Barton Mills | 717.738 | Moated Site, S. of Hawstead Lodge | 849.603 |
| Glebe Farm, Gt. Thurlow | 667.498 | **SHEET TL 78: Nil sites** | | Nowton Hall, Nowton | 861.605 |
| **SHEET TL 65** | | **SHEET TL 84** | | Moated Site, W. of Lt. Welnetham | 893.603 |
| Moat of earlier Hall, Great Bradley Hall | 675.532 | Parsonage Hall, Long Melford | 847.473 | **SHEET TL 87** | |
| **SHEET TL 66** | | *Kentwell Hall, Long Melford | 864.479 | *West Stow Hall | 817.708 |
| Moat nr. Fish Ponds, Exning | 622.653 | Park Farm, Glemsford | 833.483 | | |
| **SHEET TL 67** | | Ford Hall, Bridge Street | 879.489 | | |
| Bell Inn, Opp. Worlington | 692.735 | Balsdon Hall, Acton | 899.485 | **SHEET TL 88** | |
| Mortimer's Lane, Freckenham | 664.726 | Wood Hall, Sudbury | 877.428 | Thetford Priory, Thetford | 865.832 |
| Badlingham Hall, Freckenham | 679.709 | *Chilton Hall, Sudbury | 888.427 | **SHEET TL 93** | |
| Castle Mound (?), Freckenham | 668.718 | **SHEET TL 85** | | Smallbridge Hall, Bures St. Mary | 929.331 |
| **SHEET TL 68: Nil sites** | | Rede Hall, Brockley | 806.578 | Moat Farm, Bures Green, Bures | 919.349 |
| **SHEET TL 74** | | Gulling Green Farm, Brockley | 828.564 | **SHEET TL 94** | |
| Ganwick Farm, Gt. Wratting | 701.494 | Gulling Green, Brockley | 829.565 | Monks Eleigh Tye, Monks Eleigh | 954.485 |
| Site of Rectory, Barnardiston | 713.488 | Brockley Hall, Brockley | 828.556 | Manor Farm, Monks Eleigh | 963.480 |
| Pinhoe Hall, Moated Site of Old Hall | 734.482 | Moated Site W. of Castle Farm, Brockley | 837.556 | Brandeston Hall, Lt. Waldingfield | 914.468 |
| Houghton Hall, Cavendish | 788.467 | Moated Site at Brockley Green, Brockley | 824.548 | Nether Hall, Lt. Waldingfield | 927.464 |
| Eastcotts Farm, Kedington | 699.454 | Doveden Hall, Whepstead | 822.589 | Dyer's Green Farm, Gt. Waldingfield | 913.448 |
| Floriston Hall, Wixoe | 720.433 | Manston Hall, Whepstead | 835.568 | Wells Hall, Milden | 947.474 |
| **SHEET TL 75** | | Moated Site N. of Cages Farm, Whepstead | 838.558 | Moated Site S. of Rashbrooks Farm, Milden | 958.465 |
| The Gesyns, Wickhambrook | 738.565 | Moated Sites, Lawshall | 853.548 / 854.545 | Manorhouse Moat, Lavenham | 907.499 |
| Aldersfield Hall, Wickhambrook | 763.562 | Newhouse Farm, Lawshall | 867.535 | *Castlings Hall, Groton | 972.433 |
| Old Moated Site of Clopton Green, Wickhambrook | 767.544 | Rowney Farm, Lawshall | 851.565 | Bower House, Polstead | 984.409 |
| *Gifford's Hall, Wickhambrook | 771.538 | Barford's Farm, Lawshall | 870.553 | Moat Farm, Mill Green, Edwardstone | 952.424 |
| Fairstead Farm, Cowlinge | 723.543 | Trees Farm, Lawshall | 879.541 | Castle, Lindsey | 980.442 |
| Moated Site, Hobbles Green, Cowlinge | 705.533 | Greentree Farm, Shimpling Street | 878.527 | **SHEET TL 95** | |
| Moated Site, Pound Green, Cowlinge | 718.537 | Shimplingthorne, Shimpling | 872.515 | Moated Site E. of Church, Bradfield St. Clare | 913.578 |
| Cowlinge Hall, Cowlinge | 713.525 | Hunt's Moat, Shimpling | 882.515 | St. Clare Hall, Bradfield St. Clare | 919.577 |
| Shardelows Farm, Cowlinge | 728.562 | Moat Farm, Boxted | 806.512 | Sutton Hall, Bradfield St. Clare | 905.569 |
| Purton Hall, Stansfield | 781.536 | Truckett's Hall, Boxted | 812.501 | Felsham Hall, Felsham | 942.570 |
| Elm Hall, Stansfield | 785.517 | Hawstead Place | 843.599 | Capel Farm, Felsham | 927.563 |
| Moated Site, S. of Houghton Grove, Cavendish | 800.504 | Remains of Hawstead Hall | 856.597 | The Grange, Felsham | 938.561 |
| Blacklands Hall, Cavendish | 809.469 | Moat Farm, Ixworth | 809.589 | *Preston Hall, Preston St. Mary | 947.503 |
| Over Hall to W. Cavendish | 804.466 | Great Saxe Farm, Stanningfield | 881.552 | Brooke Hall, Felsham | 948.562 |
| Moated Rectory Site, Chevington | 785.597 | Coldham Hall, Stanningfield | 865.558 | Valley Farm, Felsham | 951.567 |
| Moated Castle Site, Lidgate | 722.582 | Pepper's Hall, Cross Green, Cockfield | 899.557 | Moated Site N. of Jay's Hall, Felsham | 948.562 |
| *Badmondisfield Hall, Badmondisfield | 748.570 | Rivett's Hall, Hartest | 846.529 | Castle Farm, Felsham | 958.559 |
| Farley Green, Stradishall | 732.533 | Langley's New House, Hawkedon | 804.538 | *Popples, Brettenham | 953.527 |
| Norley Moat Farm, Lt. Bradley | 702.524 | | | | |
| Denston Hall, Denston | 757.524 | Hall, Gt. Welnetham | 882.592 | Moated Site N. of Lower Farm, Brettenham | 964.554 |
| Wadgell's Farm, Lt. Thurlow | 705.514 | **SHEET TL 86** | | Rose's Farm, Brettenham | 958.538 |
| Barnardiston Hall, Barnardiston | 713.503 | Necton Hall, Gt. Barton | 881.675 | Ryece Hall, Brettenham | 957.547 |
| *Thurston Hall, Thurston End, Hawkedon | 794.518 | | | The Rectory, Brettenham | 967.543 |
| Moat Farm, Stradishall | 733.533 | | | | |

| Site | Map Ref. |
|---|---|
| The Poplars, Brettenham | 975.542 |
| Moated Site, E. of 'The Tuns', Cockfield | 913.549 |
| Palmer's Farm, Cockfield | 918.549 |
| Fenn Hall, Buxhall | 998.585 |
| Cockerell's Hall, Buxhall | 988.878 |
| Fazbourn Hall, Buxhall | 997.567 |
| Wood Hall, Rattlesden | 994.589 |
| Clopton Hall, Rattlesden | 984.599 |
| *Gedding Hall, Gedding | 954.586 |
| Site W. of Dairy Farm, Bradfield St. George | 908.598 |
| Hall Farm, Bradfield St. George | 908.598 |
| Water Hall, Thorpe Morieux | 934.542 |
| Moat Farm, Thorpe Morieux | 943.540 |
| Underwood Farm, Thorpe Morieux | 926.525 |
| Manor Farm, Thorpe Morieux | 932.523 |
| Manor Farm, Preston St. Mary | 928.507 |
| Priory Farm, Preston St. Mary | 938.508 |
| Kettlebaston Hall, Kettlebaston | 964.503 |
| Wetherden Hall, Wetherden | 972.510 |
| Stanslead Hall, Hitcham | 984.538 |

**SHEET TL 96**

| Site | Map Ref. |
|---|---|
| Redcastle Farm, Pakenham | 903.693 |
| Maulkin's Hall, Pakenham | 936.682 |
| Beaumont's Hall, Pakenham | 945.674 |
| Hall Farm, Gt. Ashfield | 994.678 |
| Castle Hill, Gt. Ashfield | 992.676 |
| Lea Farm, Gt. Ashfield | 999.661 |
| Little Haugh Hall, Norton | 954.668 |
| Norton Hall, Norton | 969.654 |
| Harding's Farm, Norton | 985.658 |
| Mill Hill, Hunston | 978.677 |
| Site of Hunston Hall | 972.678 |
| Rougham Place, Rougham | 923.633 |
| Moat Farm, Rougham Green | 913.619 |
| Lawney's Farm, Rougham | 925.614 |
| Site of Hessett Hall, Hessett | 931.615 |
| Moated Site, Hessett Village | 935.611 |
| Moated Site, W. of Drinkstone Village | 953.619 |
| Rookery Farm, Drinkstone | 961.609 |
| Elmswell Hall, Elmswell | 984.643 |
| Brook Farm, Boyton | 939.628 |
| Moated Site, N. of Lady's Well, Woolpit | 978.628 |
| Rockyll's Hall, Shelland | 998.605 |
| Moat W. of Church, Langham | 982.691 |

**SHEET TL 97**

| Site | Map Ref. |
|---|---|
| Moated Sites, The Lodge, Market Weston | 985.773 |
| Site of Market Weston Hall | 991.777 |
| Lynton House, Ixworth Thorpe | 916.733 |
| Moated Sites, Bardwell Village | 939.737 |
| Moat Plantation, Barningham | 969.774 |

**SHEET TM 03**

| Site | Map Ref. |
|---|---|
| Moat Hall, Layham | 023.394 |
| Little Wenham Hall, Wenham Parva | 081.391 |
| *Shelley Hall, Shelley | 027.381 |

**SHEET TM 04**

| Site | Map Ref. |
|---|---|
| Whitehouse Farm, Whatfield | 036.468 |
| Barrard's Hall, Whatfield | 024.459 |
| Old Rectory, Whatfield | 019.463 |
| Chattisham Hall, Chattisham | 086.424 |
| Moat Farm, California, Chattisham | 078.418 |
| Moated Site, Elmsett village | 059.472 |
| Rectory, Elmsett village | 055.467 |
| Moat Farm, Elmsett | 054.463 |
| Birch House, Copdock | 083.411 |
| Vauxhall, Wenham Parva | 072.409 |

**SHEET TM 05**

| Site | Map Ref. |
|---|---|
| Boyton Hall, Gt. Finborough | 029.577 |
| Moated Site, High Street Green, Gt. Finborough | 008.558 |
| Moat Farm, Lt. Finborough | 021.548 |
| Naughton Hall, Naughton | 024.491 |
| Naughton Rectory, Naughton | 025.491 |
| Fidget's Farm, Naughton | 021.487 |
| Pigeon Hall, Naughton | 032.485 |
| Holyoak Farm, Combs | 051.565 |
| Kimberley Hall, Moats Tye, Combs | 043.553 |
| Moat Farm, Wattisham | 078.523 |
| Wattisham Hall, Wattisham | 011.513 |
| Chapel Farm, Gt. Bricett | 047.517 |
| Nunnery Mount, Gt. Bricett | 037.507 |
| Offton Castle, site of | 065.493 |
| Maskell's Hall, Offton | 045.489 |
| Whatfield Hall, Whatfield | 017.473 |
| New Farm, Shelland | 009.598 |
| Onehouse Hall, Onehouse | 018.593 |
| *Roydon Hall, Creeting St. Peter | 084.585 |
| St. John's Manor House, Battisford | 046.543 |
| Loose Hall, Hitcham | 001.532 |
| Rectory, Ringshall | 004.523 |
| Chapel Farm, Ringshall | 047.516 |

| Site | Map Ref. |
|---|---|
| Moated Site, Barking Tye | 061.524 |
| Tarston Hall, Barking | 082.519 |
| *Baylham Hall, Baylham | 093.517 |
| Hall, Willisham | 069.506 |

**SHEET TM 06**

| Site | Map Ref. |
|---|---|
| Redhouse Farm, Earl's Green Bacton | 036.667 |
| Site of Rectory, Bacton | 043.661 |
| Pulham's Farm, Bacton | 055.667 |
| Bacton Hall, Bacton | 030.657 |
| Cow Green, Bacton | 054.654 |
| Kerry's Farm, Bacton | 054.654 |
| Russell's Hall, Bacton | 058.647 |
| Moated Site W. of Cock Inn, Cotton | 067.672 |
| *Hemnnall's Hall, Cotton | 082.675 |
| Moated Site, Cotton Village | 069.669 |
| Moated Site E. of Hill Farm, Cottor | 078.664 |
| Moated Site E. of Cotton Village | 079.668 |
| Cotton Hall, Cotton | 068.653 |
| Moated Site adj. Footpath W. of Hayes Farm, Cotton | 072.658 |
| Cotton Lodge, Cotton | 001.657 |
| Potter's Farm, Mendlesham | 083.662 |
| Mendlesham Lodge | 093.662 |
| Poplar Farm, Mendlesham | 098.662 |
| Old Farm, Mendlesham | 088.653 |
| Mendlesham Hall | 091.655 |
| Peartree Farm, Westhorpe | 041.698 |
| Westhorpe Hall, Westhorpe | 032.692 |
| Moat Hill, Wyverstone | 038.675 |
| Moated Site N. of Church, Wyverstone | 049.043 |
| Moat Farm, Badwell Ash | 014.683 |
| Moated Site, Hantons Lane, Badwell Ash | 003.678 |
| Moat House, Badwell Green | 013.693 |
| *Gipping Lone, Gipping | 073.643 |
| Grange Farm, Gipping | 076.641 |
| Upper Lodge, Wetherden | 014.648 |
| Wetherden Hall, Wetherden | 021.642 |
| Mutton Hall, Wetherden | 004.636 |
| New Bells Farm, Haughley Green | 036.641 |
| Wassick Farm, Haughley | 039.642 |
| Rookery Farm, Old Newton | 053.632 |
| *Columbine Hall, Stowupland | 067.608 |

**SHEET TM 07**

| Site | Map Ref. |
|---|---|
| High Hall, Walsham le Willows | 025.718 |
| Old Hall, Walsham le Willows | 026.712 |
| Crowland Hall, Walsham le Willows | 009.703 |
| Stubbing's Green, Rickinghall Sup | 063.742 |
| Facon's Hall, Rickinghall Sup | 044.736 |
| Moat at Lodge Farm, Thelnetham | 014.781 |
| Wortham Hall, Wortham | 085.789 |
| Manor House, Wortham | 078.798 |
| Burgate Hall, Burgate | 079.756 |
| Mellis Hall, Mellis | 092.742 |
| Rectory, Mellis | 096.743 |
| Moat House Wood, Mellis | 095.725 |
| Finningham Hall, Finningham | 059.701 |
| Swattesfield Hall, Gislingham | 088.719 |
| Moathouse Wood, Thornham Parva | 096.725 |

**SHEET TM 13**

| Site | Map Ref. |
|---|---|
| Tattingstone Hall, Tattingstone | 142.374 |

**SHEET TM 14**

| Site | Map Ref. |
|---|---|
| Claydon Hall, Claydon | 143.496 |
| Coles Green, Washbrook | 101.418 |
| Wherstead Hall, Wherstead | 167.408 |

**SHEET TM 15**

| Site | Map Ref. |
|---|---|
| Mowness Hall, Stonham Aspall | 122.599 |
| Broughton Hall, Stonham Aspall | 133.595 |
| Morgan's Farm, East End, Stonham Aspall | 154.598 |
| Lewis Farm, Stonham Aspall | 158.593 |
| Moat Grove, Pettaugh | 163.594 |
| Laffit's Hall, Pettaugh | 173.596 |
| Abbot's Hall, Pettaugh | 174.591 |
| Bocking Hall, Pettaugh | 179.588 |
| Site of Crowfield Hall, Crowfield | 138.575 |
| Crowfield Park, Crowfield | 143.577 |
| Birch Farm, Crowfield | 124.565 |
| Dial Farm, Crowfield | 128.562 |
| Dial Farm, Coddenham | 128.563 |
| Ivy Farm, Coddenham | 138.544 |
| Birch Farm, Coddenham | 124.565 |
| Broadgates Farm, Creeting St. Mary | 103.572 |
| Fox's Farm, Creeting St. Mary | 114.568 |
| Vale Farm, Creeting St. Mary | 117.568 |
| Moat Farm, Gosbeck | 165.569 |
| Rye's Farm, Gosbeck | 169.569 |
| Ashbocking Hall, Ashbocking | 171.547 |
| Feoffee Moat, Ashbocking Green | 184.548 |
| Berghersh House, Witnesham | 182.525 |
| *Witnesham Hall, Witnesham | 177.508 |
| Deerbolt Hall, Earl Stonham | 113.584 |
| *Helmingham Hall, Helmingham | 187.577 |

| Site | Map Ref. |
|---|---|
| Wood Farm, Otley | 195.554 |
| Moat Farm, Swilland | 192.539 |
| Whitelodge Farm, Barham | 142.512 |
| Old Rectory, Henley | 163.509 |

**SHEET TM 16**

| Site | Map Ref. |
|---|---|
| Moated Site, Thorndon Village | 142.695 |
| Thorndon Hill, Thorndon | 154.694 |
| Short's Farm, Thorndon | 143.681 |
| Hestley Hall, Thorndon | 146.682 |
| Moated Site N.E. Village, Thorndon | 153.683 |
| Lampits Farm, Thorndon | 147.673 |
| Rishangles Lodge, Thorndon | 156.683 |
| Moated Site, Hestley Green, Thorndon | 157.667 |
| Rectory, Thorndon | 143.695 |
| Wood Hall, Stoke Ash | 108.698 |
| Colsey Wood, Stoke Ash | 111.693 |
| Woodhouse Farm, Rishangles | 162.693 |
| Rishangles Lodge, Rishangles | 157.682 |
| Barnaby Farm, Rishangles | 168.681 |
| Bucks Hall, Rishangles | 167.674 |
| Moated Yards, Bedingfield | 177.697 |
| Bedingfield House, Bedingfield | 175.677 |
| *Fleming's Hall, Bedingfield | 193.679 |
| *Bedingfield Hall, Bedingfield | 198.677 |
| High House, Occold | 163.698 |
| The Grove, Occold | 169.697 |
| Old Hall, Debenham | 154.644 |
| Ulveston Hall, Debenham | 149.633 |
| Hill Farm, Debenham | 187.630 |
| White Hall, Debenham | 154.625 |
| Esther's Moat, Debenham | 163.629 |
| *Crows Hall, Debenham | 192.628 |
| Debenham Hall, Debenham | 163.637 |
| Blood Hall, N.E. Debenham | 184.648 |
| Westwood Hall, Mickfield | 107.625 |
| Read Hall, Mickfield | 128.628 |
| Mickfield Hall, Mickfield | 134.627 |
| Greenwood Farm, Mickfield | 147.629 |
| Church Farm, Mendlesham | 106.658 |
| Buses Farm, Mendlesham | 116.658 |
| Willow Farm, Thwaite | 115.685 |
| Thwaite Lodge Farm, Thwaite | 115.685 |
| Site of Thwaite Hall, Thwaite | 109.678 |
| Brockford Hall, Thwaite | 114.673 |
| Park Green, Wetheringsett-cum-Brockford | 135.645 |
| Brames Hall, Wetheringsett | 138.673 |
| Wetheringsett Hall, Wetheringsett | 134.662 |
| Moated Site, Blacksmith's Green, Wetheringsett | 142.659 |
| Green Farm, Wetheringsett | 127.645 |
| Green Farm, Winston Green | 167.613 |
| Park Farm, Winston Green | 168.611 |
| Winston Hall, Winston | 179.617 |
| Impaugh Farm, Stonham Aspall | 145.603 |
| Old East End Hall, Stonham Aspall | 155.604 |
| Aspall House, Aspall | 169.661 |
| *Aspall Hall, Aspall | 172.654 |
| Moat Farm, Kenton | 185.662 |
| Kenton Hall, Kenton | 188.652 |
| Lt. Stonham Hall, Lt. Stonham | 112.603 |
| Westwood Hall, Lt. Stonham | 107.625 |
| Moat Farm, Stonham Parva | 103.613 |
| Paradise Farm, Southolt | 195.688 |

**SHEET TM 17**

| Site | Map Ref. |
|---|---|
| Moated Site W. of Church, Hoxne | 181.776 |
| Abbey Farm, Hoxne | 185.764 |
| Redhouse Farm, Hoxne | 174.751 |
| Moated Site, Hoxne | 185.754 |
| Vicarage (Tudor), Hoxne | 181.776 |
| Chickering Corner Farm, Hoxne | 205.764 |
| Kiln Farm, Cranley | 166.725 |
| King's Farm, Cranley | 172.718 |
| College Farm, Denham | 191.748 |
| Denham Hall Farm, Denham | 179.737 |
| Low Farm, Eye | 172.732 |
| Cranley Hall, Eye | 153.728 |
| Occold Hall, Moated Site, near Occold | 149.708 |
| Benningham Hall, Occold | 168.709 |
| Stuston Hall, Stuston | 138.781 |
| Church Farm, Brome | 147.766 |
| Goswold Hall, Thrandeston | 125.757 |
| Malting Farm, Thrandeston | 128.763 |
| Moated Site, Yaxley Village | 121.743 |
| Rectory Farm, Braiseworth | 135.718 |
| The Leys and Redlingfield Hall | 185.707 |

**SHEET TM 23**

| Site | Map Ref. |
|---|---|
| Old Hall, Shotley | 238.358 |

**SHEET TM 24**

| Site | Map Ref. |
|---|---|
| Abbey Farm, Culpho | 208.493 |
| Playford Hall, Playford | 214.478 |

**SHEET TM 25**

| Site | Map Ref. |
|---|---|
| Moat Farm, Framsden | 220.593 |
| Moated Site, Framsden | 217.587 |
| Basting's Hall, Framsden | 205.578 |

## IV. Suffolk Houses the subject of articles in Country Life.

| House | Volume | House | Volume | House | Volume |
|---|---|---|---|---|---|
| Hintlesham Hall | lxiv | Parham Old Hall (Moat Hall) | x | (Shrubland Park, | |
| Ickworth Park | lviii | | xxv | cont.) | cxxvii |
| | cxvii | | lv | | cxxviii |
| | xviii | | lxxv | Somerleyton Hall | cxlviii |
| Kentwell Hall; gardens | xii | | cxvi | Sudbourne Hall; gardens | ix |
| Little Haugh Hall | cxxiii | Redgrave Hall | lxxxvii | Weaver's House, Stratford St. Mary | xcviii |
| Long Wall, Long Melford | cxxxvii | Sandhill, Aldeburgh | lviii | West Stow Hall | xxix |
| Melford Hall | lxxxii | Seckford Hall | xxvii | Wingfield Castle | xxxiii |
| | x | Shrubland Park, Ipswich | cxiv | | lxxv |
| | | | x | Wool Hall, Peasenhall | cxlvii |
| Otley Hall | lxv | | lxiii | Worlingham Hall | cxlvii |

## V. Suffolk Houses wholly or partly demolished during the last 200 years.

| House | Remarks | House | Remarks |
|---|---|---|---|
| Assington Hall | Tudor mansion — seat of Gurdons of early C17; destroyed by fire, 1957 | Ipswich, Red House | Demolished c.1935 |
| | | Lavenham Hall | Demolished |
| Barton Hall, Bury St. Edmunds | A Bunbury seat of early C17; destroyed by fire, 1914 | Livermere Hall | Demolished in 1923 |
| | | Moulton Paddocks House | Destroyed c.1950 |
| Bealings Hall | Seat of Manor; demolished c.1785 | Oakley Park, Eye | Demolished c.1930 |
| Bildeston Hall | Demolished prior to 1855 | Ousden Hall | Demolished |
| Boulge Hall | Demolished c.1958 | Playford Hall | Partially destroyed |
| Bradwell, Hobland Hall | Only a fragment remains, now offices | Redgrave Hall | Hall totally destroyed in 1960 |
| Bramford Hall | Demolished c.1955 | Rendlesham Hall | Only a few ruins of the house remain: demolished in 1949 |
| Bredfield, White House | Demolished c.1950 | | |
| Campsey Ash, High House | By Salvin, demolished c.1953 | Rougham Hall | Demolished c.1953 |
| Cavenham Hall | Demolished c.1949 | Rushbrook Hall | Destroyed by fire in 1961 |
| Chediton Hall, Halesworth | Demolished c.1953 | Sudbourne Hall | Demolished in 1953 |
| Cowlinge, Branches Park | Demolished c.1959 | Sudbury, Chilton Hall | Partially destroyed |
| Drinkstone Hall | Demolished in 1953 | Tendring Hall | Demolished in 1960 |
| Easton Park, White House | Demolished c.1924 | Thorington Hall (A12) | Demolished c.1949 |
| Edwardstone Hall | Pulled down except for gatehouse | Thornham Park | House destroyed by fire c.1945 |
| Flixton Hall | Demolished in 1953 | Tostock Place | Partly demolished |
| Fornham Hall | Demolished in 1953 | Ufford Place | Demolished in 1953 |
| Hardwick House, Bury St. Edmunds | Destroyed in 1926 | Wamil Hall, Mildenhall | Partly demolished in 1955 |

## VI. Listed Building Procedure.

The identification and protection of valuable old houses is now a statutory duty. The Secretary of State for the Environment has the job of listing buildings of special architectural or historic interest, and of keeping these lists under continual review. Each list is based upon the Civil Parish, and is supported by maps divided into sheets on each of which the position of a listed building is identified by a number. The *Sheet and No. on maps* is followed by the *Grade*; the building — its name or other description — under the heading of *Item*, and finally a column headed *Notes*. Originally there were three Grades; I, II and III, but Grade III is no longer in use. The classification now adopted is Grade I, Grade II* and Grade II. Lists must be kept available for inspection free of charge at the office of the local authority (and at the National Monuments Record, 23 Savile Row, London W1X 2HE).

The responsibility for deciding the 'grading' of a building was entrusted initially to 'an expert committee of architects, antiquarians and historians'. The principles on which they worked are still followed, and may be summarised as follows:

All buildings before 1700 which survive in anything like their original condition are listed.

Most buildings of 1700 to 1840 are listed subject to selection. Between 1840 and 1914 buildings must be of 'definite quality and character'; the principal works of the principal architects are included. Buildings of 1914 to 1939 will be selected for listing (D.O.E. says that a start is being made on this list).

Selection takes into account special value within certain types: thus the architecture, planning, or social and economic history not only of houses but of industrial buildings, railway stations, schools, hospitals, theatres, town-halls, markets, almshouses, mills, prisons and lock-ups, could qualify for selection.

Selection should also include buildings notable for 'technological innovation or virtuosity' (e.g. cast iron, prefabrication, early use of concrete); association with well-known characters or events, and *Group Value,* especially as examples of town-planning exemplified by squares, terraces, model villages, and so on.

Grade I buildings are those of outstanding interest. The Department of the Environment says that only about 4 per cent of listed buildings are so far in this grade. As things now stand the buildings at greatest risk are those formerly in Grade III, which can be altered or demolished with Local Authority approval. Innumerable Suffolk farmhouses, village houses, cottages and barns, come into this category, many of which on current standards would probably be upgraded to the Statutory List, but in the meanwhile have to await re-assessment by the Department of the Environment. It is precisely during this indefinite hiatus — whilst the districts are re-surveyed — that so much depends upon the promptitude with which any threatened buildings, formerly Grade III or otherwise, are brought to the notice of the Department. It is perhaps not generally known that the merits of such buildings can be established from photographs, and that if they are of special interest they can be listed straight away.

District authorities are required to notify the owner and occupier of a building as soon as possible after it has been included on the Statutory List or ceases to be included. They are also required to bring to the attention of the Department of the Environment at an early stage in all development proposals (including their own) any building affected which appears to them to merit listing. The fact that a building is listed does not necessarily mean that it will be preserved, but it does ensure that the case for its preservation is examined quite separately under the listed building consent procedure. Once a building is listed it is an offence to demolish, alter or extend it unless the works are authorised.

Much attention has now to be given to the selling of a building of special architectural or historic interest and in a circular dated March 16, 1977, the Department of the Environment says:

'. . . many attractive streets or villages owe their character not so much to buildings of great individual merit but to the harmony produced by a whole range or complex of buildings. Such areas require the same careful treatment when proposals for redevelopment are under consideration, even if the redevelopment only replaces a building that is neither of great merit in itself nor is immediately adjacent to a listed building. Authorities are asked to ensure that they bring fully instructed opinion to bear on any development which, by its character and/or location, might be held to have an adverse effect on buildings of special architectural or historic interest. In some cases, they may feel sure that the knowledge immediately available to them will be enough to enable them to reach a well-founded decision. In specially important cases however, it may well be advisable for authorities to consider whether they should not seek independent professional advice on the proposals before reaching a decision on them. Authorities will be aware that the advice of the Royal Fine Art Commission may also be sought in such cases.'

# Bibliographies

## General

The following is a general bibliography of works or references, either directly or indirectly touching on the subject of Suffolk Houses. There is also a bibliography relating to Sections 2-5. In the description of individual houses in Section 6 references are given in footnotes.

## Architectural

*The Baronial Halls and Picturesque Edifices of England* (2 vols.) by S.C. Hall, F.S.A. (1874. London: Chapman and Hall.) Three Suffolk houses included; Helmingham Hall, Hengrave Hall and West Stow Hall. A period piece for the general reader, not the specialist.

*Old Houses and Village buildings in East Anglia* by Basil Oliver, A.R.I.B.A. (1912. London: Batsford.) Deals with timber-framed buildings with studding exposed or plastered, brickwork, stone and flintwork, weather-boarding and tile hanging, woodwork, and wrought ironwork. Many delightful notebook sketches.

*The Minor Architecture of Suffolk* by Dexter Morand. (1929. London: John Tiranti & Co.) A brief essay, historical notes, and 48 photographic plates. A series was planned 'to give a comprehensive photographic survey of the domestic architecture of Old England', Major and Minor, but I believe only one other county — Worcestershire — was published in the Minor series.

*A History of the English House* by Nathaniel Lloyd, O.B.E., F.S.A., F.R.I.B.A. (1931; Second Impression 1949; Third Impression 1951.)

*English Cottages and Farmhouses* by Oliver Cook and Edwin Smith. (1969. London: Thames and Hudson.) Beautifully written and informative as much by letterpress as by inspired photography. Suffolk buildings are at Acton, Chelsworth, Clare, Eriswell, Framlingham, Glemsford, Hacheston, Henley, Lavenham, Long Melford, Monks Eleigh, Parham, Rendham and Tattingstone.

*Suffolk* in *The Buildings of England Series* by Sir Nikolaus Pevsner, C.B.E. (First Edition 1961; Second Edition 1974. Harmondsworth: Penguin.) Second Edition revised by Enid Ratcliffe with *Note on the Development of Timber Roofs* by J.F. Smith. Valuable essay on the background, history and details of buildings, followed by a gazetteer. A lot of houses are mentioned.

*The Provisional Lists of Buildings of Architectural and Historic Interest,* Statutory List. (Published by H.M. Government, Department of the Environment.)

## Architectural & Genealogical

*Some Old Houses in Suffolk* (6 vols.) by Rev. Edmund Farrer, F.S.A. Articles on 385 houses originally published in the East Anglian Daily Times, and later reprinted in East Anglian Miscellany (E.A.M.) 1910-1955. Collected and bound. Suffolk Reord Office, Ipswich. Architectural description followed by, often, lengthy genealogical survey.

## Country Houses

*Suffolk Country Houses.* Country Life articles 1897-1910. Bound in one Volume. Suffolk Record Office, Ipswich. The houses are at Hengrave; Sudbourne;\* Rushbrooke;\* Giffords, Stoke-by-Nayland; Campsea Ashe;\* Ickworth Park; Oakley Park;\* Parham; Glemham and Seckford Hall: those marked \* have since been demolished. *Country Life* articles on houses in Suffolk since 1910 have not been collected and bound. A list of these has been prepared and is included at Appendix iv.

*English Homes* (9 vols.) by H. Avray Tipping, M.A., F.S.A. (1910-1936. London: Country Life.) Classical articles on English Country Houses of which the following in Suffolk are covered: Period I 1066-1485; Little Wenham Hall, pages 92-100: Period II 1485-1558; Giffords Hall, Stoke-by-Nayland, pages 31-50; Giffords Hall, Wickhambrook, pages 1-10; Hengrave Hall, pages 231-243; Parham Old Hall (now Moat Hall), pages 51-58; West Stow Hall, pages 210-211: Period I and II 1066-1558; Alston Court, pages 197-206; Hadleigh, Church, Cloth Hall, and Rectory Tower, pages 343-350; Otley Hall, pages 207-212: Period III 1558-1649; Seckford Hall, pages 64-70: Period IV 1649-1714; Glemham Hall, pages 405-416: Period VI 1760-1820; Ickworth, near Bury St. Edmunds, pages 321-338.

## Gazetteers & Guide Books

*The History and Topography of Suffolk* by F Shoberl. (1813. London.) Mr. Shoberl is in D.N.B. as author, editor, historian, and translator of French and German authors (b.1775-d.1853). His book is one of the series *The Beauties of England and Wales*, and is dedicated to the great Suffolk agriculturalist, Arthur Young. He held strong views on '. . . the neglect of elegance and convenience in those gentlemen of a certain property, as well as in farmhouses', and lamented the quantity 'of lath and plaster which, decaying in a short time, caused repairs to be so heavy a deduction from the receipts of

an estate.' Generally, more informative on local history than houses, although a description of the building of Ickworth House is particularly interesting.

*History, Gazetteer and Directory of Suffolk* by William White. (1844. Sheffield.) Mr. White, preceding Kelly by two years, brought the business acumen of a Midlander to the directory trade, with a team of assistants and an office in Sheffield. His *Suffolk* was extremely popular, and ran into five editions (1844, 1855, 1874, 1884 and 1892). The wide coverage is indicated by the title page (1855 edition). An extensive history and description of Ipswich and Bury St. Edmunds is followed by the Hundreds, in which every town and village has a directory of Gentry, Clergy, Trades and Professions. (As an example of the latter, we find amongst the Surveyors of Woodbridge, an architect *Mr. Pattison*, of St. John's Street. See Mr. W.G. Arnott's interesting paper: *William Pattison, A Mid-Victorian Architect, 1805-1878* – in the Proceedings of the Suffolk Institute of Archaeology, Volume XXVIII, Part 3, pages 299-301.) William White's Gazetteer is a godsend for anyone interested in mid-Victorian Suffolk.

*East Anglia* in *Highways and Byways Series* by W.A. Dutt. (1901. London: Macmillan, and many times reprinted.) Discursive commentary on journeys, some in Suffolk: a few old houses are mentioned in a topical rather than a detailed manner.

*The Little Guides:* series on English countries. (Methuen: London.) *Suffolk* by W.A. Dutt (1904), revised by P.G.M. Dickinson M.A., F.S.A. (1957). Well informed, scholarly, pocket-size guide books. Mr. Dutt had the late Victorian preference for churches, but the balance was admirably redressed by Mr. Dickinson: in his preface he laments the passing of many of the county's famous houses, calling the demolition of *Harwick Hall,* near Bury St. Edmunds in 1926, 'a major calamity'. He refers not only to the famous but also to many lesser houses, and assiduously records *moated* houses and sites.

*The King's England:* series on English counties edited by Arthur Mee. (London: Hodder and Stoughton.) *Suffolk our Farthest East* (1941), cosy history with plentiful anecdotes, many on the old houses of Suffolk.

*Shell Guides* edited by Sir John Betjeman. *Suffolk* by Norman Scarfe (First Edition 1960; Second Edition 1976. Faber & Faber.) Mr. Scarfe is a Suffolk native and well-known historian, author of *The Suffolk Landscape,* etc., with much knowledge and love of places, people and buildings: fresh and often penetrating commentary, supported by the distinguished photography of Edwin Smith and John Piper.

## Historical Antiquities

*Historic Sites of Suffolk* by J. Wodderspoon. (1839. Ipswich: Burton and London: Smith.) Many references to halls and houses; e.g. Westhorpe Hall;\* West Stow Hall; Sparrow's House, Ipswich; Wingfield Castle; Hengrave Hall; Huntingfield Hall; Hawstead Hall;\* Melford Hall; Rushbrooke Hall;\* Lt. Wenham Hall; Mockbeggars Hall; Gedding Hall; Giffords Hall, Stoke-by-Nayland; Acton Place;\* Broome Hall;\* Somerleyton Hall; Flixton Hall;\* Cockfield Hall, Yoxford; Old Hall, Parham; and High House, Campsey\* (\* demolished, or partly demolished). Not much detailed information.

*The History and Antiquities of the County of Suffolk* (2 vols.) by Alfred Inigo Suckling. (1866. London: Weale.) The well-known antiquarian of the Suckling family of Roos Hall, Beccles. Covers the Hundreds of Wangford, Mutford, Lothingland and Blything, and mentions a number of old houses.

*Illustrations of Old Ipswich* by John Glyde, (1889. Ipswich: Glyde.) With 'Architectural Description' of the Gates and Walls, The Ancient House, the Old Coffee House, the Bridges, the Quay Custom House and port, the Black Friars, the Cornhill and the Early History of Ipswich. Large and good auto-gravure illustrations.

*Memorials of Old Suffolk* by V.B. Redstone. (1908. London: Bemrose.) An anthology, with an excellent paper by Mr. Redstone on *Historic Suffolk,* and a useful essay by Rowland W. Maitland, M.A., on *Some East Suffolk Homesteads,* mentioning Lt. Wenham Hall; Parham Hall; Seckford Hall; Crows Hall, Debenham; Boundary Farm, Framsden; Framsden Hall and Barn; Baylham Hall; High Hall, Nettlestead; Flemings Hall; Otley Hall; Ufford Hall, Fressingfield; Letheringham Hall (now demolished); Newbourne Hall and Hintlesham Old Hall.

*Suffolk and Norfolk* by M.R. James, O.M., L.D., F.B.A. (1930.

London: Dent.) Scholarly outline of principal historical and antiquarian features, with reference to some of the well-known old houses. At one time Provost of Eton, he lived (and died) at the Gatehouse, Butley Priory.

## Local History
*The Suffolk Review.* Bulletin of the local history council. Published quarterly with occasional articles on historical houses, of which the following are examples: *The West Suffolk Inventories for 1065 – Some clues to house types,* Sylvia Colman, Spring 1968, Volume 3, No. 6. *The houses of Stonham Aspall:* a survey by David Penrose and Peter Hill, Autumn 1971, Volume 4, No. 1.

## Manorial History
*History of the Manors of Suffolk* (7 vols.) by W.A. Copinger. (1905-1911.) The classical textbook on the subject. Principally concerned with the identification and ownerships of Suffolk Manors, but there are occasional interesting references to houses and quite a few useful pen and ink sketches. See also the informed critique which prefaces the *Index to Manors* by C.G.H. (Suffolk Record Office, Ipswich).

## Mediaeval and Historical Archaeology
*The English Farmhouse and Cottage* by M.W. Barley. (1961. London: Routledge). After the Legacy of the Middle Ages, Mr. Barley divides the history of housing into four periods. First and Second phases of the Housing Revolution (1575-1642), the Vernacular Tradition under Attack (1642-90), and finally, In Decay. In the first three of these periods, East Anglia is separately studied, and some Suffolk houses are mentioned (Wydard's given at 'Cratley' instead of Cratfield).
*The English Mediaeval House* by Margaret Wood M.A., D.Litt., F.S.A. (1965. London: Phoenix.) The period covered is Norman Conquest to 1540, and the approach comprehensive and meticulous. Suffolk comes in with Moyses Hall, and the Abbey gatehouse, Bury St. Edmunds; Butley Priory; Framlingham Castle; Church Farm, Fressingfield; Great Bricett Priory; The Deanery, Hadleigh; Kersey Priory; Guildhall and houses, Lavenham; Little Wenham Hall; Alston Court, Nayland; Giffords Hall, Stoke-by-Nayland; Edgar's Farm, Stowmarket; and Giffords Hall, Wickhambrook. This is already a book of standard reference on all aspects of mediaeval building, and there is a great deal of immediate relevance for students of Suffolk houses.
*The Suffolk Institute of Archaeology.* Established in 1848. Bound volumes in Ipswich Central Library, Northgate Street, both loan and reference libraries. Articles from the Proceedings of the Suffolk Institute of Archaeology on Suffolk houses are mentioned throughout this book, either in footnotes or bibliographies (Proceedings S.I.A.), with references to volume number, part, author, page numbers: the only exception being to mention here the study by the Norfolk architect J.W. Messent, A.R.I.B.A., in Volume XX, pages 244-262, *The Old Cottages and Farmhouses of Suffolk,* a useful general survey, dealing with brick and flint work, clay-lump, half timber and weather-boarding, farm buildings and dovecotes, old village shops and village types, illustrated by a number of Mr. Messent's characteristic pen and ink sketches. His companion work *The Old Cottages and Farmhouses of Norfolk* was published as a book. (1928. Norwich: Hunt.)

## Monastic Suffolk
*Index Monasticus* by Richard Taylor of Norwich. (1821. London.) An account of the religious houses in the Diocese of Norwich, with a section on Suffolk, including map. Under the headings of the four orders, Monastic, Clerical, Military and Conventual, and of the colleges, hospitals, etc., short descriptions of each foundation, valuations (the most interesting being those at the time of the Dissolution), and the names of the possessors of the properties in 1821. This is of considerable importance in a study of those religious houses which were converted into private dwellings.
*The Monastic Remains of Norfolk and Suffolk* by C.J.W. Messent, A.R.I.B.A. (1934. Norwich: Hunt.) Does not add a great deal to Taylor's work, but the latter is fairly scarce.

## Travellers and Commentaries
*The Itinerary of John Leland in or about the years 1535-1543.* First published in nine vols. at Eton and Oxford in 1710-12. (cf. *The Itinerary* edited by Lucy Toulmin Smith, 1964. The Centaur Classics: London). Leland was born into an age of ferment and ordained priest before Henry VIII's break with the Papacy; 'a parish priest of Suffolk'; was commissioned by the king to search monastic and collegiate libraries 'for the monuments of ancient writers', and made his 'laboriouse journey' of six years through England and Wales which Miss Toulmin Smith considers entitles him 'to be called the father of English topography'.
*Suffolk in the Seventeenth Century.* The Breviary of Robert Ryece, now published for the first time from the MS in the British Museum with notes by Lord Francis Harvey. (1902. London: Murray.) This is the published title of Ryece's book, often paraphrased as *A Breviary of Suffolk.* Amongst the innumerable and informative entries on the state of Suffolk in the early years of the seventeenth century, there is one oft quoted on *Mansions or Dwelling houses,* in which he contrasts unfavourably the new homesteads compared with the older halls (Lord F. Harvey's edition, pages 49-51).
*The Suffolk Traveller* by Joshua Kirby. (1735. First published Ipswich, 1764, enlarged edition with maps. 1820 Third Edition, without maps, published Smith and Jarrold; Woodbridge.) In the main text important churches and houses are the only buildings mentioned.
*Excursions Through the County of Suffolk* (2 subscription vols., published 1818-1819. London.) Described as 'A Complete Guide for the Traveller and Tourist.' Issued anonymously, although the author of this somewhat class conscious work turns out, rather surprisingly to be Thomas Kitson Cromwell, a dissenting minister, at one time of 'the literary department of Messrs. Longmans'. He is believed to have edited seven other volumes of Excursions in addition to those on Suffolk, viz. Norfolk in 2 vols., Essex in 2 vols., Surrey 1 vol., Sussex 1 vol., and Kent 1 vol. He may also have done Cornwall and Ireland in this series. One of the nicest things is the quality of the precise little steel engravings of churches and mansions, mostly after drawings by T. Higham, but also some by J. Greig, J.S. Cotman and H. Davy.
*View of The Seats of the Noblemen and Gentlemen in Suffolk* (Part I) by Henry Davy. (1827. Southwold.) Two subscription volumes were planned, but the proceeds proved insufficient to publish more than one, and this reduced the number of plates from 24 to 20. But the plates, size 6½in. by 4¾in. are well produced, and in the then fashionable taste, with mansions framed between parkland trees. The houses briefly described (although with occasional tantalising mention of the old masters in drawing-rooms and dining-rooms) are: Henham Hall;* Cockfield Hall; Worlingham Hall; Fornham Hall;* Great Finborough Hall; Gipping Hall;* Hawleigh Park (sic); Benacre Hall; Henstead House; Brampton Hall; Benhall Lodge; Glevering Hall; Plashwood (Hawleigh); Hintlesham Hall; Hurts Hall (the predecessor of the present Edwardian-Tudor house); Sotterley Hall, Rendlesham House;* Heveningham Hall; Somerleyton Hall; and Marlesford Hall. Those marked * are demolished, and how grateful one is to Henry Davy for his accurate records. (There is a good monograph *Henry Davy, 1793-1865,* by Rev. A.H. Denney, B.A., in the Proceedings S.I.A., Volume XXIX, Part 1, pages 78-90.)

## Vernacular Studies
*Illustrated Handbook of Vernacular Architecture* by R.W. Brunskill. (1971. London: Faber & Faber.)
*A Bibliography on Vernacular Architecture* edited by Robert de Zouche Hall. (1972. Newton Abbot: David & Charles.)
*English Vernacular Houses* by Eric Mercer. Royal Commission on Historical Monuments. (First Edition 1975. London: H.M.S.O.) Mr. Mercer describes houses in Barking, Beccles, Blyford, Bury St. Edmunds, Chevington, Combs, Framsden, Fressingfield, Gislingham, Great Cornard, Ipswich, Ixworth, Lavenham, Melton, Peasenhall, Ringshall, Stanton, Stonham Aspall, Stonham (Earl), Stowmarket, Walsham-le-Willows, Wickhambrook. He is particularly interesting on the so-called 'longhouse' type.

# Section 2

**Agriculture**
*A survey of the Agriculture of Suffolk* by P.J.O. Trist, O.B.E., B.A., M.R.A.C., F.L.S. County Agricultural Adviser Suffolk. Royal Agricultural Society of England, 35 Belgrave Square, London, S.W.1. 1971.
**Architecture**
*An introduction to Anglo-Saxon Architecture and Sculpture* by E.A. Fisher, M.A., D.Sc. (1959. London. Faber & Faber).
**Building**
*Building in England* – down to 1540. A Documentary History by L.F. Salzman, (1952. Oxford. Clarendon Press).
**Country Life**
*Lark Rise to Candleford,* A Trilogy by Flora Thompson (1954. London. Oxford University Press). The World's Classics.
**Gazetteers**
*History, Gazetteer and Directory of Suffolk.* William White. (See General Bibliography)
**Geology**
*A Contribution to the Geological History of Suffolk.* Parts 1-5 and Supplement. Published in the Transactions of the Suffolk Naturalist's Society as follows:– Part 1. Vol. 13 – Part 4: pub. July, 1966. Part 2. Vol. 13 – Part 5: pub. February, 1967. Part 3. Vol. 13 – Part 6: pub. August, 1967. Part 4. Vol. 15 – Part 2: pub. January, 1970. Part 5.

Vol. 15 – Part 4: pub. January, 1971. Supplement Vol. 15 – Part 6: pub. January, 1972. Papers by Harold E.P. Spencer, F.G.S.

## Landscape
*The Making of The English Landscape* by W.G. Hoskins (first published 1955. London, Hodder & Stoughton). *The Suffolk Landscape* by David Dymond in 'East Anglian Studies', ed. by L.M. Munby (1968. Cambridge, Heffer). *The Suffolk Landscape* by Norman Scarfe (1972. London, Hodder & Stoughton); a volume in *The Making of the English Landscape Series*, edited by W.G. Hoskins.

## Leys and Tracks
*The Old Straight Track* by Alfred Watkins (First published 1925 London, Methuen). *Quicksilver Heritage:* The Mystic Leys: Their Legacy of Ancient Wisdom, by Paul Screeton (1974: Northamptonshire, Thorsons).

## Maps
Reprints of the First Edition of the One inch Ordnance Survey of England and Wales with notes by J.B. Harley, Department of Geography, The University, Liverpool 7, published by David & Charles, Newton Abbot, Devon. Ordnance Survey 1:25000 First Series, published by H.M. Stationery Office, 49 High Holborn, London, W.C.1.

## Manorial History
*History of the Manors of Suffolk* by W.A. Copinger in 7 vols. Vol. 1. (1905. London. Fisher Unwin). Vols. 2-7, (1905-1911, Manchester, Taylor Garnett & Evans). *Suffolk Manorial Families*, by J.J. Muskett (1908. Exeter: Pollard).

## Miscellany
*East Anglia Miscellany*, upon matters of History, Geneology, Archaeology, Folk-Lore and Literature relating to East Anglia. Reprinted from the 'East Anglian Daily Times' from 1907 to 1958 (Ipswich. East Anglian Daily Times Co. Limited).

## Place-Names
*Place-Names of Suffolk* by W. Skeat (1913. Cambridge. Antiquarian Society, Octavo Series No. XLVI). *Place Names of the Deben Valley Parishes* by W.G. Arnott (1946. Ipswich. Adlard). *British Place Names in their Historical Setting* by Edmund McClure (1910: London. S.P.C.K.). *The Concise Oxford Dictionary of English Place-Names*, ed. by Eilert Ekwall. Fourth edition. 1960.

## Rivers
*Alde Estuary* by W.G. Arnott (1952. Ipswich. Adlard). *Orwell Estuary* by W.G. Arnott (1954. Ipswich. Adlard). *Suffolk Estuary* by W.G. Arnott (1950. Ipswich. Adlard) The story of the River Deben.

## Roman Roads
*Roman Roads in Britain* by Ivan D. Margary M.A., F.S.A. Vol. 1. South of the Foss Way – Bristol Channel (1955. London, Phoenix House).

## Sociology
*Suffolk – Some Social Trends* by R.A. Emerson and Rosemary Crompton. A Report to the Suffolk Rural Community Council. (1968 University of East Anglia). Privately printed by East Suffolk County Council.

## Suffolk Records
*Suffolk and The Great Rebellion*, ed. by Alan Everitt, M.A. Ph.D. (1960 Suffolk Records Society, Volume III). *The Letter-Book of William of Hoo*, Sacrist of Bury St. Edmunds, 1280-1294, ed. by Antonia Gransden (1963, Suffolk Records Society Volume V). *The County of Suffolk*, surveyed by Joseph Hodskinson, pub. 1783. Edited with Introduction by D.B. Dymond, M.A., F.S.A. (1972 Suffolk Records Society, Volume XV). *Suffolk Turnpikes*, compiled by W.R. Sergeant and D.G. Penrose. (1973. Ipswich and East Suffolk Record Office).

## Siting
*Aspects of Houses in Relation to Wind, Rainfall and Sunshine* by Nathaniel Lloyd, O.B.E. (R.I.B.A. Journal 20.9.24. pages 633-644).

## Topographical
*Rural Rides* by William Cobbett (1853. London. Cobbett), re-published in Everyman's Library in 2 Vols. Introduction by Edward Thomas. *Suffolk Scene* by Julian Tennyson (1939. London & Glasgow. Blackie).

## Villages
*The Structure of Villages* by the Earl of Cranbrook, C.B.E., D.L. (1971. The Suffolk Review. Autumn). *A View into the Village* by Eric Sandon (1969. Lavenham, Dalton).

## Wool Trade
*Wool: East Anglia's Golden Fleece* by Nigel Heard (1970 Lavenham, Dalton). *The Wool Trade in English Mediaeval History*, by Eileen Power – The Ford Lectures (1941. Oxford University Press). *Mediaeval People* by Eileen Power. (1924. London, Methuen).

## Section 3

### Architecture
*A History of Architecture on the Comparative Method*, by Sir Banister Fletcher, M.Arch., F.S.A., F.P.S.L., E.S.I. (First edition 1896 – numerous reprints. London: B.T. Batsford.) *A History of the English House*, by Nathaniel Lloyd, O.B.E., F.S.A., F.R.I.B.A. See General Bibliography. *England.* Introduction by Angus Wilson, photographs by Edwin Smith, notes on the plates by Olive Cook. (1971: London. Thames and Hudson.) *English Homes*, by H. Avray Tipping, M.A., F.S.A. See General Bibliography.

### Building Construction
*The Development of English Building Construction*, by C.F. Innocent, A.R.I.B.A. (First published 1916 Cambridge University Press. New impression 1971 by David and Charles (Publishers) Limited, Newton Abbot, Devon.)

### Cottages
*The Truth About Cottages*, by John Woodforde. (1969. London, Routledge & Kegan Paul.)

### Gothic Period
*Gothic England.* A Survey of National Culture, 1300-1550, by John Harvey. (1947. London: B.T. Batsford.)

### Historical
*Suffolk*, by Lilian J. Redstone, B.A. (1930. London: Knopf.)

### Ipswich
*Illustrations of Old Ipswich*, by John Glyde. (1889: Ipswich & Glyde.) *Ipswich Through the Ages*, by Lilian J. Redstone, M.B.E., B.A. (1948. Ipswich: East Anglian Magazine Limited.)

### Memoirs
*A Window in Suffolk*, by Alan Jobson. (1962. London: Robert Hale.)

### Mediaeval and Historical Archaeology
*Antiquities of the County of Suffolk*, by Suckling. See General Bibliography. *The Borough of Bury St. Edmunds*, by M.D. Lobell. (1935: Oxford.) *Smaller Post-Mediaeval Houses in Eastern England*, by P. Eden, M.A., Ph.D: an essay in *East Anglian Studies*, edited by Lionel M. Munby. (1968. Cambridge: Heffer.) *The English Farmhouse and Cottage*, by M.W. Barley. See General Bibliography. *The English Mediaeval House*, by Margaret Wood, M.A., D.Litt., F.S.A. See General Bibliography.

### Monastic
*Index Monasticus*, by Richard Taylor of Norwich. See General Bibliography. *The Monastic World 1000-1300*, by Christopher Brooke. (1947. London: Elek.)

### Suffolk Domesday
*Suffolk Domesday*, 2 vols. Translated. (1889: Bury St. Edmunds.)

### Suffolk Institute of Archaeology
*Saxon Rendlesham* Some preliminary considerations, by R.L.S. Bruce Mitford. Vol. XXIV, Part 3, 1948. *A Thirteenth Century Aisled House*, Parton Green Farm, Stansfield, Suffolk, by George and Sylvia Colman. Vol. XXX. Part 2. 1966. *The Building of Redgrave Hall 1545-1554*, by E.R. Sandeen, M.A., Ph.D. Vol. XXIX. Part 1. 1961. *Restoration of a XVI Century Farm House in Suffolk*, by Arthur Welford, A.R.I.B.A. Vol. XXIV. Part 1. 1946. *William Pattisson, A Mid-Victorian Architect, 1805-1878*, by W.G. Arnott. Vol. XXVIII. Part 3. 1960.

### Timber-framed Buildings
*The Timber-frame House in England* by Trudy West. (1975. Newton Abbot: David & Charles.) *Framed Buildings of England* by R.T. Mason. (1972. Horsham: Coash Publishing House.) *The Timber-framed Buildings of Steyning* by H.M. & V.E. Lacey. (1974. Worthing.) *Timber Building in England* by Fred H. Crossley. (1951. London: B.T. Batsford Ltd.)

### Victoria County History
History of the County of Suffolk, ed. by W. Page, F.S.A. (1907. London: Constable.)

## Section 4

### Architecture
*Some Account of Domestic Architecture in England*, by J.H. Parker. (1882.)

### Brick
*A Typology of Brick*, with numerical coding of Brick Characteristics, by L.S. Harley, B.Sc., F.S.A., F.I.E.E. An off-print from the Journal of the British Archaeological Association. Third Series, Vol. XXX VIII. 1974. *Brick Building in England*, from the Middle Ages to 1550, by Jane A. Wight. (1972. London: Baker.) *A History of English Brickwork*, by Nathaniel Lloyd, O.B.E. (1925. London: Montgomery.) *The Story of Somerleyton Brickfields*, by Audrey and Arnold Butler. Cyclostyled, obtainable for 20p. post free from Rev.

Dr. E.C. Brooks, D.D., Somerleyton Rectory, Nr. Lowestoft NR32 5PT. *Bricks to build a house* by John Woodforde. (1976. London: Routledge & Kegan Paul Ltd.) *A Select and Provisional Bibliography of works on Historical Aspects of Bricks and Brickworks in Britain*, by Terence Paul Smith (British Brick Society), March 1974. *Brickwork*: Avery Index to Architectural Periodicals (R.I.B.A. Library). (See also references to brickwork in local journals, such as Proceedings of the Suffolk Institute of Archaeology and Natural History. Lists available.)

## Building Generally
*The Pattern of English Building*, by A. Clifton-Taylor. (1962. London: Batsford.) Dr. Taylor deals with wood, stone, limestone, granite, slate, marble, flint, brick tiles, unbaked earths, thatch, plaster etc., metals and glass. *Building in England down to 1540*, A Documentary History by L.F. Salzman, F.S.A. (see Section 2 Bibliography.) Dr. Salzman has important sections on brick, wattle and daub, and the timber framed house. *A History of Technology*, edited by Singer, Holmyard, Hall & Williams. (1972. Oxford Clarendon Press.) 11. The Mediaeval Artisan, by R.H.G. Thomson (Tools). 12. Building Construction, by Martin S. Briggs. *A History of Building*, by Jack Bowyer. (1973. London: Crosby Lockwood & Staples.)

## Cottage Building
*Cottage Building in Cob, Pisé, Chalk & Clay*, by Clough Williams Ellis. (1919. London: Country Life.) *Rural Residences*, by John B. Papworth. (1818. London: Ackermann.) *Rural Architecture*, by John Plaw. (1811. London: Taylor.) Reproduction by Royal Institute of British Architects from the original (1971).

## Country Crafts
*English Country Crafts*, by Norman Wymer. (1946. London: Batsford.) Chapters on tools, blacksmith, wheelwright, carpenter, thatcher and flint-knapping.

## Dendrochronology
*Annual Rings in Modern and Mediaeval Times*, by J.M. Fletcher. Research Laboratory for Archaeology and the History of Art, Oxford University: reprinted from *The British Oak, Dendrochronology – A Reference Curve for Slow-Grown Oaks, A.D. 1230 to 1546*, by J.M. Fletcher, M.C. Tapper and F.S. Walker. *Archaeometry* 16, 1 (1974), 31-40.

## Geology
*A Contribution to the Geological History of Suffolk*, H.E.P. Spencer, F.G.S. (See Select Bibliography Section 2.) Numerous references to the Brickearths. *The Stutton Brickearth, Suffolk*, by H.E.P. Spencer, F.G.S. Reprinted from the Proceedings of the Geologists Assocation, Vol. 64, Part 1, 1953.

## History and Antiquities
*The History and Antiquities of Suffolk, Thingoe Hundred*, by John Gage, F.R.S., Dir. S.A. (1838. London & Bury St. Edmunds). Under Little Saxham, Gage makes extensive extracts from a book of disbursements 'for the reperaceyonns and building of the Manour of Hengrave, belonging unto Thomas Kytson, Mercer of London, A⁰ Dni 1525'.

## Mediaeval Builders
*The Mediaeval Builder and His Methods*, by Francis B. Andrews, A.R.I.B.A. (1925. Oxford. Reprinted by E.P. Publishing Limited, Rowman & Littlefield, 1974.)

## Plaster
*The Art of the Plasterer*, by G.P. Bankart. (1908. London: B.T. Batsford.) *Pargetting in Suffolk*, by F.A. Girling. Reprint of article in Proceedings of Suffolk Institute of Archaeology. Vol. XXIII. 1939, pp. 202-209.

## Radiocarbon Dating
*Before Civilization*, The Radiocarbon Revolution and Prehistoric Europe, by Colin Renfrew. (1973. London: Cape.)

## Suffolk Records
*Great Tooley of Ipswich*, Portrait of an Early Tudor Merchant by John Webb. (1962. Suffolk Records Society.)

## Timber-framing
*The Timber-Framed Houses of Essex*, by Harry Forrester. (1959. Chelmsford: Clarke.) *The Development of Carpentry, 1200-1700*, by C.A. Hewett. (1969. Newton Abbot: David & Charles.)

## Trees
*The Trees of the British Isles in History and Legend*, by J.H. Wilkes. (1972. London: Muller.) *Suffolk Oak* by H.J. Fane. (1954. Ipswich: Norman Adlard & Co. Ltd.)

# Section 5

## Architects and architecture
R.I.B.A. Library. Grey Book Reference Series. *Biographical*

*Dictionary of English Architects* by H.M. Colvin. (1954. London: Murray.) *Architect and Patron* by Frank Jenkins. (1961. London: Oxford University Press.) *British Architects and Craftsmen* by Sacheverell Sitwell. (1945. London: B.T. Batsford Ltd.) *Architecture in Britain 1530-1830* by John Summerson. (1953. London: Penguin Books Ltd.)

## Building
*The Making of Dutch Towns* by G.L. Burke. (1956. London: Clever-Hume.) *The Pattern of English Building* by Alec Clifton-Taylor. (1967. London: B.T. Batsford Ltd.) op. cit.

## Crafts
*English Country Crafts* by Norman Wymer. (1946. London: B.T. Batsford Ltd.) op. cit.

## Country houses
*The English Country House* by Olive Cook. (1974. London: Thames & Hudson.) *The Making of the English Country House 1500-1640* by Malcolm Airs. (1975. London: The Architectural Press.) *Country Life,* published weekly by Country Life Ltd. For list of articles on country houses in Suffolk see Appendix iv.

## Draughtsmen
*Views of the Seats of the Noblemen and Gentlemen of Suffolk* by Henry Davy. (1827. Southwold.) op. cit.

## East Anglia
*Old Houses and Village Buildings in East Anglia* by Basil Oliver A.R.I.B.A. (1912. London: B.T. Batsford Ltd.) op. cit.

## English House
*The Growth of the English House* by J. Alfred Gotch, F.S.A., F.R.I.B.A. (1909. London: B.T. Batsford Ltd.) *A History of the English House* by Nathaniel Lloyd. (1931. London: The Architectural Press.) *English Homes* by H.A. Tipping. Periods 1-6 (1 or 2 vols. each, 9 vols. in all). See also works by Christopher Hussey, e.g. *English Country Houses; Early Georgian (1955) and Mid Georgian (1956).*

## Elizabethan
*The Elizabethan Achievement* by A.L. Rowse. (1972. London: Macmillan.)

## Excursions
*Excursions through the County of Suffolk* in two volumes (1818-1819. London: Longman), see General Bibliography.

## Georgian
*An Introduction to Georgian Architecture* by Prof. A.E. Richardson R.A. (1949. London: Art & Technics.)

## Interiors
*The English Interior 1500-1900* by Ralph Dutton. (1948. London: B.T. Batsford Ltd.) *The English Interior* by Arthur Stratton. (1920. London: B.T. Batsford Ltd.)

## Jacobean
*The King's Arcadia. Inigo Jones and the Stuart Court* Catalogue by John Harris, Stephen Orgel and Roy Strong (1973. London: Arts Council of Great Britain.)

## National Trust
*The National Trust Guide* compiled by Robin Fedden and Rosemary Jockes. (1973. London: Jonathan Cape.)

## Plasterwork
*The Art of the Plasterer* by Geo. P. Bankart. (1908. London: B.T. Batsford Ltd.) op. cit.

## Regency
*The Regency Style* by Donald Pilcher. (1947. London: B.T. Batsford Ltd.)

## Renaissance
*Early Renaissance Architecture in England* by J.A. Gotch, F.S.A. (1891. London: Second Edition.)

## Reprints
*The Country Gentleman's Architect* by R. Lugar. (1897. London.) *Rural Residences* by John B. Papworth. (1818. London.) *Rural Architecture* by John Plaw. (1811. London.) *Sketches for Country Houses* by John Plaw. (1800. London.)

## Tudor
*Tudor Renaissance* by James Lees-Milne. (1951. London: B.T. Batsford Ltd.).

## Timber-framing
*Timber-Framed Building in England* Archaeological Journal Volume 122, 1965, pages 133-158, by J.T. Smith.

## Victorian
*Victorian Architecture*, Ed. Peter Farriday and introduced by John Betjeman. (1963. London: Jonathan Cape Ltd.) *The High Victorian Movement in Architecture 1850-1870* by Stefan Muthesius. (1972. London: Routledge & Kegan Paul Ltd.)

## Villages
*A View into the Village* by Eric Sandon, op. cit. *Villages of Vision* by Gillian Darley. (1975. London: The Architectural Press Ltd.)

# INDEX

Houses mentioned in the text are indexed under their names, when these are commonly known and used.

Otherwise they are indexed under the names of their towns or villages.